CONTENTS

About This Book

All the routes in this book have been carefully researched and written by experienced walks authors, and every effort has been taken to ensure accuracy. However, villages and their surrounding lands are prone to change and features mentioned as landmarks may alter or disappear completely. The changing seasons also greatly affect the appearance of the walks and paths may become overgrown during the summer months. It is of great importance to note also, that some of the routes pass close to dangerous features in the landscape and need particular care if children are in the party. Wherever possible, such hazards are highlighted in the text.

HOW THE BOOK WORKS

The position of individual villages in relation to the rest of Britain can be found on the location map on page 17.

All 165 villages in the book are divided into one of six regions: The West Country; South and South East England; Central England and East Anglia; The North Country; Wales; and Scotland. The villages within each region are arranged, where possible, in alphabetical order. Approximately a third of the villages are two pages long – the remaining two thirds are one page long.

Each walk comprises brief location details, an introduction to the village, a map of the route, walk directions and points of interest (both keyed in to the map), an information section, and occasionally a short feature on a local character, folk tale or speciality.

Symbols and an explanation of how to use the maps are given on page 18.

TERRAIN

The greater part of most of the walks lies on surfaced roads and paths, but where difficult ground or obstacles occur, this has been noted for the benefit of people in wheelchairs or for those with young children and pushchairs.

PARKING

The walks in this book should have adequate parking space available within the village area, usually in close proximity to the starting point. However, where no distinct car park exists, walkers should park carefully and considerately where they can. Individual parking details are given in the information section of each walk. Please remember that it is an offence to park in such a way that your car obstructs the highway, and a landowner can sue for damages if a car is parked on his land without permission. Remember too, that whatever the time of day or year, farm vehicles must always have clear access to field entrances and tracks.

OPENING TIMES

Opening times of places of interest in the villages or in their vicinity are given where applicable. However, it is always advisable to check the current details in advance to avoid disappointment.

REFRESHMENTS

Where possible, brief details of where to find refreshments in the villages have been given. Inclusion in this book does not necessarily mean that an establishment is approved by The Automobile Association.

USEFUL ADDRESSES

Several organisations concerned with the countryside and places of interest are referred to throughout the book and anyone wishing to learn more about them can do so by writing to the following addresses.

Council for the Protection of Rural England
4 Hobart Place, London, SW1W 0HY
Council for the Protection of Rural Wales
Ty Gwyn, 31 High Street, Welshpool, SY21 7JP
Countryside Commission John Dower House, Crescent Place, Cheltenham, GL50 3RA
Countryside Commission for Scotland
Battleby House, Redgorton, Perth, PH1 3EW
English Heritage (EH)
Fortress House, 23 Savile Row, London, W1X 1AB
Ancient Monuments in Wales are the responsibility of Cadw, Brunel House, 2 Fitzalan Road, Cardiff, CF2 1UY
Ancient Monuments in Scotland are the responsibility of the Scottish Development Office, 20 Brandon Street, Edinburgh, EH5 5DX
National Trust (NT)
36 Queen Anne's Gate, London, SW1H 9AS
National Trust for Scotland (NTS)
5 Charlotte Square, Edinburgh, EH2 4DU
Nature Conservancy Council (NCC)
Northminster House, Peterborough, PE1 1UA
Ramblers' Association
1/5 Wandsworth Road, London, SW8 2XX
Royal Society for the Protection of Birds (RSPB)
The Lodge, Sandy, Bedfordshire, SG19 2DL

THE EVOLUTION OF THE VILLAGE

Spending Christmas at Gloucester in the year 1085, William the Conqueror 'held very deep speech with his council about this land – how it was peopled and with what sort of men.' The outcome of this discussion, reported by the *Anglo-Saxon Chronicle*, was the painstaking survey of England known today as *Domesday Book*.

The *Anglo-Saxon Chronicle* was shocked that the king should lower himself to count every cow and pig in the country, but the results of the survey make it clear that the great majority of villages and hamlets in Britain were already in existence in 1086.

People had lived together in small settlements for long before that. Skara Brae, a Stone Age fishing hamlet in the Orkneys, has been dated to about 3000BC. The stone houses were furnished with stone bedsteads and cupboards, and were linked by covered stone alleys. Ensconced under a huge mound of the inhabitants' own refuse, it developed into a snug, if smelly community.

At Chysauster on the Land's End peninsula in Cornwall, it is still possible to walk along a diminutive village street of 100BC or so, with the remains of eight stone houses still standing up to 6ft high. The houses had inner courtyards, covered drains and small gardens. The villagers probably panned for tin in a nearby stream, and a hill fort a mile away provided a refuge in case of danger.

THE COMING OF THE ENGLISH

Small villages and hamlets like this continued to exist through Roman times and until the arrival, from the 5th century AD onwards, of the Anglo-Saxons. Groups of these newcomers settled at sites they found suitable, sometimes enslaving or driving out the British inhabitants. Later, Scandinavian immigrants moved into many of the eastern counties of England in the same way. Not that all country people lived in villages or hamlets by any means. There were plenty of separate, isolated farmsteads where a single farmer, with his family and slaves, hacked down trees, cleared thorns and brambles, and made a successful living.

Most villages in England have English or Scandinavian names, but there are indications here and there of older, native Celtic settlements being taken over by the new arrivals. The village of Callington in Cornwall, for instance, has a Saxon name, but it was earlier called Celliwic, meaning 'village by the grove' in Old Cornish.

The remains of 'courtyard houses' (above) at the Iron Age village of Chysauster. Inset shows surviving remnants of an even earlier Bronze Age settlement in Wiltshire.

The fishing village of Staithes, North Yorkshire (above) is a fine example of a settlement exploiting a natural feature in the coastline. The sheltered harbour provides a safe haven for the fishing fleet. Wharram Percy (left) on the other hand, failed to thrive and although extensive excavations of the site revealed several phases of rebuilding since its Saxon origins, the village suffered badly during the Black Death in 1350, and was finally abandoned in the 15th century.

BY STREAM AND FORD

Villages are sited where they are, in most cases, because of some geographical advantage. They are the product of the accumulated trial-and-error experience of many generations, hence they tend to cluster in river valleys, making use of the rich soil and shelter from the elements. Needing well-drained ground and plenty of fresh water, they were often sited close to a spring, which became the communal well.

Villages also grew up at fords, as at Kersey in Suffolk, where cars descending the main street today must still splash through the stream at the bottom of the hill, scattering the resident ducks. At Christian Malford in Wiltshire, the ford across the Avon was so dangerous and the scene of so many drownings that it was marked by a cross, or 'Christ sign', *cristelmael* (hence the village's name).

CASTLE AND COAST

Closeness to a stronghold was always an advantage. In the Middle Ages settlements sprouted near to castles, themselves sited for geographical reasons. The village would supply food and services to the garrison. At Dirleton in Lothian, Scotland, for example, a ruined fortress with a grim and bloody history looms above an idyllically peaceful village. At Rockingham in Northamptonshire a castle which goes all the way back to William the Conqueror stands on a hill, on guard above the cottages of the village below. At Manorbier in Dyfed, Wales, the village grew up on the landward side of another Norman castle, which protected it against attack from the sea.

All along the coast, fishing villages established themselves at points where a harbour or a sheltered bay offered calm water for the boats. At Clovelly in North Devon, where the houses tumble down the cliff like a cascade, the squire built a solid stone quay to improve the moorings in the 16th century. In Sussex, Bosham stands on a minor peninsular (the 'ham' in its name) jutting out into Chichester Harbour. In Wales, Aberdyfi shelters in the Dyfi estuary, shielded from Cardigan Bay. Over on the Humberside coast, the village of Flamborough stands on a high, windy headland above a sheltered fishing harbour, with huge prehistoric earthworks protecting it against attack from the inland side.

THE DESERTED VILLAGE

Some villages failed. They were founded on marginal land, or some other natural disadvantage made them impossible to sustain. The Viking coast village of Jarlshof in the Shetlands was engulfed by sand in the Middle Ages and abandoned. A few villages were completely wiped out by the Black Death, which came from the Continent and first ravaged Britain in the 14th century. From Weymouth, in 1348, the disease spread rapidly over the next two years, wiping out almost half the population. For several centuries there were localised epidemics and national outbreaks, which again took their toll of village life.

Some villages were closed down later in the Middle Ages because their landlords could make better money by dispersing the inhabitants and using the fields for pasturing sheep. There was a village called Bittesby, for instance, near Lutterworth in Leicestershire, where in 1494 the 60 inhabitants were turned out of their homes by the Earl of Shrewsbury to make room for sheep. The same phenomenon recurred in Scotland in the 19th century. In 1943 the Dorset village of Tyneham was handed over to the Army as an artillery practice ground. The empty Salisbury Plain village of Imber is used only for battle training.

Here and there across the country strange humps and bumps in the ground may be all that is left of what was once a village with people and houses and streets, and lives being lived. Lost villages like this lie away from the roads, which no longer serve them, along cart tracks or green lanes.

A ruined church and some mounds in the fields are all that remains of Wharram Percy in North Yorkshire. It is in the care of English Heritage and archaeological excavations have revealed its buried houses and farms, manor house and village green, mill and fishponds. It was abandoned in the 15th century.

THE MODEL VILLAGE

If some villages were destroyed by their landlords, others were created out of whole cloth. At Edensor in Derbyshire in the 1830s, the Duke of Devonshire became irritated by the sight of the village across his stately park – it was spoiling his view. He consequently had it removed and substituted a new, unobtrusive one.

Milton Abbas, Wiltshire, was demolished by the landowner as an interruption to his view. A 'model' village was erected a mile away in a wooded valley (above, right). Lanark (above) takes the idea of the model village a step further to the creation of the purpose-built industrial settlement, in direct contrast to the rural village.

This had comfortable houses and all modern conveniences, plus a fine church designed by Sir George Gilbert Scott, who also rebuilt the Staffordshire village of Ilam for Jesse Watts-Russell of Ilam Hall.

Other villages, if not built completely anew, were extensively reconstructed by improving landlords. Old Warden in Bedfordshire, for example, is mainly a picturesquely rustic creation of the 19th century. In Scotland, the village of Kenmure in Tayside was rebuilt in gracious 18th-century style by its Campbell lord, the Earl of Breadalbane, of nearby Balloch Castle. One of his successors added picturesque Victorian cottages. Such are the tricks of time and fortune that the castle had eventually to be pulled down, while the village still flourishes.

PLACES AND NAMES

The meaning of a placename is almost always a matter of guesswork. The main fact about village names in England is that they are in origin overwhelmingly English or Norse. This reflects the occupation of England by the Anglo-Saxons and the later settlement of much of eastern England by the Vikings.

Traces of older Celtic placenames crop up here and there, sometimes in odd ways. *Bre* was the Celtic word for 'hill' and *dun* meant 'hill' in Old English. So Breedon on the Hill in Leicestershire is named 'Hill hill on the hill.' In Scotland, Wales and Cornwall many more Celtic names have survived.

Some village names, such as 'Allen', which occurs in Allendale and Alnmouth, belong to a language so old that we do not know what it was called, or who spoke it, a tongue that is simply referred to as 'Pre-Celtic'.

Most village names seem to be related to features of the landscape. The existence of a spring, or well, inspired names like Burwell in Lincolnshire and the two Amwells in Hertfordshire, while settlement by a lake, or mere, accounts for the name of Grasmere in Cumbria. Brentwood, in Essex, means 'the burnt wood'. Another reference to clearing land by burning survives in the name of Brindley in Cheshire, 'the burnt clearing'.

Names ending in -ley (or -le, -leigh, -ly) generally come from an Old English term for a clearing in a wood. Names which end in -ton, -ham, -worth and often -wich are frequently descended from Old English words for a house, a village, a farm, a hamlet. In Norse areas the equivalents are placenames ending in -by or -thorp.

Some names ending in -ing or -ings seem to refer to the followers of an individual leader who all settled down together. Peatling in Leicestershire is translated as 'Peotla's people'. In Yorkshire, Asmunderby is explained as the village of a man named Asmundr and Helperby as the village of a woman called Hialp.

Village names were also subject to changes. Wendens Ambo, in Essex, lies in a shady vale by a winding stream, which gives rise to the first half of its name, from the Old English verb *Windan*, 'to wind'. *Ambo* is a 17th-century addition, a Latin word meaning 'both', referring to what had previously been two separate parishes, Great and Little Wenden.

New placenames have been coined right up to the present day and some names are distinctly odd. There is a Welsh village in Clwyd called Sodom, and another called Babel. Baldock in Hertfordshire was eccentrically named after Baghdad (Baldac in Old French) by the Knights Templar, who owned it in the Middle Ages. Westward Ho! in North Devon was named after a Victorian adventure novel by Charles Kingsley.

Some wonderfully poetic and magical names were created in medieval times by adding the name of the landowner to that of the village, thereby distinguishing between, say, Swaffham Prior and Swaffham Bulbeck, two villages a mile apart in Cambridgeshire. Medieval clerks introduced Latin as well, giving birth to Toller Porcorum ('of the pigs') and Ryme Intrinseca ('within'). Some names are a remarkable mixture. In Gwent the name of Llanvihangel juxta Rogiet means 'the church of St Michael' (in Welsh) 'next to' (in Latin) 'a road-gate' (in English). Placenames are a very rich tapestry.

VILLAGES: THEIR SHAPE AND APPEARANCE

Asked to imagine the typical traditional English village, most people would picture in their mind's eye a group of rustic thatched cottages set around a well-kept green – perhaps with a cricket match in progress and a venerable pub at one side. The church tower (on which the hands of the clock are set forever at teatime) and the handsome gables of the manor house rise behind sheltering trees to preside over the timeless scene.

There are certainly attractive villages which fit this picture, but they are not typical. Villages come in different patterns and varied building materials. The study of their history and development is still in its infancy, but the more closely they are looked at, the more mythical the 'typical' chocolate box specimen becomes.

Broadly speaking, there are four different types of village plan. The first is the 'nucleated' village, where the houses cluster round a centre. This may be the green, a square, the church or some other focal point, with roads and lanes leading in from outside. More complicated is the 'polyfocal' village, which has more than one nucleus. Then there is the 'street' village, where the houses lie along one main street, running in at one end and out again at the other. Finally, there is the sprawling, muddled village, with the houses set higgledy-piggledy and with no clear pattern at all.

Although these four types can be distinguished from each other in theory, in practice the distinctions are far less clear. Many villages combine characteristics of more than one type. The fact that villages grow and change as the centuries go by complicates matters. They do not stay the same shape. It is often impossible to know what a village's original ground plan was, and even when that is established, nobody really knows why it was planned in that particular way.

THE VILLAGE GREEN

Nucleated villages occur most often in lowland areas. They are found especially in southern and south-eastern England, in East Anglia, the Midlands and the North-East. There may be a link between them and the medieval lowland pattern of huge open village fields, the harvesting of which involved much communal labour and co-operation between the villagers, possibly reflected in a centrally organised village layout.

Many of these villages cluster round

A typical linear or 'street' village forms along the line of a main by-way.

a village green, whose original purpose is in considerable doubt. The theory that the green was a place of refuge, where the cattle could be kept safe in time of danger seems unlikely in most cases.

Greens were actually used for grazing the smaller livestock, including ducks and geese, which might also have a pond to dabble in. This adds to a village's picturesque quality – the pond at Finchingfield in Essex is the centrepiece of one of the prettiest villages in England.

Quite often the village well with its communal pump was on the green. The stocks and the lock-up might be erected there, and in this century it was thought a fitting place for a war memorial, at the psychological heart of the community.

The green was also used for recreation. The butts for archery practice were set up there, and the maypole to celebrate the approach of summer. Cricket and football are still played on village greens throughout the country, and there's often a playground for children.

The simple notion of a village growing up around its green may be true in some cases, but is certainly not in others. In some villages the green was not there originally, but was added later, perhaps by the local lord. He would knock down houses to clear an open space for a market, which would bring him a profit.

Some villages have more than one green. In others the green is not in the middle, but off at one side; perhaps where a stretch of land at the edge of the settlement was kept for common use when the big open fields were enclosed. Elsewhere, greens have been encroached upon, and many have disappeared altogether.

EVOLUTION AND PLANNING

Many villages have got along very well without a village green or a single centre of any kind. Napton on the Hill in Warwickshire is a typical example of a polyfocal village which has three different sections: a northern one along a road, a central one round a green, with the parish church off to one side, and a southern section which is probably a later addition. The three are linked together by a road.

Street villages sometimes grew up in that pattern simply because of geographical factors. At Combe Martin in North Devon, for instance, houses line each side of a long street running down a narrow valley to the sea. Others grew up along a road where the villagers could make a living providing services for travellers.

The conventional idea is of a village growing spontaneously, unplanned, and gently evolving over the centuries. This may well be true of many places, but there are also clear signs of deliberate planning. Appleton le Moors in North Yorkshire, for example, still keeps its medieval plan. The houses stand well back on either side of the main through-street, which was originally a rectangular green. Each house has a strip of garden to the rear, behind that is a back lane, and beyond is the countryside – in medieval days the open fields.

A.A. Milne once wrote of the sprawling, shapeless type of village, which is extremely common:

Between the woods in folded lands
An accidental village stands,
Untidily, and with an air
Of wondering who left it there.

Some settlements like this may have grown up haphazardly in the first place, with no leadership or central planning, but in other cases it is the other way round and the original pattern has been gradually worn away. Stoneleigh in Warwickshire was by 1886 a vague agglomeration of houses with four main routes leading in to a central green, but it is known that it had a far more regular plan 300 years before. Twentieth-century additions to many villages have similarly blurred earlier outlines.

The dispersed appearance of the scattered village (left) contrasts sharply with the more centralised shape of the nucleated village (above), of which, in this case, the focal point is the green. The extensive green at Elsdon in Northumberland (above, left), features the village church and an old cattle pen, lasting reminders that the site once served a far more important role in the communities life than it does today.

THE REGIONAL ROOTS

The look of a village is largely determined by the materials of which it is built. In medieval times only castles, churches and other important buildings were made of stone. Ordinary houses were constructed of sticks and mud, and when they fell down they were easily rebuilt.

With increasing prosperity, houses and cottages came to be built in a more solid fashion. The vast majority of them date from the 17th century or later. Naturally, the local stone or other materials closest to hand were used – granite in Cornwall, limestone in the Cotswolds, flint in Norfolk. Where there was no suitable building stone, houses were made of timber and plaster or mixtures of clay and straw.

The consequence was that villages in different parts of the country looked different, according to the characteristic local building materials. That was changed by the industrial revolution. New systems of transport – canals, improved roads, railways – made it cheap and simple to move bricks, tiles and slates to anywhere in the country. Mass production of bricks and tiles meant that houses were built quickly for a rapidly increasing population. Towns and villages began to bulge with rows of mass-produced, mass-designed houses which no longer had regional roots or local flavour.

People were more comfortably housed than ever before, but the individual character of most villages was severely diluted. Too much standardisation – of houses, telephone boxes, road signs and markings, rubbish bins, lamp standards – helps to destroy local identity. Even so, in the more attractive villages there is still old-style vernacular architecture to please the eye.

Brick and flint at Cley next the Sea, Norfolk (top); millstone grit at Askrigg in the Yorkshire Dales (above); and limestone at Great Tew in the Cotswolds (below).

SYMPHONIES IN STONE

Limestone and sandstone in their different local varieties are far and away the most commonly used building stones in England. The Cotswolds area is famous for its villages in mellow limestone – Snowshill and The Slaughters among them. Almost every Cotswold settlement had its own little quarry, with the colour of the stone varying slightly from one to the other. The use of the same stone, not only for houses large and small, but for churches, schools, barns, farm buildings and field walls – and often for roofs as well as walls – created a harmonious and satisfying unity.

Similarly in Somerset, Montacute and many other villages are dominated by the brownish stone quarried from Ham Hill, west of Yeovil. A harsher impression is created by villages built in the variety of sandstone called millstone grit in the Pennines and parts of the North. This is a rugged stone, difficult to work, and in places like Haworth and Heptonstall in Yorkshire and Cromford in Derbyshire, the greyish-black cottages have a *Wuthering Heights* air of grimness.

There's a similar harshness about the traditional Cornish village, built of the local granite and roofed with Cornish slate, as at Boscastle or Morwenstow. Granite crops up again in Leicestershire, and in Cumbria, where villages in shades from grey to pink granite shelter beneath the towering Lake District fells.

In Wales, Snowdonia is another area of granite and slate, while the prosperous farming valleys of Clwyd and Glamorgan yield sandstone villages of a gentler sort. In Scotland there are dour and lonely granite settlements in the Highlands, with the stone usually 'harled', or covered with a mixture of lime and crushed gravel or sand for weatherproofing. By contrast, in fishing villages along the coast to Fife, like Culross or Crail, pink and yellow sandstone walls, white harling and tiled roofs make a charming picture.

FLINT AND BRICK

Flint has probably been used as a building stone longer than any other in Britain. Impervious to weathering, it is difficult to use and the nodules have to be set in so much mortar that some flint walls contain more mortar than flint. It is often combined with brick, for support, as at Cley next the Sea and other villages in Norfolk, where flint was the only building stone. Sussex is another flint region and Steyning, for example, rejoices in buildings in flint, timber, stone, slate and brick.

The Romans built in brick, but after their time brick-making did not restart until the 12th and 13th centuries, in Suffolk. In the Tudor period, palaces and grand mansions were built in brick, but for the ordinary person it was still just as expensive as stone. Its golden age came in the 18th and 19th centuries, when brick

Box-frame construction (above) at Abbots Morton, in the Midlands. Right, Anne Hathaway's thatched cottage, Shottery, Warwickshire, sitting resplendent amidst its country garden.

The pargeted Ancient House, at Clare, in Suffolk (above). Right, brick cottages at North Warnborough, Hampshire.

dominated the South, the Midlands and the eastern side of England.

Before the industrial revolution, local bricks were just as varied as local stone. According to the clay used and the firing methods, bricks ranged in colour through every shade of red to brown, buff, yellow, grey, white, blue and purple. Midlands bricks tended to be intense, almost hostile hues of red. There were mellower shades of red in the South-East and brown bricks in the Vale of York. Besides colour, the appearance of brickwork is determined by the type of bonding used. This is the pattern in which the bricks are laid – lengthwise, crosswise or various combinations of the two.

Where suitable stone was lacking, but wood was plentiful, houses were constructed with heavy timber frames, with the walls made of wattle-and-daub (plaited sticks daubed with clay and dung) and plastered over. Hence the glittering black-and-white villages of the Welsh Marches – such as Eardisland and Weobley. Late medieval houses of this sort also survive in the South-East, and at Elham in Kent there are old timber-framed houses alongside their 18th-century successors in brick.

ROOFS AND GARDENS

The roofs of a village make an essential contribution to its appearance. Thatch of straw or reeds (or heather in moorland districts) was widely used for roofing, for its lightness and excellent insulating properties, and because the materials were readily available. A curving thatched roof clung to a house like a shawl, with attractive ornamental effects along the roof ridge and over windows.

Slates, sliced thin, grew popular in the 18th century as a more durable and fire-resistant way of covering a roof. In areas where slate was not obtainable, tiles made of baked clay were used – ordinary straight ones or ones with a curly profile (pantiles). Tiles could also be hung on timber frames to make walls, most often seen now in the South-East. Slates were used for this purpose in the West Country and the North.

A village's impact on the eye is greatly enhanced by its gardens, especially the old, traditional, brightly coloured kind, crammed with a riotous jumble of roses and honeysuckle, lavender and holly-hocks, marigolds, sweet peas and lily of the valley. There may be an old apple tree or a plum, a hedge of bee-murmurous fuchsia or a solid old wall of stone or brick.

The old-style cottage garden came to intellectual attention in the late 19th century, when the gardening expert William Robinson, reacting against the fashion for formal layouts and exotic shrubs, sang the praises of the more natural style and native English flowers. The great garden designer, Gertrude Jekyll, who loved cottage gardens, developed the herbaceous border and the principles of colour blending. Cottage gardeners themselves continued cheerfully on regardless of passing fashion, as it is to be hoped they always will.

VILLAGE SOCIETY

A place for everyone and everyone in their place. The stereotypical village of the past obeys a time-honoured social hierarchy and enjoys a harmonious relationship with nature and the land. The stereotype actually reflects and nostalgically glamourises conditions in the prosperous countryside, especially of southern and eastern England, from roughly the 1840s to the 1870s. This was also the period in which most rural parishes reached their peak in population.

At the apex of the social pyramid in a 'typical' village stood the squire. He was not one of the great grandee magnates who owned huge estates like miniature kingdoms, but belonged to the more numerous class of the country gentry, owning anything from a thousand acres to 10,000. Not very numerous, for Burke's *Landed Gentry* in the 1860s listed only some 4,000 families, but the gentry exercised power and influence out of all proportion to their numbers.

THE LORD OF THE MANOR

The squire and his family lived in the manor house, normally the biggest house in the village and often grandly called Hall, Court or Grange. A staff of domestic servants, mainly recruited from the village, looked after their comfort. Outdoors, the gardeners kept the grounds in trim, grew vegetables for the kitchens and cut flowers for the vases. The coachman and a groom or two saw to the horses and carriages.

The squire did no paid work, but lived by his rents and his farming profits. He owned all the village land, or the bulk of it. Almost all the farmers were his tenants and so were the labourers and cottagers. This put him in a position to dominate every aspect of village life.

Some squires misused their power, others were liked and respected. In most cases the squire and the villagers would have known each other since childhood; their families often went back many generations together, and they shared common experience and attitudes. A good squire felt a responsibility for his people, but well-meaning paternalistic benevolence could sometimes turn the corner into outright tyranny.

In the broader world beyond the village, the squire and his fellow magnates in the county – a network of families connected by marriage, financial sympathies and sporting ties – ran the countryside as a whole. As justices of the peace they dealt with minor crimes and quarrels, and they sat on committees which administered charities, poor relief, lunatic asylums, prisons and roads. They influenced the choice of Members of Parliament and they provided the Army and Navy with officers and the Church with clergy.

THE COUNTRY PARSON

Ranking after the squire as the village's second gentleman was the parson, attended in his comfortable rectory or vicarage by his smaller retinue of servants. If the squire was not a man of vigour, the parson might run the village. Besides conducting the Sunday services in the village church, he baptised the villagers as babies, married them as adults and buried them at life's end. He was an educated man and, like Gilbert White at Selborne, he might take a keen interest in nature and wildlife or local history. If there was no village doctor, the parson did the doctoring, with or without qualifications.

Inevitably, not all parsons were good men. Some were tyrants, some idlers or drunks, some only came alive on the hunting field. Many worked hard for their flock and took the lead in establishing village schools or in much-needed housing and sanitation improvements. The writer Charles Kingsley, for instance, who was Vicar of Eversley in Hampshire, was a vigorous campaigner for better sewage methods as well as for wildlife conservation. Some 19th-century parsons made themselves distinctly unpopular with the local farmers by their concern for the poor labourers.

INN AND SCHOOL

A farmer could be a man cultivating as little as five or 10 acres or someone with a hundred times as much. The more substantial farmers generally lived outside the village itself in their farmhouses. Some owned their own land, but the great majority were tenants, though their families might have farmed the same acres for generations.

Living in the village, but considered a cut above most of the inhabitants, were such figures as the innkeeper, the schoolteacher, the village craftsmen and one or more shopkeepers. Villages had alehouses long before the Norman conquest and these eventually developed into the familiar village inn or pub (larger villages had more than one), which might bear the name and coat of arms of the squire's family.

Most pubs brewed their own ale until the 19th century. The pub was an almost entirely male institution. Not just a place to buy a drink, it was a social centre, where men spent their evenings, gossiped and joked, shared their troubles and played such games as dominoes and shove ha'penny.

In the 1830s a few village children might be sent to a little dame school in a cottage kitchen to be taught to read. Large numbers of village schools were founded in Queen Victoria's time – many of which have now been closed down again. Village shops were mainly a product of the 18th and 19th centuries, and the typical one sold everything its customers needed, from groceries and meat to moleskin breeches and rat traps.

CRAFTSMEN AND LABOURERS

The furnace glowed and the anvil rang in the village forge, where the smith made and repaired ploughs and other implements, as well as shoeing horses – with that pungent, never-to-be-forgotten smell. The village carpenter made everything in wood, from five-barred gates to wheelbarrows and from scythe handles to coffins, but he was also often the village builder and general handyman. Many villages would also boast a miller, a cobbler, a tailor and a carrier.

The craftsmen made things to order for local requirements, from locally available materials and in the traditional local way. Most of them did not survive the impact of the industrial revolution, which brought factory-made, mass-produced articles cheaply to every village and hamlet in the country. In recent years, however, a welcome demand for handmade individual products has brought rural crafts back to life.

At the bottom of the social pile were the labourers, the lowest paid, hardest worked, least educated and most numerous group in the village. The average industrial worker earned twice what the average farm labourer was paid, and for shorter hours. 'In their daily life,' as Flora Thompson wrote in *Lark Rise to Candleford*, 'they had none of the conveniences now looked upon as necessities: no water nearer than the communal well, no sanitation beyond the garden closet and no light but candles and paraffin lamps.'

Nostalgia for the past often overlooks the poverty and drudgery of most villagers' lives and the monotony and narrowness of their experience and outlook. It also overlooks the envy, backbiting, resentments and feuds typical of these closeknit communities. On the other side of the same coin, however, were kindness, generosity and much mutual help and comfort in times of need.

The tools and reeds of the basket weaver.

THE VILLAGE YEAR

The inland agricultural village, at least until the 20th century, existed for the purpose of wringing a living from the land. Its principal activity was work – grindingly hard physical work. The pattern of the village year was set by two different calendars. One was the farming calendar of the passing seasons, as the time came yet again for ploughing, sowing and reaping. The other was the Church calendar, observing the principal Christian festivals of Christmas, Easter and Whitsun, and the major saints' days. The two calendars coalesced in a complicated, ancient and inextricably linked pattern of work, worship, social life and leisure.

THE COUNTRY FAIR

The agricultural year began in the autumn, after the harvest had been gathered in, around Michaelmas and Martinmas, which were the feast days of St Michael (29 September) and St Martin (11 November). This was one of the favourite periods for country fairs, which combined business with pleasure. The serious purpose was the sale of cattle and sheep, of horses and cheeses and geese, but there were also lively rustic amusements – wrestling, climbing the greasy pole, dancing to travelling musicians, and enjoying the antics of jugglers, conjurers, acrobats and dancing bears. There were stalls selling gingerbread and taffy, and young men would buy ribbons and trinkets ('fairings') for their sweethearts.

This was the time of year when farm workers and domestics changed their jobs if they had a mind to. At the hiring fairs, or 'mop fairs', servants and labourers hired themselves out for the coming year. To identify themselves to prospective employers, they carried the emblems of their work – a maid a mop or broom, a shepherd his crook, a carter a piece of whipcord. Sometimes there was a 'runaway mop' a week later for those who regretted their first choice of employer. (In Wales the fairs were held in early May, and in Scotland the similar 'feeing' fairs took place in August.)

PLOUGHING AND CHRISTMAS

As autumn wore on, the stubble and weeds in the cornfields were harrowed up, and root crops like mangolds and potatoes were harvested – a toilsome and heartily disliked job when winter struck and the ground froze hard. Meanwhile, as much ploughing as possible was done before Christmas, and many a ploughman and his team plodded their weary way homeward from field and furrow in the gloaming as the days shortened. Ploughmen were the aristocrats among farm labourers, the most skilful and respected. Next ranked others who worked with animals – shepherds, cowmen, carters.

Some of next year's wheat was sown in the autumn, and work continued until it was too cold or until everyone took a break at Christmas. The Church celebrated the birth of Jesus in the stable in Bethlehem, but in the background was the much older pagan tradition of the great midwinter feast, which celebrated the power of the life-giving sun in the darkest time of the year.

The Castleton Garland Day, held at the end of May. The beehive-shaped garland is carried on the shoulders of the 'king'.

Ickwell May Day. It is unusual for adults to take part in Maypole dancing.

Blazing tar barrels being rolled on Bonfire Night at Ottery St Mary, Devon.

Competitors preparing for the Haxey Hood Game, held at Haxey, South Humberside, in early January. The game resembles a giant rugby scrum which endeavours to get the 'hood' from the starting point in a field to one of several local pubs.

The Abingdon Morris Men. Ritual dances of this kind are performed at particular times of the year.

The Great Wishford Grovely Day (Wiltshire) perpetutates rights to collect firewood.

Competitors attempting to climb the greasy pole at Egremont Fair, Cumbria.

Christmas was the best-loved occasion of the year in England and Wales (after the Reformation in Scotland, the Scots made more of New Year's Eve or 'Hogmanay'). Everyone, rich or poor, reckoned to eat and drink their fill for at least one day. The carol singers made their rounds with lanterns glowing in the crisp night air. So did the mummers and the sword-dancers, and the bells pealed merrily from the church towers. Today's Christmas turkey, crackers and tree are comparatively modern innovations. In the old days families sat down to roast goose, chicken, beef or pork, with plum pudding and mince pies.

EASTER AND MAY

Ploughing recommenced after Plough Monday (the first Monday after 6 January), when the young farmhands dragged a decorated plough round the village for small gifts of food or money. The remainder of the wheat was sown, and the oats and barley. The hours of work lengthened again, as the days drew out in spring.

February or March saw the arrival of Shrovetide, another burst of feasting and merriment before the austerity of the long fast of Lent, which led directly to Easter. Fats and eggs in the larder were used up to make pancakes on Shrove Tuesday, and great mass football games heaved and struggled across country with hundreds of players a side.

Easter was the high point of the Christian year, with the commemoration on Good Friday of the Crucifixion and on Easter Sunday of the Resurrection, with its promise of life after death to all faithful Christians. A moveable feast, Easter could fall anywhere from late March to late April. Eggs were painted in bright colours and rolled down slopes, and people climbed hills before dawn to salute the sunrise. Soon after followed Whitsun, celebrating the descent of the Holy Spirit to the apostles in the upper room in Jerusalem.

A comparatively slack period on the farm was broken by the revels of May Day, another ancient pagan festival, hailing the coming of summer. Boughs and greenery were carried in from the woods to 'bring in the May', and there was dancing round the maypole on many a village green.

HARVEST HOME

Around early June, varying with the weather, the hay was cut by scythe and raked up into haycocks to be stacked. The labourers busied themselves with hedging and weeding until August, when the main corn harvest began. Armed with scythes, which they swung in unison, a line of men cut their way into the crop, followed by the women, who gathered the cut corn into sheaves and tied them round with straw. The sheaves were tossed up by pitchfork on to the waggons, to be taken to the farm and built into a stack, which was thatched against the rain.

To get the harvest in while fine weather held, the reapers would work 15 or 16 hours a day in blazing heat, and ceremony attended the final moments of the task. The last ears of wheat were shaped into a bundle called the Neck of the Mare and raised high in the air by the oldest reaper, to a bellow of triumph from all present. The corn dolly was fashioned from the last sheaf and carried back to the farm with the final load on a waggon decked with greenery and drawn by garlanded horses. The reapers rode on top, shouting and singing all the way.

In the evening, the farmer, his family, neighbours and hands all sat down to a cheerful 'harvest home' feast of roast beef and plum pudding, washed down with foaming tankards of home-brewed beer or cider. These time-honoured customs died out in the 19th century and were replaced by the modern harvest festival services in churches. The safe gathering-in of the harvest brought the agricultural year to an end.

SHEARING THE SHEEP

The lives of those who worked with animals conformed to a different pattern. The sheep-farming year had two peaks. The first came with lambing time, between January and March, which was the shepherd's most anxious time of the year, as he struggled to preserve the lives of newborn lambs in bitter winds, snow and ice. The second, which brought him his most demanding physical labour, was shearing time, in June.

Along the coastline, fishing villages worked to another different rhythm, determined by the tides and the life-cycles of fish. In mining and industrial villages the labour of the pit or the factory went on remorselessly, day by day and shift by shift.

VIEW HALLOO!

Besides the year's major festivals, there was a weekly rest on Sundays from all but the most essential work. Many villages held high revel on the feast day of the parish church's patron saint, but these largely died out in the 19th century, to be replaced by the sedate annual village flower show.

In the intervals between the hardest work periods there would be time for a spot of fishing or bird-snaring. Games like skittles and quoits were played on summer evenings. People went blackberry picking in the autumn. Football was a popular game, and cricket to a lesser extent. Cock-fighting, dog-fighting and badger-baiting were widely popular until in Victorian times middle-class opinion turned against their cruelty.

Shooting was an upper-class and middle-class sport. Hare-coursing and otter-hunting were popular, but the great country sport was fox-hunting. Starting in the 17th and 18th centuries as a development from the aristocratic hunting of deer, it took hold all over England. It attracted people of every social class above the agricultural labourers. Noblemen, squires, parsons, army officers, farmers and tradesmen all careered over hedge and ditch as the hounds gave tongue and the huntsman's horn echoed across the countryside.

In the 19th century the railways made it possible for town dwellers to join in. London businessmen took a day's hunting in Surrey and townspeople from Leicester joined the smartest hunt in all England, the Quorn. Even Friedrich Engels, one of the founding fathers of Communism, rode to hounds with the Cheshire Hunt in the 1850s.

THE END OF AN OLD SONG

The sun began to set on the old ways in the 19th century. The mechanisation of agriculture cut the need for labour, drove many families out of the countryside and into the towns and changed the character of farming. By the 1870s two-thirds of all corn was reaped by machine. An evangelical Christian revival and the powerful Victorian middle class disapproved of the boisterous rowdyism of many traditional country amusements, and frowned on the paganism of festivals like May Day.

The rural identity of the village became blurred as the bicycle and then the motorbus made it easy for villagers to travel to the nearest sizeable town, and still more as the popular press, radio and television in turn blanketed town and countryside alike with the same information and entertainment. Holiday periods lengthened and increasingly were spent away from the village. The work and leisure patterns of many villagers today are scarcely distinguishable from those of the town.

LOCATION MAP

Each regional area is colour-coded with an accompanying box which contains the villages in that area. The number before the name shows its location on this map. The one in italics refers to the page number.

THE WEST COUNTRY

1 Abbotsbury *21*
2 Avebury *23*
3 Berkeley *25*
4 Buckfastleigh *27*
5 Bishops Cannings *29*
6 Charmouth *30*
7 Castle Combe *31*
8 Cerne Abbas *33*
9 Chew Magna *35*
10 Chittlehampton *36*
11 Chulmleigh *37*
12 Clovelly *39*
13 Corfe Castle *41*
14 Cockington *43*
15 Duntisbourne Abbots *44*
16 Dunster *45*
17 Guiting Power *47*
18 Lydford *48*
19 Lacock *49*
20 Luccombe *51*
21 Mevagissey *53*
22 Minchinhampton *54*
23 Milton Abbas *55*
24 Montacute *57*
25 Morwenstow *58*
26 Mullion *59*
27 Nunney *61*
28 Slapton *62*
29 Port Isaac *63*
30 The Slaughters *65*
31 Slimbridge *67*
32 Snowshill *69*
33 South Cadbury *70*
34 Tintagel *71*
35 West Lulworth *73*
36 Widecombe *74*
37 Winkleigh *75*
38 Zennor *76*

SOUTH AND SOUTH EAST ENGLAND

39 Abinger Common *79*
40 Appledore *81*
41 Aylesford *82*
42 Ayot St Lawrence *83*
43 Battle *85*
44 Beaulieu *87*
45 Bosham *89*
46 Broughton *90*
47 Burwash *91*
48 Chiddingfold *92*
49 Castle Hedingham *93*
50 Chilham *95*
51 Clavering *96*
52 Dedham *97*
53 East Meon *99*
54 Elham *100*
55 Ewelme *101*
56 Finchingfield *103*
57 Godshill (IOW) *105*
58 Great Bardfield *106*
59 Great Tew *107*
60 Kelmscot *108*
61 Hambledon *109*
62 Ightham *111*
63 Little Gaddesden *112*
64 Minster Lovell *113*
65 New Alresford *114*
66 Newtown *115*
67 Offham *116*
68 Northiam *117*
69 Penshurst *119*
70 Pevensey *121*
71 Ringmer *122*
72 Selborne *123*
73 Smarden *125*
74 Steyning *127*
75 West Wycombe *129*
76 Westerham *131*
77 Winchelsea *132*

CENTRAL ENGLAND AND EAST ANGLIA

78 Abbots Bromley *135*
79 Acton Burnell *137*
80 Appleby Magna *138*
81 Alstonefield *139*
82 Aynho *141*
83 Berkswell *143*
84 Bourn *145*
85 Bredon *146*
86 Burnham Thorpe *147*
87 Castle Acre *148*
88 Cavendish *149*
89 Cley next the Sea *150*
90 Clun *151*
91 Coalbrookdale *153*
92 Cromford *155*
93 Dunwich *157*
94 Eardisland *158*
95 Eastnor *159*
96 Hemingford Abbots *160*
97 Ilam *161*
98 Ilmington *163*
99 Kersey *164*
100 Lavenham *165*
101 Orford *167*
102 Saxilby *169*
103 Swaffham Prior *170*
104 Turvey *171*
105 Warmington *172*

THE NORTH COUNTRY

106 Bakewell *175*
107 Bamburgh *177*
108 Blanchland *179*
109 Bowes *180*
110 Bradfield *181*
111 Caldbeck *182*
112 Castleton *183*
113 Cartmel *185*
114 Chipping *186*
115 Clapham *187*
116 Edensor *188*
117 Dent *189*
118 Elsdon *191*
119 Escomb *192*
120 Eyam *193*
121 Goathland *195*
122 Grassington *196*
123 Grasmere *197*
124 Haworth *199*
125 Hawkshead *201*
126 Kettlewell *202*
127 Hutton-le-Hole *203*
128 Ramsgill *205*
129 Reeth *206*
130 Ribchester *207*
131 Robin Hood's Bay *208*
132 Rivington *209*
133 Studley Roger *211*
134 Tideswell *213*
135 Warkworth *214*

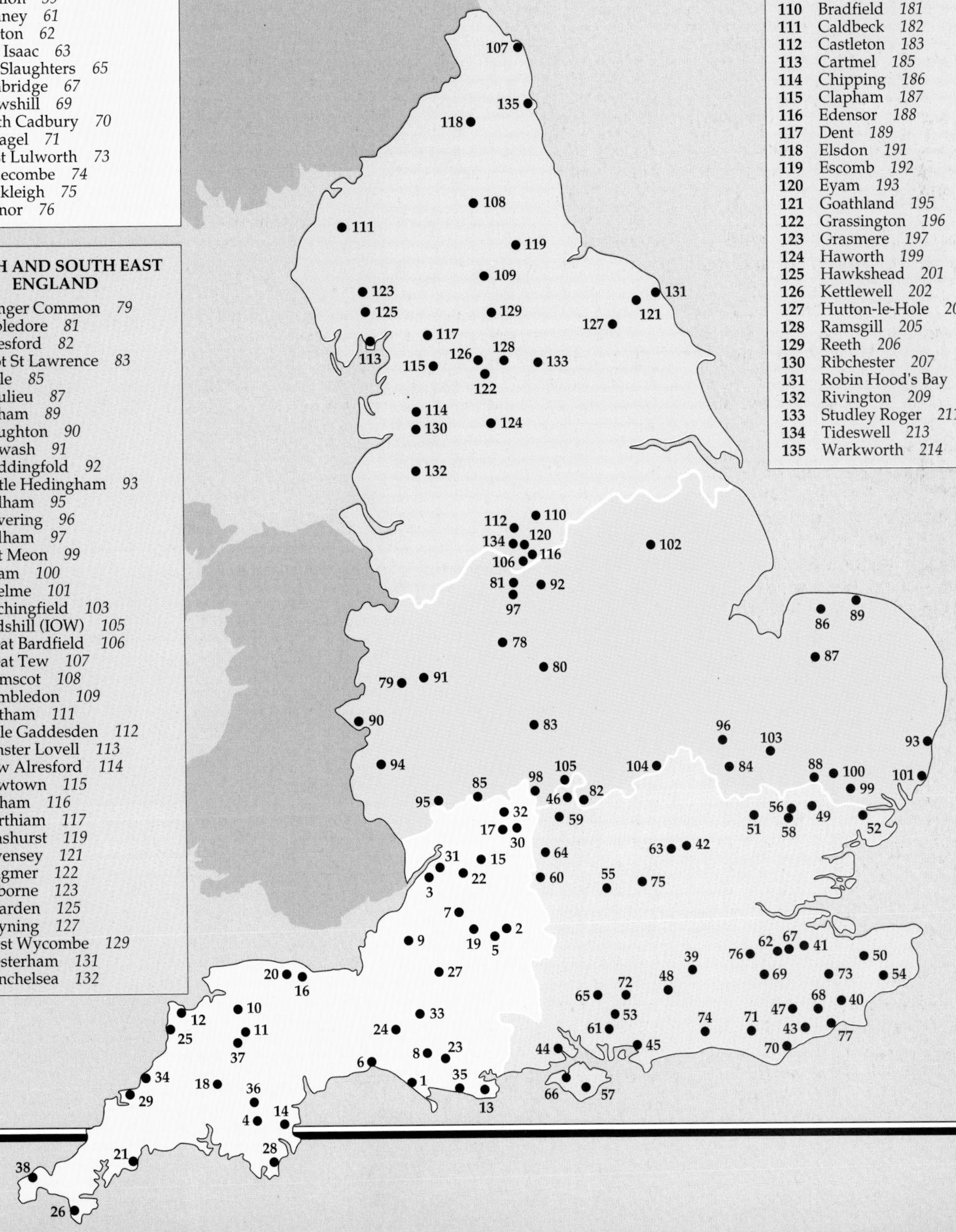

Each regional area is colour-coded with an accompanying box which contains the villages in that area. The number before the name shows its location on this map. The one in italics refers to the page number.

WALES

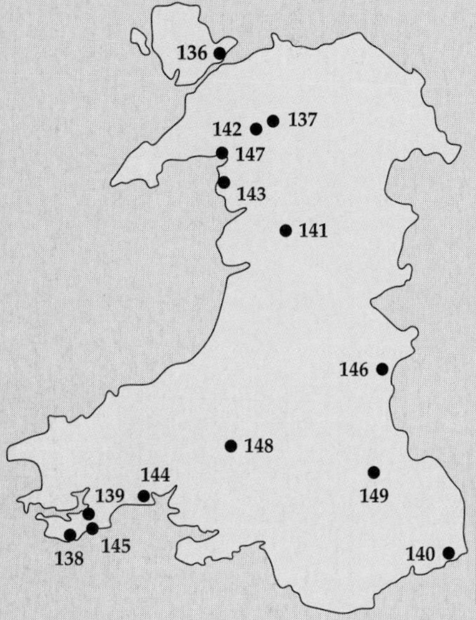

SCOTLAND

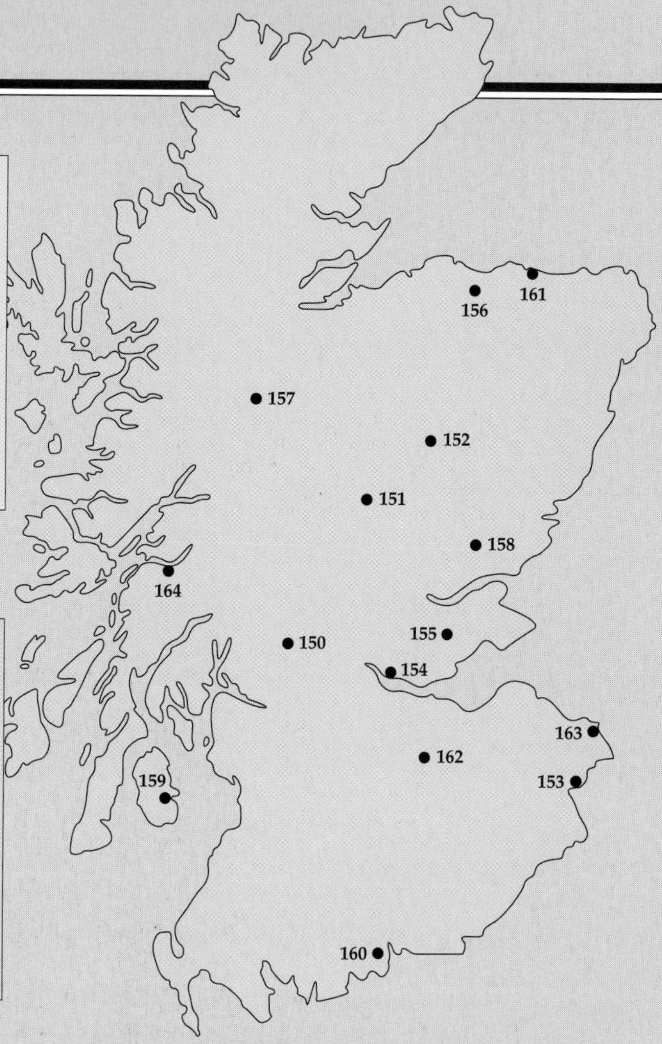

MAP SYMBOLS

EACH village map shows the route of the walk in yellow, with numbered steps along its length from start to finish. The numbers correspond with a series of directions given in the text. At various points on or close to the walk there are encircled letters marking the position of points of interest. Accompanying information can be found beneath the appropriate letter in the text.

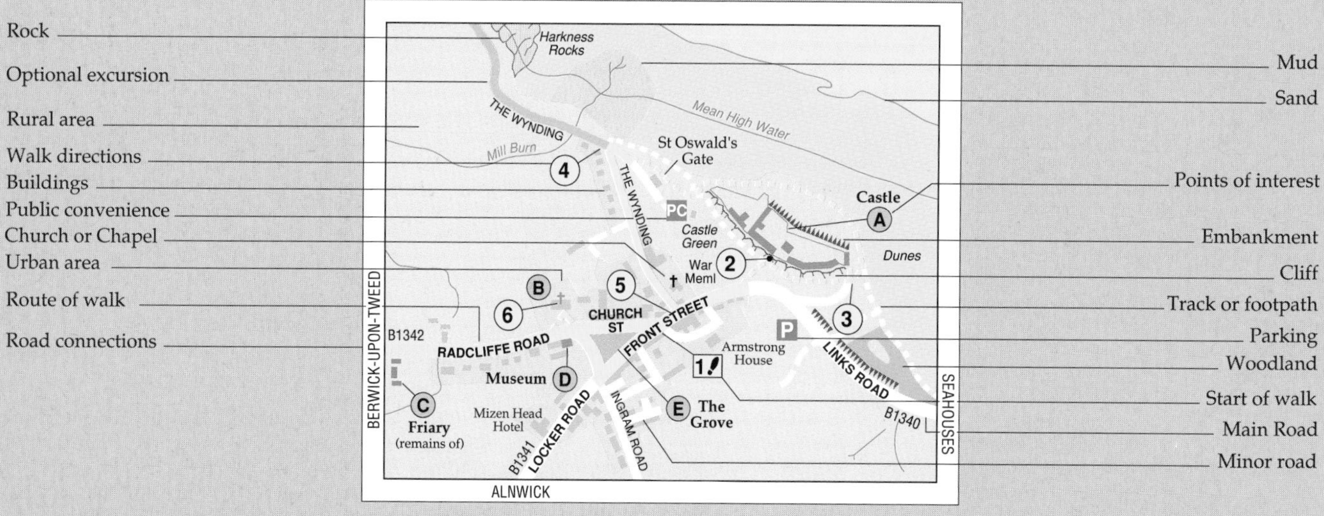

THE WEST COUNTRY

DUNSTER, SOMERSET

•

A tiny granite village nestling under high shaggy moor-hills, and a big sweep of lovely sea beyond, such a lovely sea, lovelier even than the Mediterranean . . . It is all gorse now, flickering with flowers; and then it will be heather; and then, hundreds of fox gloves. It is the best place I have been in, I think.

D H LAWRENCE – LETTER TO J M MURRY AND KATHERINE MANSFIELD, ZENNOR

•

THE WEST COUNTRY

•

•

The rare wall brown is more common in the West Country.

It was the Celtic peoples, who remained in the West Country long after the Romans had left, who determined the basic settlement pattern. Many village sites were linked with the presence of minerals, which they traded with the remains of the Roman Empire and with chapels and cemeteries set up by Celtic missionaries from Ireland, Brittany and Wales. Celts and Saxons here occupied similar sites, frequently around springs at the heads of valleys or on valley sides. Such springs were often associated with pagan spirits and later with saints, as in the case of Cerne Abbas, Chittlehampton and Morwenstow. The more level areas above the steep and wooded valley sides were necessary for cultivation in a largely self-sufficient economy.

Pastoral farming, however, predominated, and few villages grew to any size until markets developed in the Middle Ages; settlements in arable areas, on the other hand, expanded out of the necessity of pooling labour, implements and plough animals. Where villages did grow they often had large, common arable fields, but there were fewer of these further west, where soils and climate were less favourable and the population lower. Here the pattern is still very much one of scattered hamlets and farmsteads.

Tintagel, Dunster, Lydford and Corfe Castle became prominent because of their defensive position. Tintagel and Dunster are unusual in their proximity to the sea, from which much of the danger came. Few coastal villages developed until Tudor times or later. In medieval times the wealthy landowners living in their castles developed markets and trade. They also endowed monasteries, which did likewise. Most villages mentioned here had monastic lands or buildings, and Abbotsbury, Buckfast, Cerne Abbas, Lacock, Milton Abbas and Montacute largely owe their existence to their monasteries.

Medieval kings and landowners, including abbeys, increased trade by setting up boroughs and markets, from which they took rents and tolls. Saxon 'burghs', like Lydford, were fortified places which prospered because of their regional importance. Charmouth, Chulmleigh and Montacute were blessed with trade routes and Dunster was a port, but most had to improve communications. Much of the area's wealth came from wool, except in Cornwall where it was of poor quality. Some villages grew as market centres for wool, but its processing into cloth was scattered amongst farms and cottages throughout the region. With a few exceptions like Buckfastleigh, the industry failed to adapt to the industrial revolution, and villages like Dunster, Lacock and Nunney became almost fossilised after the 18th century with the draining of their commercial life-blood.

Cornwall hardly flourished at all until the industrial revolution, when demands for minerals and building materials were met by improved methods of extraction. New fish-curing and canning processes combined with faster travel to open up markets for pilchard and herring fisheries. Railways brought tourism, which is now essential to the economy of the region. Despite valiant efforts in places like Clovelly and Cockington, only a few inland villages such as Bishops Cannings, Chittlehampton, South Cadbury and Winkleigh are unscathed by it. Many have their historic cores protected as conservation areas but few remain unspoilt by unsympathetic estates of retirement or holiday homes. Abbotsbury, Corfe Castle, Luccombe and Montacute are, however, good examples of blending in the new with the old.

The West Country has a tremendous variety of building styles and materials. Sandstone and slate are the most common stones, supplemented in some places with granite and in Dorset with flint. They are usually laid as uncoursed rubble with dressings of brick, granite or limestone ashlar from the south east of the region, where the best building stone is found. Timber framing is uncommon except in Wiltshire and where building stone is poor older houses are often made of cob. This mixture of mud and straw is laid on a stone plinth or ground storey and built quickly, adding lintels and cutting out openings later. It is then given a roof of timber and thatch.

Cob needs plastering and regular whitewashing or it rapidly disintegrates in the wet climate. Many houses are carefully sited for shelter, and buildings of porous stone are often hung with slates or tiles on their exposed sides for added protection. Cornish slate still predominates in the west but is fast disappearing. Stone tiles are more common in the east and in Somerset the wavy brick pantiles once made in Bridgwater are a special feature.

One cannot easily sum up the character of such a varied region. To feel it one needs to get away from the tourist areas to where one can sense the history. In such areas are found the prehistoric granite 'hedges' of Cornwall and Dartmoor, the sunken lanes and banks of Devon and Somerset, the hills of Dorset and Wiltshire terraced by centuries of ploughing and everywhere the mark of thousands of years of sheep. Here villages look inwards upon themselves and buildings shelter one another. Cob and thatch cottages blend with the contours and seem to grow from the soil. Even the colourwash seems to fit – pink on red arable soils, cream on dairylands and white near the spray of the sea – just as the mellow, honey-coloured stones seem to match the cornfields and orchards of the east.

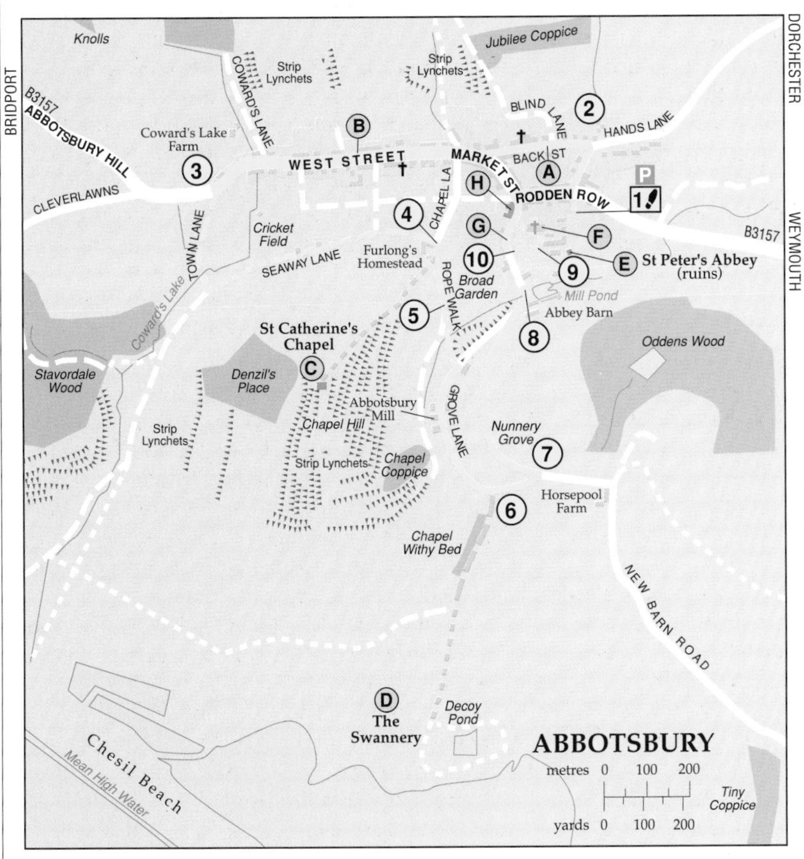

ABBOTSBURY

DORSET

On B3157, 8 miles NW of Weymouth

THE Abbot of Glastonbury owned land here before the priory was founded in 1026. The land was given by King Canute to his steward Orc, who endowed the monastery with his great wealth. It then became an abbey and the village grew with its prosperity, becoming a market town in the 13th century. Several medieval trade routes still exist: Red, Blind and Hands Lanes and Coward's Lake (from the stream which it follows).

A surviving relic of the abbey that gave Abbotsbury its name, the outer gateway originally had a pedestrian as well as a cart entrance.

Prosperity declined following the dissolution of the Abbey in 1539, despite the efforts of the Strangways family, who took over the estates. Villagers survived by a mixture of farming, fishing, smuggling and wrecking. Little changed until the arrival of toll roads and the agrarian revolution of the late 18th century. Many thatched stone cottages date from this period. Several were built by the Earl of Ilchester in 1858, a time of agricultural prosperity. Much of the village still belongs to his descendants in the Fox-Strangways family. The estate owns more than a hundred houses, many of which are let to its employees and pensioners.

WALK DIRECTIONS

1

Cross Rodden Row from the car park into Rosemary Lane.

Turn left from Rosemary Lane into Back Street and continue along Market Street and West Street. Markets were held from the time of Edward I and a market house, known as 'Tal-hal', stood in the middle of the street until the 18th century. The 17th-century Ilchester Arms became a coaching inn in the 18th century, when it had its classical façade with pediment added. At the end of West Street turn left into Town Lane.

At the next junction, turn left through a gate into Seaway Lane. Continue to the end of the lane and around Furlong's Homestead.

For an optional walk up Chapel Hill, turn right after the Homestead through a gate signposted to St Catherine's Chapel. There is a short, sharp climb to the summit. Return the same way and turn right down Rope Walk.

Keep left along Rope Walk, taking the fork signposted to the Swannery. Cross wooden and stone stiles into Grove Lane. Turn right and descend to the Swannery car park.

For an optional excursion in season, turn right and continue 500yds to the Swannery, where there is a short circular trail. Return by the same route.

7

Continue round the car park, keeping left and walking up the hill to the Abbey Barn. Tithes – rents of one-tenth of the produce of abbey tennants – were stored here. It was stone slated when built in the 15th century and twice as long as it is now – though at 276ft, the surviving half is still one of the largest and finest tithe barns in the country. It now stores thatching reed and is not open to the public.

Circuit the mill-pond to view the old granary on the far side. Turn back a few yards,

INFORMATION
Length of walk:
$2^1/_4$ miles (4 miles including options)
Approximate time:
3 hours including options

TERRAIN:
Suitable for children at all times of year, not suitable for pushchairs or wheelchairs

PARKING:
Car Park off Rodden Row, on B3157 at east end of village.

OPEN:
The Swannery. Daily May-Oct, depending upon the nesting period.

REFRESHMENTS:
Cafés and pubs in the village.

then right and up through the field with the Abbey ruins.

Pass through the gate at the top of the field and head straight across the lane into the churchyard opposite. The entrance to the church is on the far side. Return to the lane, turn right and pass under the archway.

Turn right up Church Street and right again up Rodden Row to the car park. The thatched stone tenements making up Rodden Row were built during the 17th century. Numbers 2 and 4 have been combined. The name probably comes from the last abbot, Roger de Rodden, who became vicar of Abbotsbury after the dissolution of the Abbey.

POINTS OF INTEREST

Back Street. The Fox-Strangways Estate is trying to keep Abbotsbury a viable community by providing housing for locals and attracting craft industries to the village without spoiling its character. A row of three thatched stone cottages and a detached house were finished here in 1990, but would not have looked out of place in 1790. The old single-storey thatched building nearby was a basket-maker's workshop, using withies from the Swannery.

Most of the older houses in the village have reused stones from the Abbey in their fabric. These show up as paler stones against the local orange-tinged sandstone. Some have reused carved stones as decoration, and No. 3 Back Street has an 11th-century corbel projecting from its façade.

West Street. This formerly detached western end of the village was destroyed by fire in 1706 and most of the cottages were built later that century, as datestones show. Fires were common in rows of thatched cottages and No. 48 shows its frequent rebuilding in layers of different stones in the gable end. No. 9 has a 15th-century stone carved with the inscription *vicarius de abby* over the doorway.

St Catherine's Chapel. This solidly built 14th-century chapel survived the destruction of the Abbey, probably because it was useful as a landmark for sailors. Beacon fires were lit on its tower. Formerly ruinous, it remains a shell, but its weathered, ribbed ceiling survives.

Chapel Hill is terraced with strip lynchets, formed by centuries of ploughing around the contours with ox-pulled ploughs. The medieval system of cultivating strips in open fields survived here until an Act of Parliament of 1805 forced their enclosure.

The continuous cottage-terraces and raised pavements in Rodden Row (left).
A serene picture at Abbotsbury Swannery (below).

The Swannery. Established in the 12th century as a food supply for the Abbey's Benedictine monks, the Swannery is now managed for conservation. The birds are wild and free-flying but are encouraged to nest here by the provision of suitable nest sites, nesting material and the protection of cygnets by swanherds.

The reed beds provide thatching material for cottages in the village. Most cottages were originally thatched, but slate was introduced to reduce the risk of fire spreading along terraces.

Abbey Ruins. When the Abbey was dissolved in 1539 it was leased to Sir Giles Strangways on condition that the buildings be thrown down and removed. He used some of the stone to build his home, Abbotsbury House, on the site. The house was destroyed during a Civil War battle, when it caught fire and the Royalist magazine inside blew up. The Pynion End, the most conspicuous remnant of the Abbey, is the gable, fireplace and chimney of a building originally on the south side of the cloister.

St Nicholas's Church. The church contains the 12th-century effigy of an abbot in the porch and a good reconstruction drawing of the Abbey inside. The chancel has a fine plaster ceiling of 1638 with the Strangways coats of arms. The pulpit has bullet holes in its canopy, made in 1644 when Parliamentary musketeers took the church from Royalist forces using it to protect their flank in the battle for Abbotsbury House.

Church Street. The complete archway is the 17th-century gateway to Abbotsbury House. The ruined archway straddling the street is the remains of the outer gatehouse to the Abbey. According to legend an abbot was imprisoned and starved to death here. A few carvings remain, including one of a man's head – possibly John de Portesham, abbot from 1505 to 1534.

The Old Manor House. The building has 16th- and 17th-century wings with original stone mullioned windows. The doorway on the two-storey porch has been replaced by a window. The Old Vicarage next door has a 14th-century window in the south end.

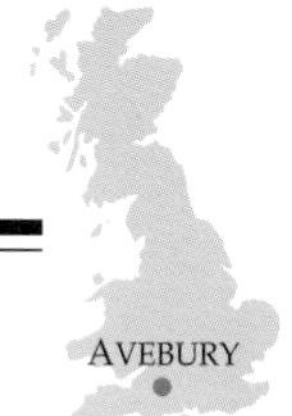

AVEBURY

WILTSHIRE

On the A4361, 10 miles S of Swindon

STANDING alone amid the vast, sweeping prairie landscape of Wiltshire, the massive prehistoric complex at Avebury tantalises the imagination. Perhaps no other village in Britain more surely illustrates our long ancestral ties with a veneration of the land, and the elements, as Avebury.

POINTS OF INTEREST

Stone Circles. A total of 37 stones remain, although only Swindon Stone is thought to have been undisturbed throughout the 4,000-year period since erection. The main Great Circle is surrounded by a deep man-made trench about 30ft deep creating a mound which is nearly a mile round. Of the two inner circles, Cove N has two central stones in place, whilst Obelisk S, behind the United Reform Church, with five ring stones, has lost its central focus.

It is not unusual to witness apparently impromptu gatherings of small groups drawing some religious sustenance from the ancient deity.

The stones of Avebury, spread throughout and beyond the village, are much older than those at Stonehenge. The 28-acre circle has a greater part of the village actually within it. Where once there would have been hundreds of upright stones, now only about 30 remain.

WALK DIRECTIONS

From the main car park follow the principal path, angling right and left to the High Street, by the outer bank of the Stone Circle. Across the road stands the striking red-brick façade of Manor Farm. Clearly enlarged, (probably early last century) it has a gambrel roof. Go right, entering the Stone Circle enclosure at a kissing-gate. The circle is cut into four segments by the converging roads which enter at original, though enlarged, gateways.

Tour the great ditch via the off-road gates on the route shown. Take your time perusing the stones, paying attention to the concise interpretive material on the strategically located panels.

The ½-mile West Kennet Stone Avenue corridor is an optional extra at this point. An opportunity, perhaps, to forge a mental 'link-back' with unknown worshippers at this mystic focus.

Turn right at the end of the fourth segment of the Stone Circle to pass between the National Trust shop and the Stones Restaurant. Enter the former Manor farmyard. Note the unusual

INFORMATION
Length of walk:
2 miles
Approximate time:
1½ hours

TERRAIN:
Access to the Stone Circle and Avenue is impeded by low steps and kissing-gates. Other than the need to approach the church via the lych-gate, the village walk is a practical proposition for pushchairs and wheelchairs. Children must be under close control.

PARKING:
Main car park off the A4361, S of the village, or the smaller English Heritage (shop) car park in the High Street.

OPEN:
Stone Circle open access. Alexander Keiller Museum (English Heritage/National Trust) Apr-Sep 10am-6pm, Oct-Mar 10am-4pm (sometimes closed 1-2pm). Charge. Telephone: Avebury 250.
The Great Barn Museum of Wiltshire Folk Life. Summer Daily 10am-6pm, winter weekends only. Charge. Telephone: Avebury 555.

REFRESHMENTS:
The Red Lion and the National Trust's Stones Restaurant.

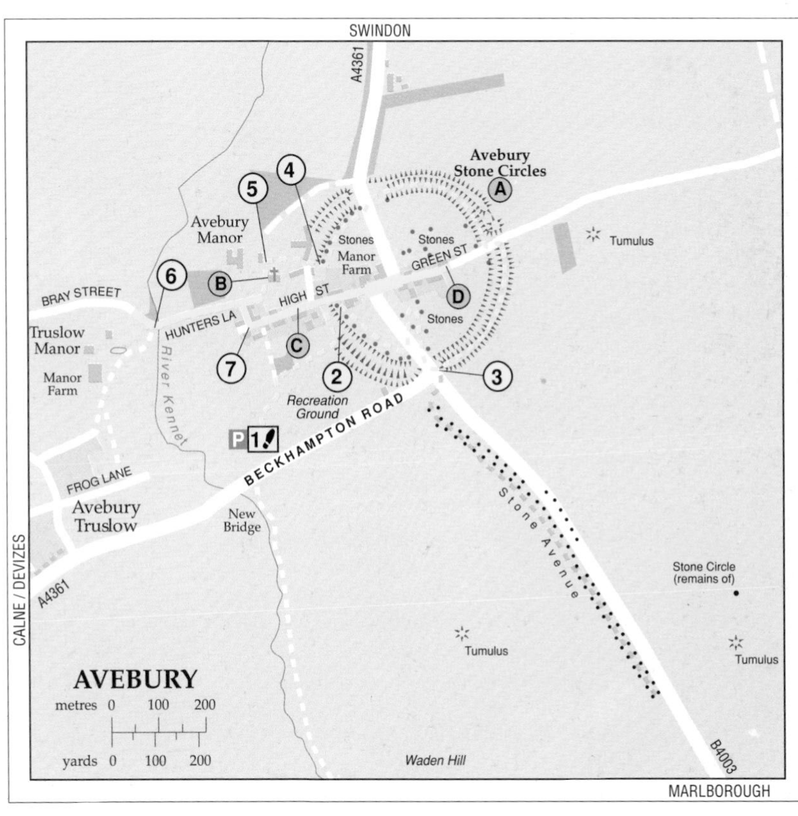

This aerial view of Avebury (above) clearly shows the Great Circle made by the ring of stones, and the deep trench dug into the chalk. Craft demonstrations can be seen at The Great Barn Museum of Wiltshire Folk Life (right).

St James' Church. Set aside time for a quiet contemplation of this fine old church. The beautiful building has taken several major architectural leaps through the centuries, notably the 15th. The painted rood screen is quite magnificent, and a spiral staircase gives access to the roof loft walkway.

High Street. The Old Vicarage stands paternally present at the west end, though visitors will probably find the mix of thatch and pantile-roof cottages lining the street to the lych-gate more appealing. On the right is Avebury Social Centre, the former National School, built in 1844 and closed in 1970: the present school having been built at its rear. Left are a further pair of Manor wrought-iron gates leading to the stable-yard drive; though a grand approach this was not the main entrance, which has been blocked off beyond Hunter's Lane.

A Victorian red-brick terrace for farmworkers nicely complements the Manor House, beyond which the car park rests on the site of old stables and the Providence Baptist Chapel, demolished in 1953. Across the road the modest post office is a re-housing from the attached Henge Gallery/Shop; there is evidence that a tannery existed on this site in the 17th century. To the left The Lodge, now Avebury's custodians' flats, was once the country home of Sir John Lubbock, first Lord Avebury.

Near the public toilets is an adaptation of an old coach-house. Red Lion Inn, established as a public house in 1822, draws a strong trade from its all-day opening. The cider-press has no relevance to Avebury's past but is a striking feature nonetheless.

Green Street. Both the United Reform Church and Silbury House (built for the minister of the chapel) were built using mutilated Circle Stones. The chapel, founded in 1670, has been the recipient of a major restoration completed in 1990. Notice the prostrate stone; in the 18th century it is said that eight stones lay in this area, fallen from the Cove and Obelisk Circles and proving irresistible to wall-builders prepared to sacrifice megaliths for mega-homes! Carpenters Cottage is the oldest house in the village, though strangely this was not faced with sarsen. The shed extension housed the saw-pit.

cart-wash pond at its midst and admire the thatched Great Barn over to the right, containing the Museum of Wiltshire Folk Life. Proceed beyond the attractive Manor Dovecote, built in the 1560s, to the Keiller Museum/Shop, former coach-house to the manor.

The handsome gates, right, invite a glance at the mid-16th century Manor House, an architecturally striking and historically important building, which has been central to the life of the village over recent centuries.

Turn left through the kissing-gate into the churchyard to view the church. At the end of the thatched wall go through a second kissing-gate and turn right to follow the walled path. Joining Hunter's Lane, take the opportunity of visiting Truslow Manor, by continuing on the broader path. This leads to a footbridge across the stripling River Kennet, known as Winterbourne, due to its summer-dry characteristic. Through this spot once strode a second avenue of stones, to rival the West Kennet Avenue, stretching south-westwards to Beckhampton.

At the path fork go right. It is only necessary to advance a few yards to catch an excellent view of the mid-16th century Manor (no public access), with newly landscaped gardens. At this point, where a footpath leads off across the meadow to the right, look north-west to the distant hilltop crowned with burial mounds. This is Windmill Hill, where evidence of settlement reaches back 5,000 years. Return, following Hunter's Lane, into the lower High Street.

Walk to the Red Lion, crossing into Green Street, the original road to Marlborough. Proceed to the last house, Carpenters Cottage, a cosy, half-timber and thatch dwelling. Return via the Manor House and approach path to the car park.

BERKELEY

GLOUCESTERSHIRE

On B4066, 2 miles off A38 between Bristol and Gloucester

SET between its famous castle and the world's first commercial nuclear power station, brick-built Berkeley lies low on the eastern bank of the Severn. To the east, the view ends at the elegant wall of the Cotswold Edge, here topped by the Tyndall monument at North Nibley, which was raised to the translator of the Bible.

Berkeley is also famous for two curiosities. First is its witch, an old woman whose body was allegedly stolen from the church by the Devil despite elaborate precautions by the villagers to prevent the theft. This supernatural event, said to have occurred in 1065, involved the revitalising of the body, the witch then riding away on a black horse whose neighing was heard for miles.

The second, and perhaps more credible, tale is that the chief mate of the East Indiaman *The Berkeley Castle* is said to have eaten the last remaining dodo!

INFORMATION
Length of walk: 2½ miles (3½ miles if Castle reached on foot)
Approximate time: 2 hours

TERRAIN:
The bank of Berkeley Pill can be muddy and slippery in wet weather and is unsuitable for pushchairs and wheelchairs. Six stiles and one footbridge.

PARKING:
The best place to park is the Castle car park, but this adds about one mile to the walk. Alternatively, park in the centre of the village.

OPEN:
The Castle. Apr-Sep. Daily except Mon. Oct Sun afternoons only. Charge.
The Jenner Museum. Easter-Sep. Daily except Mon. Charge.

REFRESHMENTS:
Several pubs and cafés in the village.

POINTS OF INTEREST

The Church of St Mary the Virgin. The church is unusual in having its tower separate from the main fabric. The church itself is of Norman, and later, origins, but is built on the site of an even earlier Saxon church. The tower was added in the mid-18th century.

Inside the church, are some modern priests' stalls, the work of Robert Thompson of Kilburn in Yorkshire, whose famous mouse trademark can be seen. Also of great interest are the alabaster tombs of Thomas, Lord Berkeley and his wife Katherine, after whom the school at nearby Wotton-under-Edge is named. Lord Thomas and his brother Maurice fought with distinction under Edward III at Crecy, which explains the two Berkeley shields in the Crecy window at Gloucester Cathedral.

Berkeley church with its detached tower.

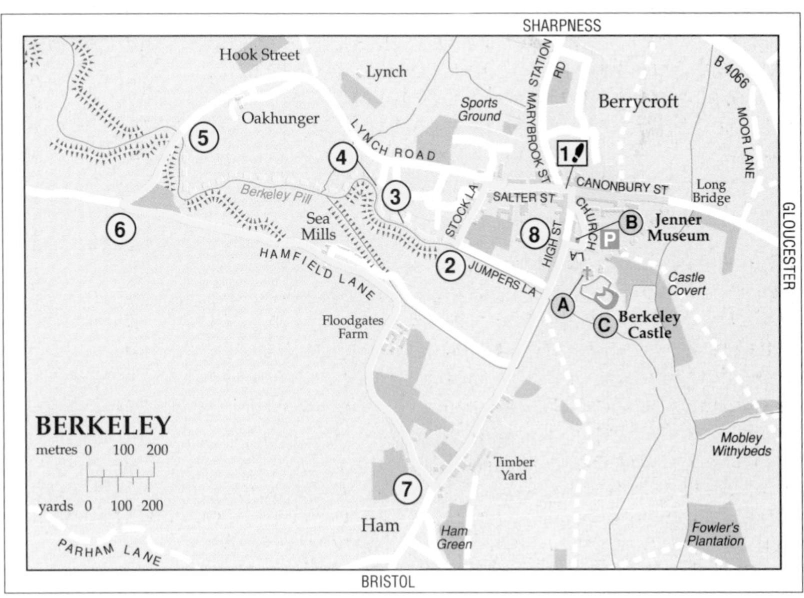

WALK DIRECTIONS

Start in the centre of the village. Go west along Salter Street, signposted for Berkeley Power Station and Laboratories, to reach a small green with the Mariner's Arms beyond it. Go left here, down Stock Lane.

At the bottom of the lane, go right after the last house to reach the bank of Berkeley Pill. From here there is a beautiful view of the village church. Go over a field stile to join and follow a gravel track near a children's playground to the right.

③

At a Y-junction of paths bear left, staying close to the Pill.

④

Bear left on a narrow, occasionally overgrown, path where a lane goes off right, again staying with the Pill. Follow the Pill closely, going over a stone footbridge, stiled at both ends, and then across fields. Berkeley Power Station is seen ahead now. The Pill turns sharply right. Stay with it, going left of a house to reach a stile. Go over this to reach a road.

Turn left along the road, going over the Pill. Soon you will reach a road coming in on the left.

⑥

Go left along the road (Hamfield Lane) – marked with an Except for Access sign – and follow it past Berkeley Sea Mills and right and left, to reach a T-junction opposite the Salutation Inn. Look for the stone cat above the door.

⑦

Turn left and follow the lane back into Berkeley itself.

⑧

Look for the sign to the Jenner Museum and turn with this into Church Lane. At the top, follow the lane left to reach the Jenner Museum. Continue to rejoin High Street. Go right to the village centre.

To reach the Castle on foot go east along Canonbury Street from the village centre, and take the access road to the Castle car park on the right.

The Chantry (above), childhood home of Edward Jenner, now houses a wealth of Jenner memorabilia. Berkeley Castle (right) home of the Berkeley family for over 800 years. In the grounds is an excellent exotic butterfly house (bottom right).

Jenner Museum. Edward Jenner was born in the Vicarage at Berkeley in 1749, son of the Rev. and Mrs Stephen Jenner. He was educated at nearby Wotton-under-Edge and then trained as a doctor. After qualifying, Edward returned to Berkeley and practised as a country doctor living, in later life, in the old Chantry that now houses the museum to his life and work. It is likely that Jenner had heard in his early days in the Vale the country belief that cowmen who had caught cowpox from their herd did not catch smallpox. Such immunity would have been providential as smallpox was the scourge of Britain at the time, killing hundreds in its routine outbreaks.

In 1796 Jenner extracted fluid from a cowpox pustule on the hand of Sarah Nelmes, a local milkmaid, and injected it into the arm of James Phipps, an eight-year-old boy. Later he injected Phipps with smallpox. Thankfully the inoculation was a success and the boy failed to catch the disease. Not everyone was impressed, however, and a local pamphlet was published complaining about the practice and suggesting that Jenner's treatment would result in village children turning into cows!

The museum has a fine collection of Jenner memorabilia, including a painting of Blossom the cow from which Sarah Nelmes caught cowpox. In the grounds is the curious Temple of Vaccinia where Jenner performed free vaccinations for the local poor.

Berkeley Castle. In the mid-12th century, Henry II granted Robert Fitzharding the right to build a castle here. The original castle forms the keep of what we see today, building having been

continuous for several centuries as the fortress/ mansion was enlarged and improved. Castle buffs hoping to find a moat will be disappointed, though it is interesting to note that much of the surrounding meadowland could be flooded by operating sluices in local rhines. (A `rhine' is the local word for a drainage ditch: it derives from the same root that gives us the River Rhine, but is pronounced rheen.)

The Castle is famous for having been the site of the murder of Edward II. The king was held in a small, airless room above a dungeon filled with rotting horse carcasses in the hope that the rising stench would kill him. When this failed, he was murdered in speedier fashion by two knights acting as jailers. Legend has it that the murder was by a method almost too gruesome to contemplate and that his screams of agony were heard all over the village.

The King's Room can be visited – it is thankfully free of mementoes of the death – as can most of the other castle rooms. The castle is a treasure house of artwork and furniture, but it is invariably the fabric of the building itself which catches the eye.

There is also a butterfly house, and a picnic area set in fine countryside.

NUCLEAR POWER

Berkeley, the world's first commercial nuclear power station, was connected to the National Grid early in 1962. The station generated about 275,000 kilowatts of power, small by today's standards but very significant at the time. In 1988 Berkeley achieved another distinction, being the first of Britain's nuclear stations to be closed down. Today the site is busy with workers decommissioning the reactors. Beside the station are the still-active Berkeley Nuclear Laboratories, research centre of what was part of the CEGB and is now Nuclear Electric.

Buckfast Abbey, built predominantly in the Early Gothic style.

BUCKFASTLEIGH

DEVON

Off A38, 20 miles NE of Plymouth

BUCKFAST means 'deer covert'. A settlement arose here around the abbey, which was endowed by King Canute in 1018, and in the 12th century a separate settlement began to develop at Legh – 'the clearing'. The dry hilly pastures were ideal sheep country and the Cistercian monks created a woollen industry, using the Rivers Mardle and Dart for processing the wool. An export trade developed and by the time the Reformation halted monastic activities there were seven woollen mills on the Mardle.

Buckfastleigh changed character when a market was granted to the abbot in 1352. It continued until the 19th century, but never greatly prospered as it was rivalled by nearby Ashburton.

Modern industries now occupy the old mills, but there is still an active fellmongery, quarry and spinning mill, making yarn for Axminster carpets from the coarse wool of moorland sheep.

WALK DIRECTIONS

From the car park turn right along Plymouth Road, then left up Bossell Road, past the Town Hall which was built in 1887 by the Hamlyn family, local mill owners and great benefactors of the village. Turn right up New Road.

Turn right down Chapel Street.

Detour down Mardle Way to view the mill buildings, then continue down Chapel Street and Fore Street, which has several covered alleys leading to attractive courtyards where houses once shared communal pumps and washing and drying areas. There is much interesting 19th-century and earlier architecture, including the King's Arms.

Keep left at the foot of Fore Street into Station Road and Dart Bridge Road, passing Church Steps. Also known as the Devil's Steps, 195 of them lead to the church. They are said to have been built to keep the church out of the reach of the Devil, who undid at night the work of its builders during the day.

Turn right where signposted for the railway, butterfly farm and otter sanctuary, which has an underwater viewing tunnel and observation holts for otters and a collection of butterflies, moths and other small creatures.

Return to Dart Bridge Road and turn right. Pass Higher Kiln Quarry and then turn left up Russets Lane, signposted to the church.

Enter the churchyard through the near gate and exit through the lych-gate. Continue ahead along Church Hill and at the road junction turn right down the path. Keep ahead along this

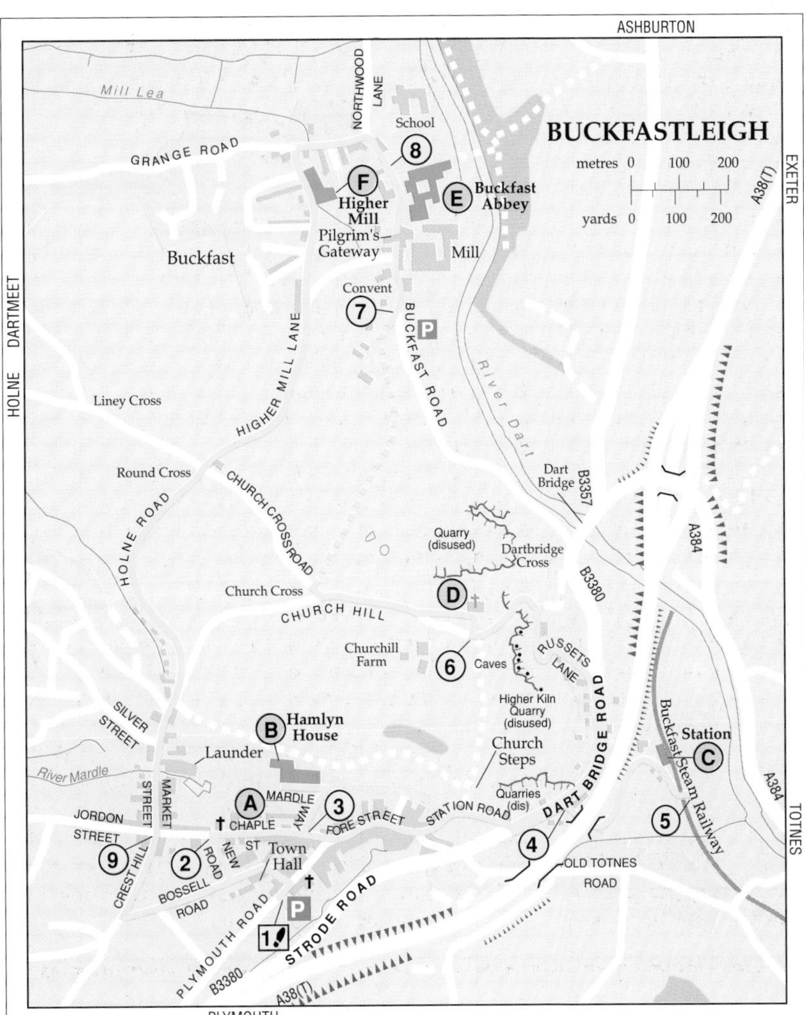

INFORMATION
Length of walk:
3 miles
Approximate time:
3 hours

TERRAIN:
Suitable for children at all times of year. Not suitable for pushchairs or wheelchairs.

PARKING:
At the bus terminus in Plymouth Road.

OPEN:
Abbey, all year except during services.
Buckfast Butterfly Farm. Mid Mar-mid Nov.
Dartmoor Otter Sanctuary. 1 Mar-mid Dec.
Buckfast Steam Railway. Easter-Sep, Daily in mid season.

REFRESHMENTS:
Cafés and pubs in the village. Tearoom at Buckfast Abbey.

path until it joins the Buckfast Road.

Continue along Buckfast Road, passing the mill, and go under Pilgrim's Gateway into the abbey precincts.

After visiting the abbey keep ahead, passing under the archway by the tearooms (not the visitor centre). Continue around to the left and at the small green turn left past Higher Mill. Keep along this road for the next mile, crossing road junctions, over the hill and down Market Street past the Launder, which took water across the River Mardle to power water-wheels in the fellmongery opposite. This started as a tannery in the early 19th century, buying sheepskins and processing the wool and pelts separately.

Markets and fairs were held from the 14th to 19th centuries. Markets were in two covered buildings, one on each side of the street (no longer surviving).

Cross the junction with Chapel Street and ascend Crest Hill. At the top turn left down Bossell Road back to the car park.

POINTS OF INTEREST

Chapel Street. So named because it contains the Methodist Chapel and Roman Catholic Church. The abbey also serves the Roman Catholic parish. The old Congregational chapel is now the John Loosemore Centre for Organ and Early Music and its patron John Loosemore made the organ in Exeter cathedral in the 17th century. The Centre contains an organ maker's workshop and provides music study facilities.

Here also is a row of four woolworkers' cottages with wool lofts over. The slatted wooden vents opened to dry the cloth hanging inside. Opposite are terraced 19th-century millworkers' cottages.

Hamlyn House. This was developed by the Hamlyn family as Town Mills woollen mill in 1846. It became the largest mill in town. The Co-operative Wholesale Society bought it in 1920 and it continued as a mill until 1975, since when several old buildings and the tall chimney have been removed to produce the present small industrial complex.

Railway Station. This was built in 1872 on the South Devon Railway Branch line from Totnes to Ashburton. It became part of the Great Western Railway in 1897. Closed by British Rail in 1962, it reopened privately 7 years later under the Dart Valley Railway Company. The line now operates as the Buckfast Steam Railway and continues to display GWR livery. There is a small railway museum.

One of the engines operating on the Buckfast Steam Railway.

LIMESTONE QUARRYING

Higher Kiln Quarry, which you pass on the walk, has three disused limekilns, a few of many constructed in this area in the 18th and 19th centuries. Here limestone was burned with culm (coal dust) which came by sea to Totnes. Limestone was also used for building and road stone. The restored buildings on the kilns belong to the Pengelly Trust for Cave Studies. Joint Mitnor Cave has yielded important finds of mammal bones from the Ice Age, including mammoth.

The King's Arms in the village is where quarry owners held their annual 'lime feasts', when customers settled their accounts. Lime was purchased by farmers, who used it to neutralise the acid moorland soils.

Holy Trinity Church. The church has a 13th-century spire, 15th-century nave, Regency box pews and a Norman font. The building with iron railings near the south porch houses the tomb of Richard Cabell of Brooke, who died in 1677. His evil reputation was such that his tomb was enclosed to prevent him rising to haunt the area. When he died black hounds were said to have run over Dartmoor to haunt Brooke – the basis of Conan Doyle's *Hound of the Baskervilles* story. The ruin to the east of the church is possibly a 13th-century chantry chapel built by the abbey for local people as their 'Chapel Without the Gate'.

A beekeeper at work on the abbey farm.

Buckfast Abbey. This became a Cistercian abbey in 1147. Little remains of the medieval buildings except the Abbot's Tower and Abbot's Lodging. French Benedictine monks bought the site in 1882 and built most of the present structure between 1907 and 1932. The working monks aim to be self-sufficient and are famous for their honey (from their own strain of bees) and tonic wine. They have a farm and boys school and are a major tourist attraction. There are souvenir sales, a bookshop, tearooms and a free audio-visual presentation.

Higher Mill. A complex of 18th and 19th-century mill buildings, the slate-hung dwellings were weavers' cottages to which a mill was added behind in 1806 when the owner purchased the Abbey site and levelled medieval ruins for the mill and his house. At the southern end can be seen the stump of a brick chimney and a wooden launder on brick piers which runs the length of the mill. The mill was later used as a plating works.

BISHOPS CANNINGS

WILTSHIRE

Off A361, 3 miles NE of Devizes

KAININGHAM ('Canning's Farm') was the largest and richest of several manors in its parish. It belonged to the Bishops of Salisbury from Saxon times and Osmund, the first bishop after the Conquest, divided it, keeping Bishops Cannings manor for himself and giving the larger manor of Cannings Cannonicorum to the Dean and Chapter. The Crown bought the church estate in 1858.

A housing shortage in the 17th century led to the erection of many of the village's timber-framed cottages.

WALK DIRECTIONS

1

From the parking area walk up Chandler's Lane to the road junction.

2

Turn left along West End past the Old School House to the Manor House, the manor farm of 1860.

3

Return to the church and go back down Chandler's Lane for ½ a mile to Horton Bridge, passing the Crown Inn and later, Chandler's, a late 16th-century cottage with stone slated oriel windows. Chandler's Lane is on the line of the Harepath, a Saxon Military road.

4

Turn left and cross the bridge. Turn left after the bridge through the wooden gate and along the canal towpath.

5

Cross the swing bridge and take the stile to the right of the track. Cut across the field in line with the tree marking a former hedgerow.

6

Cross the footbridge with stile and head across the next field towards Bourton Green Cottages, which are 15th-century, thatched and cruck-framed.

7

Cross the stile and take the track between cottage and garage. Turn right and walk a short distance until Bourton Manor Farm comes into view. Return to the junction, turn right and continue to the next road junction.

8

Turn left, walk along the road and turn left by the school. Walk down The Street.

9

Turn right along Church Walk. Pass the church and return to Chandler's Lane.

POINTS OF INTEREST

A

The Old Manor. This thatched farmhouse of the 17th century was the manor house of Cannings Cannonicorum. A deed of 1741 states that the tenant farmer had to pay to the Dean and Chapter an annual rent of £200 plus, on the Feast of St Thomas (just before Christmas), 'a well ordered chine of bacon, a young fat Hogg, a good swete turkey and two well fed young fowles'.

B

The Old School House. This timber-framed cottage dating from the 17th century is a good example of local architecture. The brickwork between the timbers is known as 'nogging' and the projecting windows with tiled roofs are oriels.

C

The Crown Inn. This is the scene of a tale illustrating the villagers' famed simplicity. A drum was made here in 1820 for the village friendly society. The maker fell ill and took the materials to his bedroom to finish it. When finished it was too big to get out of the room and future parades had to gather below the room so that the drummer could be heard.

D

The Kennet and Avon Canal. Linking the Avon at Bristol with the Thames at Reading, the canal was built in 1810 at a cost of £1 million. It was reopened in 1990 after restoration. Boats can be hired and barge trips arranged at the Bridge Inn.

E

Bourton Manor Farm. Possibly the site of a small monastic cell, it became the wealthy manor of the Ernle family after the dissolution of the monasteries in 1539. Much of the house was destroyed in the 19th century.

F

The Church of St Mary the Virgin. The connections with Salisbury Cathedral are seen in the design and grandeur of the church. It is built to a cruciform plan with an altar at the crossing. The church is rich in stone carvings, inside and out. In the south transept is an ancient monk's carrel or meditation pew with a medieval painting of a hand and Latin inscriptions on the rear panel.

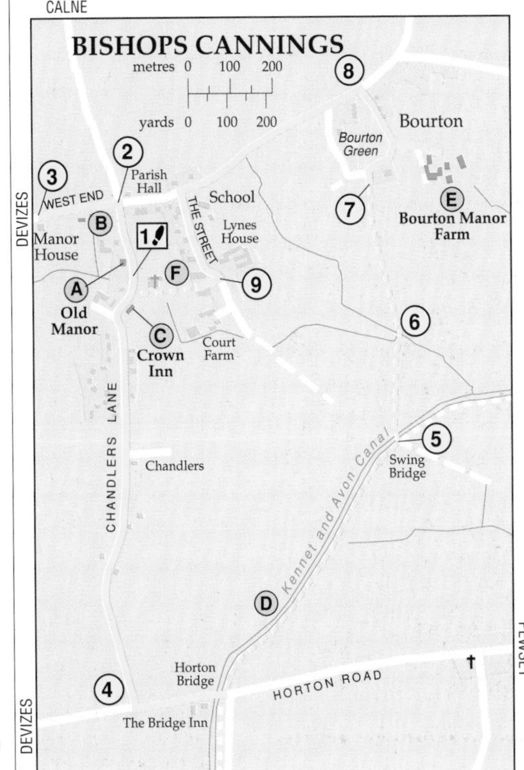

INFORMATION
Length of walk: 2½ miles
Approximate time: 2 hours

TERRAIN:
Suitable for children at all times of the year. The section between Horton Bridge and Bourton is unsuitable for pushchairs and wheelchairs.

PARKING:
In Chandler's Lane on the road verge next to the church, where indicated.

REFRESHMENTS:
The Crown Inn and the Bridge Inn.

CHARMOUTH

DORSET

Off A35, 3 miles W of Lyme Regis

CHARMOUTH was originally known as Cernemude – the mouth of the River Cerne, now the Char. It began as a new town in the 14th century when the landowner, the Abbot of Forde, created a borough – a kind of refuge from the feudal system where people were free to buy and sell property and develop their own businesses.

It grew little until the 20th century, being dependant upon trade along The Street – part of the old Roman road from Exeter to Dorchester.

POINTS OF INTEREST

(A)

St Andrew's Church. In the churchyard, near the porch, is the tomb of James Warden, who died in 1792 in a duel with a neighbour. The long inscription on the tomb is now illegible, but a full account is posted inside the church. In the aisle lies the Rev. Edward Bragge, an 18th-century incumbent who was so fond of his food he was buried in a coffin made from his dining table.

Charmouth House Hotel. The hotel is formed from a collection of 15th–17th-century buildings under one thatched roof. Its E-shaped plan can be seen from Higher Sea Lane.

Old Lyme Hill. This was the Roman branch road to Axmouth, whilst Old Lyme Road was constructed in 1825 to avoid the toll road to Lyme Regis. It was abandoned after a landslip at Black Ven in 1924. The village pound for stray animals was at the junction.

The Heritage Coast Centre. An information centre containing displays of geology, fossils and local history, it was built in the 1850s as a cement works. Limestone pebbles from the beach were ground by steam-powered millstones into a powder which was burned in kilns behind the building.

The Bridge. The bridge over the Gwyle, a tributary of the Char, was built in 1824 according to an inscription on the north parapet. On the south parapet a plaque warns would-be vandals of the penalty of transportation for damage to the bridge. Such plaques were common at that time.

The Queen's Arms. A hotel but not a public house. Despite its 19th-century facade, it is an unusually complete medieval house with original hall, solar, screens passage, fireplaces and plank and muntin partitions (tongued planks in a grooved framework). Monks from Forde Abbey came here to collect rents from villagers. Catherine of Aragon stayed here in 1501, as did Charles II in 1651 whilst trying to escape to France after the Battle of Worcester.

This beautiful beach, sandless at high tide, is 1/2m south of the village itself.

WALK DIRECTIONS

(1)

After parking look at the information board, which mentions the Old Coastguard Cottages down the lane opposite. Then walk back up Lower Sea Lane to The Street.

(2)

Turn left up The Street, passing the church and Charmouth House Hotel. Littlehurst, now the doctor's surgery, was rented in 1857 by Lord Herbert (of Crimean War fame) and opened as a convalescent home by Florence Nightingale.

Turn left along Old Lyme Road.

At the top of Old Lyme Road turn left along the Coast Path, signposted to Charmouth Beach. The tiny building with conical roof was a coastguard lookout. Smuggling was rife here in the 18th and 19th centuries.

At the Heritage Coast Centre turn up Lower Sea Lane and, after the second car park on the route, turn right up River Way and Bridge Road to The Street.

Pause to examine the bridge and turn back up The Street, passing The Queen's Arms on the left. Turn left at Lower Sea Lane to return to the car park.

INFORMATION
Length of walk:
2 miles
Approximate time:
1½ hours

TERRAIN:
Suitable for children but not for pushchairs or wheelchairs.

PARKING:
From The Street, park in the first car park in Lower Sea Lane.

OPEN:
The Heritage Coast Centre. Daily over Easter and May-Sep.

REFRESHMENTS:
Several pubs and cafés in the village.

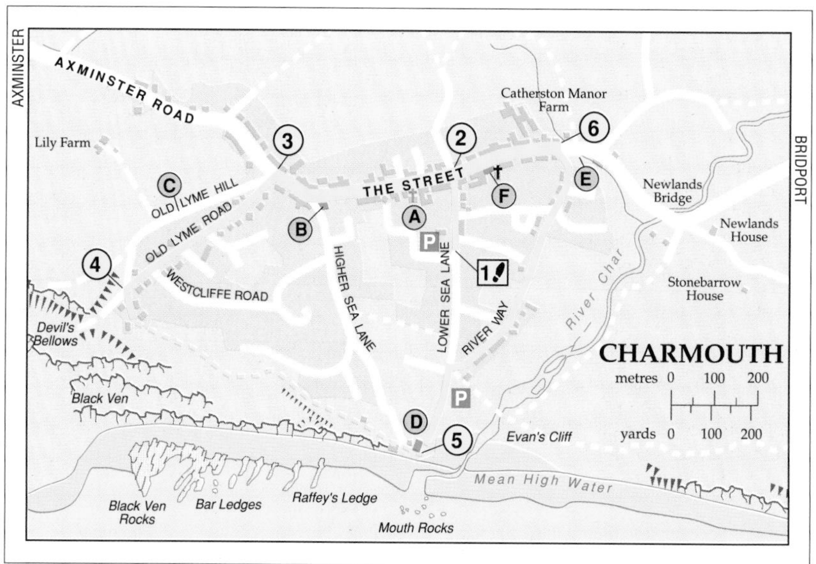

CASTLE COMBE

WILTSHIRE

Off B4039, 6 miles NW of Chippenham

CASTLE Combe, on the edge of the Cotswolds and built of its mellow, honey-coloured stone, has a strong claim to a place on the list of the most attractive villages in England. Indeed it won the title of Prettiest Village in 1962, and in addition to being a visual delight, virtually every house in the village has a story to tell.

This scene shows off the mellow Cotswold stone and the stone-tiled pitch roofs of Castle Combe.

INFORMATION
Length of walk: $1\frac{1}{2}$ miles
Approximate time: $1\frac{1}{2}$ hours

TERRAIN:
Suitable for children at all times of year; though the stiles may be a problem for push-chairs. The walk is not suitable for wheel-chairs. Three stiles and one footbridge.

PARKING:
Parking is banned in Castle Combe and visitors must use the car park close to the turn-off for the village on the B4039.

OPEN:
The Museum. Sun afternoons in summer.

BLANKET WEAVING

In the 17th century, Castle Combe was a prosperous wool village – as were many in the Cotswolds because the high wolds were excellent for sheep. The famous Cotswold breed was a hardy animal that produced a fleece that usually weighed two stones. In addition, the Cotswolds had steep valleys with streams that could power mills, and abundant quantities of fuller's earth used in the production of good quality cloth. At one stage the woollen trade was so important that it dominated the British economy.

One Castle Combe legend has it that a pair of brothers who were master weavers and lived in the Weavers' Cottages near Pack Bridge were called Blanket. The brothers were not happy with their cottages, and to keep the winter's chills at bay they wove a heavy, raised nap cloth that they wrapped around themselves. The idea caught on, and soon everyone was using the brothers' woven cloth on their beds, the new bedcloth taking the brothers' name.

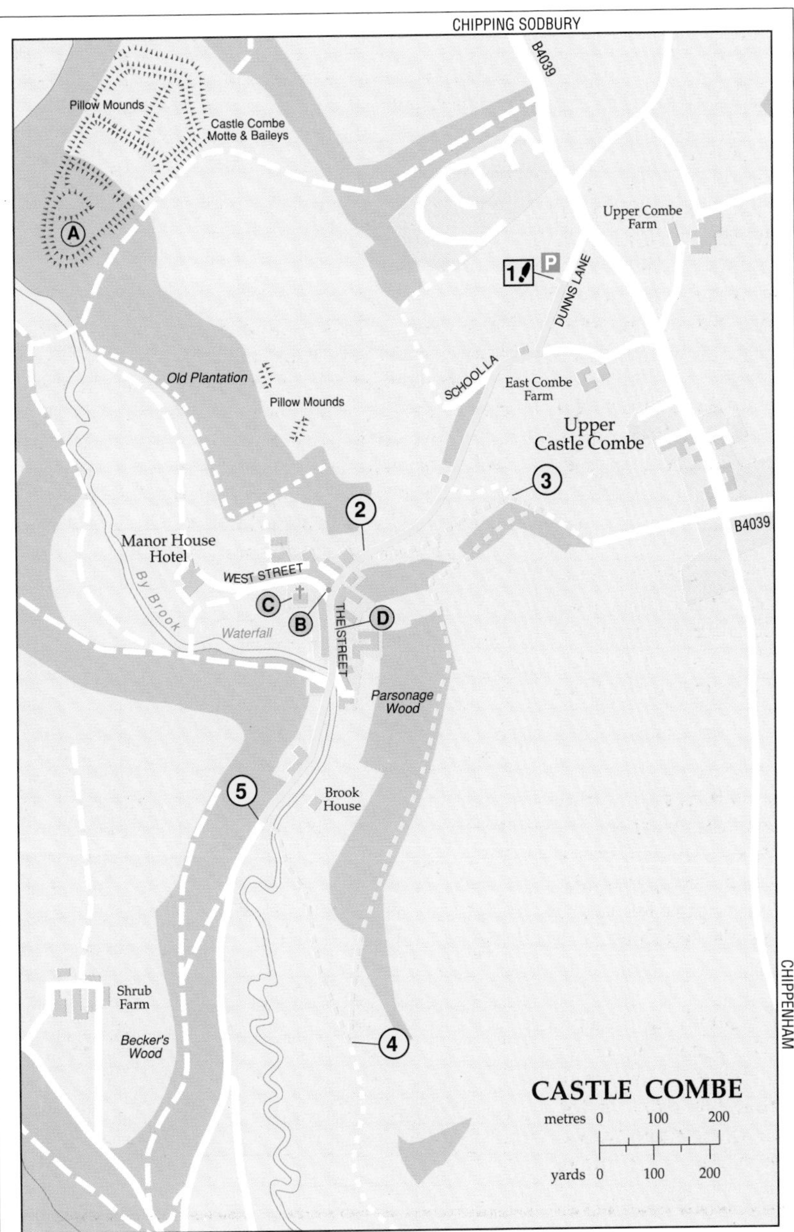

WALK DIRECTIONS

From the car park go right, downhill, along Dunns Lane, bearing right at a junction of lanes, and left where School Lane goes off to the right.

Look for the Upper Manor House (Dower House) to the right. It is easily recognised by its superb shell door lintel. Opposite the house is a path going up between trees. Follow this for about 200yds to reach a track coming in from the left.

Go right on the track and, almost immediately, right again on a clear path. From this path, before it enters Parsonage Wood, there is a good view of the village. Walk through Parsonage Wood. Beyond the wood-land stile, beside a gate elegantly set between stone pillars, there is a fine view into the valley of By Brook which flows through the village.

When the path reaches a track, go right on the track to reach a road over an old stone bridge.

Go right and up through the village along The Street to reach the outward route from the car park, passing on the way the crosses and the church.

DR. DOOLITTLE

Visitors to Castle Combe who stop at Pack Bridge may have difficulty in recognising Puddleby-on-the-Marsh, home of Dr Doolittle in the film which was made, in part, in Castle Combe in 1966, with Rex Harrison in the title role. That is no surprise as Puddleby was a seaside village and consequently the Brook in front of the weavers' cottages had to be converted into a mock harbour with a raised water level and ships at anchor. Dower House, near which our walk turned off the village road, became Dr Doolittle's house.

POINTS OF INTEREST

The Castle. Hidden among the trees beyond By Brook, to the right of a walk that begins under the arch of Archway Cottage, is the site of the castle that was added to the original settlement name of Combe. The earliest castle on this strategic site was Iron Age, but both the Romans – whose Fosse Way lies only a mile or so to the west of the village – and the Saxons had fortresses on the spur of the hill. The Saxon castle was sacked by Danish invaders, but at a decisive battle near Yatton Keynell, about two miles from Castle Combe, the invaders were finally beaten and forced to leave the area.

When the Normans came, Walter de Dunstanville, a great, great grandson of Henry I, whose family had been given the manor, built a stone castle on the hill top. Of this final fortress, which gave the village its distinctive first name, nothing but a collection of ridges and ditches remains to confirm that it ever existed.

The By Brook (above), which runs beside a row of 17th-century cottages, is crossed by the 15th-century Pack Bridge. Beyond this, at the top of The Street, sits the old market cross (right).

The Castle Combe Crosses. The Market Cross, with its stone shingled rood on a heavy stone column and its stones worn smooth by countless market goers, is one of the most delightful in Britain. Beside it is the old village pump. Estimates of its age range from the fourteenth to the sixteenth centuries. The small heap of the Butter Cross is newer, and marks the position of an older market house. The name is deceptive; it was probably erected as a mounting block.

Close to the crosses are two old inns, the White Hart Inn and the Castle Hotel.

St Andrew's Church. The village church, near the Cross, dates from the 12th century with a tower two centuries more recent, but it was largely rebuilt in the mid-19th century, the ancient habit of burying the dead under the church walls caused so much subsidence that repairs were no longer possible, and a total rebuild of the nave and chancel was required. Inside there is a superb tomb to Walter de Dunstanville. The knight is shown in full chain mail armour, the design of which proves that the carving was completed in Bristol. Sir Walter has angels at his head and a lion at his feet. The tomb is finished with six mourners said to be the children of de Dunstanville.

At the base of the tower is an early 15th-century faceless clock that is older than the more famous one in Salisbury Cathedral. It is believed that the clock was made by the local blacksmith. And to answer the most obvious question – the clock chimed, so the villagers were able to tell the hours if not the minutes.

The Street. Close to the church at the top of the village is the old Manor House, now an hotel, and a number of beautiful old cottages. Archway Cottage was an old gatehouse of the Manor House. Heading down The Street, (aptly named as it is the only village street) you pass, to the left, the Old Court House, with its overhung, half-timbered upper floor. The old wattle and daub gaol that stands behind it is now a garden shed! Further down the street, on the right, is a fine nail-studded door. At 400 years old it is the only surviving original door in The Street. Almost opposite is a house called the Old Rectory, though it is nothing of the kind.

Further on, look for the dovecote, inscribed 1617, to the right. Even this lowly building has been built with the warm Cotswold stone, and with obvious loving care. Beyond the dovecote the visitor reaches the packhorse bridge over the By Brook. Pack Bridge is certainly 15th-century and could be older. It is a delightful triple-arched bridge said to be haunted by a Roman centurion who died during the building of the valley's first bridge.

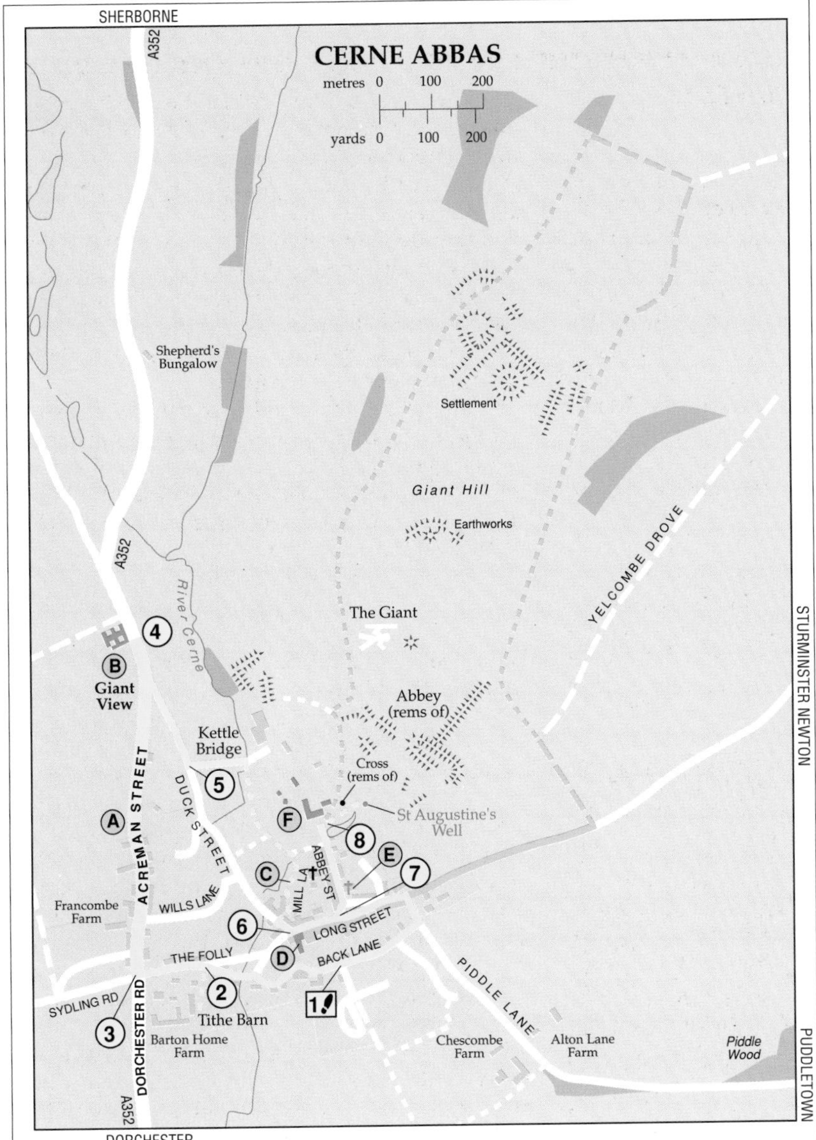

CERNE ABBAS

DORSET

On A352, 7 miles N of Dorchester

As its name suggests, Cerne Abbas was a settlement founded by monks on the River Cerne. They built the abbey in 987, rebuilt it in the 12th century and it was dissolved in 1539. A medieval market town grew up alongside it. Its shape and street pattern have changed little and are still based on a through road (Long Street) with a link to the abbey (Abbey Street) and a back road (Back Lane). Regular house plots along these streets suggest that the town was planned and grew rapidly.

Long Street is wide and has a triangular area with buildings in the middle. Here was a market place where fairs were held and there was a Corn Market, shambles (row of lock-up shops), Guildhall and market cross, now removed to the cemetery. The town had shrunk by the 17th century, when there was a large fire, and most buildings date from after that time. Earthworks to the north and south of the village mark former medieval suburbs.

Looking towards the fine 15th-century tower of St Mary's Church, with the Royal Oak in the foreground.

In the 18th century major industries were silk out-working and brewing. Quality ales from Cerne Abbas became popular in London. Large quantities of brewing malt were produced, and the malt house was busy until the late 19th century. A flourishing leather industry produced boots, gloves and hunting suits. Small housing estates have recently been built and the village is now largely a dormitory of Dorchester.

WALK DIRECTIONS

Start in Back Lane, at its junction with Chescombe. Turn left along the Lane. Pass Chescombe Cottage with its wonderful wavy thatch and, keeping to the left, cross a footbridge over a pretty part of the River Cerne.

Just before the junction with The Folly turn left through a gateway and take the way-marked track to view the tithe barn, built in 1350 for storing tithes – rents of one-tenth of the produce of tenants of abbey lands. It was converted into Barton Farmhouse in the 18th century and part was reconstructed in 1886. Keep to the left edge of the garden. Return to The Folly and turn left.

At the crossroads, turn right along Acreman Street. Drop to the side of the street to view the Old Malt House. Return to the main road and continue past the junction at Giant View for 100yds. The residential care centre was built as a workhouse in 1836. Here, in 1918, died 80-year-old Mary Ann Bell, one of the last 'reddle women' – hawkers of sheep dyes. The building became a youth hostel in 1930, then a private house before being restored for its present use.

Return to the junction and take the left fork down Duck Street.

Take the track to the left towards the picnic area and turn right at Kettle Bridge

INFORMATION
Length of walk:
1½ miles (3½ miles if option followed)
Approximate time:
1½ hours (3 hours if option followed)

TERRAIN:
Level and easy going, suitable for pushchairs and wheelchairs except for option, which has 4 stiles.

PARKING:
There is no car park, but street parking is easy and there is usually space along Back Lane. Toilets are in Long Street, opposite the Royal Oak.

OPEN:
Abbey Farm. Daily. There is a small charge to view the monastic buildings.

REFRESHMENTS:
Selection of pubs and cafés in the village.

The Pitchmarket, a row of timber-framed houses. Note the decorative lintel.

along the path by the river, continuing back into Duck Street past Mill Lane.

Turn left along Long Street, passing the New Inn.

Turn left up Abbey Street, pausing at St Mary's Church. The stocks outside the church once stood by the village pond, alongside a pillory and ducking stool used for the humiliation of petty criminals who could be punished without resort to the county court or prison. The Pitchmarket was once the home of Thomas Washington, whose nephew George became the first President of the United States of America.

Turn right after the pond for Abbey Farm and cemetery. After visiting the well in the cemetery, take the far exit into the field with the abbey earthworks. (See below for optional extra.) Return to Long Street, turn left and continue forward until you reach the junction with Piddle Lane on your right. Turn up Piddle Lane and then right into Back Lane.

For an optional route of two miles continue from 8 across the field containing the abbey remains and up to the stile under the trees.

Cross the stile into the lane and turn right. Cross the next stile and take the track to the left, which becomes one of the many sheep tracks under the Giant. It then climbs the hillside following blue way-marks.

Cross prehistoric earth-works, then a stile into a field. Follow the waymarks around two sides of the field. Pass through a gate on to a track and turn right. After about 300yds fork left down a steep track.

Fork left near the bottom of the hill and continue down the main track to the road by the playing field. Turn right and continue 400yds to the junction with Piddle Lane.

ST AUGUSTINE'S WELL

According to a legend probably originating from the abbey's Benedictine monks, this wishing-well was created by St Augustine. St Edwold, a member of the Mercian royal family, lived in a hermitage here until his death in 871. The remains of a shrine to St Catherine can be seen. It was a wishing-well at which the women would pray to St Catherine for a husband or child.

POINTS OF INTEREST

Acreman Street. The name of this late medieval street means 'farm worker' and there is a range of 10 labourers' tenements on the east side of the street dating from the 18th century at the north end to 1832 at the south. No. 6 has a carved head from the abbey set over the doorway. Until 1960 the road ended at the Old Malthouse. Here, until 1928, beer was made for the Union Arms, named after the nearby Union workhouse.

Giant View. The 180ft-high figure cut in chalk probably dates from the Dark Ages. He is a pagan fertility symbol, possibly a British version of the Roman hero-god Hercules. As late as the 19th century women slept on the hill at night to try to cure infertility. Victorians, however, were generally offended by the figure and allowed vital parts to become overgrown.

This huge turf-cut figure is 180ft long and 167ft wide and holds a 120ft long club.

Ⓒ

Mill Lane. The 18th-century cornmill at the head of the lane operated until 1933. The Miller's Brook, opposite Mill House, was a Victorian Salvation Army Citadel, becoming in turn a store, chicken house, restaurant and house. The Academy was a school built in 1793 and closed in 1860, when the forge was built in the former playground.

New Inn. One of 13 inns once in Cerne Abbas, it has carved stonework from the abbey in its east wall. The pump of 1774 dates from its rebuilding as a coaching inn. Until 1860 courts were held in the main bar, whilst prisoners were held in what are now the ladies toilets. Here until 1914 villagers paid their rents to the Pitt-Rivers estate, each tenant receiving a threepenny beer voucher in return.

St Mary's Church. The church has some walls, windows and wall paintings surviving from the 13th century. A madonna statue in a niche outside the tower has also, unusually, survived the Reformation. Wall texts were painted in 1679 and one was added in the restoration of 1960-67.

Abbey Farm. Built in 1641 for Denzil Holles, a local MP famous for restraining the Speaker in his chair to prevent the adjournment of a Parliamentary debate. The building incorporates a gatehouse and walls of the abbey, destroyed by rioters in 1580. Behind is the abbey Guest House, built by John Vanne, abbot from 1458 to 1470, for pilgrims, keeping them outside the abbey wall for fear of plague. Behind this is the mis-named Abbey Gatehouse, which was the porch to the Abbot's Hall, built for abbot Thomas Sam in 1508. The fan-vaulted porch is surmounted by a porter's lodge with large Victorian leaded window. Beyond again is the Abbey Barn, built to store grain for the Abbey Mill and now converted to a veterinary centre.

CHEW MAGNA

AVON

On B3130, about 6 miles S of Bristol

THOUGH close to the city of Bristol, the village of Chew Magna has maintained its separate identity. The quiet, compact village is a real delight, with high and wide pavements in Chew Street, fine old cottages and a couple of historic bridges, all grouped around St Andrew's Church which has medieval links.

INFORMATION

Length of walk:
2 miles
Approximate time:
1½ hours

TERRAIN:
The footpath section of the walk is suitable for children at all times of year. Not suitable for pushchairs and wheelchairs because of the kissing-gate and squeeze stile.

PARKING:
There is no car park in Chew Magna, though parking is usually straightforward near the centre.

POINTS OF INTEREST

St Andrew's Church. The church is Norman with later additions and is notable externally for its superb gargoyles, a frightening bunch, some set high on the fine tower.

Inside, the most beautiful feature is the 15th-century carved wooden screen that traverses both the nave and the two aisles. A monument, said to be for Sir John Hauteville a 13th-century knight, is a disputed curio. It is made of solid Irish oak.

Ⓑ

The Churchyard. In the churchyard, close to the entrance, is an old preaching cross – now reduced to just a shaft – set on steps. Also close to the entrance is the Old Schoolroom. The fine old building, built in 1510, was the village poorhouse in the early 19th century.

Ⓒ

Chew Court. Close to the church is the old Bishop's Palace and Courthouse. Chew Magna was once Bishop's Chew, having been owned by, firstly, the Abbot of Glastonbury and then by the Bishop of Bath and Wells. The Court is L-shaped and has a superb original gateway. Above this is the old courtroom, while the turrets to either side were once used to hold prisoners awaiting trial. The gateway dates from the 14th century.

Ⓓ

Tun Bridge. This late 15th-century bridge is a superb example of its type, with three pointed arches supporting its 60ft span. Look over the bridge on its eastern side (left with your back to the village) to see a most interesting feature. The stone trough 'well' on the top of the buttress was used when smallpox was rife in the village. Local farmers brought goods to the bridge for sale and collected their cash from the well, which was filled with disinfectant.

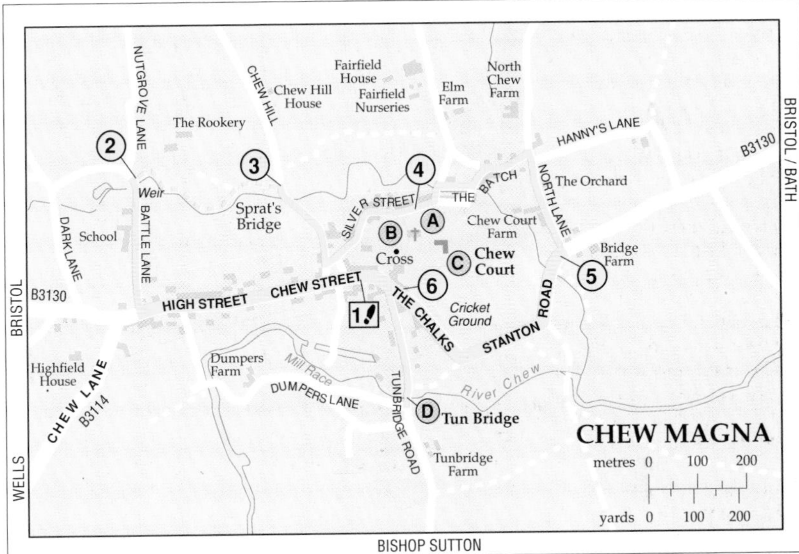

WALK DIRECTIONS

①

Start in Chew Street, near the post office. Go west, away from the Church. Chew Street soon becomes High Street. Keep walking to reach Battle Lane on the right and turn down this past the former Methodist church, now a Design Centre, to the weir bridge.

②

Just beyond the bridge a path leaves the road to the right, making its narrow way between a high stone wall, left, and rhododendrons and the stream, right. Follow the path to a kissing-gate. Beyond, follow the field path by the stream to reach a squeeze stile to Sprat's Bridge.

③

Go right along the road and near the small square turn left into Silver Street. Follow this to reach a stepped entrance, right, to the churchyard of St Andrew's Church.

④

Beyond the church go left of the Church Hall and then bear right to follow the stream which is on your right. At the T-junction turn right into North Lane and follow it to the B3130.

⑤

Walk right along the road, with care, passing the cricket field, to regain the village. Chew Court is on the right.

⑥

Turn immediately and sharply left, past the estate agent's, and follow the raised pavement to Tun Bridge. From there retrace your steps back to the village.

Looking across St Andrew's churchyard with the shaft of the old preaching cross in the foreground. St Andrew's, a mainly Norman church, is well worth a visit.

CHITTLEHAMPTON

DEVON

Off B3227, 8 miles SE of Barnstaple

MEANING 'Farm of the dwellers in the hollow' Chittlehampton is a Saxon name for a Saxon village, created early in the 8th century and still with its original plan.

In medieval times much of the land belonged to Tewkesbury Abbey and a tithe barn was set on Abbot's Hill behind the church, to collect rents in kind from tenants of the glebe land shared by abbey and church.

WALK DIRECTIONS

①

From the Square visit the church via the gate and avenue of limes. Return to the Square and turn left, between the churchyard and row of cottages. Turn right at the next track and walk down to East Street. The two thatched cottages called Rocklea were once a hotel and the outbuildings across the lane were its brewery.

②

Turn left down East Street and left again up the lane beside Rose Cottage to view the well. Return to East Street and view the pound beyond the cottage.

This beautifully preserved Victorian village pump stands in the village square.

③

Walk up East Street and take the track on the left just before the Square. Cross the field.

④

Pass under Blackmantle Cottage and turn right up the road to Townsend Cross.

⑤

Turn left along the road for a view down to Gambuston. Pronounced 'Gamston', this is a traditional cob and thatch Devon longhouse.

On the right of the road is Roger Cockram's Chittlehampton Pottery, housed in a wooden building next to Victoria House. It is a working pottery and shop, and is open to visitors. Return to Townsend Cross, and continue ahead to the Square. Turn left by the school and follow the track alongside the walled orchard to Lea Cottage.

⑥

Turn down in front of Lea Cottage and along an alley behind the Old Rolle Arms. Turn left at the main street and return to the Square.

For an optional excursion from point 5 turn left up the road, right at Biddacott Cross and on to Higher Biddacott farm. At the farm turn right, pass the farm buildings and turn right again through a metal gate. Cross the field to the next gate. Bear right, across this field to reach its bottom and then bear left along to the corner, heading towards the church tower. Cut diagonally across the next field to its right and pass through a wooden gate into a lane.

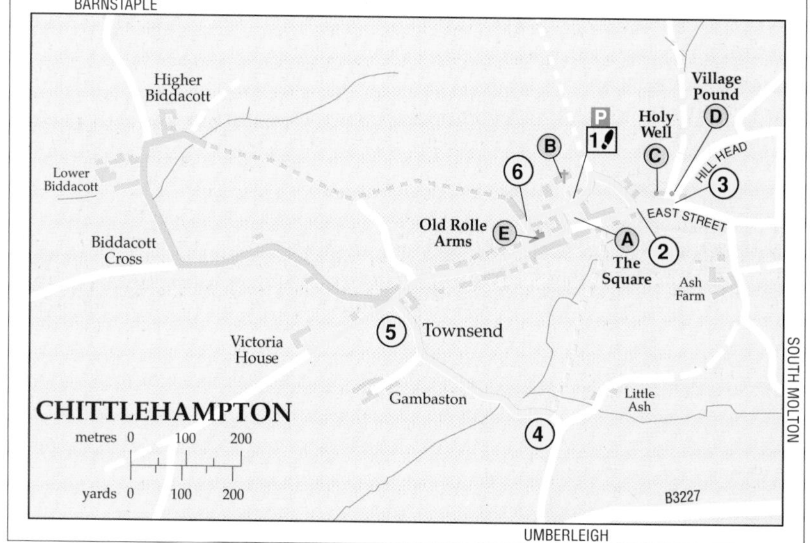

POINTS OF INTEREST

Ⓐ

The Square. This was probably the square or 'townplace' in Saxon times. It was later filled with thatched cottages which were demolished between 1876 and 1879. Opposite is the Bell Inn, built in 1888 by the Rolle estate, which owned much of the parish in the 19th century.

Ⓑ

St Hieritha's Church. 'Bishops Nympton for length, South Molton for strength, Chittlehampton for beauty' goes a local saying referring to the church's magnificent tower. For 1,000 years pilgrims came here to the shrine of St Hieritha. She is said to have been born at East Stowford, a mile to the north of the village, in the 6th century, and was converted to Christianity by missionaries. But as a Chrtistian she was made the scapegoat for a severe drought. Following a bad harvest she was killed by villagers with their scythes, and as she died water reputably gushed from the ground and flowers blossomed. A carving of her survives on the medieval pulpit.

Ⓒ

Holy Well. Said to mark the spot where St Hieritha was murdered. An ancient building around it was removed in Victorian times, when the well was capped and a pump fixed. On 8 July, the ceremony of St Hieritha's feast is held here.

Ⓓ

Village Pound. This was for retaining stray animals, which were then retrieved by their owners on payment of a fine. The area was cleared and restored in 1974 as a site for the village stocks.

Ⓔ

Old Rolle Arms. Formerly the King's Arms, this was one of seven inns which existed in the village in the 19th century. It may have been used by medieval pilgrims.

INFORMATION
Length of walk:
1¼ miles (2¼ miles if option followed)
Approximate time:
1 hour (1½ miles if option followed)

TERRAIN:
Suitable for children and pushchairs, except for option, which can be muddy at times.

PARKING:
Car park and toilets in the Square.

REFRESHMENTS:
The Bell Inn.

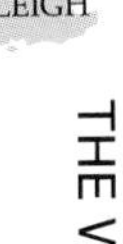

CHULMLEIGH

DEVON

Off A377, 15 miles SE of Barnstaple

CHULMLEIGH grew up at a crossing of ancient tracks near the junction of the Rivers Little Dart and Taw. Saxons came here and one, Ceolmund, settled in a clearing or leigh, giving the place its name. There is a strong tradition that King Alfred's grandson, Athelstan, stayed here and founded the church. By the time of the Domesday survey it was a prosperous sheep farming area.

The woollen industry prospered until the 18th century, when competition grew from other areas. The loss of American colonies resulted in the decline of North Devon ports and less trade passing through Chulmleigh. A new turnpike from Exeter to Barnstaple by-passed the town in 1830, as did the railway in 1854. The cattle market moved to the nearest station at Eggesford. Improvements in farming practices led to unemployment and new craft industries were started in the 1890s to solve the problem.

In recent years an industrial estate has grown up on the northern side of the town, together with housing estates, schools, library, police station and golf course. The core of the old town was destroyed by fires in 1803 and 1878, but the character of the old town was not lost; the plan survives and many old cob, stone and thatch cottages can still be found.

The old pump at the southern end of Fore Street was built for the use of the village market.

WALK DIRECTIONS

From the car park, walk into Church Street and enter the church by the lych-gate. Leave the churchyard by the gate on the north side.

2

Turn left to view Peel House, formerly the police station. The tops of two small cell windows can be seen on the west side. Turn right along New Street, passing the King's Arms. New Street was originally called Pound Street, and was renamed when it was rebuilt after the fire in 1803.

Turn right into Fore Street and continue to Academic Lane, just before which you can make a detour down Egypt Lane. This was the main road from Exeter until replaced by the gentler stagecoach route up Chulmleigh Hill. The name may refer to gypsies. Egypt Cottage retains much of its medieval character.

Turn left up Academic Lane by Turner's Garage, then left along East Street, passing the Congregational Chapel and Vicar's Stall. The modern sash windows and rendering on Silver House disguise the fact that this is an exceptionally old and complete cruck-framed merchant's house. At the road junction turn right up South Molton Street as far as the Barnstaple Inn passing the Old Bakehouse, now Philpots Tea Rooms.

Return to the road junction and turn right up Shute Street and Leigh Road.

6

Turn left down Ladywell Lane. Cross the footbridge after the cottages and follow the path up the hill and around the edge of the golf course.

Cross the stile to the alley between the cottages. Turn right and return to the car park. The Shippens was the site of the stock market and was filled with pens up to the churchyard wall. An annual sheep fair was held here each July until 1970. The fair continues, but without the sheep.

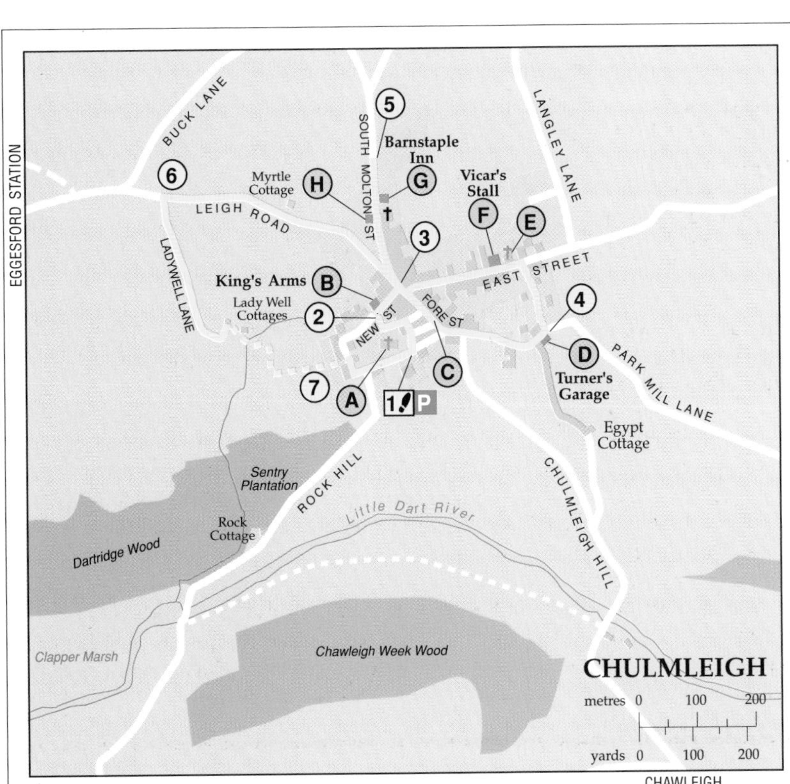

INFORMATION
Length of walk:
1¼ miles
Approximate time:
1½ hours

TERRAIN:
Easy going, suitable for children at all times of year.

PARKING:
Car park in Shippens, on south side of church. Toilets next to Town Hall.

REFRESHMENTS:
Pubs in the village.

The Barnstaple Inn (above) was once the local courthouse, with a gibbet above the main door. The medieval Egypt Cottage (right) stands in Egypt Lane, once the main road to Exeter.

THE COURTENAYS

In the 12th century the Courtenays, lords of the manor, started markets and fairs to increase trade, mainly linked with the woollen industry. However, Chulmleigh never received a charter as a borough. Although much altered externally, several cottages with cruck beams and plank and muntin (tongued and grooved) partitions have survived from this period. The church was then run on a collegiate basis, with seven prebends to serve surrounding villages without their own churches. The prebends held much land from the Courtenays and managed to keep it in 1539, when monasteries were dissolved and Henry Courtenay was dispossessed and executed for treason.

POINTS OF INTEREST

Church of St Mary Magdalene. The church largely dates from the 14th century, a time when the woollen industry prospered. Above the south doorway is an unusual Saxon stone carving of the crucifixion reminiscent of Cornish crosses and suggesting a much earlier foundation of the church. Inside is a wagon roof with fine bosses – almost 200, including a medieval king and queen – and 38 carved wooden angels on the corbels. A 16th-century screen runs the full width of the church, complete with some of its original paintwork and surmounted by 17th-century figures of the evangelists.

King's Arms. This was once a prosperous coaching inn. The extensive stables behind the inn were for coach horses on the long stage run from Barnstaple to Exeter. It was much frequented by gentry, including Jack Russell, the hunting parson who married a local lady. It lost trade with the opening of the new turnpike in 1830 and was converted into two houses in 1950.

Fore Street. At the north end of the street, the crossing of five ancient roads is the focal point and reason for the settlement, and at the south end was a market. The Town Hall was built as a market hall in 1846. A magistrates' court was held here and there were cells on the ground floor. The arcade, originally open for the market, was filled in about 1900 to make a basket-weaving workshop. Osiers were planted and skilled men brought from Somerset to teach locals and reduce unemployment. The pump outside is probably contemporary with the market for which it was used. The street suffered from the fires of 1803 and 1878; their extent can be seen by noting where slate has replaced thatch and extra storeys have been added with rebuilding.

Ⓓ

Turner's Garage. A boys' school here was replaced by the Secondary Modern school in 1937. Academic Lane was a short cut to the school, and Penny Cottage opposite reflects that it was a 'Penny School', when education was paid for by parents.

Ⓔ

Congregational Chapel. Inspired by merchant John Bowring in 1633, this is reputed to have been the second oldest foundation of its kind. The building dates from 1710 and has an outstanding interior of the period, with two galleries, minstrels' gallery and double-decker pulpit from the parish church.

Ⓕ

Vicar's Stall. This may have been built for the church as a prebend's house in the 15th century. According to legend, the original seven prebends were septuplets saved from drowning by the lady of the manor, Isabella de Fortibus. The present house is mainly 17th-century and contains fine coffered ceilings.

Ⓖ

Barnstaple Inn. A 17th-century or earlier inn with a royal coat of arms of 1633 in a bedroom where Charles I is dubiously reported to have slept. It was a court house at that time and there was a gibbet above the main door, where those found guilty of hanging offences were immediately executed.

Ⓗ

The Old Bakehouse. Now Philpots Tea Rooms, it was a 19th-century bakery and in the 16th century formed part of a wealthy merchant's house together with its two neighbours up the street. The three houses still retain the crucks, roof beams, winder staircase and plank and muntin (tongued and grooved) screens of an open hall medieval house. Many of the cottages in this block, including the Old Malthouse, are medieval in origin and are still divided by oak screens downstairs and wattle and daub ones in the attics.

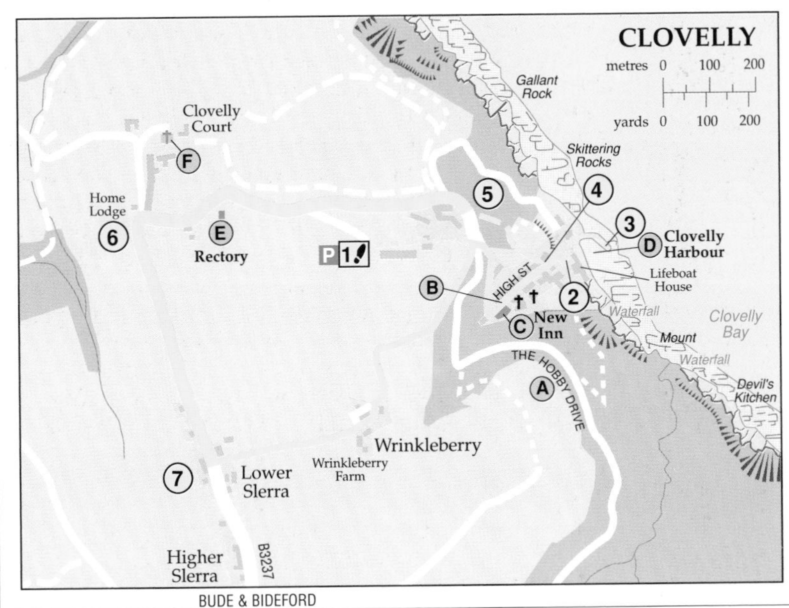

CLOVELLY

DEVON

Off A39, 10 miles W of Bideford

THE Domesday Book calls it Clovelia and the name may come from 'cleave lea' – cliff pasture. The original settlement was inland at Higher Clovelly. Medieval records show that the inhabitants gained some income from fishing.

The village really started with the building of the pier by George Carey in 1587. He diverted the stream which ran down to the harbour and put a cobbled street in its place. The Careys were lords of the manor from 1340 and the village continued in their hands until its sale in 1738 to Zachary Hamlyn. He left it to his great-nephews in the Hammet family. It was during their control in the late 18th and early 19th centuries that most of the present village was built.

The village gained fame in the mid 19th century through Charles Kingsley's *Westward Ho!*, along with several of his magazine articles and Dickens' *A Message from the Sea*. The main industry changed from fishing to tourism and the famous donkeys went from carrying baskets of herrings to carrying tourists and their luggage. Nowadays, most goods are man-handled down the steep cobbled streets on sledges.

INFORMATION
Length of walk: 2½ miles
Approximate time: 2 hours

TERRAIN:
Land Rovers convey passengers between the main road and the harbour, but the walk requires a degree of fitness and sure-footedness and is not suitable for pushchairs or wheelchairs.

PARKING:
One large car park off the road into the village. Toilets are at visitor centre, High Street and harbour.

OPEN:
Access for motorists is via the visitor centre. All year. Charge.

REFRESHMENTS:
Selection of pubs and cafés in the village.

High Street, Clovelley's main cobbled street which descends 400ft to the sea.

POINTS OF INTEREST

Ⓐ

Hobby Drive. The three-mile drive was built between 1811 and 1829 as the hobby of James Hamlyn-Williams, with help from soldiers left unemployed after the Napoleonic wars. He planted many of the surrounding trees in the romantic wilderness style new at the time. Today it is a one-way toll road which forms part of the South West Peninsula Coast Path.

High Street. This starts at the fountain erected by Christine Hamlyn for the Diamond Jubilee of Queen Victoria. The street is known as 'Up-along' or 'Down-along' according to which way you are looking. On Shrove Tuesday local children drag strings of cans up and down the street, supposedly to frighten the Devil out of Clovelly before Lent.

New Inn. Originally called The Inn, it was situated across the street until the First World War, when it was rebuilt on the site of its stables and cottages opposite. In the dining room hangs a portrait of Christine Hamlyn, who is said to haunt it.

D

Harbour. The huge stone blocks on the inner side of the quay are reputed to date from the 14th century. It was mostly built in 1587, and guns captured from the Spanish Armada were used as bollards. It was enlarged in 1808, when Clovelly was a major herring fishing port with 60-70 boats. They were mostly small boats known as 'picarooners', which could be hauled up on the beach when the tide was out of the harbour. Small ketches brought coal and limestone from Wales for the limekiln, now used as a boathouse.

Rectory. Charles Kingsley was curate, then rector here from 1831 to 1836. He had three sons, one of whom was also called Charles and became a clergyman. It was the son who returned to what is now Kingsley's Cottage in the High Street to write *The Water Babies* and *Westward Ho!*.

All Saints' Church. The church has many Norman features including the font, part of the tower and the arch of the south door with its zig-zag moulding. The 14th-century north aisle has granite pillars quarried on Lundy Island. There is a Jacobean pulpit with hourglass and unusual Jacobean pew ledges used as firearm rests. Memorials to the Carey family include a brass to Robert Carey (1540), dressed as a knight in armour.

Also in the High Street is the old surgery, a cottage whose door is decorated with carved fruit and flowers.

THE HAMLYNS

The estate was inherited through several generations of females, and both heirs and heiresses assumed the name of Hamlyn. They carefully controlled and preserved the village; particularly Christine Hamlyn, who inherited the estate in 1884.

Many houses have date plaques from 1914 to 1925 with her initials, showing when she had them restored. She ornamented cottages with carved woodwork and plaster panelling and had them modernised, improving the water supply and sanitation. However, she kept at bay the motor car and commercial developments which were likely to spoil the village. She controlled the village firmly but maternalistically and was a much-liked character, dressing herself like Little Bo Beep, complete with bonnet and shepherd's crook. When she died in 1936 the estate passed to her daughter, who married Arthur Asquith, son of Prime Minister Asquith, who was a frequent visitor. It now belongs to their grandson, Hon. John Rous.

The Peace Park was given to the National Trust by Christine Hamlyn as a war memorial. The cross is a memorial to her nephew, John Manners, who would have inherited Clovelly had he not been killed in the First World War.

Once a quiet herring fishing village, the tiny harbour here has a curving pier.

WALK DIRECTIONS

From the car park walk through the visitor centre. At the foot of the path beyond, cross to the head of the cobbled street, passing the Hobby Drive. Descend the High Street, pass the New Inn and detour right up Providence Row for St Peter's Chapel, a Church of England 'chapel of ease' for those parishioners who find the climb to the parish church too tiring. It was consecrated in 1846 and reopened in 1948 after a long lapse. Nearby is a Methodist Chapel of 1820. Continue down the High Street passing the Old Surgery, a cottage decorated with carved fruit and flowers ordered from Oberammergau in Germany by Christine Hamlyn in 1910.

Pass under the Temple Bar, home of *Westward Ho!* character Salvation Yeo, and turn right down Shamshackle Steps. Turn left at the bottom and along Fish Street, past Crazy Kate's Cottage, to the quay and harbour. The long narrow cottage with slated verandah was the home of Kate Lyall, who died in 1736. She used to watch her lover fishing at sea from the verandah and is said to have gone mad when she saw him drown.

Return up the High Street. The Red Lion inn is on the site of three cider houses which served fishermen. The bars were formerly cellars for coal unloaded on the quay.

Halfway up High Street, turn right up North Hill. The street becomes a track, passing round the Peace Park to join the main road.

Turn right and follow the road up past the Rectory to the gates at Home Lodge.

Detour right along the lane indicated to the church. Next door is Clovelly Court. Return to the road and continue up the hill.

Turn left past the village hall to Wrinkleberry. Continue past the school and down the lane, which becomes sunken and cobbled. At the bottom of the lane, turn left back to the car park.

CORFE CASTLE

DORSET

On A351, 5 miles S of Wareham

UNTIL the 14th century this was simply called Corfe, a Saxon word meaning 'gap'. The castle stands in the gap in the Purbeck Hills created by the Wicken and Byle streams.

A major ancient route, the ridgeway along the Purbeck Hills, passed through Corfe. The medieval village however, developed towards the south, whence came the limestone which made it prosperous.

The village has not prospered since the 18th century and the old part has changed little from then. The 20th-century Bankes Arms is virtually the only addition. The outlines of medieval burgage plots along West Street are still clear, whilst those along East Street were truncated by the railway, now closed. Recent development in East Street has been sympathetically undertaken.

The Ancient Order of Marblers and Stonecutters still meets at the Town Hall on Shrove Tuesday. Then they kick a football from the Fox Inn over the heath to Ower Farm at Swanage, where they pay the football and a pound of pepper for the use of Ower Quay, from which Purbeck marble was once shipped.

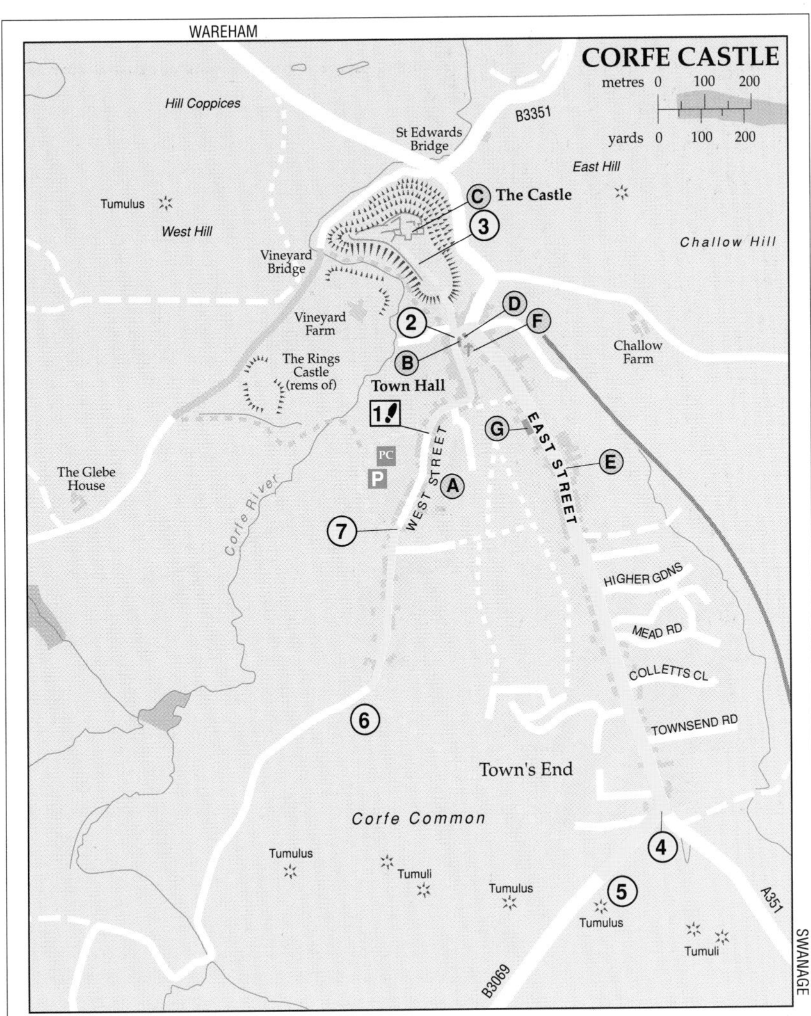

INFORMATION

Length of walk:
1½ miles (2½ miles if option followed)
Approximate time:
1¼ hours (2 hours if option followed)

TERRAIN:
Suitable for children at all times of year, easy going and mostly level except for climb to castle and option.

PARKING:
Car park and toilets off West Street.

OPEN:
Castle. Daily mid Feb-early Nov and winter weekends; National Trust. Charge.

REFRESHMENTS:
The National Trust shop and various pubs and cafés in the village.

WALK DIRECTIONS

1. Leave the car park at the cemetery end, turn left and walk down West Street, passing the Town Hall.

2. Pass the Fox Inn, dating from 1568 and probably the oldest inn in the village. It has a very narrow frontage on to West Street and the parlour wall has a 'squint' (hagioscope) through it. At The Square turn left. Reach the castle entrance, and go through to see the castle.

3. Return to the Square and continue to the junction with East Street, past the Town House. Walk the full length of East Street, passing the church and Morton's House, built around 1600 for the Dacombe family. It was later split into three tenements, which have now been rejoined as a hotel. Finally, pass John Uvedale's House.

Looking towards the ruins of the 11th-century castle, which dominates the village in the foreground.

The value of the local Purbeck marble led to the village becoming the headquarters of an ancient organisation of craftsmen. Local stonemasons (right) became influential people.

PURBECK INDUSTRIES

Purbeck marble is a limestone which will take a polish like marble and was a much-valued building stone. It was used in many medieval churches and cathedrals. Henry VIII used it to build forts, and many of London's streets were paved with it in the 18th century. Masons from Corfe Castle became wealthy and influential people, but the industry had died out by the 19th century.

An important industry which still exists is ball clay working. There were clay pits just north of the castle with tramways to quays in Poole Harbour, which were abandoned in 1954 in favour of road transport. The clay was originally dug with a curved spade, which shaped it into the 9-inch diameter balls which gave it its name. Nowadays it is dug by machine. Purbeck still supplies 15-20% of the national demand for pottery clay.

④

At the road junction turn right on to B3069. Keep to the right-hand side. In 200yds, turn right through the gate on to the common, marked with National Trust and bridleway signs.

There are several paths, but keep straight ahead towards the edge of the common. The path leads to a wooden fence and cattle grid.

Turn right by the cattle grid and walk down West Street.

Return to the car park by the coach park entrance.

For an optional excursion continue down West Street to The Square. Turn towards the entrance to the castle, but before the entrance turn left down a footpath marked with yellow waymarks.

At the road turn left over Vineyard Bridge and walk up the road. On the left are The Rings, site of a fort made by King Stephen in 1139 when he unsuccessfully besieged Corfe. It is also known as Cromwell's Battery as it was the site of a battery used to besiege the castle during the Civil War.

Shortly after The Rings, cross the stile by the gate on the left and follow the yellow waymarks. Cross the stile at the other end of the field and after the next field cross the footbridge over the Corfe River. The path leads back to the car park.

POINTS OF INTEREST

Ⓐ

West Street. This was originally the main street, now petering out across the common, still scored with tracks made by horse-drawn sledges carrying marble here, and the centre of the medieval stone cutting industry. Many 'bankers' – stone benches on which masons worked – stood in the street, which is built on up to 10ft of stone waste. Some of the 18th-century mason's houses have diamond-shaped datestones of Purbeck marble above their doorways. None are earlier than the 17th century, and some of the older thatched cottages were the homes of ball clay workers. Wayfaring Cottage, No. 49, has an unusual combination of thatch with stone tiles under the dormer windows.

Town Hall. This is reputed to be Britain's smallest town hall. The present building dates from 1770. It has a council chamber on the first floor, approached from the side, and lock-up cells on the ground floor. These are now a free museum of ball clay working, quarrying and country crafts.

The Castle. This site was fortified by the 9th century and extended as the residence of King Edgar in the 10th century. In 978 his son, King Edward (The Martyr) was murdered here by his stepmother, Queen Aelfthryth. The well in which she hid his body became known as St Edward's fountain and was said to have miraculous healing properties.

The present buildings, dating from 1080, were used to hold royal prisoners, and one dungeon could only be entered by a trapdoor in the roof. King John left 22 French knights to starve here. The castle seemed impregnable and withheld two sieges in the Civil War, when it was held for the Crown by Lady Bankes. It eventually fell in 1646 through treachery and was demolished the same year. The ruins are the focal point of an estate of more than 7,000 acres given to the National Trust by the late Ralph Bankes in 1982.

Town House. This 18th-century building overlooks the Square – the former market place with the steps of a 14th-century market cross on which a new cross was placed in 1897 for Queen Victoria's Diamond Jubilee. The first floor is entered from the churchyard behind. The large window in the central bay lit the Mayor's Robing Room. Below on the ground floor was a small house, now a bank.

East Street. Originally a cul-de-sac, this became the main through-road in the 19th century when the boggy area to the south-east was filled in. Many of the houses were rebuilt in the 18th century with stone from the castle. The oldest is No. 38, which dates from the 15th century.

Church of St Edward the Martyr. The church was damaged in the castle siege of 1646 and later repaired. Much was rebuilt in 1860, but the 15th-century tower with pinnacles and gargoyles survives. In the Chapel of the Holy Spirit are two Purbeck marble tablets of similar age with Latin inscriptions. Translations are provided together with a plan of the memorials on the floor. There are medieval carvings in local stone and there is an array of headstones and 13th-century coffin lids against the churchyard wall. Over the central aisle is a striking diamond-shaped picture of Christ in Glory painted by Ken Ward in 1982.

Ⓖ

John Uvedale's House. The house was built in 1575 for the mayor of Corfe Castle and later divided into six tenements, which are now approached from the rear, the main doorway having been blocked. The village was most prosperous in the 16th and 17th centuries, and many buildings were later split when prosperity declined.

John Uvedale's House, built as a single dwelling was then divided into tenements in less prosperous times.

COCKINGTON
DEVON

Between A379 and B3203, 1½ miles W of Torquay centre

FOR most of its history Cockington has been a hamlet overshadowed by its neighbour Torre, now Torquay. A Domesday manor, it was one of many owned by its pre-conquest lord, Alric. The lord had a chapel of ease, which was leased by the canons of nearby Torre Abbey from 1196. From then until the Abbey's dissolution in 1539 life in this agricultural hamlet was determined by the abbots and the de Cockington and Carey families, lords of the manor.

The present appearance of the village is largely due to the building and preservation of the Mallock family, lords of Cockington from 1654 until 1932.

WALK DIRECTIONS

From main car park, turn right up Cockington Lane to the almshouses.

Return to the near side of the Drum Inn and turn right up the lane alongside the inn, which was designed by Sir Edwin Lutyens and completed in 1936.

A wooden gate on the left leads into the park beside the cricket pavilion. The bank is steep here; pushchairs and wheelchairs should continue up the lane to Cockington Court. Pass in front of the Court, around the church and down the drive to the crossroads near Higher Lodge.

Pushchairs and wheelchairs should proceed from here straight to 7 to avoid steps.

Turn left down the path signposted to the Drum Inn, then right alongside the mill-pond and down the steps to the back of the mill.

Pass under the thatched archway into Cockington Lane. Turn right and walk up the hill to Higher Lodge, passing the Forge and Weaver's Cottage.

Walking up from the lodge, turn left down the track and through the arch under Totnes Road. Keep ahead to Gamekeeper's Cottage.

Turn left, passing in front of the cottage. Keeping the ponds to the left, continue downhill and go under the arch of Lower Lodge into Cockington Lane.

⑧

Turn left to the car park.

INFORMATION
Length of walk:
1 mile
Approximate time:
1 hour

TERRAIN:
Suitable for children at all times of year; suitable for pushchairs and wheelchairs except for optional loop and loop around mill-pond and mill.

PARKING:
There is a large car park in Cockington Lane to the west of the crossroads, and a smaller one in Totnes Road.

REFRESHMENTS:
Inns and cafés in the village. Wide selection of eating places in Torquay.

Thatched cottages at Cockington.

POINTS OF INTEREST

Almshouses. A row of seven houses built by the Rev. Roger Mallock in 1840, they replaced almshouses formerly built by Sir George Carey in 1620.

Cockington Court. Originally a Saxon manor, the present house was built to an E-shaped plan by the Carey family in Tudor times, but was given its 18th-century façade by the Mallock family.

Church of St George and St Mary. As it was not a parish church until 1881, it does not have a churchyard. It is largely of the 13th and 14th centuries on Norman foundations. There was considerable restoration after it was hit by a bomb in 1943.

The Flower's or Customary Mill. A mill operated here from 1435 until the Second World War, when it became an ammunition store. The waterwheel is dated 1878.

Cockington Forge. The building dates from the 14th century. The last blacksmith left in 1971, but furnace, bellows and anvils remain.

Weaver's Cottage. Since 1939 this has been a handloom weaver's workshop and craft shop. Together with the Studio next door it was part of the Home Farm for the Court. These and Higher Cottage, up the hill, are reputed to have Saxon origins.

Lower Lodge. A remarkable Gothic style gatehouse in red sandstone and grit, with an arched niche in the chimney stack.

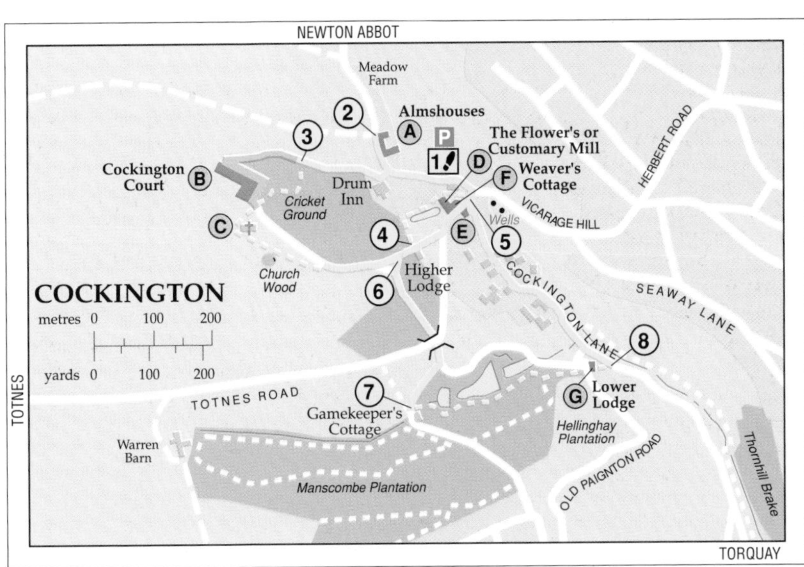

DUNTISBOURNE ABBOTS

THE WEST COUNTRY

DUNTISBOURNE ABBOTS

GLOUCESTERSHIRE

Off A417, 6 miles NW of Cirencester

The buff-coloured, weather-worn limestone of a Duntisbourne cottage (above) contrasts sharply with the bright coloured beauty of a stained glass window in St Peter's Church (top).

THE four Duntisbourne villages strung out along a tiny stream in its quiet, folded valley are among the most beautiful in the Cotswolds. We visit the upper two, Duntisbourne Abbots and Duntisbourne Leer. The next village is called, simply, Middle Duntisbourne, the last is Duntisbourne Rouse.

It is believed that the valley was named after a Saxon chieftain, Dunt, who owned the land around the valley's bourne, or stream, but the existence of two local long barrows suggest that even when Dunt came here the valley was an old site. This highest Duntisbourne village is distinguished by the addition of 'Abbots', denoting that it belonged, in medieval times, to the Abbey of Gloucester. Close to the telephone box on the route to Leer is an old iron animal drinking-trough, still in working order.

WALK DIRECTIONS

①

From the church, face down the valley with the church behind you and take the path, left, down past the post box. Go right on to a path past Devenport House and down to the telephone box. Walk on along the valley road. Soon you will reach the ford. Avoid this by following the raised pavement on its right. Walk uphill slightly to reach Duntisbourne Leer.

②

Turn right at the unsigned T-junction and bear right at the Y-junction and right again (signed Duntisbourne Abbots ½-mile) soon after. On the new lane the poppies and cornflowers are a delight in summer and there are superb views of Duntisbourne Abbots over the hedge on the right.

③

At a T-junction turn right (signed Birdlip 6, Cirencester 6) and bear right at the next junction (signed as before) to reach the top of the village. Now either take the first right, passing a thatched outhouse (an unusual sight in the Cotswolds where few buildings are thatched, most being roofed in Cotswold slates) or continue to the Youth Hostel and turn right in front of it.

POINTS OF INTEREST

St Peter's Church. The Abbots church is reached through a swinging lych-gate. A path between wired yews leads through a churchyard dotted with fine table tombs to reach an Early English doorway. It is a surprise to find that it is not in its original position, having been dismantled and carefully re-erected when the church was widened. Inside there is a fine timbered roof and an interesting memorial to Dr Matthew Baillie, a famous London doctor who died in the village in 1823.

Duntisbourne Ford. The ford is unusual for running along the stream rather than across, and comes as a great surprise to drivers who round the bend expecting a few yards of shallow water and instead find themselves confronted by a long stretch of deep stream. Some have suggested that the road was deliberately run along the stream bed so that carts would benefit. It was the old practice to soak wooden cartwheels in water to prevent shrinkage – a walled tip can still be seen near Chipping Campden church further north – and what better way than to run them through a stream? Others say that the Duntisbourne valley was so tight there was no choice but to run the road here, pointing out that this ford, though the best, is not the valley's only example.

Ⓒ

Duntisbourne Leer. The smaller village of Leer is also named for its possessor church, though here it was not local, the Normans having given the village to the Abbaye of Notre Dame de Lyre in Normandy.

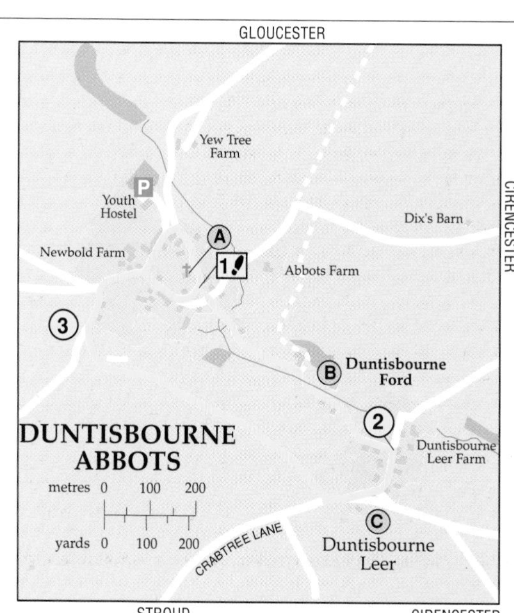

INFORMATION
Length of walk:
1½ miles
Approximate time:
1 hour

TERRAIN:
Suitable for children, pushchairs and wheelchairs at all times of year.

PARKING:
There is limited parking in Duntisbourne Abbots, at the top of the village by the Youth Hostel (the old Rectory) or in front of the church.

Looking towards the yarn market with the castle in the background.

INFORMATION
Length of walk:
2 miles
Approximate time:
1½ hours

TERRAIN:
Mostly level and easy going, with some uphill walking on the Grabbist section. Conduit Lane can be wet in places. Not suitable for pushchairs or wheelchairs.

PARKING:
Car park and toilets in Dunster Steep, near the junction of A39 and A396.

OPEN:
Dunster Castle. (National Trust) Apr-Oct Mon-Thu and Sun.
Dunster Mill. Apr-Oct Sun-Fri (Daily Jul-Aug).

REFRESHMENTS:
Selection of inns and cafés in the village.

DUNSTER

SOMERSET

On A396, 2 miles SE of Minehead

AFTER the Norman conquest, William de Mohun was given 69 manors in the West Country. He chose to make Dunster the administrative centre of his estates and the village grew in the shelter of his castle. By the 12th century it was a borough and by the 13th it had markets and fairs. It was sold to the Luttrells in the 14th century.

The village became a busy centre for manufacturing a heavy cloth known as Dunsters. Most households were involved in spinning or weaving and there were several fulling mills and dyeworks by the river. Trade prospered until the 18th century, when the area was outcompeted by mechanised centres in the north and east of England. Trades such as millers, tailors, saddlers, wheelwrights, smiths, watchmakers and candle-makers continued until recent years. Minehead and Taunton are now the service centres and Dunster's shops are given over to tourism. However, its comparative lack of recent development has preserved the village.

WALK DIRECTIONS

1

From the car park, turn left up Dunster Steep. Keep round to the left and walk down High Street, passing the Luttrell Arms and the Yarn market. Go straight up Castle Hill to the castle.

Return to the High Street and turn left into Church Street, passing the Nunnery, which was built soon after 1346, when the site was granted to the Abbot and Convent of Cleeve. It was called High House until the 18th century and was never actually used by nuns. Continue to the end of the street to reach the church. Leave the church and turn right, walking through the churchyard and out through the lych-gate. Turn right to the Priory. Take the doorway in the wall opposite the dovecot into the memorial garden.

Return to Church Street. (It may be possible to short-cut back through the church via its north door.) Turn right and follow West Street to its junction with Mill Lane. Turn left and follow the leat to the mill. This working mill is possibly on the site of one of the two mentioned in Domesday Book. The present building dates from the 17th century, and was extensively restored in 1780 and in 1980. Unusually, it has two overshot wheels.

Return up Mill Lane for 100yds and take the path between the bungalows to the left. Keep to the left and continue on to Gallox Bridge.

Return straight up Park Street to West Street. Turn left and keep to the edge of this busy road, noting the village pound on the left and the toll house on the right.

At the road junction turn right and take the path doubling back through the woods. Keep ahead without forking. The path is joined by Goosey Path and gradually climbs through woodland along Ducky Path.

Turn right down Conduit Lane. Just past the double bend you see St Leonard's Well on the right. Water from here was taken along pipes to the priory and through to the arch in the churchyard wall, later occupied by stocks. It still feeds a well in St George's Street. The wellhouse is 16th-century. At the junction, turn left up St George's Street.

At the Butter Cross, turn right and take the footpath over the field behind it. The cross once stood in the market place at the foot of Castle Hill where dairy produce was sold (hence the name) but was moved here about 1825 when wooden shops known as The Shambles and other market buildings were demolished. Continue along Priory Green and The Ball to return to the car park.

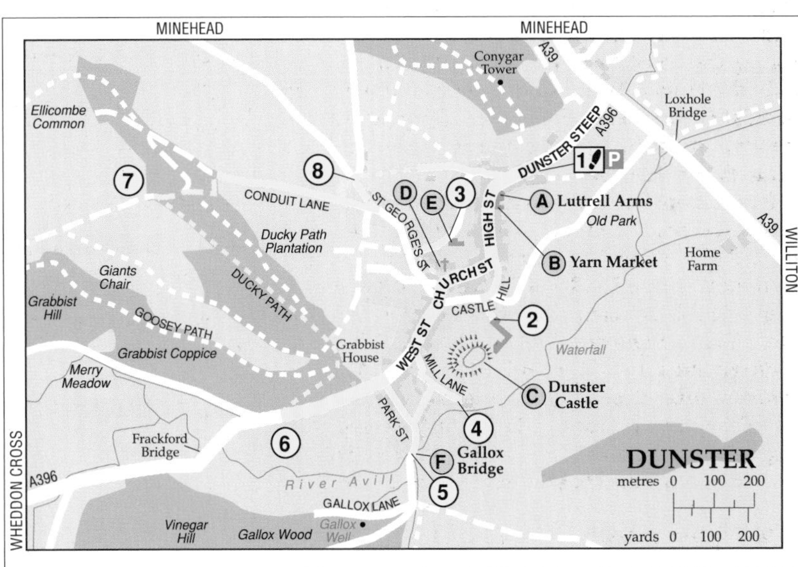

POINTS OF INTEREST

A

Luttrell Arms. This was built in the 15th century as the guest house of the abbots of Cleeve Abbey. Many medieval features include the hall and yard with carvings around the windows to the abbot's kitchen. In the 17th century it became an inn, and stone from the ruined castle was used to build the entrance porch.

B

Yarn Market. This was probably built in 1547 by George Luttrell; it was restored in 1647 after being damaged in the siege of Dunster Castle. There is still a hole in one beam made by a cannonball fired from the castle. The belfry was used to signal the start of the day's market, and merchants spread their cloth on the wide oak-topped walls.

Dunster Castle. Started by the de Mohuns soon after 1066, the oldest surviving part is the 13th-century gateway. Many of the medieval buildings were remodelled in the 17th century when the house was enlarged. The castle was besieged during 1645 and 1646 and was held for the King. Its defences were demolished but the house was saved and in the following century the grounds were landscaped by artist Richard Phelps, who built ornate bridges and Conygar Tower opposite. Reconstructed in the 1860s under architect Anthony Salvin, the internal features of the house are largely Victorian in character. In 1975 it was acquired by the National Trust, after 600 years of occupancy by the Luttrell family.

St George's Church. The church was conveyed to Bath Abbey by William de Mohun in the late 11th century and was rebuilt by the monks early in the 12th century as a priory church. Inside is an exceptional fan-vaulted rood screen, the longest in England, built about 1500 to separate the chancels of the parishioners and Benedictine monks.

Priory. Looking from the gateway, to the left is the Norman dovecot, restored in 1988 but still containing its original woodwork. Inside are about 500 nest holes for pigeons, which provided fresh meat in winter. After the dissolution of the priory in 1539 it became the property of the Luttrells, who would serve several hundred squabs (young pigeons) at castle banquets.

Ahead is the 16th-century tithe barn, used for storing rents in kind from church and priory tenants – mainly wool in this case. To the right is a garage built for storing lime from kilns in Alcombe. Beyond is the prior's house, now a private house. Adjacent is the walled cloister garden, still with herbs as would have been used by monks, and the castle kitchen garden, now a park.

Gallox Bridge. Several packhorse bridges were built in this area from medieval times until the 18th century, mainly resulting from the woollen trade. This one was known as Doddebridge in the 14th century; its name was changed when gallows were erected at the crossroads beyond the bridge during the reign of Henry VIII.

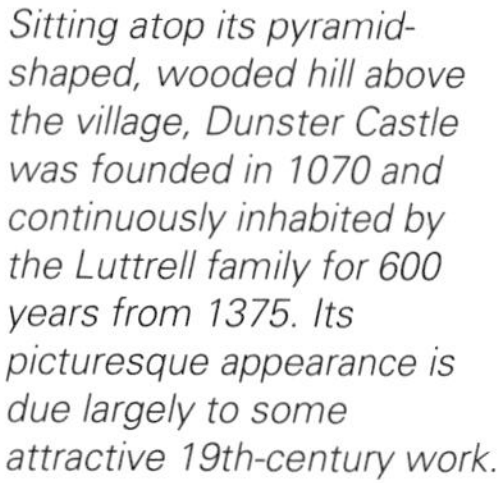

Sitting atop its pyramid-shaped, wooded hill above the village, Dunster Castle was founded in 1070 and continuously inhabited by the Luttrell family for 600 years from 1375. Its picturesque appearance is due largely to some attractive 19th-century work.

MARSH STREET

This suburb, to the north-east of Dunster, ran alongside the Fowler's Marsh in the Avill estuary, and its inhabitants made their living from fishing and shipbuilding. An 18th-century packhorse bridge and several old cob, stone and thatch cottages survive. Peep Hole Cottage has 'squints' from the living room through a porch to provide a view up the street.

Lower Marsh House, now the Old Manor, was built on an area of firm ground before the 13th century, although the present home with its own chapel dates from the 16th century. It belonged to wealthy families who were merchants or castle officials.

The station was built in 1874, when the West Somerset Railway was extended from Watchet to Minehead. The line was closed by British Rail in 1971, but re-opened privately in 1976.

The 16th-century yarn market in the centre of High Street.

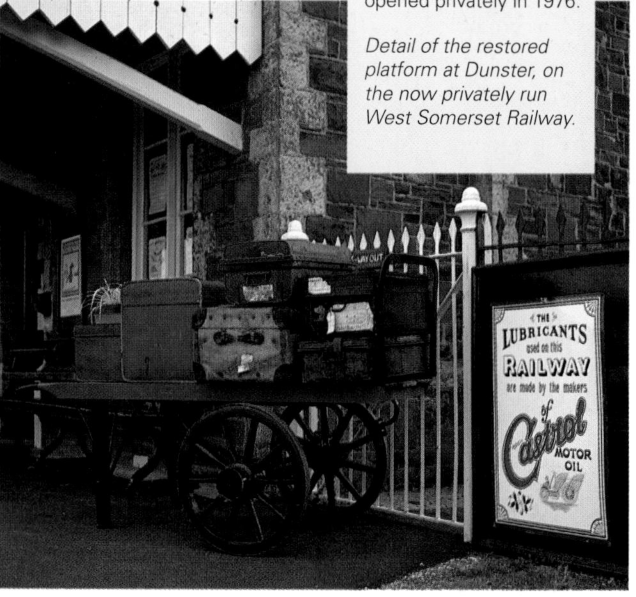

Detail of the restored platform at Dunster, on the now privately run West Somerset Railway.

GUITING POWER

GLOUCESTERSHIRE

Between B4068 and B4077, 6 miles W of Stow-on-the-Wold

Of modest size, the village is set upon a gently swelling ridge above the River Windrush, surrounded by higher wolds. It is blessed with a significant social vitality, which has at its roots the foresight stemming from the 1930s when houses were purchased and held exclusively for village people. In 1977 a Trust was formed to secure the future of the village lands, reserving half the housing stock for the local community.

POINTS OF INTEREST

Ⓐ

Saxon Village Site. The site, in the 'close' adjacent to the Old Manor House, has revealed what appears to be the original Saxon nucleus of Guiting. It is thought this could even be the stronghold of Alwyn, the last Saxon Lord of Guiting. The clear outline of the church has been found together with evidence of Roman and Iron Age use.

Ⓑ

The Green. The banked Green features a pleasing surround of traditional Cotswold-style village houses. The War Memorial replaced a market cross; several stones from the cross lie beneath.

Ⓒ

Th'ollow Bottom. Ye Olde Inne has been a public house for two centuries. Linked to it is Cloud Hill Cottage, with a smiling sun Fire Union plaque on the wall. By displaying this device, if fire broke out the Victorian householder could call the fire brigade.

Ⓓ

Well Lane. Above the spring, notice the wall which lines the road to the right. It contains one solitary pipe-like stone, a remnant of the ill-fated 19th-century pipe-making venture in the parish: Manchester Corporation lost nearly £40,000 after laying the pipes to carry a water main in the city, only to see it burst under pressure.

Ⓔ

St Michael's Church. This old church has undergone major changes, most notably in the 19th century. Both the north and south transepts were lengthened, creating a cruciform plan, upon the 15th-century tower. A Norman doorway was reset as the entrance in the south transept.

WALK DIRECTIONS

①

From the village hall turn left along Church Road past the village school. Reaching The Green, turn left and follow Winchcombe road, to Th'ollow Bottom. (See below for optional extra.)

②

Return towards the small banked green and turn left down the 'tewer' (narrow path), to the right of 'Chestnuts'. Entering Castlett Street go left, turn right at Close Cottage, go along the path to a stile, then down the pasture locating the stile at the foot of Well Lane.

③

Cross the stile and follow Well Lane up to The Green. Turn left, following the main road past the guesthouse, Farmers Arms and Greenfield House. The Saxon Village site is on your right.

④

Beyond the stone barn turn right at the gates, and follow the footpath up to St Michael's Church, passing through the churchyard to conclude the walk.

The War Memorial cross on Guiting Power green, flanked by a neat row of cotswold stone cottages with stone roofs.

INFORMATION
Length of walk:
1 mile
Approximate time:
½ hour

TERRAIN:
One flight of steps makes part of the basic route unsuitable for pushchairs and wheelchairs. Suitable for children.

PARKING:
Village Hall Car Park ('trust the motorist' charge).

OPEN:
Cotswold Farm Park.
1 Apr-31 Sep 10.30am-6pm. Charge.

REFRESHMENTS:
Ye Olde Inne, The Farmers Arms and the Cotswold Farm Park.

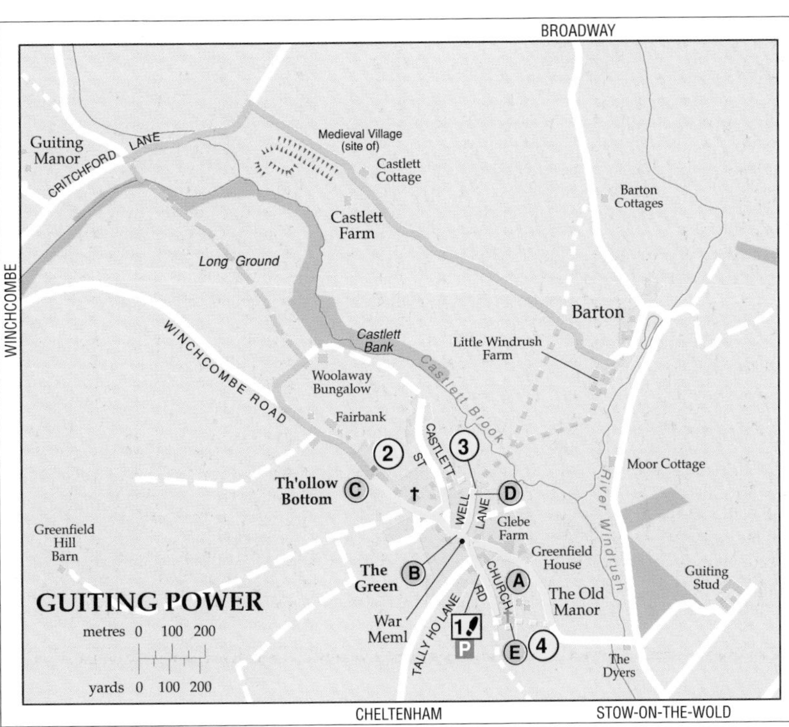

For an optional route of two miles from 2: continue beyond Ye Olde Inne at Th'ollow Bottom, branching right down the track, signed 'unsuitable for motors'. Go left opposite Woolaway Bungalow, along the unenclosed track, through Long Ground. Beyond the gate ascend to the road directly below Guiting Manor.

Go right along the road via the road gate and ford, rising to turn right, signed Castlett Farm. Follow this for ¾ mile.

Where a stile invites a right turn go down beside a new hedge: alternatively continue into Barton, there turning right along a footpath, crossing four stiles to meet the earlier path. Cross the Castlett Brook footbridge, to enter Well Lane at point 3.

LYDFORD
DEVON

Off A386, 8 miles SW of Okehampton

IN a naturally defensive position above a gorge and on the edge of the Saxon kingdom of Wessex, Lydford was fortified by Alfred the Great around AD880. It became a *burh*, one of the five Saxon towns in Devon, and remained a royal borough until 1239, when it became part of the Earldom (later Duchy) of Cornwall.

Harsh stannery (tin mining) laws and savage 'justice' protected the Duchy's hunting and mineral rights. For instance, a man found adulterating tin would have three spoonfuls of the molten mixture poured down his throat.

INFORMATION
Length of walk: 1½ miles
Approximate time: 1 hour

TERRAIN:
Mixed: main streets level and easy for pushchairs and wheelchairs, but steep hills are encountered on visits to the gorge and lych way and the gorge is precarious in places.

PARKING:
Car park and toilets off main street opposite Castle Inn.

OPEN:
Lydford Gorge. Daily Easter-Oct. Charge.

REFRESHMENTS:
Castle Inn.

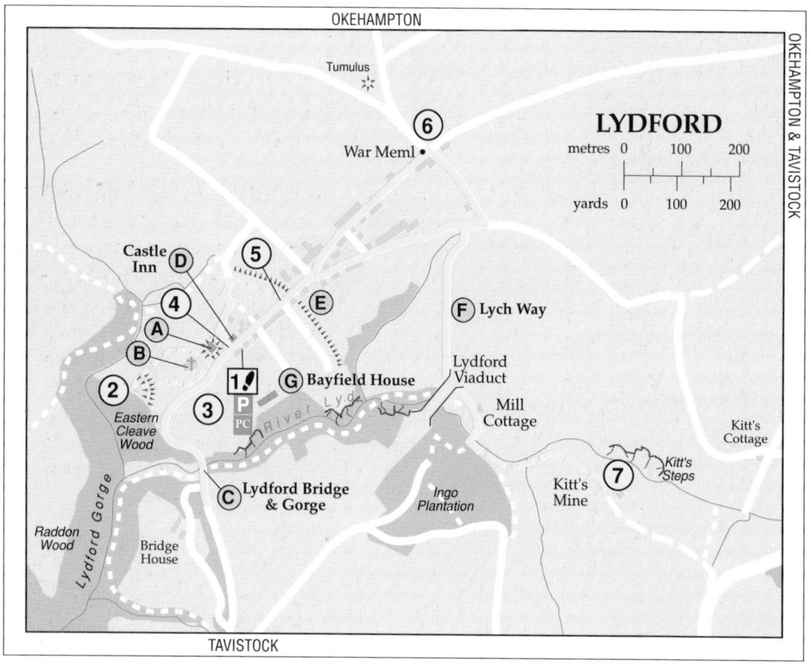

POINTS OF INTEREST

Ⓐ

The Castle. A castle was built on this site about 1195. It is now hidden under the mount of the present castle, which was built in the 13th century. It became a prison in the 14th century and continued as such until the 17th century. It is supposed to be haunted by a black pig, reputedly a reincarnation of Judge Jeffreys, who held court here.

Ⓑ

St Petrock's Church. St Petrock was a 6th-century Welsh prince who studied in Ireland and came to Devon and Cornwall as a missionary. His oratory here was covered by the church, which in turn was rebuilt in the 11th and 13th centuries.

Ⓒ

Lydford Bridge and Gorge. The single-span bridge existed before 1478, but has been rebuilt and widened since. It towers 60ft above the Devil's Cauldron, a pot hole in the River Lyd.

Ⓓ

Castle Inn. The inn dates from the 16th century. Displayed inside are four Lydford pennies, coins of locally mined silver struck by the Lydford royal mint between 975 and 1050. They were paid as Danegeld – a tax imposed by Viking invaders.

Ⓔ

Saxon Defences. These are best preserved where they cross the neck of the promontory between two arms of the gorge and are cut by the main street. The narrow side lanes, follow the Saxon town plan.

Ⓕ

Lych Way. Coffins were carried along this route to the church from outlying parts of this vast parish.

Ⓖ

Bayfield House. The vicarage was built for the Rev. Chafry in 1870 by the architect of London's law courts. The arch bears the arms of the Inns of Court.

Lydford Castle and the Castle Inn.

WALK DIRECTIONS

①

Leave the car park, turn left and cross the road to the castle. Enter the castle from the rear, then cut across the field to the rear of the church to view the earthworks of the earlier castle.

②

Return to the road. Turn right and enter the churchyard to view the church.

③

Continue down the road to the bridge. The entrance to the gorge is to the right of the hill on the far side. Return to Castle Inn.

④

Take the track through the inn car park and behind the inn. Take the second track to the right along the line of the Saxon Defences, back to the main street.

⑤

Turn left and continue up the street to the war memorial.

⑥

Turn right. Cross the next crossroads and take the track under the viaduct and over a bridge by Mill Cottage. This is part of the Lych Way. Cross another footbridge and continue uphill until the path joins a wide track.

⑦

Return to the last crossroads. Turn left down Silver Street and continue straight down the main street to the car park from where you can see Bayfield House.

LACOCK

WILTSHIRE

Off A350, 3m S of Chippenham

LACOCK lies on the Bide Brook near its confluence with the Avon. Saxons called it *lacuc*, meaning little stream. In Domesday times it had mills, meadows, vineyard and wood. It was on the edge of the Royal Hunting Forest of Melksham. The king stayed in the parish at the manor of Lackham in 1086. Lacock Manor then belonged to Edward of Salisbury. His great granddaughter, Ela, Countess of Salisbury, founded Lacock Abbey in the 13th century.

The Abbey, a nunnery for Augustinian Canonesses, owned much of the village in the Middle Ages. It had large sheep pastures and the village, being on the 'cloth road' from Bath to London, prospered with the woollen industry. Houses were built with wide first-floor rooms to accommodate looms. The size of the buildings generally reflects the prosperity of the inhabitants.

The woollen industry died in the 18th century and few houses were built after that time, although crafts such as chair and hurdle making and tanning continued to thrive. Roads were turnpiked in the 18th century and the Wiltshire and Berkshire Canal ran alongside the River Avon from 1810 to 1914. The Talbots did not wish the railway to spoil the village and later development grew around the station a mile to the west. Most of the village was given to the National Trust by Matilda Talbot in 1944 and remains remarkably unspoilt.

WALK DIRECTIONS

Take the path opposite the car park and walk up the street to the entrance to Lacock Abbey, which is next to the Fox Talbot Museum.

After visiting the Abbey and the Museum continue to the tithe barn at the head of East Street. The barn, which has a magnificent cruck framework, dates from the 14th century. It was later used as the market hall.

Turn left along High Street and right along West Street.

At the end of the street, detour left to Cantax Hill and Cantax House, which was the vicarage until 1865. It is early 17th-century but the classical brick façade was added later. Retrace your steps and turn left down Church Street.

At the end detour right for the church, ahead for the tanyard and left for the packhorse bridge, built over the Bide Brook by Thomas Drummer in the early 18th century. From here, return to Church Street, turn left up East Street past the Blind House, a windowless 18th-century jail, and continue around the tithe barn to regain the car park.

For an optional walk continue over the packhorse bridge to the end of the lane.

Take the kissing-gate on the right, follow the path and go through the gate to the cottages and road. Turn right over Rey Bridge.

From the floodwalk turn right over the stile. The river is prone to flooding in winter. Cross the field to the stile on the far side and follow the river to the gate and stile in the next field.

Roughly follow the line of telegraph poles across two more fields and stiles, then turn across the large field to the steps and stile on to the right-hand bridge, which is medieval.

Turn right over the bridge and follow the floodwalk and road back to the car park.

POINTS OF INTEREST

Lacock Abbey. This dates from the mid 13th century, when records show stone coming from near Box and oak from Royal Forests at Chippenham and Melksham. Many medieval parts remain, including 15th-century cloisters, sacristy and chapter house. It was the last abbey to be dissolved by Henry VIII in 1539 and was purchased by Sir William Sharington. He demolished the abbey church and used the materials to convert the rest of the abbey into his house. His niece Olive inherited the abbey which, following her marriage to John Talbot, has been lived in by the Talbot family ever since, although ownership passed to the National Trust in 1944.

The cloisters (below) together with other features, survived the abbey's adaptation to manor house.

The abbey-mansion (bottom) was altered to the Gothic style of architecture in 1753.

Ⓑ

Fox Talbot Museum of Photography. A 16th-century barn was converted in to the museum in 1975. It is devoted to the life and work of William Henry Fox Talbot (1800-77), who lived at the abbey from 1827. He was a pioneer of photography and invented the negative/positive process. He took many pictures of the abbey and its life, and his earliest surviving negative dates from 1835.

The timber-fronted and stone-mullioned Sign of the Angel inn in Church Street.

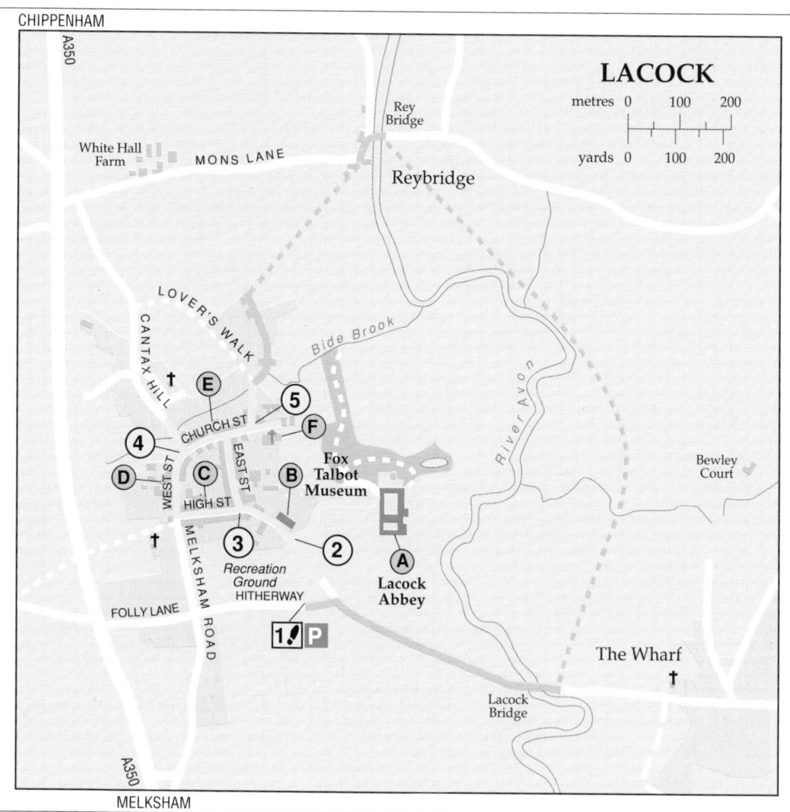

High Street. The width of the street reflects its former use for markets and fairs. The market cross was moved from in front of the Red Lion to the schoolyard in the 19th century to aid the flow of traffic. The Red Lion has a 1730s façade on a much older building. Next door the National Trust has retained a shop, once a coffee tavern, as a museum piece. The car park beside the inn was once a farmyard with a pond and the enclosure beyond it was the village pound for stray animals. The houses are mainly of the 16th and 17th centuries, including the imposing timber and stone Porch House at the far end.

West Street. The war memorial was made from the stone framework of the tomb of Sir John Talbot, taken from the church. The building where the ground floor has been gutted for a bus shelter housed a smithy at the beginning of the century. The George was known simply as The Inn for centuries and was renamed in the reign of George II. It has a fireplace with 17th-century dog spit.

Ⓔ

Church Street. At the west end of the street is the 14th-century Cruck House, with exposed cruck beam. Originally thatched, such houses were quickly built and date from times when people could acquire land if they could erect a house on it within a day. Beyond is the Sign of the Angel inn, built in 1480 and named after a gold coin called an angel. Behind its 16th-century doorway is a 'horse passage', used to lead horses through the house to the yard behind.

At its east end the street widens into the 13th-century market place. Here is King John's Hunting Lodge, now a tea and gift shop. It is possible that King John did indeed stay here on a trip to his Royal Forests. Beside the church the street opens out to the tanyard, which closed in 1928. Here skins were cured in a solution of oak and elm bark which was collected by local boys. The skins were then washed in the brook and hung up in the open barn to dry. Next door the pottery is housed in the old workhouse, which operated from 1833 to 1861.

Church of St Cyriac. The unusual dedication is to a three-year-old Sicilian boy martyred in AD303. The church is mainly of the 15th century, with soaring aisles and a beautiful east window in Perpendicular architecture. It is a 'wool church', built on a grand scale with profits from the woollen industry. The Talbot Chapel, containing ornate memorials to the Talbots and Sharingtons, has a beautiful lierne vaulted ceiling, and the Lackham Aisle has an unusual brass of 1501, a memorial to Robert and Elizabeth Baynard and their 18 children. Within a tomb decorated with heraldic carvings of painted angels and odd lizard-like creatures, lies Sir William Sharington, who converted Lacock Abbey into a house.

INFORMATION
Length of walk:
¾ mile (2 miles with option)
Approximate time:
1 hour (3 hours with option)

TERRAIN:
Easy going and level in the village, suitable for pushchairs and wheelchairs, except optional excursion, which has stiles and muddy patches.

PARKING:
Off Hither Way, to south of village. Toilets in car park opposite Fox Talbot Museum.

OPEN:
Lacock Abbey (NT). Easter-early Nov, Wed-Mon 1-5.30pm. Charge.
Fox Talbot Museum of Photography (NT). Daily Mar-early Nov 11am-5.30pm.
Both closed Good Fri. Charge.

REFRESHMENTS:
The Red Lion, The George, and the Sign of the Angel inn and seasonal tea shops.

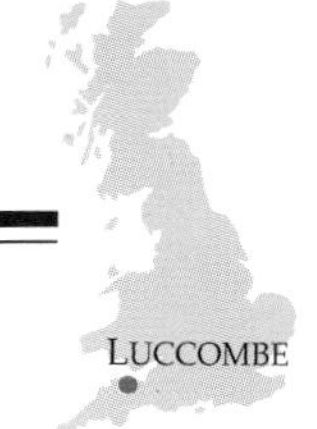

LUCCOMBE

SOMERSET

On minor roads off A39, 4m SW of Minehead

This cottage is a typical dwelling in a village where most are rustic, cream-washed and thatched.

INFORMATION
Length of walk:
1½ miles
Approximate time:
1½ hours

TERRAIN:
Quiet country roads (but beware of traffic) and lanes, moderate slopes.

PARKING:
On green next to village hall, where there are toilets.

REFRESHMENTS:
None in village. Dunkery Hotel at Wootton Courtenay, 2 miles to the east, or seasonal tea gardens at Horner or Selworthy.

Luccombe, meaning 'enclosed valley', lies in a corner of the fertile Vale of Porlock. It was a Domesday manor, becoming a manor of the rectory in the 13th century, the house probably standing on the site of the present vicarage. There was also a manor at Wychanger, which has a thatched 16th century farmhouse. From medieval times it has been a prosperous cereal farming area, with orchards since Tudor times.

In the Civil War, Parliamentary troops were garrisoned in the Royalist village. They tried to arrest the vicar, Henry Byam, but he escaped with his sons to join Charles I. His wife and daughter were drowned whilst escaping across the Bristol Channel. After many exploits he escaped to Jersey with the Prince of Wales, later Charles II. There was much local festivity at the Restoration, when Byam was returned as vicar of Luccombe, Canon of Exeter and Prebendary of Wales.

There were iron workings on Knowle Top and Huish Ball, and ore was shipped to South Wales via Porlock Weir and Minehead. In 1745 much of the area became property of the Aclands of Killerton near Exeter, and thrived under their ownership for two hundred years. Thomas Dyke, 10th Baronet Acland, lived at Holnicote from 1794, spending much effort in improving the estate.

Many 16th- and 17th-century cottages were extended from their simple two-room longhouse plans by raising the roofs and making attic rooms with semi-dormer windows. Most three-room cottages were 17th-century with fireplace and tall chimney on the front wall centrally placed to heat the whole house. Cloam (clay-lined) bread ovens project from the backs of the fireplaces and small openings in the chimneys ventilate curing chambers. Most buildings are of undressed local red sandstone rubble. The 10th Baronet destroyed some vernacular features by ornamenting cottages in the Romantic fashion. At the end of the 19th century the population declined and the village shrank by 20 houses, mostly ones of cob, which deteriorates rapidly with lack of maintenance.

Between the 1920s and 1940s the novelist Eleanor Helme lived here and wrote about the village. In 1947 it was subject to a Mass Observation survey, recording its life in great detail in the book *Exmoor Village*.

The Holnicote Estate, including most of Luccombe, was given to the National Trust in 1944 by Sir Richard Acland. The Trust lets 23 cottages to families with local connections and attempts to retain a balance of young and old.

POINTS OF INTEREST

Village Green. The car park is on the site of a former saw pit. A track leads to a field where the village pound for stray animals once stood. At the other end of the green is the village hall, built in 1881 as the school, which closed in 1946. Education was financed by subscription and assistance from the church and Acland family until 1891. School holidays were started at the whortleberry picking season and there were half-days for children to pick the berries, which were taken by horse and cart to the railway at Minehead for the dyeing industries. Several entries in the records show cases of children truanting to take part in stag hunting. The green is surrounded by walnut trees, a feature of the Estate. A huge specimen near the hall was uprooted in a storm of 1950.

Church View. This cottage has a date 1680 and initials HLI over the doorway. It was one of a row of thatched cottages which burned down at the end of the 19th century. The slated bread oven of the middle one remains, but the building was replaced by Glebe and School Cottages. Church View was originally built to a simple plan of two rooms divided by a cross passage. A second storey and tiled roof were added after the fire. School Cottage was the teacher's house for the new school and Glebe Cottage was a farmhouse. Its milking shed and outbuildings were in Stoney Street.

The village post office, once Ketnor's shoemaker's shop.

Post Office. This stands in The Square, where the village pump stood. Mains water and sewerage did not come to the village until the 1960s. The post office with Victorian post box is a 16th-century cob, rubble and thatch cottage. The 'Ketnor' sign remains from when it was Robert Ketnor's shoemaker's shop in the 1880s. Kitnor is another name for the neighbouring parish of Culbone, of which the family were medieval lords. The shop became a general stores in the 1890s, adding a post office in the 1960s, when there was still a shoemaker in the village.

In the 19th century, much thatch was replaced with Bridgwater tiles; note the low-hung roof.

Ⓓ

Church Gate Cottage. The original 17th-century cottage is between the chimneys. The original longhouse plan was extended in the early 19th century to provide a schoolroom at one end and teacher's cottage at the other.

Ⓔ

Church of St Mary the Virgin. The church has a 13th-century chancel and some tiles and stained glass from that time are preserved in the Chapel of Quiet. The 15th-century wagon roofs have fine painted bosses. There is a brass of 1615 to William Harrison of Wychanger and memorial of 1669 to Henry Byam, its Latin inscription giving details of his eventful life. The church is depicted in Samuel Palmer's painting *Coming out of Evening Church.*

New Houses. Three new houses were erected here in 1990, where cob and thatch cottages stood a hundred years before. They were built for a local housing association, providing much-needed accommodation in an area where few people can afford it. Two cottages were built further up the street in 1988. Sympathetic but functional modern designs were chosen.

Ⓖ

Stoney Street. The street was originally rough and stony, hence the name. Inglenook Cottage was two one-roomed cottages and Rose Tree Cottage two two-roomed cottages. Along with Oakapple Cottage they are 16th-century and many others are 17th-century. The Cottage and Oakapple Cottage were originally farmhouses and Post Cottage was the post office between the two World Wars. All have been extended from simple two or three-room plans.

St Saviour's Chapel. Foundations of a 20ft by 30ft chapel with doorways in south and west walls can be seen. Excavations showed it to be of Early English style and there is mention of a chantry chapel in the 14th century. The chapel was probably abandoned in the 16th century.

WALK DIRECTIONS

From the green pass the village hall and Church View.

Turn right at The Square and pass through the lych-gate opposite the post office and next to Church Gate Cottage. Visit the church, return to the lych-gate and turn right. Pass the new houses and continue up Stoney Street to the gateway beyond Hill Gate Cottages.

Turn right along the track signposted to Chapel Steep. From here there are views across the village to Knowle Top with its small plantation and mine spoil heap; Selworthy with its white-washed church; and beyond Stoney Street to Wychanger. The conifer plantation above the track was started in the 1920s for Sir Francis Acland, one of the original commissioners when the Forestry Commission was formed in 1919. Continue to the crossroads at Chapel Cross.

Detour left for 60yds to view the remains of St Saviour's Chapel beyond posts in the lay-by. Return to the cross-roads and turn left down Chisland Lane. Turn right at the next junction, along Huish Ball Steep. Turn left past East Luccombe Farm and return to the green.

MEVAGISSEY

CORNWALL

On B3273, 5m S of St Austell

THE small religious community of Lamorrick sprang up around a church dedicated to Saints Meva and Issey. A fishing hamlet grew around the nearby harbour at Porthilly and the Saints' names were used to unite the two settlements in the 14th century.

The village expanded to become a major fishing port. Good years for fishing resulted in rebuilding and improvements to the harbour, although few structures earlier than the 18th century survive. Pilchards were the main catch, caught by drift netting. They were salted for a month in quayside pits, then pressed into barrels and sold to the Navy or the oil extracted and exported for lamp oil. The processing went on in 'cellars' on the ground floors of fishermen's cottages. Communal cellars were built when the harbour was enlarged in the 18th century. From these, barrels of fish were carried through narrow streets by mules or on poles between two men.

Smuggling was rife in the 18th and 19th centuries. Fast local luggers were suited to this trade, which was mainly with Roscoff in Brittany.

INFORMATION
Length of walk:
2 miles
Approximate time:
2 hours

TERRAIN:
Up and down moderate hills with steps in places.

PARKING:
Car park and toilets in Valley Road (part of B3273).

OPEN:
Mevagissey Museum. Daily Easter-early Oct (afternoons only on Sun).

REFRESHMENTS:
There are several inns and cafés and seafood is a speciality.

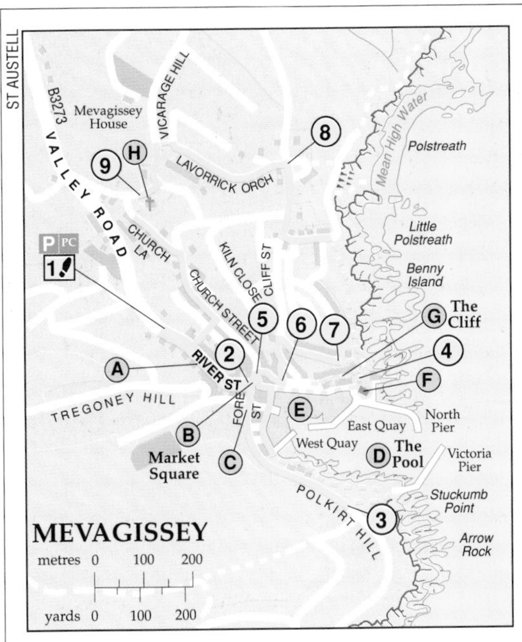

WALK DIRECTIONS

From the car park turn left and walk down Valley Road into River Street and Market Square.

Turn right along Fore Street and continue up Polkirt Hill to the park, passing 18th-century shipowner's residences including the imposing Polkirt House.

Turn left through the park and go down the steps to Victoria Pier. Turn left along the quayside and continue right around the harbour to the museum.

Return above the quayside along The Cliff, past The Hoss and back along the quay, but keeping straight ahead to the square with the War Memorial.

Turn right and keep right up Cliff Street, passing the Fountain Inn, one of only two inns remaining from the 10 that were here in the 18th century. The covered 'Shill-alley-opp' alongside leads to Bank Street, site of a 19th-century bank.

Turn left up cobbled Mount Street, passing between 18th- and 19th-century fishermen's cottages and continuing up Cliff Street to the handrail. Turn right along The Battery, site of a battery of six canons during the Napoleonic Wars.

(7)

Pass in front of Seapoint Hotel and left up the steps past the Ropewalk, which is now overgrown and fenced off. Ropes were made here by the Robins family for over a century until the 1940s. Cross the recreation ground and turn left along Beach Road. Turn right up Cliff Street.

Turn left along Lowcrick Orchards, down the steps at the end and down Vicarage Hill to the church.

Take the path through the churchyard into Church Lane and continue down Church Street. Turn right, then right again into Valley Road.

POINTS OF INTEREST

River Street. The river, now underground, flowed to the east of the street and the mill leat alongside it. The mill stood where the Midland Bank stands today. Opposite were netmakers' lofts and pilchard stores.

Market Square. This area, known as Town Bridge, was the village centre. The village pump outside the Ship Inn was used until 1944, when mains water arrived.

Fore Street. Several alleys or 'opes' lead from here to the harbour. Lining these are buildings which were once boat stores, net lofts and fish cellars with their wide doorways.

(D)

The Pool. This is the outer harbour, which was created by building two piers in the 1880s. Destroyed in a storm of 1891, they were rebuilt in 1897, when the lighthouse became the first in the country to be lit by electricity.

(E)

Inner Harbour. There was a pier and harbour here in the 15th century, but the present jetties date from the 1770s, when many of the quayside buildings were built.

(F)

Museum. This is on Island Quay, which was an island until this century. The museum, started in 1968, is housed in a boatbuilder's workshop of 1745. Its roof is supported by three masts and the walls have many timbers taken from ships repaired on the premises. Some of the boat-builders' tools and machinery are exhibited.

(G)

The Cliff. No. 14, 'Seaview', or 'Glanville House', is 17th-century and reputedly the oldest cottage in the village. No.1, 'The Hoss' dates from the 18th century and is built from timbers of a wrecked grain ship called *The Horse*.

(H)

St Peter's Church. On a Saxon site, this is mainly 13th century, with a Norman font. The north aisle was built in the 16th century of Pentewan stone.

MINCHINHAMPTON

THE WEST COUNTRY

MINCHINHAMPTON

GLOUCESTERSHIRE

Off A419, 3m SE of Stroud

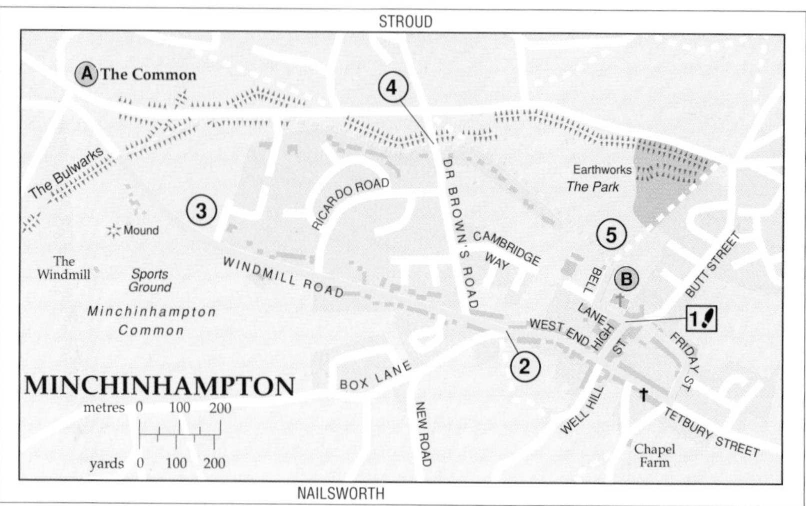

THIS fine old village occupies one of the last remaining stretches of common on the Cotswolds. Its high position on the southern ridge of the Golden Valley means it commands expansive views over Stroud and the high Wolds to the north.

Rising to prominence during the Cotswold wool boom of the 17th and 18th centuries, Minchinhampton's centre is an almost untouched example of the period village market. The Market Hall was built in 1698 for wool trading and is a most elegant structure with its outer stone columns and inner, bobbin-like wooden ones. Close by, the Ram Inn is early 18th-century. Narrow Friday Street is delightful, as is Tetbury Street, in which virtually all the houses date from the village's heyday.

POINTS OF INTEREST

Ⓐ

The Common. Minchinhampton Common is the largest piece of remaining Cotswold common land south of Cleeve Hill. Those with rights of common must live in one of approximately 250 houses that comprise the Ancient Parish of Minchinhampton. That the commoners do still exercise their rights can be seen from the number of cattle grids in roads into the village: and you can still meet cows in High Street.

A major part of the common is occupied by The Bulwarks, a large Iron Age defensive earthwork consisting of a massive rampart and ditch almost one mile long. Defending some 600 acres it encloses Amberley Camp, an Iron Age hill-fort of 50 acres. Pottery found at the site suggests that both the fort and The Bulwarks were constructed at, or just before, the Roman Conquest of AD43.

A few yards from where the route of this walk reaches the common is a point where six roads meet. There stands Tom Long's Post. Legend has it that the post is all that remains of the gallows where Tom Long, a notorious local highwayman, was hanged, though it is more likely to mark the grave of a suicide, as such unfortunates were commonly buried at crossroads.

Holy Trinity Church. Matilda, wife of William the Conqueror, asked her husband to present the Manor of Hampton to the newly founded Abbaye-aux-Dames in Caen, Normandy. The original church was consequently rebuilt or enlarged in the 12th century and in 1415 it passed to the nuns of Syon Abbey until the Dissolution.

The church is one of the most distinctive in the Cotswolds with its curiously truncated spire. The 16th-century records show that the original full-height spire had to be part-demolished as it was too heavy for the tower. The 14th-century font was restored to the building after spending many years in active service as a flower pot in a local garden. At the west end of the north wall are three fine brasses, the best of which shows John Hampton and his wife, with their children grouped below them. The brass is 15th-century.

INFORMATION
Length of walk:
2 miles
Approximate time:
1½ hours

TERRAIN:
Suitable for children, pushchairs and wheelchairs in all but the very wettest weather when the common can become a little muddy.

PARKING:
Parking is straightforward on the common to the west of Minchinhampton itself, and it is also possible to park in the centre of the village, close to the Market Hall. The directions assume the village centre is used.

REFRESHMENTS:
Selection of pubs and cafés in the village.

The market cross in the square, with the fine Market House to the right.

WALK DIRECTIONS

①

From the Market Hall walk down High Street, away from the church, to a T-junction. Turn right into West End, a compact, narrow street.

②

Bear right into Windmill Road and follow this on to the common.

③

Once the common is reached, take time to explore the ramparts and ditches of The Bulwarks. The walk goes right, across the common, keeping close to the final boundary walls of Minchinhampton, and following these, right, around the northern end of the village. The views across the Golden Valley are superb.

④

Reach and cross Dr Brown's Road – named after a well-loved local doctor – then stay with the garden walls on a metalled private lane that leads to a wide turning circle.

Go right from the turning circle, walk down Bell Lane between the church, left, and a school, right. At the T-junction turn left, still on Bell Lane, to reach the entrance to the church and the Market Hall. Now go along Friday Street to the left of the Hall, following it to its T-junction with Tetbury Street. Turn right and follow Tetbury Street back to High Street. Go right, back to the Market Hall.

MILTON ABBAS

DORSET

On minor roads off A354, 11m NE of Dorchester

ON the banks of Milborne Brook were three settlements; Hewish, Bagber and Milton – the 'middle farm'. A monastery founded here in 938 was converted by King Edgar in 964 to a Benedictine abbey of 40 monks. The abbey became the centre of a populous manor. Norman terraces, possibly for vineyards, line the hillside above the abbey and lynchets from medieval open fields continue down the valley.

In 1252 a market and fair were granted and the village became a prosperous agricultural market town, with the Market Square and cross outside the abbey gates. By the 18th century there were about 100 houses, a Grammar School, shops, a brewery, almshouses and three inns: The George, King's Arms and Red Lion. Plans of the village as it was during this period can be seen in the abbey church and parish church.

The abbey was dissolved in 1539 and sold to John Tregonwell, the lawyer who arranged Henry VIII's divorce from Catherine of Aragon. The estate remained in the Tregonwell family until 1752, when it was sold to Joseph Damer, later Lord Milton and Earl of Dorchester – a local landowner who never looked back after marrying a daughter of the Duke of Dorset.

After converting the Tregonwell mansion, Damer decided that the village spoilt his view. He had it gradually demolished between 1770 and 1790 after an unsuccessful attempt at flooding it with a seven-acre lake originally intended to cover the 25-acre site. He bought back leases or waited for them to expire, but one sitting tenant was flooded out and sued him. Damer employed Lancelot 'Capability' Brown to landscape the area and rehouse inhabitants in a 'model' village out of sight in the next valley.

Apart from a new housing estate, the village remains little changed.

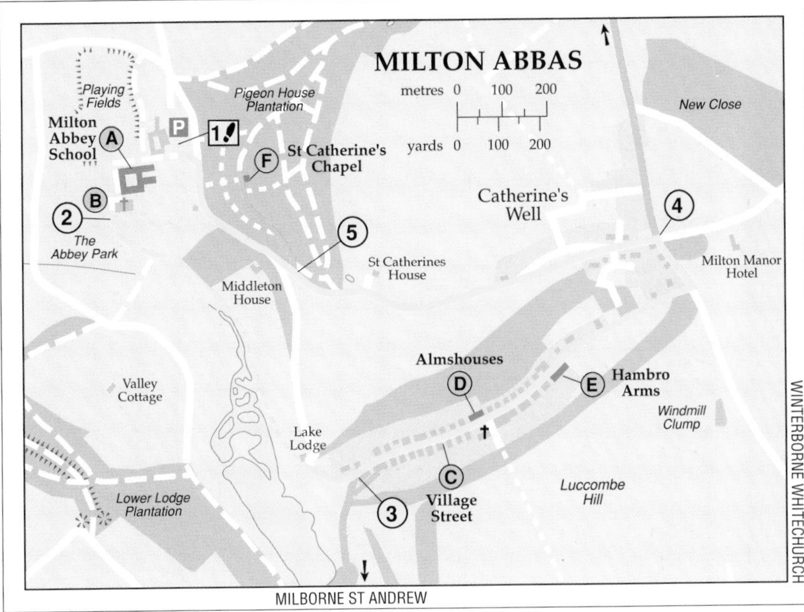

WALK DIRECTIONS

From the car park at Milton Abbey School, turn right to the abbey church, passing the 15th-century Green Walk Cottage, the only dwelling to survive from the old village.

From the church continue around the edge of the green to the track leading alongside the brook. Low mounds in the field across the brook mark the site of the former village. Pass Lake Lodge and continue to the foot of the main street. An optional detour can be made right to the lake dam, from which can be seen the cob-and-thatch Dale Cottage. Its kitchen window has a pane inscribed 'The first light which I ever made, which was in 1831, Thomas Longman.'

Turn up the village street past the Vicarage with its stone slated roof, opposite The Maltings. This range of thatched cottages incorporates a former brewery and stables dating from 1770. The brewery was run by the Fookes family from 1849 until 1950, when it became a museum. Continue up the main street past the Almshouses to St James' Church, built in 1786 using stone from the old tithe barn. It was restored and enlarged in 1889 by Charles Hambro.

Carry on past the Hambro Arms and turn left at the top of the street.

④

At the crossroads, detour ahead for an optional visit to Park Farm Museum. Housed in a thatched 18th-century stable block, it has displays of village history, old implements, farm animals and pets and sells farm produce. For the main walk, turn left by Catherine's Well and go down the track beyond.

Turn right opposite the pair of metal gates for a detour along the woodland track to St Catherine's Chapel. Return and continue down the track and road to return to the car park.

The Abbey's main house, once part of the mansion, is now part of a school.

POINTS OF INTEREST

Milton Abbey School. In 1540 the former abbot's hall became the mansion of Sir John Tregonwell. Other monastic buildings, apart from the church, were demolished in 1769 and the house was reconstructed by Sir William Chambers, architect of Somerset House. He did not like his employer's brief and, finding the house ugly, resigned in 1774, when James Wyatt and 'Capability' Brown were employed to finish the job. A Grammar School founded here in 1520 was closed after complaints from the Earl of Dorchester that the building was dangerous and pupils were stealing his eggs and fruit. One famous pupil here was Thomas Masterman Hardy, later Nelson's flag captain.

The abbey church, part of a 10th-century foundation, became the parish church following the Dissolution.

Abbey Church. The church dates mainly from 1309, when the original building was destroyed by lightning. Rebuilding continued until the dissolution in 1539, when construction of the nave ceased and the 26 figures on the reredos of 1492 were destroyed. A wooden tabernacle designed to accompany the reredos hangs on a wall of the chancel, uniquely surviving the Reformation. A tomb to John Tregonwell (died 1680) states that he fell from the church roof when aged five, only to be saved by his petticoats acting as a parachute. A white marble monument to Lady Milton (died 1775) is by Robert Adam. Sir Giles Gilbert Scott carried out a sensitive restoration in 1789.

Village Street. The 20 pairs of cob-and-thatch cottages were painted yellow when built between 1771 and 1790. Each has a central doorway with vestibule leading to doors to the tenements, each of which has a staircase lit by one light of a two-light window. Some have been altered or combined, but most retain the original bread ovens. The Old Forge has a brick-and-flint forge to the rear and the Old Bakery a cob-and-thatch outbuilding said to have been a factory for window glass. The windows are scratched with inscriptions of 1793 to 1830. The rowans lining the street replaced chestnuts felled in 1953.

Almshouses. Originally built in the old village in 1674, these were removed here in 1779 – an early example of the Romantic fashion of preserving old buildings. There are three tenements and a central hall with coats of arms of the Miltons and Sackvilles.

Hambro Arms. The original cob building of 1780 was extended to the rear in the 19th century and joined to its stable block under a continuous thatched roof. It was first called the Milton Arms, then Dorchester Arms and Portalington Arms and finally Hambro Arms after a member of the banking family purchased the estate from Lord Milton.

St Catherine's Chapel. A Saxon chapel was built here on the spot on which King Athelstan camped on his way to battle with Danes. In thanks for his victory, and in memory of his brother Edwin, he founded Milton Abbey. The chapel was rebuilt in the 12th century and the contemporary Latin inscription by the doorway suggested that a pilgrimage here would mean 120 days less in purgatory after death. In the early 19th century it was converted to a labourer's cottage and later a carpenter's workshop, only to be restored by Everard Hambro in 1901 and reconsecrated. The 111 grassy steps leading down to the abbey are closed to the public.

INFORMATION
Length of walk:
2¼ miles (3¼ miles with option)
Approximate time:
2 hours (3 hours with option)

TERRAIN:
Moderate slopes, suitable for children and pushchairs.

PARKING:
Car park and toilets adjacent to Milton Abbey School, or parking in main street.

OPEN:
Park Farm Museum.
Daily all year, 10am-dusk. Charge.
Milton Abbey School.
During school holidays.

REFRESHMENTS:
Hambro Arms or The Tea Clipper tea shop in the main street.

These evenly spaced, thatched, cob cottages are part of the Earl of Dorchester's 'model' village.

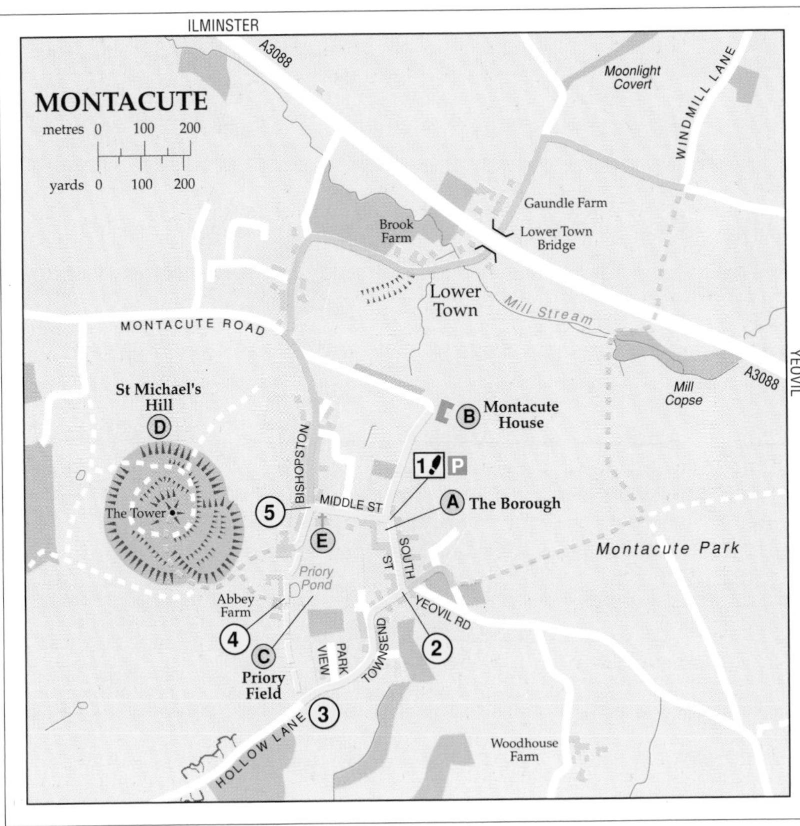

MONTACUTE

SOMERSET

On A3088, 4m W of Yeovil

MONTACUTE was named after the *mons acutis* – pointed hill – above it. It was given by William the Conqueror to his half-brother, Robert, Count of Mortain. His son William established the borough of Bishopston but, facing a charge of treason, was forced to give the village to the French Abbey of Cluny for a priory. Under the priory the village grew into a prosperous market town and woollen centre.

POINTS OF INTEREST

(A)

The Borough. The name refers to the new borough which was added to Bishopston in 1240. Here is the medieval market place, originally with guildhall and 'shambles' or lock-up shops. Many 17th- and 18th-century buildings include the Phelips Arms, an inn since 1698.

(B)

Montacute House. This was built in the 1590s for the Phelips family, who lived here for over 300 years, after which they leased to a series of tenants. The house became dilapidated and would have been demolished had it not been purchased by the National Trust. Its 180ft-long gallery houses paintings from the National Portrait Gallery.

(C)

Priory Field. Under the field, farm and churchyard lie the remains of the Priory of St Peter and St Paul. The priory, founded in 1102, became run down in the 13th century and after the dissolution in 1539 its buildings were demolished. The fishpond and square dovecot remain from medieval times.

(D)

St Michael's Hill. King Canute's standard bearer, Tofig, found the supposed remains of the Holy Cross here. A motte-and-bailey castle was built here for the Count of Mortain. The folly tower was built in 1760 by the Phelips family.

WALK DIRECTIONS

From the car park in The Borough, cross to the drive to Montacute House. With Montacute Cottage, The Chantry forms part of a house dating from 1500.

Continue to Montacute House. Return to The Borough and walk down South Street, where numbers 7 and 9 are parts of a 16th-century manor house.

(2)

Turn right up Townsend to Hollow Lane.

(3)

After Park View, turn right through a gate and down the track to Priory Field.

(4)

An optional detour can be made to St Michael's Hill. Marked routes start from between the buildings opposite the pond or from behind the priory gatehouse, which bears the initials of Thomas Chard, the penultimate Prior (1514-32), and has superb oriel windows.

On either approach, keep left to the base of the hill, where a stile leads to the steep path to the tower. Return the same way, passing the gatehouse and continue to the church. Leave the churchyard through the main gates, opposite which is the Old Vicarage, of 1715.

(5)

Turn right down Middle Street to return to The Borough, or, as an optional extension, continue ahead up Bishopston, passing the Monks' House on the right. This 16th-century building was probably the priory hospital, built some way from the priory to avoid the spread of disease.

As the road bends left, take the fork on the right, through Lower Town, under the bridge and turn right towards Lufton.

At the next junction take the stile to the right, waymarked Leland Trail. Cross the main road and the stile at the foot of the embankment.

Cross the stiles on either side of the mill stream, which fed one of the three mills on the Montacute Estate in the 18th century. Keep uphill, following the waymarks and crossing three more stiles. Turn right and head towards the village across the park. Pass through a small enclosure to a kissing-gate. Turn right into Back Lane and right again into South Street and The Borough.

(E)

St Catherine's Church. This contains parts of the Norman chapel, including chancel arch. It has a 16th-century tower with similar details to The Chantry and priory gatehouse. The north transept has monuments to the Phelips family dating from the 15th century.

INFORMATION
Length of walk:
3/4 mile (3 miles with options)
Approximate time:
1 hour (3 hours with options)

TERRAIN:
Village circuit suitable for pushchairs and wheelchairs. Options have several stiles, occasional muddy patches and a steep climb to the tower on St Michael's Hill.

PARKING:
In The Borough. No toilets except at Montacute House.

OPEN:
Montacute House, Park and Garden. House Apr-4 Nov, daily (ex Tue) 12-5.30pm. Park and Garden daily, all year (ex Tue) 11.30am-5.30pm. Charge.

REFRESHMENTS:
Inns, cafés and restaurant.

MORWENSTOW

CORNWALL

On minor roads off A39, 9m N of Bude

MORWENSTOW was named after St Morwenna, a Celtic saint. The original church probably marked her grave. The name is first mentioned in the 13th century, when the church and tithes were granted to the monks of the Hospital of St John the Baptist at Bridgwater.

Morwenstow's chief claim to fame is that the Rev. Robert Stephen Hawker was vicar here from 1834 until 1875. He was a poet and author well known to Cornish people for writing *The Song of the Western Men*, which contains the lines: 'And shall Trelawney die? Then twenty thousand Cornishmen – Will know the reason why!' He also invented the Harvest Festival service. An eccentric who wore a fisherman's jersey and seaboots under his cassock, he was so fond of animals he allowed pets in church during services.

Hawker also collected and embellished local folk stories, such as the legend of Cruel Coppinger, leader of a vicious band of local smugglers and wreckers in the 18th century who arrived and left mysteriously in a ship in a storm.

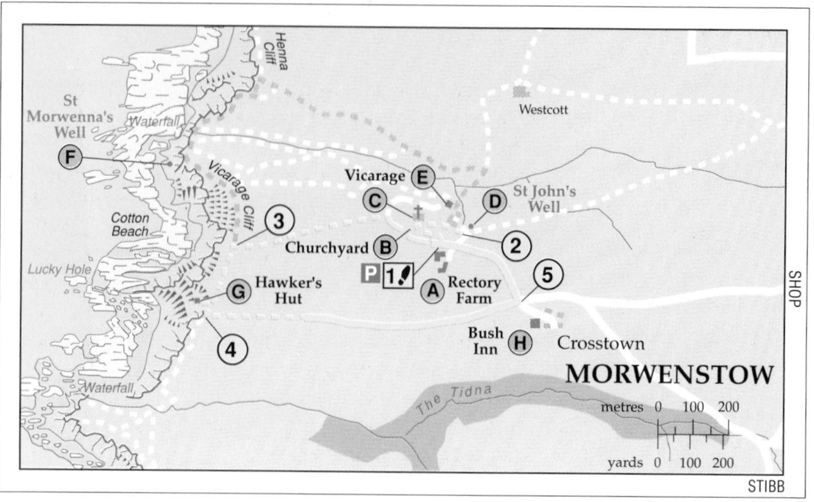

WALK DIRECTIONS

(1)

From the car park near Rectory Farm, cross to visit the church. From here a level path leads to the east end of the churchyard.

If option is followed, take the waymarked path which drops from the east end of the church over a stone stile and alongside the vicarage. It crosses a footbridge and ascends to a waymarked post in the field beyond. Turn left along the edge of the field, through a pole barrier and head towards 450ft-high Henna Cliff. Turn left and descend into the valley, noting the cliff waterfall near what use to be the site of St Morwenna's Well. Ascend Vicarage Cliff to the stile, point 3.

If not following the option, return to the track by the car park and turn right. The track, noted as being ancient in the 13th century, passes through two kissing-gates and along the edge of a field to a stile by the cliff edge.

Cross the stile and follow the cliff edge to the next stile, detouring right to Hawker's Hut as signposted.

(4)

Cross the stile and turn left, keeping to the edge of the field and then along the high banked lane to the Bush Inn.

(5)

Turn left and walk down the road back to the car park.

POINTS OF INTEREST

(A)

Rectory Farm. Parts of the house date from the 14th century, when it belonged to the monks of the Hospital of St John. After the dissolution of the monasteries in 1539, the church lands passed to Sir Richard Grenville.

Churchyard. The lych-gate was constructed in 1641. Beside it the lych house, now a store, was a mortuary which Hawker used to store the bodies of shipwrecked sailors. Outside the gate are buried three men hanged for sheep stealing, who could not be buried on consecrated ground. Just inside the gate is an ancient Celtic cross brought by Hawker as a memorial to his first wife in 1851.

St Morwenna's Church. The church contains some of the most outstanding pieces of Norman sculpture in the country. These include the carved south doorway and three arches in the north arcade of the aisle. The central arch is similar to the doorway, being carved with alternating heads of men, birds and beasts.

St John's Well. This is in a private garden. It is a holy well which provides water for baptisms. It was first recorded in 1296, when its dedication was changed to that of St John, along with the church.

(E)

Vicarage. When Hawker came to Morwenstow the old vicarage had not been used for a century and was a ruinous barn. He built the new vicarage at his own expense in 1837 and never recovered financially. The chimneys are supposed to represent two Oxford colleges and three churches associated with his family and the large kitchen chimney is shaped like his mother's tomb.

St Morwenna's Well. According to legend St Morwenna was one of 24 children of Welsh King Brychan. She came here in the 5th or 6th century and established her cell by a spring on the cliff.

(G)

Hawker's Hut. Hawker made this shack from timbers of the wrecked ship *Alonzo*. He used it as a study, where he meditated, composed verse and smoked opium.

(H)

Bush Inn. A traditional inn and range of farm buildings dating from the 12th century. It is well known for several ghostly happenings.

INFORMATION
Length of walk:
1½ miles (2½ miles if option followed)
Approximate time:
1½ hours (2½ hours if option followed)

TERRAIN:
Level, except option, which is steep in parts. Two gates, two stiles. Not suitable for push-chairs or wheelchairs.

PARKING:
Between Rectory Farm and churchyard. No toilets.

REFRESHMENTS:
Bush Inn and Rectory Farm for teas (in season)

MULLION

CORNWALL

On B3296, 8m S of Helston

MULLION is named after the patron saint of its church, but nobody is quite sure who he or she was. The name may come from St Melina, a Roman lady who died in AD438, St Mellanus or Malo, a 6th-century Breton bishop, or the Welsh St Mullion, who died in AD570. Pilgrims came here along paths marked by ancient stone crosses like one surviving at Pradannack, one of four hamlets in the parish. The hamlet around the church became known as Churchtown.

Many buildings are of the local serpentine rubble dressed with granite. This beautiful green-streaked stone takes a good polish and is used decoratively. A factory that worked large pieces for buildings had to close due to the difficulties of transporting such brittle stone. Workshops now turn small pieces for the souvenir trade. Copper was found in local rocks but attempts at mining it were unsuccessful.

The area was renowned for smuggling in the 18th and 19th centuries, mainly from Roscoff in Brittany. Cottages in Mullion still have cupboards with false backs or bottoms, hidden chambers in walls or wells underneath double flooring for concealment of goods. Smuggling was last recorded in 1840, when coastguard patrols put an end to it.

In the 19th century improvements were made by the main landowners, Lords Robarts and Falmouth. Cereal farming prospered and there were three mills, masons, smiths, carpenters and shopkeepers. The railway came to Helston in 1887, bringing tourism. Large clifftop hotels were built at Poldhu and Polurrian in 1901 with much smaller development since. The air base at Culdrose is now the main local employer.

INFORMATION
Length of walk:
3$\frac{3}{4}$ miles
Approximate time:
3 hours

TERRAIN:
Fairly level and dry, except along the coast, which is steep in places; 2 stiles. Not suitable for pushchairs or wheelchairs.

PARKING:
Car park and toilets in Lender Lane in village centre.

REFRESHMENTS:
The Old Inn and several cafés and restaurants.

POINTS OF INTEREST

Church of St Melanus. The serpentine and granite church dates from the 13th century. The tower was built for the vicar, Robert Luddra, in 1500. The wooden studded north door is Norman and has been brought from another building and cut to size. It is known as the 'Devil's Door' from the custom of opening it for the Devil when driven out during baptisms. The south door contains a small dog flap to allow shepherds to release their attendant dogs during services. There are remarkable 16th-century bench ends and panels along some pews, supposedly carved from oaks from the now treeless Goonhilly Downs. The carvings were covered for many years until restoration in 1870, reputedly because they show naked bacchanalian figures, but most are symbols of the Passion. A 17th-century vicar, Thomas Flavel, was a famous exorcist of ghosts. By the porch is a medieval granite cross with a 19th-century base and inscription 'To him who raised this cross and to all faithful people pardon and peace.'

The road descends 200ft to Mullion harbour, where solid granite piers weather Atlantic storms.

THE FISHING INDUSTRY

The area around Mullion prospered with the expansion of the pilchard industry in the 18th century. Fish were seine netted and taken across Mounts Bay to Newlyn for packing. Lookouts were posted on clifftops during the autumn pilchard season. When they spotted the shoals they called 'Heva, Heva', which is probably Cornish for shoal, but linked (with seine netting) to the mythological Heva, a nymph who was supposed to have diverted the waters of the River Seine. Pilchards and herrings have gone now and mackerel are fast disappearing, but crab and lobster continue to be profitable. In the 19th century these were loaded at sea into a regular ketch bound for Southampton.

WALK DIRECTIONS

From the car park, cross Lender Lane to walk up the western arm of Churchtown. The thatched part of the Old Inn is 17th-century with a cob first floor on a stone ground floor. The two wings date from the 19th century. Detour left opposite the 17th-century stone and cob Mullyon House through the 19th-century lych-gate to the church. Return and continue along Churchtown.

At the Cottage Restaurant, formerly the King's Arms inn, turn left up the eastern arm of Churchtown. Examine Chapel Place behind Stock's Restaurant and the Methodist Church opposite Willow Cottage, whose delicate Regency fanlight door is overwhelmed by a modern porch.

Turn left back on to Lender Lane and continue along The Commons to the start of Poldhu Road.

Turn left as signed to Angrouse Farm and take the small gate ahead by the footpath sign into Parc Venton.

At Poldhu Point there is a memorial marking the site of the Marconi radio station which received the first transatlantic morse signals in 1901.

⑤

Cross the field and the two stone stiles on the far side.

⑥

Take the gate on the far side of the next field and turn left, then right through the Meres Valley estate. Turn left at the bottom, then swing right down Laflouder Lane. On the left, pass Laflouder Thatch, a row of 17th-century stone, cob and thatch cottages restored as one house in the 1970s, and, on the right, Meres with its horizontal and vertical sash windows. Keep straight down the lane towards the sea.

Cross the footbridge and ascend the serpentine steps past the hotel to Polurrian. Follow the Coast Path signs to the Cove Hotel.

Take the zigzag path by the old cannon in front of the hotel down to the Cove.

Follow Nansmellyon Road up the valley past Criggan Mill, which although disused, still has its 30ft overshot wheel and the complete machinery inside. Continue for nearly a mile on this road to Churchtown (the old school contains a model museum) and so back to the car park.

Chapel Place. The small brick Methodist Chapel was built here in 1791. Wesleyans and Methodists separated in 1834 and in 1840 the Wesleyans built a new chapel across the road at Tremenhee, a Celtic name indicating a sacred site. The present Methodist Church was built in 1877 and the old chapel became a barber's shop, now a cottage. The Wesleyan Chapel became the Methodist Hall when the two groups reunited in 1932.

Angrouse Farm. When rethatched in 1961, 15 layers of thatch were removed from the cob and stone farmhouse – a layer for each 20 years of its age. Its roof beams include deck planks from wrecked ships. To its ancient simple plan of hall and service room were added a dairy, pantry and second fireplace in the late 17th century. At the same time the sliding sash windows, popular in Cornwall because they do not blow open, were added. In 1787 the farmer, Thomas Triggs, bequeathed 'the chamber above the hall' to his wife, Ursula, for her use during widowhood. She held early Methodist meetings and invited John Wesley here.

Parc Venton. The name means 'field with a spring'. Inside the gate is a serpentine boulder with the inscription S.T. 1762. This and the modern granite plaque above mark the spot where John Wesley preached. Parc Venton House, adjacent, was built in the 1820s for Commander Drew, a Customs and Excise officer.

Polurrian. Here was Huel Fenwick copper mine and engine house, erected in 1853 but closed within a year. The cliff is fast eroding and the remains of a fallen house can be seen. From here you can look across the Cove to the memorial of Poldhu Point. Erected in 1937, it commemorates the first transatlantic wireless transmission sent from here by Marconi in 1901. His wireless station stood here until 1933.

Mullion Cove or Porthmellin. The harbour looks across to Mullion Island and Gull Rock. The island, now a bird sanctuary, grew nothing but tree mallow and beet, according to the antiquary Borlase. The piers were built between 1893 and 1895. They provide scanty protection from southwesterly Atlantic gales, which can tie up boats for weeks. Harbour and buildings were given to the National Trust by the Meyers family in 1945.

The old lifeboat house held the county's largest lifeboat from 1867 to 1909. The 19th-century Winch House at the top of the slipway is still used. Harbour Cottage is an early 19th-century fish cellar built into rocks on the south side of the harbour.

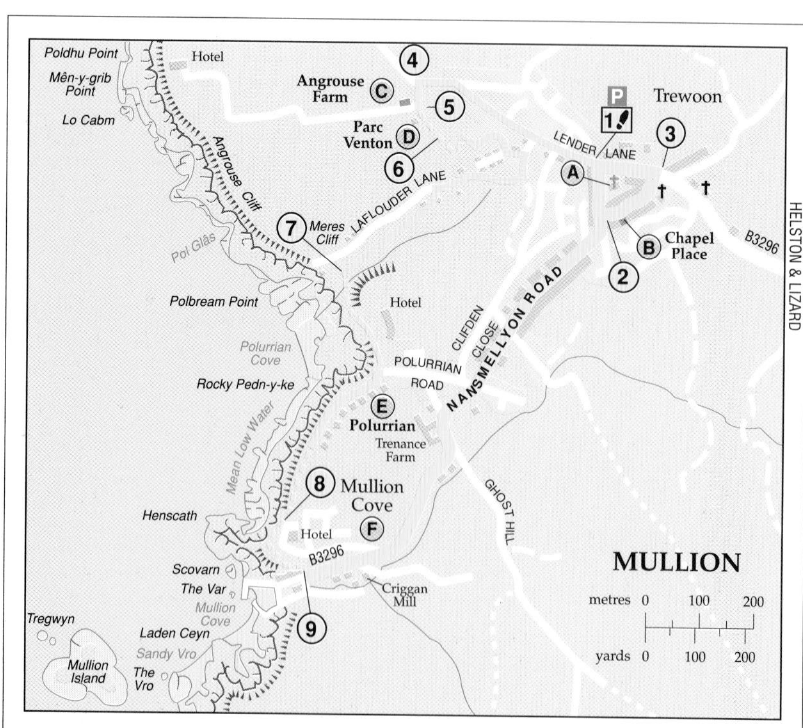

NUNNEY

THE WEST COUNTRY

NUNNEY

SOMERSET

On minor roads off A361, 3m SW of Frome

NUNNEY grew near prehistoric trackways, including the Ridgeway, referred to as 'the olden wei' in a Saxon charter. After the 7th-century conquest of Somerset by Saxons, one called Nunna settled on the island in the brook, now a bird sanctuary. Its name has also been associated with a nunnery, but there is no evidence of this.

Nunney prospered with the woollen industry centred on Frome. Wool was washed in Nunney Brook from the sloping pavement in front of the church. Master clothiers had weekly rounds delivering wool and collecting spun yarn. A woollen mill and the whole local industry disappeared in the late 18th century, outcompeted by northern mills.

Nunney Brook provided power for Fussel's ironworks, producing scythes and other edge tools. The business grew up in the late 18th century and became the largest employer in the 19th century. Established at the same time were quarries in the local blue lias, a hard building stone which takes a polish like marble.

NUNNEY
metres 0 100 200
yards 0 100 200
Nunney Brook
Combe Farm
Fullwell Farm
Nunney Castle
FROME ROAD
FROME
Manor Farm
Castle Hill Farm
CASTLE HILL
CHURCH ST
HORN ST
Rockfield House
PRIMROSE HILL
HIGH STREET
BERRY HILL
Mill Race
The Combe
HORN ST
Holwell Valley
DALIMORES LANE
SHEPTON MALLET & FROME

POINTS OF INTEREST

Church Street. The George Inn alone survives from Nunney's four 18th-century inns, plus the Theobald Arms, which was built on the new turnpike. The sign across the street is a modern imitation of the traditional village sign. Praters, much altered but with some original mullioned windows, is one of several early 18th-century houses, including Court Farmhouse, which is on the site of the 15th-century manor of the Mawdley family. The ruins of its gatehouse form the base of the present gateway.

All Saints Church. The largely 13th-century church was restored in 1874. It has a Norman font and fragments of a Saxon cross. Above the nave arcade is a painting of St George with background motifs including the White Hart of Richard II. There is a fine oak screen and monuments to the De la Mere family, whose key and knotted cord emblem appears on the west face of the tower.

Nunney Castle. This was not so much a fort as a fashionable manor house, built in imitation of the Bastille; a complete residence on four floors. It was altered in Elizabethan times and slighted after the Civil War. The large double-entranced barn to the east of the castle dates from 1500.

(D)

Manor Farm. This was built for William Whitchurch as the new manor house after the destruction of the castle. A vaulted cellar and stable block survive from the mid-17th century, but the present house was built about 1720 in the fashionable Palladian style.

(E)

Horn Street. Here, weavers' cottages in Doulting stone date from a prosperous period of the cloth industry in the late 17th and early 18th centuries. Some are built in vernacular style and some in the classical fashion of the time. The Bell House was created in the 1940s from cottages dating from 1699 and occupies the site of dwellings which housed Parliamentary troops during the castle siege. Further up on the right is The Old Weaver's Cottage, dated 1693 and initialled SRA. Adjoining cottages, dated 1724 and 1736, are initialled SIA, possibly referring to the Ashe family.

(F)

High Street. Side Hill Farmhouse is dated 1731. The initials LIS on the old house and later extension refer to the Samborne family. From 1790 to 1816 it was the home of Jane Folliott who, unusually for a woman in those days, became a wealthy yeoman farmer. Opposite is the 16th-century Cherry Tree Farmhouse with its 17th-century oak mullioned window.

INFORMATION
Length of walk: ¾ m
Approximate time: 1 hr

TERRAIN:
Moderate slopes, steps and a stile. Unsuitable for pushchairs and wheelchairs.

PARKING:
In streets, limited parking in Market Place, no toilets.

OPEN:
Nunney Castle (EH). Any reasonable time. No charge.

REFRESHMENTS:
George Inn or Bridge House teashop.

WALK DIRECTIONS

Start from Market Place with its thatched bus shelter. Henry de Montfort obtained a license from the Crown for a market and fair in 1259, and this area soon became the focal point of the village. The fair was revived on its 700th anniversary in 1959.

Walk down Church Street to the church and the 13th-century market cross, which stood in the churchyard for many years. It was dismantled in 1869, allegedly because children playing around it were too noisy. Pieces were salvaged by Mr J.H. Shore, who kept them until the cross was restored.

(2)

Return up Church Street.

(3)

Turn right after the church and cross the footbridge to the castle gateway. Circle the moat, entering the castle from the rear. Continue back to the gate, passing Manor Farm.

(4)

Walk down Castle Street and cross Castle Hill to the Guard House, a windowless lock-up built for the parish overseers in 1824. Continue ahead down Horn Street.

(5)

Turn left down the lane passing in front of the restored Penny's Mill. Cross the footbridge and ascend the steps beyond to the stile. Cross the field to the farm buildings, skirting the edge of them, and walk down the track to the gate.

(6)

Pass through the gate and turn left down High Street back to Market Place.

SLAPTON

DEVON

Off A379, 8m E of Kingsbridge

SLAPTON, meaning 'wet or slippery settlement', grew around the stream running from Pool to the Ley. Pool, the main manor, was owned by the de Brien family from the 12th century. In the early 17th century it belonged to Admiral Sir Richard Hawkins, kinsman of Elizabethan 'sea dog' Sir John Hawkins. The old house was destroyed by fire in 1800.

Farming was supplemented by sea and freshwater fishing, lime burning and quarrying. Most of the buildings are of slate rubble from quarries at Charleton. Local slate and reed from the Ley were used for roofing and there are many timber-framed, cob, stone and thatch buildings dating from the 17th century or earlier.

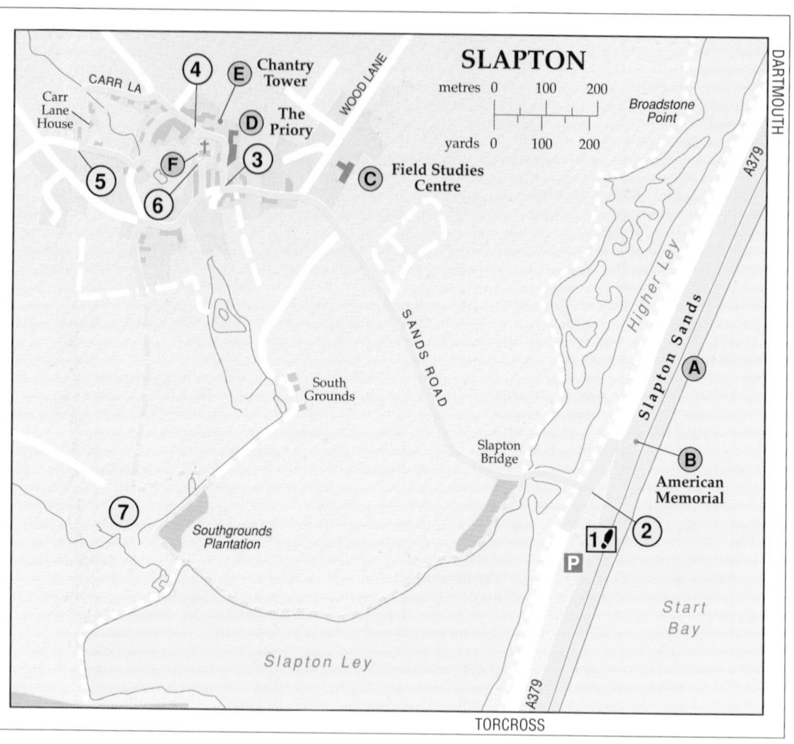

POINTS OF INTEREST

Slapton Sands. The car park stands on the site of 19th-century fish cellars, a shipyard and two limekilns. After the road was built in 1856 the cellars were converted to the Royal Sands Hotel. The hotel was ruined in 1940 when a dog set off six coastal defence mines as he walked by.

American Memorial. The memorial was erected by the American Army for the inhabitants of seven parishes, including Slapton, who were evacuated so that the area could be used for military training from December 1943 until D Day, June 1944.

Field Studies Centre. This is based around the old vicarage, which was built in 1906 for the Rev. H.G. Warner at his own expense. It now belongs to the Field Studies Council.

The Priory. This large house incorporates remains of the chapel of St Mary, demolished when the adjacent College was dissolved in 1547. It became the property of the Arundell family from then until 1786.

E

Chantry Tower. The 80ft-high tower is all that remains of the College of St Mary, founded in 1372 by Sir Guy de Brien. The College was for a Rector and nine clerics, one of whom was parish priest, to sing masses for the de Brien family.

F

Church of St James the Great. The church dates mainly from the 14th and 15th centuries, with a medieval broached spire on a Norman tower. The north door has a sanctuary ring and over its porch is the Parish Chamber, once the priest's room and school. There is a full-length oak screen and a tomb to Lady Judith Hawkins (died 1629), wife of Sir Richard. Not known for her modesty, Lady Judith liked to walk to church preceded by two negroes, who rolled a red carpet in front of her.

WALK DIRECTIONS

From the car park on Slapton Sands turn right up the road to the American Memorial and return to the road junction.

2

Turn right and cross the bridge over the Ley. There was a drawbridge here in the 16th century. Walk up Sands Road to the village centre, passing the Field Studies Centre on the right and Gospel Hall of 1868 on the left. Ahead at the next junction are the 18th-century Assembly Rooms, (left) now a store, and on the right Tithe Barn Gardens in front of the former Chantry barn.

3

Turn right, passing the Queen's Arms. It probably began as the Church House, which was like a combination of an inn, village hall and almshouse run by the church. It was renowned for its white ale.

4

At the Round House turn right to view the Chantry Tower from the yard of the Tower Inn, which was the College's guesthouse. Return to the road, continue uphill and turn left along Carr Lane with its reed-thatched cottage and farmhouse which once produced renowned local cider.

5

At Mingoes, turn left then left again opposite Sloutts Farmhouse. Pass the Old Workhouse on your left. Turn right at the road junction and right again to the church.

6

Continue to the lych-gate beyond the church. Walk down the steps to the old houses in Church Lane. Turn right and walk up the road past thatched Vale Cottage. Turn left down the public footpath by the nurseries. Continue along the edge of the fields and over the stile by the sewage works.

Turn left along the boardwalk, then right and along the edge of the Ley, over five stiles to the gate on to the road by Slapton Bridge. Return to the car park.

INFORMATION
Length of walk:
2½ miles
Approximate time:
2 hours

TERRAIN:
Easy going with moderate gradients, but 6 stiles and wet patches along edge of Ley. Not suitable for pushchairs or wheelchairs.

PARKING:
Off A379 on Slapton Sands, no toilets.

REFRESHMENTS:
Queen's Arms and Tower Inn pubs.

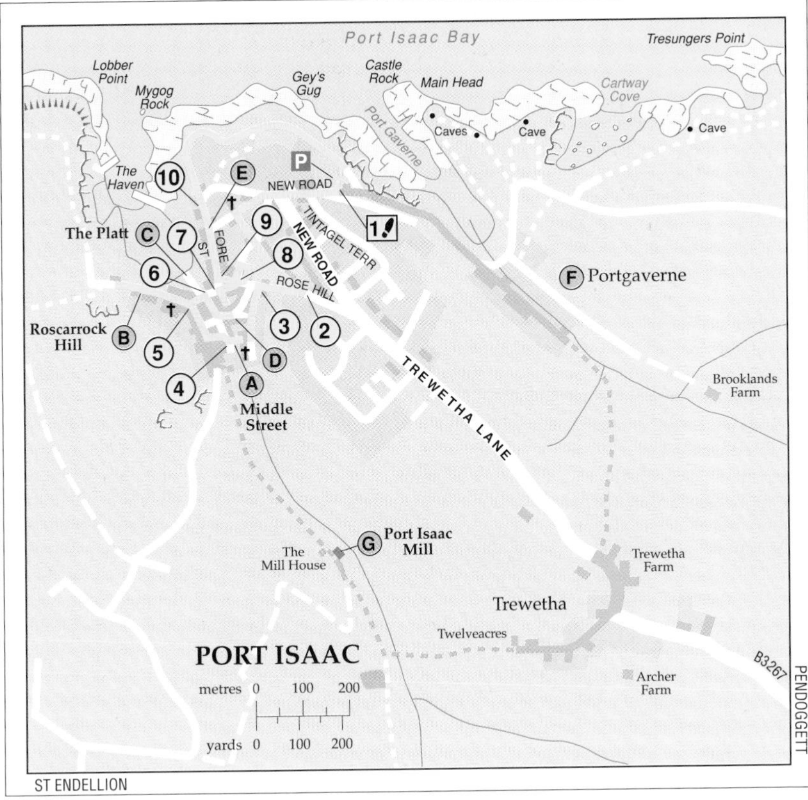

PORT ISAAC

CORNWALL

On B3267, 8m N of Wadebridge

PORT Isaac developed in medieval times. It was once known as Porthissick, which probably means 'corn port', although from the beginning it was mainly a fishing port.

The present piers date from the 1930s, but the remains of one built in the reign of Henry VIII can still be seen. A plethora of fish cellars and houses followed its buildings and the village flourished with the pilchard fishing industry. During this time Delabole slate was first exported from the port – mainly to France and Belgium. The slate trade continued until the 19th century, when ships of 50 to 80 tons were plying a more local coastal trade. This was lost to the railways in the 1890s, which fortunately brought the tourist trade to replace it.

The fishing industry declined from about 1820, when herring shoals began to decrease in size. In 1850 there were about 50 fishing boats, each bringing in 200-300 fish at a time. These were sorted in four fish cellars. Fish were sold locally or sent to Billingsgate and pilchard oil sold to Italy. Herrings were smoked in kipper lofts, but there were few by the 1870s, when railways made it possible to substitute fresh mackerel and shellfish by reaching markets more rapidly.

There were boat building yards on both sides of the harbour. The population grew during the 19th century and a school was built in 1804 and a

WALK DIRECTIONS

From the car park follow New Road and Back Hill towards the harbour. At the church turn left up Trewetha Lane.

Turn right down Rose Hill.

Turn left just before Chicago House, a tall weatherboarded dwelling typically built into the hillside with entrances at different levels. Although one property now, it was built as three houses on top of one another, which are not connected internally. Walk down Back Lane into Middle Street.

Turn left at the butcher's shop and right down Church Hill, past The Slipway Hotel, which dates from the 16th century and was until recently a chandlery selling paint, ropes and preservatives for nets.

Detour up Roscarrock Hill as far as Northcliff House and return to the Platt (harbour slipway).

6

Turn right up Middle Street, then left for Dolphin Street and left again under Temple Bar to Fore Street.

Turn right up Shuggy's Ope, a wonderful alley across which buildings nearly touch, to Rose Hill and turn up the hill.

Turn left up Margaret's Lane, left around the Birdcage, an odd, three-storey, 19th-century house belonging to the National Trust, and return down Rose Hill to Fore Street.

Turn right up Fore Street and pass the post office on the left.

Turn left at Cliff Cottage and follow the Coast Path back to the car park.

If option is followed continue past the car park and down the hill to Port Gaverne.

Turn right up the lane past the fish cellar and toilets. Cross a slate stile, then a wooden stile. Along the stream withies were planted to provide twigs for making lobster pots.

Turn right up the hill as signposted to Trewetha. Follow the waymarks, keeping to the left-hand side of the field.

Cross the stile and continue along the road past Trewetha Farm and cottages.

Take the track downhill signposted to Port Isaac.

Cross the stile and tiny footbridge and immediately turn right, skirting around the former pond.

Take the small gate on to the track and continue downhill past the mill to church Hill. Return to car park via Fore Street, Back Hill and New Road.

A fishing harbour since the Middle Ages, Port Isaac is protected by high headlands, which are in turn protected by the National Trust. Despite its popularity as a holiday resort, the village has managed to retain its Cornish character.

church in 1889. This was a chapel of ease to save the villagers the two mile walk up Church Hill to the parish church at St Endellion, until Port Isaac became a parish in 1913. John Wesley visited several times between 1748 and 1789. He had a rough reception at first, partly because of his views against smuggling, but Methodism gained great popularity and Methodist and Wesleyan chapels still exist.

Despite tourism and many new houses at the top of the hill, down in the old part of the village the character has changed little since Wesley's time. Cottages, whitewashed or slate-hung and roofed with pale grey Delabole slate are separated by 'opes, drangs and courts'. They cluster around the small harbour and mill stream which threads through and under them.

Here, at the centre of the village, the fishermens' catch was landed, then stored or sold.

POINTS OF INTEREST

Middle Street. Wesley House stands at the top of the street. Early Methodist meetings were held at 'church houses'. The owner of the first house barred Wesley from it, lest it be attacked by villagers. The first Wesley chapel was built near here in 1750. A window in the shed of No.31 opposite may have come from this.

Down the street is Pump Cottage, with its housed pump in use for drinking water until recently. Further down is The Bakehouse, one of two operating in the 19th century with large cloam (clay-lined) ovens where housewives brought their meals to be baked.

Roscarrock Hill. 'Northcliff' stands on the site of the former carpenter's yard for boat repair. In an exposed position at the top of the street, its roof timbers are tied to the foundations with an anchor chain. Below this 'Halwyn' stands on the site of the main boatyard whose last boat, *Bessy Jane*, was built in 1850. The yard was converted to a house after the First World War.

The Platt. This is the centre of the village where boats were hauled up, fish landed, lobster pots stored and markets held. The Market House incorporates 15th-century corner stones of Lundy granite. The Wheelhouse is an old meeting house with galley inside. Opposite, the fish cellars are still used for storing and processing fish and to house the inshore lifeboat. They were built for curing herrings and salting pilchards, which were pressed in barrels to extract the oil. This was done by levering down the lids with poles using holes in the cellar walls as anchor points, the lids as pivots and boulders from the beach as weights. One weight has been built into the wall below Port Isaac Stores. To the east of the harbour old fishermens' 'linneys' or stores lean against the 'Pentus', a wall supporting Fore Street above.

(D)

Dolphin Street. The street took its name from the Dolphin Inn now a private house. Opposite this is Trevan House, named after a Doctor Trevan, who owned it in the 19th century and probably built Bark House, which partly blocks it, and Vesta Cottage next door. Bark House was the Doctor's coach house and surgery, later converted for 'barking' fishing nets – preserving them in a hot solution of oak bark. Further up is Temple Bar, an alley under Temple Cottage commonly known as 'Squeeze-ee-belly-alley'. At an average width of 18 inches, it is claimed to be Britain's narrowest thoroughfare.

Fore Street. The post office is in what was the lifeboat house from 1869 to 1927. The boat was guided down the narrow street on a carriage held back by many men with ropes. Corners of buildings were cut away to help it round the bend in the street and the wall of the newsagents was scored by the ropes. Cliff Cottage was built in 1868 with ships timbers.

Port Gaverne. In the 19th century slates came by ox cart from Delabole along the 5-mile Great Slate Road. Women loaded them into sailing boats, which brought in coal and lime for the limekiln which can still be seen. It was a boat-building centre and busy pilchard fishing port with four cellars. The Rashleigh cellar is preserved by the National Trust. The cottage named Chimneys, backing on to the stream, was where the fish were salted.

Port Isaac Mill. Now just a farm, this was a corn mill and bakery in the 19th century. The owner had a shop in Middle Street, to which he carried his produce by donkey.

INFORMATION
Length of walk:
1 mile (3 miles with option)
Approximate time:
1½ hours (2½ hours with option)

TERRAIN:
Suitable for children at all times of year, except option, which has steep and muddy sections. The walk is unsuitable for wheelchairs and pushchairs are limited to the village.

PARKING:
Car park and toilets at top of Port Gaverne Hill.

REFRESHMENTS:
Several inns and restaurants. Takeaway seafood and pasties a speciality.

THE SLAUGHTERS

GLOUCESTERSHIRE

Off A429 (Fosse Way), 1m N of Bourton-on-the-Water

IN the heart of the Cotswolds on the tributary of the River Windrush, and separated by ridge and furrow meadows, these two streamside villages hold great appeal. In Saxon times the centre of a 'hundred', in modern times their beauty makes them the pilgrimage of hundreds. The two villages have but the River Eye in common; in layout and development they are quite different. The placename Slaughter derives from *slohtre* meaning 'marshy place'. There remains evidence of this in the higher village, where a path treads a Mesopotamian course through the watermeadow.

WALK DIRECTIONS

①

From the roadside parking place in Lower Slaughter, follow the River Eye upstream. Keep right at the road bridge, advancing beyond The Green to follow the curve of the river, passing round by Collett's Mill to a footpath and two kissing-gates. Proceed beside the millstream to a further kissing-gate.

Cross the ridge-and-furrow pasture; the footpath initially angles half-right before advancing to another kissing-gate. Descend, half-left, to a kissing-gate and footbridge over the Eye, following the confined path winding up to the road. On the opposite bank rises the mound of an early Norman motte; there is no record of its occupation.

Go left, passing the entrance to the Lords of the Manor Hotel, formerly the parsonage. Cross Bagshot's Square, and proceed through the churchyard to view the church.

④

From the Old School House descend, left, along the road to the ford/footbridge over the River Eye. The attractive upstream scene incorporates Way's End, the rectory during the first half of the present century. Notice the gable-end dovecote in the adjacent barn, clearly constructed above a lower roofline. Either follow the road right, from the former Primitive Methodist chapel (now a pottery workshop), or cross the stile immediately right and follow the causeway path through the watermeadow to the stile beside the old sheep wash. Go left to the road junction.

Leave Upper Slaughter along the road uphill. At the sharp left corner, go right, through the gate. Advance to rejoin the approach path through the pastures.

⑥

Retrace your steps back towards Lower Slaughter. Keep straight ahead through the horse paddocks via the fenced corridor, leading back into the village, passing the Hatch Patch, Manor Hotel and St Mary's Church to finish the walk.

POINTS OF INTEREST

Washbourne Hotel, Lower Slaughter. Formerly Washbourne's Place and in more recent years a school, its name derives from its 15th-century owner. Notice the heavy buttress, clearly an attempt to hold in check an old wall. In the last few years the current owner has transformed it from a charming, private residence, into a thriving hotel.

Collett's Mill, Lower Slaughter. The striking red-brick chimney and static waterwheel of the still-active bakery (originally a 19th-century mill running until the 1960s) make a pleasing feature at the upper end of the village. Beneath it flows the clear water of the millstream and River Eye.

Lords of the Manor Hotel, Upper Slaughter. The earliest parts of this house date from 1680. During the 19th century it became the home of the Witts family, who were first rectors and then lords of the manor. The Rev. Francis Witts was notable for his compassion and pastoral care; he wrote the still popular *Diary of a Cotswold Parson*.

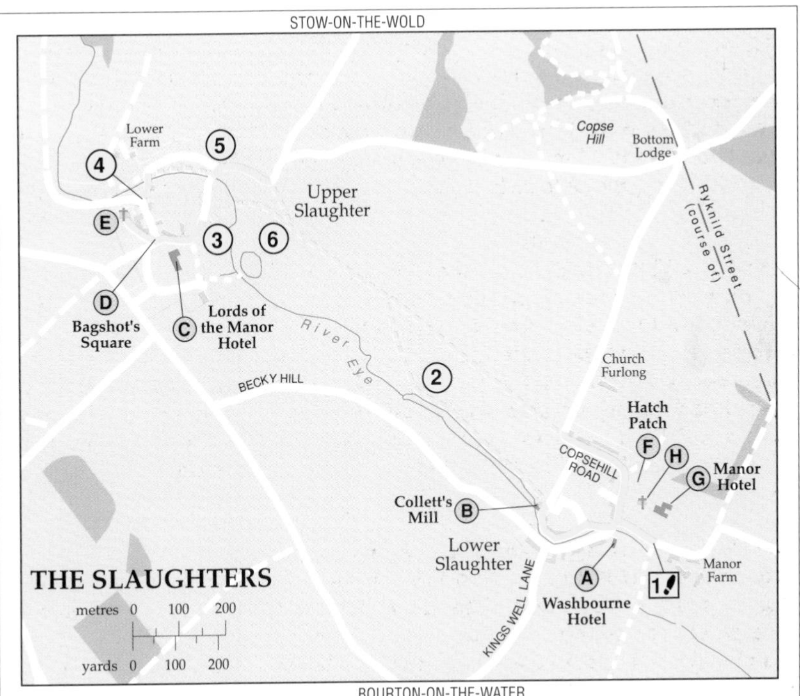

A stone footbridge in Lower Slaughter.

CHARACTERISTICS OF COTSWOLD STONE

The oolitic limestone of the Cotswold region has excited masons since the days of the Romans. Its colour varies from near-white to rich honey. When freshly quarried, as a 'free-stone', it can be sculpted. Exposure to the elements makes it hard, though eventually prone to flake. Stone taken from near the surface was less likely to be friable and came into its own during the great period of stone building, from the mid-16th century, as a roofing material. Later, as the Enclosure Acts of the late 18th century drew the wolds into great square fields, it was raised to create drystone walling.

A tributary of the River Windrush runs beside the tree-shaded main street of Lower Slaughter.

Bagshot's Square, Upper Slaughter. The cottages grouped near the entrance to the churchyard were remodelled by Sir Edwin Lutyens in 1906. From that time the village saw no new building until the current decade, with the expansion of the Lords of the Manor Hotel and the conversion of the farmyard flanking the Square.

Ⓔ

St Peter's Church, Upper Slaughter. A subtle Victorian refurbishment of an early Norman church, picturesquely approached via a sunken path. The three brasses in the chancel belonging to the de Slaughters, owners of the Old Manor House in the 16th century, are of special interest, as is the rather grim canopied mortuary chapel dedicated to Rev F E Witts, rector from 1808-54. Underneath the structure is a chest tomb with a cross and text in its matrix. The chapel floor has good Victorian tiles, and the small window is dedicated to the parson's wife by their son Edward.

Hatch Patch, Lower Slaughter. Approached through the churchyard, this wildlife conservation garden was created in 1987. Featuring a pond stocked with iris and lily, a wildflower meadow and a diversity of trees, this innovative scheme deserves high praise. It provides a tranquil haven for all forms of wildlife (see the information board for precise details of the project).

Manor Hotel, Lower Slaughter. The house was built in 1640 by Valentine Strong of Little Barrington for Sir Richard Whitmore. The Whitmore family remained influential in village life up until as recently as 1964. In the hotel grounds, tucked in close by the churchyard, is a dovecote built like a typical Cotswold cottage. It is one of the largest in Gloucestershire.

St Mary's Church, Lower Slaughter. In the main this shows Victorian restructuring in early post-Norman style. The upper portion of the spire is a deft use of fibreglass, set in place with a helicopter in 1968.

INFORMATION
Length of walk:
$1^3/_4$ miles
Approximate time:
$1^1/_4$ hours

TERRAIN:
The sequence of kissing-gates make the inter-village section impractical for push-chairs and wheelchairs. Children will have no difficulty, though be watchful beside the millstream.

PARKING:
Roadside parking beside the River Eye opposite the Manor Hotel, Lower Slaughter.

REFRESHMENTS:
Lower Slaughter. Manor Hotel, Washbourne Hotel and Collett's Shop. Upper Slaughter. The Lords of the Manor Hotel, or the generous range of facilities in nearby Bourton-on-the-Water.

Upper Slaughter stands on a hill overlooking Slaughter Brook, once dominated by a Norman castle.

INFORMATION
Length of walk:
2½ miles (4 miles if the Wildfowl Trust site is visited)
Approximate time:
2 hours (a long half-day if the Wildfowl Trust is visited)

TERRAIN:
Suitable for children at all times. Not suitable for pushchairs or wheelchairs. Many stiles and footbridges.

PARKING:
Parking is very easy at the Wildfowl Trust site, and relatively easy near Shepherd's Patch on the canal. In Slimbridge itself there is no car park, but it is possible to park tidily.

OPEN:
The Wildfowl Trust. Daily (except Christmas Day and Boxing Day). Wheelchairs are available inside. Strictly no dogs, except guide dogs. Charge.

The fine Early Gothic church of St John with its three-stage tower, is faced with blocks of tufa.

Pleasure boats moored up along the banks of the Gloucester to Sharpness Canal.

SLIMBRIDGE

GLOUCESTERSHIRE

1m W of A38, between Gloucester and Bristol

SET in the Vale of Berkeley, Slimbridge is famous as the home of Sir Peter Scott's Wildfowl Trust, and also for the nearby Gloucester and Sharpness Canal, an unexpected waterway so close to the Severn.

The original, tiny village grew up among the fertile watermeadows of the Vale of Berkeley. Traditionally, William Tyndale, the translator of the Bible into English, was born at Hurst Farm, to the south-west of the village. It has to be said, though, that other sites are also held to be his birthplace. Tyndale was executed for heresy though later ages have seen him as martyr rather than as an agent of the devil. A memorial tower to him dominates the Cotswold Edge at North Nibley, south of Slimbridge. More locally the Cotswold Edge is dominated by two 'outliers' near Cam, north-east of Slimbridge. The tent-shaped hummock is Cam Long Down, while the conical peak is Cam Peak.

POINTS OF INTEREST

St John's Church. By common consent this is the finest Early Gothic (13th-century) church in Gloucestershire. It is believed that there was a 9th-century church on the site, but nothing earlier than 1200 now exists. Before going in, notice the two stone corbel heads on the wall to the right of the entrance porch. They are of Edward I, commemorating a visit the King made to Berkeley Castle, and an abbot who was living in Slimbridge at the time. Look too for the old sundial above the porch door. Inside, the eye is drawn to the beautiful nave arcade, but do not miss the lead font, dated 1664 and one of the few that remain in England.

Behind the church is the old Rectory, and separating the two is the remains of a moat that once helped protect the vicar from his flock!

The Gloucester to Sharpness Canal. Gloucester suffered as a dock from the fact that large ships could only reach it on spring tides, which severely limited its trade. It was therefore decided, in 1783, to dig a canal from Berkeley to Gloucester. Not until the Manchester Ship Canal was built in 1885 was there a bigger waterway in Britain and still today only the Manchester canal is larger. Digging began in 1793, though it was soon decided to reach the Severn at Sharpness rather than Berkeley, to save money and time. Even so it was not until 1827 that the canal, and the Sharpness docks, were

opened, due to the fact that there was no heavy machinery at that time and the waterway was entirely dug by hand. The men who did the digging of such navigations were called navigators, soon shortened to 'navvies', a name that remains in use today.

The bridge at Shepherd's Patch is a swing bridge, like all the others on the canal, the ships for which it was designed being tall masted.

As the years went by larger and larger ships arrived at Sharpness. Many were too big to use the canal, so their cargo had to be transferred to barges for the final leg of the journey to Gloucester. In 1960 over one million tons of trade passed up the canal, though today it is quieter, most of the cargo being unloaded at Sharpness for rail or road transport.

Ⓒ

The Wildfowl Trust. Slimbridge is the home of the first Wildfowl Trust site, founded by Sir Peter Scott in 1946. In its earliest days visitors were, virtually, personal guests of Sir Peter, viewing the over-wintering geese and swans through his own picture window. Times have changed considerably, the site now boasting an excellent visitor centre, restaurants, hides out on the estuary and a collection of penned birds. The wildfowl collection is the largest in the world, with around 200 different species, many of which breed here. Slimbridge has had notable success with endangered wildfowl such as the Hawaiian Goose, saved from extinction and then re-introduced to the wild after breeding here. The larger reserve on the tidal mudflats of the Severn covers 2,000 acres and is home to over-wintering flocks of white-fronted geese and Bewick swans.

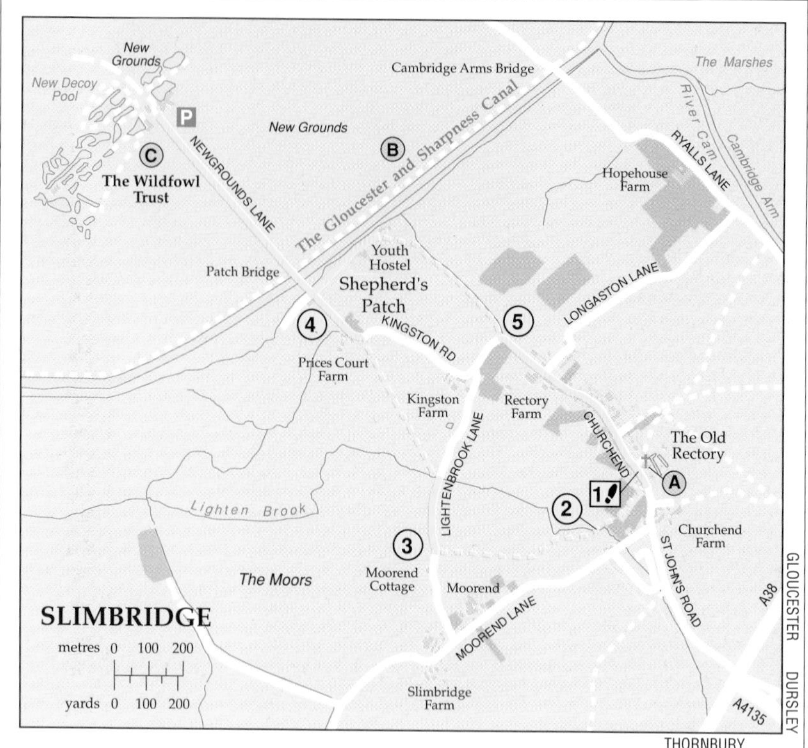

The Wildfowl Trust has six other sites in Britain: at Arundel in Sussex; Peakirk and Welny in East Anglia; Martin Mere near Southport; Washington in Tyne and Wear and Caerlaverock on the Solway Firth.

Geese feeding at the Wildfowl Trust, where fowl can be observed from hides.

WALK DIRECTIONS

①

From the church, walk towards the A38 for about 50yds to reach a stile, right, beside Malthouse Farm. Climb over and cross the field. Go through a gate and follow the left hedge to a footbridge.

②

Walk over the footbridge and bear right across the field, passing to the right of some iron fencing. Go over a stile and follow the fence, right, to a corner. Now turn left and cross the field to a gate. Go through and turn right to cross a big field to a stile by a large tree. Go over and cross the next field to a footbridge on to a lane.

③

Turn right along Lightenbrook Lane for about 300yds to a stile on the left, just beyond a field opening, also left. Climb over the stile and walk diagonally across the field towards a tall tree to reach a stiled footbridge. Go diagonally across the next field, under the power lines. Occasionally there is a paddock in the far corner of this field entered by a stile and crossed to a final stile on to a lane. Turn left along the lane to Shepherd's Patch.

④

To visit the Wildfowl Trust, continue along the lane, going over the canal and down Newgrounds Lane to the site. To return, retrace the route to Shepherd's Patch.

Take the lane signed for the Youth Hostel and bear left past it. Go over a stile, right, before the bungalow and cross a field to another stile. The route is marked with yellow arrows. Walk diagonally over the next field, under the power lines, to reach another stile. Now follow the field edge, left, over two further marked stiles, heading towards a building – an electricity substation. Just before it there is a stile in the left hedge that gives access to a plank bridge over a ditch. Cross and go right along the track to reach a lane.

⑤

Go left along the lane back into Slimbridge.

SNOWSHILL

GLOUCESTERSHIRE

Off A44, 2m S of Broadway

SNOWSHILL is located on a pent shelf just beneath the head of a deep tuck in the Cotswold escarpment, facing north to the fertile Vale of Evesham. The scenic outlook is enhanced by wood-draped slopes and verdant pastures. Historically linked to Stanton, during the early medieval period the village formed part of Winchcombe Abbey's vast sheep estate.

A settlement has existed here over many centuries. Its connections with the outside world were via the ancient ridgetop trackway network, only in 1872 did the road to Broadway come into being.

INFORMATION
Length of walk:
¾ mile
Approximate time:
½ hour

TERRAIN:
Almost entirely on roads, though as the village is built on steep banks, wheelchairs will need good brakes. It is quite suitable for push-chairs and children.

PARKING:
National Trust car park at the northern tip of the village, off the Broadway road.

OPEN:
Snowshill Manor (NT). Easter Sat-Mon 11am-1pm, 2-5pm, Apr and Oct Sat-Sun 11am-1pm, 2-5pm, May-Sep, Wed-Sun, 11am-1pm, 2-6pm. Limited access to ground floor and part of garden for wheelchairs. Charge. Broadway Tower Country Park. Apr-Oct 10am-6pm. Charge.

REFRESHMENTS:
The Snowshill Arms, or a range of visitor orientated facilities in Broadway.

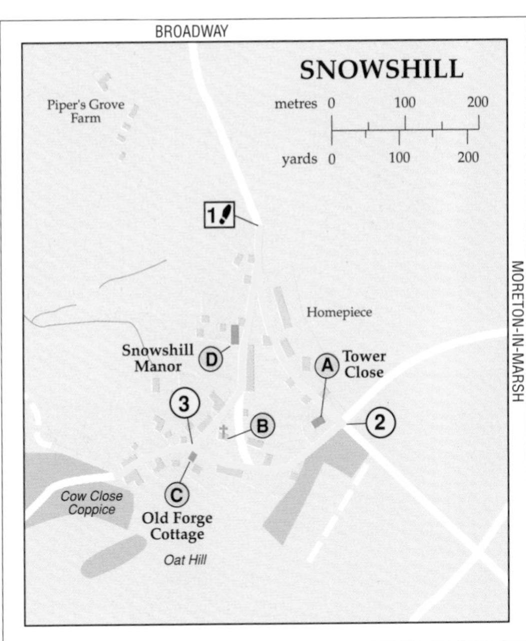

POINTS OF INTEREST

(A)

Tower Close. Tower Close, formerly three cottages, was established in 1917 by Sydney Russell, owner of the Lygon Arms in Broadway and father of Sir Gordon Russell, the famous furniture designer.

St Barnabas' Church. Rebuilt in 1864 the church is composed of quality Cotswold stone, yet it fails to beguile. Funds were apparently insufficient to complete the intended spire, so a temporary pointed roof was erected. This was removed in 1958, the entire roof being renewed in 1990. The pulpit is Jacobean, probably salvaged from the preceding church, of which there is no record.

In the churchyard, beside the porch, is a 'primitive' double chest tomb of early date. The tombstone leaning against the holly tree by the fenced Marshall tomb is inscribed to Mary Stanley, who died in 1797, at the grand old age of 97.

Old Forge Cottage. Until 1929 this had a workshop adjacent. It caught the eye of Henry Ford, a guest of Sydney Russell's, who had it shipped to the USA and re-erected in his outdoor museum.

The Snowshill Arms, near the entrance to the manor of this tiny, close knit upland village.

(D)

Snowshill Manor. The original early 16th-century farmhouse saw numerous alterations during the succeeding two centuries. Below the hipped roof the south front has an odd symmetry, with the mixture of windows either side of the pedimented door. In the grounds, close to the Manor, are a dovecote and a house thought to have been built upon the site of a priest's residence, from the time when Winchcombe Abbey held the manor. In 1919 Charles Paget Wade purchased the dilapidated house, restoring it extensively to display his eccentric collections of gadgetry and artefacts and landscaping the rustic farmyard into a beautiful tiered garden.

WALK DIRECTIONS

From the NT car park follow signs for Snowshill Manor, keeping left at the road fork. Ascend beyond the council houses to the Tower Close crossroads.

Go right, signed 'Snowshill and Ford 3'. The lane descends steeply, curving to the expanding village prospect, centred upon St Barnabas' church. Pass straight down through the churchyard via wicket gates. On the left is Old Forge Cottage. The War Memorial, a beautiful creation of Frederick Griggs, is suffering the effects of weathering. It stands within the church-yard upon the site of the wheelwright's shop.

Go left along the street. Admire the staddle stones built in 1922 into the former farmyard wall adjacent to Old Barn. The 12 stones originally supported a thatched granary. Follow the road to Oat Hill (formerly Snowshill) Farm. You may like to temporarily escape the possible torment of cars by detouring right at the broad wicket gate, down the footpath (concrete plinth waymark), to a galvanised gate. From here the rough landslipped banks of the combe come into view. Retrace your steps, forking left at the church to pass the Snowshill Arms and Snowshill Manor entrance. An attractive row commences on the right with the manor farmhouse. The Malthouse, in the middle, appears to have been raised to form a malting floor. Return to the car park.

SOUTH CADBURY

SOMERSET

On minor roads off A303, 9m NE of Yeovil

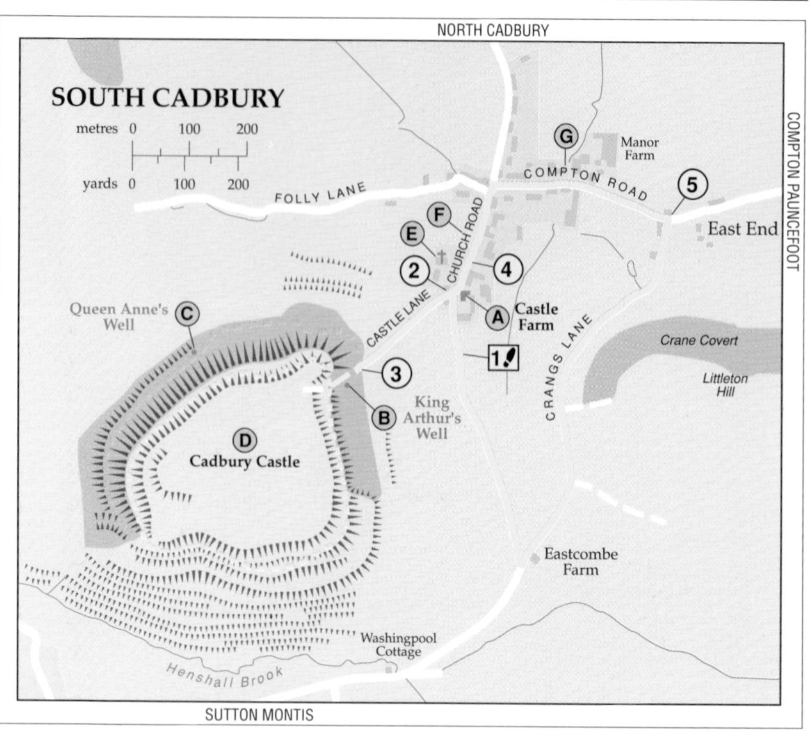

THE attractive village of South Cadbury grew at the junction of ancient trackways. Its early history entirely concerns the fortification on the hill above it.

Here was an Iron Age town of industrial and commercial importance. The town of wood, wattle and thatch buildings was destroyed by the Romans after a battle at its gates in AD70. The Romans built a temple here but it was in the Dark Ages that the settlement became most important.

It was then that tradition has it that King Arthur used the castle as his base to defend the area against the Saxons. It was frequently called Camelot by early topographers.

The Saxons finally overwhelmed the castle, which was not used again until the 11th century, when Ethelred the Unready fortified it against the Vikings.

POINTS OF INTEREST

Ⓐ

Castle Farm. The farmhouse has a datestone of 1687 and retains some of its original four light stone mullioned windows. It is thatched and of mellow Cary stone with Doulting stone dressings.

Ⓑ

King Arthur's Well. This circular, brick-lined well is topped with a small stone arch set into the bank. It is said to never run dry, but is choked with debris. It is supposed to be haunted by King Arthur's hounds, which drink from the well before following their master on ghostly rides along the old track to Glastonbury known as Arthur's Hunting Causeway. He and his knights are said to sleep in a cavern in the hill, emerging occasionally on moonlit nights to ride around the hill on silver shod horses.

Ⓒ

Queen Anne's Well. It is also disappointingly filled with debris and its former elegant semi-circular stone basin has been replaced with one of brick and corrugated iron. It is a wishing well and pins dropped into it before sunrise are supposed to foretell one's luck in romantic matters. A pin aligning with another gives promise of marriage.

Ⓓ

Cadbury Castle. This covers 18 acres with four sets of ramparts nearly a mile in diameter, and three entrances. In places the tops of the ramparts are 40ft above their ditches. Below the southern side these are supplemented by 'The Linches' – cultivation terraces last used in the 18th century. On a clear day it is possible to see Glastonbury tor, and the Mendip, Quantock and Blackdown Hills.

Ⓔ

Church of St Thomas à Becket. St Thomas à Becket was martyred in Canterbury Cathedral in 1170. The church was built in the mid 13th century when his cult was at its height.

Ⓕ

Church Road. Opposite the church is South Cadbury House, the former rectory. It was built in the 18th century of local Lias stone and enlarged in 1835 to form a U-shaped plan.

Ⓖ

Compton Road. At the head of the street a carpenter's workshop looks across to an old well. There are several old cottages and farm buildings in Cary stone. Thatched Eiston Cottage has a variety of casement windows, original beams and fireplace with oven and curing chamber.

INFORMATION
Length of walk:
2 miles
Approximate time:
2 hours

TERRAIN:
Easy going around village, but Castle Lane is steep and muddy at times and the option to Queen Anne's Well is overgrown and muddy in places.

PARKING:
No car park or toilets, but parking is possible in the main streets and the lay-by to the south of Castle Farm.

REFRESHMENTS:
The Red Lion inn.

WALK DIRECTIONS

①

Walk towards the village from the Castle Farm layby.

②

Turn left up Castle Lane, opposite Castle Farm.

③

Pass through the kissing-gate and continue uphill past King Arthur's Well, which is to the left of the track near a cattle trough. Circuit the castle ramparts on the top of the hill and return down Castle Lane. Turn left along Church Road to the church.

For the option turn right immediately after the kissing-gate and take the path which follows the ditch of the lower rampart around the base of the hill past Queen Anne's Well. It ascends the hill on the far side, from where the circuit can be completed on the top rampart.

④

From the church continue up Church Road. At the crossroads turn right down Compton Road.

⑤

At East End Cottage turn right down Crangs Lane and after Eastcombe Farm turn right up the road back to the lay-by.

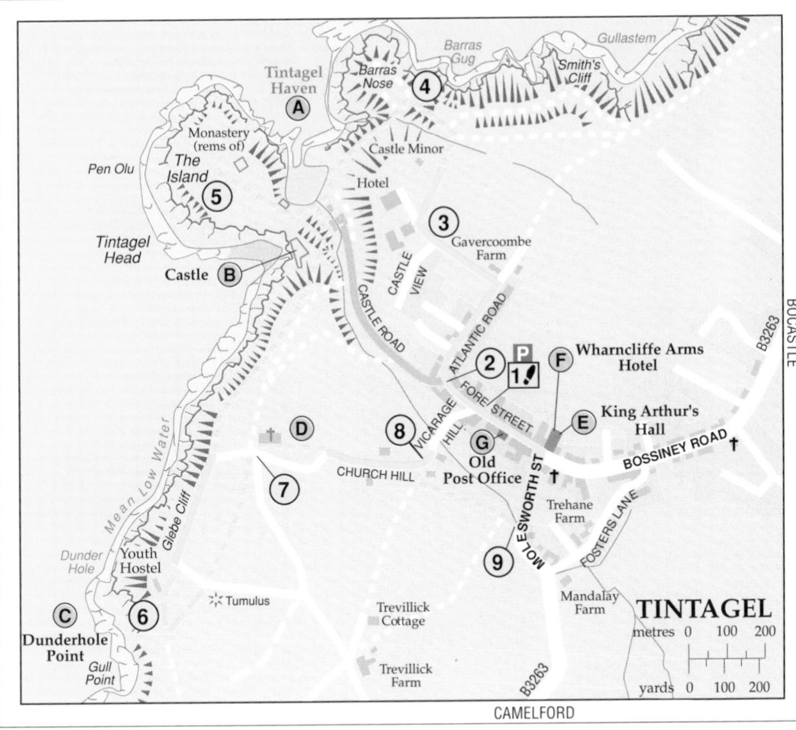

TINTAGEL

CORNWALL

On B3263, 5m NW of Camelford

TINTAGEL parish contains 13 hamlets, one of which, Trevena, became the main village. It took the name of the parish in this century to identify itself with the castle of the same name, which is Cornish for 'fortified neck of land'.

Field patterns show cultivation since Celtic times and there are medieval lynchets or cultivation terraces at Bossiney, which then was the more important hamlet with a 13th-century charter. It was a 'rotten borough' where a few easily corruptible voters returned two members of Parliament. In 1584 one of these was Sir Francis Drake, and in 1784 the one eligible voter returned both members.

Trevena, now linked with Bossiney, ended at the top of Fore Street, where stood the Town Hall and Market House (demolished in about 1840), the village stocks and pound for stray animals. There was a sheep and cattle fair in October, when the whole street was filled with stock.

According to legend embellished by Geoffrey of Monmouth in the 12th century, Arthur was the son of Ygraine, wife of Gorlois, Duke of Cornwall. She was seduced by Uther, disguised as Gorlois with the help of Merlin. New interest in the legend was sparked by the Romantic movement in the 19th century. Hawker wrote his *Quest of the Sangraal* here in 1823 and Tennyson his *Morte d'Arthur* in 1842 and *Idylls of the King*

WALK DIRECTIONS

From the car park turn right down Fore Street. Near the end a short cut option may be taken down Castle Road to the castle.

If following the longer route, keep round to the right, along Atlantic Road and left at the end down towards King Arthur's Castle Hotel, an outstanding landmark erected in 1899 on Fire Beacon Hill.

Turn right by the hotel entrance, walk down the footpath and cross the stile to Barras Nose, the second-ever acquisition of the National Trust in 1896. There are good views to the castle and, on a clear day, north as far as Hartland Point.

Cut back down and along the Coast Path to the footbridge which crosses the stream dropping into the Haven. From here an option at low tide is to descend to the beach to view Merlin's Cave. This is only for the agile as rocks are slippery on the path and in the cave. Facing the Haven from the Coast Path, detour to the left to visit the Island part of the castle.

Retrace your steps and walk up the valley past the shop and exhibition centre and turn right up the Coast Path to the mainland section of the castle. Continue up the path and along Glebe Cliff to Dunderhole Point.

Follow the Youth Hostel drive around a bend and when the church comes in sight cut across the old golf course towards it.

Cut through the churchyard via lych-gates at each end and down Church Hill as far as the vicarage. Note the magnificent old stone dovecote in the garden.

Return to the bend in the road, pass through the gateway and take the path to the left signposted to Molesworth Street.

Turn left down Molesworth Street and left at the end, facing the Hall of Chivalry and Wharncliffe Arms Hotel. Continue down Fore Street, passing the Old Post Office and return to the car park.

INFORMATION
Length of walk: $2^3/_4$ miles
Approximate time: 3 hours

TERRAIN:
Quite easy going except in area of Haven and castle, where paths are steep.

PARKING:
Several car parks, main one with toilets in Fore Street opposite Old Post Office.

OPEN:
Castle (EH). Daily Apr-Sept, Oct-Mar, Tue-Sun except Bank Hols. Charge.
Old Post Office (NT). Daily Apr-end Oct. Charge.

REFRESHMENTS:
Several inns and cafés.

The village post office is a very rare, small 14th-century manor house.

in 1859. Swinburne wrote a poem here; it also inspired Elgar's Second Symphony and Arnold Bax's tone poem *Tintagel*.

Relying on the tenuous link with King Arthur, the tourist industry grew with the coming of the railway to Camelford in 1893. Slate quarrying operated on a large scale for at least three centuries, the last quarry closing in 1937.

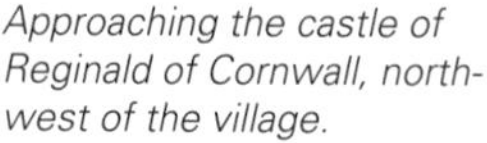

Approaching the castle of Reginald of Cornwall, north-west of the village.

POINTS OF INTEREST

Tintagel Haven. Small sailing vessels called here until the 19th century, bringing in coal and taking out slate. They entered the difficult inlet by 'hobbling' – a combination of towing by rowing boat and warping (using ropes around bollards like pulleys). A cable was stretched across the harbour from a gantry called a 'poppet head' on the cliff. Slate was lowered to vessels from a pulley on the cable operated by horses or donkeys via a capstan behind the gantry. The circular platform for the animals to turn on can still be seen.

Running through the headland of the Island is Merlin's Cave, reputedly haunted by the magician. The baby Arthur is supposed to have been washed ashore here.

Tintagel Castle. The island has 6th-century ruins, possibly of a Celtic monastery. Excavations in the 1930s revealed 4th- to 7th-century pottery from North Africa, Turkey and Greece. The Romans may have traded for tin here and the finds suggest continuing trade with their empire after they left.

The castle was built centuries later by the Earl of Cornwall, son of Henry I. Parts dating from 1145 are on the Island and the mainland site dates from the 14th century, when it belonged to Edward the Black Prince. Later that century it became a prison and by the 16th century it was derelict.

Dunderhole Point. The remains of Long Grass Quarry are to the north of the Point and Gull Point Quarry to the south. These slate quarries operated until the 1930s. Quarrymen at Gull Point were lowered on ropes to drill the best slate at the base of the cliff. It was winched to the top to be split and then dropped by poppet head and whim into ships hazardously moored against the cliff. At Long Grass the slate was split in sheds and steam winched on a tramway to a stacking area from which it was carted to the Haven. The Youth Hostel, still surrounded by slate waste, was the quarry office, blacksmith's shop and engine house.

Church of St Materiana. St Materiana may also be St Madryn, a princess of Gwent who evangelised this area in the 6th century. The church may be on the site of an oratory served by monks from her shrine at Minster, a few miles away. Recent excavations in the churchyard have revealed Dark Age graves and pottery similar to that found at the castle. A Roman stone in the south transept, inscribed with the name of Emperor Licinianus, who died in AD324, suggests a nearby fort.

Among much Norman work in the church are the north wall, windows and doorway and the font, which has roughly carved heads at the corners. Another Norman font by the south wall is from St Jullita's chapel at the castle.

The churchyard has a Cornish 'hedge' or bank faced with slate in the local 'curzyway', herring-bone fashion. Its two lych-gates have granite cattle grids known as 'Cornish stiles'. Some of the headstones are buttressed against the wind.

King Arthur's Hall of Chivalry. Sir William Glassock built this between 1928 and 1933 as headquarters for his Fellowship of the Round Table of King Arthur, which was dissolved when he died in 1934. Built mainly of granite with oak vaulted ceiling and granite Round Table, it incorporates 92 types of Cornish stone and, for a fee, shows the story of King Arthur in 10 paintings and 73 stained glass windows.

The ruins of a 12th-century castle, built on 'The Island'.

Wharncliffe Arms Hotel. In front stand two ancient granite crosses. The larger, rescued from being a gate post, is of the 9th century with a Latin inscription which translates: 'Elnat made this for the repose of his soul.' The Wharncliffes were local landowners of influence in the days of the 'rotten borough.'

Old Post Office. This small 14th-century manor house has a deceptively spacious interior with parlour, bedchamber and hall which reaches the full height of the building to sooty rafters. It was the village post office from 1844 to 1892 and the National Trust, who purchased it for £100 in 1900, have preserved the post room as it was then.

WEST LULWORTH

DORSET

On B3070, 9 miles SW of Wareham

FAMED for its scenery, the area has attracted authors, poets and painters since the 18th century. Here Keats wrote his last sonnet and Thomas Hardy called it Lulwind, using it as the scene for the drowning of Sergeant Troy in *Far from the Madding Crowd*. Rupert Brooke stayed here with literary friends known as the 'Neo-Pagans'.

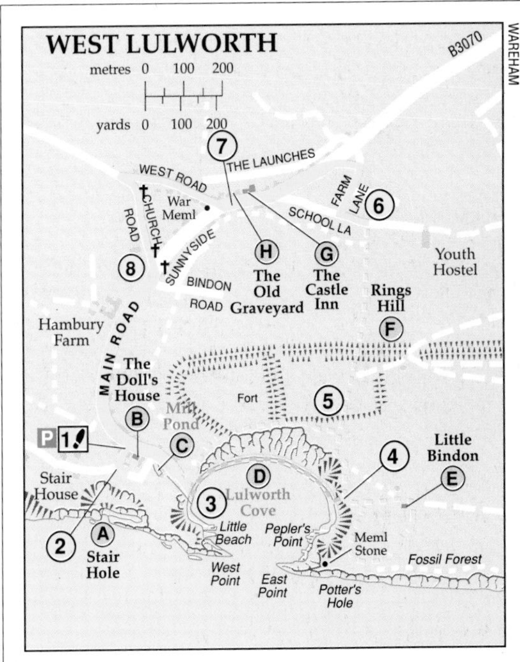

POINTS OF INTEREST

A

Stair Hole. A collapsed cave system of arches and cove exhibiting the contorted structure in Portland limestone known as 'Lulworth crumple'. As in the formation of the cove, the hard band of limestone has been breached by the sea to wear out the softer chalk behind.

B

The Doll's House. The frame of a Canadian log cabin was brought here on the deck of a sailing ship in the early 9th century. It was given a brick skin and chimney stack and two tiny bedrooms were added over the roof. Now decayed, it once had a garden ornamented with plates, figures and crockery.

C

Mill Pond. The cob and thatch mill fell down years ago. Its pond is fed by a spring which for centuries has been the village's main water supply. The pond was used by villagers to wash their clothes and farmers to wash their sheep.

D

The Cove. This was once a busy fishing harbour. Paddle steamers from Weymouth called here from 1879 until 1955. To the right are the remains of a stone jetty which enclosed an oyster pond

E

Little Bindon. This is the site of a 12th-century Cistercian abbey. A chapel and cottage were built from the remains in 1250. They were re-roofed in 1500 and faced with brick in the 18th century. Carved corbel stones project from the east wall. The chapel, open to the public, has 18th-century sailing ships scratched on the wall plaster and a ceiling painted with stars and planets.

F

Rings Hill. For 1½ miles along this and Bindon Hill run a vast series of Iron Age earthworks called Flower's Barrow. At its western end, now eroded by the sea, is a fort enclosed by double ditches and ramparts. Romans camped here following their conquest of the Veneti, the local tribe. To the NE can be seen Lulworth Camp.

G

The Castle Inn. Named after Lulworth Castle, this 18th-century thatched inn has been known as the Jolly Sailor, Traveller's Rest and Green Man. Opposite is the Olde Malt House, its former brewery.

H

The Old Graveyard. The tiny Norman church was hemmed in here between two cottages. Although extended in 1842, it was too small and dilapidated for the needs of the parishioners and was demolished in 1869, when the new church was built.

WALK DIRECTIONS

1

Leaving the car park, keep to the right and walk around past the Heritage Centre. Built in 1990 with the new post office, it houses an exhibition of natural and local history and smuggling. Go up the lane and in 100yds turn left to the clifftop to view Stair Hole.

2

Return to Main Road and turn right, passing the Doll's House and Mill Pond, to reach the Cove.

3

Take the steps behind the Old Boathouse. Passing over a stile, take the steep track around the back of the Cove. It comes to a fence and drops to a signpost to Pepler's Point and the Fossil Forest. Alternatively, at low tide, the beach can be followed to the far end of the Cove, where steps rise to this signpost.

4

Fork right towards the memorial stone and head along the cliff to the range gateway. If closed, return to point 4 and fork right to Little Bindon; if open, go through the gate and take the steps down to the Fossil Forest. Here were found fossils of pine trees which grew around a lagoon 120 million years ago. The fossils have been removed to museums, but the impressions of their trunks and the algae which grew around the stumps can still be seen.

Return up the steps and head inland along the track to the next range gateway. Exit through the gate to view Little Bindon and continue back to point 4. Return up the steep path, but where the village path leaves the fence, continue up by the fence towards the Youth Hostel.

5

Pass over a stile and walk over Rings Hill straight down to another stile and into School Lane.

6

Turn down School Lane and go right at the next T-junction. Pass the Old Farmhouse on your left and turn left at the next junction. Keep left and then ahead down Main Road past the Castle Inn and the old graveyard.

7

At the war memorial turn right up West Road. Turn left down Church Road and through the lych-gate to view the church, built in 1869 to replace the old Norman church in the village.

8

Turn right into Main Road and return to the car park.

INFORMATION
Length of walk:
3 miles
Approximate time:
2 hours

TERRAIN:
Strenuous and best suited to fit adults.

PARKING:
Use the large car park on the south-west side of Main Road at the Cove end of the village.

REFRESHMENTS:
Pubs and cafés in the village.

WIDECOMBE IN THE MOOR

DEVON

On B3387, 6 miles NW of Ashburton

W*IDECOMBE* is a huge parish with six Domesday manors but, due to its moorland location and small population, it has never really prospered.

Tin mining provided sporadic income until the 19th century, when the population reached its peak, and there were woollen mills from the 17th to 19th centuries.

The song *Widecombe Fair,* may be based on fact, as Tom Cobley, Tom Pearse and Bill Brewer lived in the district in the late 18th and early 19th centuries. The Fair is still held on the second Tuesday of September.

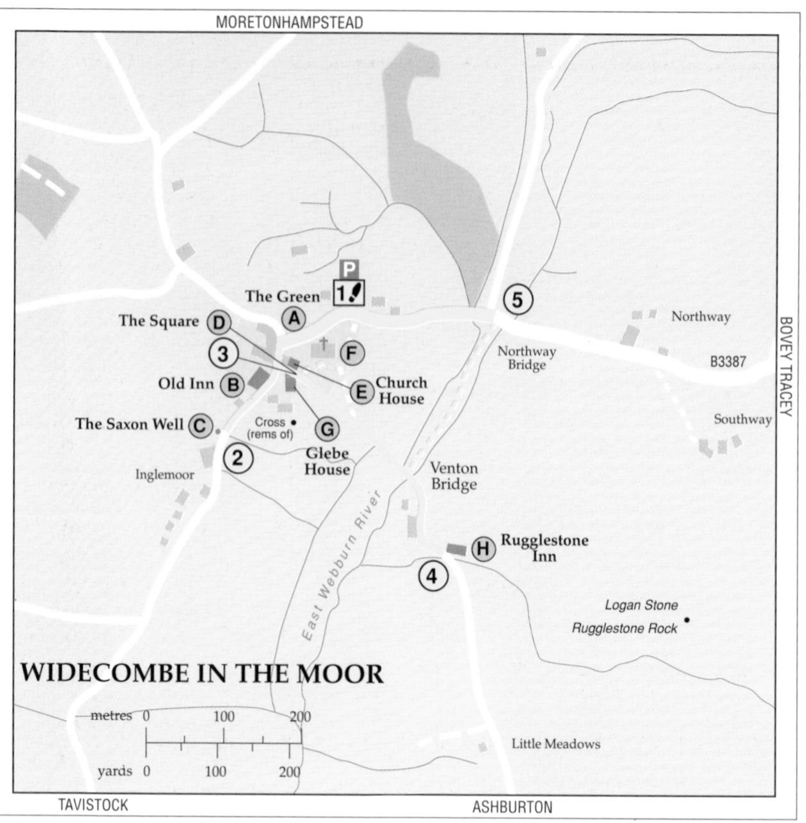

POINTS OF INTEREST

The Green. Formerly known as Butte Park, archery was practised here in the days of the longbow. A law of 1466 made it compulsory for every man to own a bow and practise regularly, on penalty of one halfpenny for failing to do so. The Act has never been repealed! Most bow wood came from Spain, but yew trees were grown in the churchyard for this purpose.

The Old Inn. Its name distinguished it from the New Inn, which no longer exists. Originating in the 14th century, the present building is 16th-century with 18th-century wings. It has two ghosts - a man who disappears into a room and a child crying in a bedroom.

Ⓒ

The Saxon Well. This old well was the main source of water in the village and is reputed never to run dry. Unfortunately the water is no longer drinkable. The well housing is mostly 17th-century.

Ⓓ

The Square. There were two trees here. Only a stump remains of the upper one, a large and beautiful elm which died of disease in 1979. It was planted in 1822 and had a girth of 18ft. It was pollarded to bear a platform on top for dancing on and was known as the Dancing Tree. The second is a yew planted in 1860. It was used to display all the foxes killed in the parish, for which there were bounties paid out of local rates.

Ⓔ

Church House. This was built about 1500 for people from outlying parts of the parish to rest before church services. Ale was served and it continued in this use until the 17th century. In the 19th century the ground floor was used as an almshouse whilst the upper floor was used for the village school. The National Trust acquired the building in 1933.

Ⓕ

St Pancras's Church. The present church dates from the 14th century. The 120ft tower was built in the 16th century with endowments from tin miners. One of the colourful roof bosses over the cancel shows a triangle of three rabbits - a common tin miner's symbol.

In a famed storm of 1638 the church was struck by lightning during a service, killing four people and injuring 62. A legend arose that the Devil had visited the church to claim the lives of four men playing cards during the service.

Ⓖ

The Glebe House. This largely 19th-century building started as a farmhouse in 1527 on land rented from the church. Many old internal features include an open fireplace with bread oven and a 16th-century chair said to belong to Tom Cobley.

Ⓗ

The Rugglestone Inn. This 18th-century inn is very simple and traditional, with no bar or spirit licence and serving beer from the barrel. It is named after the Rugglestone – a large granite rock in an adjacent private field.

INFORMATION
Length of walk: ½ m
Approximate time: 1 hr

TERRAIN:
Suitable for children at all times of year

PARKING:
Adjacent to The Green.

WALK DIRECTIONS

From the car park turn right along the main road and keep down the hill to the well beyond the post office.

Return uphill to The Square. Pass through The Square and lych-gate into the churchyard. Enter the church by the west tower.

③

Return to The Square and turn left down the road. Cross Venton Bridge to the Rugglestone Inn.

④

Return to Venton Bridge. Step over the railings by the footpath sign. Walk through the field by the river.

⑤

Cross one stile over the wall, turn left and walk up the road to the car park.

WINKLEIGH

WINKLEIGH

DEVON

On B3220, 12 miles SE of Great Torrington

WINKLEIGH was formed as a nucleated village early in the Saxon occupation of Devon. At the time of the Norman Conquest it was known as Wicheleia and belonged to an important and romantic-sounding Saxon named Brictric of the Golden Hair. It had a 500-acre wood and the only park in Devon.

William the Conqueror gave it as a gift to his wife Matilda. Soon afterwards it was split into two manors, Wynkelegh Keynes and Wynkelegh Tracey. The families constructed fortified manors at each end of the village. Known as Croft Castle and Court Castle, they were reputed to be linked by a tunnel. The houses did not survive but in between developed a medieval borough.

INFORMATION
Length of walk:
$1^3/_4$ miles
Approximate time:
$1^1/_2$ hours

TERRAIN:
Mostly easy going with some moderate slopes. Suitable for both push-chairs and wheelchairs.

PARKING:
There is no car park, but it is usually possible to park in Fore Street or Castle Street, where there are toilets.

OPEN:
Inch's Cider Factory, Mon-Fri 9-5.30pm, Sat-Sun 9-4.30pm (not open on BHs).

REFRESHMENTS:
Three inns and a restaurant.

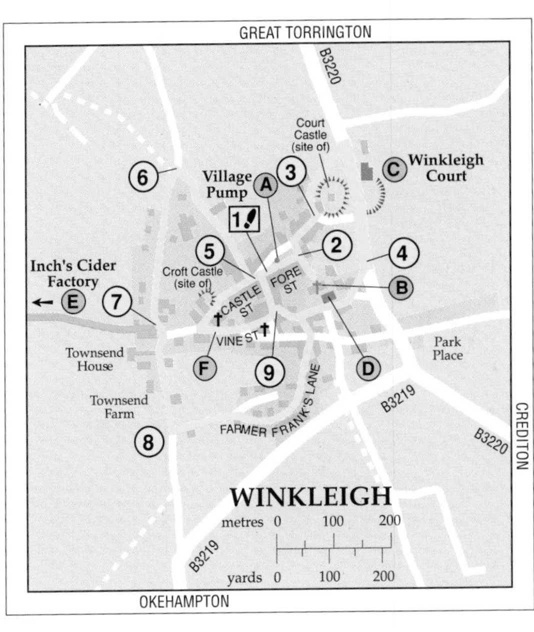

WALK DIRECTIONS

Start at the western end of Fore Street, pass the pump and the King's Arms, an old inn rethatched in 1990 at a cost of £53,000, and turn right to detour to the church.

2

Return to Fore Street and continue up High Street.

3

Turn left along Chulmleigh Road, past Court Castle. Turn right down B3220, with Winkleigh Court opposite.

4

Turn right along Queen Street and go ahead past Church Hill and Church House. Turn right up Coopers Hill and back to Fore Street via South Street, where you pass Linden House, a fine late 18th-century building with original portico and delicate fanlight.

5

Turn left. Ahead is Keswick House, originally called Kings; an old cob-and-thatch house with 17th-century façade. Turn right up Barnstaple Street.

6

Turn left at Folly and walk down to Townsend Cross.

7

Detour right for the cider factory at Western Barn. Return to Townsend Cross and continue downhill to the school.

8

Turn left and walk along Farmer Frank's Lane. Cross Exeter Road and climb Coopers Hill.

9

Turn left down Vine Street. Continue ahead and turn right up Castle Street past Croft Castle, and back to Fore Street. The mound of Croft Castle was partly levelled for the building of Castle School in 1840.

POINTS OF INTEREST

Village Pump. The pyramid-shaped pump-housing and water trough were erected in 1832 at the time of the great Parliamentary Reform Act. Its inscriptions commemorate William IV and the reformers of the time – Grey, Brougham, Russell and Althorp.

B

All Saints' Church. The church is mainly of the 14th and 15th centuries, but underwent extensive restoration in 1870 and 1975. The magnificent 14th-century tower is in three stages with battlements, part buttresses, pinnacles and octagonal lantern. The fine wagon roofs are supported by 70 carved angels and many interesting bosses include one thought to represent Catherine of Aragon. The chancel has a beautiful ceiling with gilded cross ribs and bosses including a capstan, cassock and the Five Wounds.

C

Winkleigh Court. The site includes the remains of Court Barton, the Keynes' manor which replaced Court Castle opposite. Here they, and later the Lethbridge family, held manorial courts. The present building is 18th-century and is now a residential home.

Winkleigh village pump – a memorial to the 1832 Reform Act.

D

Church House. This was built in 1535 at a cost of £28.14s.4d and was later split into two dwellings. The almshouse was founded by Bartholemew Gidley in 1681 for four poor widows. It has been considerably altered and restored in recent years.

E

Inch's Cider Factory. The enterprise was begun in 1900 by Sam Inch as a small farmhouse cider press set up to make use of a glut of apples. It has grown to a factory producing 150,000 gallons per year. The factory shop is open to the public.

F

Vine. Street. The street contains a number of 17th and 18th-century cottages. The Old Malthouse and adjoining cottage were originally three cob and thatch cottages dating from the mid 17th century.

ZENNOR
CORNWALL

On B3306, 4 miles SW of St Ives

ZENNOR is named after St Sennara, one of a number of missionaries who converted the Cornish to Christianity in the 6th Century. According to legend she was the wife of King Goello of Brittany and was exiled in Ireland when accused of infidelity. She returned via Zennor after being found innocent, and the present church may be on the site of a chapel erected for her.

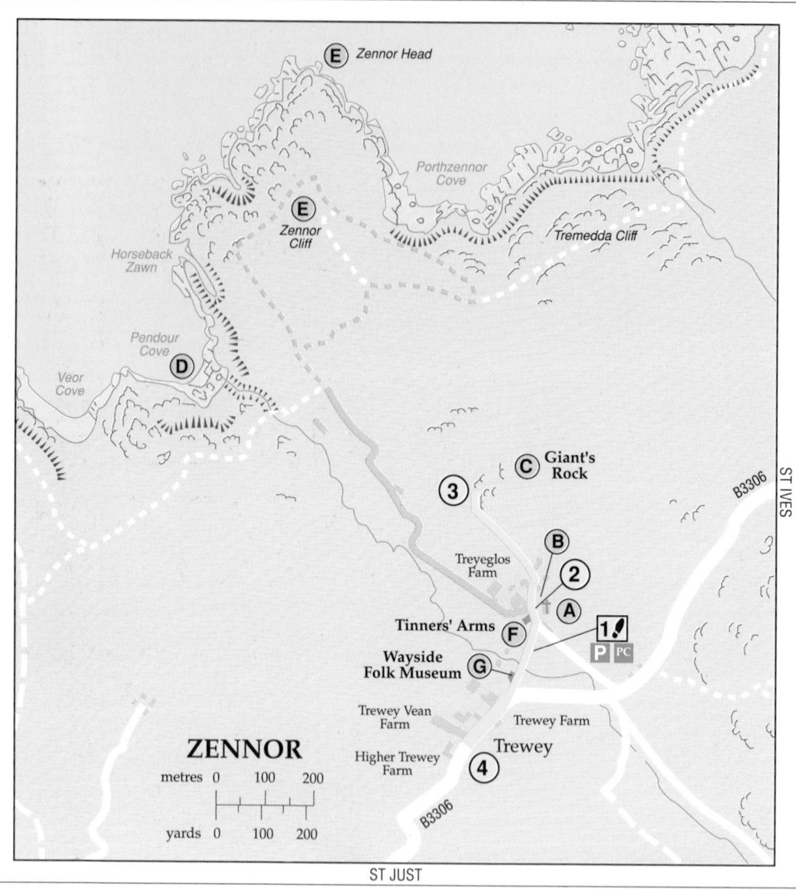

POINTS OF INTEREST

Ⓐ

St Sennara's Church. The church dates from the 12th century and was enlarged three centuries later and restored in 1890. In the side chapel is the famous mermaid chair, made from two medieval bench ends which survived the Victorian restoration. One has a carving of a mermaid holding a mirror and comb. She may represent the two natures of Christ – human and divine.

Church Path. By a ruined mill a gateway with a granite cattle grid marks the end of the path from St Ives which links outlying hamlets with the church. Coffins were carried along the path, and bearers rested at 12 Celtic stone crosses which marked the route. Three are now in the church-yard, two marking a grave.

Giant's Rock. To the SE is a huge boulder now inaccessible in the midst of a patch of thorns. It appears immovable, but is a logan stone, which can be rocked by a few people together. Women who jump on the stone nine times are said to become witches.

Pendour Cove. According to legend Matthew Trewhella, the squire's son and tenor in the church choir, was bewitched by a beautiful woman who appeared in church each week. She was a mermaid and lured him to this cove. He was never seen again, but on stormy nights his voice is said to be heard singing with her beneath the waves.

Zennor Cliff and Head. This area was given to the National Trust in 1954. The path is scattered with stones containing the blackish tin ore cassiterite, and several ruined tin workings can be seen.

Ⓕ

Tinners' Arms. D.H. Lawrence stayed here for a week and wrote the poem *Kangaroo* before he rented a cottage at Higher Tregerthen, a mile to the east. He and his wife stayed there during the First World War while he wrote *Women in Love*.

Wayside Folk Museum. This is housed in Old Trewey Mill and miller's cottage. The wheel has gone but the axle, machinery and millstones are still in place. The miller's cottage is very small, and started as a one-roomed cottage in the 16th century. It had a raised sleeping platform known as a 'talfat' with a 'spence' underneath – a space for a dairy and store.

INFORMATION
Length of walk:
$^{3}/_{4}$ mile ($2^{1}/_{2}$ miles if option followed)
Approximate time:
$^{3}/_{4}$ hour (2 hours if option followed)

TERRAIN:
Suitable for children and pushchairs except for option.

PARKING:
Off the road between the church and Trewey.

OPEN:
Wayside Museum. Daily Easter-Oct.

REFRESHMENTS:
Village pubs and a café.

WALK DIRECTIONS

①

Turn right from the car park entrance and walk up the road to the village church. Enter the churchyard by the main gate.

②

After visiting the church, leave by the gate on the far side of the churchyard and enter the small square. Church Path is on the right. Keeping the Vicarage to your left, continue along the track between granite buildings, which ends in a field at Giant's Rock.

③

Return to the square. Continue past the Tinners' Arms and car park to the museum, then turn right up the road to Trewey to look at the old cottages and the collection of granite troughs, rollers and staddle stones.

④

Return to the car park, passing Wesley's Rock, a large granite boulder from which John Wesley preached.

For an optional excursion from the square turn right around the farm buildings and along the track to a granite stile. Below to the left is Pendour Cove.

Cross the stile and continue ahead. The path winds around Zennor Head and goes up to a mine adit.

Beyond the adit is a waymarked post. Turn right here. The track follows a field boundary and returns to the stile. Cross the stile and return to the square.

SOUTH AND SOUTH EAST ENGLAND

ALRE MILL AT ALRESFORD, HAMPSHIRE

An historic patina covers their buildings more deeply than any others, in England at least. Indeed, I know of no place save for Paris, where memories seem so thick on every stone.

FORD MADOX FORD – RETURN TO YESTERDAY (RYE AND WINCHELSEA)

SOUTH AND SOUTH EAST ENGLAND

•

•

Just as cattle can be seen grazing in fields only ten miles from Trafalgar Square, so can roaming pigs be found during the pannage season in the New Forest just a few miles from the growing Bournemouth and Southampton conurbations. Villages and their agricultural industries can be discovered a short distance from the populous centres in the South and South East.

The South and South East embraces such diverse counties as flat Essex, the more lush Hertfordshire, the mainly rural counties of Buckinghamshire and Oxfordshire, wooded Hampshire and Surrey, hilly Sussex and England's 'Garden' – Kent. Not to be forgotten is the rewarding Isle of Wight, which only recently secured its independence from mainland Hampshire as part of the wish to retain its own character as much as possible.

The Essex countryside is so treeless that the Countryside Commission is creating a brand new forest linking the villages in the South. Yet further into East Anglia and the open coastal and river creeks, such landscape with lonely church towers and sparse trees is part of the county's tradition and attraction. Indeed it is there that the best of Essex is often unfairly attributed to Suffolk. Such is the fate of John Constable's Dedham, which has the finest surviving example of a medieval factory.

Upland Essex has the East Anglian knapped flint buildings, while to the south there are Kentish rag and weather-boarded houses which might well be on the opposite bank of the Thames estuary. Kent is rich in timber-framed buildings, best appreciated in groups such as at Smarden or in Chilham where they face each other across the Pilgrims' Way.

Wooded Surrey naturally has many half-timbered houses but there tile-hanging has long been preferred to weather-boarding. The famous 'stockbroker' wealth has preserved and imitated the style which can be found framing impressive commons or greens such as the grazing land in the centre of Chiddingfold.

Sussex has flint houses and churches and in the west the county seems to merge imperceptably with its neighbour on the chalk ridge near Gilbert White's countryside around Selborne and the cradle of cricket at Hambledon. Hampshire is a vast county as much influenced in architecture by its five neighbouring counties as by the former brickfields in the south. It does, however, have a higher than average number of thatched buildings.

Hertfordshire's excellent local tiles meant that thatch gave way to mellow roofs early on. Indeed the quality of the clays discovered by the Romans has given the villages some pleasing bluish-grey walls as well. Buckinghamshire is a small county with plenty of Georgian buildings. From the Robert Adam market hall in High Wycombe a straight road leads west to the almost completely Georgian village street at West Wycombe. This is the old coaching road to Oxford whose county retains its stone buildings in the west where the Cotswolds begin rather than in the Chilterns which it shares with Buckinghamshire.

Many of the region's villages owe their growth if not their entire existence to invasion, or fear of it, from France. William the Conqueror landed at Pevensey and saw that it was left defended by a castle. In Essex Castle Hedingham has the country's finest Norman keep. The remaining mounds of disappeared castles provide the clue as to why a village has been sited in such an odd location. At Abinger in Surrey the village clusters round the mound away from the main road, but at Chilham the castle still stands on the old main road ready to check subsequent arrivals from abroad.

Battle in Sussex is, of course, the result of an invasion. The village has grown up at the gates of the abbey founded to keep alive the memory of the Battle of Hastings. In a remote corner of the New Forest, Beaulieu is the successor to the spot the Normans called 'the beautiful place'. Later it became the home of the largest Cistercian abbey in the country, and when the buildings were turned over to the aristocracy in the 16th century the village continued to thrive. The 18th-century round towers and moat, however, are a reaction to another feared French invasion.

However, villages do not always have a big house to justify themselves. Dedham and Smarden are examples of villages which were once small towns 'built on wool'. A sudden change in the national economy put a stop to their expansion but left behind some handsome buildings. Appledore's wide main street is designed to accommodate a large market and only the sudden natural diversion of the river estuary in a great storm robbed the village of its port status.

The great contrast in this region is between east and west. In the east there is the more open Essex and the ordered patchwork of Kent regularly stamped with its oast house logo. In the west is the 145 square miles of New Forest, which must be the nearest this country has to a free-range game reserve dotted with villages. William I founded this Royal hunting ground at the same time as he fortified the east.

The South and West of England had a head start when it came to the distribution of Norman heritage and successive generations have been as generous with their history. Today's visitors will find the past well guarded in the incomparable village settings.

ABINGER COMMON

SURREY

Off A25, 4 miles W of Dorking

ABINGER Hammer, with its famous clock bell hanging over the A25, is well known by motorists. Missed by most of the traffic is Abinger Common, where a notice warns drivers to watch for ducks crossing from the pond to the pub. It has been called 'England's oldest village' due to the discovery of a pit dwelling used by Mesolithic hunters some 7,000 years ago.

Behind the church is an early Norman motte and its successor, a 17th-century manor house built by the diarist John Evelyn. As recently as 1933 there was an annual fair on the green on St James' Day to mark the church's patronal festival. Now an Old Fair is held on the second Saturday in June, when villagers wear medieval costume.

SIR EDWIN LUTYENS (1869-1944)

The leading British architect during the first half of the 20th century, Sir Edwin Lutyens is best known for New Delhi's city centre, Castle Drogo and Queen Mary's Dolls House. Yet first he had undertaken a noted series of country houses. One is Abinger's Goddards built in 1898-9 with the garden court laid out by Gertrude Jekyll, whose work often complemented a Lutyens building. The Abinger War Memorial in the churchyard was designed by Lutyens soon after he had completed work on The Cenotaph in Whitehall.

The well of St James on the west side of the village's triangular green.

WALK DIRECTIONS

①

The walk begins at the church. A detour leads through the gates beyond the church door to give a glimpse of the manor house before curving round the base of the motte. Beyond a stile, the path runs across a field giving a panoramic view down into the Tillingbourne Valley and then to the left of the hut protecting the Mesolithic site.

②

Back at the church, turn right to pass The Abinger Hatch and the pond. Follow the road past two turnings to the houses. Beyond the remains of a gateway the road reaches the common. Ahead is St James' Well.

③

The main route turns right at the side of Pasture Wood Cottage. (See below for option.) The enclosed path runs downhill to enter Pasture Wood. At once go right on a path which runs along the edge of the wood.

④

After a field comes into view, the path bears left to join another path. Here go right and climb up to a stile. Walk up a field to another stile at a lane. Opposite is the village green and church. For a detour to Friday Street from point 3, turn left on to a track. Where it curves left, switch on to the narrow path and cross the road. Follow a path through the wood, ignoring a branch to the left. At a firm crosspath, go left. At a 5-way junction take the second left to reach a road. Go right to a pond. The lane at the side leads to the Stephen Langton pub.

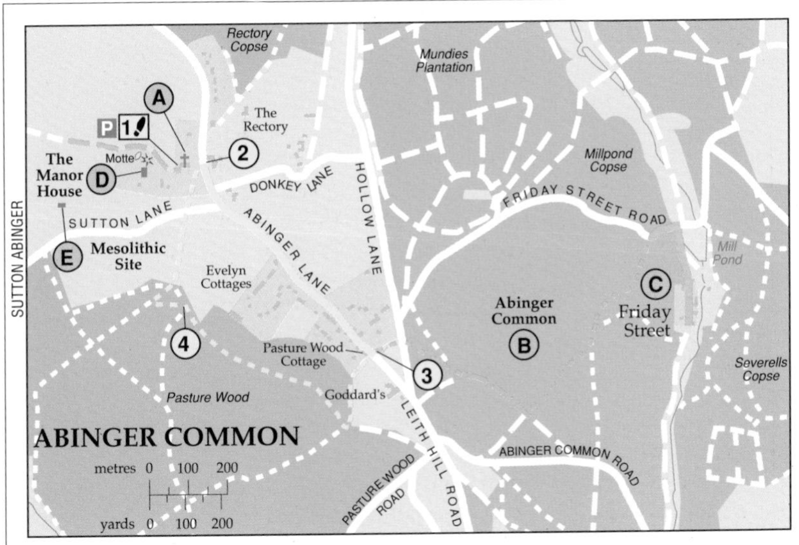

POINTS OF INTEREST

Ⓐ

Abinger Church. Dating from the early 12th century and the picture of a traditional Surrey church, has twice been restored this century. It was the only church in the Guildford Diocese to suffer serious war damage in the 1940s and in 1964 the building, the second highest church in the county, was struck by lightning. Consequently only two wooden tie beams in the roof are original and the modern replacements were cut nearby on Leith Hill. The striking east window, showing the Cross as a living tree, by Laurence Lee was installed in 1967. Under the main altar is the tomb of Thomas Crawley who was both Rector and chaplain to Charles II and a contemporary of diarist John Evelyn who lived at the manor. Look in the north chapel for the carved chest dating from about 1515 which comes from a Normandy church. The flag in the corner is an Order of the Bath standard. The church is thought to have been dedicated to St James the Great due to the proximity of the Pilgrims' Way used by those going to St James's shrine in Spain as well as St Thomas à Becket's at Canterbury.

Ⓑ

The Common. The remains of a gateway on the road mark the boundary between the glebe land where the houses stand and the common. The house on the east side of the gateway is called Glebe Gate. Most of the common is now wooded,

ABINGER HAMMER

Although the most famous part of the parish, Abinger Hammer is often considered to be a separate village down on the main road with the cricket field and post office. Its focal point is the Jack the Hammer figure striking the hour on his anvil. The clock was erected in memory of Lord Farrer who died in 1899 and lived at the nearby and now demolished Abinger Hall – a Victorian rival to the Manor House at Abinger Common. The memorial serves more as a reminder of the iron industry which once dammed the Tilling Bourne to create hammer ponds. Cannon balls and the gates of Fleet Street's Temple Bar came from the local iron furnaces. Later the water was used to feed watercress beds. Now there is Frog Island Trout Farm (open for teas). To the east, on the corner of Raikes Lane which links the two communities, is Crossways Farm built in 1610 for a wool merchant. The house, noted for its Dutch style windows,

features in George Meredith's novel 'Diana of the Crossways'. Piney Copse in Beggars Lane was given to the National Trust by E.M. Forster who lived nearby and called it 'my wood' after replanting following First World War felling. In 1936 he published his collected essays under the title 'Abinger Harvest'.

but on grass near the village is St James's Well. Five years later, Goddards, a ladies' holiday home designed by Sir Edwin Lutyens, was built opposite the Well. After a decade he was asked to convert the building into a private house but the skittle alley survives.

Friday Street. This village has been compared with Switzerland due to its large mill-pond and steep wooded valley. Among the cluster of buildings are a number of cottages and The Stephen Langton pub. Its sign depicts the mitred head of Archbishop Langton who helped force King John's assent to Magna Carta.

The Manor House. The house was rebuilt, next to the village church, St James's, on the site of an earlier hall by the 17th-century diarist John Evelyn who inherited the estate. The family are still the lords of the manor. Abinger Manor Cottage was home of author and caricaturist Sir Max Beerbohm during the Second World War. Nearby is the manor's cattle pound dating from John Evelyn's time. The 15th-century tithe barn was moved in 1934 to stand in the grounds of the Burford Bridge Hotel below nearby Box Hill.

Mesolithic Site. Lying to the west of the Manor House, the site is marked by a protective hut covering the 3ft deep pit measuring 10ft by 14ft. When Dr L.S.B. Leakey excavated the greensand soil in 1950 he revealed a hearth and post holes as well as over a thousand worked flints including weapons and tools. This was in an area where flint is not natural. Other artifacts have been found near the pond. The pit, which may have had a bracken or sapling roof, is thought to be just part of a village built here about 5,000BC.

Tranquil Friday Street – a few cottages beside a pond in a pine-wooded valley.

Abinger Manor House. Only the old floors and Jacobean porch hint at its origins.

INFORMATION
Length of walk: 1½ miles
Approximate time: 1½ hours

TERRAIN:
Suitable for children at all times of the year; not suitable for push-chairs or wheelchairs. 3 stiles.

PARKING:
Park in the car park behind the church.

REFRESHMENTS:
The Abinger Hatch, where cream teas are served on summer Sunday afternoons; the Stephen Langton pub in Friday Street.

APPLEDORE

KENT

On B2080, 10 miles S of Ashford

APPLEDORE was once a port with tidal waters, but a great storm and gradual silting up has left the village more than eight miles from the English Channel. The southern approach to the Romney Marsh village is like crossing a drawbridge and entering a fortification, as the road comes off the old seabed into Appledore's hidden main street. This attractive thoroughfare is wide enough to accommodate the fair licensed by Edward III, which was last held in 1899.

INFORMATION
Length of walk:
1¼ miles (1¾ miles if detour followed)
Approximate time:
1 hour (1¼ hours if detour followed)

TERRAIN:
Suitable for children at all times of the year; suitable for pushchairs; not suitable for wheelchairs. 3 stiles.

PARKING:
Park in the main street near the church.

REFRESHMENTS:
The Red Lion; The Swan; Sentry Box Tearooms.

WALK DIRECTIONS

The walk begins at the church. Turn left to follow the narrow approach road as far as the canal.

Before the bridge, go through a kissing-gate on the left to walk along the high canal bank. After bearing left the bank becomes part of the Saxon Shore Way and later there is a choice of stiles to cross. After running into trees the canal turns sharply right.

At the bend go left down to a stile by a National Trust sign. A path runs inland on a bank to another stile. Bear half left across a field to reach the village recreation ground. Continue in the same direction to the main street and turn left for the church.

A detour to the Mill Mound viewpoint goes along Court Lodge Road opposite the church on the Saxon Shore Way. At the top of the hill, go left through a gateway and at once right through another gate. Keep to the right of the mill mound ahead for the view of the Isle of Oxney, with the Ferry Inn visible in the foreground on the very tip of the island.

POINTS OF INTEREST

Appledore Church. The church had to be rebuilt following its burning during a French raid in 1380. In the south chapel there is glass showing the Black Prince on a charger. Buried there – although the body is now lost – was Philip Chute, Henry VIII's Standard Bearer. In the south aisle Appledore's history is illustrated in a long and colourful tapestry. Stand in the middle of the church facing the west door to see medieval paintings of St George in the spandrels of the left-hand arches. The north chapel has a window showing St Nicholas, patron saint of sailors, looking like Father Christmas.

Royal Military Canal. This artificial waterway largely follows the old Kent coastline, bringing water back to medieval ports such as Appledore. The 27-mile waterway between Seabrook, east of Hythe, and the River Rother near Rye, was hurriedly dug as a defensive measure rather than as a transport artery, over three years from 1804, when a Napoleonic invasion was feared. At the same time the famous Martello Towers were erected elsewhere. The canal was designed with a kink every third of a mile so that the entire stretch could be covered by cannon fire. This plan was again revived in the Second World War when pillboxes were built. But in the early 19th century there was an additional scheme to open sluices and flood Romney Marsh if the enemy appeared. At Hythe the water provides the perfect setting for the bienniel Venetian fête where illuminated floats glide past spectators at night.

Ⓒ

Mill Mound Viewpoint. This provides an excellent view of the Isle of Oxney with The Ferry Inn visible in the foreground on the tip of the island.

THE SAXON SHORE WAY

This long-distance footpath is a 140-mile coastal walk which follows the old Kent coast between Gravesend on the Thames estuary and Rye on the south coast just inside Sussex. The name is derived from the Roman forts (still existing at Reculver and Richborough) which were built as a defence against Saxon 'pirates'. These huge forts were impervious to any artillery the Saxons possessed and retained a large number of highly disciplined Roman soldiers. At Appledore the Way follows the old shoreline by staying near the canal before making a dramatic exit from the village by going down the Mill Mount cliff on to the old seabed to reach the Isle of Oxney.

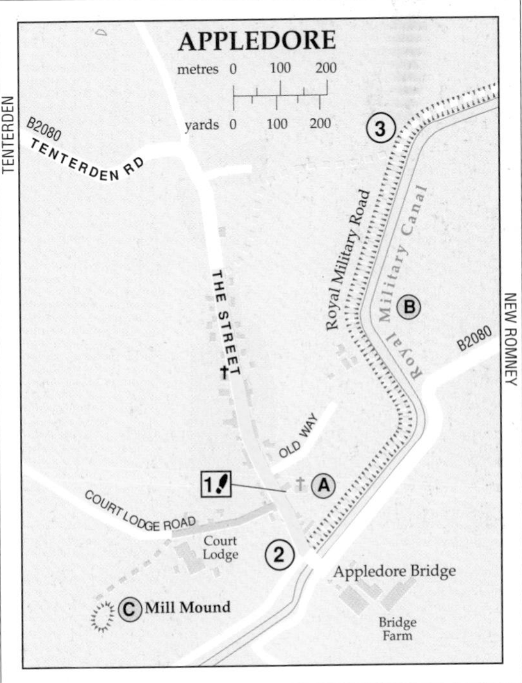

The peaceful setting of Appledore's 14th-century church, where the village's history is illustrated in a tapestry.

AYLESFORD

KENT

Off M20 between junctions 4 and 5, 3 miles NW of Maidstone

AYLESFORD is one of Kent's oldest and most picturesque villages, and the scene of several historic battles. The village with its steeply gabled, half-timbered cottages has changed little over the centuries, and the view from the 14th-century bridge which spans the broad River Medway is deservedly one of the most photographed in the county.

A pottery plaque in Aylesford priory.

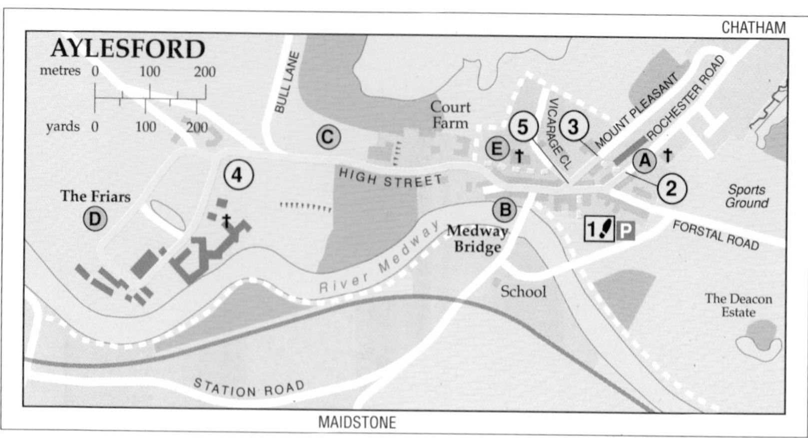

POINTS OF INTEREST

Ⓐ

Sedley Almshouses. These were built in 1605 with an endowment from John Sedley. A new wing was added in 1892. There is an ancient priests' door leading into the walled garden at the rear which originally came from the church.

Ⓑ

Medway Bridge. This 14th-century, 300ft-long bridge of Kentish flagstone replaced an earlier bridge recorded in 1287. Originally composed of eight arches, the central two were replaced by a single 60ft span in 1824 to allow larger vessels to travel upstream to Maidstone.

Ⓒ

Aylesford Battlefields. Jutish invaders led by Hengist and Horsa defeated the Britons here in AD455. Horsa was killed but Hengist survived and his victory led to the creation of the English nation. Alfred the Great defeated the Danes here in 893, and in 918 Canute and the Vikings were routed by Edmund Ironside. The running battles were fought in the fields and woods surrounding the village, mostly to the north.

Ⓓ

The Friars. The Carmelites (White Friars) started work on the Great Priory in 1240 and it was completed two years later. It was the Order's first Chapter in Britain. The Priory flourished until the Dissolution when the house and its lands were given to Ann Boleyn's lover, Sir Thomas Wyatt of Allington. The estate stayed in private hands until 1949 when the Carmelites bought it back and restored Friars as it is now known. Worth seeing are the 14th-century cloisters, 15th-century Pilgrims' Hall and gatehouse, crafts workshops and pottery. Open free to the public.

Ⓔ

Cage Hill. The site two centuries ago of a lock-up cage for miscreants. The cage was partly set into the wall beneath the graveyard. Law breakers were kept in the cage until they could be taken before the Magistrate at West Malling. The cage ceased to be used in 1870 and was bricked up. It was not rediscovered until 1975 when the wall started to subside and there were fears that graves in the churchyard might be exposed. The cage is now preserved in Maidstone museum and a plaque marks the site.

INFORMATION
Length of walk: 2 miles
Approximate time: 2 hours

TERRAIN:
Paved all the way; steps and some short hilly sections. Suitable for children and for pushchairs with a little effort. Not suitable for wheelchairs.

PARKING:
Use the car park between the High Street and the River Medway.

OPEN:
The Friars. Daily. No charge.
Cobtree Manor Park. Daily. No charge.
Kent Rural Museum. Daily. Charge.

REFRESHMENTS:
Several pubs and cafés in the village.

WALK DIRECTIONS

①

Starting from the car park, walk north towards the village, and cross the little bridge over the stream into the High Street. Turn right and then first left into Rochester Road to view the Tudor Alms-houses from the pavement.

②

Cross the road and take the diagonal path to the left corner of the Almshouses, turn right and climb the steps to Mount Pleasant.

③

Turn left and follow the road down into the High Street, then right past the traffic lights and on to The Friars, clearly signposted and approached by a drive running left from the High Street as it turns sharply right to become Bull Lane.

④

Explore The Friars then return along the High Street down Cage Hill. This was the site of a lock-up for miscreants. Carry on until you reach the church steps on your left. The church of St Peter and St Paul is 14th-century with the original Norman tower. Roman tiles found locally were embedded into the building. The path at the top of the steps runs alongside the churchyard and then down the hill back into the High Street.

Cross over to explore the Little Gem, a small but delightful oak-beamed pub with a tiny gallery upstairs and an even tinier front door, before returning to the car park to finish the walk.

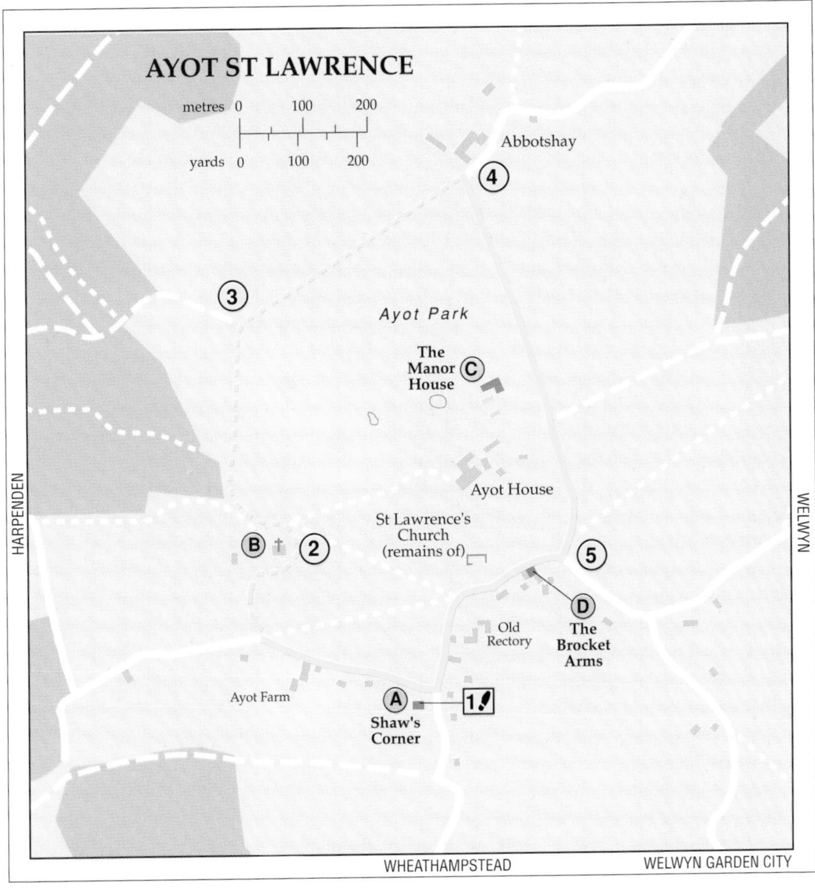

AYOT ST LAWRENCE

HERTFORDSHIRE

2½ miles W of Welwyn

AYOT St Lawrence is a scattered village with no obvious centre, containing many fine houses, a ruined church that was replaced by one designed in the form of a Greek temple, and some attractive tiled cottages. It is chiefly famous as the home of George Bernard Shaw, the cantankerous man of letters who still delights theatre-goers with his sparkling wit, and who lived at Shaw's Corner for the latter part of his life. The name of the village is probably derived from the Anglo-Saxon *Aega's gaet*. *Aega* is a personal name and *gaet* means 'a pass', and probably refers to the valley between Ayot St Lawrence and Ayot St Peter.

POINTS OF INTEREST

Shaw's Corner. George Bernard Shaw lived at Shaw's Corner from 1906 until his death in 1950. It is a large, architecturally undistinguished family house in the care of the National Trust, which has preserved it exactly as Shaw left it. Originally, it was known as the New Rectory but GBS, with becoming modesty, renamed it after himself. Among the contents are many fascinating personal mementos of the great man and his literary friends.

GEORGE BERNARD SHAW

The playwright George Bernard Shaw.

'GBS' was born in Dublin in 1856 but came to live in London at the age of 20 and spent the rest of his long life in England. He started his career as a music critic and wrote a number of long forgotten novels before he achieved lasting fame as a dramatist.

From 1884 onwards, almost to his death, he wrote a series of memorable plays enlivened with his sparkling barbed wit and quirky sense of paradox. Among his most famous were *Man and Superman* (1902), *Pygmalion* (1913) and *Heartbreak House* (1919). Many were vehicles for his unconventional, and sometimes unpopular views on subjects as diverse as prostitution and the exploitation of women, vegetarianism (of which he was a keen advocate), socialism, pacificism and the armaments race, and religion. Many of his polemical plays contained a preface, which in some cases was longer than the play itself, in which he allowed himself to comment on subjects that interested him.

Shaw was his own best publicist and the popular press could rely on him for a memorable quote or an idiosyncratic opinion. He was an effective public speaker, a journalist of rare talent, and had a gift for lucid exposition. The world became a duller place with his passing.

'GBS' moved into the New Rectory in 1906 and renamed it Shaw's Corner.

THE OLD CHURCH

The old church of St Lawrence is now in a ruinous state and cannot be visited. Its decline is reputed to have started in the 1770s when the lord of the manor, Sir Lionel Lyde, wanted to improve his park by making the church a ruin in the fashionable 'picturesque' style. He managed to remove the roof before the Bishop of Lincoln obtained an injunction against him, but the church was never rebuilt. It dates from the 12th century, but the tower was not added until the 15th century. A tiny war memorial garden has been created on the edge of the churchyard adjacent to the road.

WALK DIRECTIONS

Begin by visiting Shaw's Corner. Leave the house and turn left along the lane for 300yds. At a footpath sign, turn right along a gravel track that will take you to the church. Just before reaching the church, turn right, walk to a gate, then turn left and walk to the church entrance.

After visiting the church, turn left and walk to a gate which gives access to a broad path that crosses at right angles. Continue forward for a few yards to a stile. Cross the stile and follow the hedge on the left to another stile. Do not cross this stile but bear right and follow a hedge on the left. After 60yds the hedge turns sharply left. At this point, leave the hedge and continue forward, aiming for a prominent Scots pine at the top of the field, beyond which you will find a stile at the point where the fence meets the hedge.

Cross the stile and turn right, keeping the hedge on your right.

On reaching the farm that is visible ahead (Abbotshay), turn sharp right at a footpath sign and follow a broad bridleway that runs past the Manor House and Ayot House – a fine early Georgian mansion now divided into several residences – and then becomes metalled before reaching the road at a lodge.

Turn right and walk past the Brocket Arms, the half-timbered Old Post Office and the picturesque ruins of the church of St Lawrence to Shaw's Corner.

The New Church. This is an unusual and fine example of a village church built in the Palladian style in 1778. It was designed by Nicholas Revett on the instructions of Sir Lionel Lyde in order to provide a classical view from his house. The church itself is a copy of the Temple of Apollo at Delos, but the side colonnades and outer aedicules are not in the Grecian style. Because Sir Lionel wanted the church essentially as a decoration for his park, the altar had to be placed at the west end instead of at the east end, as tradition normally dictates.

Sir Lionel is buried in one aedicule and his wife in the other, a result, it is said, of marital differences. Apparently, he believed that as the church had united them in life, it should make amends by separating them in death.

The Manor House. Originally a Tudor building, the front was rebuilt in the 18th century, giving it a Georgian appearance. It is now divided into separate dwellings. An unlikely legend has it that Henry VIII locked Anne Boleyn, his second wife, in the attic while he courted Catherine Parr, who became his sixth wife, in private downstairs.

The Brocket Arms. This gets its name from the family who were lords of the manor in the 16th century and again in the years before the Second World War. It is a good example of a Tudor half-timbered building, and has a king pin that supports the roof, and an enormous open fireplace. During the war, the Sunday school was held in the public bar. By a curious irony, Lord Brocket was noted as a friend of leading Nazis and was interned for a while.

INFORMATION
Length of walk:
$1^1/_2$ miles
Approximate time:
$1^1/_2$ hours including a visit to Shaw's Corner and the new church.

TERRAIN:
A level route over lanes and paths. Suitable for children and push-chairs but not for wheelchairs because of stiles and kissing-gates. Shaw's Corner and the new church are accessible to wheelchairs.

PARKING:
There are no public car parks. Limited parking is possible in the lane near the Brocket Arms. Shaw's Corner has a car park for visitors.

OPEN:
Shaw's Corner. Apr-end Oct from 2-6pm; Wed-Sat, and bank hols 12noon-6pm. Visitors in wheelchairs are requested to telephone first.

REFRESHMENTS:
The Brocket Arms serves bar meals throughout the year, and cream teas on Sundays in the season.

A Tudor cottage flanked by the Brocket Arms.

BATTLE

SUSSEX

On A2100, about 6 miles NE of Hastings

BATTLE is a thriving community which derives its name and existence from the best-remembered event in English history, the Battle of Hastings, hard fought throughout the day on 14 October 1066. The victorious William, Duke of Normandy, established an abbey on the site, placing the altar of the abbey church on the spot where King Harold fell. The altar site is now marked by the 'Harold Stone'.

The village, now perhaps better described as a small town, has grown up around the abbey, and stands on a high wealden ridge. The Great Gatehouse, reconstructed in sandstone during the 14th century, still rises intact, beside the Market Place at the end of the High Street, and provides the focal point of the town and of the walk.

To inspect the ruins of the abbey church and tour the battlefield site, you will have to pay an admission charge, which includes an opportunity to experience an audio-visual account of the Battle of Hastings.

The busy High Street in Battle, at the head of which stands the massive gatehouse to the abbey.

WALK DIRECTIONS

①

Start from Battle Station. Walk up the station approach road and turn right. After approximately 350yds, bear left into Upper Lane. Walk beneath the walls of Battle Abbey, passing St Mary's Church and Buckley's Shop Museum with its remarkable collection of bygones on the right to reach the abbey gate house and Market Place.

②

Continue along High Street. Turn right into Mount Street and follow it past a car park on the right. Continue as far as Lewins Croft, a substantial 16th-century timber-framed house, now converted into cottages.

③

Retrace your steps to High Street and turn left, back towards the abbey.

④

In front of the gatehouse, fork right into Park Lane for an optional excursion to the abbey and the battle site. The entrance is through a car park on the left. Otherwise, return to High Street and turn right.

⑤

By the Chequers Inn, bear right, retracing your outgoing route to the station. The station building was designed by William Tress in 1852 in the Gothic style.

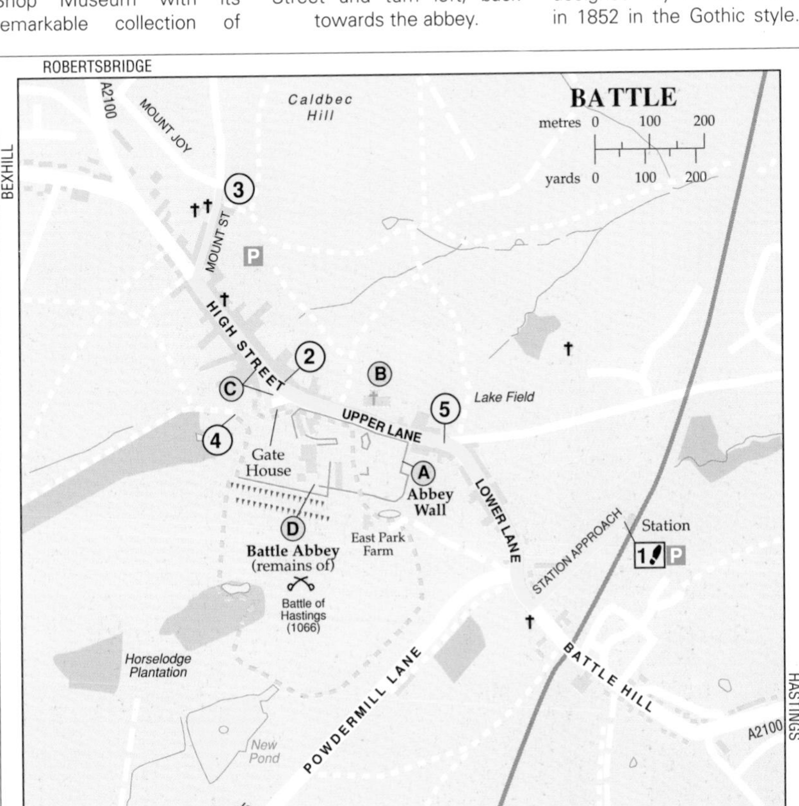

POINTS OF INTEREST

Ⓐ

Abbey Wall. The northern wall of the abbey precinct towers above the street. Visitors to the abbey site can enjoy a walk along the top of the wall with good views over the town and the parish church.

Ⓑ

St Mary's Church. The original church, founded by the Abbot of Battle Abbey in about 1120, has gone, apart from a single arch in one of the chapels. The present church dates from the 12th to 14th centuries. The nave arcades are Norman, the chancel was rebuilt in the 13th century and the tower was added about 1450. Further restoration occurred in the 19th century.

Inside, on the north wall of the nave, can be found the remains of 13th-century wall paintings depicting the life of Margaret of Antioch. The Norman font is made of Petworth marble and there is a fine modern Sussex oak screen. In the south aisle, the Senlac Memorial Window was dedicated as recently as 1984 in memory of those who fell at the Battle of Hastings.

Between the north chapel and the chancel lies Sir Anthony Browne, once the tutor of the future Elizabeth I. His elaborate tomb, on which he and his first wife lie in full size effigy, is made of alabaster. Sir Anthony, later master of the King's Horse to Henry VIII, was rewarded by the King, at the dissolution in 1538, with a gift of Battle Abbey, one of the richest in the country. He was responsible for the destruction of the abbey church and the conversion of the abbot's lodging into his residence.

The red brick Deanery, behind the church, is Elizabethan in origin.

The Market Place and High Street. The triangular market place is dominated by the magnificent 14th-century abbey gatehouse, still virtually intact and one of the finest in the country. It was built in 1338 by Abbot Retlynge, on the site of an earlier gatehouse, and consists of a square sandstone tower, pierced by a double archway with ribbed vaulting, and framed by octagonal turrets at each corner. To repel raids from across the channel, a common occurence in the 14th century, the gatehouse was designed to double as a small fortress, complete with portcullis and holes from which to launch missiles on to intruders.

The square, was once the scene of bull-baiting and a brass plate marks the place where the bulls were tethered. The Pilgrim's Rest, beside the Market Place, is a 15th-century timber-framed building, once a hostel for abbey visitors.

Further along the High Street is the Old Pharmacy dating from 1500 and the 18th-century George Hotel. The Museum of Local History, on the right, houses a replica of the Bayeux Tapestry and a diorama of the Battle of Hastings. No. 27, at one time the Bull Inn, but which now houses *La Vielle Auberge*, is built from stone salvaged from the Abbey when it was destroyed in the 16th century.

Western Avenue which starts opposite the junction of Mount Street with the High Street, is lined by an attractive row of weather-boarded cottages.

Battle Abbey. Consecrated in 1094 the abbey was run as a Benedictine house until the dissolution in 1538, when the abbey church was destroyed. Some of the remaining buildings house a school and are not normally open to the public. The Abbot's House can be viewed during school holidays, and several other rooms are always open.

The abbey terrace fronts the ridge on which Harold's army faced William's attacking forces. From the western end of the terrace, a circular battlefield walk is punctuated by displays, charting the course of the conflict. The marshy dip which separated the two armies has now been drained into several small lakes, first dammed by the monks as fish ponds, then used to provide water power for the manufacture of gunpowder during the 18th and 19th centuries.

INFORMATION
Length of walk: $2^3/_4$ miles (including battlefield walk)
Approximate time: 2 hours

TERRAIN:
Generally easy; suitable for children. Abbey and battlefield circuit suitable for pushchairs.

PARKING:
Park at Battle Station, or alternatively in the car park east of Mount Street.

OPEN:
Battle Abbey. Good Fri-30 Sep, 10am-6pm, 1 Oct-Maund Thu, 10am-4pm.
Battle Museum of Local History. Easter-Oct, 10am-1pm, 2-5pm, Sun 2.30-5.30.
Buckleys Shop Museum. Mon-Sat 10am-5pm.

REFRESHMENTS:
Several pubs and cafés in High Street and Mount Street.

THE BATTLE OF HASTINGS

When Edward the Confessor died without immediate heir on 5 January 1066, the stage was set for the most famous confrontation in English history. On his deathbed, Edward had named Harold of Wessex, brother of Edward's wife, as his successor and he was crowned king on the following day. However, William of Normandy laid prior claim to the throne through Edward's grandmother and on 27 September he crossed the Channel, with the blessing of the Pope, to claim his inheritance.

After a series of remarkable forced marches from the north, Harold brought his army to the battle site on the evening of Friday 13 October, occupying a commanding position on the ridge where Battle Abbey now stands. The two armies were equally matched in numbers, estimated at about 7,000 on each side. The English infantry included some of the finest professional warriors in Europe, armed with battle axes and spears, but were ex-hausted after their long journey.

Battle commenced at 9am on 14 October. William's infantry, advancing up the hill, were repelled at first and his horsemen faired little better, retreating in disorder. Harold's infantry, sensing victory, gave chase, but in small groups and without coordination. William's horsemen wheeled and cut them to pieces. After re-grouping, William's knights and infantry attacked again. By nightfall, Harold was dead and William victorious. On Christmas Day 1066, King William I was crowned in Westminster Abbey.

The Abbey's beautiful arched undercroft.

Battle Abbey, built on the rise of Senlac Hill.

BEAULIEU

HAMPSHIRE

On B3054, 8 miles S of Southampton

BEAULIEU is perhaps best known for being the home of the National Motor Museum, but the village itself has much to recommend it. Far smaller than you might think, it is a gem of an English 17th-century village at the centre of events which over the centuries have shaped its unique character.

The great Beaulieu Abbey was the seat of power here for hundreds of years. When the days of the monasteries were ended by Henry VIII the lords of the manor became the rulers of everything they overlooked. This was undoubtedly feudal but it led to certain standards having to be observed by those who wanted to live, work and build in Beaulieu. It is these standards that have preserved Beaulieu for us to enjoy today.

The walk described here is through land owned by the Montagu family. The peace and tranquility of the oak-covered banks of the Beaulieu River cannot have changed a great deal since the monks held sway at the Abbey.

Beaulieu Tide Mill with the Abbey gateway in the background.

WALK DIRECTIONS

 1

From the public car park in Beaulieu, walk into High Street, turn left and walk to the Montagu Arms. Go down the lane at the side of the inn, passing the fire station and Curtle Cottage.

 2

Go through a wooden gate at Tayler's Close into a wide lane with a good surface. Walk towards Sevilles Copse, where the path draws close to the river and oak trees go down to the water's edge.

 3

Pass between Sevilles Copse and Jarvis's Copse in a pleasant shady lane.

4

In open fields, keep trees on the left. Arrive at Keeper's Cottage, with a brickyard behind it. Continue for a short distance in a wide lane in woodland and go right at a T-junction and left almost immediately on a straight, narrow path.

 5

After 200yds bear right and turn left into the woods beneath an oak tree to reach the path beside Beaulieu River. If you wish to extend the walk, this path follows the river's edge all the way to Buckler's Hard, a round trip of about three miles. Otherwise, after taking time to enjoy the river scenery, retrace your steps to the Montagu Arms. Scenes for the film *A Man For All Seasons* were shot here because it was felt Beaulieu River today was the place most likely to resemble the Thames in the 16th century.

 6

At the B3054 turn right and walk out to the village green. From here you can see the water being released from the Mill Dam, by way of the tide mill. Ahead is the Beaulieu Estate.

 7

Walk back into High Street where the 17th-century houses are all worth closer inspection.

POINTS OF INTEREST

 A

Tide Mill. On the eastern edge of the village stands the tide mill, the earliest parts of which date from the early 16th century. For hundreds of years after that, tenants grumbled at being forced to pay the extortionate charges at the Lord of the Manor's mill. After many years in decay, the mill was brought back into use during World War Two.

 B

Beaulieu Abbey. Few English places sound more French than this, and with good reason. In 1204 King John granted permission to 30 Cistercian monks from France to establish an abbey on this site. It took its name from a hunting lodge called Beau Lieu (beautiful place), pronounced in Norman French much the same as it is in English today. The Abbey was conceived on the same grand scale as Winchester Cathedral and took 40 years to build. The remains are still imposing.

HYTHE
LYNDHURST
National Motor Museum
Palace House
Beaulieu Abbey
Tide Mill
Mill Dam
Bignalls Wood
Home Farm
Dock House
DOCK LANE
HIGH STREET
Mean High Water
Carpenters Dock
Beaulieu River
The Lodge
Sevilles Copse
Jarvis's Copse
Bailey's Hard
Keeping Copse
BUCKLER'S HARD
B3054
B3056
BEAULIEU
metres 0 100 200
yards 0 100 200

The Montagu family home, Palace House, beside the mill dam.

INFORMATION
Length of walk:
2 miles
Approximate time:
1½ hours

TERRAIN:
Suitable for children at all times of the year. Suitable for pushchairs but not for wheelchairs. Where there are stiles there are also gates that open. Several plank footbridges, all easy to negotiate.

PARKING:
There is free parking off the High Street in Beaulieu.

OPEN:
National Motor Museum and associated displays; Palace House, home of the Montagu family; Beaulieu Abbey and exhibition. Charges to all three. Open all year, Easter-Sep 10-6pm; Oct-Easter 10-5pm.

REFRESHMENTS:
Inns and cafés in both Beaulieu and Buckler's Hard.

Ⓒ

National Motor Museum. One of the world's great motor museums, Beaulieu was an innovative idea when it was set up by Lord Montagu in the 1950s. Since then it has grown steadily and now houses some 200 fine vehicles reflecting the history of the motor car in Britain over the past 90 years. From early Rolls-Royce limousines to modern racing cars, there is a fascination here for anyone with a feel for superb machinery. Supporting displays tell the story of man's motoring achievements through the ages.

Ⓓ

Palace House. Home of Lord and Lady Montagu, Palace House has been in the family since 1538, when it was acquired after the Dissolution of the monasteries. The building is a combination of three architectural styles. It began as a 14th-century gatehouse to the abbey (the outline of the main entrance, on the south side, can still be seen). In the 1730s it was modified by the 2nd Duke, and in the 1870s converted and extended as a 'Scottish baronial' mansion by the architect Andrew Bromfield for Henry, 1st Baron Montagu of Beaulieu.

The house has collections of fine paintings and furnishings, with costumed wax figures showing generations of the Montagu family.

Ⓔ

High Street. Beaulieu's character derives from the use of mainly 17th-century brick in the buildings in its High Street. A warm red colour, with some purple, the bricks were made locally, probably at a works on the site of the present brickworks near Keeper's Cottage.

Eighteenth-century cottages at Bucklers Hard.

SHIPBUILDING

To the long-established New Forest industries of tanning, forestry, brick and salt making, was added another in the 18th century – that of shipbuilding. It proved the most famous industry of all, and the one for which Buckler's Hard is remembered today, and will be remembered for years to come, thanks to the steps being taken by the Montagu Estate.

Protected at the western end of the Solent by Henry VIII's Hurst Castle, surrounded by huge forests of oak, and with iron smelting a well-established local industry, Buckler's Hard was ideally suited for warship building.

Its heyday was the 18th century, when one of England's foremost boat builders, Henry Adams, lived in a fine house there from 1749 to 1806 and supervised the work which went on beneath his windows. Three of the ships which fought in the Battle of Trafalgar were built in his yard, the best-known being the 64-gun Agamemnon. In fact the Agamemnon was probably the Navy's most famous battleship of the day, being Nelson's favourite command in which he established his reputation in the Mediterranean during the early years of the French Revolutionary Wars.

Henry Adams' house is now an hotel, but a Henry Adams room has been created in the style of the period, and this can be viewed from the village street. Contrasting with the elegance of Adams' home is that of Thomas Burlace, a shipwright who worked for him and whose cottage is open to visitors, partly reconstructed as it was in the 18th century.

A Maritime Museum at Buckler's Hard tells the whole story and there are associated displays and exhibitions. River cruises depart from Buckler's Hard each day from Easter to September.

BOSHAM

BOSHAM

SUSSEX

1 mile S of A259, 3 miles W of Chichester

BOSHAM (the 'h' is silent) is one of the prettiest villages in Sussex, and as a result has often been drawn, painted and photographed. Here King Canute proved to be only human and could not turn back the tide. Later, in 1064, King Harold sailed from Bosham for his visit to Duke William of Normandy. The Bayeux Tapestry shows him going to pray in Bosham church before sailing.

Today the great events of the world pass Bosham by; it is a quiet backwater, one of the handful of sailing villages dotted around the edge of Chichester Harbour.

POINTS OF INTEREST

Holy Trinity Church. The tower and, inside, the chancel arch date back to before the Norman Conquest – the long and short stones on the corners of the tower are a feature of Saxon architecture. Legend has it that a child's coffin, discovered in 1865 below the floor, is that of King Canute's eight-year-old daughter, who drowned in the millstream. Don't miss the crosses cut in the stone doorway of the inner porch. They are said to have been made by crusaders blunting their sword points on church walls as a dedication to peace on their return from the Holy Land.

(B)

Quay Meadow. This is said to be where Canute, King of England, Denmark and Norway tried unsuccessfully to turn back the tide. It was probably from here that King Harold set sail for Normandy in 1064, where he was tricked into swearing support for Duke William's claim to the English throne.

(C)

Bosham Mill. This is a fine building now used as the headquarters of the local sailing club. Notice how the water in the mill-race was carried in to operate the machinery.

(D)

Bosham Quay. The tile-hung, timbered building at the end of the quay is called the Raptackle - a store for ropes and tackle. In the plague year of 1665 the citizens of Bosham saved Chichester from starvation when the city was sealed off. They put fish in buckets, which could be hauled up the city walls. Payment was made in a bucket of sea water to prevent the spread of infection.

WALK DIRECTIONS

Walk from the car park to the water's edge, at the junction with High Street. Go round the northern edge of the creek to a point opposite to where you are standing. If the tide is in, use the footpath opposite High Street.

(2)

Pass the National School (dated 1834 and now a private house) at the head of the creek and walk as far as Creek House, or further if you wish.

(3)

Retrace your steps. If the tide is low you may be able to walk across a causeway. Return to the beginning of High Street.

(4)

If the tide is out, continue round the edge of the creek as far as the mill, and then retrace your steps until you reach High Street.

(5)

Walk along High Street. The Anchor Bleu public house is on the left. Further on is the Holy Trinity Church. The village's long and sometimes sad association with the sea is recorded, often very graphically, on many of the tombstones in the churchyard.

(6)

Leave the churchyard and walk out to Quay Meadow, then turn left and walk along the millstream towards Bosham Mill and on to Bosham Quay.

(7)

Leaving the quay, walk across Quay Meadow and back into the churchyard by the gate. Go round the back of the church and leave through the gates at the eastern end.

(8)

Continue along the lane to Bosham Lane, coming out at Bosham Walk.

(9)

Turn left and walk as far as Moreton Road opposite the Millstream Hotel.

(10)

Go left here and at the signpost after about 80yds, go left on a footpath down to the creek. If the tide is out you can walk back to Quay Meadow.

INFORMATION
Length of walk:
$1\frac{1}{2}$ miles
Approximate time:
$1\frac{1}{2}$ hours

TERRAIN:
Suitable for children at all times of the year. Suitable for pushchairs and wheelchairs if the last two walk directions are left out. No stiles.

PARKING:
There is adequate public parking off Bosham Lane. Do not be tempted to park on the creek edge. The tide regularly catches motorists unawares.

Bosham waterfront juts into an inlet of Chichester Harbour.

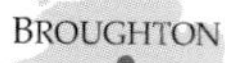

BROUGHTON

OXFORDSHIRE

On B4035, 2 miles SW of Banbury

SET in a parkland landscape little changed from at least Saxon times, Broughton Castle is a sensational Tudor manor having strong ties with Roundhead intrigue during the Civil War. It has been the continuous home of the Fiennes family, Lords Saye and Sele, from the 14th century. Understandably it is prized as a film location, from the production of Shakespeare's *Henry VIII* in 1969 through to the comedy *Three Men and a Girl* with Tom Sellick in 1990.

Broughton Castle sitting amidst its uncommonly large moat.

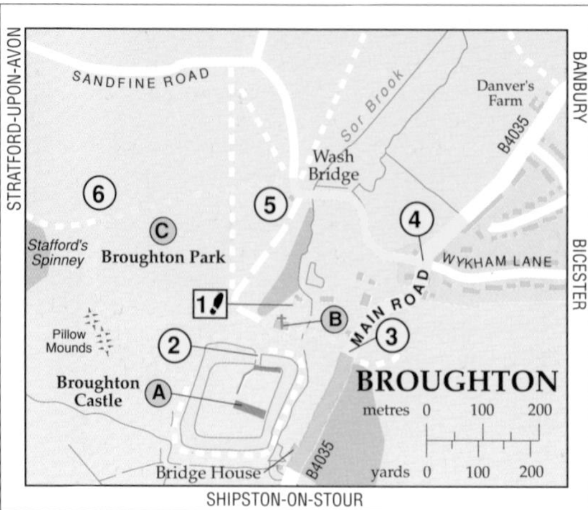

INFORMATION
Length of walk:
1 mile
Approximate time:
½ hour

TERRAIN:
One stile and 2 wicket gates make this a walk of minimal hindrance suitable for children and pushchairs, but not wheelchairs.

PARKING:
When the castle is closed, park in the lay-by in Main Road opposite the walled path to the church. Visitors who time their arrival to coincide with the Castle opening will be able to park in the private car park, tucked behind the church, approached from the Castle drive.

OPEN:
Broughton Park. Pedestrian access at any time, by kind permission of Lord and Lady Saye & Sele. Broughton Castle. 18 May-14 Sep, Wed and Sun. (Also Thu in Jul-Aug and Bank Hol Sun and Mon (including Easter) 2-5pm. Charge.

REFRESHMENTS:
The Saye and Sele Arms.

POINTS OF INTEREST

Ⓐ

Broughton Castle. Broughton means `farmstead on a brook'. The large moat fed by Sor Brook predates the present `castle', for prior to Sir John de Broughton's stone manor of 1300, which forms the eastern core of the present Tudor `court', there was a timber hall. A carving of the early manor is set into the oak linenfold panelling in the undercroft, dating from before the remodelling of the castle by Richard Fiennes during the mid 16th century.

The castle is full of delightful features, such as the original kitchen garden, which was turned into a geometric formal garden in Elizabethan times. Notice the spying head peering down as a reminder to the servants that stealing will be found out!

Ⓑ

St Mary's Church. Dating largely from the 14th century, St Mary's contains memorials from Sir John de Broughton, accredited with building the church, through the family line of Fiennes, Wykeham and Twistleton, the Lords Saye & Sele.

Ⓒ

Broughton Park. The survival of the burial mounds, well in excess of 2,000 years old, is the most tangible evidence that the park has experienced little disturbance over several millennium. The Fiennes medieval wealth was founded upon the `golden fleece'. In the 18th century the northern portion of the park was annexed and called Sainfoin Park (hence Sandfine Road), for the practise of sheep pasture `improvement'. The present estate extends to 1,700 acres of tenanted farmland: two-thirds of the original medieval estate, defined by the parish boundary, was enclosed as early as the 1590s.

WALK DIRECTIONS

①

Walk past the church to a kissing-gate/cattle grid, and cross over the moat to enter the castle island through the gatehouse, built c.1405.

②

Following a tour of the castle, re-cross the moat and pass through the churchyard right, via wicket gates, progressing over the Sor Brook along the roughly flagged path to the B4035.

③

For an optional excursion turn right to Bridge House and the adjacent old estate corn mill with millpond and backwater secreted outside the moat. However, with the distinct advantage of a pavement the main route turns left, passing Warren Lodge (1877); the wooded bank across the road having, in medieval times, been an enclosed rabbit warren. Beyond the well-screened Rectory of 1694, reach the crossroads where stands the Saye & Sele Arms (public house).

Advance briefly beyond the Turnpike Toll lodge to glance at the Elizabeth Bradford Wyatt almshouses, Gothic villas of 1859. A little further along are the triple Tudor-styled estate cottages of 1841. The enclosure closer to the crossroads, known as Pound Close, is clearly `where stray animals were impounded'. Return to the crossroads.

④

From the crossroads go right, the road dipping through a rock cutting to cross Wash Bridge, the site of an ancient sheep wash. The farm in view to the right is called Woadmill, associated with the herb used for dyeing cloth purple.

⑤

To the right of the lodge enter Broughton Park via a stone stile. The footpath ascends the closely cropped turf, an estate map of 1803 shows this as `foot road', its destination the old fulling mill.

⑥

Approaching Stafford's Spinney slant left from the barely discernible path, and cross the old dykes to locate a pair of pillow burial mounds reclining on the declining slope. Continue down the slope to the recently dredged moat. Go left to conclude the walk.

BURWASH

SUSSEX

On A265, 5 miles E of Heathfield

BETWEEN the 15th and 17th centuries, Burwash was one of the main centres of the Wealden iron industry, a fact which is reflected by the number of substantial old houses along the High Street. The village is well situated on a narrow ridge separating the valleys of the Rother and Dudwell rivers.

Rudyard Kipling spent the last 33 years of his life at Bateman's, to the south of the village in the Dudwell valley. The surrounding landscape provided the inspiration for some of his finest poems as well as the settings for *Puck of Pook's Hill* and *Rewards and Fairies*.

WALK DIRECTIONS

The walk starts through a gap in the fence in the far-left corner of the car park, to the left of a wooden scout hut. After a short enclosed path and a stile, walk downhill with a hedge on your right.

After 150yds, bear right across a field to a second stile beside a massive oak tree. Keep to the right of the field beyond until you can go right over a stile. Walk diagonally down across the next field to a stile and descend to join a lane.

③

Turn right and walk along to Bateman's. In front of the house, turn left along the drive to Park Farm.

After 300yds, a path on the right leads to Bateman's Mill and millpond. Retrace your steps to point 3 and carry on along the lane.

At the next road junction, turn left, signposted to Burwash. Walk up this road (Bell Alley Road) for ½ a mile to its junction with High Street, and turn right to visit the church.

Opposite the Bell Inn, turn left and follow the High Street to return to the starting point.

INFORMATION
Length of walk:
2 miles
Approximate time:
1½ hours

TERRAIN:
Easy. Suitable for children. Suitable for pushchairs and wheelchairs if field path section (Points 1-3) is avoided, using Bateman's Lane to the west of the village.

PARKING:
Park in the car park to the south of High Street, behind the Bear Hotel.

OPEN:
Bateman's: Apr-Oct.
Sat-Wed 11am-6pm.

REFRESHMENTS:
Several pubs in village.
Tearooms at Bateman's and in the High Street.

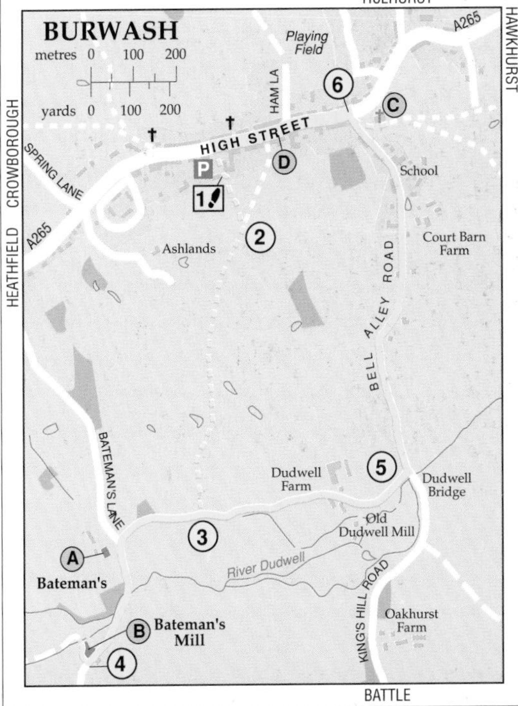

POINTS OF INTEREST

Bateman's. This 17th-century stone house with brick chimneys was built in 1634 for a local ironmaster. Rudyard Kipling lived here from 1902 until he died in 1936. The house is now in the hands of the National Trust and Kipling's study, packed with personal mementoes, has been left just as it was when he used it.

The 300-acre estate was laid out by Mrs Kipling, who stayed on in the house after her husband's death until she died in 1939.

Bateman's Mill. The watermill at Bateman's dates from about 1750. In 1903, Rudyard Kipling installed a turbine which generated electricity for the house for 20 years. After recent restoration, the mill now grinds corn again on Saturdays during the summer season and can be inspected in detail by visitors to the house.

St Bartholomew's Church. Although rebuilt in the 19th century, the church still incorporates a solid early Norman tower. Inside can be found one of the oldest iron gravestones in Sussex. From the sloping churchyard and the church meadow beyond, there is a fine view across the Dudwell valley to Brightling Needle, an obelisk erected by an 18th-century eccentric, Jack Fuller.

In the 18th century, Burwash lay on one of the smugglers' routes from Pevensey Bay and it is said that they used a vault beneath one of the tombstones to hide their goods. Could this tradition have inspired Kipling's *Smugglers' Song?*

``Five and twenty ponies,
Trotting through the dark -
Brandy for the Parson,
'Baccy for the Clerk.''

High Street. The attractive High Street is lined by a raised pavement and a row of pollarded lime trees. The Bell Inn, opposite the church, was another smugglers' haunt. To the south of the High Street, `Rampyndene' is a distinguished William and Mary house with striking tall chimneys, built in 1699. Further along, look out for a 16th-century barn in the grounds of Mount House.

Bateman's, a lovely 17th-century stone mansion.

CHIDDINGFOLD

SURREY

On A283, 6 miles S of Godalming

THE milestone on Chiddingfold Green reads '38 miles to Hyde Park Corner', which has proved far enough from London to save the village from over-development. In 1347 even the Black Death by-passed Chiddingfold which lies in a hollow or 'fold' with a church, pond, inn, smithy and shops nestling in one corner of a large green. All around are sweet chestnut and ash trees, grown for the making of walking sticks and umbrella handles at nearby Witley. For its size, the village maintains a remarkable number of shops and two banks. The butcher's behind The Crown Inn is famous for its award-winning sausages.

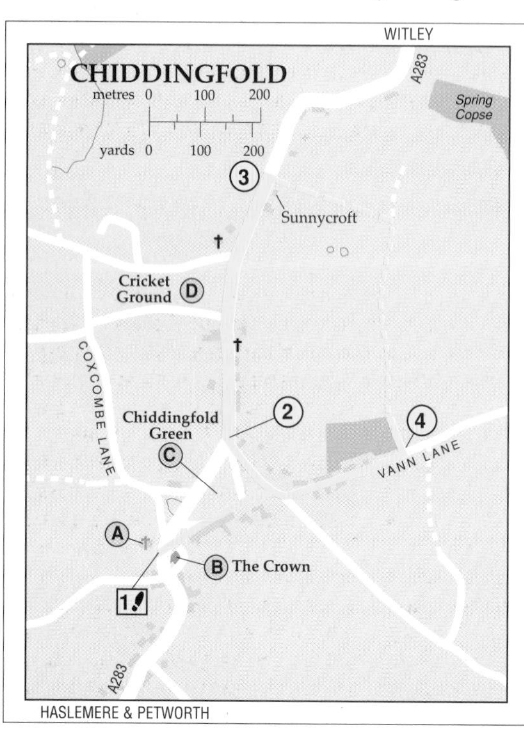

GLASS MAKING

Glass Making was an important industry in Chiddingfold from 1300 until it was suppressed by Elizabeth I after complaints about the village's French and German owned furnaces. In the 14th century glass was supplied to Westminster's St Stephen's Chapel, which later became part of the House of Commons, and St George's Chapel at Windsor. The remains of the glassworks lie on several sites to the south from which 427 fragments dating from 1325 have been collected together to make the window at the back of the church.

INFORMATION
Length of walk:
1¼ miles
Approximate time:
1 hour

TERRAIN:
Suitable for children at all times of the year; not suitable for push-chairs or wheelchairs.

PARKING:
Park outside the shops on the south side of the green.

REFRESHMENTS:
The Crown; The Swan; Roberts Stores.

Looking across the village pond to the southern corner of the green with the church and its superb lych-gate.

POINTS OF INTEREST

Chiddingfold Church. The church dates from 1190 and the chancel retains its 13th-century roof. Buried in the chancel is Dr Robert Taylor, who worked on the translation of the Authorised Version of the Bible for James I. Look on the west wall, by the Chiddingfold glass window, to find the tablet to Sir William Bragg, who invented the iron lung when trying to help a sick villager. The churchyard has been a sea of wild crocuses every spring for over a century. The lych-gate has a rare high coffin rest, illustrating the original reason for the traditional roofed gate outside churches.

B

The Crown Inn. Timber framed and partly covered in wisteria and lilac, it was built for Cistercian monks and may date from as early as 1258. The Crown is Surrey's oldest licensed house, and past customers include Edward VI and Elizabeth I. Its telephone box is a converted sedan chair.

C

Chiddingfold Green. The impressive green remains the size of a meadow large enough to graze a herd of cattle; in 1552 around 4,000 men accompanying Edward VI camped on it. The greatest gathering now is for the annual bonfire (on the nearest Saturday to 5 November), which has been held for at least 150 years. As recently as 1929, 150 policemen had to protect the magistrate who arrived to read the Riot Act. The working forge is in a 17th-century building opposite the pond. On the east side of the green are several noted timber-framed buildings.

D

Cricket Ground. This second, smaller green is reserved for cricket, which has been played here for more than 150 years. One of the first professional players, Alfred Hoar, played for Chiddingfold as a teenager. The ground is over-looked by St Theresa's Church, built in the 1960s.

WALK DIRECTIONS

1

The walk starts at the church. Walk past The Crown and along the row of shops. Turn left up the east side of the green passing Botley House.

2

At the signpost, leave the green on the main road to reach the cricket ground. Continue past the church and where the houses on the right end, turn right up a track.

3

The path passes Sunnycroft and then gently climbs to a gate. Keep forward up the side of a field and before the top turn right over a (probably) broken stile in the trees to reach another field. Bear right with the field boundary, which soon falls away whilst the path stays on high ground to join a hedge on the left. Beyond a gateway the now wide path becomes enclosed as it runs down to a lane.

4

Turn right to pass Rose Cottage and Pound Cottage opposite the post office. On reaching the green keep ahead to the church.

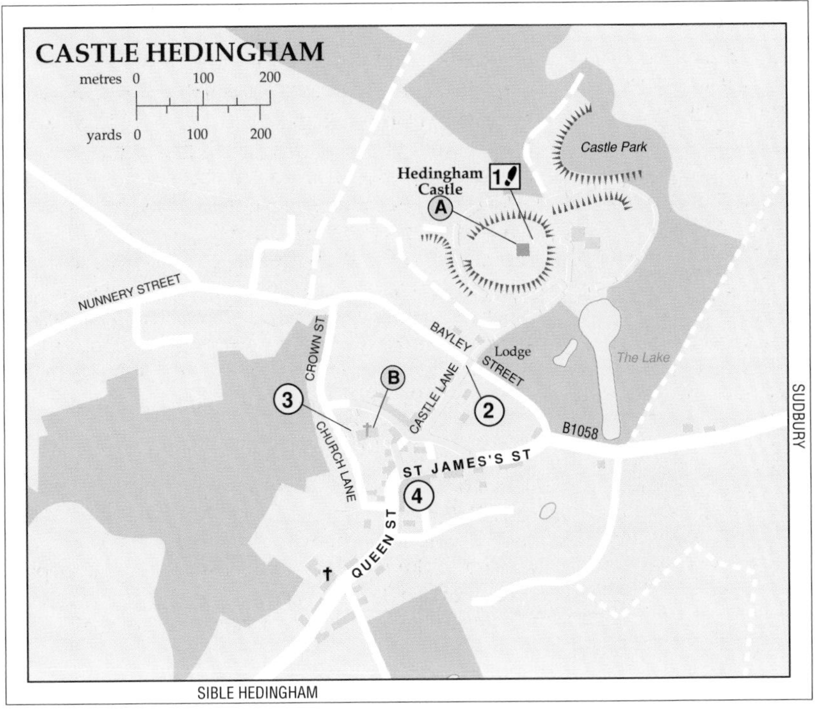

CASTLE HEDINGHAM

ESSEX

On the B1058, 9 miles N of Braintree

A compact village containing a delightful mixture of buildings including black-and-white half-timbered medieval houses, pink-washed thatched cottages and handsome Georgian dwellings in mellow red brick. On the hillock to the north is the magnificent Norman keep that continues to watch over the village.

Castle Hedingham has derived its wealth from wool. In the 12th century. Lucy, the third wife of Aubrey de Vere, 1st Earl of Oxford (known as Aubrey the Grim due to his stern features) founded a Benedictine nunnery on the site of the present-day Nunnery Farm. In the following century, King John laid siege to the castle and granted the village a charter to hold a market.

NORMAN CASTLES

After William the Conqueror defeated Harold at the Battle of Hastings in 1066, William parcelled out the lands of England to his chief military leaders. In turn, these tenants in chief, as they were termed in the feudal system, sub-divided their huge landholdings to their vassals in return for 'homage and services'. Castles were built by both tenants-in-chief and vassals to serve as a home, a power-base from which they could police their lands, and as a refuge in times of strife.

No complete examples of Norman castles survive but we know that the vassals built small structures known as motte and bailey castles. The motte was a circular earthwork and the bailey a wooden defensive tower built on or within the motte.

The castles of the great Norman lords were much more elaborate affairs. They were large enough to house the lord and his family in some splendour as well as providing barracks for a considerable number of troops. If time, labour and materials were available, castles were built of stone. There was usually storage facilities for food and a well that enabled the castle to withstand a lengthy siege.

The first line of defence was the moat. The attackers then had to scale or breach the curtain wall and possibly other defences before reaching the keep. Elaborate siege techniques were developed. These included scaling ladders, enclosed battering rams that protected the soldiers from the hail of arrows and boiling oil while they were attempting to breach the walls, and portable towers that could be pushed alongside the keep so that the roof could be attacked. Providing that the castle was well stocked it could hold out for a considerable period, but if time was on the side of the attackers, then ultimately the defenders could be starved into submission.

The 12th-century castle was built by the powerful de Vere family to dominate the Colne Valley.

POINTS OF INTEREST

Ⓐ

The Castle. There are castles that appear to be more complete, but the keep (i.e. the central fortification) at Castle Hedingham is reckoned to be one of the best preserved in Europe. After the Norman Conquest, the Lordship of Hedingham was taken from Ulwine, its Saxon owner, and given to Alberic de Ver (the name was later spelled 'de Vere'), one of William's most successful knights. Alberic's son Aubrey, a noted Crusader, built the castle in about 1140. Originally, the castle mound was protected by a curtain wall but this, together with the keep tower, was demolished in 1592. The dry moat originally had a drawbridge, which was replaced by the existing Tudor bridge. To the right of the bridge will be seen a splendid Georgian house dating from 1719 in which the castle's owners now reside.

The keep is entered by a flight of steps which were once protected by a tower. To the left of the steps can be seen the dungeon into which prisoners were lowered through a trap in the ceiling. You enter the Garrison or Guard Room which housed the soldiers. In the corner farthest from the entrance will be found a *garderobe* or privy. A spiral staircase beside the door goes down to the food store and also provides access to the upper storeys.

The next floor up is the Banqueting Hall or Armoury which is dominated by a timber ceiling supported by the largest Norman arch in Europe.

These colour-washed houses are just one of the many types of building to be found in the square.

WALK DIRECTIONS

After visiting the castle walk back towards the car park. Just before the entrance to the car park, turn left along a broad grassy path that runs past the top of the lake (note the gazebo at the lakeside). Continue forward until meeting the earth banks of the outer bailey, which should be kept on your left. Follow the earth fortifications, bearing left wherever the path forks. Once beyond the outer bailey you will find yourself walking in the moat, which will lead you to the car park.

②

Return to the entrance and take the road opposite (Castle Lane). It will bring you into Falcon Square, which contains an interesting mixture of buildings including a fine half-timbered black-and-white house. Turn right and walk almost to the end of Church Ponds. Turn left and climb the steps into the beautifully kept churchyard (visitors in wheelchairs should return to Falcon Square, turn right and then enter the churchyard).

③

After visiting the church, continue across the churchyard, noting the Saxon cross with Norman carvings on your left, to a lane (King Street). Turn right and walk to St James Street.

④

Turn left and walk past the half-timbered Moot House (now a restaurant) until opposite a half-timbered house. At this point, turn sharp left along a metalled footpath that will return you to Falcon Square. Turn right along Castle Lane to the castle entrance.

The medieval church of St Nicholas was built 50 years after the castle.

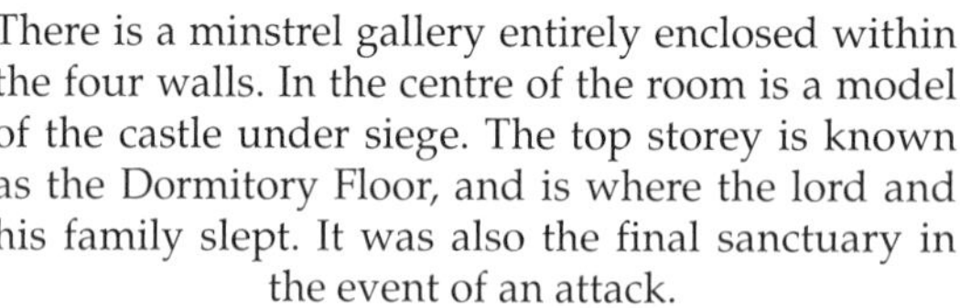

There is a minstrel gallery entirely enclosed within the four walls. In the centre of the room is a model of the castle under siege. The top storey is known as the Dormitory Floor, and is where the lord and his family slept. It was also the final sanctuary in the event of an attack.

The Church of St Nicholas. St Nicholas' is one of the most interesting churches in Essex. The exterior appears to be Tudor with a Norman chancel but only the tower, with its charming cupola and vane on the newel staircase is Elizabethan. Apart from the late medieval double hammer-beam ceiling, the rest of the church is Norman, although early in the 17th century, many of the windows were enlarged and crenellations added to the tops of the walls.

The church is entered by a huge Norman self-closing door that still swings on its massive iron C-hinges. The pillars of the nave are Norman with Transitional (i.e. Norman to Early English) capitals. The east window above the altar is a very rare example of a Norman wheel window. The rood screen, with its fine ogee arches, dates from about 1400. To the right of the altar is a remarkable three-seater sedilia and piscina. To the right of the chancel, in the south wall of the side chapel on the right-hand side of the altar, is a small carved stone, known as the Saxon Stone, which depicts the head of a woman or a saint. There is a Norman cushion stoup for holy water in the south wall near the main door.

INFORMATION

Length of walk:
1½ miles
Approximate time:
1 hour. Allow plenty of extra time for the castle and church

TERRAIN:
Suitable for children and pushchairs. It is not possible to get wheelchairs into the castle, but they can make the circuit of the moat and village.

PARKING:
There are no public car parks. The castle has a car park (for visitors only). Street parking is possible in the main street (St James Street) and in Bayley Street, which gives access to the castle.

OPEN:
Castle. Daily Easter-Oct 10am-5pm.

REFRESHMENTS:
Light refreshments, afternoon teas, etc. available in the castle and the Magnolia Tea Rooms. The Wheatsheaf and the Bell Inn serve bar meals, and Hugo's and the Old Moot House are restaurants.

CHILHAM

KENT

On A252, 5 miles SW of Canterbury

CHILHAM is a film set village, dominated by its church and castle, which face each other across the village square. The Pilgrims' Way used by travellers from both Winchester and London ran through the square and today its 20th-century successor, the North Downs Way, passes through the churchyard on its more tranquil way to Canterbury.

INFORMATION
Length of walk:
¾ mile
Approximate time:
45 minutes

TERRAIN:
Suitable for children at all times of the year; suitable for pushchairs and wheelchairs.

PARKING:
Park in the village square.

OPEN:
Chilham Castle. Mid-Aug-Sep; Tue-Thu, and Sat. Charge. Chilham Castle Gardens. Daily mid-Apr–mid-Oct. Charge.

REFRESHMENTS:
The White Horse; The Woolpack; Jacobean Tea Room at the Castle.

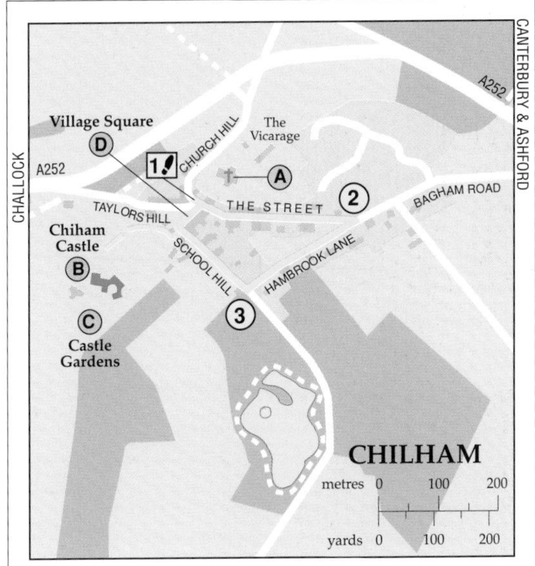

WALK DIRECTIONS

①

The walk begins at the church. Turn left out of the church by The White Horse to walk downhill along The Street past the shops to The Woolpack.

②

Turn right along the far side of The Woolpack. Walk down Hambrook Lane to its junction with School Hill.

Go right up School Hill to the square, turning left on reaching the square to visit the castle and gardens, before returning to the church.

St Mary's Church has a fine stone and flint tower.

POINTS OF INTEREST

Chilham Church. The church is pre-Reformation but the 68ft tower was never a landmark for pilgrims as it was only completed in the 1530s, when the Canterbury shrine was being shut down by Henry VIII. The door is riddled with holes said to have been caused by bullets, although a more prosaic explanation is simply nails for notices. Inside on the left are the figures of the Hardy children, who died at the castle in 1858. Their toys and an illustrated book can also be seen.

Chilham Castle. This, the seat of Viscount Massereene and Ferrard, comprises a keep built by Henry II and a Jacobean mansion. King John and Archbishop Langton, who were on opposite sides in the Magna Carta negotiations, met at the castle. Sir Dudley Digges, who built the house in James I's reign, still has his birthday celebrated by a peel of bells at the church.

Castle Gardens. The gardens were laid out for the new house by Charles I's gardener, John Tradescant, but his work was obliterated 150 years later by 'Capability' Brown, who is responsible for today's parkland views and the ha-ha. However, the evergreen oak on the upper lawn was planted in 1616 and later that century the mulberry trees which survive provided cuttings for the USA's Mulberry Island. There is a bird of prey sanctuary and the falconer gives flying displays at 3.30pm on most afternoons when the gardens are open.

Chilham Village Square. Said to be the most photographed in Britain, it has often been used by film makers. When not serving as a movie location, the square is the visitors' car park. Both the long distance walker coming in on the North Downs Way and the motorist are usually amazed to find such well-preserved timber-framed buildings on two sides of a square. Where there are no half-timbered houses and shops there is the church tower and the Tudor-style castle lodges added this century by architect Sir Herbert Baker who sensitively removed Victorian embellishments to the Jacobean castle behind.

FALCONRY

The art of training falcons to attack wild fowl or game, was practised in the east-especially Persia and Arabia – at the time of Christ's birth and introduced in to England about 200 years before the Conquest. In medieval times barons would have had falcons whilst knaves made do with a kestrel. Falconry was the country's leading sport until the Civil War in the 17th century, after which the recovery of interest at the Restoration was hampered by the invention of better and better sporting guns.

Although there has recently been a renewed interest in falconry, the world's birds of prey are declining in numbers. Falconry was reintroduced to Chilham in 1971 and now any injured bird of prey in the south-east is likely to be brought to the Castle to be looked after by Lord Massereene's falconer who runs a bird sanctuary.

CLAVERING
ESSEX

On B1038, 7 miles N of Bishops Stortford

THE parish of Clavering is very large and scattered and includes a number of hamlets, but its centre remains unspoiled because all development has taken place outside the old village. This allows the visitor to stroll in peace and enjoy the pleasing vernacular architecture, which includes a medieval Guildhall and one of the smallest houses in Britain.

POINTS OF INTEREST

Ⓐ

The Parish Church of St Mary and St Clement. The church gets its unusual dual dedication because the parish tithes went to the Priory of St Mary at Prittlewell, which was a daughter foundation of the Benedictine abbey at Cluny in France that claimed to possess a relic of St Clement.

The present building replaces a Saxon church in which miracles associated with King Edward the Confessor are reputed to have occurred. The chancel dates mostly from the 14th century and the nave, timber roof, porch and tower from the 15th century, so it is built very much in one style. The fine 15th-century screen has a series of figures of saints along the bottom including St Anthony and his pig and St Agnes and her lamb. There is some medieval glass in the windows of the north aisle.

Among the interesting memorials are those of the Barlees, an important local family, at the back of the north aisle. Haynes Barlee's memorial shows seven of his 13 children kneeling, but the six that died in infancy are represented by skulls.

Ⓑ

Clavering Castle. Built in 1052 by Robert Fitzwimarc, the castle has completely disappeared except for the moat and associated earthworks. Robert, an interesting man, was a French adventurer who held high office under both Edward the Confessor and William the Conqueror.

Tiny thatched and weather-boarded Chestnut Cottage.

WALK DIRECTIONS

①

Walk down Church Lane. The recently restored medieval Guildhall was for many years the parish poorhouse. Reach the churchyard and visit the church (this is not accessible to wheelchairs as there are three steps down from the porch). Come out of the church, turn right and immediately right again to follow a path through the churchyard to a kissing-gate. To your right is the moat and castle mound. (Wheelchair visitors should turn right just before the kissing-gate, go through the churchyard and follow the gravel drive into the centre of the village.)

②

Pass through the kissing-gate and follow the path to a lane. Turn right for 600yds to the first turning on the right and pass through a ford (there is a footbridge on the left). Follow the road (Middle Street) through the centre of the village admiring the handsome houses and attractive cottages (note the old pump on your right). Opposite the footbridge is Chestnut Cottage which dates from the 17th century, measures just 10 x 8ft, and is one of the smallest houses in Britain.

③

Where Middle Street makes a sharp bend to the left, leave the road by turning right to follow a gravel track that will take you past The Bury to the churchyard. The Bury is the Manor house. Its 17th-century exterior conceals a rare 13th-century aisled hall. Walk through the churchyard, keeping the church on your right, to the lane, and return to the main road.

INFORMATION
Length of walk:
2/3 mile
Approximate time:
1 hour

TERRAIN:
A mainly level route over lanes and paths. It is suitable for push-chairs and children. Visitors in wheelchairs can follow a modified route that avoids both a kissing-gate and the narrow footbridge.

PARKING:
There are no public car parks. There is parking for about five cars in a lay-by on the B1038 opposite the lane leading to the church. It is also possible to park near the ford in Middle Street, and in the housing estate that turns off the B1038 by the telephone box.

REFRESHMENTS:
The Fox and Hounds, on the B1038 on the Saffron Walden side of the village, serves morning coffee and bar snacks.

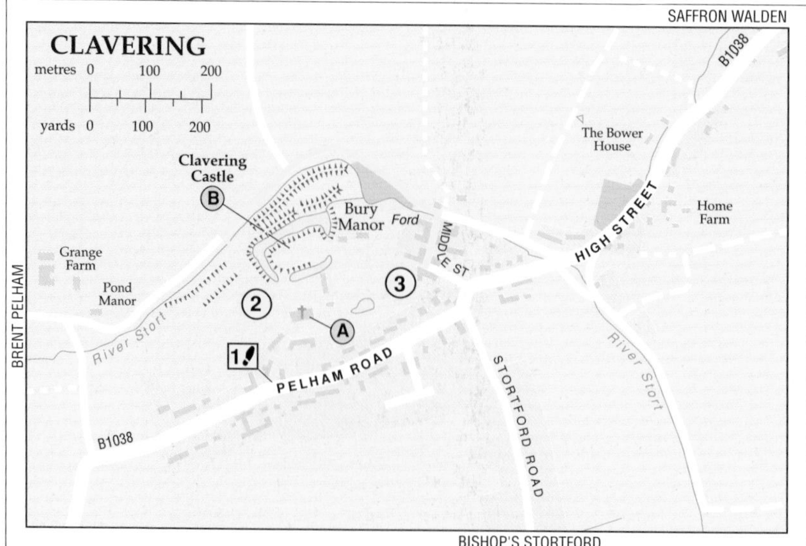

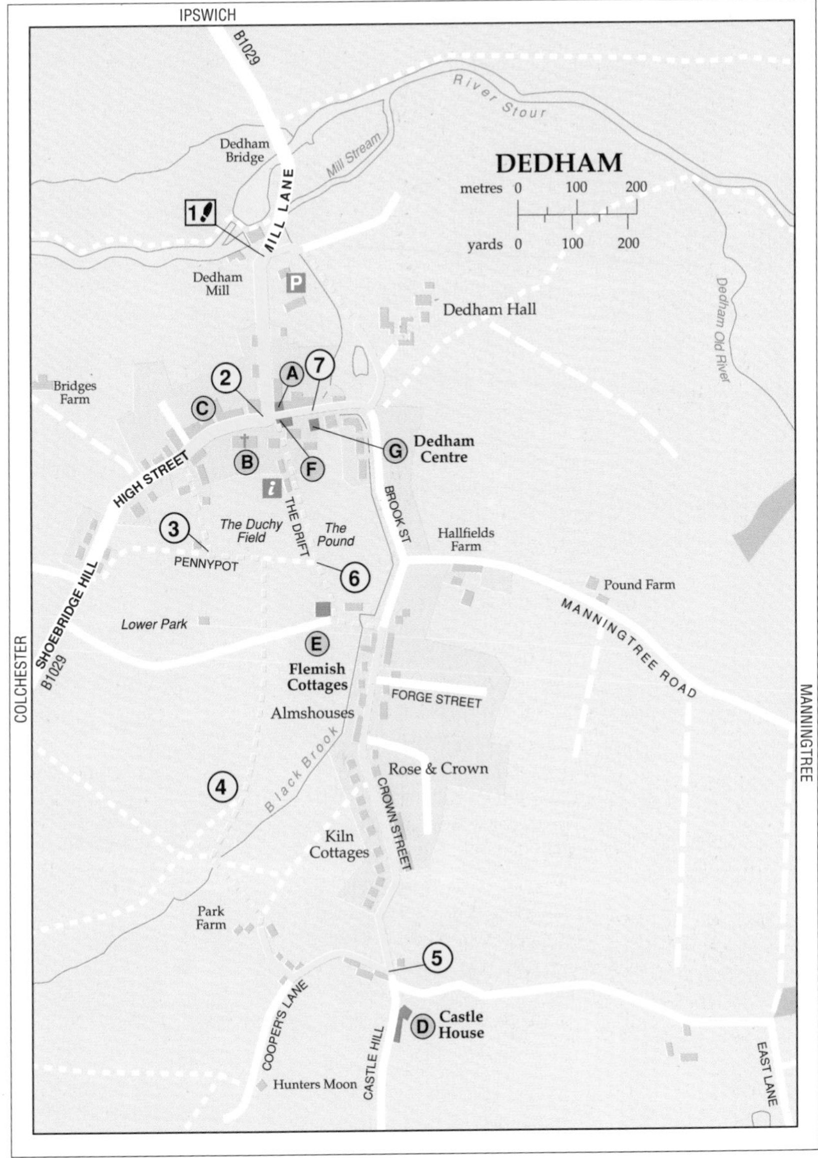

DEDHAM

ESSEX

On B1029, 6 miles N of Colchester

THE painter John Constable, who was born and brought up in Dedham Vale, claimed in later life that he loved 'every stile and stump and lane'. These lanes – School Lane, Pennypot Path and The Drift – are still walked by artists seeking new angles on Dedham Church tower as well as those just wanting to see how little the scenery has changed since Constable recorded it over 150 years ago.

Although often believed to be in Suffolk, Dedham is just inside Essex, since the River Stour is the county boundary. However, the village is also part of the Duchy of Lancaster, with the head of that estate – the Queen – being joint patron of the church, and the Tourist Information Office housed in Duchy Barn.

WALK DIRECTIONS

①

From the car park, turn left up Mill Lane to the village centre.

②

Go right to visit St Mary's Church. Continue along the High Street and go left just past the post office. The lane passes a half-timbered cottage and the Old School House. Keep left where the path divides.

③

Turn left along the edge of Duchy Field and before reaching the end go right to a set-back stile. A path crosses two fields and goes through two kissing-gates. At a third field keep ahead past an oak tree to a stile on the far side.

④

From the stile bear half left to a point just beyond the pole (or go left round the field as waymarked) to find a footbridge leading to a stile. Go up the side of the farm buildings and over a stile to follow a drive. Turn left along a lane which curves round to a junction by pink-painted Castle House.

⑤

Turn left along Crown Street to pass the Rose & Crown public house and two rows of almshouses. Where the houses on the left end, go left up a lane towards the pink half-timbered Flemish Cottages.

St Mary's was built with the wealth of prosperous clothier families.

⑥

Follow the lane across Duchy Field and past Duchy Barn to the village square. Turn right past the former Grammar School to the Dedham Centre.

⑦

Cross the road outside the Dedham Centre and turn right to go left up the Dedham Hall drive. Go over a stile on the left and walk between the drive and the pond to a gate. Bear half left to a stile and follow a path to two stiles to cross a ford on a footbridge. At Mill Lane turn left for the car park.

POINTS OF INTEREST

Ⓐ

Marlborough Head. The L-shaped, timber-framed corner house, is in the most commanding position facing the square and the church. This 15th-century pub, which some suggest is as early as 1430, was designed as a cloth merchant's house with the Mill Lane frontage intended as the storage chamber. A spacious cellar contained woad vats.

After the decline in the wool trade in the 1660s the house was divided into an apothecary's and a dyer's. In 1704 the partitions were removed for the building to become an inn named after the Duke of Marlborough, who that year had won the Battle of Blenheim. Four years later the church bells rang out to mark his success at Oudenarde over the French. The pub's central lounge has finely carved woodwork and another beamed room is now the Constable Bar. The inn, well known for its food, and popular with locals, has a hidden garden at the back.

St Mary's Church. The church dates from 1492, the year Columbus discovered America, and recently the people of Dedham, Massachusetts contributed towards restoration here. The 131ft tower features in many Constable paintings. On the north wall is a tablet to Judith Eyre, who died in 1747 after swallowing a pin in a Christmas pudding. Look at the pew ends to find a pair of rugby boots. Buried in the churchyard (NW corner of plot behind Duchy Barn) is art forger Tom Keating, who could produce a 'Constable' on demand.

High Street. Many of the buildings are older than their Georgian appearance. In the Sun Inn yard is an early 17th-century exterior covered staircase. The Marlborough Head was built in the 1430s as a wool market. Opposite is the former Grammar School where Constable was a pupil.

Castle House. The house has a Tudor entrance hall leading into the Georgian addition where there is a Gothic staircase. Painter Sir Alfred Munnings called the pink-washed building 'the house of my dreams' when he bought it in 1919. In the studio can be seen his early poster work including one of girls in large hats advertising Caley's Chocolates. The firm was his first patron and in the main house is an oil painting of Daniel Tomkins, father of the Caley's director. The scene includes a dog but it was horses that were to make Munnings famous. The dining room is hung with his Newmarket equestrian paintings which brought comparison with George Stubbs.

The house, including furniture, is much as Munnings left it at the time of his death in 1959, and modern art is nowhere to be seen. In a famous speech as President of the Royal Academy of Arts, he condemned all modern art along with Picasso.

Flemish Cottages. This is a converted medieval cloth factory still retaining its dye house. No part of the building is later than early 15th century and part has been standing since the 12th century.

The Grammar School. Founded in 1574 by a wealthy cloth merchant, the school moved into the building in the square in 1732. The headmaster's study was to the left of the front door and the dining room beyond looked on to the main street. On the top floor were the dormitories.

John Constable, who had been unhappy at school in Lavenham, was a day boy here. His daily walk across the water-meadows from East Bergholt had a lasting influence on his later work. One of his early paintings was of his headmaster, who had encouraged his artistic leanings.

Ⓖ

Dedham Centre. In a converted chapel, the Centre continues Dedham's artistic tradition with displays by resident artists and craft stalls. There is also a toy museum and a health food restaurant.

INFORMATION
Length of walk:
2 miles
Approximate time:
2 hours

TERRAIN:
Suitable for children at all times of the year; not suitable for push-chairs or wheelchairs. Seven stiles and 3 footbridges.

PARKING:
Park in the car park in Mill Lane.

OPEN:
Castle House. May-Sep Sun, Wed and bank hols. Charge.
Dedham Centre. Daily except Christmas hols and Mon in Jan-Mar. Charge.

REFRESHMENTS:
The Marlborough Head; The Essex Rose Tearoom: Bridge Cottage at Flatford (Jun-Aug).

JOHN CONSTABLE

Britain's most influential 19th-century artist grew up in Dedham Vale and first exhibited in London in 1802. Thanks to an inheritance, he was able to marry in 1816 and continue painting the scenes of his boyhood. His famous painting of Salisbury Cathedral came about through his friendship with the rector of Langham, near Dedham, who became Bishop of Salisbury.

From Dedham, the towpath of the River Stour provides a direct walk of just over a mile to Flatford Mill, where Constable painted a number of his most famous scenes, including *The Haywain.* Bridge Cottage at Flatford is a National Trust tearoom and there is also a field studies centre there.

Constable's painting of the Valley of the Stour and Dedham village.

The unusual white brick façade of the Early Georgian Grammar school.

EAST MEON

EAST MEON

HAMPSHIRE

On minor roads between Petersfield and West Meon. Take signposted minor road from A32 at West Meon or from A272 at Langrish, near Petersfield

TIME, good taste, and a remoteness from the commercial scene have combined to produce a near-perfect Hampshire village in East Meon, lost in a tangle of lanes to the west of Petersfield.

INFORMATION
Length of walk:
2 miles
Approximate time:
1½ hours

TERRAIN:
Suitable for children at all times of the year. Mostly suitable for pushchairs, which could be carried for short distances if necessary. Easily amended, by leaving out field sections, to accommodate wheelchairs.

PARKING:
There is no public car park. Seek parking space in Chapel Street, Temple Lane, or at The George or Izaak Walton pubs if you are patronising them.

REFRESHMENTS:
Two pubs in village.

The parish church of All Saints', East Meon.

The Izaac Walton public house on the High Street.

THE WORKHOUSE

A great fire raged through East Meon in 1910, destroying many buildings, including the old workhouse. This institution was created in the early 1700s from two low thatched cottages, probably similar to the two on the other side of Workhouse Lane today. Records show that the old East Meon workhouse was quite unusual in being a humane place where kindness and consideration were paramount, unlike the dreadful Union workhouses inflicted on the poor in Victorian times.

WALK DIRECTIONS

①

Start the walk from the church. For a bird's-eye view of the village and East Meon valley, take the path which goes up left from the churchyard through the trees. Go up some steps, right, at the top and over a stile on to Park Hill; where the view is rewarding and it is an ideal place for a picnic. Return to the church and go right on Church Road to the western edge of the village.

②

Turn left into Workhouse Lane at a signpost which points one way to West Meon and the other to Petersfield. Follow the road round to the left, passing on the left a pair of low thatched cottages and the black oak-beamed Tudor House, one of the oldest in East Meon, and on the right the timber-framed Heycroft House.

③

Turn left and walk through the narrow street called The Cross. Go right at the top (back on Church Road) and right again into Church Street.

④

Turn left and walk along High Street beside the River Meon. Pass the Izaak Walton inn and between two cottages, one wood-beamed and the other tile-hung, take the footpath with a No Cycling sign.

⑤

Walk beside gardens, allotments and the riverbank to Frogmore. Go left and at Bottled Ale Cottage go right over a stile on to a fieldpath.

⑥

In 200yds turn right again and walk through fields back to the village recreation ground and into High Street at The Forge.

⑦

Turn right and walk back into the village, passing two ancient cottages and a shop, all 500 years old or more. The tiny green triangle on the right is called Washers Triangle; it is thought that the women of the village did their washing here in olden days. Make your way back to the church by whatever road you fancy.

POINTS OF INTEREST

Ⓐ

All Saints' Church. This impressive place of worship has sat on the side of Park Hill for the last 900 years, and was probably designed by the architect responsible for Winchester Cathedral. The church is mostly in the Norman and Early English styles and has the Arms of King James I over the door. Its greatest treasure is a carved black Tournai marble font, brought from Belgium around 1150.

Ⓑ

The Courthouse. The 14th-century courthouse to the left of the church is a symbol of the feudal power that ruled here in medieval times. The Bishops of Winchester held their courts here.

Ⓒ

River Meon. There are many little bridges in East Meon, all crossing the young River Meon, one of Hampshire's famous fishing rivers. Izaak Walton, the father of English angling, who wrote *The Compleat Angler* knew this river well and fished it.

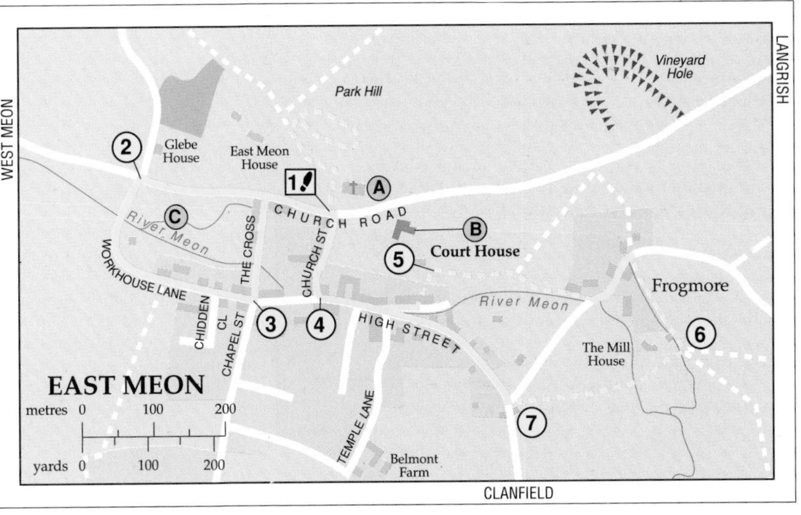

ELHAM

KENT

On B2065, 6 miles N of Hythe

A lovely sprawling Downs village, built on the site of a neolithic settlement and really off the beaten track in the pretty Nailbourne Valley. Elham has many fine old buildings, from the medieval timbered houses, with their overhanging upper storeys, to elegant red-brick homes built in the 18th century. Charles II is reputed to have hidden in the village from pursuing Roundheads.

The award-winning Elham Valley Vineyard and winery can be visited a short distance away. There are many fine walks in the area.

POINTS OF INTEREST

The Square. Elham's market charter was granted by Prince Edward in 1251, 21 years before he was crowned Edward I. The Square has been used for the market for centuries. The King's Arms was built in the Middle Ages, but the medieval timbers are now hidden beneath a tile-clad façade.

The Church of St Mary the Virgin. A 12th-century flint-and-ragstone Norman church, St Mary's is noted for its tall spire atop a fortified tower with battlements. The church underwent alterations in the 13th and 19th centuries, which account for the rather unusual front entrance.

The church has an alabaster Becket triptych, and a wonderful stained-glass window depicting Carlyle and the opera singer Mme Patti, attended by Gladstone, Disraeli and three of Queen Victoria's daughters.

Ⓒ

Rural Heritage Centre, Parsonage Farm. Rare native farm animals are bred here. There is also a collection of old farm machinery.

Ⓓ

The High Street. Abbot's Fireside, a large half-timbered house built in 1614, used to be the Smithies Inn, and was the headquarters of the Duke of Wellington during the Napoleonic Wars. The female figures (caryatids) supporting the over-hanging upper storey provide a very unusual feature. The Rose and Crown opposite was a coaching inn on the road between London and the Channel ports. It was used by the Scarlet Pimpernel as he travelled between London and Paris. There are other fine houses in the High Street, including The Master's House and the row of terraced cottages opposite, dating from 1742. The imposing Methodist Church was built in 1839.

Ⓔ

Elham Manor House. The Row was used by a weaver in the 17th century, and then by the Wotton family. Well Cottage and Updown Cottage used to be part of a medieval hall house. There is a well in the front garden of Windlass Cottage in Cullings Hill – a feature of many houses. According to local lore, Christian and pagan priests used their powers to locate the wells in a bid to win the souls of the villagers during a bad drought.

A rare Tamworth pig, one of the residents at Parsonage Farm Rural Heritage Centre.

Abbot's Fireside stands in a prominent position in the High Street, its timbered upper storey resting on brackets carved into figures.

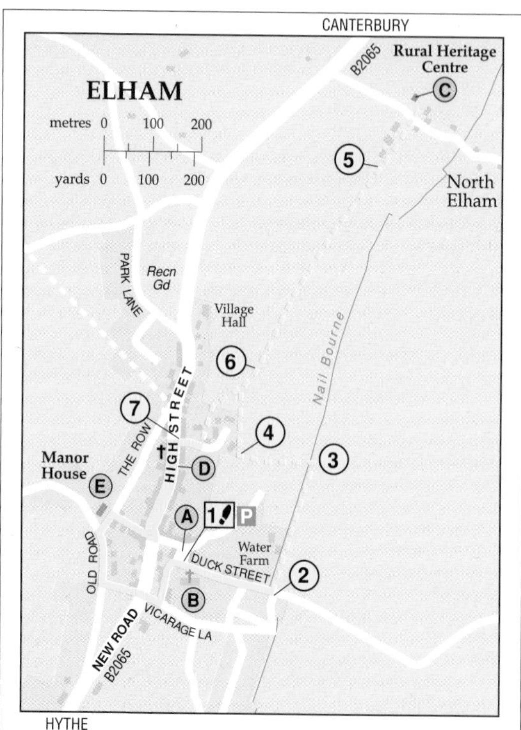

INFORMATION
Length of walk:
2 miles
Approximate time:
2-2½ hours to explore the village and Parsonage Farm

TERRAIN:
Flat paths across farmland, 3 stiles to negotiate.

PARKING:
Park in The Square. Enter via Pound Lane and exit via Vicarage Lane.

OPEN:
Parsonage Farm Rural Heritage Centre. Daily except Mon, 10.30am-5pm. Charge.

REFRESHMENTS:
Parsonage Farm Rural Heritage Centre.

WALK DIRECTIONS

Walk down Duck Street to turn left along the well-signposted footpath just beyond Water Farm.

②

The path follows the course of a disused railway line to the right of a stream.

③

Cross the stile on your left at the end of the first field and head towards the houses.

④

Turn right at the houses and follow the path with farm buildings ahead of you. There is a stile to cross.

⑤

Go through the gate, past the farm buildings, and cross the road to Parsonage Farm. Return the same way until you reach the stile.

Cross the stile and cut diagonally right across the field to the gate into Cherry Gardens and then into the High Street.

Explore the High Street, turning right into Cullings Hill and then left in to The Row before cutting back across the High Street into Vicarage Road and the car park.

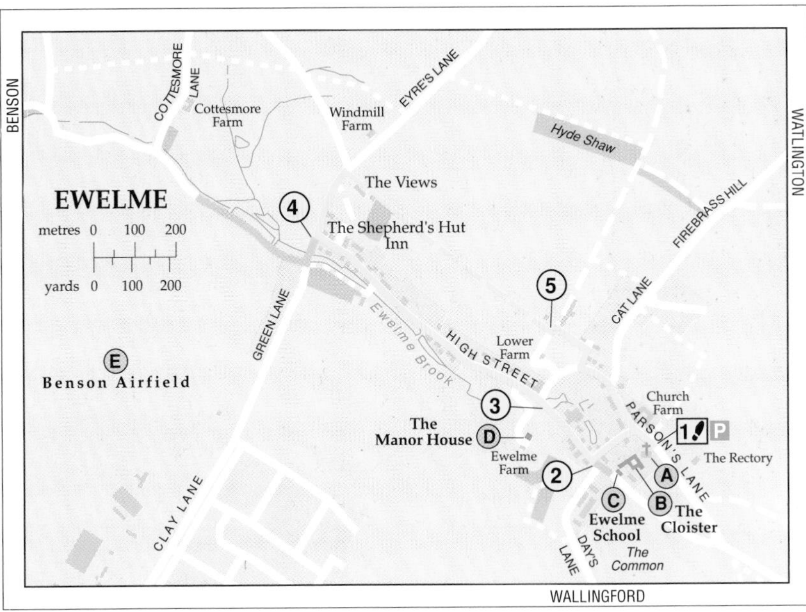

EWELME

OXFORDSHIRE

Off B4009, 1 mile E of Benson

EWELME'S location away from any main road and on the 'wrong' side of an airfield has left the old village largely intact in its own valley. The main street follows the Ewelme Brook, which feeds watercress beds at the western end. Ewelme appears in the Domesday Book but owes its attractiveness to the Chaucer family, whose connections built the almshouses, school and church in the 15th century.

A visit to the church, with its original cloister which has remained in daily use despite the attentions of Henry VIII and Cromwell, will be highly rewarding. It has served as a film set, but your only guide is likely to be a cat who likes snoozing on the Chaucer tomb.

WALK DIRECTIONS

①

From the north gate of the church, a path runs downhill outside the churchyard to the main street.

A detour to the left leads to the village school. The main route turns right along the High Street to pass Day's Cottage, with its ancient warning against dumping 'anything injurious to health' in the clear water which later joins the Thames – an early example of awareness of the dangers of pollution.

③

Continue along the street, passing the lane leading to the post office, the unmarked Manor House entrance on the left and a ford before reaching The Shepherd's Hut inn. (A detour to the left over the brook and then right leads to a road running across the end of the main RAF Benson runway and a vantage point for watching aircraft on certain days.)

The main route turns right at The Shepherd's Hut to go up Eyre's Lane, which gives a view across part of the airfield to Wittenham Clumps. At a junction, turn right along a straight, rough track to pass the back of a house known as The Views. Soon there are more views of Wittenham Clumps over the hidden village below.

At the far end of the track, go left by a house and at once right to continue in the south-easterly direction. At the residential Chaucer Court road turn right. Go left up Parson's Lane to return to the church beyond the Cat Lane turning.

POINTS OF INTEREST

Ⓐ

Ewelme Church. Little changed since it was built between 1430 and 1435, locals claim that the church retains its screen and figures thanks to the Roundheads being unable to find the village. The $10\frac{1}{2}$ft high font cover dates from about 1480. In St John's Chapel is the tomb of Geoffrey Chaucer's son Thomas and his wife, who are seen on top in brass. Nearby, and separating the two sanctuaries, is the tomb of their daughter Alice, Duchess of Suffolk. Her body lies between her effigies in life and emaciated in death. Look on her arm for the Garter, which she had special permission to wear, and then lie down on the floor to see the hidden roof painting over the lower body.

The church was used in the filming of John Mortimer's *Paradise Postponed* in which the Rector is called Simeon Simcox – Henry Simcox was incumbent here in the 1890s. On the path to the Old Rectory is the grave of *Three Men In a Boat* author Jerome K. Jerome, who lived a mile to the south and worshipped here.

The Cloister. Beyond St Mary's west door, steps lead down to a cloister built with the church in the early 1430s. Here almshouses provide accommodation for 13 men who meet together daily and pray for their foundress Alice, Duchess of Suffolk, and her husband. Since 1605, Oxford's Regius Professor of Medicine has been the Master of the community.

An impressive brick entrance to the Almshouse, 'God's House in Ewelme', with the church close by.

The original structure and organisation of the cloister has changed very little during the five and half centuries through which it has stood.

Ⓒ

Ewelme School. Also part of the 15th-century church complex is the village school, the oldest in the state system and still in its original building. Elsewhere, such schools have often become public schools; a notable example is Eton, which Henry VI founded three years later.

The Manor House is mainly Georgian but incorporates the remains of the Chaucer family's moated brick and stone residence. Geoffrey Chaucer's granddaughter enlarged the house after marrying the Earl of Suffolk and from her home planned the village's magnificent almshouses and school. One of her guests was Margaret of Anjou, Henry VI's Queen. The house was grand enough for Henry VIII to choose it for his honeymoon with fifth wife Catherine Howard. Elizabeth I came as a very young princess and then as Queen. The building was already much reduced in size when Prince Rupert took up residence during the Stuart period.

Benson Airfield. When the runways were built, a quantity of cannon balls, believed to be Cromwellian, were found.

FAMILY PRIDE

The tomb of Alice Chaucer in Ewelme church is one of the finest heraldic monuments in the country. Her alabaster effigy with its hauty-faced aristocratic lineaments lies beneath an elaborate canopy adorned with angels. Beneath her is a stone tomb chest and under it can be seen a grisly, half-shrouded corpse. On the sides of the tomb chest are eight winged figures in niches, each holding a shield.

The coats of arms painted on these shields identify her own and her husband's ancestry and amount to a glowing statement of family pride by their son, who had the monument built. Alice's father's and mother's arms are there with the badge of the De la Poles, Dukes of Suffolk – three golden leopard's faces above and below a horizontal band. They also appear quartered with the lion of Alice's rich Burghersh mother. Also on display are the arms of Alice's previous husband, the Earl of Salisbury, and the royal arms of England, which refer to her son's marriage to the Princess Elizabeth, sister to two kings – Edward IV and Richard III.

There is deliberately no inscription to say that this is the tomb of Alice de la Pole, (nay Chaucer), Duchess of Suffolk. The cultivated visitor of the day would know her by her heraldry.

The cloister within the Almshouse shows a very early use of brick in Oxfordshire.

THE CHAUCER CONNECTION

Ewelme owes much of its character today to the granddaughter of the poet Geoffrey Chaucer, author of *The Canterbury Tales*.

The poet earned his living as a civil servant and was often hard up, but his son Thomas stood high in the favour of Henry IV and Henry V, and made himself a fortune. Through his marriage to an heiress, Matilda Burghersh, he acquired substantial estates, including the manor of Ewelme. He was an MP for many years and was chosen Speaker of the House of Commons in 1407. He died in 1434 and was buried at Ewelme.

The manor passed to his 30-year-old daughter Alice, who had already been widowed twice and was now married to William de la Pole, Earl of Suffolk. He moved to the village, bringing with him the technique of building with brick which was fairly uncommon in Oxfordshire at that time. Alice and her husband built the magnificent almshouse, which still survives, and also the school and church. The earl fought in the wars in France and on one occasion was taken prisoner by Joan of Arc. These were troubled times and although he was created Duke of Suffolk in 1448, two years later his enemies succeeded in having him banished. On his way abroad by boat he was seized and beheaded, and his corpse was dumped on the beach near Dover.

Alice lived on at Ewelme comparatively undisturbed until she died there in 1475. Her son John, Duke of Suffolk, built her the splendid tomb in St Mary's Church. The property of the Suffolk family was later seized by the Crown.

INFORMATION
Length of walk:
$1^1/_2$ miles ($1^3/_4$ miles if detours followed)
Approximate time:
$1^1/_2$ hours (if detours followed)

TERRAIN:
Suitable for children at all times of the year; suitable for pushchairs; not suitable for wheelchairs.

PARKING:
Park outside the church in Parsons Lane.

OPEN:
The church and almshouse cloister.

REFRESHMENTS:
The Shepherd's Hut pub.

FINCHINGFIELD
ESSEX

On B1053, 9 miles NW of Braintree

FINCHINGFIELD is everybody's idea of an archetypal English village. It has everything; a fine old church that dominates the village, a windmill, a green with a duckpond, almshouses, attractive pubs, and a wealth of charming thatched cottages. Most of the modern development is on the outskirts, leaving the centre virtually unspoilt. The large, undistinguished houses at the top of The Green are screened by mature trees. It is a showplace and can become very crowded on fine summer weekends.

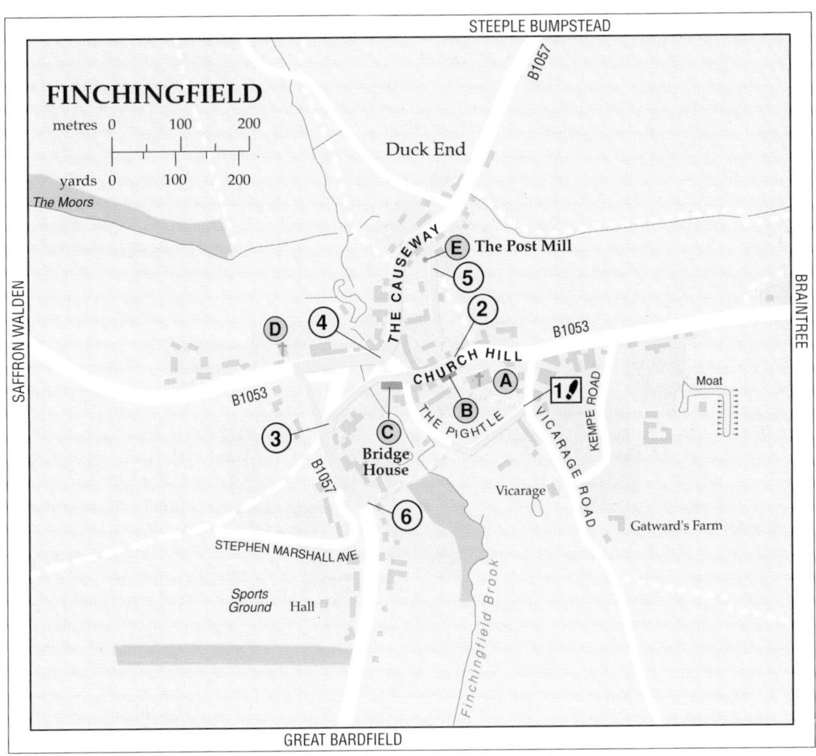

WALK DIRECTIONS

①

Begin the walk by visiting the church, using the Vicarage Lane entrance (visitors in wheelchairs should now follow the instructions in paragraph 6). Turn right out of the church and walk across the churchyard to the 15th-century Guildhall and almshouses.

Turn left and walk down the steep hill towards the pond.

③

Cross the footbridge and walk to the top of The Green to admire the view of the village. To the left is the Nonconformist chapel. Turn right and walk towards the bridge past the Fox and the Old Manse.

④

Turn left beyond the bridge, climb to the top of The Causeway and walk along the pavement past some attractive cottages. Just beyond the windmill, turn right along a gravel path which will bring you close to the windmill.

Continue along the footpath to reach the road opposite the church. This brings you back to point 2. Turn right and walk down the hill, cross the footbridge and turn left along The Green back to point 3. When 75yds beyond the post office, turn left along a path.

Continue ahead over a footbridge and reach a lane at a squeeze stile. Turn right along the lane and return to the back of the village church.

Alternative route for wheelchairs.

To begin the walk visitors in wheelchairs should turn left out of the church and proceed to the road. Turn left and left again at the T-junction and go down the steep hill past the church to the Guildhall.

To finish the walk visitors in wheelchairs should return along The Causeway, cross the road in which the Guildhall stands, and follow the narrow lane opposite that will bring you to the back of the church.

The increasingly rare sight of the old traditional-style village shop, Finchingfield.

POINTS OF INTEREST

Parish Church. The church of St John the Baptist dates mostly from the 12th and 14th centuries. The tower is the oldest part and has a fine Norman doorway, which can be seen on the side facing the Guildhall. The cupola on the tower, which replaced the steeple blown down in 1735, houses a 15th-century angelus bell.

The beautiful rood screen across the chancel dates from the early 15th century and is an outstanding example of the craftsmanship of medieval woodcarvers. The south aisle contains the 16th-century tomb and brasses of Sir John Berners and his wife Adelaide. Close examination reveals that there is a monkey near Sir John's head, which recalls that Sir John's son was saved by the screeching of a pet monkey when his house was destroyed by fire.

Scratched into one of the windowsills in the south aisle are some concentric squares that are believed to have been used in the medieval game of nine men's morris The chapel in the north aisle contains memorials to the Kempe and Ruggles-Brise families, who lived at Spain's Hall, 1 mile away. The one to William Kempe records 'that he did hold his peace for seaven yeares' because he falsely accused his young wife of unfaithfulness.

Patrick Brontë (see page 199-200) was curate of Finchingfield from 1806-08.

Ⓑ

The Guildhall. Situated on the edge of the churchyard, the Guildhall dates from the 15th century. In 1630, Sir Robert Kempe of Spains Hall endowed the almshouses and a school for the poor children of the village. The Guildhall now houses a small museum and the old schoolroom above is sometimes used for exhibitions.

The 15th-century tower of St John the Baptist, topped by an 18th-century cupola.

Finchingfield's stream-fed pond and green backed by its cottages and windmill.

Finchingfield Post Mill restored to its former working beauty.

INFORMATION
Length of walk:
1 mile
Approximate time:
1 hour

TERRAIN:
A hilly route along roads and footpaths that is suitable for children and push-chairs. An alternative route is given for visitors in wheelchairs, but it does include some steep hills.

PARKING:
There are no public car parks. Parking is possible on the roads bordering the village green and on the B1057 Steeple Bumpstead and Haverhill road (The Causeway). Probably the best place is in Vicarage Road, which turns off the B1053 between the Three Tuns Inn and the church.

OPEN:
The gardens of Spains Hall, a fine Elizabethan mansion, 1 mile NW of the village. May-Jul, Sun and bank hols.

REFRESHMENTS:
The Red Lion, the Finch, the Fox, and the Three Tuns Inn all serve bar meals. The Old Nosebag is a licensed restaurant, and there are tearooms on The Green and The Causeway.

(E)

The Post Mill. The 18th-century post mill, which last worked in 1890, was bought by the village in 1949 and has recently been restored by Essex County Council. Windmills made important contributions to village life until well into the 19th century. There has been a windmill on this site since the early 12th century.

Bridge House. Lying next to the pond, Bridge House dates from the 16th century, and from 1767 was used as the workhouse for 30 inmates. It has a massive chimney stack with four octagonal shafts. A contemporary describes it thus: 'There, old people and young children, ne'er-do-wells and imbeciles were all crowded together, the able-bodied paupers being let out to work in the hop grounds. The Master, a native of the parish, was a stern and much feared man who dressed in a kind of smock, with grey breeches and stockings, and went in search of fugitives with a whip'.

The Nonconformist Chapel. The chapel was built in 1779. Next to it is the Lecture Hall and what was once the chapel day school, which dates from 1865. Nonconformist schools are rarely found in villages.

BORSTAL PIONEER

There are memorials in Finchingfield church to several generations of the Ruggles and Ruggles-Brise families of Spains Hall, the handsome Elizabethan mansion outside the village. One of them commemorates Sir Evelyn Ruggles-Brise, who has a claim to fame as the pioneer of the Borstal training system for young offenders.

Sir Evelyn was born at Spains Hall in 1857, one of twelve children, and had a long and distinguished career as a civil servant in the Home Office. From 1895 until 1921 he was chairman of the Prison Commission and in 1902 he received a knighthood in recognition of his many reforms to humanise penal treatment. He believed that it was wrong to send young law-breakers under the age of 21 into the adult prisons, which turned too many of them into hardened criminals.

He was instrumental in setting up a new type of reformatory, for youths of 16 to 21, intended to rehabilitate them as decent citizens. The experiment began at a former convict prison at Borstal, near Rochester in Kent, which eventually gave its name to the whole system. The reforms were introduced under the Children Act of 1908.

Ruggles-Brise died in 1935, aged 77. An inscription in his memory was placed over the gate at Borstal which said: 'He determined to save the young and careless from a life of crime. Through his vision and persistence a system of repression has been gradually replaced by one of leading and training. We shall remember him as one who believed in his fellow men.'

INFORMATION
Length of walk:
2½ miles
Approximate time:
2 hours

TERRAIN:
An excellent walk for children at all times of the year. Not suitable for pushchairs or wheelchairs; 5 stiles and 3 gates.

PARKING:
Large free public car park on Shanklin Road.

OPEN:
(Enquire locally as to opening times):
The Old Smithy; Toy Museum; Nostalgia Toy Museum; Model village; Isle of Wight Natural History Centre. Charge to all places listed.

REFRESHMENTS:
Several cafés plus The Griffin inn.

Picturesque Godshill, exemplifies rural England.

GODSHILL

ISLE OF WIGHT

On A3020, between Newport and Shanklin

MORE holiday attractions are gathered together in a small part of Godshill than in any other comparable area of the Isle of Wight, and that is saying something! There are shops, gardens, cafés, toy museums, a model village and a natural history centre. Add to that a handsome church surrounded by warm greystone cottages with thatched roofs and you have a setting like a picture postcard.

POINTS OF INTEREST

Ⓐ

The Church of All Saints. Godshill's glory is its Church of All Saints which sits majestically on the hill overlooking the village. It was built in the 14th century and stands on the site of earlier churches. Legend has it that when the stones for a Saxon church were taken to the building site a mile away, they moved miraculously in the night to the top of God's Hill. This was taken as a sign and the church was built there.

It is unique among English churches in having a 500 year-old wall painting, *Christ on the Lily Cross.* Similar paintings exist in a handful of churches in mainland Europe.

Ⓑ

Old Houses. At one time most of the houses in Godshill were built of mellow grey stone with thatched roofs. Nowadays there is more of a mixture of styles but a number of thatched cottages remain, including a 'picture postcard' group around the church on God's Hill. They can be reached by a steep road or a long flight of steps.

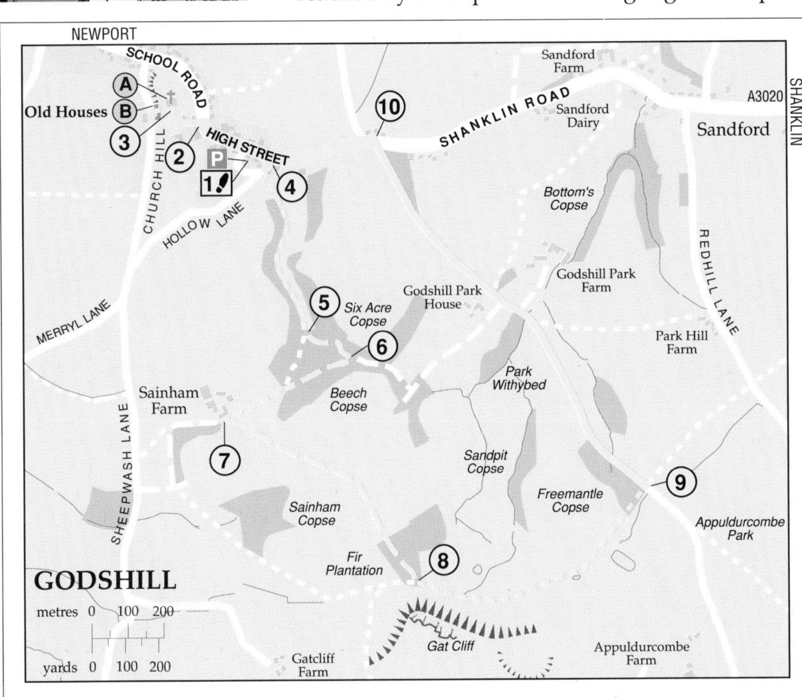

WALK DIRECTIONS

①

From the car park walk along the High Street. Pass the Old Smithy on the right, and farther along the Natural History Centre, then on the left the model village in the gardens of the old vicarage, and the two toy museums.

②

Go left and take the steep, narrow road up to the church. It meets Church Hill at the top and turns round amid thatched cottages into the churchyard.

③

On leaving the church either trace your steps back to High Street, or go past the sundial in the churchyard opposite the church door, through a gate and down a flight of steps. Walk back along the High Street as far as The Griffin inn.

④

Turn right into the lane immediately before the pub. Go left over a stile at footpath sign GL57, walk through a field, over another stile into a second field, and on into the woods.

⑤

Take the path on the left going uphill among oak, beech and birch trees and continue until reaching a definite track from the left.

⑥

Turn right here and walk along the contour of the wood out to open farmland with Sainham Farm ahead on the right. Carry on a few yards past it, and go through a gate.

⑦

Turn left at footpath signpost GL58. Walk uphill along a sandy lane with views of Godshill and the church to your left. Continue along the lane and eventually walk into a small wood, after going up the edge of a field.

⑧

Walk through the wood and at the other side of it take footpath GL49, which goes left through a wooden gate. Walk in open country with views over Shanklin and Sandown to the chalk-white Culver Cliff. The village on the right in the valley is Wroxall. Behind, on the right, is Stenbury Down with the Worsley Obelisk on top. Go through a gate at trees to arrive at a lane.

⑨

On the right is a massive wrought-iron gate known as the Freemantle Gate. The drive beyond once led to Appuldurcombe House, the home of the Worsley family. Turn left and walk downhill to Godshill on the Worsley Trail (GL44), one of several long-distance trails which cover the Isle of Wight.

⑩

On reaching the Shanklin Road, cross it and walk back along the pavement to return to the starting point.

GREAT BARDFIELD

ESSEX

On B1057, 7 miles NW of Braintree

GREAT Bardfield is a large, thriving nucleated village of considerable charm containing a mixture of vernacular architectural styles.

POINTS OF INTEREST

Ⓐ

St Mary's Church. Built on a hill on the outskirts of the village. The tower is Norman with an 18th-century spire, and the large clock commemorates the coronation of George V in 1911. The interior is dominated by a fine 14th-century rood screen.

Ⓑ

Gibraltar Mill. The windmill, of about 1690 was in use until 1930.

Ⓒ

Lock-up. The village cage or lock-up of 1816, was designed to hold drunks and other petty criminals.

Ⓓ

'Gobions'. A private house not open to the public, it is a striking example of a medieval hall house.

Ⓔ

Town Hall. The unusual Victorian town hall was built in 1859, for £750 raised by the village.

Ⓕ

The Bardfield Cottage Museum. A tiny, primitive thatched cottage containing a collection of bygones, it was lived in until 1958.

Ⓖ

Place House. Built in 1564 by William Bendlowes, local benefactor. He was a Member of Parliament, Judge of Assize, Recorder of Thaxted, Governor of Lincoln's Inn, and a Serjeant-at-Law serving under both Queen Mary and Queen Elizabeth.

Ⓗ

The Meeting House of the Society of Friends. Built in 1804, a walled graveyard can be seen.

Ⓘ

William Bendlowe's Cottage. Once owned by the eponymous charity that still helps the poor and needy of Great Bardfield.

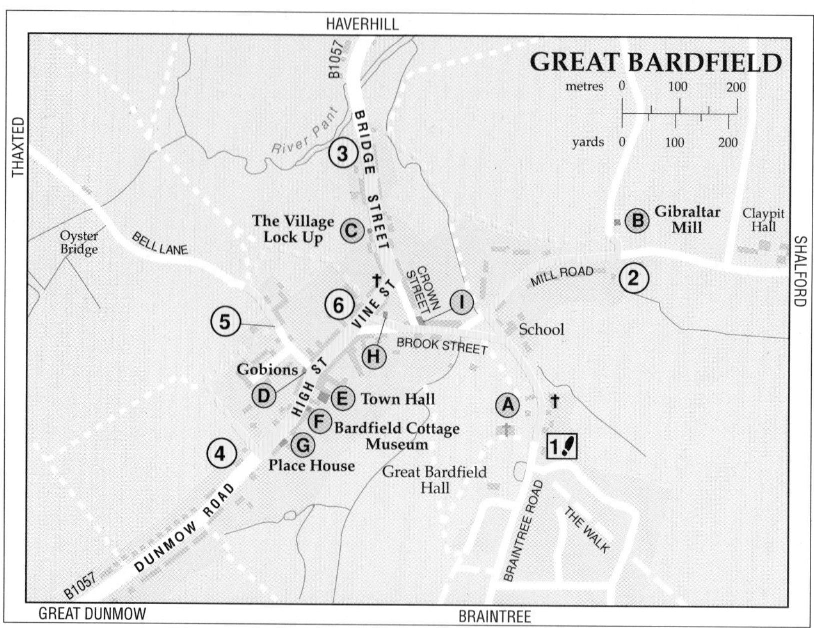

Great Bardfield is a mixture of old cottages and shops.

WALK DIRECTIONS

①

Start by visiting the church. Return to the road, turn left, walk past the modern Roman Catholic church, and take the first turning on the right by the school. In a few yards turn right and follow the lane for 300yds to a windmill on the left.

②

Take the access road to the windmill for 30yds and then turn left into a field and follow the path that runs down the left-hand side. After 300yds the path turns sharp left and then right. Continue round the field edge for another 250yds, then cross the brook on your left by a plank bridge that leads to an alleyway which runs beside restored Victorian cottages to the road.

③

Turn left and walk past the lock-up to the road junction in the centre of the village. Turn right and walk towards the end of the village to Place House on the left.

④

Continue to the next house, then cross the street and follow a short lane beside a white house. Enter the field at the end and take the path down the right-hand edge. 30yds before the first corner, turn right through a kissing-gate.

⑤

Turn left at the road and walk for 120yds to a footpath sign beside a gate and stile. Climb the stile and follow the path diagonally across a field to a hurdle, hidden in the hedge. Cross the hurdle and continue to a gate and stile with access to a track that leads to the road by the Vine.

⑥

Cross to the other side of the road, turn right and almost immediately left. At the War Memorial, cross to the other side of the road, turn left and walk down the road past the village green. Bear right at the school and return to the church.

INFORMATION
Length of walk:
1½ miles
Approximate time:
1½ hours

TERRAIN:
Undulating lanes and paths. The walk is suitable for children but the paths are not accessible to push-chairs or wheelchairs.

PARKING:
There are no public car parks. Parking is possible in the Dunmow Road and near the church (but not during services).

OPEN:
The Cottage Museum and the Cage. Easter-end Sep Sat-Sun and bank hol 2-6pm.

REFRESHMENTS:
The Bell and The Vine serve bar meals.

GREAT TEW

OXFORDSHIRE

On B4022, 6 miles E of Chipping Norton

THIS village displays a rare and endearing marriage of traditional stone cottages with 19th-century model farm landscaping. The resulting rustic harmony of thatch and Cotswold tiles, ashlared and rubble ironstone walls, box-hedges, blooming gardens, green valley pastures and enclosed parkland trees make for an unforgettable, arcadian image of rural England.

WALK DIRECTIONS

From the car park walk into the village. Follow Brook Road left, passing the early 17th-century Porch House.

At the foot of the hill, opposite Bee Bole Cottage, turn right signposted Brookside Cottage. Approaching the cottage, fork right by the shed, following the stream between hedges to a wicket gate. Ascend the pasture to the gate.

Walk up the track flanked by the cottages of The Square. Thatched with wheat straw, the cottage at the top has not only horseshoes hanging on its wall, but circular ox-shoes! Turn right, back towards the village.

Emerge into the village street between The Falkland Arms and Hornbeam House. Go left along Old Road, branching right on the path immediately after the last house on the right and before the communal tap.

The path climbs to join New Road. Go left along the pavement, passing the entrance to Tew Park. On reaching the Vicarage go left, through the archway along the shrub-lined path, to hidden St Michael's Church. Return, retracing your steps as far as the old estate office.

Follow the lane left to a gate and on to the open track known as Old Norton Way, formerly the thoroughfare to Chipping Norton, Tew's principal market town. Do not enter the estate timber yard, The Crimea. Its distinctive chimney was formerly connected to a beam engine.

At the kissing-gate, go right down the Butcher's Hill road, turning right into The Lane to return to the car park.

POINTS OF INTEREST

The Falkland Arms. Formerly known as The Horse and Groom, The Falkland Arms' popularity is founded both upon its wide range of beers and peculiar snuffs, and its atmosphere.

Tew Park. Sir Lawrence Tanfield, Lord Chief Baron of the Exchequer to James I, created a Jacobean manor here early in the 17th century which in 1626 his maternal grandson Lucius Cary, Viscount Falkland, inherited. The romantic Falkland cultivated artistic and scholarly society, but his allegiance to Charles I brought him early death fighting the Cavalier cause at the Battle of Newbury.

During the next 200 years the estate was sold three times through the Keck, Stratton and Boulton families. Under Colonel Stratton the decrepit Jacobean pile was largely demolished. In 1815 Matthew Boulton, son of the great Birmingham industrialist, obtained the estate.

The Boulton family continued a sensitive Gothic elaboration of all the houses, built substantial farmsteads, and Gothic primary school, and enlarged Tew Park.

St Michael's and All Angels Church. There has been a church on this site since the mid-11th century, when the village became known as Church Tew. The building is noted for its seclusion, exterior elegance, spacious interior and adherence to high-church practice. The unusual Italianate stone gateway at the beginning of the path to the church is probably mid-17th century, and is thought to have been moved to its present position from the grounds of the original manor house early in the 19th century.

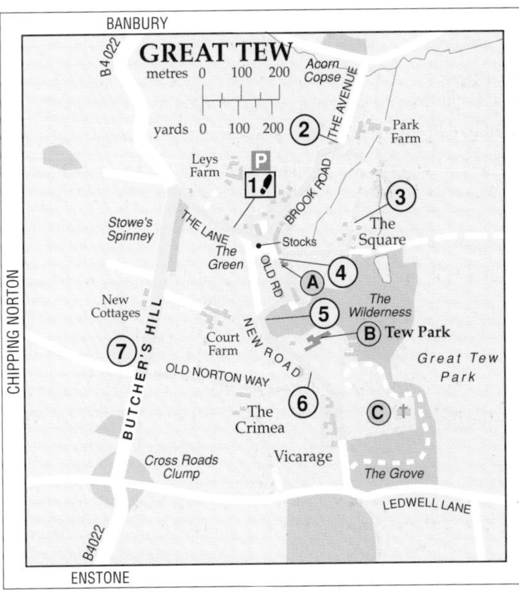

Even the post office in Great Tew is built of traditional thatched stone.

INFORMATION
Length of walk:
2 miles
Approximate time:
1¼ hours

TERRAIN:
Field and kissing-gates. The off-road sections are not suitable for pushchairs and wheelchairs.

PARKING:
Park in the recently created car park in Leys Farm orchard, off The Lane.

OPEN:
Tew Park is not open to the public.

REFRESHMENTS:
The Falkland Arms and the post office shop.

KELMSCOT

OXFORDSHIRE

Off A417, 3 miles E of Lechlade

A Cotswold stone-built farming community in the quiet meadows of the upper Thames valley, Kelmscot will for ever be remembered for its association with William Morris, the 19th-century social visionary and founder of the Arts and Crafts Movement.

POINTS OF INTEREST

Ⓐ

St George's Church. Dating from about 1190, the church is a small cruciform building very much in scale with its setting. It contains notable 14th-century wall paintings depicting Cain and Abel in the north chapel, while tucked away on the east side of the churchyard the grave of William Morris may be found, designed by Morris' lifelong friend Philip Webb to the pattern of a Viking tomb.

Ⓑ

Memorial Cottages. Built in 1902 by Morris's widow, Jane, to the design of Philip Webb, the carving over the front door depicts 'William Morris reclining in Home Mead', the work of George Jack created from a drawing by Webb.

Ⓒ

Kelmscott Manor. The earliest elements of Kelmscott Manor (correctly Lower Farm), date from around 1570, with major and elegant additions a century later. The pale grey complexion of the Taynton stone, brought from the Windrush valley 10 miles away, gives the house remarkable architectural expression.

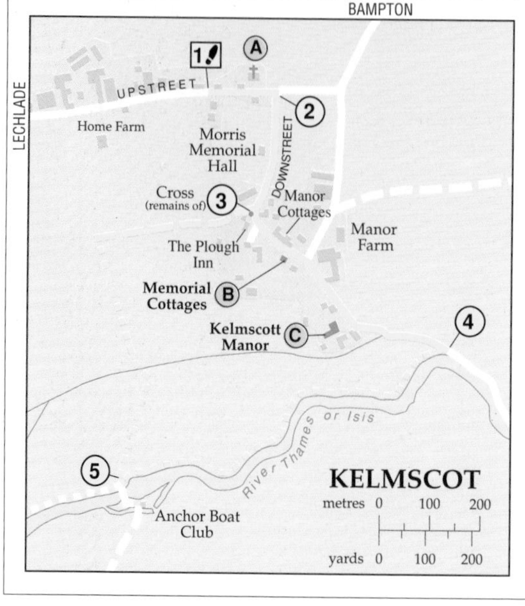

The exterior exhibits a mixture of traditional features. For example, the lead and wood water-spouts and graduated stone tile roofing are coupled with classical embellishment. The tapering twin-gabled east wing and the window pediments, ball finials and angled chimneys, combine to give this small country house a rare dignity and stature.

WALK DIRECTIONS

①

Begin the walk in Upstreet, and admire St George's Church, approached along a path lined with limes.

②

Turn right following the road, Downstreet, into Kelmscot village. Pass the Morris Memorial hall, designed by Ernest Gimson, a disciple of Morris. The Hall was opened by George Bernard Shaw in 1934.

③

Reaching the stump of an old preaching cross, follow the road left. To the right stands The Plough. To the left, the late 17th-century Lower House farmhouse. Pass the Memorial Cottages and Manor Cottages, on either side of the road.

From the road junction looking left see the late 17th-century Manor Farm; a free-standing dovecote stands adjacent. A splendid stone fence flanks the road to the right, and where this ends is the charming Kelmscott Manor Cottage with built-in bread oven. Stay on the track beyond Kelmscott Manor, winding towards the banks of the River Thames, passing a Second World War pill-box.

④

Go right, over the footbridge, and follow the river bank beyond the moorings. After the next footbridge/gate pass a second pill-box.

Kelmscot's Tudor manor-house became the retreat of William Morris from 1871, until his death in 1896.

INFORMATION
Length of walk:
$1\frac{1}{2}$ miles
Approximate time:
1 hour

TERRAIN:
Level walking throughout, with only one stile to negotiate. The open riverbank means children need to be under close control. This section would not be suitable for pushchairs and wheelchairs.

PARKING:
Park discreetly in Upstreet, possibly near the church (when Kelmscott Manor is open, Home Mead is preferable).

OPEN:
Kelmscott Manor (the property of the Society of Antiquaries). Apr-Sep. Wed 11am-1pm, 2-5pm. Charge. Parties (maximum 20) at other times, written application necessary.

REFRESHMENTS:
The Plough Inn.

The carving over the front door of Memorial Cottages shows William Morris, as drawn by Webb.

⑤

Coming alongside the Anchor Inn moorings (the only footbridge over the Thames between Radcot and Lechlade), go right, with the fence to the left, guided by the red signs to The Plough. Cross the ditch via a plank to the stile, and continue, now with the hedge to the right, entering a lane leading right, conveniently to The Plough Inn. Return via Downstreet and Upstreet to the starting point.

HAMBLEDON

HAMPSHIRE

Off B2150, 8 miles N of Portsmouth

HAMBLEDON has a long history. The name is Saxon, so it must have been there when the Normans came in 1066. The village is most renowned as the home of cricket. In June 1777 the Men of Hambledon defeated the Men of All England by a massive margin, thus ensuring its place in history. Yet it has much else besides cricket. It has fine houses, charming streets, interesting historical links and lies amid pleasant rolling countryside.

Hambledon inhabits a tranquil valley between two partly wooded ridges, criss-crossed by walks radiating from the village centre. The one described here takes a look at the church, the old village square and some of the interesting buildings in the main streets. It then takes a turn into the countryside to the north of the village and returns by way of farmland, a vineyard, the school and churchyard.

WALK DIRECTIONS

Start the walk at the Church of St Peter and St Paul. It is a 13th-century building with later additions but is remarkable for being built around a Saxon church, several hundred years older, most of which is still intact inside. Walk down and out of the churchyard into High Street, which is Hambledon's showpiece, and is more in the nature of a village square than a street. It is hard to believe that in 1830 William Cobbett described this as 'a tumbledown rubbishy place'.

When you reach East Street and the post office ahead (a fine old building itself), turn and walk back up the cobbled street, viewing the buildings on the eastern side. Return to the post office and walk a few yards right into West Street to look at perhaps Hambledon's most celebrated building, Manor Farm.

Walk back past the post office and continue along East Street. From the shop at the corner of High Street, all the buildings as far east as the Bakery were destroyed by fire in 1726. The attractive and varied houses here date from around that period.

On the other side of the road is The George, an evocative link with the past. It dates from the 18th century and it is easy to imagine stage coaches wheeling into its stable yard. Note the magnificent iron bracket holding the inn sign.

At Yew Tree Cottage, on a small crossroads, turn right and immediately take the left fork, uphill. The lane is called Whitehill, because it is cut deep in the chalk, but soon becomes Glidden Lane. A hoard of Roman coins was found here some years ago.

The lane enters the wood known as The Hangers. After ½ a mile, turn sharp left and walk back down through the woods into Dogkennel Lane to reach the crossroads at Park House and Park Farm, which have stood there for nearly 500 years.

A stained glass window in Hambledon Church.

(6)

Continue along Brook Lane for 300yds to the edge of the village cricket ground (this is not the famous Broadhalfpenny Down ground). Turn left along a path and cross three fields to Hambledon Vineyard.

(7)

Go left and walk by the fence for 150yds, then take a signposted path right, through the vineyard. The path reaches Hambledon school, built by public subscription in 1849. Continue and cross the churchyard at the back of the church.

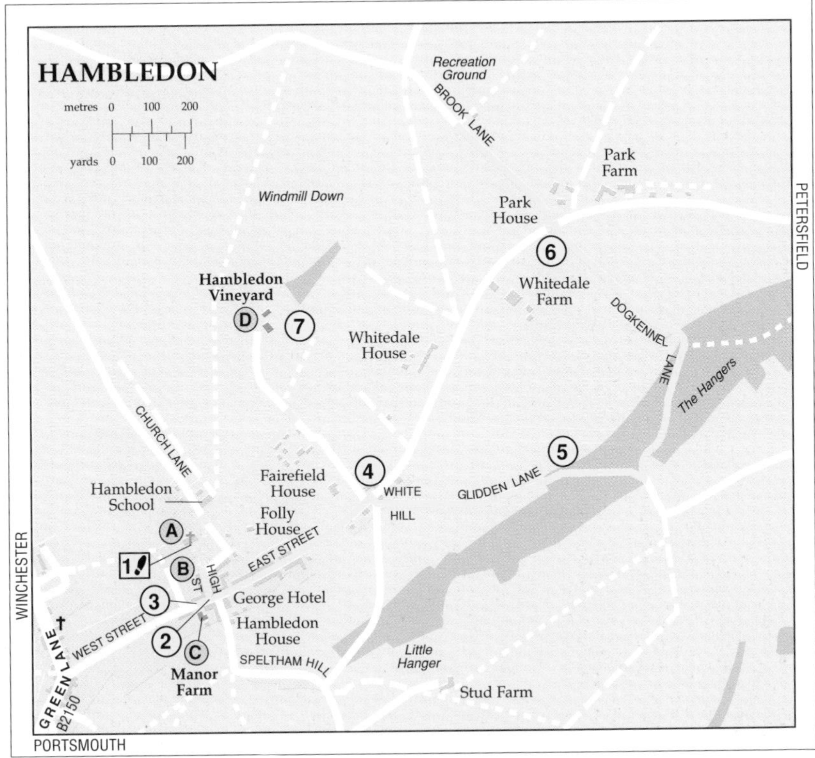

POINTS OF INTEREST

Hambledon Church. The church of St Peter and St Paul at the top of the High Street somehow contrives to be bigger and more impressive inside than it looks from the outside. The core of it is a diminutive Anglo-Saxon church, fragments of which survive in a much larger medieval church. The oddity of it is that the nave and the aisles are cut in two halfway along their length by arches. The tower was added in the 13th century.

The church with its cool whitish-grey pillars has seen the centuries of village life pass slowly by. The faded banners hanging above the south aisle were once the blazing colours of the Hambledon Volunteers in the wars against Napoleon. The wooden ceiling of the chancel is brightly painted and there's some pleasant Victorian stained glass. Outside in the churchyard where generations of Hampshire families lie in their last sleep – Merrets, Goldsmiths, Pratts – are gravestones adorned with skulls and winged cherubs' faces.

The High Street. The buildings are described in the order in which you walk past them. No.s 1 and 2 Church Gate have attractive 18th-century fronts but it is likely that much of the work behind the façades is considerably older. This is common to a number of houses in High Street.

The next building down is Langtry's, the butcher's, no longer used as a shop but retaining the old features. It is over 500 years old and was built before houses had chimneys. The smoke escaped through a hole in the gable, still clearly visible although long since filled in.

The shop at the bottom on the eastern side dates from 1726, the year in which a great fire swept through this part of the village, actually starting on this site. Notice on the store houses next door the unusual iron wall brace in the shape of a serpent with head and tail.

Tower House was once the Red Lion inn and retains a fine metal bracket that once held the inn sign. The smaller bracket would have held an oil street lamp. At the top of High Street, Church Lane goes off to the right. The first house has a fine blue iron-studded door nearly 400 years old.

Manor Farm. This is a rare example of a manor house of the early 13th century in stone and flint. The years have wrought many changes, and the Victorians, with typical self-confidence, gave it a new west front. Despite this it retains its splendid shape and quiet dignity.

Hambledon Vineyard. Started on a hill at the eastern end of the village 40 years ago, the grapes grown in the vineyard's present sunny position produce a fine dry white wine which is enjoyed far beyond the boundaries of Hampshire and has increased the fame of Hambledon.

INFORMATION
Length of walk:
2 miles
Approximate time:
2 hours

TERRAIN:
Suitable for children at all times of the year. Suitable for pushchairs and wheelchairs if the return to the centre of the village is made from Park Farm.

PARKING:
There is no public car park in Hambledon, but street parking is much easier than in many other places.

High Street (below), where the market was held, is the original heart of the village. It runs uphill to the flint-and-rubble church of St Peter and St Paul.

Grape vines reaching maturity in the summer sun at the Hambledon Vineyards (bottom).

THE EARLY DAYS OF CRICKET

In 1744 the London Cricket Club drew up the first set of authoritative rules for the game. The Hambledon club was established in the 1760s by a group of wealthy landed gentry and the village has since been dubbed, erroneously, 'the birthplace of cricket'. The club reached a peak of importance after a famous match played at Broad-halfpenny Down in June 1777. The Men of Hambledon defeated the Men of All England by the massive margin of an innings and 168 runs. Memories of this golden age are preserved in the 17th-century Bat and Ball Inn, which stands opposite the ground. The club once used the inn as a clubhouse.

Control of the game later passed to the Marylebone Cricket Club in London (more familiarly known as MCC), but the name of Hambledon is still revered by cricket lovers the world over.

If you want to see the famous ground, it is a couple of miles east of the village on the Clanfield road and can easily be visited by car while you are in the area. For those with energy to spare, the walk described here could be extended to take in Broadhalfpenny Down.

Broadhalfpenny Down cricket monument.

IGHTHAM

KENT

On A227, ½ mile E of Borough Green

IN 1555, a certain Thomas Skynner broke planning regulations by erecting his new house partly on the road. Today, traffic still has to slow down when it reaches the Ightham hollow filled with the timber-framed houses that followed Skynner's example.

Although not mentioned in Domesday Book, the village is believed to date back to the invasion of the Jutes in the 5th century. In 1643, the Rector of Ightham led a Royalist rebellion against Roundhead troops, who withdrew after killing a villager.

Although surrounded by a moat, Ightham Mote does not appear forbidding.

WALK DIRECTIONS

From the church, turn right out of the lych-gate to join the main village road.

Reach the Town House and the tight squeeze caused by The Forge to enter the square. Continue through the square. Stay on the left and ignore the turning to the right. Keep ahead up Bates Hill.

At The Rectory turn left into Mill Lane. Just past Mill Lane House, go left over a stile to follow the fenced path down hill. At a junction go left and at the bend keep ahead to follow a narrow path up a slope.

④

The enclosed path soon runs down hill by the side of a house. On reaching Trycewell Lane, go down Busty Lane. At the bottom of the hill go ahead over the stream and along a footpath to the main road. Go right to the garage and cross the road to enter a footpath running up the side of the end house, Beresford Villa.

Follow the path to Fen Pond Road. Turn right for the church.

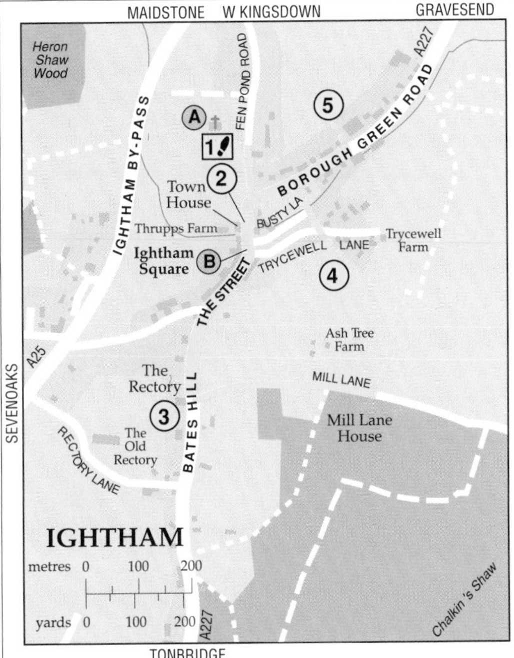

INFORMATION
Length of walk:
½ mile
Approximate time:
45 minutes

TERRAIN:
Suitable for children at all times of the year; suitable for pushchairs; not suitable for wheelchairs.

PARKING:
Park outside the church in Fenpond Lane.

OPEN:
Ightham Mote. Apr-Oct Sun-Mon, Wed-Fri, Nov-Dec Wed-Sat. Charge.

POINTS OF INTEREST

Ightham Church. Two Norman windows survive outside the east end of the building, which is mainly 14th and 15th century. Only the Jacobean box pews and 1639 north aisle are later. The oldest memorial is that to Sir Thomas Cawne of Ightham Mote who provided the window above his memorial. He is laid out in armour and appears about to be tipped on to the floor. He died in 1374. Opposite is the memorial to Sir William Selby, who lived at Ightham Mote in James I's reign. He was knighted by the Scottish king on the border as he came south to accept the English Crown. To the right of the altar is Dame Dorothy Selby's memorial, whose inscription seems to suggest that she had advance warning of the Gunpowder Plot.

Ightham Square. The timber-framed Town House is 15th century. The Forge opposite was built during Mary I's reign as a home for Thomas Skynner, who was fined for obstructing the 'Ightham Streyt highway'. The attractive square was last closed to traffic in 1988, when the Coxcombe Fair licensed by Edward II was revived.

IGHTHAM MOTE

One of Britain's best medieval manor houses, it only survives in its wooded cleft because Oliver Cromwell's troops failed to realise that it lies two miles south of the village. In 1985 the National Trust took possession of a sensitively restored 72 room building dating back to 1340.

Although there are examples of six centuries of architecture the result is still a tightly-knit house with an array of Tudor chimney stacks. The water-filled moat, an irregular square, may not have given the house its name – which is more probably derived from 'moot' meaning meeting place. A local council was held here in Medieval times. Ightham has been home to Robert Cawne who fought with the Black Prince at Crécy; courtier Sir Richard Clement who added the pomegranate decorations in honour of Catherine of Aragon; and Lord Mayor of London Sir John Allen, whose Roman Catholic wife needed a safe retreat during Elizabeth I's Protestant rule. Look to the left of the gatehouse for a medieval letterbox where callers could pass a note and identify themselves.

The little house in the cobbled courtyard is a St Bernard dog kennel made in 1891.

LITTLE GADDESDEN
HERTFORDSHIRE

On a minor road, 6 miles NW of Hemel Hempstead

LITTLE Gaddesden lies in the Chiltern Hills, surrounded by glorious woods and commons. It is an unusual, secretive village built on the north-east side of a long lane. Many of the houses are set well back from the road and concealed behind high hedges. The parish church is nearly half a mile outside the village. Ashridge, to the south-east is an immense Gothic Revival structure built on the site of the College of Bonhommes, a monastery dissolved during the Reformation. Little Gaddesden is mentioned in several Saxon charters, and in the Domesday Book.

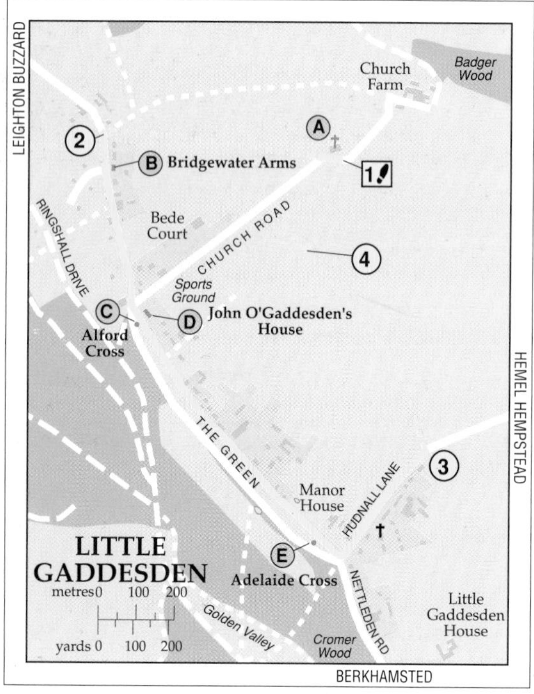

POINTS OF INTEREST

Ⓐ

St Peter & St Paul's. The parish church which dates from the 13th century, was thoroughly restored in the 1870s. It contains a number of interesting memorials to the Bridgewater family.

The Bridgewater Arms. This inn dates from the 18th century and became a public house in 1815. In 1853, one room was used as a school and the pupils had to climb in through the window to avoid passing through the door of the licensed premises.

Ⓒ

Alford Cross. The cross that lies at the junction of the lane to the Ashridge estate was erected in 1891 as a memorial to Lady Marian Alford, who lived at Ashridge House. Below the cross is a fountain, a drinking trough for horses, and at ground level, another for dogs. Opposite is the War Memorial.

Ⓓ

John O'Gaddesden's House. This structure dates from the 15th century. John O'Gaddesden was a noted doctor who wrote the *Rosa Medicinae* in 1314 and may have lived in an earlier house on this site.

Ⓔ

The Adelaide Cross. A memorial to the wife of the 3rd Earl Brownlow who lived at Ashridge. Just beyond is the fine Elizabethan Manor House.

WALK DIRECTIONS

①

Begin by visiting the church. Turn right at the church gate and walk down the outside of the churchyard to a kissing-gate. Follow the well-defined path to a road.

②

Turn left and walk along the road past the Bridgewater Arms, and the Alford and Adelaide crosses to Hudnall Lane (the second turning on the left). Walk along Hudnall Lane for 300yds to a footpath sign and stile on the left.

③

Cross the stile and follow the hedge on your left to a gap. Pass through into the next field and go forward, with the hedge still on your left, to a stile in a fence.

④

Cross the stile and continue forward. Just before the next stile ahead, you will see a stile on your left. At this point, turn right and walk parallel to the fence towards the top of the field. When opposite the church, turn left through a kissing-gate and walk to a stile at the road.

Ashridge House was designed by James Wyatt in 1808 for the seventh Earl of Bridgewater.

INFORMATION
Length of walk:
2 miles.
Approximate time:
1½ hours

TERRAIN:
A level route over lanes and footpaths. It is suitable for children and pushchairs, but not wheelchairs.

PARKING:
There are no public car parks. There is limited parking on the grass verge of the lane that runs through the village. The best place to park is near the church (but not during Sunday services).

OPEN:
Ashridge. National Trust. Grounds accessible by a toll road.

REFRESHMENTS:
The Bridgewater Arms is a free house, has a restaurant and serves bar meals.

An ornate detail from Little Gaddesden's War Memorial.

MINSTER LOVELL

OXFORDSHIRE

On B4047, 3 miles W of Witney

A charming mix of traditional Cotswold cottage styles in the village street perfectly compliments the romantic riverside ruins of Minster Lovell Hall and Manor Farm's exquisite specimen Dovecote.

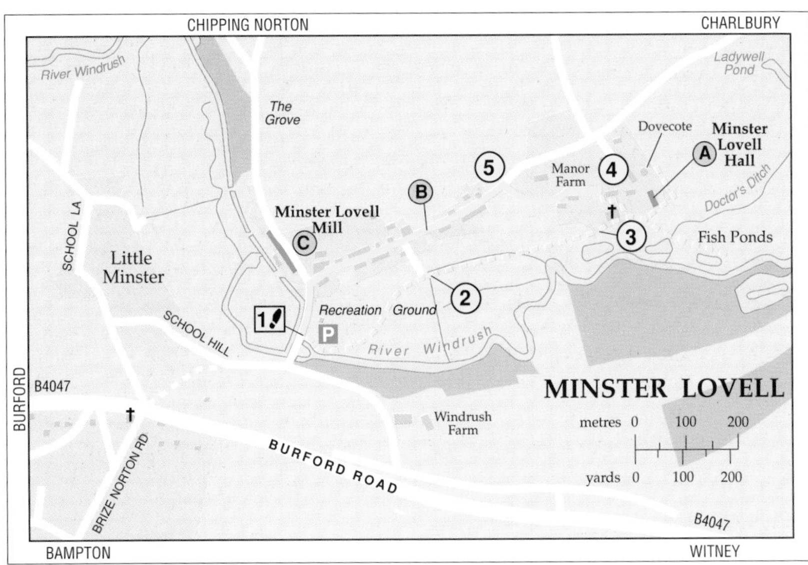

INFORMATION
Length of walk:
1mile
Approximate time:
3/4 hour

TERRAIN:
Two stiles and kissing-gates to negotiate in the approach to and vicinity of Minster Lovell Hall make this walk unsuitable for pushchairs and wheelchairs, but it is fine for children.

PARKING:
Park at the recreation ground car park beside the River Windrush in Old Minster.

OPEN:
Minster Lovell Hall and Dovecote (in the care of English Heritage). Apr-Sep Daily 10am-6pm, Oct-Mar Tue-Sun 10am-4pm. Charge.

REFRESHMENTS:
The New Inn, The White Hart and The Swan Hotel.

POINTS OF INTEREST

Ⓐ

Minster Lovell Hall. From the 12th century the Lovells had lived on this site, on the southern boundary of the Royal Forest of Wychwood. The ruins principally belong to the stately residence of William Lovell, seventh Baron of Tichmarsh, and date from 1430s.

The ninth Lord Lovell, Francis, was a prominent Yorkist during the time of the Wars of the Roses. Following the defeat of Richard III at the Battle of Bosworth Field in 1485, the Lovell estates were confiscated by the Crown. Francis is thought to have hidden in a secret chamber where he was sustained by a faithful servant. For some reason the servant ceased plying him with food and some 200 years later, during modifications, the decomposed body was discovered slumped over a desk (this story cannot be corroborated as both the skeleton and chamber were lost). The Earls of Leicester became the owners early in the 17th century, and a century later laid the Hall waste by 'quarrying' for building stone.

The scant remains of Minster Lovell Hall.

Ⓑ

Village Street. Towards the pound road junction, admire the Old Post House and as the lane descends and broadens, The Old Bakehouse with shutters and an espalier pear tree on its west wall. Then glance left into a former ox pen where a rare thatched hovel is raised upon stone pillars.

Ⓒ

Minster Lovell Mill. The Old Swan Inn has been incorporated with the Mill, across the way, into a hotel complex. The much embellished mill buildings date from at least 1526. When last in service in the 1920s, two wheels drove four pairs of cullen stones (now to be seen in the mill courtyard laid in the paving, the term 'cullen' refers to the hard stone imported from Cologne).

Domesday Book records the unusual number of five mills, worth 60 shillings, working at 'Minstre'. There is no trace of the monastery inferred by the Domesday name, Minstre, though during the 13th and 14th centuries a tiny alien priory dependent on the Benedictine abbey at Ivry in Normandy existed somewhere in the vicinity of the church.

WALK DIRECTIONS

①

Follow the cricket field boundary downstream beside the river to the wooden seat. Leave the river and cross the football pitch diagonally, making for the right end of the stone wall. An opening here gives access to a stile ahead. (Ignore the track to the left.)

②

Cross the stile and follow the footpath as it hugs the edge of the watermeadow to a metal stile, left, then rises invitingly towards the church.

③

Enter the churchyard via the stone stile. Pass beneath the yews, keeping to the right of the church, to the entrance to Minster Lovell Hall and tour the ruins. From the kissing-gate strike diagonally left to another kissing-gate. Follow the narrow path to visit the beautiful circular dovecote situated next to the Manor Barn. Backtrack to just before the first kissing-gate, cross the stile on the left and follow the green track diagonally, left, to the footbridge over old bridge abutments (former main eastern approach to the Hall). Return, viewing the old fishponds, to the front of the church.

④

Leave St Kenelm's churchyard and follow the lane past the Rectory.

⑤

At the road junction go left and walk along the village street. At its end on the right is the Minster Lovell Mill complex. Return to the car park upon The Causeway path to finish the walk.

NEW ALRESFORD

HAMPSHIRE

Off A31, 7 miles E of Winchester

EIGHT hundred years of prosperity are reflected in New Alresford – prosperity built on its abundant supply of water. Watercress has been grown here in beds for centuries and continues to flourish, but the milling, fulling and tanning industries which brought riches in the past exist no longer.

New Alresford was marooned in a swampy waste until about the year 1200 when Bishop Godfrey de Lucy of Winchester decided that where there was so much water there could be wealth. He built a great weir which contained the water in one place, and made it available to drive many watermills. His 'great weir' is today's B3046 road, which runs north of the village.

New Alresford Fulling Mill on the River Alre.

POINTS OF INTEREST

A

The Swan Hotel. The building dates from the 18th century, and up until the coming of the railway in 1865, it would have been the busiest place in the village as stagecoaches came and went through the huge front entrance to the stable yard behind. The front door is now built into this entrance, which can still be seen.

The Church of St John the Baptist. The walk ends at St John's Church: large, imposing and Norman. Its history indicates that there was probably a church here from as early as the 7th century, when the site was given to the Bishop of Winchester by Kenwale, King of Wessex.

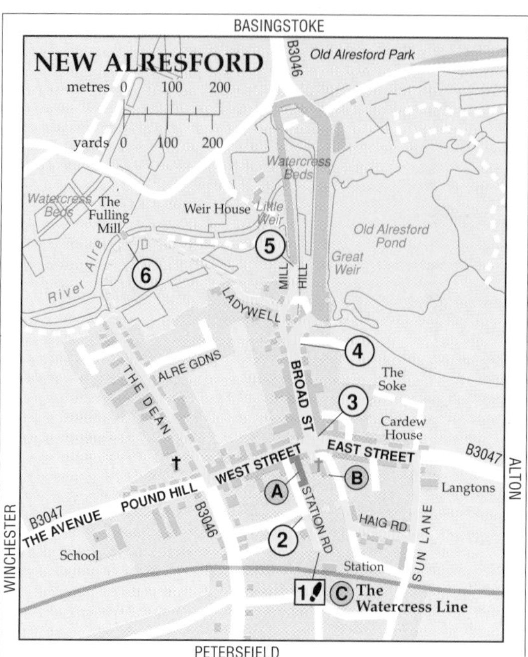

C

The Watercress Line. The Mid Hants Railway first connected New Alresford to the outside world in 1865. Today, affectionately known as the Watercress Line, it offers visitors a splendid 10-mile ride between New Alresford and Alton on a beautifully preserved steam train. The line operates on most days in June, July and August, and at other times as advertised.

WALK DIRECTIONS

1

Start at the railway station. Walk past the Railway Mill in Station Road and take the footpath going right into the churchyard.

2

Go right, and then left and right at the flint churchyard wall, past several cottages and left into Haig Road, leading to Sun Lane. Go left along a brick wall and then left again into busy East Street. For hundreds of years sheep were driven this way to fairs and markets. Cross the busy road when you can, and continue to the newsagents on the corner of East Street.

3

Turn right into Broad Street, which is of exceptional width considering it was laid out 800 years ago. At the bottom on the right is the old fire station.

A tranquil scene on the waters held back by the Great Weir.

Go briefly right into The Soke and take the lane between the cottages at the side of The Globe for a glance at Old Alresford Pond, where Bishop de Lucy contained the water 800 years ago. Retrace your steps to the bottom of Broad Street and go left into Mill Hill.

This is where the industry formerly was. Note the houses on the left which are among the oldest in the village and escaped the fires which ravished it regularly until the 18th century.

Walk down to the Town Mill, rebuilt 100 years ago on the site of an older mill, and continue past it to look at the mill stream.

You may at this point continue along Little Weir past Alre Mill, and turn right and right again to return along the Great Weir. Alternatively, from the Town Mill, retrace a few steps, and go right into Ladywell. Walk down a shady lane past the War Memorial gardens to the River Alre and the 13th-century fulling mill.

Continue on the riverbank to emerge at The Dean. Walk along this street to reach West Street. Turn left and walk uphill crossing the road at the pelican crossing to reach the church.

INFORMATION
Length of walk:
2 miles if weirs included
Approximate time:
2 hours

TERRAIN:
Riverbank paths can be muddy. Suitable for children with supervision near river. Not suitable for wheelchairs beyond point 5.

PARKING:
Park at the railway station, or use the two-hour metered parking in Broad Street.

REFRESHMENTS:
Several cafés and pubs.

NEWTOWN

SOUTH AND SOUTH EAST ENGLAND

NEWTOWN
ISLE OF WIGHT

Off A3054, 6 miles W of Newport, IOW

It is hard to imagine how things were hundreds of years ago when Newtown was a bustling town, the 'capital' of the Isle of Wight, and one of the most important ports on the south coast. Bishop Valance's original master plan for the 'new town' of 1256 laid out roads and 73 plots available for houses, each at a rent of one shilling (5p today) per year.

The town has existed for 1200 years. It was often raided by the Danes and later the French, who in 1377 left most of it burnt to the ground.

C
Newtown Quay
5
Newtown River
Newtown Nature Reserve
Mean High Water
Clamerkin Lake
4
Marsh Farm
7
6
B
Hart's Farm
Taylor's Coppice
Town Copse
HIGH STREET
2
3
Mean High Water
Causeway Lake
A Town Hall
1
P
Walter's Copse
NEWTOWN
metres 0 100 200
yards 0 100 200
Newtown Bridge
Fleetlands Copse
YARMOUTH
NEWPORT

WALK DIRECTIONS

From the car park at the Town Hall walk towards the sea. 40yds on the right is the house which was once the Franchville Arms, an indication that the village was once called Franchville.

Turn left and walk along the High Street, the only short street of houses in Newtown.

After the church go right, walk past the front of Marsh Farm and continue on a grassy lane towards the sea. Go through a wooden gate into the Newtown Nature Reserve at an area known as The Scrape, and turn left.

4

Go through another gate and turn right. Ahead is a wooden bridge which, as the notice says, you use at your own risk! It leads to Newtown Quay and the Estuary.

After exploring the quay, retrace your steps but this time do not walk back to Marsh Farm. Instead walk straight up a field with the hedge on your left until you reach some houses.

At the bend in the road, go over the stile on the left. This wide green lane was once Gold Street, a busy village area.

Leave the green lane at the road and turn right to return to the old Town Hall.

Newtown's Gothic-style church is light and airy.

INFORMATION
Length of walk: 1½ miles
Approximate time: 1½ hours

TERRAIN:
Good at all times of the year, suitable for children but not for pushchairs or wheelchairs. One footbridge and 2 stiles.

PARKING:
Two free public car parks.

OPEN:
The Town Hall. Charge.

POINTS OF INTEREST

Town Hall. This 300-year-old building is the only remaining symbol of Newtown's former eminence in returning two Members of Parliament. Elections were held until the Reform Act of 1832 declared the place a 'Rotten Borough' and ended its parliamentary status. In the early years of this century the building was in a poor state, but in 1933 an anonymous group of benefactors, calling themselves 'Ferguson's Gang', rescued it, restored it, and gave it to the National Trust.

Church of the Holy Spirit. The building of the Church of the Holy Spirit was a touching act of faith. For it was built in 1837, at a time when Newtown had been in decline for centuries, and there was no indication that the decline would be arrested. Nor was it, and the scattering of houses around the new church grew less with the years.

There was a church here in 826, and others followed it. A roll of early vicars can be seen in the church and goes back to 1306 when it was dedicated to St Mary Magdalen.

C

Newtown Quay and Estuary. Once an important commercial and naval base, with the largest ships of the day lying alongside. Oysters have been grown at Newtown for hundreds of years, and the trade still exists. The salt-making industry has gone, but the shallow, square pans in which the sea water was collected still exist to some extent.

These shallow ponds banked by grass dykes and topped with footpaths are remnants of the old salt industry.

OFFHAM

KENT

1 mile S of A20, between West Malling and Wrotham

THIS charming Kent village grew up alongside a Roman road which ran through the Weald to London. Today it is surrounded by orchards and farmland and there are marvellous sweeping views of the Downs. The village is most famous for the Quintain, a medieval jousting post – the only one remaining in England.

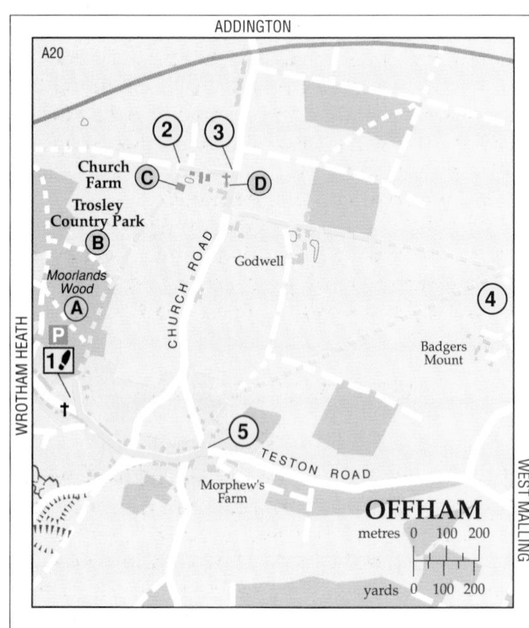

POINTS OF INTEREST

Ⓐ

Moorlands Wood. A perfect example of the ancient craft of coppicing, in which the older trees are cut down to the stumps to allow another crop of wood to grow. The coppice provides shelter for a wide range of flora and fauna.

Ⓑ

Trosley Country Park. There are lovely views over the 160-acre Trosley Country Park with the Weald in front and the North Downs as a backdrop to the north. A number of well-marked walks exist in the park, and as the ground is quite flat, you can use the church as a beacon.

Ⓒ

Church Farm. The farm has a wonderful collection of well-preserved old buildings and a glorious row of mature weeping willows.

Ⓓ

St Michael's Church. Typical of many churches in the area, St Michael's stands some distance from the village because it was built to serve a scattered community of farmsteads before Offham existed. Closer inspection reveals several different styles of church architecture. The herringbone work on the north wall dates from Saxon times, but the two Norman windows at the top of the wall show that it must have been completed after the Norman Conquest. The original chancel was rebuilt in the 13th century at the same time as the tower.

The village church of St Michael shows a variety of architectural styles.

In the centre of the village green, the quintain is a survivor of medieval times.

QUINTAIN

The oddly-shaped triangular green marks the centre of the village, surrounded by cottages built of brick and Kent ragstone, Georgian houses and the pub. The Quintain in the centre of the green is unique. In medieval times the pole was used by knights on horseback to practise tilting; introduced to Britain by the Romans and especially popular during the Middle Ages.

The tilting post has a revolving arm with a flat target at one end and a sandbag at the other. The knight had to strike the target with his lance and get out of the way before the arm spun round and he was struck by the sandbag. Tilting was once a favourite sport on English village greens, and survived until recently at Offham.

ST LEONARD'S TOWER

To the south east you can spot St Leonard's Tower, one of the best preserved Norman keeps in England. It was built in ragstone around 1100 by Bishop Gundulf, who also designed Rochester Cathedral. It is thought that the tower was part of a chapel, but it is more probable that it was Gundulf's home. Over the centuries it has been used as a prison and a hop store.

The tower and many of the old houses in Offham were built of ragstone, a sandy limestone which is very hard wearing. It is very close to the surface in this area, making the farmland difficult to work, and it is mined in a number of places around the village, mostly, today, for road construction.

To the north are the Downs, which were cleared of trees to provide grazing land.

WALK DIRECTIONS

①

Exit into Pepingstraw Close and then take the footpath on the left hand side of the road just beyond The Orchard House. Follow the path alongside Moorlands Wood towards St Michael's Church.

②

Turn right beyond Church Farm and follow the path behind the church until it runs into Church Road.

③

Turn right and then take the track on the left past Godwell. Continue along the track across two fields until you come to a 'crossroad' of footpaths in the far corner.

④

Turn right and follow this path, which skirts the fields back to the village.

⑤

Turn right into Teston Road and walk to the Green to see the Quintain and then follow the road back to the car park.

INFORMATION
Length of walk:
$2^1/_2$ miles
Approximate time:
2 hours to enjoy the views and places of interest

TERRAIN:
Paved or flat footpaths.

PARKING:
Use the car park next to the recreation ground in Teston Road.

NORTHIAM

SUSSEX

On A28, about 14 miles N of Hastings

NORTHIAM sprawls on either side of a two-mile section of the A28 Hastings to Ashford road, and straddles a low hill above the valley of the River Rother.

The Rother, now quiet and navigable only by small craft in these upper reaches, was once a substantial waterway. In 1822, a well-preserved Danish ship, 65ft long and 14ft wide, was discovered in a field by the river close to Northiam. It probably sank in the 9th century.

The Kent and East Sussex Railway runs along the Rother valley. In its heyday, it carried thousands of hop-pickers from London to the hop fields of Kent. After many years of disuse, the line has been renovated by a private company and you can arrive at Northiam by train once more, steam hauled from Tenterden.

The village contains a rich variety of buildings in various styles, a recurring feature being the white weatherboarding so commonly found in villages along the Kent-Sussex border.

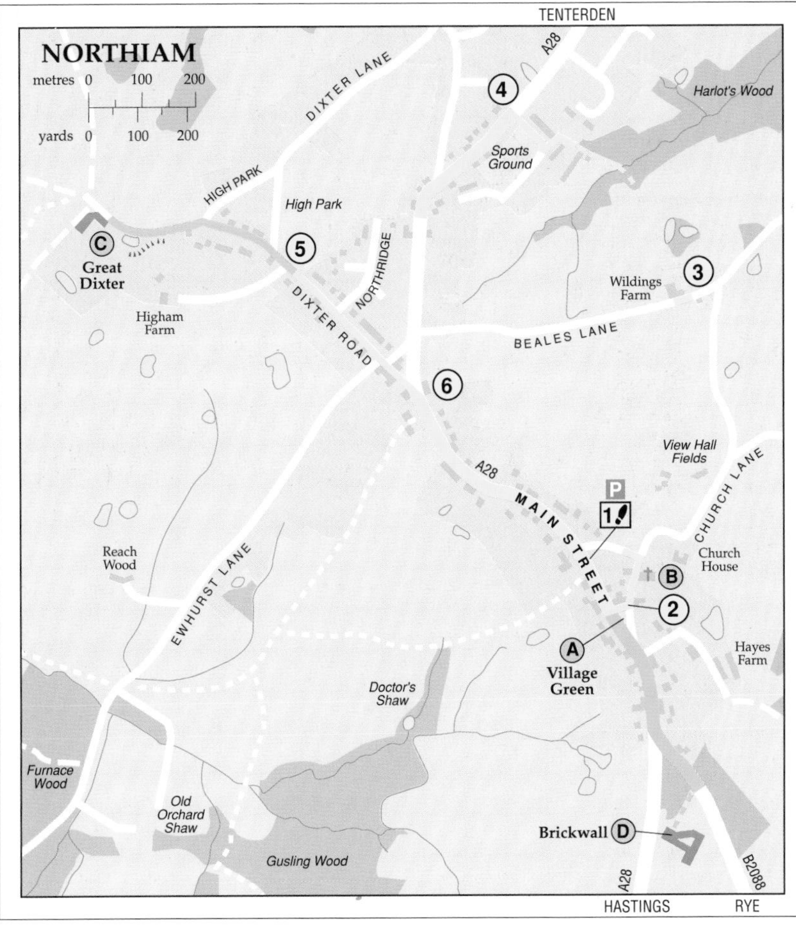

WALK DIRECTIONS

From the car park, turn left along the A28, walking in a southerly direction. Very shortly, go left again, leaving the small, sloping village green on your right.

In a few yards, turn left at a lane junction and walk up past the church. At a junction of lanes immediately beyond the church, turn left and, in 10yds, go right over a stile and forward along a field edge. Beyond another stile in the next field corner, cross a field and continue for 100yds between fences to a lane.

Cross the lane and walk through a concreted yard, almost opposite, passing between two barns, Go ahead over a stile and continue on a fenced path. Descend through a wood to a stream crossing and climb again to leave the wood, passing to the right of a scout hut to join a road. Go forward, bearing left and right with a sports ground on your left, to join the A28.

Turn left. After 300yds, just past the weatherboarded Pear Tree Cottage on the left, turn right over a not very obvious stile. After a short enclosed path, keep to the left of a field, through to another lane.

To visit Great Dixter, turn right, keeping left at the next junction of lanes. It is less than 1/4 of a mile away and well worth the detour. Retrace your steps and carry on down the lane (Dixter Road).

The road joins the A28. Carry on along this road to reach the entrance to the car park. To visit Brickwall, continue for 1/4 of a mile and then fork left along the B2088 on the outskirts of the village. The entrance is a few yards further, on the right. Retrace your steps back to the car park.

A white weather-boarded house in Northiam.

POINTS OF INTEREST

Village Green. On the corner of the Green stands an ancient and much-battered oak tree, possibly over 1,000 years old. Queen Elizabeth I didn't sleep at Northiam but did, at least, stop long enough to change her shoes and have lunch, when on her way to Rye in 1573. The green silk shoes are still preserved in the village.

St Mary's Church. The church of St Mary is notable for its lofty ironstone spire, one of five in Sussex. The lower stages of the tower are Norman, and inside the arcades of the nave date from the 14th century. The chancel was rebuilt at the time of major restoration in 1837.

There is a mausoleum to the Frewen family who lived at Brickwall. Two members of the Frewen family, John and his son Thankful, held the post of rector of Northiam in succession for a total of 102 years. Another member of the family, Accepted Frewen, became Archbishop of York in 1660.

Great Dixter. This magnificent half-timbered manor house dates from 1460, and contains a remarkable great hall with an unusual roof construction. The property came into the hands of the Lloyd family in 1910 and the house was restored

QUEEN ELIZABETH WAS HERE

Elizabeth I was adept at public relations. The travels she made every summer were as much to let her subjects see her as for her to see them, and she had a coach specially constructed to give people a good view of her. Long distances and poor roads meant that she never travelled north of Norwich or west of Bristol, but she covered the south of England very thoroughly and these journeys and her charm contributed to the immense affection in which she was held.

Hundreds of carts creaked and trundled along behind as the queen, her ladies and courtiers made their way from town to village to stately home, pausing for meals, addresses of welcome, presenting of petitions and to stay the night. Putting her cavalcade up was an expensive business. In 1591, for instance, when she stayed for a week at Cowdray in Sussex on her way to the south coast, three oxen and 140 geese were slaughtered for Sunday breakfast.

Queen Elizabeth's Oak Tree.

Great Dixter Manor with the original house in the background and the 1910 extension in the foreground.

INFORMATION
Length of walk:
3 miles (not including extension to Brickwall)
Approximate time:
2 hours

TERRAIN:
Roads and undulating field paths. One short overgrown path, requiring a squeeze through a wooden fence. Not suitable for pushchairs or wheel-chairs. Older children should have no problems.

PARKING:
Park in the large car park beside the A28 near the village green.

OPEN:
Great Dixter. 1 Apr-14 Oct Tue-Sun, 2-5pm.
Brickwall House and garden. Summer Sats, 2-5pm.
Kent and East Sussex Railway. Daily steam trains from Tenterden in high summer. Variable service at other times.
Northiam Station is on the A28, 1 mile N of the village. Telephone (05806) 5155 for information.

REFRESHMENTS:
Crown and Thistle pub at junction of main street and Dixter Road. Hayes Hotel beside the village green.

by Sir Edwin Lutyens. By removing floors and partitions he opened up the hall for the first time since 1595. He also incorporated, as an extension, a medieval house which was moved 8 miles from Benenden. The house is richly furnished and adorned with a variety of needlework.

Lutyens also designed and laid out the unusual garden, in which several farm buildings as well as an oast house have been carefully preserved within the overall plan. The contrasting sections range from an elaborately formal topiary lawn to a wild meadow garden. Great Dixter is a mecca for gardeners in search of the unusual plants grown there by Christopher Lloyd, the gardening writer.

Brickwall. Now a school, this imposing, large scale, half-timbered mansion, dates from the early 17th century.. The formal garden contains an 18th-century bowling alley and a chess garden, in which shaped yews, still at an early stage of development, will one day form the pieces.

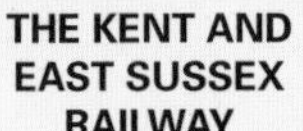

THE KENT AND EAST SUSSEX RAILWAY

It was not until as late as 1900 that the railway first reached Northiam. In this year the first passenger trains ran between Robertsbridge and Tenterden, operated by a small independent company.

In 1905, the line was extended to Headcorn, but never made a profit and the Company went into receivership in 1932. Between 1948 and 1954, British Rail maintained a passenger service, and hop pickers were brought to Bodiam as late as 1959.

In recent years the line has been acquired by the Tenterden Railway Company and, in May 1990, the restoration of the line to Northiam was completed. For the first time in 35 years, regular steam hauled services now operate during the summer months on the 7 miles of track linking Tenterden and Northiam.

With steam locomotives dating back to the 1870s and a large collection of vintage carriages and freight wagons, the railway recaptures the flavour of a rural line in the Edwardian era.

The Kent and East Sussex Railway at nearby Tenterden Station.

PENSHURST

KENT

On junction of B2176 and B2188, 5 miles NW of Tunbridge Wells

SET in a bowl of green hills, the village is dominated by Penshurst Place, one of the great private houses of England. With its graceful array of turrets, the house overlooks magnificent parkland to the north, but has formal gardens to the south and east where poets and princes strolled, while Elizabeth I danced with Dudley in the great baronial hall.

The heart of the village forms a pleasing aspect whichever way you approach it. Although the buildings represent many different styles and periods, all happily co-exist with a sense of harmony. This walk takes you virtually through the whole village. It also explores the countryside immediately to the south where the young River Medway casts its spell on the landscape.

INFORMATION
Length of walk:
$2^1/_4$ miles
Approximate time:
1 hour

TERRAIN:
Roads, farm tracks and footpaths, some rather narrow. One footbridge and some rough ground under foot make this unsuitable for pushchairs or wheelchairs. Otherwise fine for a family outing.

PARKING:
Lay-by car parking beside B2176 on the N side of the village.

OPEN:
Penshurst Place. Apr-Sep. Daily except Mon, 1-5.30pm. Charge.
Penshurst Vineyards. Apr-24 Dec. Daily, 10am-6pm.

REFRESHMENTS:
Cafés and pub in the heart of Penshurst.

The Church of St John the Baptist is remarkable mainly for the Sidney family chapel which was rebuilt in 1820. Around the approach to the churchyard is a charming group of cottages.

WALK DIRECTIONS

Facing Leicester Square a few paces from the entrance archway to Penshurst Place, head to the left along the main street, ignoring the turning to the right (to Leigh) and follow the Fordcombe Road out of the village, passing on the left-hand side the garage with the horse-shoe-shaped doorway.

Continue beyond Grove Road, a turning off to the right leads to one of the largest vineyards in the south of England, and go as far as South Park Farm at a junction with a country lane leading to Smarts Hill.

Turn left on to a farm drive and walk along it, passing first New Cottage on the right, and on to Ford Place.

④

Just before the house turn right along a grass track which slopes gently downhill, and on the continuing footpath to reach a pill-box beside the River Medway. Walk ahead along the river bank for about 40yds to a footbridge.

Cross the footbridge over the Medway and bear left on a narrow winding path that skirts a hop garden.

Having gone round two sides of the hop garden the footpath then swings left and brings you to a track. Walk ahead along this, and you soon come in view of Penshurst church, village and Place together in a neat collection.

On coming to a road bear left and walk downhill, over a hump-backed bridge across the Medway and up the slope to Leicester Square by the entrance to Penshurst Place.

The lych-gate entrance into Leicester Square.

POINTS OF INTEREST

Leicester Square. The entrance to Penshurst Church is under an old cottage propped up on stilts and shakily supported by other veteran dwellings on each side. Beside them are more cottages, designed about 1850 by the architect George Devey. Immediately to the east is the Tudor-style lodge of Penshurst Place, also by Devey. This collection of half-timbered and tile-hung Tudor cottages forms a three-sided courtyard called Leicester Square, named after the Earl of Leicester, who was a favourite of Elizabeth I. (The better-known Leicester Square in London was named after the second Earl, who built a mansion there in 1631). A few yards along the road is a brick bridge, by Devey again. Looking back up the road from the bridge, you get a pleasing view of the composition of lodge, cottages and church which Devey intended. In his youth he trained under John Sell Cotman, the Norwich School artist, and he had a painter's eye.

The Church of St John the Baptist. Drastically restored and reconstructed in the 19th century, the church has an odd appearance outside, with its top-heavily pinnacled tower. Inside, the lords of Penshurst Place lie buried in the Sidney chapel, which was gracefully rebuilt in 1820. There's a heraldic ceiling and the monuments include a chilly figure of Lady Sophia FitzClarence, illegitimate daughter of King William IV. A tablet commemorates a later chatelaine of Penshurst,

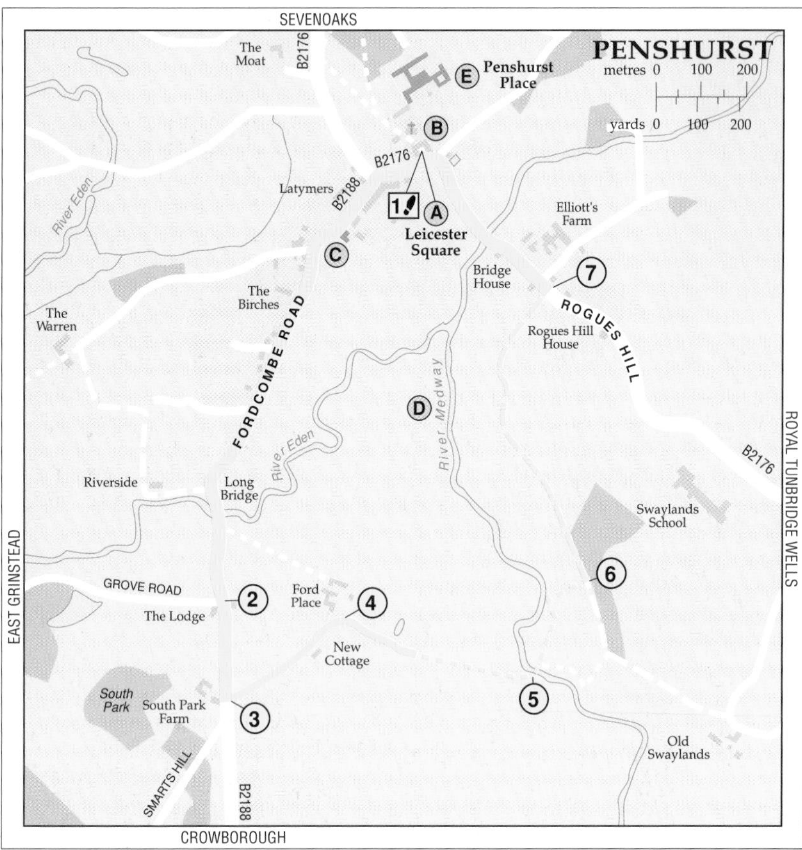

who died in 1962. Daughter of Field Marshal Lord Gort and married to the 1st Viscount De L'Isle, she had the unusual distinction of being the daughter of one VC and the wife of another.

Beneath the tower is the 13th-century stone coffin lid of 'the smiling lady of Penshurst'. A window was installed in 1970 to commemorate Archbishop Thomas Becket and another 1970 addition is a tapestry in honour of St Luke, designed by a local doctor. In the churchyard is an unusual tombstone to Thomas and George Weller of Penshurst, who on 18 November 1834 'suddenly passed into eternity by descending a well before the foul air was expelled.' Above the inscription are crossed torches and a snake swallowing its own tail, a symbol of eternity.

Ⓒ

Former Smithy. One of the most attractive garages in Kent stands beside the Fordcombe Road. This one-time smithy has a doorway in the shape of a huge horseshoe, and hammer and spike symbols on its gable.

Ⓓ

River Medway. Meandering through the water-meadows below the village, Kent's major river is joined by the Eden. Here the Medway is an innocent stream – except when it floods after heavy rain. The river is navigable from its estuary to Tonbridge, but in the 19th century attempts were made to extend that navigation for barges as far as Penshurst. Work was abandoned, however, short of the village. Where the walk crosses the river you can see a war-time pill box, one of many such defences built along the Medway's banks at a time when invasion was feared during the last War.

Ⓔ

Penshurst Place. Described by Sir Philip Sidney – courtier, poet, statesman and soldier – as 'handsome without curiosity and homely without loathsomeness' Penshurst Place counts as one of the great houses of England and is set in a vast acreage of parkland.

PENSHURST PLACE

This 14th-century manor house was designed during the reign of Edward III for a wealthy merchant who was Lord Mayor of London on four occasions between 1331 and 1337, Sir John de Pulteney. In the centuries since, it has expanded considerably from its original size into an impressive collection of mellow stone walls and towers containing a superb Great Hall, considered by many to be the finest of its kind in Britain.

Penshurst Place amidst Tudor style gardens.

In 1552 Edward VI gave Penshurst Place to his chamberlain and chief steward, Sir William Sidney, and it has been in the hands of the Sidney family and their descendants ever since. The most famous family member, Sir Philip Sidney was born here in 1554. He gained fame at the Battle of Zutphen in Holland when, mortally wounded he refused water and gave it to a wounded soldier. There are staterooms and a minstrels' gallery and a collection of 16th- and 17th-century portraits on show, while the 10-acre walled garden is a delight. Of this the poet sang "The blushing apricot and wooly peach/Hang on thy walls, that every child may reach . . ."

The extensive parkland to the north of the great house has several footpaths offering further walks of charm, and within sight of Penshurst Place stands an oak tree where, it is said, the last bear in England was killed.

Constructed mostly of local sandstone, Penshurst place has grown to impressive proportions.

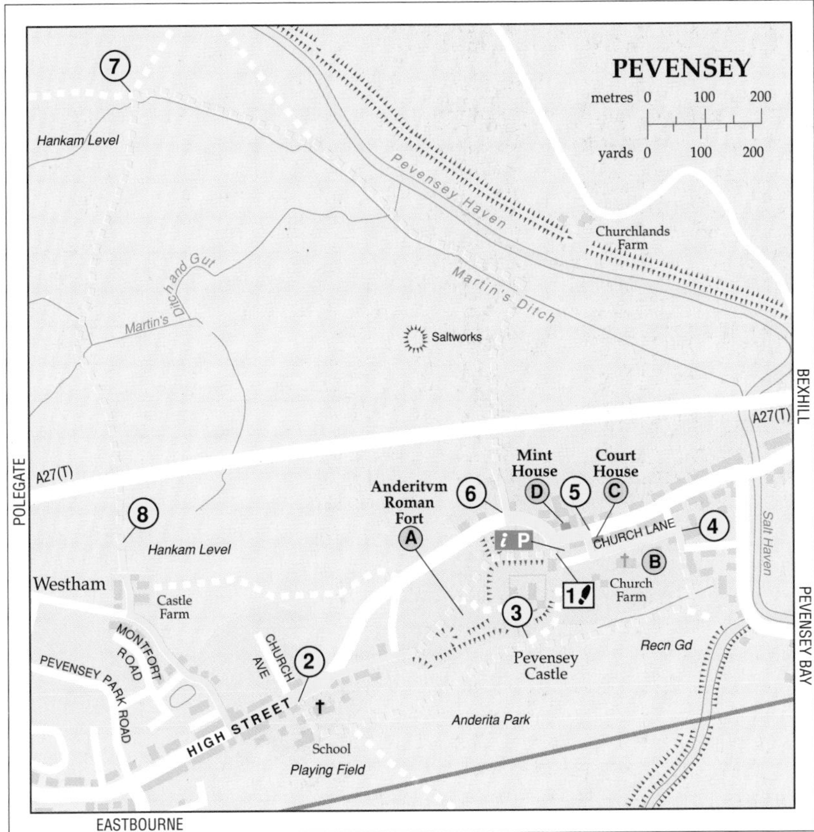

PEVENSEY

EAST SUSSEX

On A227, 5 miles E of Eastbourne

PEVENSEY developed on the site of the Roman harbour where William the Conqueror landed in 1066. The village is dominated by the massive walls of the ruined castle. The Romans and the Normans both recognised the defensive importance of the site; a peninsula which at that time lay surrounded by marshes, at the mouth of a river.

Pevensey Castle was built in the early 12th century

POINTS OF INTEREST

Ⓐ

The Roman Fort of *Anderida*. One of a chain along the south coast, this fort was built to fend off the Saxons. The remaining walls, enclosing an area of nearly 10 acres, stand to a height of 20ft in places.

William of Normandy gave Pevensey to his half-brother, who built a fort of his own, making use of part of the Roman wall. The castle was, in turn, besieged by Simon de Montfort in 1264, given to John of Gaunt in 1372, neglected by the Tudors, patched up to help repel the Spanish Armada, and finally abandoned as beyond repair.

Ⓑ

The Church of St Nicholas. The original Norman church, probably established on an even older Saxon site, was destroyed, except for the font, when Simon de Montfort laid siege to the castle. The present church, built in 1270 has survived with some Victorian restoration.

Ⓒ

The Court House. This tiny building has been described as the smallest town hall in England. The gaol occupied the ground floor, with the courtroom above.

Ⓓ

The 'Mint House'. A medieval building, much altered since, is a reminder that William the Conqueror established a mint at Pevensey in 1076.

INFORMATION
Length of walk:
$2^3/_4$ miles.
Village and Castle loop:
1 mile
Pevensey levels loop:
$1^3/_4$ miles
Approximate time:
2 hours

TERRAIN:
Easy, level walking.
Village and Castle loop: suitable for pushchairs.
Pevensey Levels loop: suitable only for walkers.

PARKING:
Park in the car park at the eastern end of the Castle area where there is an information centre.

WALK DIRECTIONS

①

Start the walk through the east gate in the outer Roman wall and walk along a metalled path which skirts to the right of the keep. After leaving through the west gate, follow an access road to join the A27 near Westham church.

②

Turn left into the churchyard and walk round behind the church in an anti-clockwise direction. Where the path leaves the main churchyard, fork left on a fenced path which leads you beneath the walls of the castle.

③

Ignore a left fork and go forward along the edge of a sports ground. Beyond a cricket pavilion, turn left over a concrete bridge and along a path to join Church Lane.

④

Go forward for a few yards, then bear left to Pevensey church. Opposite the church gate, turn right along a narrow lane to reach the A27. The Old Court House is on the corner.

⑤

Turn left and walk back to the car park.

⑥

For Pevensey Levels, follow the main road round to the right, beneath the castle walls. After about 100yds, turn right along a signed bridleway. Cross the new bypass and, after another 60yds, go over a wide culvert and turn left.

⑦

After about $^1/_2$ mile, turn left over a stile and head out across a field, aiming a little to the right of a barn with a white roof. Cross a culvert in the first hedge and maintain the same direction to a gate in the one beyond. Recross the bypass, go over a bridge and head for the barn.

⑧

Pass left of the barn and go ahead to join a lane. Turn left and follow this lane to the A27. Turn left, and retrace your steps to the start.

RINGMER
EAST SUSSEX

On B2192, 3 miles NE of Lewes

THE first settlement at Ringmer can be traced to the 12th century or earlier, when the land now occupied by the village green was cleared for grazing, and habitations were established around the area. The green is still the focal point of the village, which has expanded southwards in modern times towards the foot of the Downs.

South of Ringmer, paths lead up to the top of Mount Caburn and down to Glyndebourne; now world famous for its opera house, founded by John Christie in 1934. The Elizabeth mansion at Glyndebourne is not open to the public, but is visible from the lane.

Ringmer has strong American associations. John Harvard, the founder of the university of the same name, and William Penn of Pennsylvania, both married Ringmer girls.

POINTS OF INTEREST

Ⓐ

The Village Sign. Unveiled in 1923, this commemorates two 17th-century women, Ann Sadler and Gulielma Springett, who married Americans; and Gilbert White, who used to visit his aunt at Delves House.

Ⓑ

The Church. Dedicated to St Mary the Virgin, the church has been much restored, but retains features which are over 700 years old. The nave, with piers raised on pedestals, rises in a series of arcades dating from the 14th century and the exceptional organ was the gift of John Christie of Glyndebourne.

Ⓒ

Delves House. Delves House was visited frequently by the Hampshire writer and naturalist, Gilbert White. It was here that he found and immortalised Timothy the Tortoise. Timothy appears on the village sign; his shell is in the British Museum.

The church of St Mary at Ringmer (below left).
The village sign (below).

WALK DIRECTIONS

①

For the start of the walk, cross the green to the Anchor Inn and set out along the main road in Lewes' direction, passing between the village pump and the war memorial.

②

Cross the road to the village sign, and proceed along Vicarage Way to the church. Bear right through the churchyard out on to the green and turn left along the edge.

③

Turn right along Bishops Lane, follow it out to the B2192 and turn left, passing the Green Man public house on the left.

④

Turn right along a metalled drive. Beyond an industrial site entrance it becomes a pleasant lane. In front of a house, bear left and, in 100yds or so, beyond a stile by a gate, bear right across a field, heading for a white weather-boarded cottage. Join Potato Lane over a stile and turn right.

⑤

After $\frac{2}{3}$ mile, on the edge of the village, bear left into Gote Lane. After another $\frac{1}{4}$ mile, turn right along Springett Avenue and follow it back to the start.

INFORMATION
Length of walk:
$2\frac{3}{4}$ miles
Approximate time:
$1\frac{1}{2}$ hours

TERRAIN:
Easy; suitable for push-chairs and wheelchairs.

PARKING:
Park along the northern edge of the village green. Between May and September it is possible to park nearby, on the green.

REFRESHMENTS:
Two pubs in Ringmer.

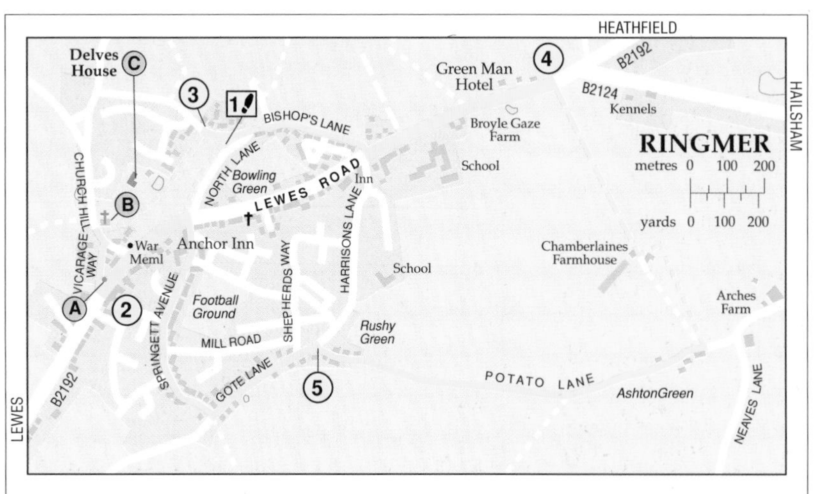

The old Mill Post is an excellent vantage point.

NOTE: From a point opposite the junction of Gote Lane and Springett Avenue, the walk can easily be extended southwards via a stiled path across two fields to climb to Glyndebourne Mill Post, $\frac{1}{2}$ mile each way.

SELBORNE

HAMPSHIRE

On B3006, 4 miles S of Alton on A31

SELBORNE is a living celebration of the life and work of the Revd Gilbert White (1720-93), the outstanding amateur naturalist who spent most of his life in the village and loved it so much that he gave up ambition and advancement to remain there. A one-street village of great character, pretty in places, it is traversed by the busy B3006, which means the visitor wandering in the main street must be ever watchful. The countryside around the village is especially beautiful on fine autumn days.

WALK DIRECTIONS

From The Plestor (village green) go through the churchyard into Church Meadow. There are beautiful views ahead of the wooded valley, with timbered Dorton Cottage at the valley bottom.

Walk down and cross the stream by the footbridge, then go over a stile and into the woods of the Short Lythe (Lythe rhymes with 'with'). There is a brief open stretch of undulating field between the Short Lythe and Long Lythe. Walk into the Long Lythe.

Continue on a flat, easy path through beech and poplar trees and at the end of the Long Lythe reach Coombe Meadow. Go 100yds into the meadow, using single plank bridges if the weather is wet, then turn right into Great Dorton Wood, where a wooden bridge crosses Oakhanger stream.

Go half-right up through the woods. Reach a wide path following the contour above the stream. Walk back to Selborne, via Huckers Lane.

The Zig-Zag at Selborne

From the Selborne Arms take the path marked to Selborne Common. It leads to the bottom of the wooded steep scarp slope. The Zig-Zag, cut by Gilbert White and his brother in 1753, leads, up the steep slope to the top.

Take the Bostal path on the right, reach the top, walk along the edge of the hanger, and return to the village either by retracing your steps, or by going on to Wood Lane and Gracious Street. Any path down takes you back to the village.

The Romany Folklore Museum at Limes End Yard vividly recreates gypsy life.

INFORMATION
Length of walk:
2½ miles
Approximate time:
2 hours

TERRAIN:
Suitable for children at all times of the year. Not suitable for push-chairs or wheelchairs. Numerous stiles and footbridges (easy).

PARKING:
There is a public car park behind the Selborne Arms.

OPEN:
Gilbert White/Oates Memorial Museum. Formerly White's house and later the family home of Oates family and Captain Oates who perished on Scott's Antarctic expedition. Museum and gardens Wed-Sun and Bank Hol. Mon, 11.00-17.30. Charge. Romany Folklore Museum and Workshop at Limes End Yard. Features traditional Romany living wagon and an exhibition of gypsy history, traditions and crafts. Most weekends Easter-Sep. Charge.

POINTS OF INTEREST

The Plestor. An unusual name for a village green, it stands between the road and the church and is edged by some fine period buildings. It has a stately oak tree, no doubt a worthy successor to that mentioned in one of Gilbert White's letters. This was blown down by a great wind in 1703 and so great was the general concern that it was 'set in place again'. White records that all the care and attention was of no avail and it died. Will history repeat itself with the Selborne Yew of 1990?

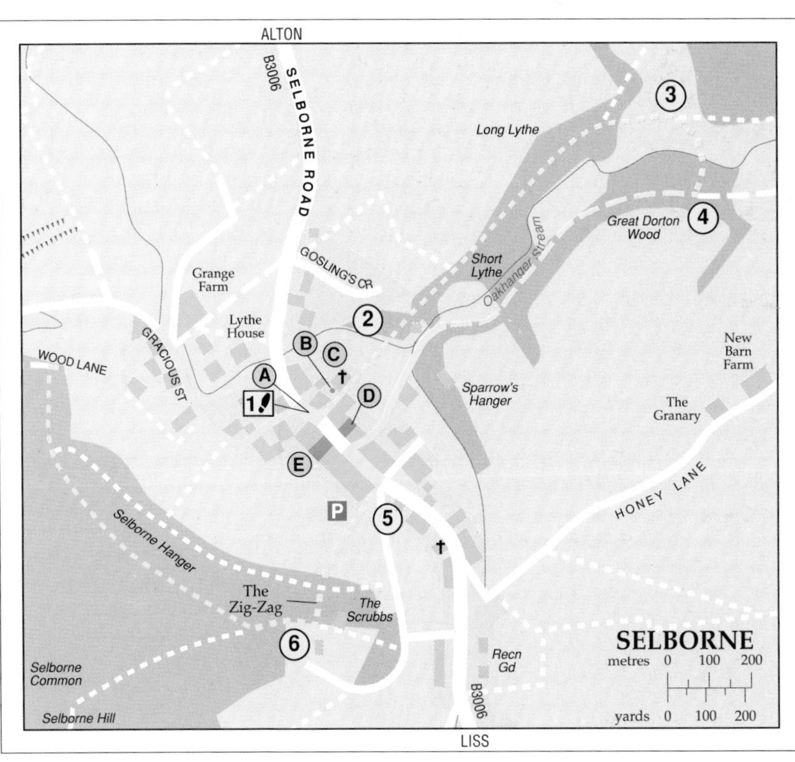

The Wakes at Selborne. Gilbert White lived and died here. Today both the house and the extensive gardens are open to visitors.

The Selborne Yew. Nearly 1,400 years old and 35ft in girth, it was blown down in the churchyard by a gale on 25 January 1990 and split in two. The best specialist advice available was brought in, and resulted in the tree being shorn of its branches, winched upright and replanted.

It is believed yews have a strong power of natural regeneration, but it will be 1993 before it is known for certain it is alive or dead.

Gilbert White's Grave. White's tombstone in the churchyard is so simple and plain that not even his name appears on it, in accordance with his wishes. The small headstone bears only this inscription: 'G.W. 26th June 1793'.

The Old Butcher's Shop. Opposite the Gilbert White house, the butcher's shop has two pollarded lime trees in front of it. These are two of the four that White planted on 31 March 1756 'to hide the sight of blood and filth from ye windows'. Some meat hooks are still visible on the wall fronting the road.

The Selborne Cottage Shop. The shop has an unrivalled stock of country books, crafts and bygones, including the Mallinson collection of rural relics.

GILBERT WHITE

The year 1789 witnessed two major events in the history of civilisation. The noisier one was the outbreak of the French Revolution. The other was the publication of a book called *The Natural History and Antiquities of Selborne*. One of the best-loved volumes in the English language, it has gone through more than 200 editions since its first appearance and it originated the special genre of country writing as fine literature. With its graceful style, gentle humour, humanity and patiently meticulous accuracy of observation, the book helped to fix love of nature firmly into the English national character.

The author, Gilbert White, was a clergy-man and a fellow of Oriel College, Oxford, who lived almost his entire life in the village of Selborne, where he was curate. He was born there in 1720, in the days of George I. A lifelong bachelor, he passed a quiet, uneventful existence deep in the Hampshire countryside, ministering to his rustic flock and assiduously cultivating his beloved garden. On walks he carefully noted the life of the meadows, woods and hedgerows of his parish. Rooks and swallows, rabbits and hedgehogs, crickets and grasshoppers, all came under his keen and patient eye and he recorded the wind and the weather and the changing seasons of the year. As a pet he had a venerable tortoise named Timothy, whose doings were watchfully minuted. Timothy's pulse was taken, he was weighed in the village shop and to test his hearing he was bawled at through a speaking trumpet. White also faithfully noted the births of his own 63 nephews and nieces.

On his expeditions White liked to plant acorns and beechnuts at suitable spots and some of Selborne's oaks and beeches today have him for a forebear. In 1771 he told a friend of his plan for 'a natural history of my native parish... comprising a journal for a whole year', but it took almost another 20 years to bring it to completion. The book is in the form of a series of letters and White's blend of painstaking accuracy with an easy, vivid style is evident on every page. He writes, for instance, about a pair of owls which ever since he could remember had nested under the church eaves:

> 'I have minuted these birds with my watch for an hour together and have found that they return to their nests, the one or the other of them, about once in five minutes...'

Gilbert White died at The Wakes in 1793, a few weeks short of his 73rd birthday. He is buried in Selborne churchyard.

Visitors can enjoy a wonderful view over Selborne (above) from the top of Gilbert White's zig-zag path. White is shown studying a partridge (below).

SMARDEN

KENT

On B2077, 10 miles W of Ashford

AN attractive scattered village in the garden of Kent, set on the River Beult, Smarden has won the award as Kent's Best-kept Village a number of times. Many Weald villages have names ending in 'den' meaning 'clearing in the forest'. 'Smar' means 'butter valley and pasture'. Smarden received its market charter from Edward III, who encouraged the manufacture of broadcloth from the plentiful wool. The industry survived until the last century, when hops were introduced.

Most visitors to Smarden are heading for the famous Bell Inn and, as this can be reached without passing through the village, they often miss the half-timbered and weatherboarded houses in the main street and the huge church, reached through a cottage archway.

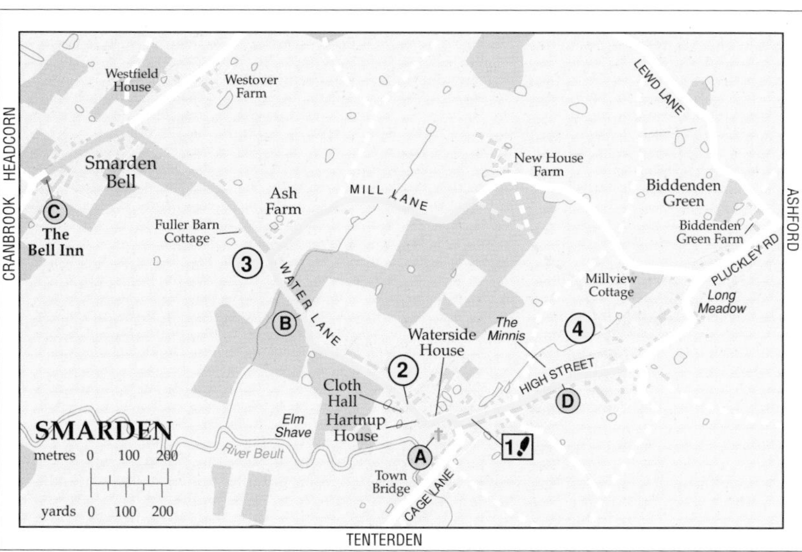

INFORMATION
Length of walk:
1½ miles (2¼ if detour followed)
Approximate time:
1½ hours if detour followed

TERRAIN:
Suitable for children at all times of the year; only lanes suitable for pushchairs and wheelchairs as far as The Bell. Three stiles.

PARKING:
Park outside the post office in The Street, which leads to the church.

REFRESHMENTS:
The Bell at Smarden Bell; The Chequers in Smarden.

WALK DIRECTIONS

Walk down the side of The Chequers past the church to follow Water Lane round a double bend, passing Waterside House, Hartnup House and Cloth Hall.

Beyond Cloth Hall and the oasts stay on the lane as far as a T-junction. Continue ahead only to visit The Bell which is 225yds to the left at the second T-junction.

The main route turns right at the first T-junction off Water Lane to pass Ash Farm and soon the isolated, timber-framed Little Ash. Later there is a view of the church tower. Where the road bends sharply left (north-east), look for a lay-by on the right and go over the stile. A path runs across a large field to a stile.

Go ahead across the grass and up an enclosed path to cross a stile to the High Street. Turn right to the post office and church.

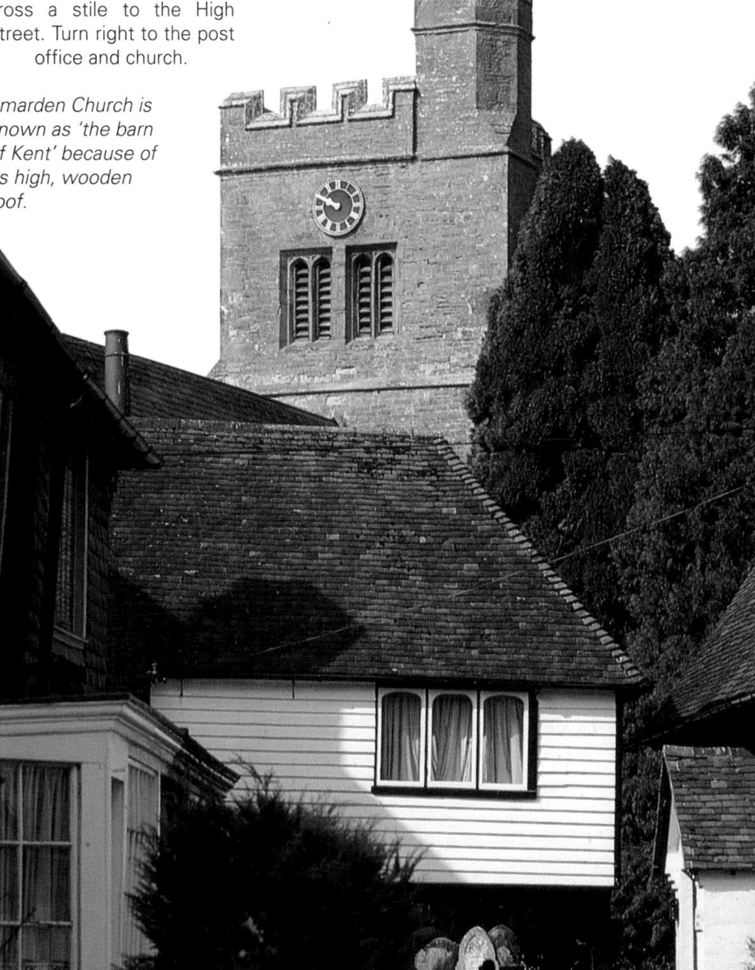

Smarden Church is known as 'the barn of Kent' because of its high, wooden roof.

POINTS OF INTEREST

The Church. Known as the 'Barn of Kent' due to its width and lack of any aisles to support the roof, the church was built between 1325 and 1350 of local Bethersden marble. The tower was added a century later. Notice the fossilised snails in the stone path outside. To determine the wall's thickness, lean up the rood steps on the right of the chancel arch.

The early 20th-century wall paintings, featuring villagers as models for the figures, replace lost medieval paintings. Beyond the wall seats to the right of the high altar is a very rare wafer oven, and the north wall has a mysterious grotesque head. Children can ride on the wooden rocking horse made in 1990 by Stevenson Brothers, the fairground furniture makers at Bethersden.

MARCHING WITH CADE

Nostalgia for the English countryside of the past overlooks its legacy of hardship, suffering and violence. In the 15th century, when Smarden was a small cloth town, more than 60 Smarden men joined the rebellious army of Jack Cade. Respectable citizens and tradesmen, they marched with him to protest against high taxes and high prices. So did many hundreds of others, all over the county of Kent.

Very little is known about Jack Cade, but in late May 1450, when Kentish discontent boiled over, the protesters chose him as their general. He led them to Blackheath, where they camped on 1 June. They then retreated, defeated a government force just outside Sevenoaks, and marched back to London in triumph, reaching Southwark early in July. Cade seized two royal officials and had them beheaded. He now had 40,000 men at his back, or so it was estimated. The City of London, nervous of disorder and disliking his demands for money, closed its gates against him, and after fierce fighting he failed to force his way over London Bridge.

The government now offered concessions and pardons all round, and most of Cade's men went home. Cade was given a pardon, but it was then declared invalid. He was soon hunted down and mortally wounded near Heathfield in Sussex.

Smarden is a pretty village in the Weald of Kent. Many of its buildings have Kentish weather-boarding.

Water Lane. Still liable to flooding from the River Beult, a ferry sometimes has to operate between The Chequers and Hartnup House. Waterside House, which can be cut off, was built in Elizabeth I's reign. Hartnup House is probably older than the 1671 date on its fascia showing the Apothecaries' Company rhinoceros (indicating a doctor's surgery). Next door is Cloth Hall, built about 1420 as a farmhouse but later turned into the wool warehouse. Bales were hoisted up at the west end, where the loft doors can be seen from the road.

The Bell Inn at Smarden Bell. This is older than the two pubs in the village, having been in business since 1400. Today its exceptional range of real ales and local Biddenden cider attracts customers from far afield. Part of the front bar is set aside for families with children who can enjoy home-made chocolate crunch cake or real ice cream there and in the garden,' where roses cover the old building. Rupert Croft-Cooke, famous for producing the longest autobiography, wrote that The Bell was 'all that I most value in the tradition of the English inn'. On the second Sunday of the month vintage and classic cars rally outside at lunchtime.

The High Street. This has changed little over the centuries and two ancient shops survive including the butcher's. Next to the village pump is The Dragon House, built in 1331 for the Pell family, who were brought here from Holland by Edward III to manufacture broadcloth. Notice the 17th-century Wyvern heraldic device - a play on the word weaver - which gave the house its present name. Wool spun by single women - spinsters - was sent here for weaving. Near the delightful 1841 Zion Chapel is Chessenden, once Smarden House, built in 1462 and formerly the village hall and workhouse.

The weather-boarded butcher's shop at Smarden (above) is an evocative reminder of times past.

Church Street (left) displays a wide variety of building styles.

The last remaining wall fragment of Bramber Castle (below left) is almost 80ft high.

STEYNING
WEST SUSSEX

On A283 about 10 miles NW of Brighton

STANDING to the north of the gap in the Sussex Downs carved by the River Adur, Steyning (pronounced 'Stenning') was a major port in Saxon times. After the Norman Conquest, the silting of the river led to a decline in trade.

The walk along Church Street and High Street provides a rich variety of fine old houses, ranging from medieval timber framed to Georgian brick, a delightful medley of contrasting styles in perfect harmony. Indeed, the village provides a remarkable concentration of the fine buildings, with over 100 of them officially 'listed'. Steyning is framed to the south by a natural, thickly wooded downland amphitheatre.

A little to the west, Chanctonbury Ring, a small Iron Age fort marked by beech trees planted in 1760, stands on the crest of the Downs, much battered by the Great Gale of 1987, but still a recognisable landmark.

The walk extends to the edge of the neighbouring village of Bramber for a visit to the ruins of Bramber Castle, and the church, both built at a time when they were part of the parish of Steyning.

INFORMATION
Length of walk: 3 miles
Approximate time: 2 hours

TERRAIN:
Suitable for children. Suitable for pushchairs but use Maudlin Lane between points 8 and 10, avoiding field paths. Main village walk (points 1 to 5) suitable for wheelchairs.

PARKING:
Park in the large car park to the south of the church, signposted from the High Street.

OPEN:
Village Museum. Apr-Oct Tue, Wed and Sat: 10.30-12.30 am, 2.30-4.30pm: Sun 2.30-4.30pm. No charge.

REFRESHMENTS:
Several pubs and cafés in the village.

WALK DIRECTIONS

1

From the south-western corner of the car park, walk westwards along School Lane and turn left into Church Street and then right into the High Street.

Walk along the High Street as far as the point where it veers to the right. Continue along Mouse Lane to see the Workhouse Cottages.

Retrace your steps along the High Street for 200yds before turning left into Tanyard Lane.

At a road junction where Shooting Field goes left, turn right, and in a few yards go left into Vicarage Lane. On the left is the church and to the right, behind the library, is the museum.

A few yards short of a phone box on the right, turn right along a path. In 200yds, at a path junction, turn left for a few yards out to a lane. Follow Holland Road, opposite.

6

At the next road junction, go forward on a narrow fenced path which crosses the bypass. Beyond the bridge, go right for five yards, then left, still along an enclosed path. Go ahead past the end of the cul-de-sac.

At the next junction, turn right into Roman Road. After 200yds the road narrows to a lane. A few yards short of a roundabout with the A283,

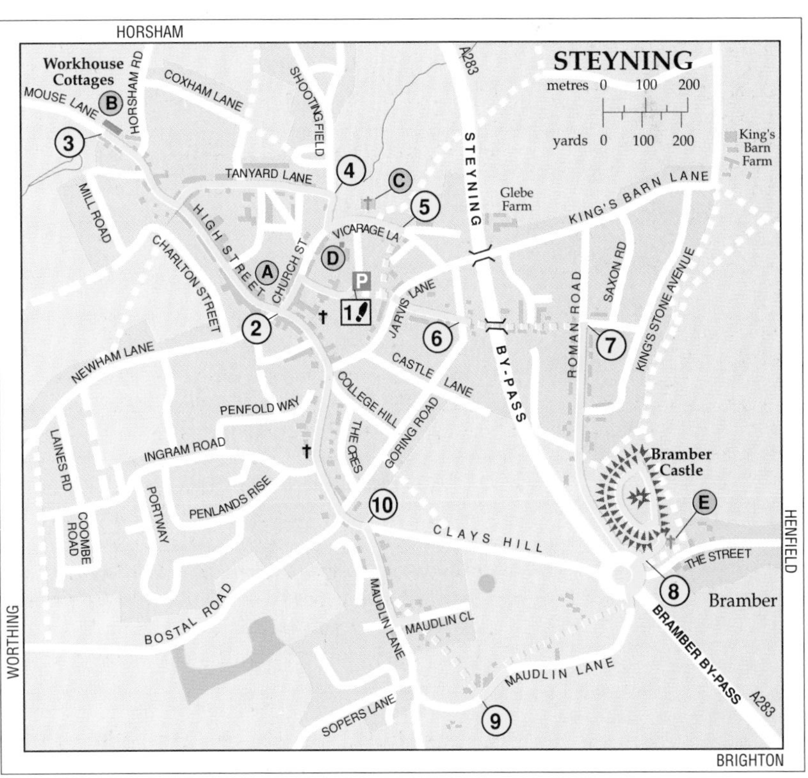

The Old Market House (above) with its clock tower serving as a reminder that this was once the town hall. (Above right) For 150 years the Workhouse Cottages were home to the parish poor. (Right) A well-kept timber-framed house.

turn left up to Bramber Church and Castle.

After completing a circuit of the castle mound, return to the roundabout and take the third exit (Maudlin Lane). About 10yds along the lane, turn right, down steps, over a stile and across a paddock, walking parallel to the hedge on the right. Veer slightly left across a second field to rejoin Maudlin Lane over a stile to the left of a house and garden. Turn right.

After about 100yds, a camouflaged sign to the left of the lane indicates a path to the right, through a gate and to the left of a flint and metal barn, where the path is overgrown. After another gate, veer left across pasture to a stile and a narrow path between gardens. At Maudlin Close, turn left for a few yards to rejoin Maudlin Lane and turn right.

Turn left along Clays Hill, then straight ahead over the crossroads back into Steyning. At point (2), turn right into Church Street and retrace your outgoing route to the car park.

POINTS OF INTEREST

(A)

Church Street and High Street. Several of the finest buildings in the village can be found within a short distance of the junction of Church Street and High Street. No.s 1, 3 and 5 Church Street form a harmonious group, dating from the 14th/15th centuries. Next door, the Grammar School, endowed in 1614, still houses part of a large Comprehensive School. Opposite the junction is Stone House, once the local gaol.

On the way along the High Street, the Old Market House, surmounted by an attractive bell tower has, in turn, served as Town Hall, Police Station and Fire Station. George Fox, the founder of the Society of Friends, once addressed a Quaker meeting here.

Workhouse Cottages. These are a fine example of the 15th-century 'wealden' style of timber-framed building, characterised by curved central braces supporting the roof, and overhanging end bays. They were built in 1684, and were used to house the poor of the parish until 1834.

The Parish Church of St Andrew. This is the oldest building in the village and one of the best examples of Norman architecture in the country. It is a substantial structure, but, even so, is only a small part of the grand cruciform church built by the monks of Fecamp after the Norman Conquest. The richly carved nave arcades and lofty clerestory are particularly impressive.

The once busy port of Steyning probably occupied a site to the north and east of the church.

Village Museum. The enterprising museum has recently moved to new premises behind the library, and provides a useful introduction to a tour of the village.

Bramber Castle and St Nicholas' Church. Built in the 11th century, the castle occupied a strategically placed natural chalk mound overlooking the gap in the Downs formed by the River Adur. At that time the water extended right up to the foot of the mound, with the port of Bramber nearby.

The castle was destroyed in 1641, during the Civil War, but a mighty remaining wall fragment gives an indication of the size and scale of the original structure. The rim of the castle mound, and the central *motte*, now in the hands of the National Trust, provide a series of viewpoints through the trees to the Downs and across the Adur valley.

The Church of St Nicholas, beside the Castle, dates from 1073. It was first used as a chapel by a group of Benedictine monks and only later as a parish church. Badly damaged when used as a gun emplacement by the Parliamentarians during the castle siege, it was subsequently restored in the 18th and 19th centuries.

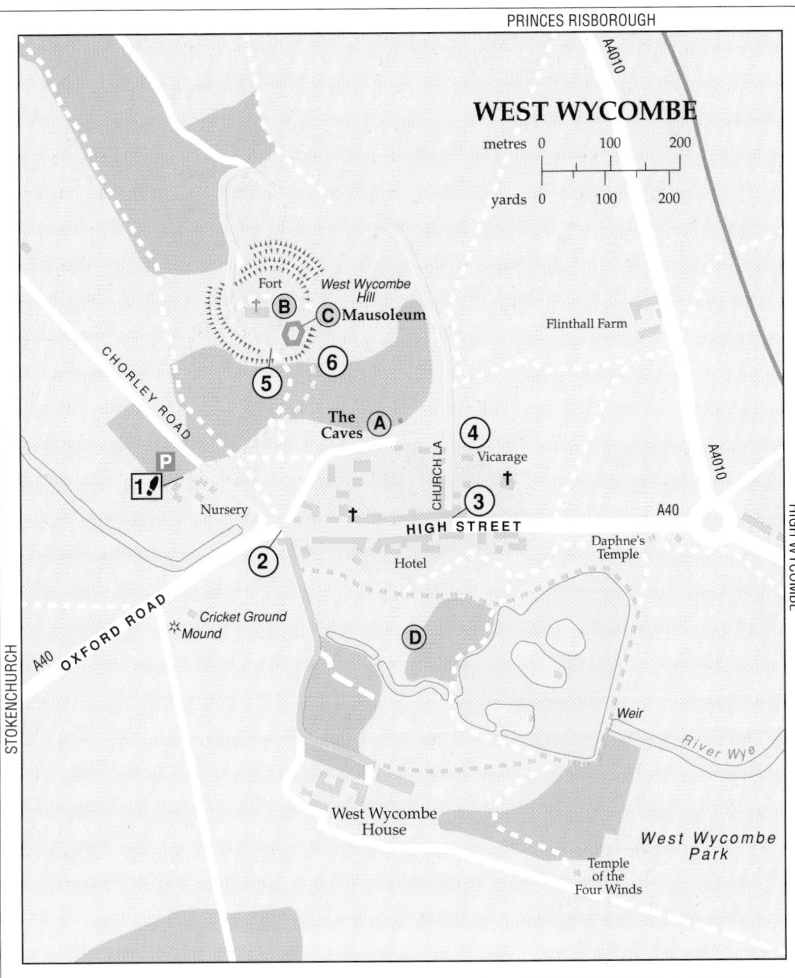

WEST WYCOMBE

BUCKINGHAMSHIRE

On A40, 2 miles NW of High Wycombe

A mid 18th-century Chiltern village, West Wycombe narrows the old Oxford road. Practical joker Sir Francis Dashwood, who built the Palladian mansion, laid out the Park, over-embellished the hill-top church and dug the caves, would still feel quite at home in the main street where zebra crossings are forbidden and a cobbled courtyard stands ready to receive the Oxford-London mail coach.

In 1929 West Wycombe was bought for safekeeping by the Royal Society of Arts and later passed to the National Trust. Among the interesting buildings is the timber-framed Church Loft, (next to the newsagent) built in 1417 for two monks who looked after passing pilgrims on their way to St Frideswide's shrine at Oxford. Look for the worn stone outside, where travellers knelt below a cross, the outline of which is still visible. At the back of the building is a workshop maintaining the dying Chiltern chairmaking trade. The George & Dragon displays its original early 18th-century inn sign.

WALK DIRECTIONS

①

From the car park, cross the road and walk down to the junction by the Wycombe Park gates.

②

Turn left across the end of West Wycombe Hill Road and walk down the village street. The Swan and The George & Dragon are on the far side of the road.

At Church Loft go through the archway and up Church Lane. At the end of the row of cottages follow a narrow path round to the left to join another lane and see the elaborate Caves entrance.

Retrace your steps to bear left, and continue up Church Lane. The way is now rural, and soon there is a view across a meadow to the Mausoleum. Where the way divides at a gate, bear left to walk along the ridge towards the church.

Go through the gateway and beyond the church. Stay on the path below the wall to reach the Mausoleum. Do not curve round the Mausoleum with the main path, but keep forward down the line of horse chestnut trees.

⑥

Soon there is a spectacular view over the village to the West Wycombe Park. Go down the steps and follow the path to the Garden Centre and car park.

⑦

On certain days a detour can be made around West Wycombe Park. Walk through the gates at the end of Chorley Road and go left along the Broad Walk. On approaching the lake, go left round the edge. After the Cascade bear right up to the mansion, and follow the drive back to the village.

INFORMATION
Length of walk:
1¼ miles
Approximate time:
3 hours if Caves and Park visited

TERRAIN:
A gentle hill and steps. Suitable for children; suitable for pushchairs and wheelchairs only as far as the church.

PARKING:
The car park next to the Garden Centre in Chorley Road.

OPEN:
The Caves: Daily, Mar-Oct and winter weekends. Charge. West Wycombe Park Jun-Sep, daily except Fri-Sat. Charge.

REFRESHMENTS:
The Swan and George & Dragon inns. There are cafés at the Caves' entrance and the Garden Centre.

West Wycombe Caves (above), the supposed venue for the Hell Fire Club's black magic practices.

POINTS OF INTEREST

Ⓐ

The Caves. In the 1750s Sir Francis Dashwood, who wanted to provide local employment, extended the caves to a ¼-mile in depth. The chalk spoil was used for the new straight road from High Wycombe. The chambers now contain life-size figures of Sir Francis and some of his Hellfire Club friends, such as reformer John Wilkes and Sandwich, who occasionally met here.

The unusual golden ball atop West Wycombe church (right).

Church of St Laurence. On the site of a 5th-century Iron-Age fort and all that remains of a village once called Haveringdon, St Laurence's is essentially medieval, but was made Georgian by Sir Francis Dashwood.

Most surprising is the golden ball he placed on top of the 14th-century tower after he had seen the Customs House in Venice. The ball seats six, and John Wilkes called it 'the best globe tavern I was ever in' after Dashwood entertained him there with 'divine milk punch and jolly songs very unfit for the profane ears of the world below.'

The Mausoleum. The open-air Portland stone and flint hexagonal building was erected in 1765 by Sir Francis Dashwood with a bequest from Lord Melcombe Regis. Inside are monuments to the Dashwoods and others, including Paul Whitehead, the Hellfire Club steward. His heart is in an urn which was placed here amid much ceremony and firing of cannons at the end of a two-hour long funeral. The Mausoleum, like the village church, has long been a landmark of the old London-Oxford road.

The Dashwood family mausoleum (above).

West Wycombe Park. The House was built for Sir Francis Dashwood, who filled it with Italian marble, paintings and ceilings copied from Rome. Dashwood is seen in a portrait here as a successful Postmaster-General, holding the first American prayer book which he and Benjamin Franklin prepared together at West Wycombe Park.

Another well-known feature is the unusual two-storeyed colonnade at the south side of the house. Humphry Repton was employed to landscape the grounds and the lake, where Dashwood had a small fleet for mock battles, was created by damming the River Wye. There are eight Temples in the grounds, including a Temple of Music on an island in the lake. Visitors can step inside the parlour of the recently rebuilt Temple of Venus.

HELLFIRE CLUB

Sir Francis Dashwood's infamous club, also known as the 'Society of St Francis of Wycombe', met among the ruins of Medmenham Abbey, 8 miles away, and at Wycombe Caves, which are sometimes still called the 'Hellfire Caves'. The club motto was 'Do whatever you like', which fuelled rumours of strange rituals. These appear to be confirmed in Hogarth's portrait of Sir Francis, in which he is shown dressed as a monk holding a naked Venus. John Wilkes is said to have once let loose a baboon representing the devil during a mock religious ceremony conducted by another member of the club, Lord Sandwich.

An engraving of Sir Francis Dashwood.

WESTERHAM

KENT

On A25, 6 miles W of Sevenoaks

AN historic village picturesquely grouped around a sloping green, Westerham honours two local heroes: General James Wolfe, of Quebec fame, and Sir Winston Churchill, who lived at nearby Chartwell.

This walk explores the best of 'old' Westerham. It has a number of interesting buildings along the route, as well as a lovely country section with a one-time mill pond and a clear stream for company.

Squerryes Court overlooking attractive grounds.

INFORMATION
Length of walk: 1³/₄ miles
Approximate time: 1 hour

TERRAIN:
Roads, tracks and footpaths. Two stiles, narrow footbridges and some steps make this walk unsuitable for pushchairs and wheelchairs. Otherwise it is ideal for a family outing throughout the year.

PARKING:
Park in the Market Square.

OPEN:
Squerryes Court. Open Wed, weekends and Bank Hol. Mon, Apr to Sep, from 2pm-6pm. Charge.
Quebec House (NT). Open daily (except Thu & Sat), Easter to Oct, 2pm-5.30pm. Charge.
Chartwell (NT). Open daily (not Mon or Fri), Easter to Oct, 12 noon-5pm (closed on Tue following Bank Hol. Mon). Charge.

REFRESHMENTS:
Cafés, pubs and hotels line the main street.

POINTS OF INTEREST

Westerham Green. Backed by the Parish Church, a row of attractive cottages, tearooms and shops, the Green is adorned by two statues: one of a defiant General James Wolfe, whose early home was in Westerham, the other of Sir Winston Churchill, a bronze created by Oscar Nemon and given by the people of Yugoslavia in 1969.

Squerryes Court. A William and Mary house built in 1681, Squerryes has been the home of the Warde family for 250 years, and it was in the grounds that James Wolfe received his first commission. The house contains Wolfe memorabilia.

Pitts Cottage. This small 13th-century cottage, is named after William Pitt, who in 1783 became Britain's youngest Prime Minister at the age of 24. Pitt lived for a while in this cottage while repairs were being made to his home in Keston.

Quebec House. Wolfe spent his childhood in the multi-gabled house formerly known as Spiers, but renamed Quebec House after his famous victory against the French. In the old stable block at the rear, the National Trust has created an exhibition detailing the Battle of Quebec.

WALK DIRECTIONS

From the green walk uphill on the right-hand side of the road to the junction with B2024, the Croydon Road.

Turn right, then left on to a tarmac footpath which leads to Westbury Terrace. Continue to a junction with Granville Road, and go straight ahead on a hedge-lined footpath passing allotments, to reach the edge of Farley Common.

Bear left here and follow a narrow road for about 150yds, and on reaching Farley Lane go left again and walk downhill to reach the A25.

Turn left, passing Goodley Stock Road on the right. This leads in 5 minutes to Squerryes Court – see opening times. Continue alongside A25 past Pitts Cottage, until the road curves to the left.

An imposing bronze statue of General James Wolfe (above).

Cross the road with caution and go down Mill Lane as far as a pond.

⑥

Turn left opposite the pond and over a concrete footbridge across the young Darent stream. Walk ahead through meadowland on a footpath which follows the course of the stream.

⑦

When the path brings you to another footbridge, go over it, cross a corner of meadowland to a stile, and onto a footpath which leads to a row of cottages in Mill Street. (This and Mill Lane were both named after watermills that were powered by the Darent. Both mills were demolished prior to the Second World War.)

⑧

On coming to the main road opposite The Old House at Home, note that the house next to it is Quebec House (NT). Turn left and walk up Vicarage Hill to Westerham village green.

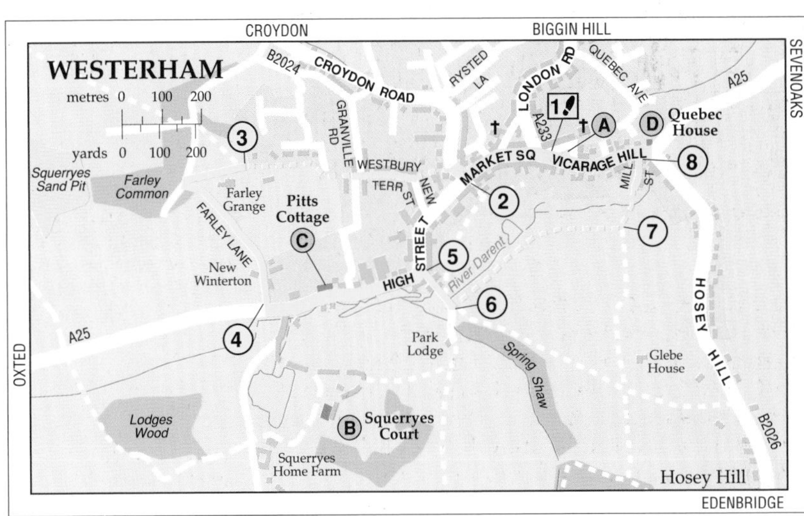

WINCHELSEA

EAST SUSSEX

On A259, $10\frac{1}{2}$ miles E of Hastings

WINCHELSEA was, with Rye, admitted to the confederation of Cinque Ports in 1191. Once the most important port in Sussex, the old town was drowned by the sea in the 13th century. The present village is all that exists of the 'new town', designed by Edward I in a regular 'chequer-board' pattern, and laid out on higher and drier land at the end of a sandstone ridge.

Before the town could be finished, attacks by the French, silting of the harbour compounded by the great storm of 1287 which altered the course of the River Brede, and finally the Black Death led to commercial collapse and a steady decline into what has been aptly described as `a town in a trance, a sunny dream of centuries ago'.

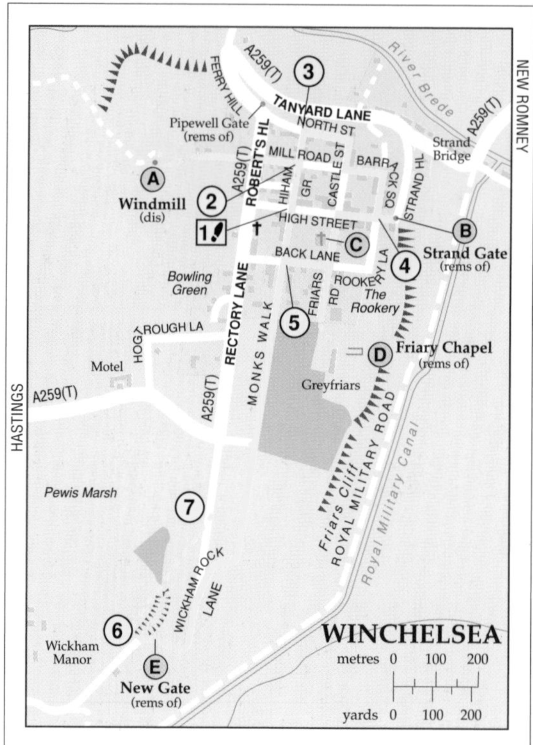

INFORMATION
Length of walk:
2 miles ($2\frac{1}{2}$ miles including detour to windmill site)
Approximate time:
At least 2 hours

TERRAIN:
Easy walking. Suitable for pushchairs and wheelchairs, except for footpath back from New Gate (which can be avoided by reversing your outgoing route).

PARKING:
Roadside parking is available to the north and west of the church.

OPEN:
Court Hall Museum:
Apr-Sep – weekdays 10.30-12.30pm, 2.30-5.30pm, Sun 2.30-5.30pm. Charge.

POINTS OF INTEREST

Ⓐ

Winchelsea Mill. Literally blown away in the Great Gale of October 1987, only the brick footings and two millstones remain. The view from the site, along the Brede Valley, is magnificent.

Ⓑ

The Strand Gate. So-named because it originally stood beside the River Brede. Ellen Terry, the silent film actress, once lived in the house next door. The nearby look-out was used to spot marauding Frenchmen. You can see across to France on a very clear day.

Ⓒ

The Parish church of St Thomas. As it stands today, it is but a fragment of the large-scale building originally conceived - but what a splendid fragment. The impressive interior is in the 14th-century Decorated style. John Wesley preached his last open-air sermon in the churchyard in 1790.

Ⓓ

Friary Chapel Ruins. In the grounds of a 19th-century house called Greyfriars stands the ruin of the chapel of a Franciscan friary, built about 1310. All that survives are the walls of the chancel.

Ⓔ

The New Gate. Situated about $\frac{3}{4}$ of a mile away from the village, it was built by Edward I as the southern entrance to the town and reminds us of the large scale of the original design. This part of the town was laid out but never built.

WALK DIRECTIONS

①

Start the walk from the north-west corner of the churchyard where you will find the Court Hall museum and the New Inn. Walk north along Hiham Green.

②

At the next crossroads, go ahead. (To visit the site of Winchelsea Mill, turn left, cross the A259 and follow the lane opposite. Return the same way).

③

At the junction with North Street, turn right (the Pipewell Gate is within sight to the left along the North Street). The road then bends right. About 50yds past the butcher's shop, turn left into Barrack Square and follow the road round to the right.

④

At the next junction, the Strand Gate is a few yards to the left. Turn right along the High Street. At the next crossroads, by a useful tourist information board and map, turn left, with the church on your right. At the south-east corner of the churchyard, turn right. (The road ahead takes you to Greyfriars).

⑤

At the next crossroads, turn left along the tree-lined Monks Walk. After $\frac{1}{4}$ of a mile, where the main road veers right, go ahead along Wickham Rock Lane.

⑥

A few yards beyond the New Gate, go right through a modern gate and follow a fence with the deep town ditch to your right. At the next field corner, cross a stile by a gate and bear slightly right, uphill, across undulating pasture to a second stile.

⑦

Go over a green lane and the stile opposite. Bear left up towards a ruin. Cross a stile to the left of this ruined building and turn right. Follow Monks Walk back to the start of the walk.

The Strand Gate is one of three old gateways still standing in the village.

CENTRAL ENGLAND AND EAST ANGLIA

APPLEBY MAGNA, LEICESTERSHIRE

•

As one who long in populous city pent,
Where houses thick and sewers annoy the air,
Forth issuing on a summer's morn to breathe
Among the pleasant villages and farms
Adjoin'd, from each thing met conceives delight.
MILTON – PARADISE LOST

•

Central England and East Anglia

•

•

The goldfinch, a common bird of hedgerows and open country.

The great belt of Central England covered by this section of the book comprises 13 counties; Shropshire, Staffordshire, Hereford & Worcester, West Midlands, Warwickshire, Derbyshire, Northamptonshire, Leicestershire, Bedfordshire, Cambridgeshire, Lincolnshire, Norfolk and Suffolk. These glorious counties have little in common, beyond the indefinable quality of being English. Any foreigner driving across them from the North Sea to the Welsh border would soon learn what every Englishman knows - that you don't have to travel far in Britain for the scenery to change quite dramatically, and with it the appearance of the local villages.

The most abrupt change occurs in the west, where the higher land rises. Visitors to the Shropshire villages of Acton Burnell, Clun and Coalbrookdale will find themselves among mighty hills, though the three settlements are very different in history and appearance. But from the bony ridge of The Wrekin, near Coalbrookdale, from the Malverns above Eastnor, or from the Cotswold plateau behind Ilmington - all villages described in the following pages - it is possible to gaze eastwards across lowlands that reach beyond vision to the cold North Sea.

The Peak District villages - Alstonefield and Ilam in Staffordshire, Cromford and Eyam in Derbyshire - lie also amongst the hills. At the last two we are caught up in the broader stream of history, for at Cromford we find Sir Richard Arkwright's great mill from the early years of the Industrial Revolution, and Eyam is for ever associated with the Plague of London in 1665, the last of the plagues that ravaged England from the Middle Ages. Alstonefield claims one of the oldest gravestones in England (that of Anne Green, who died in 1518), and at Ilam walkers can stay overnight in a great hall above the lovely River Manifold for the modest price of a youth hostel.

Another Staffordshire village, Abbots Bromley, has an historical association of a different kind: its annual Horn Dance. One of the oldest ceremonies surviving in England, it may have been performed for a thousand years. At Turvey in Bedfordshire, by the stone-built bridge that marks a prehistoric crossing place of the River Great Ouse, it is easy to imagine the arrest, said to have taken place there, of one of the partners in the Gunpowder Plot in 1605, and at Swaffham Prior in Cambridgeshire the original 'Hobson's' choice had to be made at a local livery stable.

Further east, in Norfolk, Castle Acre has a triple endowment: the great earthworks of its Norman castle, the ruins of the priory founded about 1090, and its fine church in the Perpendicular style. In the same county, Cley next the Sea is noted for its picturesque windmill of 1713, and at Bourn in Cambridgeshire is found what is claimed to be the oldest windmill in Britain (records go back to 1636).

Some of these Midlands villages were once more important places that have come down in the world. Abbots Bromley used to be a busy market town, and a great barn at Acton Burnell was the reputed setting for an early Parliament in the 1290s. Cley next the Sea, now inland, was once a prosperous port, and Dunwich in Suffolk, which was a cathedral city in Anglo-Saxon times, was bigger when the Domesday survey was taken than it is now, much of it having simply toppled off the crumbling cliffs into the waves. In the same county Kersey, one of East Anglia's loveliest villages, was a cloth-producing town as late as Shakespeare's day, and Lavenham also declined with the East Anglian cloth trade.

There is much to discover about these country villages. The squires or Lords of the Manor, from whom their names were sometimes taken (such as the distant Burnells of Acton Burnell), or who influenced their later development (as did the numerous Higgins family at Turvey and the Cartwrights at Aynho), played their parts. So did local building materials and economic forces. Britain is fortunate in possessing thousands of lovely villages of all sizes. In Central England just twenty-eight of the best have been selected for readers of this book to explore.

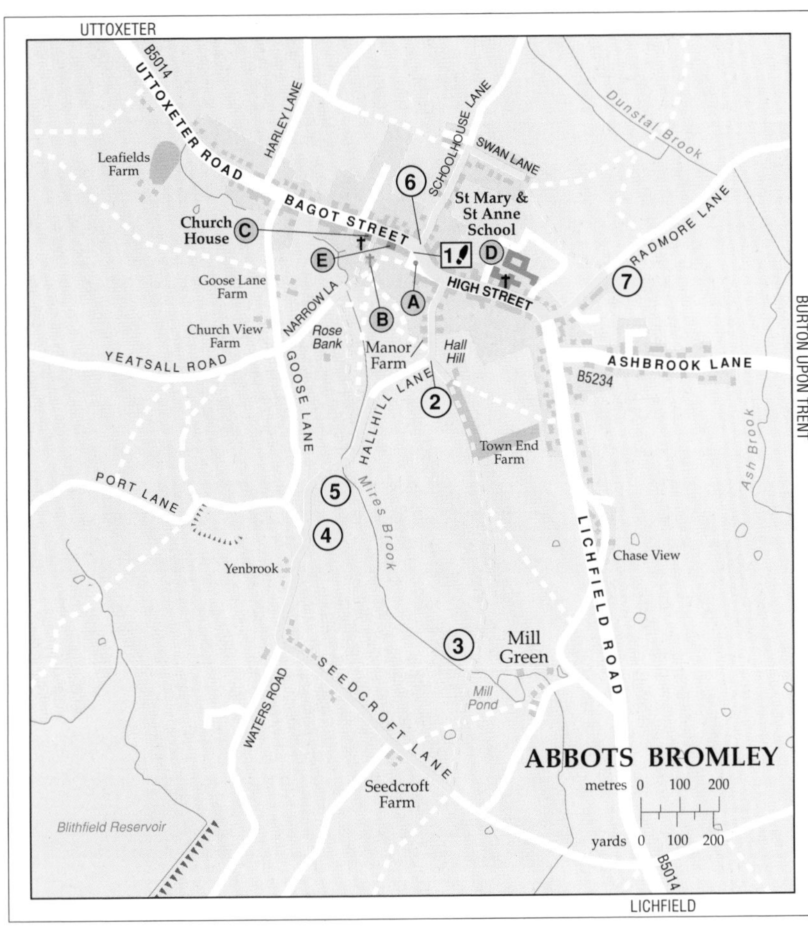

ABBOTS BROMLEY

STAFFORDSHIRE

At junction of B5014 and B5234, 4½ miles NE of Rugeley

THE gentle hills and quiet lanes in this part of Staffordshire are a delight to both drivers and walkers. Abbots Bromley is best approached along the B5013, which crosses the lovely Blithfield Reservoir by a causeway. This route provides a view of Blithfield Hall, the home for 600 years of the Bagot family, though heavily Gothicised in the early 19th century.

The village, once a busy market town, now lies peacefully in charming countryside. Only once a year does it wake up – on the Monday in September when the annual Horn Dance is held. There is a pleasing blend of brick-built and timber-framed houses, and its focal point is a tiny green beside the ancient Butter Cross.

POINTS OF INTEREST

The Butter Cross. There is uncertainty about the age of this small hexagonal-shaped and pyramid-roofed building beside the Green. The village map on its central post states that the Butter Cross was probably built in 1339, but some authorities have suggested that it is actually 300 years younger. However, Abbots Bromley, though now only a

INFORMATION
Length of walk:
2½ miles
Approximate time:
1½ hours

TERRAIN:
Suitable for children at all times of year. Not suitable for pushchairs or wheelchairs; 8 stiles and 2 footbridges. Some of the walking is on the waymarked Staffordshire Way long-distance footpath.

PARKING:
Park at the roadside in the village centre or in one of the inn car parks.

OPEN:
Fishers Pit Rare Breeds Farm is open daily from Easter to Oct and at weekends in winter. Charge.

REFRESHMENTS:
Inns in village.

THE HORN DANCE

Abbots Bromley's annual Horn Dance was first recorded by the historian Dr Plot in 1686, but probably dates from long before that. The characters represented in the dance are Robin Hood on a hobby horse, Maid Marian, a jester, a boy with a bow and arrow, two musicians, and six men wearing antlers. The six pairs of reindeer horns have been carbon-dated from Norman times, so the medieval dress worn by the 12 male dancers is relatively modern.

In Dr Plot's time the dance was performed on Christmas Day, New Year's Day and Twelfth Day; now the dancers are to be found about the village or at Blithfield Hall on the Monday after the first Sunday after 4 September. The dance is believed to have originally marked certain rights in Needwood Forest.

Locals participating in Abbots Bromley's annual Horn Dance, thought to be derived from a pagan ceremony.

THE STAFFORDSHIRE WAY

Abbots Bromley lies on the long-distance footpath that meanders through Staffordshire for 90 miles. Starting at the 1,100ft-high Mow Cop, north of Stoke-on-Trent, it heads east to Uttoxeter, before turning south to cross Cannock Chase and passing west of Wolverhampton to terminate on Kinver Edge. Part of the network of trails established by local authorities, the Countryside Commission and independent organisations over the past 20 years, the Staffordshire Way connects with Cheshire's Gritstone Trail at its northern end. Its southern end connects with the Worcestershire Way and the North Worcestershire Path.

The pyramid-roofed Butter Cross (above) marks an ancient market place. Close by, Church House (below) displays highly attractive timbers.
Brocton Coppice (right) on nearby Cannock Chase.

village, was certainly a market town in the 14th century, and butter was an important local product. It is not difficult to imagine those busy market days when the Butter Cross (or Market House) was the centre of activities.

St Nicholas's Church. Built about 1300 in the Gothic style, the church was restored by the architect G.E. Street in 1845. The classical tower dates from 1704, following the collapse of a previous spire. The reindeer horns used in the famous Horn Dance are hung in the north aisle.

Church House. A fine example of a 17th-century timber-framed town house, Church House was built in two stages in 1619 and 1659. It stands in Bagot Street, at a junction west of the Green. The Bagot Street end of the building is gabled and has decorative panelling above the ground floor. Probably many of the brick-faced houses in the village conceal similar half-timbering, covered over when brick became fashionable. Church House is now used as a meeting room for the church.

St Mary and St Anne School. Originally separate girls' public schools founded in the 1870s, the buildings on opposite sides of High Street and in several neighbouring houses became one school in 1921. The fine chapel of St Mary's, by R.H. Carpenter, rises sheer from the street. Behind it is the 18th-century house from which the great complex has grown.

The Bagot Almshouses. The row of brick-built almshouses in Bagot Street, between the Green and Church House, were constructed in 1705 by the Bagot family of Blithfield Hall. The Bagots

originally lived in a moated manor house at Bagot's Bromley, a mile north-west of the village. Richard II used to stay there while hunting in Needwood Forest, but in the 14th century the Bagot family moved to their present home, Blithfield Hall. Though outwardly of Gothic appearance, the Hall is mainly Elizabethan and occupies a fine situation 2 miles from the village, overlooking the large Blithfield Reservoir. It is not open to the public.

WALK DIRECTIONS

①

From the Goat's Head Inn walk past the Butter Cross to High Street and turn right up Hall Hill Lane. Notice the lovely village gardens and the interesting backs and gables of houses, before passing through the yard of Manor Farm. Mary, Queen of Scots spent a night under guard at Hall Hill House, when being taken for imprisonment at Fotheringhay Castle. Soon the rough lane dips, giving a distant view of Cannock Chase.

②

Fork left to a stile at the end of a short track and bear to the right along a hedge. Drop to a lower field and again follow the right-hand hedge. At the bottom of the field the path follows a wooden fence to a stile on the right, then goes left beside a hedge to a stiled footbridge over a stream. Beyond it, to the left, Mill Pond makes a charming scene, with its resident geese and the old mill.

Cross the field diagonally, passing left of a small pond, to an exit stile at the far corner. Bear right along a quiet lane, passing Seedcroft Farm, to a T-junction, and turn right.

After about 350yds join the Staffordshire Way by climbing a stile beside a gate on the right, and follow the right-hand field-edge to a gate and squeeze stile.

Keep ahead along a concreted lane and cross a bridge. The way becomes a green lane, and soon there is a stile on the left, with a footbridge beyond over Mires Brook. From it turn right, towards the church tower, and look for a stile into a hedged path leading to the churchyard. There, the Wildflower Heritage Area, beside the path, is a riot of colour in summer. Leave the churchyard by the north gate and follow a short lane ahead to emerge on Bagot Street by Church House. Turn right, past almshouses of 1705, to the Butter Cross.

To continue the walk, climb Schoolhouse Lane and pass the old school house of 1606, which hides behind a Victorian successor. Turn right along Swan Lane, and at the end bear right to a kissing gate. Cross to the far corner of a school playing field, where a shaly path leads through trees and between tennis courts.

Emerging onto Radmore Lane, turn right. Go right again at the junction with High Street to return to the Butter Cross past the St Mary and St Anne School to finish the walk.

POINTS OF INTEREST

Acton Burnell Castle. The roofless but impressive shell of the fortified manor house was built by Robert Burnell, Lord Chancellor of England and Bishop of Bath and Wells, at the end of the 13th century. Its walls and towers are 40ft high.

Ⓑ

St Mary's Church. Mainly 13th-century, with a modest Victorian tower, it is neat and bright inside, having been substantially restored in 1960 by the Lees of Virginia. There is a good, high, timber-beamed roof, a brass of Sir Nicholas Burnell (1382) and effigies of Sir Richard Lee and his wife (1591).

Ⓒ

Castle Barn. In a field beside the Castle two great stone gable ends stand over 150ft apart. They are remains of a tithe barn said to have been the scene of a Parliament called in 1283, during a visit by Edward I to the powerful Bishop Burnell.

Ⓓ

Acton Burnell Hall. The Hall, now a college, was rebuilt in its original Georgian style after a disastrous fire in 1914. The previous house had been built by the Smythes. Its large park is now mainly arable land.

INFORMATION
Length of walk: 2 miles
Approximate time: 2 hours

TERRAIN:
The bridleway to Barn Cottage is suitable for children at all times of year, and for push-chairs and wheelchairs. The latter should return by the same route, rather than attempt the footpath along arable field edges.

PARKING:
Park in the car park at Acton Burnell Castle.

OPEN:
Acton Burnell Castle is open daily. English Heritage. No charge. Wheelchair access. Langley Chapel. Admission by arrangement. Ring English Heritage on Wolverhampton 765105.

REFRESHMENTS:
The nearest inn is 1 mile W at Frodesley.

ACTON BURNELL

SHROPSHIRE

On unclassified roads midway between A49(T) and A458, 7 miles S of Shrewsbury

THE village lies amid quiet lanes, just north of the magnificent Shropshire hill country. The Romans knew the area well, for one of their roads passed only half a mile to the west. The original Lords of the Manor, the Burnells, were succeeded by the Lees of nearby Langley, whose American branch included the famous US Civil War general, Robert E Lee.

Acton Burnell Castle, built between 1284 and 1293, one of the oldest fortified houses in England.

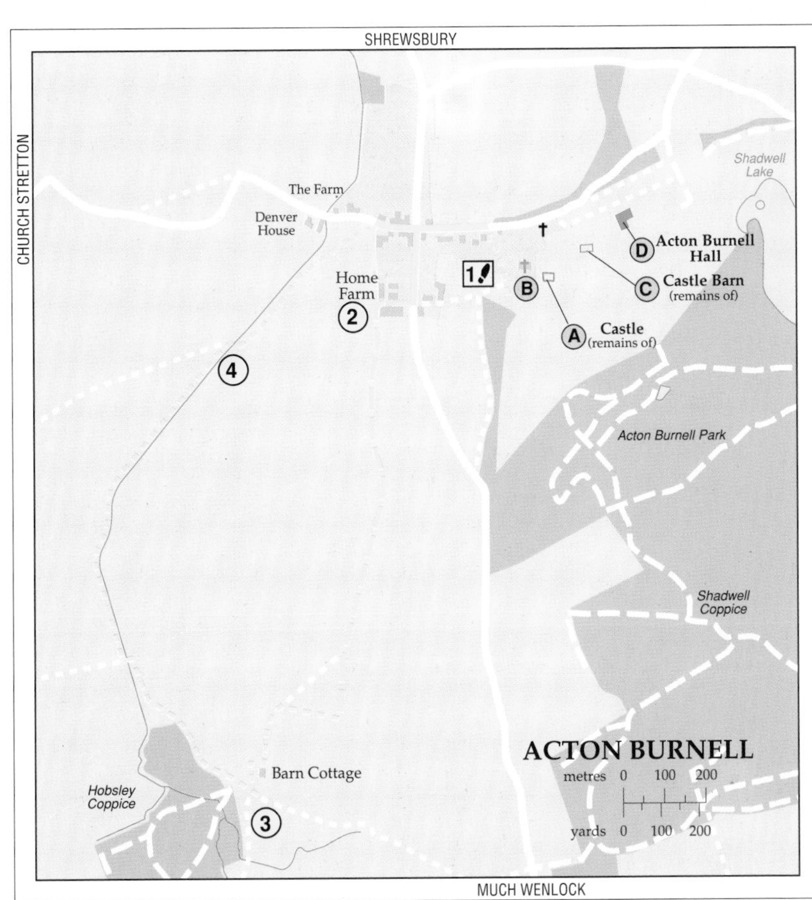

WALK DIRECTIONS

After visiting the Castle and Church, walk back to the crossroads and bear left for 150yds to a farm on your right. Enter the first farm gate on the right and walk through a covered area to join a bridleway track from a gate on the left.

②

Follow the track through several gates. There is a fine view ahead of the wooded Lodge Hill and of The Lawley, an impressive pyramid of 1,250ft. The way turns sharp right and then left to Barn Cottage, a brick- and stone ruin.

③

Turn right and descend beside Hobsley Coppice to a gate at the right-hand field corner. The footpath then follows the hedge for 100yds to a railed footbridge on the left and turns right beside the stream. Continue along the footpath for ½ mile, going past two stiles, before eventually recrossing the stream at a railed footbridge with stiles.

Follow the other side of the hedge to a gate, and in the next field veer away from it to a gate ahead. Cross a small field to a stile in the far right-hand corner and you will see a second stile on the lane beyond. Turn right towards the village crossroads, passing an attractive row of black-and-white cottages on the way, and then retrace your steps to the Castle car park.

APPLEBY MAGNA

LEICESTERSHIRE

½ mile E of the M42–A453(T)–A444 junction, 9 miles NE of Tamworth

NEAR the most westerly point of Leicestershire (neighbouring No Man's Heath, in Warwickshire, used to be the meeting point of four counties), the village of Appleby Magna lies in gently undulating countryside. Pleasantly old-fashioned, the village has attractive buildings in both brickwork and timber-framing. From the late 17th century the local squires were the Moores, the first of whom, Sir John, made his fortune in the East India Trade and became Lord Mayor of London. Their home – Appleby Hall at Appleby Parva – is now demolished, and the Moore Arms on the A444 has been renamed The Appleby Inn.

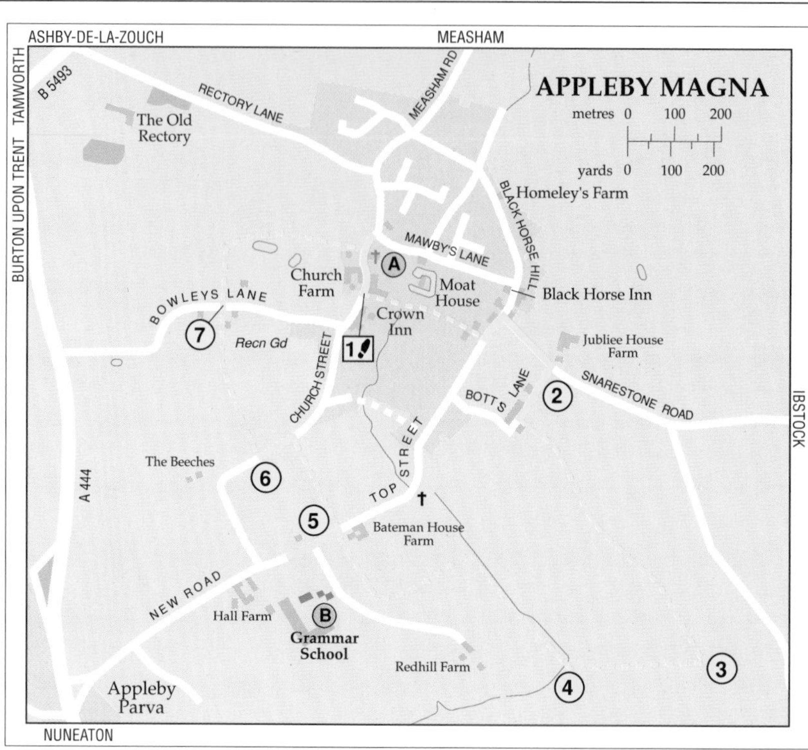

POINTS OF INTEREST

A

Parish Church. Impressive and tall-spired, dating from the 14th century, though its interior was revamped in Victorian times. There is a gallery built for the Grammar School boys, and an alabaster effigy of a knight in chain-mail and his wife. He is believed to be Sir Edward de Appleby, who fought at Crécy in 1346.

B

Grammar School. Now the Sir John Moore CE (Aided) Primary School, it was built by Sir John in the 1690s from plans drawn up by his friend Sir Christopher Wren.

The main street at Appleby Magna, showing the Crown Inn in the foreground with the parish church behind.

WALK DIRECTIONS

1

At the Crown Inn in Church Street, a fenced path leaves the car park. After crossing a railed footbridge, bear left to look at Moat House. It was originally the gatehouse of a medieval manor, and is still surrounded by a moat. Return to the fenced path and follow it to Top Street. Bear left further along Top Street, and then right along Snarestone Road.

From Snarestone Road turn right into Botts Lane. Immediately before the first house on the left a path is signed to a stile. It continues down a field edge to a stile leading into a vast sheep pasture, which may be divided by temporary fences. Aiming for the right of Upper Rectory Farm, on the skyline, cross to a yellow marker in the hedge.

Now angle back to the right across the pasture to another marker post and short plank footbridge. Please follow the rights-of-way as indicated, rather than cut across the field from the entry stile to the footbridge.

Turn right over a broader bridge to another post indicating a path along a field edge. At the next post, cross the field on your left to a post and bear right to a stile. Walk through a field to a stile on Top Street.

There is a stile opposite, but first turn left and walk along the lane a little way to admire the old Grammar School's classical facade. From the stile, cross a field to a stile on a lane and turn left to a stile by a gate.

Follow the right-hand hedge to a stile, and half-way down the next field climb a stile into a cricket field. Keep left to a kissing-gate on a lane.

Appleby Magna is as its name suggests: scenic, tranquil and charming.

INFORMATION
Length of walk: 2 miles
Approximate time: 1 hour

TERRAIN:
Suitable for children at all times of year. Not suitable for pushchairs or wheelchairs; 12 stiles and 3 footbridges. The route is indicated throughout by signposts, waymarks and yellow direction posts.

PARKING:
Park at the roadside or at an inn car park.

OPEN:
Twycross Zoo. All year except Christmas Day. Charge.

REFRESHMENTS:
Inns in village.

Almost opposite is a stile. Take the path through to the next stile and bear right, past a marker post, to another stile. Cross to a kissing-gate, from which an enclosed path emerges opposite the church. Turn left for a few yards to the corner of Mawby's Lane, before returning past the church to the Crown Inn.

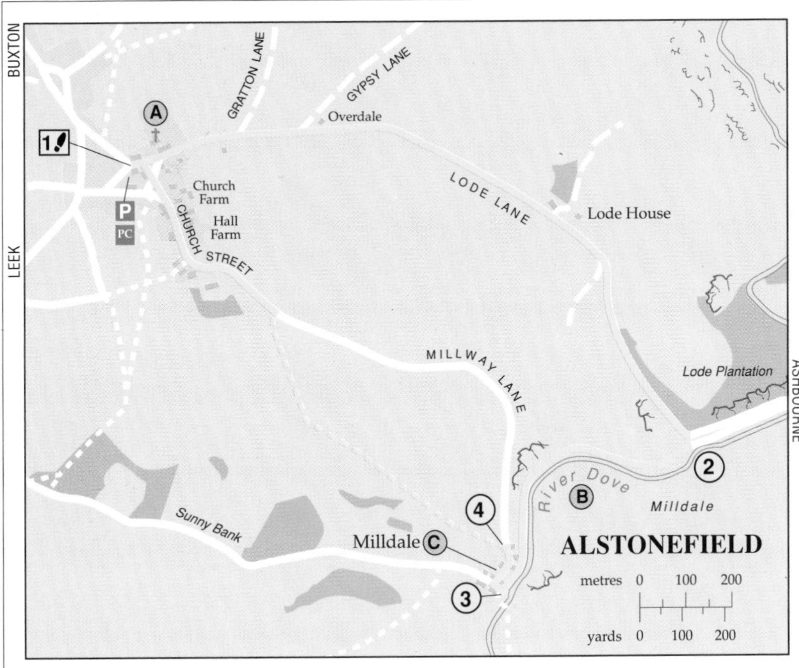

ALSTONEFIELD

STAFFORDSHIRE

On unclassified roads, 1½ miles W of A515, 6 miles N of Ashbourne

AT 900ft above sea-level Alstonefield stands high in the southern Peak District, between the rivers Manifold and Dove. It is just within the Midland county of Staffordshire – by a mile or so, for the Dove marks the county boundary – yet the bare, stone-walled fields tell us that, in character at least, we are already in the north of England, at the southern tip of the Pennine chain.

Two small triangular greens near the George Inn are the focal points of Alstonefield's straggling settlement of old stone-built houses. For two centuries from 1308 a market was held here. Later, the Cottons of Beresford Hall (now demolished) were the squires. Best remembered of this family is Charles, the bosom friend of Izaak Walton, who wrote *The Compleat Angler* in 1653. Hall Farm of 1587 – in Church Street, which leads to St Peter's Church – was once the rectory.

INFORMATION
Length of walk: 2 miles
Approximate time: 2 hours

TERRAIN:
Suitable for children at all times. Not suitable for pushchairs or wheelchairs. There is a steep climb up the field path from Milldale.

PARKING:
Use the car park on the Hulme End and Hartington road.

OPEN:
Orchard Stable at Milldale (National Trust). Daily. No charge.

REFRESHMENTS:
The George Inn (bar meals), and The Old Post Office (café) – both in village. Polly's Cottage, Milldale.

WALK DIRECTIONS

1

From the car park, turn right and follow the road left. You pass two left forks and the road (now Lode Lane) passes Lode House and descends to the River Dove.

2

Turn sharp right and walk alongside the river for ½ mile to the hamlet of Milldale.

3

At Milldale turn right and immediately right again, past the door of Polly's Cottage (refreshments), to a stepped path on the left, just beyond a telephone box. By keeping to the unmade road, Millway Lane, the steeper climb can be avoided.

4

When the enclosed path emerges through a squeeze stile into a field, bear left up to the next stile and climb steeply to a stile at a top right field corner. The path takes a line well left of Alstonefield's church tower to reach another corner stile. Here, arrowed to the right, it crosses to a stile, by a gate, on Millway Lane. Turn left to return to Alstonefield.

The Victorian village pump (below).

POINTS OF INTEREST

A

St Peter's Church. A building of great interest, fully described in the free guide leaflet provided. The tower is probably late Tudor, the nave and chancel are of the Decorated and Perpendicular periods, the chancel arch is Norman, and fragments of Saxon crosses are built into the Victorian porch. Box pews dominate the nave, and there is a great carved pulpit of 1637. Beside it is

Part of the tree-shaded village green forming the centre of Alstonefield.

the Cotton family pew. As the guide leaflet confesses, its pea-green colour is not to everyone's taste, but Charles Cotton's association with Izaak Walton earns it a place in literary history.

Outside the church, on each side of the East window, the date 1590 and the initials L.B. (Laurence Beresford) refer to the rebuilding of the chancel. The churchyard claims one of the earliest gravestones in England - that of Anne Green, who died in 1518. It stands near the wall, opposite the porch, as does that of Margaret Barclay, who died aged 107 in 1731. Unfortunately the latter is now so badly weathered that it cannot be deciphered.

Ⓑ

River Dove. Though the Dove rises high on Axe Edge, near Buxton, and meanders south for 45 miles to its lowland rendezvous with the Trent, near Burton-upon-Trent, it is the 7 miles downstream from Hartington that have made it famous. Beresford Dale, Wolfscote Dale and Dovedale (the last being the stretch south of Milldale) constitute prime, yet easy, walking country through dramatic limestone scenery, a small sample of which is offered by the described here.

Milldale. Squeezed in beside the Dove, the tiny hamlet of Milldale is at the head of Dovedale, $2^1/_2$ miles upstream from the stepping stones that mark the southern end of the best known of the Derbyshire dales. Here you can cross the river - and change counties - by Viator's Bridge. The old packhorse bridge gets its name from the character in *The Compleat Angler* who described it as being 'not two fingers broad.' A nearby barn, the National Trust-owned Orchard Stable displays local information, and there are refreshments, toilets, and a restored sheepwash in the river.

A tranquil stretch of the River Dove (left) between Alstonefield and the hamlet of Milldale (below left). The presence of limestone rock is evident everywhere, both in building materials and landscape.

PEAKS OF CONTRAST

The Peak District is where the North begins, as the high Pennines loom up above the gentler landscape of the Midlands. Set between the two great urban and industrial complexes of Manchester and Sheffield, the national park covers 542 square miles of farming country and moorland, largely in Derbyshire and Staffordshire. Within it are the two contrasting landscapes of the White Peak and the Dark Peak. The White Peak, to the south, is a country of deep valleys and green pastures criss-crossed by drystone walls. To the north lies the harsher, wilder area of the Dark Peak, broken by sheer walls of gritstone rock, with peaty grouse moors studded with isolated tors.

Although much of the landscape is meadow and moor, there are vast limestone quarries in the White Peak. The most celebrated of the park's rivers is the Dove, which rises north of Hartington in the White Peak and flows south through a famously scenic gorge. The Derwent rises in the north, among the solitary moors of Bleaklow, and runs south through three enormous reservoirs and an agreeable wooded valley to pass Chatsworth. East of Buxton is the delightful valley of the Wye, which flows east to join the Derwent.

The Valley of the River Dove with Thorpe Cloud, centre.

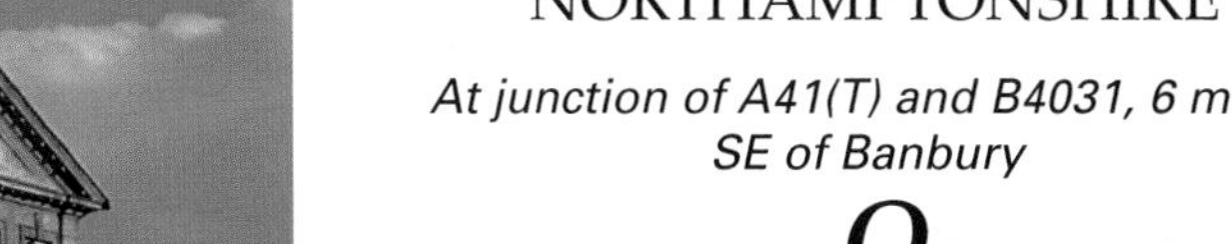

AYNHO
NORTHAMPTONSHIRE

At junction of A41(T) and B4031, 6 miles SE of Banbury

OCCUPYING a hilltop position above the River Cherwell, Aynho, the most southerly village in Northamptonshire, is dominated entirely by buildings of local limestone. To the west of the village the Oxford Canal and the railway lines from Oxford and Bicester to Banbury are channelled along the Cherwell valley; to them has now been added the M40 motorway.

There is a great deal of beauty and interest in the village, with its steep, narrow lanes and network of alleyways. Inexpensive but information-packed guidebooks to the parish church and the village, produced by local school children, are on sale in the church.

St Michael's Church was altered in 1723 to match the Grecian style of Park House.

WALK DIRECTIONS

Follow the main road west, towards Banbury, and turn first left to the church. Return to the A41(T) and follow it eastwards, towards Buckingham, passing the former Grammar School.

At a crossroads take the lane to the left, and at the T-junction with Charlton Road turn left again. Enter a recreation ground at a gateway on the left and cross diagonally to an exit on Portway.

Turn left and immediately right along a fenced path. An old right-of-way known as the Black Path, it runs through new housing to Butts Close.

Turn right past Barn House (formerly a malthouse) to Charlton Road. There is a fine view over the Cherwell valley, taking in Banbury, Edge Hill and the Cotswolds.

INFORMATION
Length of walk: 1mile
Approximate time: 1½ hours

TERRAIN:
Suitable for children at all times of year, and for pushchairs or wheelchairs. There are no stiles on this walk.

PARKING:
Park in the village near the Cartwright Arms, or in The Square, which lies to the left of the inn. There is also unlimited parking in Charlton Road.

OPEN:
Park House open Wed-Thu, 2.00-5pm, May-Sep.

REFRESHMENTS:
The Cartwright Arms at Aynho.

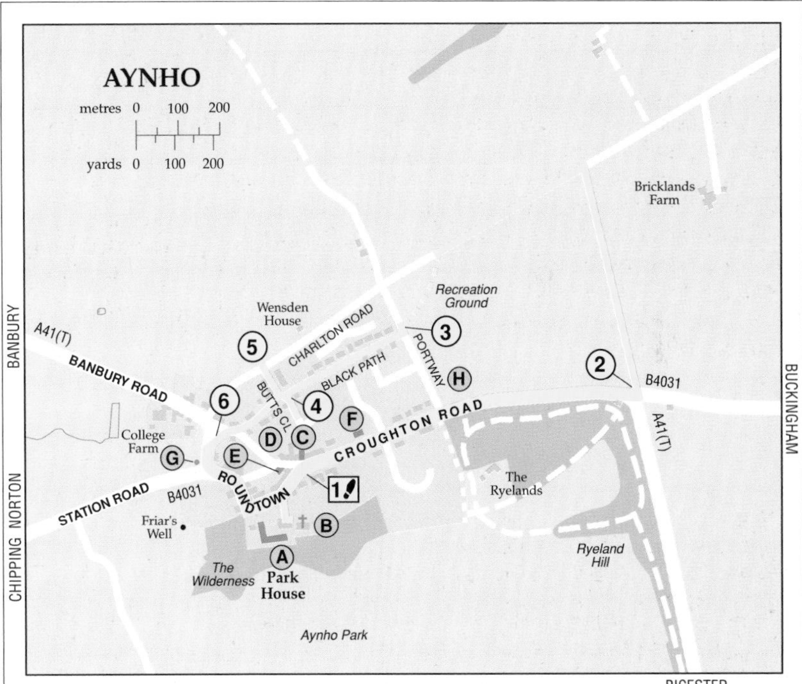

(5)

Go back along Butts Close and turn left beyond the Black Path to see the eight two-storied almshouses of 1822. They were built by an Oxford glazier, John Baker, to accommodate '4 poor men and 4 poor women'. The beneficiaries were required to attend church twice on Sundays. Turn back again and bear left into Blacksmiths Hill, where the village's oldest cottages stand to the right. Pass Skittle Alley and keep left to the A41(T) junction.

(6)

Turn left, passing the stocks on a green. There is a view of Park House from the main road, which leads back to the Cartwright Arms.

POINTS OF INTEREST

Park House. The great mansion beside the main street was the home of the Cartwrights from 1616 until 1954, when the death of the squire and his son in a car accident brought the line to an end. Coincidentally, Richard was the Christian name of both the first and last squires, the former being a barrister of the Inner Temple. Though burned down by retreating Royalist troops after the Battle

APRICOTS

Legend has it that at one time villagers paid their rent to Park House in the form of apricots. The introduction of guttering and paving stones meant that many of the once-thriving apricot trees died from lack of water, but others survive in the village, or have been introduced as replacements, and some are watered by drainpipes. The best examples are to be seen outside a house on the main road, opposite Park House.

of Naseby in 1645, the house was rebuilt in the Classical style and was added to in the 18th and 19th centuries. It is now divided into apartments. The great landscape architect, Capability Brown, designed Aynho Park, south of the house, in 1761-3. It is possible to get a glimpse of the former deer park by following an enclosed footpath south from the A41(T), opposite Portway.

Ⓑ

St Michael's Church. An uncommon building that looks more like a minor stately home, for added to the 14th-century tower, in place of the original nave and chancel, are large 18th-century ones designed in the Grecian style to match Park House. The architect was locally-born Edward Wing, who was also responsible for several London churches. When, in the 17th century, there were two candidates for the post of village rector, each was requested to preach a sermon, following which a vote was taken. Later, when asked the result, the successful candidate replied that he had got the Ay and his opponent the No – a neat pun on the village name.

The Cartwright Arms. The stone-built pub by the green at the centre of the village was once a coaching inn on the London to Birmingham stagecoach route.

The Square. West of the inn is the charming little village Square, surrounded by cottages and old houses, with intriguing byways leading off. Two of them are called Little Land and Hollow Way. The latter, as its name suggests, has been gouged deep by centuries of use. From it the narrow Skittle Alley climbs to Blacksmiths Hill. Opposite the Alley, the former village bakehouse still has an insurance plate on its wall, issued as evidence of premium payment in the days when fire brigades were run by insurance companies. At the far end of Little Lane is a house with a window blocked up to avoid the Window Tax (1697-1851). Other village names that take us back in time are The Glebe (former church land off the main road), The Butts (beside The Black Path), and Butts Close. Archers practised in the Butts in medieval times.

The Village Hall. The Hall, opposite the inn, was built in 1920 with stones from the ruined plague house that had stood since medieval times in Pesthouse Wood, a mile east of the village. Villagers suffering from plague were isolated in the wood and food was left for them daily at the boundary fence.

The Grammar School. A Jacobean stone-built house, now a private residence, it stands behind pollarded limes on the main road, east of the Cartwright Arms. Note the mullioned windows and sun-dial.

The Stocks. On the site of the former village green at the junction of A41(T) and B4031 are the stocks which were erected about 1700 and remained in use until the mid-19th century. The site of the original village is behind the nearby stone wall.

Portway. This road at the eastern edge of the village is part of a Romano-British track from Borough Hill, near Daventry, to Alcester, near Bicester.

Apricot trees (top left) are associated with Aynho. The Cartwright Arms (left) is an old coaching inn.

BERKSWELL
WEST MIDLANDS

On unclassified roads, 1 mile E of A452, 2½ miles S of A45(T), 6 miles W of Coventry

THIS former Warwickshire village, now in the West Midlands, is one of the loveliest in the area. It lies in pleasant, rolling countryside between Birmingham and Coventry, and visitors will find it difficult to believe that the latter's western suburbs are only two miles away. The Heart of England Way long-distance footpath, linking Cannock Chase with Chipping Campden, runs through Berkswell.

Compact, but full of many interesting features, the village is gathered around a little green, near the well where the monks who brought Christianity to the village baptised their first converts. Berkswell has red-roofed white cottages with weathered timbers. one of its most delightful buildings is the Bear Inn. Church, almshouses, museum and inn are all within a short walk of each other.

INFORMATION
Length of walk:
2½ miles
Approximate time:
2½ hours

TERRAIN:
Suitable for children at all times of year, though the path past Lavender Hall Farm can be overgrown in summer. Not suitable for pushchairs or wheelchairs. Eleven stiles, one footbridge and a long wooden causeway. The return path to the village is part of the waymarked Heart of England Way long-distance footpath. The walk can be reduced to two miles by following Lavender Hall Lane from Berkswell and re-joining the longer route at Park Lane.

PARKING:
Park beside Meriden Road, north of the Bear Inn.

OPEN:
Berkswell Village Museum is open on Easter Sun and Mon, and from May-Sep on Sun and Bank Hols., 2.30-6pm.
Berkswell Windmill is open Sun, May-Sep, 2.30-5.30pm. Charge.

REFRESHMENTS:
The Bear Inn, Meriden Road, Berkswell; afternoon teas on summer Sundays in the Reading Room, Meriden Road, Berkswell.

The Parish Church of St John the Baptist at Berkswell boasts an unusual gabled and timbered porch (above). Dating from the 16th century, it is two-storeyed, with a priest's room above. This is reached by an outer stair.

WALK DIRECTIONS

Follow Lavender Hall Lane, opposite the inn, to the village green. Fork right at the green and turn left to pass the well and a gate to the museum. Cross Lavender Hall Lane to a path through an archway, left of bungalows, leading to a stile. (To shorten the walk by ½ mile, turn right along the lane and re-join the longer route at Park Lane.)

2

Continue to a stile and gate, and ascend left of a hedge, passing another stile and gate before crossing to its other side at a stile. At the end of the field turn right to a stile and gate, and climb to Ram Hall Farm.

Pass a stile and gate, but keep left of the next gate to a fence stile opposite the house. Follow the drive out to Baulk Lane and turn right for ¼ mile.

Just before a bridge is a stile on the right. Follow the left-hand field-edge to a railed footbridge and cross to a stile at the far right corner of the next field. The path runs left of a hedge and, from a stile, passes right of Lavender Hall Farm to a lane. Turn left to see the long, timber-framed Tudor barn. Its roof was destroyed on Bonfire Night in 1983, but has since been restored.

Turn back along the lane and enter Park Lane on your left. At the end of a long spinney turn right through a kissing-gate, waymarked for the Heart of England Way. Leaving the trees at a gate, descend the left side of a sloping field to a copse by the great lake of Berkswell Hall, which stands in rising parkland beyond. The Hall is noted for its rhododendrons and is best seen across the lake, from a footpath on the left.

Go through a kissing-gate to the right of a track and continue to a wooden causeway, beside a marshy stream, leading to a stile. After two more gates, with woodland between, re-enter Berkswell through the churchyard.

FACING THE MUSIC

Stocks and whipping posts are mute reminders of a time when punishment for fairly minor offences was swift and public. An unpopular character in the stocks would be pelted with filth and missiles, and left half-dead. For the night-time drunk and disorderly there was often a village lock-up, basically a single stone cell, to hold them secure until the morning.

Villagers had effective unofficial methods of punishment, too, from the cold shoulder to 'rough music', when a crowd gathered outside an offender's house to make the night hideous with catcalls, clashing saucepans and the blowing of whistles. It occurred especially in cases of adultery or incest, and the victim's humiliation was deeply felt.

In Victorian times the new national police force replaced the village constables. Fines and prison sentences became the norm, and the countryside crime rate fell. The old ways of punishment were abandoned.

The five-holed stocks on the green were said to have been built for a one-legged man and his two companions.

POINTS OF INTEREST

Parish Church of St John the Baptist. Dating from the 12th century and among the most beautiful in the Midlands, it has a double crypt, now restored, and a 16th-century timber-framed vestry in a former priest's room over the porch. On entering the church, look out for the carved mice – the trademark of Robert Thompson, a wood carver from Kilburn in Yorkshire, who has done much modern work here. There are eleven of them scattered about the building. In the churchyard, there is a symbolic broken pillar above the grave of James Owen, whose head was cut off in a sawmill accident in 1898. The grave of James Weetman, who died in 1840 'of a broken heart', was prominently situated near the porch, so that the young lady who had trifled with his affections could not miss it. Carved on another gravestone are two loaves, 21 eggs and 18 rashers of bacon - the grave's occupant is believed to have died of over-eating!

The Village Green. Enclosed by cottages, a shop with Georgian windows and a row of Victorian almshouses, the green is famous for its set of five-holed stocks. They are said to have been built for a one-legged reprobate and his two boon companions, though cynics maintain that part of the original woodwork has rotted away. Walkers can fittingly end their day by resting on a bench installed 'In memory of Jack Schatz (E.J.S.) Author, Poet and Rambler, 1907-80', who for 25 years wrote a *Weekend Walk* column in the *Birmingham Evening Mail.*

The Well House. A 17th-century former rectory, glimpsed through ornamental gates, the Well House was the childhood home of Maud Watson, the first Wimbledon Ladies' Champion in 1884 (the runner-up was her sister Lilian). Maud developed her game against the Cambridge undergraduates who came to study mathematics with her father. There were thirteen competitors that first year, and it is recorded that the champion wore a white ankle-length skirt with a small bustle, a long-sleeved silk jersey blouse and a sailor hat. Her prize was a silver flower basket worth 20 guineas. She is buried in the parish churchyard, near the nave of the church.

Berkswell Village Museum. A small local museum, behind the almshouses, run by volunteers. The collection includes farm implements, household items and many church and parish documents.

The Bear Inn. Formerly the Bear & Ragged Staff, taking its name from the emblem of the Earl of Warwick, who was Lord of the Manor. The 16th-century building has a Russian cannon standing outside, captured during the Crimean War in 1855 by Captain Arthur Wilmot, whose family lived at Berkswell Hall.

Berkswell derives its name from this 16ft-square tank walled with stone, with clear water running inside.

BOURN

CAMBRIDGESHIRE

Off B1046, 7m W of Cambridge

NOWADAYS Bourn is probably best known for Bourn Hall Clinic, where pioneering work with test-tube babies takes place. The Hall itself, an Elizabethan mansion, was built on the site of a former castle built by the Sheriff of Cambridgeshire after the Norman conquest. It has, however, been added to and altered, first in Jacobean style, and later Victorian, so that its Tudor aspects now appear more like quaint imitations than the real thing!

Outside the village, near Caxton, is Bourn Windmill, the oldest windmill in the country. Dating from 1636, it is a post mill, a wooden structure clad in dark weather-boarding, with the entire mill – sails and machinery – revolving on a central post. There is a small car park, the entrance to which is very easily missed in the hedge lining the Caxton-Bourn road, and a short walk down one side and to the back of a private dwelling brings you to the windmill.

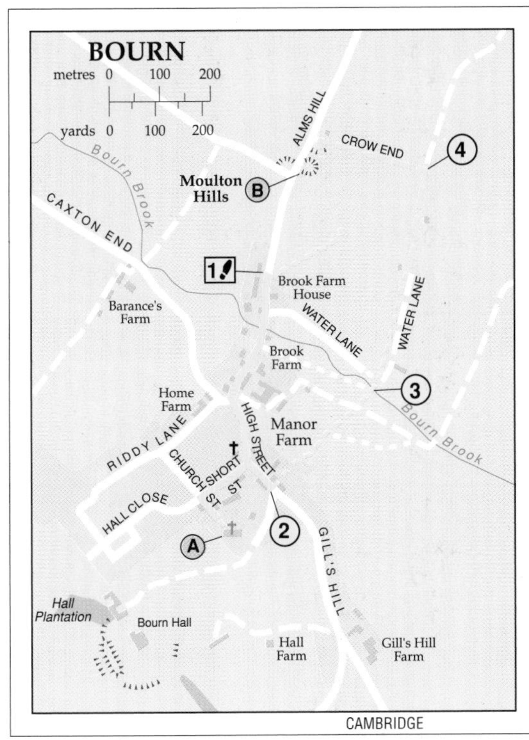

INFORMATION
Length of walk: 1¼ miles
Approximate time: 1 hour

TERRAIN:
Route includes crossing open fields and several stiles, so appropriate footwear is advisable. Not suitable for pushchairs or wheelchairs.

PARKING:
Bourn is not the easiest village in which to park, so park carefully where you can.

OPEN:
Bourn Mill. Accessible for external viewing any time of year. Inside Apr-Sep last Sun in the month 2-5pm. Charge.

REFRESHMENTS:
Inns in the village.

WALK DIRECTIONS

Turn right from the Duke of Wellington pub car park on to Alms Hill. Walk along the road, past Riddy Lane. The church can be reached by walking up Short Street, to the right. After visiting the church, continue along High Street.

At the Golden Lion pub, turn left on to a footpath, sign-posted for Crow End and Caldecote, and almost immediately, cross over a stile. Follow the path to another stile bearing a yellow waymark arrow. Continue over a field to another stile, and cross the drive which goes to Manor Farm.

Cross the footbridge (a path goes down beside it as well, as the stream is nothing more than a trickle). A few yards on, another stream is crossed by a single railway sleeper, followed by a stile bearing two yellow arrows. Once over the stile, keeping to the right-hand side of a large field, head towards a thatched cottage. Here, in the far corner of the field, cross over two stiles and a footbridge, and continue along a track until you reach a junction marked by a Ramblers Association post bearing two red waymark arrows.

Go left on to Crow End, a track lined on either side with hedges. Just before the track emerges on to the road (Alms Hill), take a sharp left over a stile. Follow the direction of the yellow arrow past Moulton Hills, keeping to the left of them. The arrow on the next stile which crosses the fence points out the way back towards Alms Hill. Continue to the gate at the corner of the field, which is directly opposite the Duke of Wellington.

POINTS OF INTEREST

Bourn Church. The large cruciform church of Saints Helen and Mary is Norman and early English. It has some elegant arcading around the belfry, and inside, there are imposing arches in the nave, and a fine hammerbeam roof in the chancel. The floor of the tower is decorated with an unusual maze constructed in red and blue tiles, rare in English churches, although a recent example can be found in Ely Cathedral.

Moulton Hills. Rather small for hills, but significant none the less. They are three tumuli, two passed by the route, the third on the other side of the road heading into the village. Excavations of two have revealed remains dating from the Roman occupation, including pottery fragments and a coin, with the intriguing complication of one mound covering an earlier barrow containing Romano-British remains.

Bourn's post windmill, bought and sold by deed in 1636, was restored 300 years later.

BREDON

HEREFORD AND WORCESTER

On B4080, 3½m NE of Tewkesbury

THE village lies in beautiful countryside on a curve of the broad River Avon and to the south-west of Bredon Hill, a domed outlier of the Cotswolds almost 1,000ft high. Church, Rectory, Manor House and an ancient stone barn form its nucleus. There is much else of interest, though the village turns its back on the river, which can only be reached by descending Dock Lane.

POINTS OF INTEREST

Ⓐ

The Reed Almshouses. The eight homes provided by the Reed family in 1696 for 'Bredon residents of limited means' stand at the junction of Church Street and High Street. The picturesque buildings are one-storeyed, with an attic above, and have projecting wings on the Church Street side, where there is a pleasant little garden. The rent for 1990 was £15 per week.

Bredon Barn. Though it has traditionally been called a tithe barn, the huge stone outbuilding at Manor Farm, 132ft long by 44ft wide, is believed by its owners, the National Trust, to have been a manorial barn (i.e. a barn belonging to the manor, rather than to the church). Built by the Bishop of Worcester about 1350, it was acquired by the Trust in 1951. Fire destroyed much of the timber-work in 1980, but it has been fully restored. An unusual feature is the Reeve's Chamber, reached by an outside staircase.

Looking down the village street towards the church from the 16th-century Fox and Hounds.

Rectory House. This Elizabethan stone building was the summer residence of the Bishops of Worcester. One of them, John Prideaux, died there in poverty in 1650, 'after being driven from his See in the Great Rebellion'. The two small figures silhouetted on the roof are Charles II and Oliver Cromwell. According to tradition, if they ever meet it will mean the end of the world.

Ⓓ

St Giles's Church. A slender 160ft-high spire signals the presence of the large church of Norman origin, standing in a spacious green churchyard. Above the Norman porch is a room that, when discovered in 1911, appeared to have been mysteriously sealed up without being completed. The sanctuary is noted for its early 14th-century heraldic tiles which represent the arms of many noble English families. Also in the sanctuary is a 14th-century coffin lid, and the south aisle contains the enormous monument to Sir Giles and Lady Reed (1611). A large panel in the nave details the bequest of William Hancocke, who died in 1718. (The Hancocke Endowed School stands on the north side of Church Street.)

INFORMATION
Length of walk:
1¾ miles
Approximate time:
2 hours

TERRAIN:
Suitable for children at all times of year; only suitable for pushchairs in dry weather; not suitable for wheelchairs.

PARKING:
Free car parks at junction of B4079 and B4080, and near River Avon in Dock Lane.

OPEN:
Bredon Barn (NT). Mar-Nov. Wed-Thu, Sat-Sun 10am-6pm or sunset. Charge.

REFRESHMENTS:
Inns, shop and café.

WALK DIRECTIONS

Start at the Dock Lane car park. From the neighbouring grassy area a broad and pleasant sweep of the River Avon is visible, though tranquillity is somewhat marred by the noise and movement of the M5 less than ½ a mile away. Turn towards the village, but almost immediately climb to the left up a signed path between houses, leading to Back Lane. Keep ahead to Church Street, emerging between the Fox and Hounds, a lovely thatched inn dating from the 16th century, and the Hancocke Endowed School.

②

Bear left, passing buildings in stone and half-timbering, to the junction with Back Lane, opposite the Reed Almshouses. Follow Back Lane to Perwell Close and take the public footpath signed on the left from a gate and stiles. It descends, then rises to an old stone-stepped stile, from which you cross a field diagonally to reach the corner of an apple-orchard.

The path turns right and crosses a stone railway bridge to the B4080. Follow the grass verge to the right for 70yds and go through a wooden squeeze stile on your left to a wooded area. Cross a little brook beside a culvert and skirt the edge of playing fields to a car park.

Re-enter the village by turning right along the B4080 and pass the Royal Oak Inn of 1761 to the Reed Almshouses at the High Street–Church Street fork. Bear left along High Street, passing The Old Cider House, where there are stables visible at the rear. On a small green to the right a curious stone pillar of 1808 indicates the mileages to six nearby towns.

Just beyond the pillar enter the drive of Manor Farm to visit Bredon Barn. Return to the pillar and follow the unsurfaced track from it to the churchyard. Rectory House can be seen over the wall and between the church and the barn is the 18th-century Manor House. After visiting the church go out on the far side, turn left past the Old Mansion House, built in the 17th century on the site of a monastery, and descend Dock Lane to the car park.

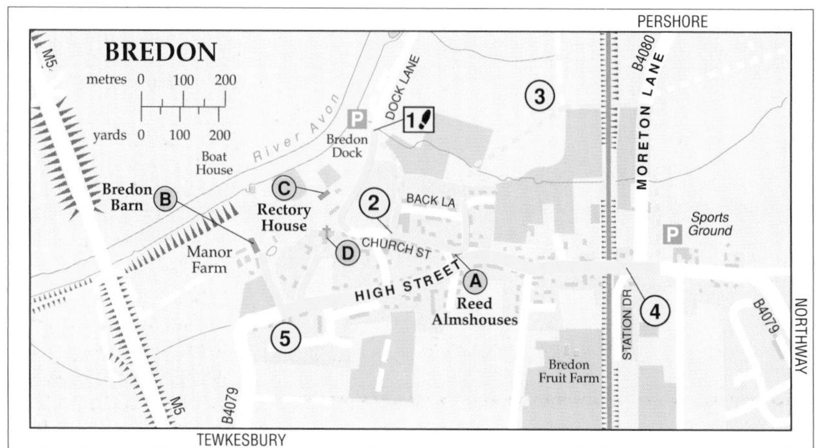

BURNHAM THORPE

BURNHAM THORPE

NORFOLK

Off A149, 6m W of Wells-next-the-Sea

THERE are no less than six British villages with the prefix of Burnham. Whilst not the biggest (this is Burnham Market, 1 mile to the north-west) Burnham Thorpe is perhaps the most significant, as it was Nelson's birthplace. It is thought that the village originally lay closer to the church. Hummocks in the church meadow could indicate the original site, and it has been suggested that an outbreak of plague frightened the villagers into burning the houses and moving further away.

To the east of Burnham Thorpe is Holkham Hall, the Norfolk home of the Earls of Leicester. A magnificent Palladian stately home, it was built between 1734 and 1759 by William Kent. During its early years, the estate was something of a wasteland, until it was inherited by Thomas Coke. He knew nothing about farming, but utilising some of the ideas of 'Turnip' Townsend, he made a success of it, and inspired an agricultural revolution in the process. Just to the north of the park is the pine-fringed expanse of Holkham Dunes Nature Reserve, the largest National Nature Reserve in England.

WALK DIRECTIONS

Start from the Lord Nelson public house, turning right from the car park. Walk down Walsingham Road, with the playing field off to your left.

At the first junction, take the left-hand turning signposted for Burnham Overy Staithe. Here, too, is the village sign, commemorating Nelson, and presented on behalf of the Royal Navy in 1975. Pass the end of the playing field and the turning for the church, continuing up the hill on Lowe's Lane.

At the junction at the top, turn left, on to Mill Lane and carry on until the road is crossed by a stony track.

Go left here, catching a glimpse of the church tower. Follow the track down the hill, where, as you round the bend, the decorative flint-work of the east façade of the church is revealed in all its glory.

After visiting the church, leave the churchyard by the exit just past the war memorial, and join the surfaced lane curving round to the left.

Turn left where the road forks, and left again on to Walsingham Road. The Lord Nelson is on the right.

The church, some distance from the village, was restored in the 1800s.

HORATIO NELSON

Lord Horatio Nelson was born in Burnham Thorpe in 1758, the son of a rector. He was educated in North Walsham and Norwich and joined HMS *Raisonable* in 1771. Just seven years later he was semi-retired, living on half-pay in Burnham Thorpe with his wife, Fanny. For the next five years, he farmed some 30 acres of glebe land, and took time off to visit his various relatives around the county.

When war broke out in 1793, Nelson was appointed Captain of HMS *Agamemnon*, and a good number of his crew were Norfolk men. The next 12 years saw Nelson rise to become Britain's greatest sailor; inflicting defeats on Napoleon at the Battle of the Nile, the Battle of Copenhagen, and the Battle of Trafalgar, where in 1805 he lost his life.

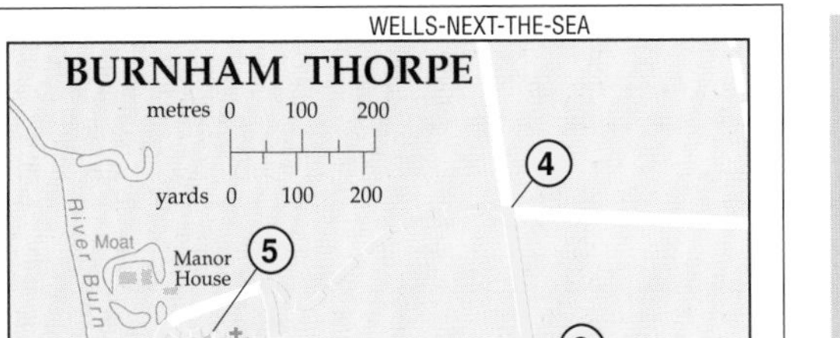

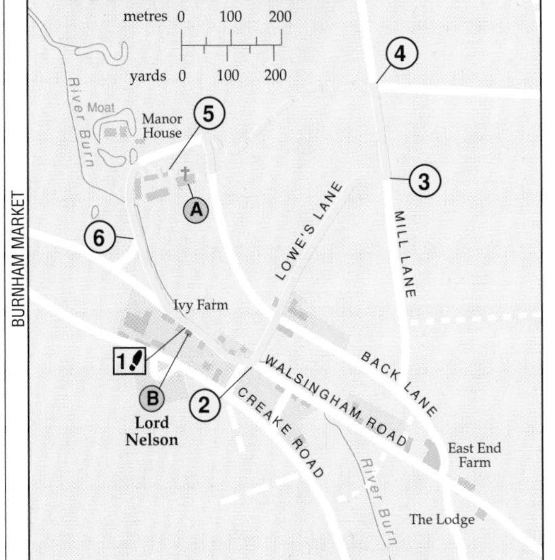

INFORMATION
Length of walk: 1 mile
Approximate time: 45 mins

TERRAIN:
Mostly surfaced road, with one stretch of stony track. Suitable for pushchairs and wheelchairs, except perhaps for the stony track between points 4 and 5.

PARKING:
Park carefully where you can, close to the Lord Nelson if possible. The walk starts at the pub.

OPEN:
Holkham Hall. Jun-Sep Sun-Thu. 11.30am-5pm. Charge.

REFRESHMENTS:
Lord Nelson public house.

POINTS OF INTEREST

All Saints' Church. The 13th-century church contains several mementoes of Lord Nelson. The rood beam and lectern are made from timbers taken from HMS *Victory*, Nelson's flagship at Trafalgar, and an exhibition about the man can be found in the south aisle. Nelson's parents, Edmund and Catherine, are buried in the chancel, and above is a bust of their famous son. Nelson himself expected to be buried here, but in fact lies in St Paul's Cathedral in London.

Lord Nelson Public House. In Nelson's day, it was 'The Plough', and he held a party here before boarding HMS *Agamemnon*, and setting off for the Mediterranean in 1793. Inside, little has changed over the last 200 years. The walls are covered with Nelson pictures and memorabilia. The bar is a small room with benches lining the walls, and the landlord fetches each drink from the cellar while entertaining the clientele with his encyclopaedic knowledge of the pub's most famous customer.

CASTLE ACRE

NORFOLK

Off A1065, 4m N of Swaffham

ALTHOUGH it takes its name from the once-important Norman castle, of which very little now remains, Castle Acre is better known for its ruined Cluniac priory.

Arguably one of the most imposing villages in Norfolk, Castle Acre was originally at the head of navigation on the River Nar, and the site of an important ford across the river. Though the Nar is now nothing more than a stream, it is possible to gauge the size of the castle on learning that much of the village stands within the bailey.

Today, Castle Acre is a popular overnight halt for walkers on the Peddars Way. It is the only village of any size on the route, and for anyone who has attempted the 26 miles from Knettishall in one day, the final stretch up Bailey Street can be the most tiring, but also the most cheering!

INFORMATION
Length of walk:
1 mile
Approximate time:
1 hour

TERRAIN:
Surfaced roads other than one short stretch of track leading to the castle. Suitable for pushchairs and wheelchairs with the exception of the castle ruins.

PARKING:
Park carefully where you can as there is no car park.

OPEN:
Castle Acre Priory (EH). Daily Easter-Sep 10am-6pm, Oct-Maundy Thu Tue-Sun 10am-4pm. Charge.

REFRESHMENTS:
Village inns.

The Priory ruins, set among paths and lawns. The Prior's Lodging is the only part still roofed.

POINTS OF INTEREST

Ostrich Inn. An 18th-century coaching inn, the Ostrich is a well-known stopping point for walkers on the Peddars Way. The interior displays fine beamed ceilings and huge fireplaces.

St James's Church. Set in a spacious churchyard, much of the church is in the Perpendicular style, although there are parts which date back to the early 1300s. The 13th-century font has a very tall cover, made in the 15th century and the wooden wine-glass shaped pulpit is painted with the four Latin Fathers of the Church.

Priory Ruins. William de Warenne, the son-in-law of William the Conqueror, was so impressed by the abbey at Cluny in Burgundy, that he founded a Cluniac priory at his main castle in Lewes. The priory at Castle Acre was founded in 1090 as a daughter priory of the one at Lewes, but it later became independent. Whilst the priory suffered from the ravages of the Dissolution, the west front, with its elaborately ornamented blind arcading, gives perhaps the best impression of the former magnificence of the building.

Castle. Built shortly after the Conquest by William de Warenne, the castle was occupied by his family until the line died out in the 14th century. What remains now is the outline of the walls, some very impressive earthworks, and the only building which has survived intact, a 13th-century gateway with pointed arch and towers on either side.

WALK DIRECTIONS

①

Start from Stocks Green, with the church as your first stop.

After visiting the church, rejoin Priory Road, carrying on to the left-hand turning which leads to the priory.

After visiting the Priory, return towards the village along Priory Road, and turn right on to South Acre Road. Continue down the hill.

Turn left in to Chimney Street, and at the next T-junction, turn left into Blind Lane and then left again into Bailey Street.

Walk up the hill. Turn right at the old chapel, and follow the track to the castle.

Return along the same route, and continue up Bailey Street, through the Bailey Gate, and left on to Stocks Green.

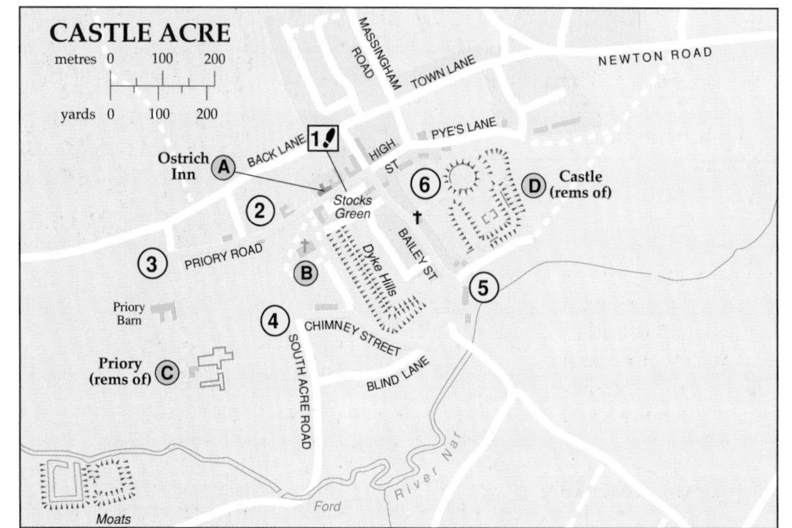

PEDDARS WAY

A pre-Roman track, the Peddars Way is now an ancient monument, and one of the few on which visitors are encouraged to walk! What exists today is by no means complete, but the 50 miles or so which run from Knettishall Heath on the Suffolk border, to Holme-next-the-Sea on the North Norfolk coast follow the line of the original track fairly closely except where recent development has obscured it.

The Peddars Way is now a National Trail, officially opened by HRH the Prince of Wales in 1986, and funded mainly by the Countryside Commission. It joins up with the Norfolk Coast Path to provide a 93-mile long-distance walk taking in a wide spread of rural and coastal scenery.

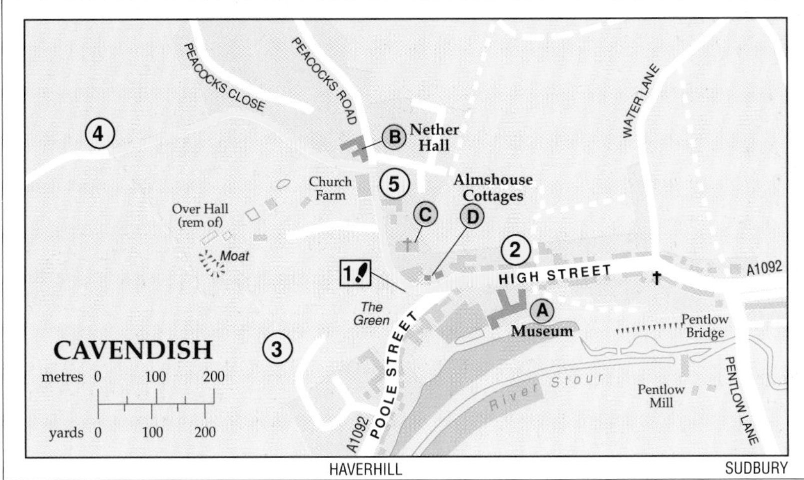

CAVENDISH

SUFFOLK

On A1092, 6m NW of Sudbury

A picturesque village in the Stour valley, photographs of Cavendish often adorn the covers of guidebooks and calendars. Sir John Cavendish, whose bequest enabled the chancel in the church to be built, received some rough justice when his son stabbed and killed Wat Tyler at Smithfield. Tyler was the leader of the 1381 rebellion, but had already been given amnesty by the king when the young Cavendish murdered him. Bent on revenge, a mob descended on Sir John's home in Cavendish. He fled, but was caught later and beheaded.

POINTS OF INTEREST

Sue Ryder Foundation Museum. Based in the old Rectory, a fine timber-framed house, the headquarters of the Sue Ryder Foundation contains a museum which explains the work of the foundation. It charts the misery inflicted on people during the war years, the most poignant exhibit being a small bar of soap made from human bones, taken from a concentration camp. It also highlights the hope which the foundation has given to thousands since, with displays showing its successes.

Ⓑ

Nether Hall. Once home of Jane Colt, wife of Sir Thomas More, who was 'A Man for All Seasons', 500-year-old Nether Hall is a fine early Tudor house, and boasts one of the few vineyards in England. The historical connection explains why Basil Ambrose's award-winning dry white wine is called 'a wine for all seasons'! Cavendish Manor Vineyards also produce a non-alcoholic drink of grape and apple juice called, appropriately enough, Ambrosia. The house and grounds are open for tours and wine-tasting.

St Mary's Church. A lovely church with a jutting stair turret. The ringing chamber in the tower was formerly a priest's room, and has a fireplace. The 14th-century tower dominates the entire village. The church itself has a bright interior, with hardly any stained glass. It contains a brass eagle lectern, and a fine altarpiece depicting the crucifixion.

Almshouse Cottages. Known locally as 'Hyde Park Corner', this small group of thatched cottages with pink plaster walls has been rescued twice within 20 years from near dereliction, due to fire and general dilapidation, by Tom Ambrose of Nether Hall. It won an architectural award after the most recent renovation, in 1973.

INFORMATION
Length of walk:
1 mile
Approximate time:
1½ hours

TERRAIN:
Surfaced road and footpaths, one stile. Only the road section of the walk is suitable for pushchairs and wheelchairs.

PARKING:
Park carefully near the green.

OPEN:
The Sue Ryder Foundation Museum. Daily, 10am-5.30pm. Charge.
Cavendish Manor Vineyards. Daily 11am-4pm. Charge.

REFRESHMENTS:
Village inns and a tea shop.

WALK DIRECTIONS

Start from the green, and head east first of all along High Street, to visit the Sue Ryder Foundation Museum, on the right-hand side.

②

Return the same way, and cross the green to the far corner, between the cemetery and the school. Climb the stile and follow the path beside the cemetery.

③

At the far end, the path comes to an open field, and bends right to follow the field edge. Stay with the path as it curves round to the left, and goes through a hedge into the next field, and on to a road.

Turn right here, and follow the road back towards the village. On your left is Nether Hall, the home of Cavendish Manor Vineyards.

Turn right at the junction, and follow the road back to the green, with the church and Almshouse Cottages on your left.

Across the village green.

SUE RYDER FOUNDATION

Sue Ryder served with the Polish section of the top secret Special Operations Executive during the Second World War. It was then that she saw the extent of human suffering which had been inflicted on the people in Europe, and she was inspired by the fortitude of so many. After the war, she threw herself into relief work, first in Europe, and then in Third World countries. The Sue Ryder Foundation was set up in 1953, as a living memorial to the millions who died in two World Wars, and to those still suffering as a result of persecution.

In 1959, she married Group Captain Leonard Cheshire, VC, whose homes for the disabled form a completely separate charity. There are now over 80 Sue Ryder homes – 24 of which are spread throughout in the UK – caring for sick and disabled people of all ages in 14 countries and 380 Sue Ryder charity shops help provide the necessary funds.

CLEY NEXT THE SEA

NORFOLK

On A149, 8m W of Sheringham

THE village (pronounced 'Cly') was once an important port, like several other places along the north Norfolk coast, but continual silting up along the coastline has gradually moved Cley more than a mile from the sea. The customs house on the old quayside stands as a reminder of the huge trade that would have been done in the days when East Anglian wool went far and wide, and the proliferance of Dutch gables are reminiscent of the Low Countries with whom so much trade was done.

Cley Marshes, to the north of the village, became the first nature reserve in the country, set up in 1926 by the Norfolk Naturalists Trust.

Traces of the old quay at Cley are dominated by the now converted windmill, looking across marshes and mudflats.

POINTS OF INTEREST

Ⓐ

St Margaret's Church. The church and green once formed the centre of the village, but after a fire in the 17th century, new houses were built around the harbour area. The church is a magnificent testimony to the former wealth of Cley, even though the arrival of the plague prevented the planned west tower from being built. A tomb in the churchyard commemorates James Greeve, who on 14 June 1676 assisted Sir Cloudsly Shovel in 'burning y Ships in y Port of Tripoly.'

Ⓑ

'Made in Cley'. Hand-thrown pottery is made here, the products on sale in a shop dating back to Regency times, with a broad timber counter and lines of wooden drawers behind.

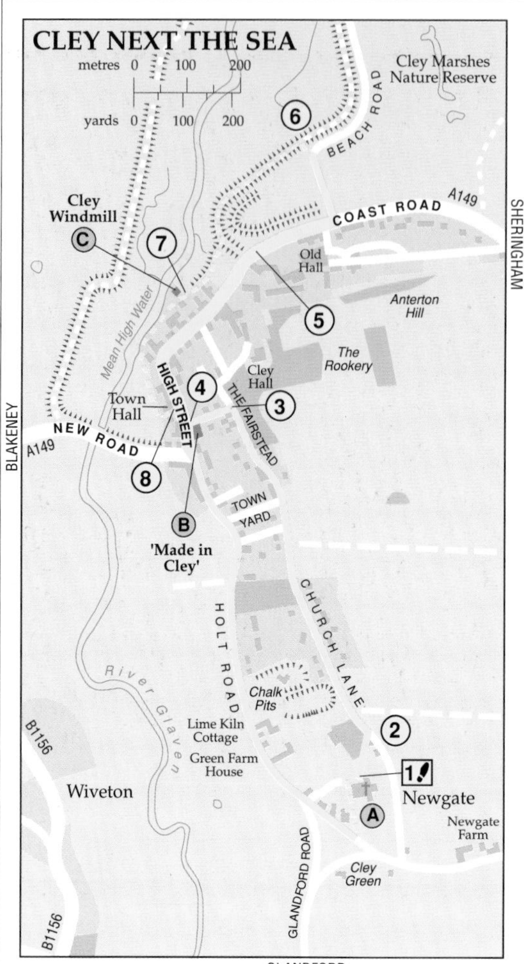

Ⓒ

Cley Windmill. Built in the 18th-century, the five-storey brick-built tower now has no internal machinery. It was used as a mill up until 1910, and converted into a holiday home in 1921.

INFORMATION
Length of walk:
2 miles
Approximate time:
1½ hours

TERRAIN:
Mostly surfaced, but embankments can be muddy in wet weather. Pushchairs and wheelchairs, southern loop of the walk only.

PARKING:
Park near the church.

OPEN:
Cley Windmill. Daily Jun-Sep, 2-5pm. Charge.
'Made in Cley' Pottery. Daily 10am-6pm. No charge.
Glandford Shell Museum. All year, Mon-Thu 10am-12.30pm and 2-4.30pm, Fri and Sat 2-4.30pm (closed pm, Nov-Feb). Charge.

REFRESHMENTS:
Village inns.

GLANDFORD SHELL MUSEUM

Sir Alfred Jodrell was the epitome of a Victorian benefactor. He rebuilt Glandford church in memory of his mother, and endowed it with all manner of carvings and stained glass windows. The shell museum displays the same eccentric charm, with its collections of shells and fossils from all over the world, as well as relics from the buried city of Pompeii. It is located two miles inland from Cley on the B1156 at the village of Glandford.

WALK DIRECTIONS

①

Start at the church at the southern end of the village. After looking inside, go out of the opposite entrance, taking a track straight ahead.

②

At the road (Church Lane), turn left, and continue along it past the village hall.

③

Turn left into a narrow alley with flint walls on either side, following the sign for the pottery.

④

Turn right on to the main road, and follow it round through the village. Be careful as there are no pavements.

⑤

Follow the road out of the village, and turn left where it is signposted Beach Road. Just as the road curves into an 'S' bend, take the path to the left on to the embankment, where you can see the cast-iron dome of an old gun emplacement.

⑥

Keep left on the embankment, heading towards the mill. Just before the mill, a stile and steps takes the path down below the embankment.

⑦

Pass the mill along a wide track, and where it goes over a steep ramp, take the path to the right (signposted Norfolk Coast Path). The path winds round at the back of houses. Go left down a short alley, which brings you out next to the old Town Hall.

⑧

Turn right on to the main road, past the pottery, and where it bends right for Wells, go straight on (signposted to the church). The road takes you back to the green where you started.

CLUN

SHROPSHIRE

At junction of A488 and B4368, 14m NW of Ludlow

THE large, mainly stone-built village nestles among the Shropshire Hills in a designated Area of Outstanding Natural Beauty. It has much to offer the casual stroller, the walker on its nearby footpaths and the motorist exploring the little-used roads that lead to it. Once a busy market town, Clun has declined in the present century to village status. With a population of about 700, against 1,200 in 1851, it is perhaps even more peaceful today than when the following often-quoted lines were published by A.E. Housman a century ago:

Clunton and Clunbury,
Clungunford and Clun,
Are the quietest places
Under the sun.

The crumbling ruins of the castle, set among grassy earthworks above the point were the River Unk flows into the River Clun.

WALK DIRECTIONS

Start from the car park and cross the River Clun by the narrow medieval bridge on the A488. Note the recesses for the safety of pedestrians, and ponder the mysterious saying that 'He who crosses Clun bridge comes back sharper than he went.' Climb Buffalo Lane to a gate on the left, from which a path runs to a stile and gate into the castle grounds. A footbridge from the car park to the castle grounds is proposed.

After exploring the ruins and earthworks of the castle, leave by the gate near the bowling green and immediately step over a stile on your left. The path swings through a gap on the right and bears left along the hedge to an exit stile on a lane. Turn right to the A488 and left along it. The following attractive walk through fields north of the village is recommended, but can be omitted by continuing ahead from the castle exit to a road junction by Castle House (once the Castle Inn). Bear left for 40yds, then right along a path between buildings, passing a children's play area and the Memorial Hall to reach Mill Lane, where the longer route can then be rejoined.

For the longer route, follow the A488 past the village boundary sign and fork right along an unsurfaced lane. At the top turn right into a hedged green lane and enter the gate on your right at the end. Cross the high-level field, with lovely views all round, to a former gateway at the far corner and turn right along a hedge. Bear left at the bottom to another former gateway at a corner and cross a railed footbridge and a stile to Mill Lane. A large marshy area to the right of the path was the site of a lake that drained away in the 1930s during an ambitious attempt to enlarge it. In a hollow to the left along the lane lies the solid, stone-built 18th-century Clun Mill, a youth hostel since 1932.

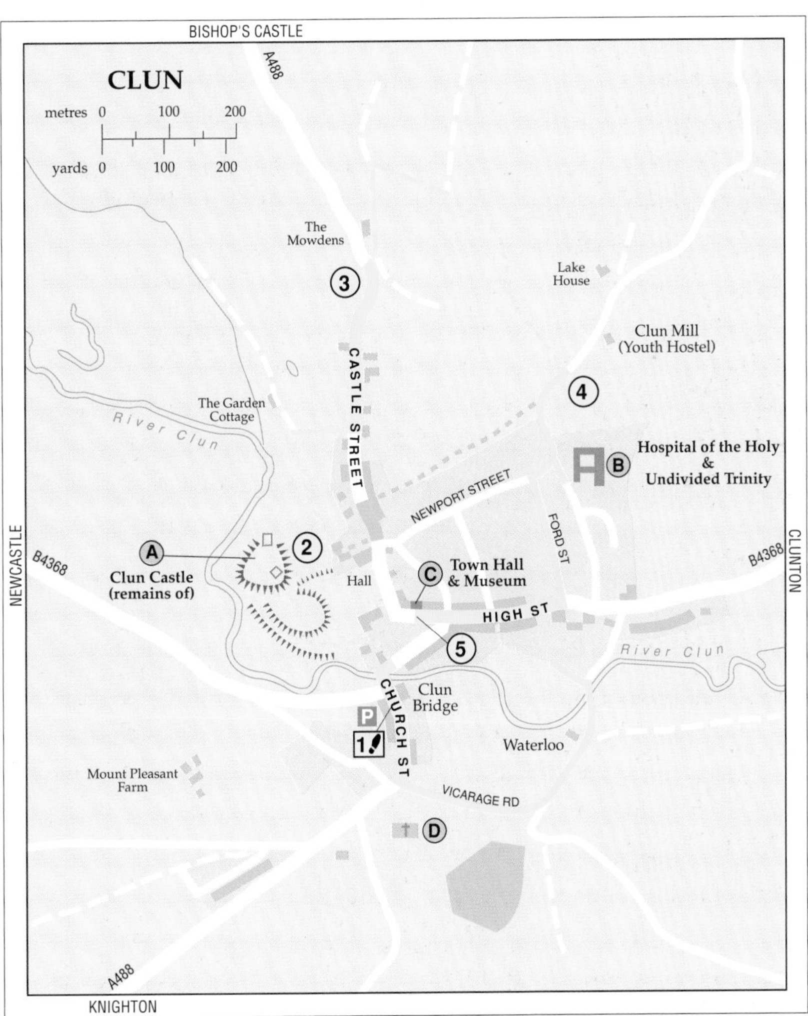

INFORMATION
Length of walk: $1\frac{1}{2}$ miles
Approximate time: 2 hours

TERRAIN:
Suitable for children at all times of year; only suitable for pushchairs in dry weather; suitable for wheelchairs, though hilly, if the longer route to north is omitted. Four stiles and two footbridges.

PARKING:
Free public car park and toilets by the bridge.

OPEN:
Clun Castle. At all times. No charge.
Town Hall Museum. Easter-1 Nov, Tue and Sat 2-5pm. Also Bank Hol Mon and following Tue, 11am-1pm, 2-5pm. No charge.
Trinity Hospital. Garden and chapel. Daytime.

REFRESHMENTS:
Three inns; tearoom.

This narrow medieval bridge crosses the river at the bottom of Church Street.

Follow the lane to the right, passing the entrance to the Memorial Hall, and at a junction keep ahead along Hospital Lane to visit Trinity Hospital. Return to the junction and bear left and left again into Ford Street. The Thatch, on the right, was the last thatched cottage in Clun, and at the junction with High Street is another former inn, Ship House, once the Royal George. To the right along High Street note the date 1682 on Lower House, set back on the north side. Continue past the Sun Inn to The Square, where the town hall and museum building stand, together with the village's other two inns.

Return to High Street and descend a path to the right. Beyond public lavatories fork left down a tarred path leading to an unmetalled road. Bear right and cross a railed footbridge on the River Clun. This attractive spot is known as Waterloo, though it seems to have been originally called Waterlow. Climb to the right and bear right into Vicarage Road, where the cottage high on the left was once the Dame School. Before reaching the church, pass the former vicarage of 1700, and complete the walk by descending Church Street to the bridge, near which the one-time Home Farm is now the Clun Bridge Tea Room.

CLUN'S INNS

Today Clun has three inns: the 16th-century Sun, in High Street, and the White Horse and the ancient Buffalo Head Hotel in The Square. Sir Walter Scott stayed at the latter whilst writing *The Betrothed*, and is believed to have based the novel's Garde Doloureuse on Clun Castle. During its years of prosperity as a market town, Clun had many more inns. In the late 19th century there were at least 14, including four or five in Bridge Street. Some of the former hostelries can still be identified, and two are indicated in the walk directions. To balance things a little a Temperance Hall was built at the south-east corner of Clun Bridge in 1870. It is now a shop.

POINTS OF INTEREST

Clun Castle. For 750 years the great, gaunt keep has stood sentinel over the village from its vantage point above the river. The mound on which Picot de Say raised the original castle of timber was probably formed during the Ice Age. This building proved insufficient to keep the Welsh at bay, so Picot's grandson Helias constructed the stone fortress about 1140, and it saw much action in Border conflicts up to the time of the Owain Glyndwr uprising.

Early occupiers were the Fitzalans, whose line ended in 1580. The castle and lands then passed to the Dukes of Norfolk, who to this day include the Barony of Clun among their titles. The present Duke leases the castle to the parish council for recreational purposes. A leaflet which explains the full story of the castle can be purchased at the museum.

Parliamentary soldiers occupied St George's during the Civil War. It was attacked by Royalists.

The Hospital of the Holy and Undivided Trinity. The lovely gabled almshouses in Hospital Lane were built in 1614 by the Earl of Northampton, the Duke of Norfolk's brother. They originally provided accommodation for 12 old men of good character; provision was made later for married couples. A list of the wardens, on the wall of St George's Church, shows that the vicars of the parish have filled the post since 1900.

Town Hall and Museum. Though the Duke of Norfolk is Baron of Clun, the Lord of the Manor is the Earl of Powis. The fact that the Earl is a descendant of Clive of India explains the elephant in his coat of arms on the exterior west wall of the Town Hall. The building was constructed in 1780 by the 2nd Lord Clive, using stone from the Court House, which stood on the present site of the bowling green at the castle. The ground floor was originally open and prisoners were chained inside. Later the arches were filled in and markets were held there. The small museum has many items of local interest and is noted for its collection of flints.

St George's Church. A no-nonsense, fortress-like Border church, where the medieval inhabitants of Clun sheltered from Welsh invaders. It has a broad, buttressed Norman tower, topped by a 17th-century pyramid roof, and a vast stone porch. The nave arches have thick pillars with dog-tooth carving, and there is a fine, high, timbered roof. An ancient carving of an heraldic shield and some strange figures can be seen on the east wall of the north aisle chapel. In the nave a painting (1913-1916) of St George by an Abyssinian artist depicts the saint in the costume of that period and with the features of the Emperor Lu Yasu. The building was restored by G.E. Street in 1877.

Abraham Darby III's famous cast iron bridge across the River Severn, built in 1779.

COALBROOKDALE

SHROPSHIRE

On A4169, 4m S of exit 6 off M54 at Telford

THE setting for the cradle of the Industrial Revolution (the 'Silicon valley of the 18th century', as it has been called) is unexpectedly green. The old buildings nestle deep in the wooded Severn Gorge, where they survived long after the industrial flowering of the 18th century had withered; thankfully no one bothered to knock them down. The Ironbridge Gorge Trust began restoring them in 1959, since when the area has prospered.

In 1986 the Gorge was declared Britain's first World Heritage site by UNESCO, a mark given to fewer than 250 worldwide attractions. There are six major sites belonging to the Trust spread over as many square miles, plus a number of smaller ones, including a reconstructed Victorian village and museums of iron and steel making. Since it is impossible to do justice to them all in a day, this walk concentrates on the western side of the area.

WALK DIRECTIONS

After visiting the Museum of the River follow the main road (The Wharfage) westwards and turn right into Dale Road, signposted for the Museum of Iron. Pass the half-timbered Rose Cottages and the Upper Forge picnic area and continue up the wooded gorge, which becomes Wellington Road, to Coalbrookdale. On the right is the former Coalbrookdale Institute, now a youth hostel and study centre. When built by local ironmasters in 1859 to house literary, art and science classes, its many up-to-date facilities included central heating.

Pass the Coalbrookdale Company works and enjoy the fine view back to the Severn valley. At a junction on the left a lamp with a Corinthian capital celebrates Queen Victoria's Diamond Jubilee of 1897. Continue past traffic lights, where the road narrows, and note Carpenters Row, the long line of cottages on your right. Some of the dwellings have been restored by the Trust to represent ironworkers' homes of different periods from 1780 to 1930, and these can be viewed by appointment.

Turn left down Darby Road, pass under the railway arch and bear right, climbing the lane to Rosehill House, the home of the Darby family in the 18th and 19th centuries. Further uphill a footpath sign by a pottery shop indicates the short but steep climb to the small, sloping Quaker Burial Ground. Abraham Darby II was the first to be buried here, in 1763, but there are no indications of individual graves. Instead, beneath tall redwoods, there are numerous small, square memorial stones propped against the walls, several of them bearing the name Darby. The elevated situation provides a good view of the gorge below.

INFORMATION
Length of walk:
3 miles
Approximate time:
5 hours (plus lunch/rest breaks)

TERRAIN:
Suitable for children at all times of year; suitable for pushchairs and wheelchairs if the steep climb to the Quakers' Burial Ground is omitted and the return to the Museum of the River made by the same route as the outward journey. There are stairs to climb at the Museum of Iron and the Elton Gallery. No stiles or footbridges, but the footpath ends with a long, steep descent of steps into the gorge.

PARKING:
Park at the Visitor Centre car park off A4169, 250yds W of the Iron Bridge. There are free car parks at all the Ironbridge Museum Trust sites.

OPEN:
The Museum of the River, the Museum of Iron and the Elton Gallery. Daily 10am-6pm during British Summer Time, otherwise 10am-5pm. Rosehill House. Daily, 11am-5pm, mid-Feb-end Oct.
A passport ticket covering all Ironbridge Gorge Museum Trust sites is available and has no time limit.

REFRESHMENTS:
Inns at Coalbrookdale and Ironbridge; cafés at Ironbridge; light refreshments at the Museum of Iron.

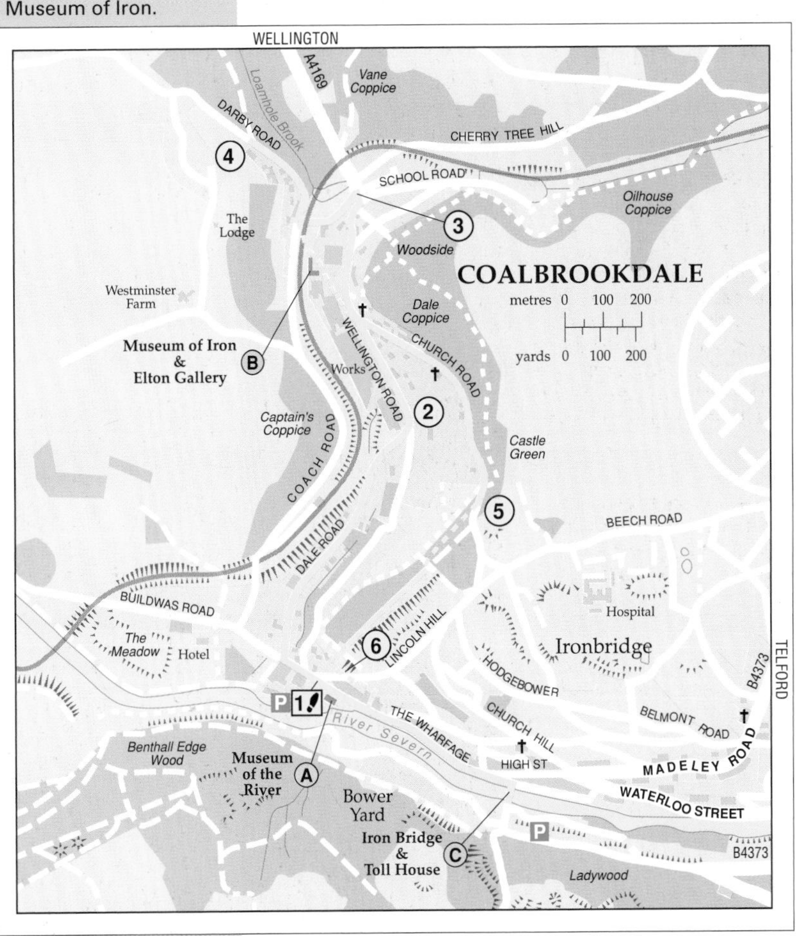

POINTS OF INTEREST

The Museum of the River Visitor Centre. Built in the 1840s as the Severn Warehouse, this turreted and crenellated building housed the Coalbrookdale Company's products before they were shipped downstream. The Museum, declared open by Prince Charles in 1989, contains a fascinating exhibit recalling an earlier royal visit – a 40ft-long, detailed model of the Gorge as it was when William V of Orange and Queen Wilhelmina embarked from The Wharfage in 1796. Today's visitors are shown an audio-visual display about the history of the Gorge, the various museum sites and the use and abuse of water, a theme taken up by the museum's exhibits.

Ⓑ

The Museum of Iron and the Elton Gallery. A modern building in the yard of the museum houses Abraham Darby's coke-powered furnace of 1709. Nearby, a full-scale model of the world's first steam locomotive circles a replica of the track used by its inventor, Richard Trevithick, to display the original in Euston Square. The Great Warehouse of 1838, containing the main museum collection, tells the story of the Darby family and the history of iron. Paintings, prints, drawings and commemorative pieces are on display at the neighbouring Elton Gallery, an important centre for the study of industrial history.

The Iron Bridge and the Toll House. A tourist attraction since its opening on New Year's Day 1781, the world's first cast-iron bridge, slung across the Severn by Abraham Darby III at a cost of £2,737-4s-4d, is perhaps the most potent symbol of the Industrial Revolution. A toll bridge, it was the main local crossing point of the river until 1931, since when it has been open to pedestrians only, and is now free of charge. A board listing the former tolls can be seen outside the Toll House, south of the magnificent bowed structure. Inside, visitors can read the full story of the Iron Bridge.

This turreted building (above), originally a warehouse, was opened as a museum in 1989. Its recurring theme is the River Severn and its gorge. The beautiful cast iron fountain (right) can be seen in the Ironbridge Gorge Museum.

Return down the lane and bear right for the Museum of Iron and the Elton Gallery. Leave by the opposite exit and climb to Wellington Road. Cross to Church Road and follow it past Holy Trinity, a prominently sited Gothic church of 1854. The large monument of Abraham Darby IV lies immediately beyond the building.

Near the top of the road take a wooded path on the right. Beyond a viewing point for the Severn Valley and the Iron Bridge it plunges down steep steps. At a cross-path go right for a few yards before turning off down more steps, which end at a wall. Bear left to a stile and join a track leading from a house to Lincoln Hill, a surfaced road.

The road descends to The Wharfage, near the Visitor Centre, but to continue the walk turn left along it for a few yards and take a path on the right down to the main road. Bear left for the Iron Bridge and the Toll House, the Tourist Information Centre and the Trust's Shop in The Square, before walking back beside the river to reach the Visitor Centre.

Overlooking the beautiful tree-lined gorge of the River Severn.

THE BIRTH OF THE INDUSTRIAL REVOLUTION

It was the discovery in 1709 of a technique for smelting iron with coke that started the Industrial Revolution. Previously, charcoal had been used for smelting, but the supply of this commodity was restricted by the fast-disappearing woodlands, whereas sources of coal for the manufacture of coke seemed infinite. Thus the door was opened for the mass production of iron, a key product in the development of industry.

Abraham Darby began it all in the unlikely rural setting of Coalbrookdale, which had a coal-producing tradition, water-power and a broad river for transport. Beginning his experiments in 1708, he had achieved success by the following year and began producing pots and pans. The River Severn, which has been called the M1 of that time, bore them away to hungry markets. Industry – both iron at Coalbrookdale and china at nearby Coalport – flourished throughout the 18th century. Many 'firsts' were achieved – the first cast-iron steam engine, iron wheels, iron boat, iron aqueduct, iron bridge, metal-framed building and steam locomotive, yet the Shropshire equivalent to Birmingham or Manchester failed to emerge. Not only were new techniques developed elsewhere, but the River Severn, often too low in summer and too swift in winter, was unable to cope with its cargo. The thriving valley that an early 19th-century visitor called 'The most extraordinary district in the world' died. It has come alive again only with the recent upsurge of interest in industrial archaeology.

CROMFORD

DERBYSHIRE

On A6(T), 2m S of Matlock

AN early industrial village lying beside the clear waters of the River Derwent and among the hills of the Peak District National Park. There is a great deal to see here, most of which can be attributed to one man, Sir Richard Arkwright, who began the development of Cromford when he built his first mill in 1771.

It was the power of the Derwent (right) which drew Arkwright to Cromford where he set up the first water-powered cotton mill (above).

SIR RICHARD ARKWRIGHT

Born in Preston in 1732, the man who has been called the father of the factory system began his working life as a barber and wigmaker. He travelled the country making and selling wigs, before joining up with a clockmaker, John Kay, in his native town in 1768. Together they perfected a roller spinning machine known as the water frame, and Arkwright, in partnership with others, opened a mill in Nottingham. This invention was the first machine that could produce cotton-thread of sufficient tenuity and strength to be used as warp. In 1771 he came to Cromford, where there was water-power and a local work force, and built Cromford Mill in 1771. His methods were immensely successful and brought him great wealth, although animosity arose against his labour saving invention. In 1786 he was knighted and became High Sheriff of Derbyshire. He died in 1792, unfortunately without seeing the completion of his ambitious new Cromford residence at Willersley Castle.

POINTS OF INTEREST

Cromford Bridge. One of the oldest bridges in Derbyshire, its 15th-century arches are rounded on one side and pointed on the other. An old inscription on the downstream parapet records the involuntary leap in 1697 of Benjamin Hayward of Bridge House on his mare, which failed to take the sharp turn on to the bridge and soared over the parapet instead. Amazingly, in view of the long drop to the river, the mare landed safely, Mr Hayward kept his seat, and they scrambled to safety up the far bank. Bridge House, of the Jacobean and Georgian periods, stands to the right beyond the bridge. Nearby are the gates of Willersley Castle, built by Sir Richard Arkwright but not completed until 1793, a year after his death. It is now a Methodist Guild Holiday and Conference Centre. Beside the bridge stands a pyramid-roofed 18th-century fishing pavilion and below it the remains of a 15th-century chapel.

St Mary's Church. Built near Cromford Bridge by Sir Richard Arkwright as a private chapel for Willersley Castle, the building was consecrated as the village church five years after his death. Though he was buried at Matlock, his remains were later moved to St Mary's. Originally Georgian in style, the church was Gothicized in 1858. Dry rot forced its closure in 1977, and it has subsequently been under restoration.

Cromford Canal. Opened in 1793 the canal linked Arkwright's works with the major Midland and Northern cities. It was profitable in its early decades, but declined after being taken over by a railway company in 1852. The collapse of the Butterley Tunnel in 1900 meant its closure to through traffic. Finally all traffic ceased in 1944. Derbyshire County Council bought the Cromford-Ambergate section in 1974, since when restoration

The wash mill wheel at Arkwright's mill, restored.

has been carried out by the Cromford Canal Society, which runs horse-drawn boat trips during summer weekends.

Cromford Mill. From Mill Road the mill has an almost fortress-like appearance, having been built by Arkwright in 1771 to withstand the possible attacks of cottage weavers put out of business by the new machinery. Some 200 workers were employed here, but it ceased to be a cotton mill in the mid-19th century, and was a dye-works from 1927, during which time great damage was done. Today the site belongs to the Arkwright Society. With the support of English Heritage a million pounds has been spent on restoration since 1979. The work will continue for many years to come, ensuring visitors come back again and again.

The Greyhound Hotel. Originally the Black Greyhound Inn, built by Arkwright in 1778, it faces the Market Place and has been likened to a town hall in appearance. Its clock, the first public one in Cromford, was intended to help the mill workers with their timekeeping. A Saturday market established by Arkwright in 1790 continued until about 1880. Behind the Hotel is the Greyhound Pond, the lowest of a series of reservoirs along Bonsall Brook that regulated the water supply to Cromford Mill.

Millworkers' Houses. The village contains some of the earliest houses provided by an industrialist for factory workers. The best examples are in North Street, off the Wirksworth road. Built by Arkwright in 1776-7, they have outlasted many later examples elsewhere and are far superior to much 19th-century industrial housing. The three-storeyed gritstone terraces had weavers' workshops on their upper floors, the long windows of which can still be seen. Further uphill on the Wirksworth road are two and three-storeyed Arkwright houses of later date, some with their original windows.

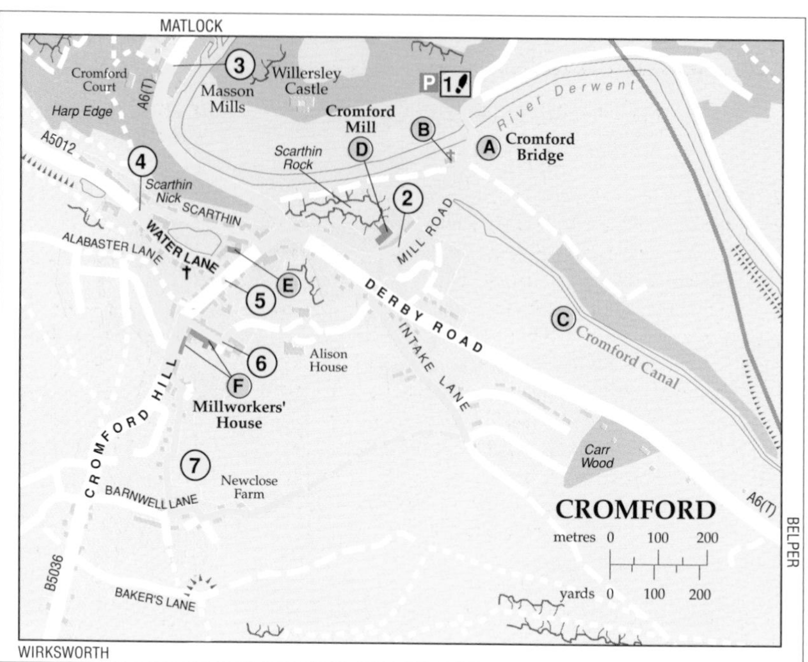

WALK DIRECTIONS

Park at one of the Mill Road car parks and walk along the lane to Cromford Bridge over the River Derwent. After crossing the bridge and bearing right for Bridge House, return to Mill Road. Pass the end of the Cromford Canal to reach Cromford Mill, opposite which stands the 18th-century mill manager's house.

Leave the mill and bear right to A6(T), passing under a cast-iron aqueduct (locally known as a launder) built in 1821. Turn right for 1/4 mile, through the limestone gorge of Scarthin Nick, to Masson Mill. The six-storeyed middle section of the building, with its Venetian windows, is Arkwright's third mill, completed in 1784.

Return along A6(T) and bear right into Cromford village. From the Market Place pass to the right of the Greyhound Hotel to Scarthin, originally a lead-mining settlement. There is a good secondhand bookshop on the right and the Boat Inn, formerly the Hit or Miss, is on the left, with the Greyhound Pond visible beyond. Pass the Primitive Methodist church of 1853 to A5012, known as the Via Gellia, constructed up the lovely wooded gorge in the 19th century. Uphill and across the road is the 18th-century Cromford Corn Mill, owned and in the course of being restored by the Arkwright Society.

Descend the A5012 past the remains of another mill, which retains a mid-19th-century overshot waterwheel, 14ft 7in in diameter, restored by the Arkwright Society in 1975.

Cross the Wirksworth road to an alley, where the café on the corner was once the Crown Inn. The alley leads to a large sluice built in 1785 to regulate another Cromford Mill water source, the Cromford Sough. A path continues up to the school built by Richard Arkwright II at the end of North Street.

Following North Street out to the Wirksworth road, where the Bell Inn stands at the corner, turn left uphill, and enter Bedehouse Lane on the left. Fork right and climb to the Bedehouses, or Almshouses, built with money left by Lady Armine, Lady of the Manor, who died in 1662.

Continue uphill to the junction with a lane and turn left. Beyond a bend is a signed path along an unmade road leading to a gate and squeeze stile. The village is laid out far below, and Willersley Castle nestles among woods on the hillside beyond. The path, with lovely views, passes two more stiles before reaching a road. Follow this downhill to A6(T). Cross to a walled path, which winds down beside the garden of Rock House, Arkwright's residence, to return to Mill Road.

INFORMATION
Length of walk:
2 miles
Approximate time:
3 hours

TERRAIN:
Suitable for children at all times of year; only suitable for pushchairs in dry weather. Though hilly it is suitable for wheelchairs, if the walk is shortened by turning left to the Market Place after descending past the waterwheel. Three stiles, no footbridges.

PARKING:
Free car parks at Cromford Mill, Cromford Canal and by Cromford Bridge.

OPEN:
Cromford Mill. Weekdays 9.30am-5pm. Weekends 10am-5pm in summer. Daily 10am-4.30pm in winter. Slide shows and guided tours start on the hour.

REFRESHMENTS:
At Cromford Mill; inns and café in village.

DUNWICH

DUNWICH

SUFFOLK

Off A12, 6m E of Yoxford

DUNWICH'S history testifies to the awesome power of the sea. Once a Roman settlement, later an Anglo-Saxon city and then a medieval port, traces of all three have now vanished beneath the waves. Dunwich was the centre of Christianity in East Anglia in the 7th century, when St Felix was installed as the first bishop. The Danish invasion prompted the bishopric to be moved to North Elmham in Norfolk, but even after that, Dunwich remained an important port. At its height, there were nine churches here, and a base for 80 ships.

INFORMATION

Length of walk:
1½ miles (extended route just over 2 miles)

Approximate time:
¾ hour to 1 hour (1½ hours if walking extended route)

TERRAIN:
May be muddy in wet weather, so appropriate footwear would be sensible. Unsuitable for pushchairs and wheelchairs.

PARKING:
Park at the beach car park.

OPEN:
Dunwich Museum. Mar-Oct Sat-Sun. May-Sep Daily except Mon and Fri. 2-4.30pm. No charge.

REFRESHMENTS:
Village inns.

POINTS OF INTEREST

Grey Friars. The Black Friars (Dominicans) had a monastery at Dunwich, but it was lost to the sea in the 14th century. The remains of the Grey Friars (Franciscans) priory stands on the clifftop, once at the very western outskirts of the town. It was actually their second attempt at a priory here – the first having been washed away with a sizeable part of the town within 12 years of its erection. Of the building which they started the year after the loss of the first, only part of the wall and two flint-dressed gatehouses survive. Most of the masonry was removed for use in other houses following the Dissolution.

Dunwich Church and Leper Hospital. St James's Church was built in the 19th century, and the churchyard contains the remains of All Saints, the last of the churches to fall into the sea, as well as the ruins of the Leper Hospital. The Leper Hospital, built well outside the western ramparts of the town, survived the ravages of the sea, but nevertheless fell into ruin. The remains of the chapel, with its Norman arcading, stand next to the modern church.

(C)

Dunwich Museum. Dunwich Museum houses an interesting collection of archaeological finds, scripts and illustrations which chart the history of the ancient town and its decline. Upstairs, there are sections devoted to the more recent history of the village, and also to the natural history of the surrounding area.

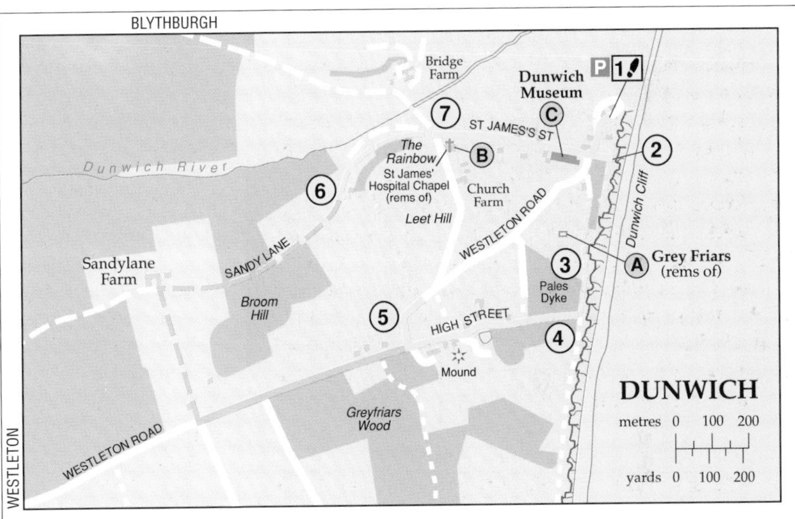

Once a great port, Dunwich's remaining street now leads to the quiet shore, with its fishing boats, huts and shore winches.

WALK DIRECTIONS

From the beach car park, walk towards the junction, where the Westleton Road meets St James's Street. Turn left on to a footpath marked by a post with a yellow band, and go through a kissing-gate. The narrow path arrives at the cliff, where there are steps leading down to the beach.

(2)

Turn right here, on to the clifftop path. Just past a wooden seat, head in towards the trees, and pick up a well-worn path. To your right is a gate leading to Grey Friars.

(3)

Carry straight on to a T-junction with another path.

(4)

Carry straight on, underneath a small bridge. The path broadens out into a track – marked on the map as High Street – as you pass some houses and emerges on to the Westleton Road. Turn right here, for Dunwich.

To extend the walk, turn left on to Westleton Road, and continue ahead until you reach a track going off to the right, signposted Sandylane Farm. Follow this track to the bottom, and turn right at the farm on to a narrow path – marked on the map as Sandy Lane. The path rejoins the main route which emerges at the junction with the church, Point 7.

(5)

On the shorter walk the road bends round to the right. Soon afterwards, look carefully for the public footpath sign which indicates a gap in the hedge on your left. The path follows the edge of a field, and crosses straight on through a hedge into another field. At the bottom corner, follow the path round to the left.

Go through a gap in the hedge (public footpath sign), and turn right on to a small track. The track broadens out with a gravel surface, and continues to the road junction on which the church stands.

Take the road for Dunwich Beach and Museum, at the end of which is the turning for the beach car park.

EARDISLAND

HEREFORD AND WORCESTER

On unclassified road (formerly A44), 5m W of Leominster

THIS charming little village of stone-built and black-and-white cottages makes splendid use of its riverside setting, especially around the bridge. A stroll through it is much more pleasant now that its main road is no longer the busy A44. It is one of a cluster of beautiful Herefordshire villages included in a signposted circular drive.

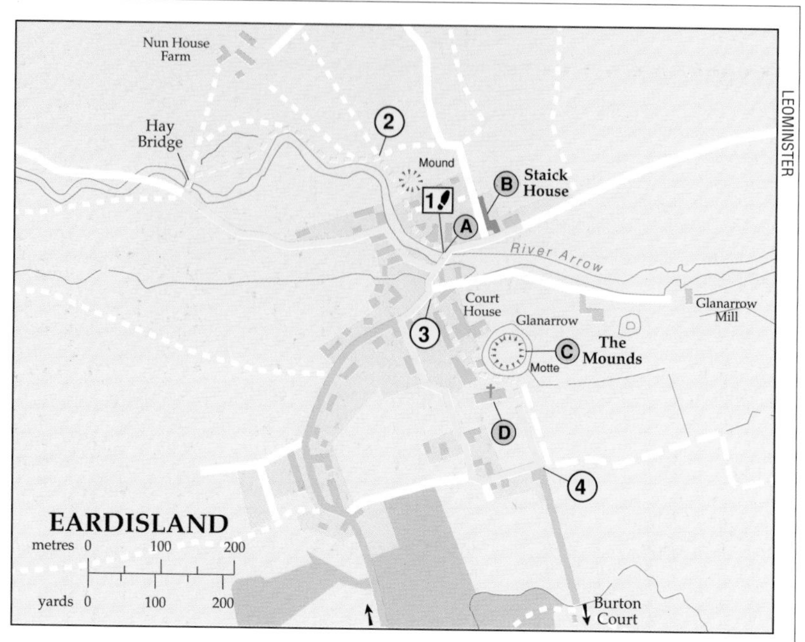

POINTS OF INTEREST

River Arrow and Bridge. The swift-flowing river, ancient bridge and surrounding buildings in half-timbering or stone make up a scene of striking beauty. Millstream Cottage, beside the bridge, was once the Grammar School. At the end of it nearest the bridge is the former whipping post, with manacles attached. Opposite, the millstream emerges from under the Old Mill House, stone-built in Georgian times. The timber-framed manor house, to the west, is 17th century with a Queen Anne brick extension. A tall, eye-catching but ramshackle red-brick building with four gables, by the bridge, is a dovecote from the same period.

Staick House. A domestic building of great antiquity, the house was built about the year 1300 as a yeoman's hall. Sprawling and gabled, its great sandstone-tiled roof sagging with age, it advances a 17th-century dovecoted wing towards the road, beside which is a topiary garden.

The Mounds. There are two ancient mounds at Eardisland. The moated Castle Mound is 94ft in diameter and 17ft high. It stands on private land, but can be viewed over the north wall of the churchyard. A document in the church suggests that it held a timber-built Saxon stronghold or was used by villagers and cattle as a refuge from Welsh marauders. A low, flat circular mound, immediately north of the village, is described as 'a puzzle to antiquarians', but monks may have held court there for their tenants.

Church of St Mary the Virgin. Though the church dates from the end of the 12th century, it was heavily restored in 1864. The tower was built in 1728 at a cost of £155, replacing one that had collapsed. Much local history can be gleaned from the copy, on the nave wall, of a learned paper written by a former vicar, the Rev. Barker, towards the end of the 19th century.

INFORMATION
Length of walk:
1 mile (1¾ miles if Burton Court is included)
Approximate time:
1½ hours (3 hours if a visit to Burton Court is included)

TERRAIN:
Suitable for children at all times of year; only suitable for pushchairs in dry weather; not suitable for wheelchairs. Two stiles and one footbridge.

PARKING:
Roadside on main road.

OPEN:
Burton Court. Spring Bank Hol.-end Sep. Wed-Thu, Sat-Sun and Bank Hol. Mon, 2.30-6pm.

REFRESHMENTS:
Two inns, tearoom.

Once clustered around its castle, the village has gradually spread along the banks of the River Arrow.

WALK DIRECTIONS

Start from the bridge over the River Arrow and follow the main road east for 30yds to Staick House. Return towards the bridge and take the lane to your right on the near bank. At a bend, a public footpath continues between a stone wall and a private garage to a stile. Beyond is one of the village's two ancient mounds.

Turn left, beside the river, to a second stile and follow a track into a caravan park. Bear left and return to the river at Hay Bridge. To the left the lane leads back to the bridge on the main road.

Take the signed footpath to the churchyard from the gate opposite and turn left to look over the north wall at the Castle Mound. After visiting the church leave by the gate at the south-east corner and follow a hedged path to a surfaced lane. It is possible to extend the walk to Burton Court by continuing past the village hall to a footbridge, where a path bears half-right to join the lane at the far field corner. Turn left to Burton Court, and afterwards walk back past this point to the main road, following it to the right to reach the bridge.

For the shorter walk turn right from the hedged path along the surfaced lane, which leads back past the Eardisland Tea Room and Garden towards the main road. Bear left along the road for the Cross Inn and the White Swan. Beyond them is Knapp House, an early 15th-century hall of cruck construction. Return to the bridge.

Eastnor Castle, a creation of the prosperous early 19th century, is a Norman style mansion with tall turreted towers. It has turrets at each corner and a central keep, and remains in the family who built it.

EASTNOR

HEREFORD AND WORCESTER

On A438, 2m E of Ledbury

EASTNOR is a delightful little Herefordshire village near the southern tip of the magnificent Malvern Hills. There are a few black-and-white and stone-built cottages, an old school, a green on which stands an ornamental well, and the parish church, but the major interest lies in the castle and its grounds.

INFORMATION
Length of walk:
2 miles (3¼ miles if ascent to obelisk is made)
Approximate time:
1½ hours (2½ hours if ascent to obelisk is made)

TERRAIN:
Suitable for children at all times of year, and for pushchairs and wheelchairs. No stiles; 1 kissing-gate and 1 footbridge (both avoidable by using A438 for last 200yds of walk).

PARKING:
Eastnor Castle car park (for visitors) when open; off-road parking opposite Castle main gates.

OPEN:
Eastnor Castle. Late May-mid-Sep Sun 2.15-5.30pm, Jul-Aug Wed-Thu, and on Bank Hol Mons. Charge.

REFRESHMENTS:
At Eastnor Castle when open.

WALK DIRECTIONS

①

The walk can be started by visiting the Castle, if it is open. Return to the main gates and follow the lane left into the village. Note the lovely thatched post office on the corner, the stone-built Eastnor Estate houses, and the school designed by Sir Robert Smirke. Pass right of the green, with its roofed well, and visit the church before returning once more to the castle gates.

②

Follow the surfaced drive opposite into the deer park and continue until two small lakes appear below. Take the right-of-way that passes between them and climbs the hillside beyond.

③

On reaching a vehicle track either turn right along it to Tinker's Grove Cottage, and the shorter route back to the castle, or cross and climb steadily for nearly ¾ mile, veering right towards the top of the hill to reach the tall obelisk. The great switchback of the Malvern Hills is seen running north as you approach the site, from which the magnificent westward views include the Black Mountains in South Wales. Return from the obelisk to the vehicle track and bear left to Tinker's Grove Cottage.

④

Turn right down the surfaced road. After crossing a cattle-grid near the A438, go through a kissing-gate on your right and cross over a railed footbridge. Walk parallel to the main road, passing a bowling green, and then veer right to join the surfaced way by which you came.

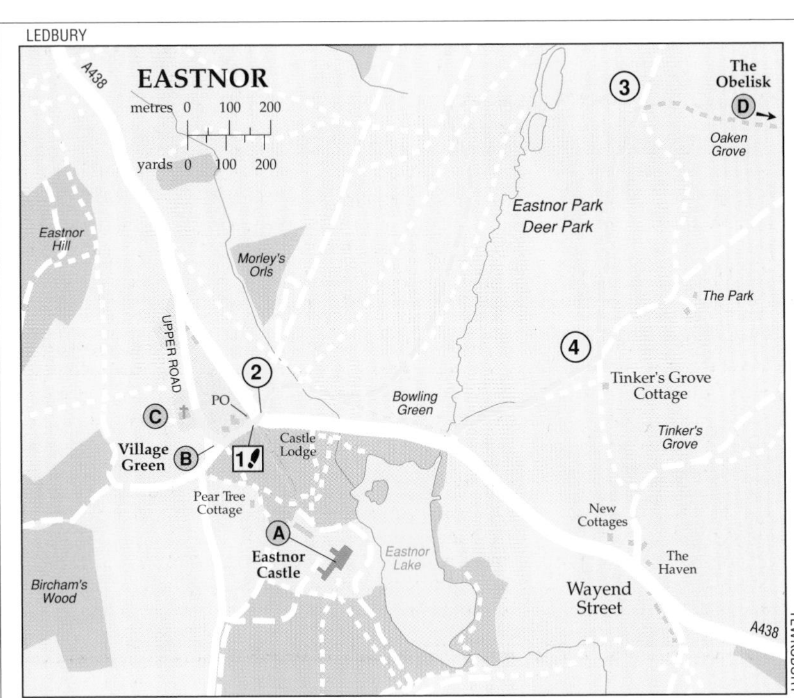

POINTS OF INTEREST

Ⓐ

Eastnor Castle. The massive stone building in the Norman style has no history of medieval battles and sieges; its construction was begun by the second Lord Somers only in 1812, when the Romantic Movement was well under way. Sir Robert Smirke, designer of the British Museum, was the architect. Its showpiece is the Great Hall, 60ft long, 30ft wide and 57ft high. Noted for its collection of armour, the castle also contains several tapestries and many paintings.

Ⓑ

Village Green and Well. The small village green contains a pyramid-roofed well, with terracotta panels depicting Christ and the words 'If any man thirst let him come unto me and drink.' The shelter is believed to have been erected by the third Earl Somers' daughter, Lady Henry Somerset, who was a notable worker for the Temperance Movement.

Ⓒ

Church of St John the Baptist. The tower is 14th century, but the rest was virtually rebuilt in Victorian times by Sir Gilbert Scott. In the north transept is the Somers Cocks mortuary chapel; its tombs and memorials can be viewed through a grill. From the churchyard can be seen the rectory.

Ⓓ

The Obelisk. Whilst Eastnor Castle was being built, Lord Somers' eldest son, the Hon. Major Edward Charles Cocks, was killed at Burgos during the Peninsular War. The great obelisk on a spur of the Malvern Hills was erected in his memory. It also recalls Ensign James Cocks, who 'preferred honour to security', and while fighting for his country, fell in battle on the coast of France, in 1758, before he had reached the age of 20. 'John, Lord Somers, Baron of Evesham, Lord High Chancellor of England in the reign of William and President of the Council in that of Queen Anne,' is also honoured.

HEMINGFORD ABBOTS

CAMBRIDGESHIRE

Off A604, 3m E of Huntingdon

UNTIL the 13th century, Huntingdon was a port on the River Great Ouse. Then the powerful Abbot of Ramsey built a weir across the river on his land at Hemingford Abbots, persuading the lord of neighbouring Hemingford Grey to do likewise. The reason for their actions being, to block navigation to Huntingdon, and increase their own rents and tolls.

The village of Hemingford Abbots is an attractive collection of brick, timbered and thatched cottages and houses, which originally started as just a small hamlet gathered around the church, but which subsequently grew westwards, towards Godmanchester.

Down the road to the east is Hemingford Grey, with its much-photographed church surrounded by willows at the river's edge. The moated manor house, dating from around 1160, is claimed to be the oldest inhabited house in England.

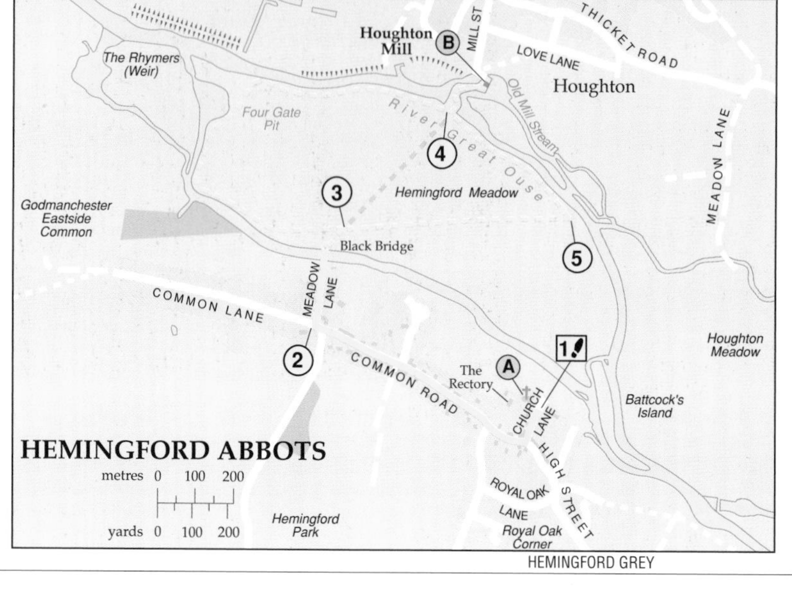

WALK DIRECTIONS

Starting from the church walk down Common Road, which is lined with delightful houses. There is a particularly grand one standing at the junction with Meadow Lane; its name 'Thatched Cottage' is rather an understatement.

Turn right down Meadow Lane. Go over the footbridge (Black Bridge) and through a gate, and follow the tarmac path for a few yards until a path heading off to the left along the riverbank comes into view.

Follow the path, left, all the way round, past a weir, until it reaches the River Great Ouse, and joins the Ouse Valley Way. Continue along the riverbank path to rejoin the tarmac path which runs across the meadow.

Turn left across the bridge to visit Houghton Mill. To continue the walk, keep to the path along the riverbank.

Where the tree-fringed former railway embankment comes closest to the river, turn sharp right and follow the path along its top. The embankment slopes down just before Black Bridge and Meadow Lane.

POINTS OF INTEREST

Hemingford Abbots Church. The tall-spired Perpendicular church contains a Roman coffin, and a painted east bay to the nave roof. Parts date from the 14th century but the chancel, of yellow brick, is probably of the 19th century.

Houghton Mill. Built on an island in the River Great Ouse, 17th-century Houghton Mill is a timber-built watermill with much of its early Victorian machinery still intact. Its waterwheels have been replaced by flood gates, and the works are now turned by an electric motor. During the season, corn is ground on the first and third Sundays in the month.

The tall-spired church around which this village grew.

CHEERY MONKS

The Hemingfords and surrounding area have long provided haunts for a number of artists. During the Romantic era of the late Victorian period, pictures of cheery monks with rosy cheeks and jolly cardinals were popular subjects. It was the River Great Ouse which provided the setting for local artist Dendy Sadler's 'Thursday' and 'Friday' pictures of jolly friars fishing one day, and heartily tucking into the results the following day.

INFORMATION
Length of walk: 2½ miles if starting from Church Lane, just over 1½ if starting from Meadow Lane. Approximate time: 1½ hours

TERRAIN:
Surfaced road and grassy paths. The path which cuts straight across Hemingford Marshes is surfaced, so this route to Houghton Mill and back could be an alternative for a pushchair or wheelchair.

PARKING:
Park near the Axe and Compass pub, at the junction of Church Lane and Common Road, or near the footbridge at Meadow Lane.

OPEN:
Houghton Mill (NT). Apr-May, Sep-mid-Oct, Sat-Sun 2-5.30pm, Jun-Aug, Sat-Wed, 2-5.30pm. Charge.

REFRESHMENTS:
Pubs in the village.

ILAM

STAFFORDSHIRE

On unclassified roads, 5m NW of Ashbourne

THIS tiny village, situated where the Peak District National Park ventures into Staffordshire, consists of little more than a handful of Alpine-style estate cottages, a great early 19th-century Hall and many acres of broad parkland beside the winding River Manifold. The National Trust owns the Hall and park, as well as many of the surrounding hills and the beauty spot of Dovedale, only 1 ½ miles away. The settlement dates back to at least 1004, when the Benedictine Abbey at Burton-upon-Trent acquired Hilum, as it then was. In 1546, after the Dissolution of the Monasteries, John Port became Lord of the Manor, and his family lived at Ilam until 1809. In 1820 the estate was inherited by Mary Watts Russell, whose husband Jesse was responsible for most of what we see now, including the estate cottages and the rather quaint school, all built in 1857.

WALK DIRECTIONS

From the National Trust car park beside Ilam Hall descend to St Bertram's Bridge, which spans the River Manifold. Restored in 1839, it was the main local crossing point before the bridge in the village was built. Turn right along the near bank, soon passing two boil holes, where underground streams emerge into the river, and the grotto in which the hermit Bertram is said to have lived.

Further on climb steps to reach Congreve's Grotto. The stone seat and table overlooking the river are believed to have been used by the 19-year-old William Congreve when writing his first play, *The Old Bachelor,* in 1689.

Restoration of this medieval church was Russell's last project.

Return to the path, known as Paradise Walk, which was laid out for the occupants of the Hall. It passes the Battlestone, a Saxon battle cross that probably marked the site of a battle between Saxons and Danes. The cross was discovered in the foundations of an old cottage when it was demolished to make way for the present estate houses.

Continue along the path, now moving away from the river, with Hinkley Wood cloaking the high bank beyond. The wood, noted for its large and small-leafed limes, is a Site of Special Scientific Interest. A steep alternative path climbs through it from St Bertram's Bridge and descends to a footbridge before joining Paradise Walk.

5

Follow the path until it regains the riverbank. Opposite a footbridge take a faint path angling back up a bank and cross Ilam Park, bearing left of the trees and aiming for the distant flat-topped Thorpe Cloud. Note the undulating grassland – the remains of a medieval ridge and furrow system.

The remains of a once vast Ilam Hall.

6

Join a green track leading to a gate and stile opposite the school at Ilam. Follow the road right, past the village green to the cross and river bridge. Turn back as far as the entrance to the Country Park and enter a gate on your left. A path runs past the church to the Hall. For the tearooms go through an archway in the tower ahead and turn left.

INFORMATION
Length of walk:
1¼ miles (3¼ or 3¾ miles with options)
Approximate time:
1½ hours (2 or 2¼ hours with options)

TERRAIN:
Suitable for children at all times of year; only suitable for pushchairs in dry weather; not suitable for wheelchairs. One stile, no footbridges. Easy walking.

PARKING:
National Trust pay car park and toilets at Ilam Hall (free for Trust members). Free car park for youth hostel guests.

OPEN:
The National Trust Shop and Information Centre, including a permanent exhibition, in Ilam Hall Country Park. Daily Apr-Oct and weekends during the rest of the year.
Ilam Hall is a youth hostel and is not open to the general public.

REFRESHMENTS:
Tearooms in the stable block, Ilam Hall; the Izaak Walton Hotel, 1m E.

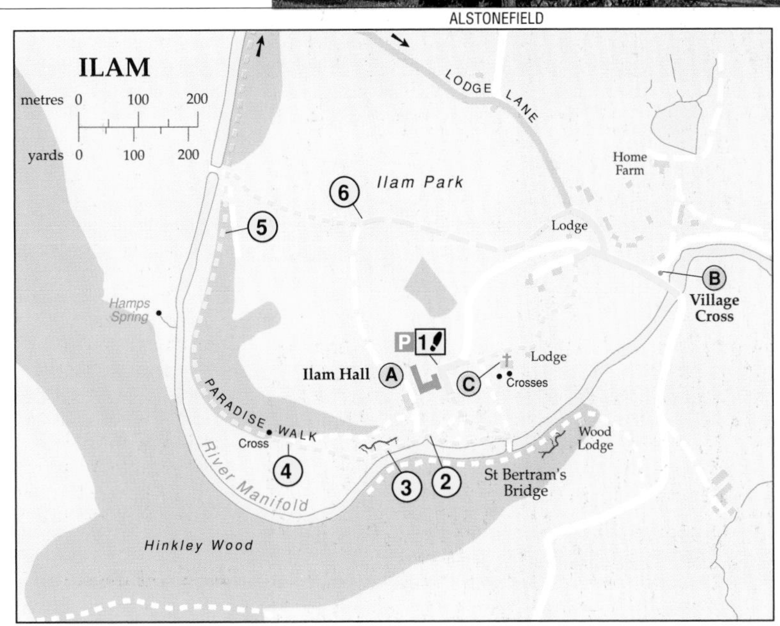

The broken shaft of an Eleanor Cross, erected as a memorial to Mary Watts Russell, wife of Jesse.

The River Manifold emerges from the cliffs as a stream, in the grounds of Ilam Hall.

POINTS OF INTEREST

Ilam Hall. Large though the building is, there remains today barely a quarter of the vast Gothic house built by Mary Watts Russell for her husband Jesse in the early 1820s. On his death in 1875, the Hall passed to the Hanbury family, who sold it in 1927. After failing as a restaurant, it was purchased by a demolition contractor. About three-quarters of the massive pile had been knocked down before Sir Robert McDougall bought the estate and gave it to the National Trust, specifying that the Hall should be leased to the Youth Hostels Association. The oldest surviving part is the stable block, behind the Hall, which is believed to date back to the Port era. Immediately south of the Hall, though partly lost to the car park, are the Italian Formal Gardens. To the north is the Pepper Pot, a tall octagonal tower built as a dovecote. The estate, now a country park, consists of 84 acres of parkland and broadleaved woodland.

The Village Cross. The centrepiece of the village is the 30ft-high Eleanor Cross erected in 1840 in memory of Mary Watts Russell. This type of decorated cross takes its name from Queen Eleanor, wife of Edward I, who died in Nottinghamshire in 1290. The King set up such crosses at each place where the funeral cortège rested on its way to London, the last of them being Charing Cross.

Church of the Holy Cross. The church, with its saddleback tower, is of the 13th century, though restored by Sir Gilbert Scott in 1855. It contains a Saxon font and the Watts Russell Mausoleum, built in 1831. Mary Watts Russell's father, David Pike Watts, is represented on his deathbed, surrounded by his daughter and grandchildren, in a fine group of statuary by Sir Francis Chantrey. The church also contains the Chapel of St Bertram, built in 1618 to house the saint's tomb.

For an optional longer walk of 2 miles from point 5, instead of crossing Ilam Park continue beside the Manifold to River Lodge. Since the path is concessionary walkers are asked to put 2p each in a box in the Lodge garden. An inscription tells us that 'The first Stone of River Lodge was laid on the 6th of May 1840, by Jemima, Countess of Montgelas'. From the Lodge either follow the lane to the right to reach Ilam village, or go left for an extra ¼-mile to where Rushley Bridge crosses the river, before turning back and continuing to Ilam.

THE RIVER MANIFOLD

A curiosity of the Manifold, and of its tributary the Hamps, is that they are often found to be dry-bedded in summer, due to their tendency to disappear underground; a characteristic of rivers in limestone country. Like the more famous Dove, with which it merges below the village of Ilam, the Manifold rises high on the wild Axe Edge, near Buxton, and descends to a gentler, more tranquil setting at Ilam.

From 1904 to 1934 the Manifold Valley was traversed by the Leek & Manifold Light Railway. Today its track has been lifted and the line converted to a broad path used by walkers and cyclists, especially those who take advantage of local cycle-hire schemes.

ST BERTRAM

Also known as Bertelin, the Saint lived in the 8th or 9th century and may have been a son of a king of Mercia. He is said to have gone to Ireland, where he eloped with a beautiful princess, who bore him a child whilst sheltering in a forest on their way home. There, the mother and child were killed by wolves, and the distraught prince retired to live the life of a hermit in a cave at Ilam. His shrine, now in the church, was believed to be the scene of many miraculous cures, and the holes in its sides had to be blocked by railings to prevent pilgrims from crawling through.

ILMINGTON

WARWICKSHIRE

On unclassified roads 7½m S of Stratford-upon-Avon, 3m W of A34(T)

THE large, stone-built village stands where the Feldon, or southern Warwickshire plain, meets the Cotswolds. A chalybeate spring turned it into a minor spa for a while, a century ago, but today's visitors come to visit Ilmington's picturesque lanes and alleys, or to walk its many lovely fieldpaths. Nearby attractions, just across the Gloucestershire border, include the National Trust's Hidcote Manor Garden and the privately owned garden at Kiftsgate Court, both about 2½ miles away.

INFORMATION
Length of walk:
2 miles
Approximate time:
1½ hours

TERRAIN:
Suitable for children at all times of year. Not suitable for pushchairs or wheelchairs. Eight stiles and one footbridge.

PARKING:
At roadside in Back Street, W of the church.

OPEN:
Hidcote Manor Garden. Gardens only Apr-Oct, daily (except Tue and Fri), 11am-8pm. Charge.
Kiftsgate Court Garden. Apr-Sep, Wed, Thu, Sun and BH, 2-6pm. Charge.

REFRESHMENTS:
Inns in village.

WALK DIRECTIONS

From Back Street take the path through to the churchyard. After visiting the church, continue to a gabled stone cottage and bear right along an orchard wall to reach a road.

Turn right, passing a drinking fountain of 1864 and a war memorial high on the sloping Upper Green. At a junction, bear left along Campden Street and go through a gate on the left, immediately beyond Hill House. The path drops through allotments and crosses two stiles to reach a green track.

Turning right and immediately left, follow a garden fence to a stile leading into a meadow and skirt its lower edge to cross a railed footbridge on your right, with stiles at each end. Go left to another stile and climb a field-edge. Walkers wishing to return to the village without climbing further can do so by crossing two stiles to the left leading to a green lane, which will bring them down to rejoin the full route at Crab Mill.

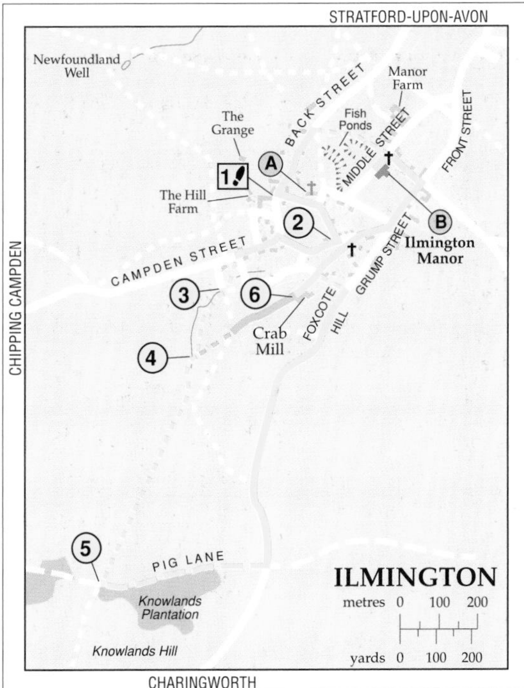

④

Long views north over the Warwickshire plain open out as you continue through a hedge-gap and over two more stiles to the unsurfaced Pig Lane at the top of Knowlands Hill, about 700ft above sea-level. Foxcote House can be seen far below in the valley away to the south.

Bear left along the lane and left again to descend a metalled road, with fine views eastwards. On the outskirts of Ilmington, turn left through a vehicle barrier and, on reaching a road, go left to view the stone-built Crab Mill of 1711.

⑥

Turn back and follow the road along the top of Upper Green. Bear round to the left, into Church Street, passing the manor house gate, and immediately before the Red Lion go left along a 'No Through Road'. Emerging on Middle Street, opposite a kissing-gate, bear left to see the manor house. Return to the kissing-gate and follow a path below a large embanked pool to a gate, from which the path veers left to a kissing-gate on Back Street. Turn left to return to the start of the walk.

POINTS OF INTEREST

St Mary's Church. A cruciform building, tucked away from the village streets. You enter by a Norman doorway, with an empty niche above, and find Norman arches to the tower and chancel. An ancient stone effigy survives in the bell tower and, as at Berkswell, there are 11 carved mice by Robert Thompson of Kilburn in Yorkshire. Near the porch is an unusual tomb in the form of a Gothic church and a gravestone to a parishioner who reached the grand old age of 106 years, 9 months and 11 days.

Ilmington Manor. Hidden, like the church, from the casual passer-through, the 16th-century manor house has mullioned windows, gables and a lovely garden, glimpsed from the narrow, pedestrianised Middle Street. It has known bad times – the indignity of squatters, a working life as a post office – but now resumes its place as one of the attractions of the village. The large pool on the other side of Middle Street occupies the site of fish-ponds belonging to the manor in its early days.

The beautiful gardens of the 16th-century manor.

FOXCOTE HOUSE

Just 1½m SW of the village and visible from the highest point of the walk, the fine, three-storeyed, early 18th-century mansion was probably built by Edward Woodward of Chipping Campden. It was later occupied by such leading local families as the Cannings and the Howards. The latter gave their name to the Howard Arms, the inn by Lower Green, at the north end of Ilmington.

KERSEY

SUFFOLK

Off A1141, 10m W of Ipswich

KERSEY is an oddity amongst East Anglian villages in that it is built across a valley, rather than along it. The single main street, lined with picturesque timber-framed weavers' cottages, runs north-west/south-east, with its famous and much-photographed watersplash down the middle. Kersey was a weaving town, producing a coarse-ribbed cloth often used in the Middle Ages for stockings, and the stream which runs across the street would have been used for washing the wool. Shakespeare had Berowne, in *Love's Labour's Lost*, deciding to avoid the company of women, with the words: 'Henceforth my wooing mind shall be express'd in russet yeas and honest kersey noes.'

Running steeply down a single road to a water splash, and up again, Kersey is a peaceful, multi-coloured village.

Just to the north-west is another wool village, Lindsey, which also gave its name to a coarse textile of mixed wool and flax – linsey-woolsey. Nearby St James's Chapel is the shell of a medieval chapel once attached to the local castle.

The wool industry came to an end in East Anglia in the 17th century, and Kersey then became dependent on agriculture for its livelihood. Now, although the village is surrounded by huge arable fields, very few of Kersey's 350 inhabitants work on the land.

POINTS OF INTEREST

St Mary's Church. Set in a beautiful position overlooking the village, the church stands as a fair indication of Kersey's wealth as a weaving centre. Apart from its sheer size, the decoration within, although much ravaged at the hands of 17th-century iconoclasts and 19th-century restorers, still bears witness to former splendour. The ornate flint flushwork of the south porch is particularly impressive, and inside, the south wall displays faded traces of a painting showing St George slaying the Dragon.

Kersey Watersplash. This is the focal point of the village, where the main street fords a tributary to the River Brett, which in turn is a tributary to the River Stour. Car owners driving through may feel inclined to test their brakes – in times past, the watersplash would undoubtedly have been the local cart-wash! The ducks take precedence here, but pedestrians need have no fear about getting their feet wet, as there is a footbridge on one side of the road.

INFORMATION
Length of walk: 2/3 mile
Approximate time: 3/4 hour

TERRAIN:
Surfaced road and unsurfaced footpath. Unsuitable for push-chairs and wheelchairs.

PARKING:
Park as near to the church as possible.

OPEN:
St James's Chapel (EH), Lindsey, is open all year from dawn to dusk.

REFRESHMENTS:
Village inns in main street.

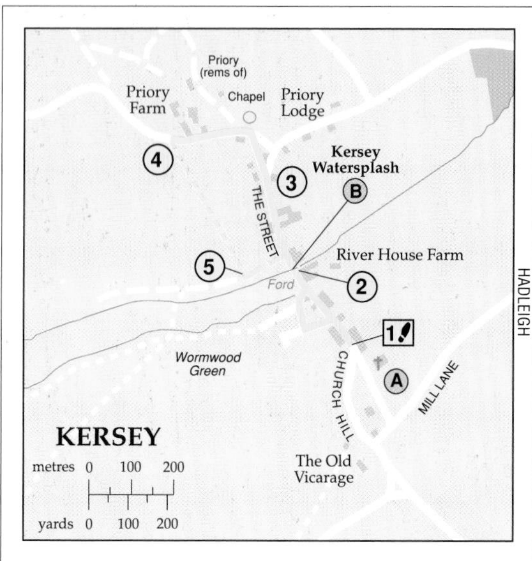

WEAVERS' COTTAGES

There is scarcely a house in Kersey without character. Timber-framed cottages with leaning colour-washed walls, overhanging gables and some thatched, but mainly pantiled roofs (and sadly some are covered in non-indigenous slate) abound. The old weaving industry of the Middle Ages was literally a cottage industry, and each weaver's cottage would have had a loom clattering away inside, producing the cloth which made Kersey's fortune, whilst the larger houses would have belonged to merchants. Although most of Kersey's houses, and its two pubs, are exceedingly pleasing on the eye, the 500 year-old River House, by the ford, with its huge oak door, is particularly attractive.

WALK DIRECTIONS

1

Start from the top of the hill, close to the church. Walk down the hill and just past a house on the right sporting an old AA sign, take the left turning. The road curves round in a short loop, taking in some delightful cottages, before rejoining the main street close to the water-splash.

Go over the watersplash (using the footbridge) and head up the other side. Just opposite the White Horse public house, embedded in the pavement, is a pudding-stone; a large conglomerate stone which because of its scarcity, would have been placed somewhere significant, as a marker for an ancient track.

Where the road bends round to the right, continue straight on along the surfaced path to the junction with the road at the top, and there turn left.

Continue along the road, and turn left on to a public footpath (signposted) down the side of a field. At the bottom corner of the field, continue straight on, following the path through the allotments.

Turn left on to the track, which emerges on to the main street near the water-splash. Cross over, and return along the main street to the church.

LAVENHAM

SUFFOLK

On A1141, 7m NE of Sudbury

LAVENHAM is the finest and most complete surviving medieval town in England. The mere mention of its name conjures up visions of timbered houses in rows, with leaning walls, overhanging upper storeys, and scarcely a true vertical or horizontal line to be found anywhere. Yet, it would be wrong to imagine Lavenham as a typical town of the era. The timbers, studded closely for decorative effect rather than any structural requirement, indicate enormous wealth, particularly so in the 15th century, when mature oak was already expensive.

Such extravagance was paid for by the woollen cloth trade, of which Lavenham was a leading centre. Here, weavers and merchants continued an industry started in the 14th century, producing the heavy woollen broadcloth which was common to all the wool centres. Lavenham's reputation was built on its fine quality broadcloth, where both warp and weft were made from carded wool. An influx of Flemish weavers during the reign of Elizabeth I brought new techniques. Technology killed off the wool industry in East Anglia. Cottage looms were unable to compete with the mechanical ones powered by fast-flowing Pennine water.

The black and white, timbered splendour of the Swan Hotel is typical of Lavenham's extravagant buildings.

WALK DIRECTIONS

Start from the free car park near the church. Turn right down Church Street, passing Bear's Lane on the right.

Turn right into Water Street, with the Swan Hotel on the corner. The Priory is found on the right, opposite the junction with Lady Street. Continue up Water Street.

Just past Lavenham Press, turn left into Shilling Street. Up the hill on the right is Shilling Old Grange, home of the Taylor family, one of whom, Jane, wrote the famous children's nursery rhyme *Twinkle, Twinkle, Little Star*.

At the junction at the top of the hill, go right into Bolton Street (down again), left at the bottom and then left again up Prentice Street, emerging for a brief glimpse of the market place.

Go left round the Great House Hotel on the corner, and walk down Barn Street, turning right, back into Water Street.

Turn right into Lady Street, with the Old Wool Hall on your left, and continue up the hill once more to the market place. The Guildhall is on the right.

Just across the market place, go left down Market Lane (vehicles prohibited sign), and turn left on to High Street, then right on to Hall Road.

8

Just before the road bends round to the right, take the public footpath signposted to the left. Follow a pleasant, shady path down to a small footbridge, and pass through a gate into a field. Head across to the opposite corner, and continue on into the churchyard. The entrance to the village church is on the other side, and the car park can be found just across the road.

INFORMATION
Length of walk:
$1^1/_4$ miles
Approximate time:
$1^1/_2$ hours

TERRAIN:
All surfaced except for one short footpath section near church. Suitable for pushchairs and wheelchairs, except for the path between points 8 and 1.

PARKING:
Use the free car park near the church.

OPEN:
Lavenham Guildhall (NT). Daily Easter-Oct, 11am-1pm, 2-5.30pm. Charge.
The Priory. Daily Easter-Oct, 10.30am-5.30pm. Charge.
Little Hall. Easter-Oct, Sat-Sun and Bank Hols, 2.30-6pm.

REFRESHMENTS:
Village inns.

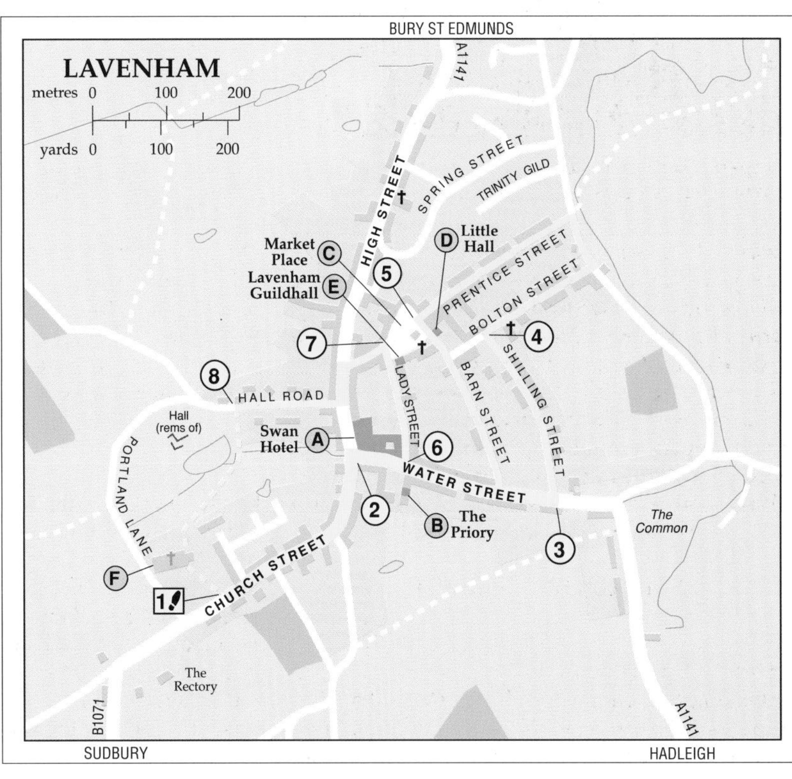

POINTS OF INTEREST

The Swan Hotel. This superb timbered building was a favourite meeting place for American airmen based in the area during the Second World War. There is a large collection of memorabilia from this era, including one section of wall in the bar inscribed with many signatures.

The Priory. A timber-framed house which was, at various times, the home to Benedictine monks, medieval clothiers and an Elizabethan rector. Only a few years ago, the building was on the brink of collapse, but it was rescued from ruin by its current owners. A great deal of original detail was uncovered during the restoration, exposing the frame, and Elizabethan wall paintings.

At the rear of the house is a courtyard, and a herb garden with an unusual design.

Market Place. A triangular space crowning a hilltop, surrounded almost entirely by timber framed buildings, including the Corpus Christi Guildhall, the Angel Hotel, and Little Hall. The cross in the market place has stood there since 1502.

Little Hall. This 14th-century house is now the home of the Suffolk Preservation Society. The main door is decorated with an arrangement of pointed arches, common to several houses in Lavenham. Inside is the Gayer-Anderson Collection of antique furniture, pictures, ceramics and books.

The beautiful Guildhall was built in 1529.

Lavenham Guildhall. Originally the hall of the Guild of Corpus Christi, the early 16th-century timber-framed Guildhall dominates the market place. Over the years, the building has been used as a store, shop, school, prison and community centre. Inside, is a display about local history, with an emphasis on the 700-year woollen cloth industry, including an original loom in working order, and there is a room devoted to the Taylor family of *Twinkle, Twinkle Little Star* fame.

Ⓕ

Church of St Peter and St Paul. A smaller church originally occupied this site, but it was replaced by the present building between 1444 and 1525. It is a splendid example of late Perpendicular architecture, and its mass of clear windows provides an unusually bright interior. The church was financed by two families, the Springs, the leading cloth merchants in the area, and the de Veres, the Earls of Oxford. For the time, it was an unusual partnership between the bourgeoisie and the aristocracy. Each family has its own chantry chapel in the church. Although already a soaring 141ft, the tower was never completed.

THE SUFFOLK WOOL CHURCHES

The glory of the Suffolk wool churches is inextricably linked to the industry which made East Anglia the wealthiest region of the country during the Middle Ages. Up until the 14th century, most of England's wool was exported as raw material. Very little was woven here, and most woven products were imported. In 1326, Edward III decided to encourage home production by banning the import of foreign cloth, and offering franchises to weavers, dyers and fullers.

This encouragement alone was not enough to establish a cottage industry, and it was only when he allowed in immigrant craftsmen that it started to take off. Enterprising Dutch and Flemish weavers, keen, no doubt, to save the expense of shipping raw material across the North Sea, settled in East Anglia. Here was a ready market for woollen cloth, in areas where they already had trading connections – around Ipswich and Colchester, and along the Stour valley.

The weavers and cloth merchants celebrated their wealth, and perhaps eased their consciences too, by building magnificent churches. Many of them were built using materials shipped from afar, and unlike the major cathedrals of the area which were planned close to navigable waterways, the wool churches did not all have such a convenience, so the transportation of building material by land would have added considerably to the cost.

Fourteenth-century Lavenham Little Hall (far left), and the village church (left) of Saints Peter and Paul.

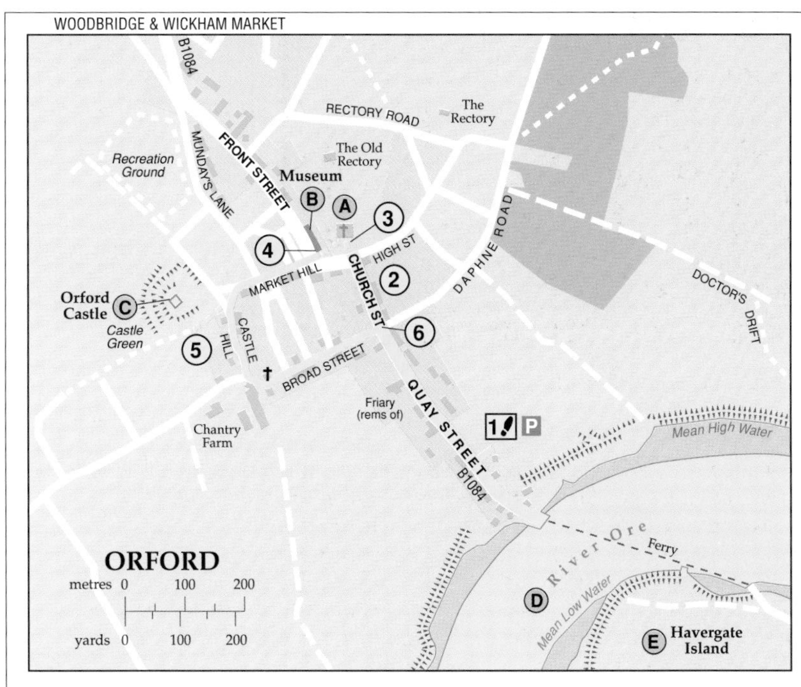

ORFORD

SUFFOLK

On B1084, 10m E of Woodbridge

SET amidst miles of lonely marsh, with forests inland, Orford occupies an undeniably peaceful setting. Despite the fact that both Rendlesham and Tunstall forests were severely battered by the Great Storm of October 1987 and subsequent gales, the drive to Orford along winding roads east of Woodbridge is a pleasant one. As you arrive in the market square, the keep of Orford Castle rises above trees and houses. It was built by Henry II as a foothold in East Anglia, dominated by the powerful and rebellious Bigod family, the Dukes of Norfolk.

At the time the castle was built, and right up to the 16th century, Orford was a thriving port, with access to the open sea. It began to decline with the build-up of the shingle spit which starts six miles further up the coast. The result of a tidal action called longshore drift it still continues at an average rate of 16yds per year. Today, the quay is a base for fishing boats and pleasure craft.

Beyond Havergate Island is Orford Ness, a six-mile spit of shingle which deflects the course of the River Alde from its more natural point of entry to the sea at Aldeburgh. It was used by Robert Watson-Watt during the Second World War for his radar research station, and afterwards for secret work connected with the development of nuclear weapons. At the north end, the multiple aerials of the US Air Force 'Cobra Mist' radio research station are clearly visible. Used between 1967 and 1970, it was an experimental 'over-the-horizon' radar for early warning of ballistic missiles. The aerials which transmit the BBC World Service are also sited here.

INFORMATION
Length of walk:
1 mile
Approximate time:
1½ hours

TERRAIN:
Surfaced roads. No special footwear needed. Suitable for pushchairs and wheelchairs.

PARKING:
There is a small amount of free car parking on Market Hill, but it is often full in summer. The walk starts from the pay and display Town Marsh car park in Quay Street, opposite the Jolly Sailor inn.

OPEN:
Orford Castle (EH). Daily Easter-Sep 10am-6pm. The rest of the year: Daily except Mon, 10am-4pm. Charge. Dunwich Underwater Exploration Museum. Daily all year. Charge. Havergate Island (RSPB). Access by permit only, obtainable in advance from the RSPB.

REFRESHMENTS:
Village inns.

WALK DIRECTIONS

Start from the Town Marsh car park. The site of the car park was under water in the 16th century, when the creek and harbour extended the length of Quay Street. Turn right, heading up Quay Street, continuing on beyond the junction with Broad Street.

Walk up Church Street, and straight ahead into the churchyard.

After visiting the church, take the other path out of the churchyard into Front Street, beside the King's Head Inn. The craft shop containing the Dunwich Underwater Exploration Museum can be found next door.

Return to Market Hill, and turn right, past the Crown and Castle Hotel, and head towards the castle.

After visiting the castle, turn right out of the entrance into Castle Hill, and turn left into the aptly named Broad Street. Chantry Farm House on the corner has typical examples of Dutch style bell-shaped gables.

At the crossroads, turn right, heading back down Quay Street. Before returning to the car park, continue down to the quay for a fine view of the river, Havergate Island and Orford Ness beyond.

The unique irregular eighteen-sided tower of Orford's once large castle – built by Henry II during the 12th century.

OYSTERS

The Butley River, which feeds into the River Ore near the southern end of Havergate Island, is a prime breeding ground for a large, flat variety of oyster. They have been a popular food for hundreds of years and the shells have even turned up in prehistoric refuse heaps. Oysters from here and other East Coast estuaries such as the River Colne were particular favourites of Julius Caesar, who used to send them home by the shipload. They spawn during the summer months, and traditionally cannot be eaten when there is no 'R' in the month. Oysters grown in the estuary waters can be tasted at the Orford Oysterage, on Market Hill.

THE ORFORD MERMAN

According to legend, local fishermen once caught a naked wild merman in their nets. They took him to the castle, where, despite being hung up by the heels and tortured, he refused to speak, nor would he show any signs of reverence when taken into the church. The people of Orford kept him prisoner, allowing him to swim about in the harbour, cut off from the sea by suspended nets.

The merman outwitted his captors by diving beneath the nets, and so made good his escape to the sea.

The Oysterage (top) just off the village square on Market Hill. Orford is now famous for its smokery which does not only smoke fish. In summer pleasure craft come up the River Ore (above) from the North Sea.

POINTS OF INTEREST

Ⓐ

St Bartholomew's Church. Like much of the castle, the church is built from the rough-looking septaria, a soft local stone. The original chancel, now in ruins, was probably built at about the same time as the castle. The broad nave dates from the 14th century, when the growth of the town necessitated a larger church. In recent years the church was 'put on the map' when it became the setting for the first performance of Benjamin Britten's *Noye's Fludde*, and a dedication to Britten can be found in the floor at the west end.

Dunwich Underwater Exploration Museum. Whilst the former capital of East Anglia may have become an English Atlantis, divers are still able to explore the remains on the sea-bed. The museum, above the craft shop in Front Street, contains exhibits detailing the exploration, and some of the finds which have been brought to the surface. The building itself was a 19th-century coach house, operating services to Felixstowe and Ipswich up until 1910.

Orford Castle. Built by Henry II in the late 1160s, Orford Castle has two major claims to fame. It is the oldest castle for which any documentary evidence exists – in this case, the Pipe Rolls, the financial records of the King's Exchequer. Secondly, it was the first castle to be built with a keep which is cylindrical inside, and polygonal outside. This 'inside out' structure, reinforced by three projecting rectangular turrets, was designed to make the castle better to defend all points around its circumference, and also made it less likely to collapse if its foundations were undermined during a siege.

The River Ore. Were it not for the long strip of shingle which has built up over the centuries, the River Ore might not exist. Further upstream, at Slaughden, where it once entered the sea, it is the River Alde. And indeed, for a few hours during the terrible flood of 1953, Orford Ness was breached by the sea at Slaughden.

At the beginning of the 19th century, a scheme was suggested to revive Orford as a port. It involved damming the river at Havergate Island, and cutting a channel through the spit of Orford Ness. The idea never got off the ground, and just as well!

During the 18th century, the seclusion of this stretch of coast made it an ideal place for smugglers to operate, and thousands of gallons of illicit gin and brandy came ashore here. Margaret Catchpole was one of the most notable local smugglers, but in the stories that surround her exploits, it is not clear whether her accomplice, Will Laud, reputedly shot dead by the Preventive men on Orford Beach in 1800, really existed or not.

Havergate Island. Much of the Suffolk coast provides superb opportunities for watching waders and wildfowl. Access to the Havergate Island reserve is limited to those who apply to the RSPB for a permit, and numbers per visit are restricted to 12 persons, the maximum allowed in the boat, which departs from Orford Quay.

The lagoon at the southern end of the island came about as the result of a chance hit during the Second World War, when the island was used as an artillery range. One of the shells damaged the sluices which controlled the water level, allowing the area to flood. In some ways the flooding proved fortunate, as shortly after the end of the war, avocets returned here and to nearby Minsmere to breed following an absence of nearly a hundred years.

SAXILBY
LINCOLNSHIRE

Off the A57, 6 miles NW of Lincoln

SAXILBY lies on the banks of a Roman canal; a position which has over the centuries brought wealth to the village and left a row of attractive and interesting buildings alongside the waterway. It is a village with two centres; St Botolph's church occupies higher ground half a mile away from the canal, and in the past must have cast a disapproving eye over the antics of its commercial waterside twin.

INFORMATION
Length of walk: 1½ miles
Approximate time: 1 hour

TERRAIN:
Suitable for children and pushchairs; some mud after wet weather. The path is narrow and not suitable for wheelchairs. No stiles.

PARKING:
Follow the Village Centre signs from the A57. Use the car park on Sykes Lane, which is signposted from High Street.

OPEN:
St Botolph's church is open during daylight hours.

Good coarse fishing is possible on the Fossdyke at Saxilby. Other centres are Lincoln and Torksey.

POINTS OF INTEREST

The Village Sign. A touching tribute to a local councillor, Geoffrey Ford, the village sign shows the parish church, a Lincoln Red cow, a sailing keel, and the ubiquitous Lincolnshire poacher.

(B)

Fossdyke. This is possibly the oldest canal in Britain. A statuette of Mars, the god of war, found in the canal bed at nearby Torksey confirms its Roman origin - an artificial cut to link Lincoln to the River Trent and thence by the Humber and Ouse to York. Unlike its cousin, the Car Dyke, this canal was not totally forgotten after the Romans left, and the route was re-opened in 1121 by Henry I. The last commercial cargo passed this way as recently as 1971.

The Swing Bridge. For almost a century this bridge carried the main Lincoln road over the Fossdyke - it was built around 1846 by the Great Northern Railway, who at that time owned the canal. With the coming of the motor age the bridge proved to be a liability: weight restrictions were imposed and buses had to unload their passengers before crossing. Its days were numbered and it was superseded in 1937 by the modern bypass.

Picnic Site. The 'no-man's-land' on the south side of the Fossdyke, between the canal and the railway, was the scene in 1987 of a conservation project by British Waterways and the District Council. The area is now overhung by willows.

St Botolph's Church. This enigmatic building has great 'Perpendicular' windows, which give the impression that the church dates from the 15th century. However, in the north wall there is a little round-headed Norman doorway which is over 300 years older. Inside the church are copies of sheet music five centuries old.

WALK DIRECTIONS

From the car park, return to High Street. Turn right along the village street, passing the village sign on the right.

Follow the road as it bends to the left alongside the Fossdyke.

Cross the metal footbridge opposite The Ship public house to explore the remains of the old swing-bridge and the picnic area on the far side of the canal. Retrace your steps over the bridge and take the footpath which leaves Bridge Street directly opposite the bridge.

Follow the path through the Recreation Ground and past the War Memorial gates. Pass to the left of a *Leylandii*-hedged tennis court and where the tarmac path goes left, bear right into a snicket between gardens. Cross Highfield Road and continue along the surfaced path to emerge on to Manor Road opposite a shop.

(5)

Turn right and first left into Meadow Rise; a signposted footpath leaves the road on a sharp right-hand bend.

(6)

Reach Church Road beside a telephone box and turn right and then immediately left to enter the churchyard of St Botolph's church.

(7)

After visiting the church, retrace your steps to the edge of the churchyard and turn right down Church Road, passing the telephone box once more. Carry on down the road, past a half-timbered house, and back into the village centre.

Turn right into Sykes Lane to return to the car park.

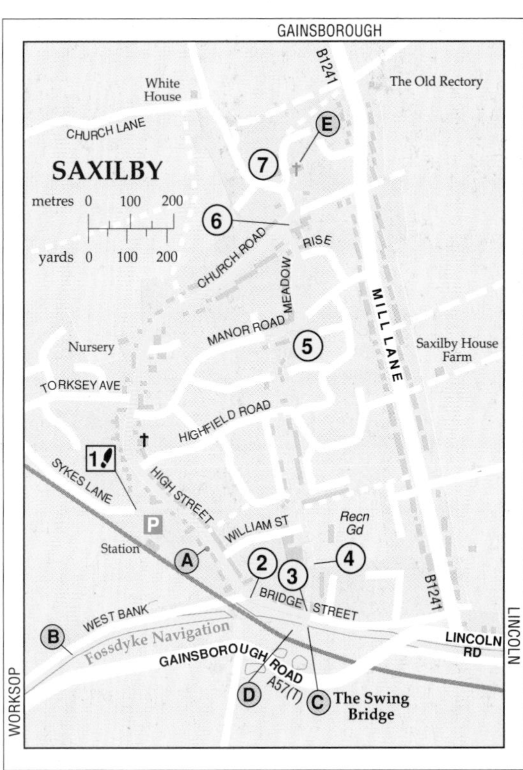

SWAFFHAM PRIOR

CAMBRIDGESHIRE

On B1102, 6 miles W of Newmarket

CAMBRIDGESHIRE can boast little in the way of hills, but Swaffham Prior occupies one of the few, its two churches standing over a main street lined by Georgian houses and cottages.

To the north of the village is Devil's Dyke, an 8th-century defensive earthwork constructed by the East Anglians against Mercia, to the west.

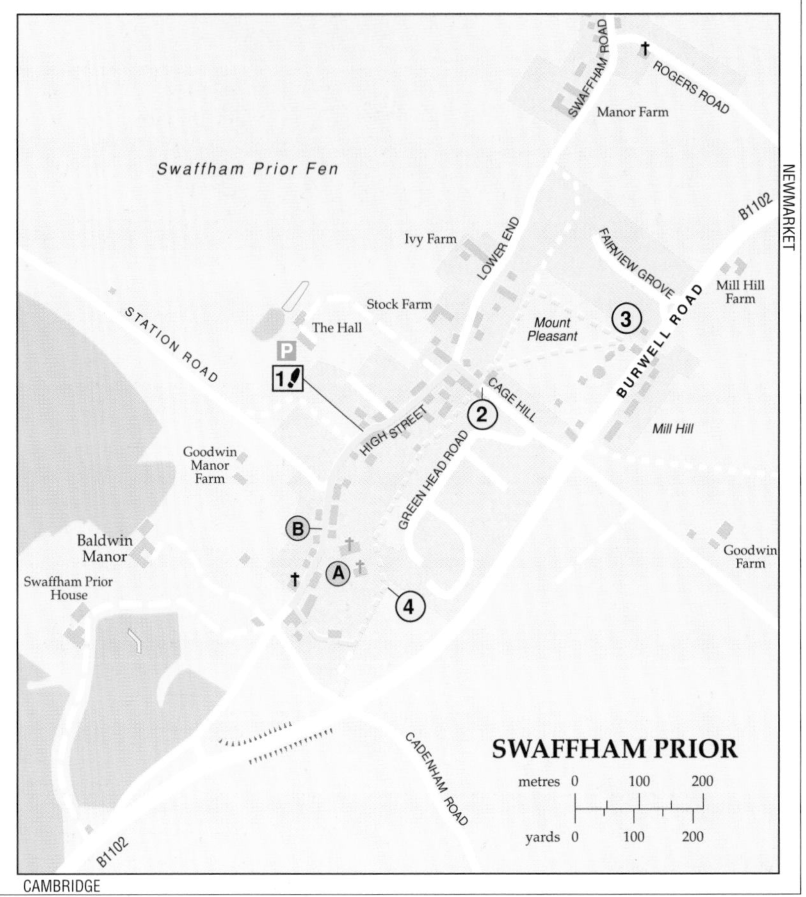

POINTS OF INTEREST

Ⓐ

St Mary's and St Cyriac's. This attractive Fenland village has two churches side by side in one Saxon churchyard. This is not unheard of, but in most other cases, one of the churches will have fallen into ruin, or disappeared altogether. The village was once split into two parishes, each with its own church. The parishes were united by Act of Parliament in 1667, and the nave of St Cyriac's was demolished, leaving the tower and bells intact. But when, a hundred years later, the spire of St Mary's was struck by lightning, the parishioners refused to worship there and St Cyriac's was rebuilt.

After another hundred years, St Mary's had fallen into an advanced state of deterioration. Restoration began, and the main work was completed at the turn of the century. In the meantime, St Cyriac's had fallen into disrepair once more, but it was restored in 1976 by the Redundant Churches Commission.

Ⓑ

The High Street. The curved High Street is a mixture of demure cottages and Georgian houses, some up against the road, others set back in shady gardens. Visible from the road at the south-western corner of the route is Baldwin Manor, a beautiful example of a Tudor timber-framed house.

WALK DIRECTIONS

①

Turn left from the car park on to the High Street. Just past the telephone box, turn right on to Cage Hill.

Turn left at the post office (public footpath sign), and almost immediately after, take the fork on to the right-hand path. Follow the path through the allotment, straight for a windmill, and out along a gravelled drive to the road.

Follow the road down to a small housing estate, and where the road bends left, take the path straight ahead. Follow the fence around until you come to a T-junction with another path, and go left. Follow the path back to Cage Hill. Go straight over the road, and on to the path ahead, which runs between domestic gardens. Cross a small green, with a stile for the churchyard in the right-hand corner, to view the two churches.

④

Walk through the churchyard to a gate in the south-east corner. Take the grassy track ahead, passing between wooden barriers. The track swings round to the right, bordered by trees to the left, and a hedge and house beyond to the right. The track emerges on to the High Street, where you turn right. Carry on down the road, with the Red Lion pub on the right. The turning for the car park is just past the junction with Station Road.

INFORMATION
Length of walk: Just over 1 mile
Approximate time: ½ hour

TERRAIN:
Easy. Some unsurfaced paths might be a little muddy in wet weather. Suitable for children but for pushchairs only in dry weather.

PARKING:
Park in the signposted car park off the High Street.

OPEN:
Anglesey Abbey and Lode Water Mill: weekends from Easter to Oct. (Charge). Stevens Mill, Burwell (2½ miles NE of Swaffham Prior): Every other Sun, or by arrangement (tel: (0223) 811233 office hours). No charge but donations welcome.

Two churches in one churchyard: Swaffham Prior.

TURVEY

BEDFORDSHIRE

On A428(T), 7 miles W of Bedford

THIS Bedfordshire village lies amid rich and gently undulating farmland immediately east of the River Great Ouse, which here marks the county boundary with Buckinghamshire. Perhaps as far back as 1800BC the Beaker people settled here at the river crossing; much later came the Romans. The Mordaunts, Lords of the Manor in the late Middle Ages, have their great monuments in the parish church, though they are far outnumbered by the later Higgins memorials.

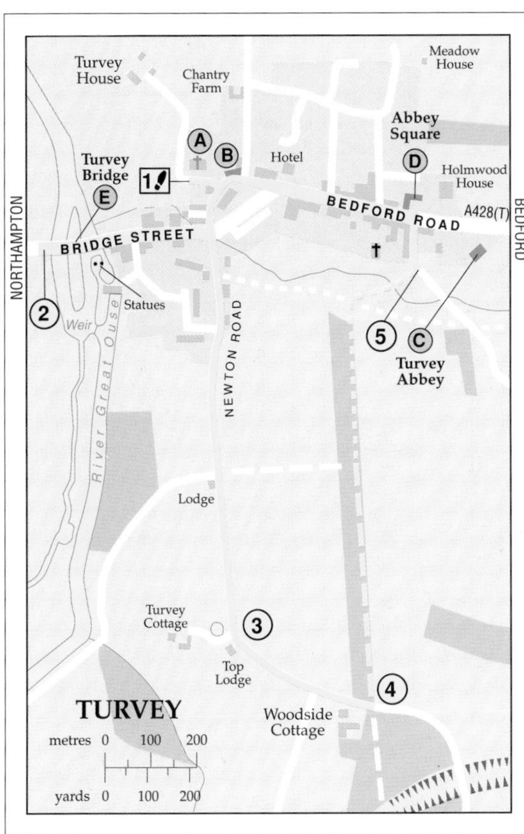

WALK DIRECTIONS

①

From the church, walk past the Three Cranes Inn to Bridge Street (noting the old rectory at the junction with the Carlton road) and turn right to the Three Fyshes Inn and Turvey Bridge. From just beyond the bridge there is a good view of Turvey House.

②

Return along Bridge Street and enter Newton Lane on your right.

③

Where the lane bends right, keep ahead of a bye way, soon there are good views across the valley of the Great Ouse. Pass the brick-built woodside cottage on your right and the end of a long strip of woodland on your left.

④

Turn left through a gap immediately beyond the woodland and descend beside the trees to a stile and gate at the lower end of the wood. Cross to a junction of paths in the small field beyond and make for a stile and footbridge at the far right corner of the field.

⑤

The path exits to Jack's Lane beside the Greene King Inn. Bear left for the main road and cross to its footpath. Go right to look at Turvey Abbey, before turning back to re-enter the village past Abbey Square to finish the walk.

INFORMATION
Length of walk:
1½ miles
Approximate time:
1½ hours

TERRAIN:
Suitable for children at all times of year, and for pushchairs in dry weather. Not suitable for wheelchairs.

PARKING:
Park near the church, in the loop of the old High Street north of A428(T).

REFRESHMENTS:
Inns in village.

Turvey House (above) built by Charles Higgins (1794), then lord of the manor. Turvey Bridge (below).

POINTS OF INTEREST

Ⓐ

All Saints' Church. A Saxon church was built on the site about AD980. Some of its stone-work remains in the western nave and adjoining tower. The medieval church was restored and extended eastwards by Sir George Gilbert Scott in 1852. It is entered through massive 13th-century oak doors covered with ornamental ironwork. The Mordaunt tombs are impressive and there is a large Higgins mausoleum in the churchyard.

Ⓑ

The Rectory. A house of Tudor origin, it has curious figures of saints on Tudor brickwork panels at the far side from the church.

Ⓒ

Turvey Bridge. An ancient stone-built bridge of 16 arches, widened in 1935. On an island to the south are two large old statues. 'Jonah', on the left, was brought from Ashridge House in Hertfordshire in 1844; his un-named companion joined him in 1953. In the background is Turvey Mill and to the left has stood the Three Fyshes Inn since 1622. It is said that one of the Gunpowder Plotters was arrested nearby.

Ⓓ

Turvey Abbey. Though always known as the Abbey, the former home of the Longuet Higgins family was never truly one until purchased by Benedictine monks in 1980. The Jacobean house stands close to the road at the east end of the village.

Ⓔ

Abbey Square. Almost opposite the end of Jack's Lane, the lovely 17th-century cottages built for agricultural labourers on the Abbey estate are set back from the main road.

WARMINGTON
WARWICKSHIRE

On A41(T), 5½ miles NW of Banbury

WARMINGTON is on the boundary between Warwickshire and Oxfordshire. That the village was large in early times is shown by Domesday Book (1086), which recorded a population of about 250. Nearly 600 years later, Charles I's army marched confidently through, *en route* to Edgehill. Places of interest nearby include the National Trust properties of Farnborough Hall, Upton House and Burton Dassett Country Park.

Warmington's cottages are of creamy Hornton limestone.

POINTS OF INTEREST

Ⓐ

St Michael's Church. Though mainly 14th-century, it has Norman arches in the nave. An ogee-arched doorway in the chancel leads to the sacristy, above which is a medieval priest's room. One of the weather-worn 17th-century gravestones near the porch commemorates Alexander Gourdin, a Scottish captain killed at the Battle of Edgehill. The parish register also refers to the burial of Richard Sannes, 'Captaine of Foot companie a gentleman of Worcestershire ... and Seven other ... whose name I know not.'

Ⓑ

Warmington Manor. Its broad stone face, divided by a central chimney-breast, has stared down the lovely village green for almost four centuries. Originally the King was Lord of the Manor, but after the Norman Conquest the property was granted to the Earl of Warwick, who gave it to the monks of Preaux in Normandy. Later the title passed to Wytham Abbey in Somerset, and through various private hands after the Dissolution of the Monasteries.

Ⓒ

The Village Green. Unusually large, the Green has a small, lily-flagged pond, known as the Town Pool, originally used for sheep washing. The Rectory, a large 18th-century house with stone gateways, also overlooks the Green, as does the 17th-century Grove Farm House.

WALK DIRECTIONS

①

After parking your car enter the churchyard to visit the church. To start the walk, turn left from the church porch and descend the flagged path to the junction of Church Hill and the unsurfaced Soot Lane, on the right.

②

Take Soot Lane and descend past two modern houses and through a vehicle barrier to the village green. Walk anti-clockwise round the Green, noting in particular the Manor House at its upper end and the Rectory, on the far side from where you entered.

Climb the road and pass right of the Manor House to the 17th-century Plough Inn. Continue uphill to see the old houses in Court Close just above it. Descend again and enter Chapel Street, which leads past the Wesleyan Chapel of 1811 to School Lane. Go right to view fine thatched stone cottages and turn back to climb the lane to A41(T).

Below a stone-built house on the far side of the road is a public footpath. Climb it and look for a stile on the right, from which a fieldpath continues uphill. Soon the village is spread out below. To the north are long views over the Feldon, as Warwickshire south of the River Avon is known.

Climb past a stone cottage and go through two gates to follow a green track ending at a stile. Turn left and cross a field to a hedge-gap on Camp Lane, the B4086.

To return to Warmington bear left for about 600yds and fork left along a byway signed to Cherry Tree Farm. Where the lane bends left a path continues ahead and winds gently down a steep bank to the A41(T).

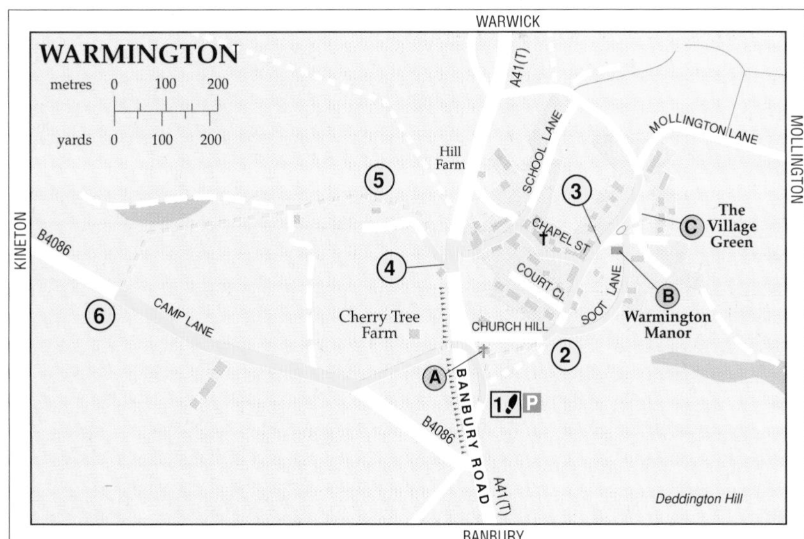

INFORMATION
Length of walk:
1½ miles
Approximate time:
1¼ hours

TERRAIN:
Suitable for children at all times of year. Not suitable for pushchairs or wheelchairs.

PARKING:
Park in the lay-by beside A41(T) above the church (but please do not obstruct parking for services).

REFRESHMENTS:
Plough Inn in village.

THE NORTH COUNTRY

BAMBURGH CASTLE, NORTHUMBERLAND

•

The crowded graveyard, the tall solemn trees,
The dark tower and the narrow climbing street,
At every turn the grim blue distances,
The gray roofs and the hill-winds blowing sweet-
WILFRED ROWLAND CHILDE – HAWORTH IN MAY

•

THE NORTH COUNTRY

•

•

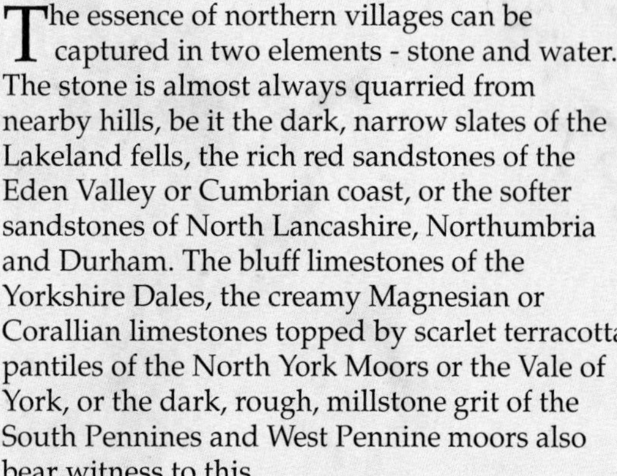

Although absent from most of southern England, meadow cranesbill is frequently found in meadows and hedgerows in northern England.

The essence of northern villages can be captured in two elements - stone and water. The stone is almost always quarried from nearby hills, be it the dark, narrow slates of the Lakeland fells, the rich red sandstones of the Eden Valley or Cumbrian coast, or the softer sandstones of North Lancashire, Northumbria and Durham. The bluff limestones of the Yorkshire Dales, the creamy Magnesian or Corallian limestones topped by scarlet terracotta pantiles of the North York Moors or the Vale of York, or the dark, rough, millstone grit of the South Pennines and West Pennine moors also bear witness to this.

Until the era of cheap transport - rail and later road - the cost of transporting bricks, slates and tiles was prohibitive, and local builders used whatever material was to hand. The services of an architect were usually prohibitively expensive, even if one could be found, so houses were built to traditional patterns which often had a strongly localised style. This is why so many north country villages seem to have almost grown out of the landscape, reflecting the colours of the seasons like the crags and outcroppings of the hills themselves - a harmony of roofs and walls, of farmhouses and barns and miles of drystone walls that criss-cross Northern fellsides.

Stone, too, has different qualities which affect the way buildings look. Slate splits easily, so Lakeland buildings exploit the use of narrow blocks of stone for walls and even chimneys. Gritstone, on the other hand, is difficult to work, and Pennine cottages and farms retain their rough exteriors. Softer sandstone and limestone can be dressed or cut into smooth, neat shapes, and became more popular for the elegant houses of Georgian and Victorian times with their decorative sash windows and mock-classical porches.

Water is perhaps a subtler influence. Many villages were built close to the sea, a river or lake as a source of water supply and transport, or even at a significant bridge across a river, where for centuries travellers had to cross and villagers could earn a living servicing their needs.

More common, in the uplands, are hamlets and villages alongside a fast-flowing stream which provided a source of power for early mills. These often began life as corn mills, were developed from Tudor times onwards into weaving or fulling mills, and then had a new lease of life in the Industrial Revolution when steam-power – another form of water-power – enabled the growth of larger factories with mills around them. Even though, by the late 20th century, the village mill may have long since closed, defeated by cheap imports, the mill building, perhaps with its defiant chimney, almost always survives, often with a deep, old mill pond where sinister pike lurk. The mill itself may well have metamorphosed to meet a quite different need as fashionable apartments, craft workshops, or a restaurant.

Another feature of many North Country villages, which is an indirect yet significant influence of water, is to be found in the steep-sided valleys, carved out by glacier and river, where human settlement has to compete for scarce, level valley-bottom land. Houses were built wherever a reasonably flat surface was available, as hill slopes are difficult and unstable. So in hillier areas villages crowd into a small area of valley floor or hillside terrace, sometimes with miners' or millworkers' cottages packed into what had originally been the gardens of larger medieval house crofts, filled with cramped little dwellings during the boom years of the early 19th century. In the cities and larger towns, such cottages were long cleared away by the planners as slums. Here they have survived and gained a patina of age, restored as little bijou weekend or retirement cottages or perhaps specialist shops or boutiques, helping to give tourist appeal which the original poverty stricken inhabitants, crammed several to a room, could never have imagined. The great charm of such villages is that they were not planned, they just happened as people used what skills and materials they had to hand to create the shelter and living space they needed.

Yet there are some handsome villages which *have* been planned, examples of which can be seen in the north. These were mainly estate villages, often created when a local landowner, grown newly rich in the 18th century on trade or the booming industries such as iron, textiles or coal, desired to rebuild his existing estate and enclose his Park. The ancient manor house at the edge of the village was abandoned in favour of a handsome new country house, architect designed and in neo-Classical style. Often an entire village was replanned and transplanted some distance away to secure aristocratic privacy and a pleasing view of the countryside. The architects of the grand houses were employed to build fine villages to match, using local stone and local craftsmen to produce an effect which two centuries later we can still admire.

The North of England is fortunate in that such villages, remote from the large centres of population and the pressures of development, have been allowed to keep their individual character, and have been spared from the worst excesses of standard modern urban development and sanitised concrete, pebbledash and brick.

It is an inheritance to cherish.

BAKEWELL

DERBYSHIRE

On A6, 8 miles N of Matlock, 12 miles SE of Buxton

COMMANDING a natural crossing place of the River Wye, Bakewell has occupied an important place in Peak District history at least since AD924, when it was mentioned in the *Anglo-Saxon Chronicle*. It was known then as *Badecean Weillon* (Beadeca's Springs or Wells) after the warm springs which issue from the junction between the limestone and the shale.

Bakewell is still the biggest and most important village in the Peak, the charter for its busy Monday market having been granted as long ago as 1330. It is also famous for its unique delicacy, the Bakewell pudding, and its large annual agricultural show, held during the first week in August.

INFORMATION
Length of walk:
2½ miles (with shorter alternatives)
Approximate time:
2 hours

TERRAIN:
Mostly easy walking on good paths, suitable for pushchairs but no wheelchairs. A few short climbs.

PARKING:
Park in the main car park behind the Information Centre in Market Street.

OPEN:
The Information Centre in the Old Market Hall. All year except Thu during winter. No charge. The Old House Museum. Apr-Oct. Charge.

REFRESHMENTS:
A good selection of pubs, cafés, etc, in the village.

A Saxon cross in All Saints' churchyard.

POINTS OF INTEREST

The Old Market Hall. This arcaded late 16th or early 17th-century sandstone building was once the centrepiece of Bakewell's street market. It later became shops and the village library and was restored and converted to an information centre in 1968. Notice the coats of arms of local families on the south wall and the timbered roof, now exposed inside.

Monsal Trail. The latest of the Peak's 'railway trails,' the Monsal Trail follows the line of the former Midland Railway between Bakewell and Buxton. Opened in 1863, it closed down in 1968 and was bought by the National Park authority. There are long-term plans to bring steam trains back to the line.

Old House Museum. The oldest house in Bakewell, the core of which dates back to 1534. Later it housed workers from Sir Richard Arkwright's Bakewell Mill (now demolished). It was rescued from imminent demolition by a group of local enthusiasts who formed the Bakewell Historical Society which now runs it as fascinating museum of local history.

All Saints' Parish Church. The distinctive octagonal tower and steeple date from an 1841 restoration, but Bakewell's church rests on Saxon foundations. Evidence of this is found in the two Saxon crosses now found in the churchyard, and the collection of carved fragments of stone from earlier buildings now stored in the south porch. Inside the church are Norman arches and a font, and many monuments to the Vernon and Manners families, owners of nearby Haddon Hall.

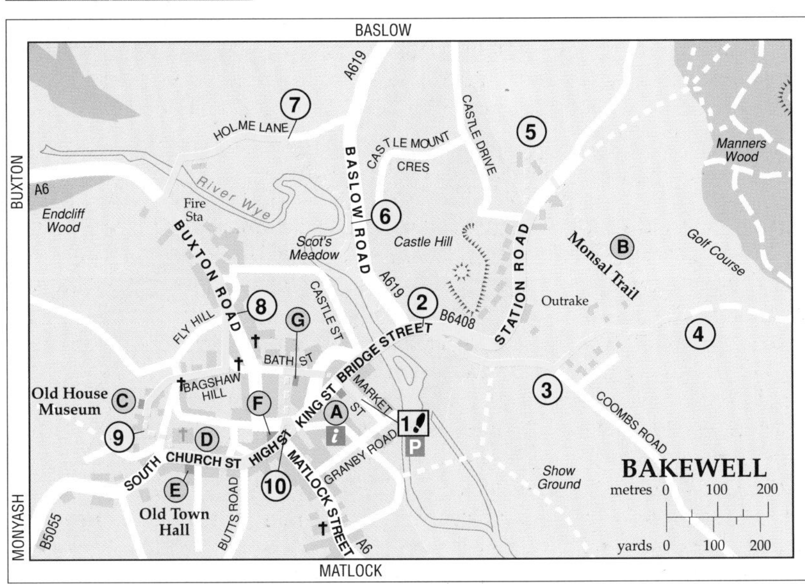

The Parish Church of All Saints.

Ⓔ

The Old Town Hall, Avenel Court. Built in 1709, the upper floor of this lovely old building has been used for quarter sessions, a Grammar School, a working men's club, and finally an antiques showroom. The lower floor has housed a fire engine, the village butter market, and a fish shop over the years.

Ⓕ

The Rutland Arms Hotel. Bakewell's internationally famous delicacy, the Bakewell pudding, was first made by accident in the kitchens of this fine old inn. It is claimed that Jane Austen stayed in the hotel in 1811, and based the town of Lambton in *Pride and Prejudice* on her impressions of Bakewell.

The Bath House. Built in 1697 by the Duke of Rutland, of nearby Haddon Hall, the Bath House (private) was fed by the warm springs which may have first attracted the Romans to the valley of the Wye. A Roman milestone found near Bakewell is on show at Haddon Hall, 2 miles down the A6.

The Rutland Arms (left), home of Bakewell's famous pudding (above). Holme packhorse bridge (far left).

FRUITFUL ERROR

The Bakewell Pudding,for which the place is celebrated, was first made by mistake, so the story goes. Some say it happened in the 1860s, others date it 200 years ago, when Bakewell's principal coaching inn was the White Horse, in The Square. It has since been renamed the Rutland Arms (Haddon Hall, the Duke of Rutland's Derbyshire manor house, is nearby).

The landlady usually did the cooking, but on this particular day she was away or busy, so an inexperienced assistant filled in. Trying to make a strawberry tart, the assistant mistakenly spread strawberry jam on the puff pastry and then put the egg-and-sugar mixture, which should have gone into the pastry, on top. To everyone's relief the customers liked it, and Bakewell Pudding was born.

You can buy one at the Old Original Bakewell Pudding Shop, or the Gingerbread Shop on Matlock Street. Both establishments claim to have the original recipe.

WALK DIRECTIONS

From the car park, turn right along Bridge Street, cross the Wye by the ancient bridge and go straight ahead into Station Road.

Turn right in a few yards into Coombs Road, which leads past the flood-meadows of the Wye.

After 300yds, turn left up a track past Outrake. In another 300yds, the track meets the Monsal Trail, which runs along the former Midland Railway track.

Turn left on to the Trail and walk along it to the former Bakewell Station. There are fine views left across the showground to Bakewell, its church spire prominent, and across the golf course to Manners Wood (right).

From Bakewell Station, descend Station Road back to Bakewell Bridge, turning right through a metal gate just before crossing it, on to the riverside path leading through Scot's Meadows.

Through a pair of kissing gates, follow the path across meadows to a squeeze stile giving access to Holme Lane.

Turn left along the lane past Lumford Cottages to reach the ancient Holme packhorse bridge. Cross this and turn left at the main road.

Re-entering Bakewell past the Fire Station and Victoria Mill, turn right and climb steeply up Bagshaw Hill, past Bagshaw Hall. Cross straight over the crossroads into Cunningham Place, and up to the Old House Museum.

Take the narrow alley left opposite the museum to descend to Church Lane, and enter the churchyard by the lych gate to look at the church. Through the churchyard, take the steps down to South Church Street, past the Old Town Hall and the Rutland Arms.

Cross the busy roundabout and go left into Bath Gardens, past the old Bath House, and into Bath Street. Turn right and then right again through a narrow alley which takes you back to the Information Centre and car park.

Bakewell (above), sitting amidst the Wye Valley, dominated by the spire of its parish church.

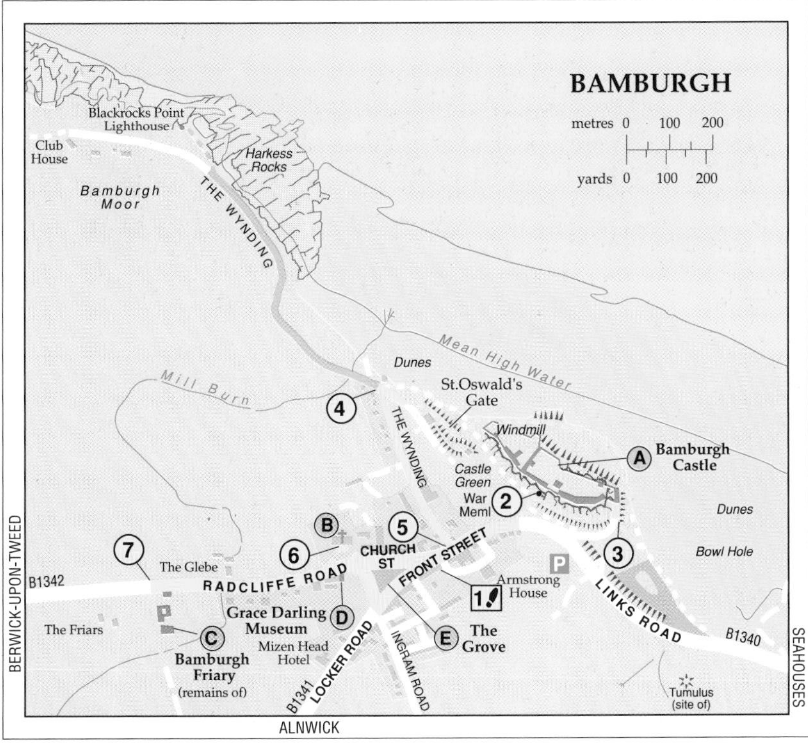

BAMBURGH

NORTHUMBERLAND

On B1340, 17 miles N of Alnwick

DOMINATED by one of Britain's most impressive castles and bordered by Northumberland's finest Heritage Coast beaches, Bamburgh village provides a wealth of historical and wildlife interest in a designated Area of Outstanding Natural Beauty. The nearby Lindisfarne National Nature Reserve and the Farne Islands (a short distance offshore) are internationally noted for their birdlife, whilst in the village itself, St Aidan's Church and the Grace Darling Museum represent the cradle of northern Christianity and the life of a national heroine respectively.

POINTS OF INTEREST

Bamburgh Castle. Built on a massive outcrop of the igneous whin sill rock, Bamburgh's castle is today the home of Lady Armstrong and houses, in addition to industrial exhibits relating to the first Lord Armstrong (an engineer and inventor), collections of arms and armour, china, paintings and furniture, within its many public rooms.

A fortified centre for Northumberland's royalty by AD547, the defences were rebuilt in stone in Norman times and remained intact until the advent of gunpowder and artillery fire in the 15th-century Wars of the Roses. More recently, the castle has been extensively renovated, initially by the Lord Crewe Trust and then by the first Lord Armstrong, who purchased it in 1894.

St Aidan's Church. Having successfully introduced Christianity to Northumberland's pagans with the support of King Oswald, St Aidan, a monk from Iona, established a wooden church on this site in AD635. The present church is largely of 13th-century origin, although a wooden beam in the baptistry is reputedly that against which St Aidan rested prior to his death in AD651. Church guides are available inside the building.

Bamburgh Friary. Hidden amongst farm buildings to the east of The Friars are the remains, which include fragments of a church, of a 13th-century Dominican Friary. Subsequent to its dissolution, the friary estate was converted into a farm.

Standing on a rocky outcrop, Bamburgh Castle towers 150ft above the sea and spreads for a quarter of a mile along the cliff top. The present castle was rebuilt by Henry II.

D

Grace Darling Museum. At the age of 22, the lighthouse keeper's daughter Grace Darling won the hearts of the nation with her brave contribution to the rescue of nine survivors from the *Forfarshire*, wrecked on the Farne Islands in 1838. The museum, opened on the centenary of the event in 1938, houses the original coble in which she and her father put to sea, in addition to other relics of the family, the *Forfarshire* and the rescue.

Grace died just four years after the event. She is buried in St Aidan's churchyard, where a memorial to her has also been erected. Opposite the church is the cottage in which she was born.

E

The Grove. The wooded, triangular green around which Bamburgh village is clustered is known as The Grove. In order to preserve its character, which includes the long-established rookery, a management programme of tree felling and replanting has been undertaken by the Bamburgh Castle Estate.

WALK DIRECTIONS

1

The walk begins outside the village post office in Front Street. Walk downhill along Front Street towards the castle, and where the road begins to bear right, cross and follow the tarmac path across Castle Green to a war memorial at the base of the castle rock.

2

At the war memorial, turn right and walk uphill on a grass path, bearing left to meet the castle access road. Turn left across the bridge to visit Bamburgh Castle, or right to continue the walk.

3

Cross into the viewpoint car park and after 30yds turn sharp left along a sandy path above the dunes. Continue on this path to the far end of the castle, beyond which bear left up low stone steps and then right on a clear, narrow path to join a stone track after 150yds.

4

At the junction turn sharp left into The Wynding to walk back into the village.

A painting of Grace Darling (above) in the museum bearing her name.

Note: At this point there is an optional 1 mile loop out to Blackrocks Point lighthouse and return. If you wish to take this loop, simply follow The Wynding north from the junction and return to this point to continue the main walk.

5

At the foot of The Wynding, turn right up Front Street and continue along Church Street. Bear right through a gate into the churchyard, then left at the church entrance.

6

After visiting the church, go through a second gate on to Radcliffe Road and turn right. Walk on past The Glebe and cross the road opposite The Friars.

7

Return on the same road back into the village. Beyond the Grace Darling Museum bear right around a red brick wall into The Grove, then left down Front Street to the post office.

St Aiden's Church with the tomb of Grace Darling in the foreground.

INFORMATION
Length of walk: 2 miles (3 miles if lighthouse detour is taken)
Approximate time: 1½ hours (2¼ hours if detour is taken)

TERRAIN:
Surfaced roads and paths and a sandy beach. Two gates in the churchyard. Village Centre, Castle Green, and the Wynding accessible for wheelchairs and pushchairs, with a viewpoint car park situated at the castle entrance. Whole walk suitable for children.

PARKING:
Park either in the village centre (limited space) or in the public car park opposite the castle entrance.

OPEN:
Bamburgh Castle: Easter-Oct, daily. Charge. Grace Darling Museum: Easter-Oct, daily. No charge, but donations to Royal National Lifeboat Institution appreciated.

REFRESHMENTS:
Inns and cafés in village, tearoom in castle.

WONDERFUL WILDLIFE

Established in 1964 to safeguard a wetland site of international importance, the Lindisfarne National Nature Reserve stretches north from Budle Bay past Holy Island to Goswick Sands. In winter particularly you can see large flocks of seabirds and waders here. Access on foot is permitted, but visitors are asked to avoid disturbing the wildlife. The southern part of the reserve, at Budle Bay, is accessible from the B1342 – 2 miles N of Bamburgh.

The Farne Islands are also noted for their diverse seabird population and seal colony.

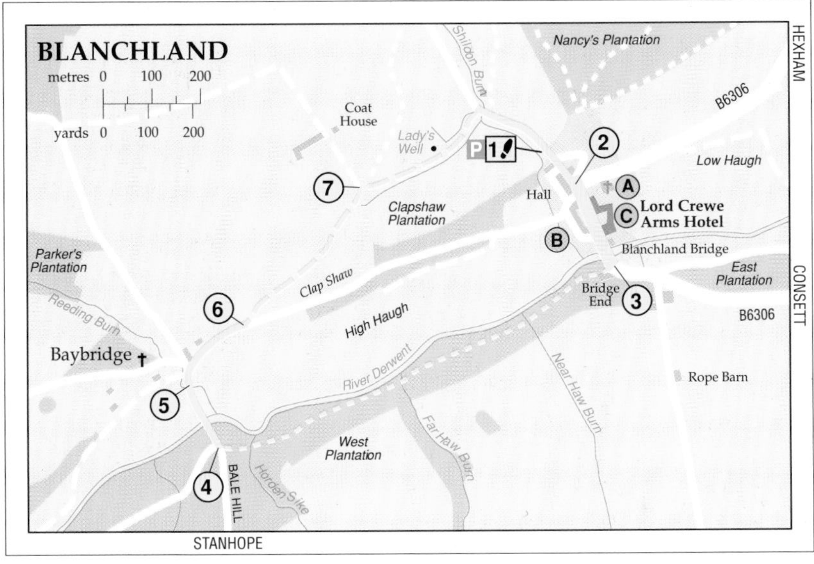

BLANCHLAND

NORTHUMBERLAND

On B6306, 10 miles S of Hexham

AN attractive wood-ed valley surrounded by the magnificent heather moorlands of the north Pennines provides a perfect setting for this charming village. Historical interest abounds, from the monastic foundations of Blanchland to the more recently abandoned lead mines, and a short walk through woodland and enclosed farmland offers much to interest the naturalist.

INFORMATION
Length of walk: 1½ miles
Approximate time: 1 hour

TERRAIN:
Tarmac roads, a woodland path and enclosed farmland. Four gates. Unsuitable for pushchairs and wheelchairs but suitable for children.

PARKING:
Park in the public car park at the north end of the village.

REFRESHMENTS:
Public house and tea-room in village. Picnic site at Baybridge.

EVENTS:
Blanchland and Hunstanworth Show (August).

POINTS OF INTEREST

St Mary's Church. In 1165 Walter de Bolbec granted land on the north bank of the Derwent to an order of 'White Canons' (hence the origination of *Blanche Lande*), who founded a monastery. St Mary's was rebuilt in the 18th century on the site of the original abbey church, and features of particular interest include medieval tombstones of two of the abbots.

Blanchland Village. Following the dissolution of monasteries by Henry VIII in 1536, the domestic building associated with Blanchland Abbey became part of the Forster family's estate. In 1699 Dorothy Forster married Lord Nathaniel Crewe, who took control of the estate. On his death in 1721, control was handed to trustees who, in the mid 18th century, constructed a beautiful grey-stone village on the site of the old medieval abbey and its buildings.

Today, the former abbey gatehouse incorporates the village post office, and the courtyard, which formerly fronted the monks' living quarters, is surrounded by cottages initially built to accommodate lead-mining families.

Lord Crewe Arms Hotel. Formerly both part of Blanchland Abbey's domestic quarters and the manor house of the Forster family, the hotel is steeped in history. Behind one fireplace there is a priest's hole, reputedly the hiding place of General Thomas Forster following his escape from capture by government troops during the Jacobite rebellion of 1715.

Blanchland holds an isolated position, deep in the Derwent Valley.

WALK DIRECTIONS

From the public car park at the north end of the village, turn right and walk downhill, passing a row of terraced cottages on your right, towards the main road and village centre.

At the road junction, cross towards the Lord Crewe Arms Hotel and the gatehouse, enter the village square through the gatehouse arch, and continue along the main street to the bridge.

Cross the bridge and turn immediately right to walk in front of a stone cottage. Continue up a grass slope on to a clear woodland path, pass through a narrow gap in the fence and continue through the woods for approximately ½ mile (with the river down to your right) to a gate.

Go through the gate and turn right downhill along the road to the hamlet of Baybridge.

Continue on the road as it bears right away from Baybridge, passing an old barn on your left, and approximately 100yds further along the road bear left into a field through a gate.

From the gate bear diagonally right up the field on a clear grass track to reach a second gate (with Coat House Farm to your left). Go through this gate and after a short distance bear right along the farm track.

Continue to the end of the farm track, go through a gate, and turn right along the road to Blanchland car park and village.

BOWES
CO DURHAM

Off A66 and A67, 4 miles W of Barnard Castle

THIS village of stone houses lies beside the main road. To the west the road begins the ascent of Bowes Moor, still today one of the trans-Pennine routes to be most easily blocked by snow. The Romans built a fort here to guard the route and a thousand years later Bowes Castle was built for the same purpose. In the 19th century, Charles Dickens came to Bowes to collect background information for his book *Nicholas Nickleby*, published in 1839.

The great square, stone keep of Bowes Castle, built for Henry II, stands resiliently upon its moated island.

POINTS OF INTEREST

Ⓐ

Ancient Unicorn Inn. The inn retains the atmosphere of a coaching inn, with a cobbled yard outside and an interior with thick walls, low beams and an open fire. One of the regular coaches to use the inn was `The Post' from London to Carlisle via Ferrybridge.

Ⓑ

Church and Churchyard. The church was restored in 1864 but retains two Norman doorways and 14th-century transepts. There are two fonts, one of which rests on a possibly Roman altar. In the churchyard is the gravestone of George Ashton Taylor, who died at Shaw's Academy when he was 19 years old. Dickens was inspired by this to creat the character Smike in *Nicholas Nickleby*. Also in the churchyard is the grave of William Shaw, the headmaster of the Academy.

Ⓒ

Dotheboys Hall. The former school was used by Charles Dickens as the setting for *Nicholas Nickleby*. He set out to reveal the scandal behind boarding schools; places where children could be sent on payment of 20 guineas a year, ostensibly to be educated, but where they often received bad treatment or even cruelty. Here on the windswept Pennines, with poor food and the possibility of regular beatings, it was a miserable life for a child. Dickens set out to expose the corruption that existed through his writing. Bowes Academy (Dotheboys Hall), run by William Shaw, was chosen as the setting for the book because Shaw had earlier been taken to court for ill-treating pupils.

Ⓓ

Bowes Castle and Roman Fort. The keep of the castle stands over 50ft high and occupies a strategic position overlooking the River Greta. The walls are 12ft thick and contain narrow passages and a spiral staircase. The building of the castle was started in 1171 and completed in 1187. Much of the stone came from the Roman fort *Lavatris*, which lies under the castle and part of the village.

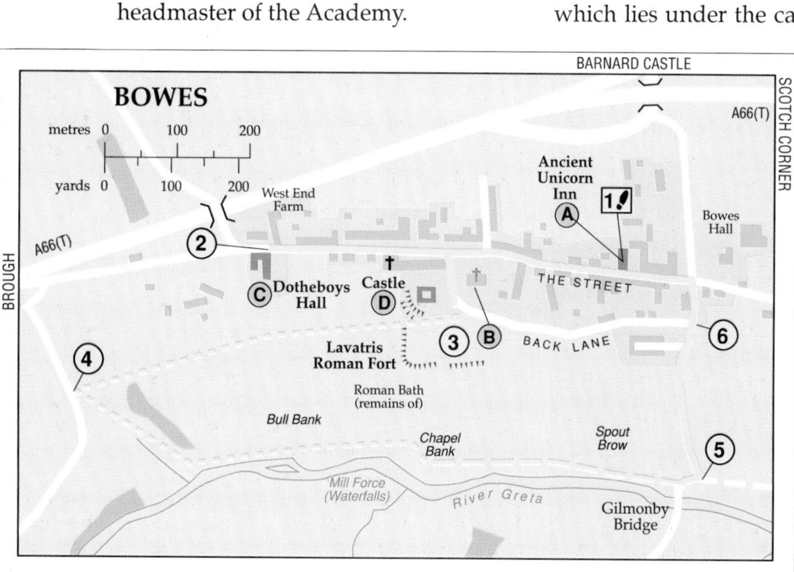

INFORMATION
Length of walk: 1¾ miles
Approximate time: 1½ hours

TERRAIN:
Good surface in village. The section between points 3 and 6 is unsuitable for pushchairs and wheelchairs due to stiles.

PARKING:
Park in the main street.

OPEN:
Bowes Castle is open daily. No charge.

REFRESHMENTS:
One inn.

WALK DIRECTIONS

From the Ancient Unicorn Inn, walk up the main street to the church on the left. Continue to Dotheboys Hall, the last building on the left in the village.

Return down the main street and turn right into Back Lane, signposted Bowes Castle. At the corner of Back Lane you can turn right to visit Bowes Castle.

Return to Back Lane and turn right through two gates then turn right, keeping the boundary wire of the castle on your right. Cross six fields using the stiles set in the walls until you reach a stile that gives access to a road.

Don't cross this stile but turn back left down the valley to the river. Bear left to a stile which leads to a track along the riverside, and continue until you reach theroad above the bridge.

Turn left up the road to pass the end of Back Lane on your left.

Continue to the crossroads and turn left back to the Ancient Unicorn Inn.

INFORMATION
Length of walk:
2 miles
Approximate time:
1½ hours

TERRAIN:
Easy lane and field walking. Not suitable for pushchairs or wheelchairs because of stiles.

PARKING:
Use the village car park in Low Bradfield.

REFRESHMENTS:
Pubs in both High and Low Bradfield.

BRADFIELD

SOUTH YORKSHIRE

Off B6077, 4½ miles NW of Sheffield

THERE are really two Bradfields – High and Low – with Low Bradfield in the valley of the Dale Dike and High Bradfield up on the ridge. Both warm gritstone villages are dominated by the fine Parish Church of St Nicholas, which stands 860ft above the sea and has extensive views down Bradfield Dale.

Evidence of Bradfield's past importance is not hard to find. The extensive earthworks known as Bailey Hill north-west of the church may be of Saxon origin, later converted to a Norman motte and bailey, while the origins of Castle Hill, half a mile to the south-east, have never been satisfactorily explained.

POINTS OF INTEREST

Ⓐ

St Nicholas's Parish Church. A superb example of Perpendicular architecture dating mainly from the 15th century, it has a Saxon cross, some Norman work and a 14th-century tower. The reason for the church's disproportionate size was that it was endowed and staffed by monks from nearby Ecclesfield Priory. There are superb views from the south porch down the valley over the Agden and Danflask Reservoirs, built to supply Sheffield. The Watch House is an unusual feature; it was built in 1745 to allow watchers to keep an eye out for potential body-snatchers.

Ⓑ

Damflask Reservoir. This is one of four reservoirs in the quiet valley of Bradfield Dale; the other three are Strines, Dale Dike and Agden. The most famous is Dale Dike, because in 1864 it was the scene of one of the greatest flood disasters in Britain. About 240 people died and 4,500 homes were flooded when the dam was breached, and the waters rushed down as far as Sheffield.

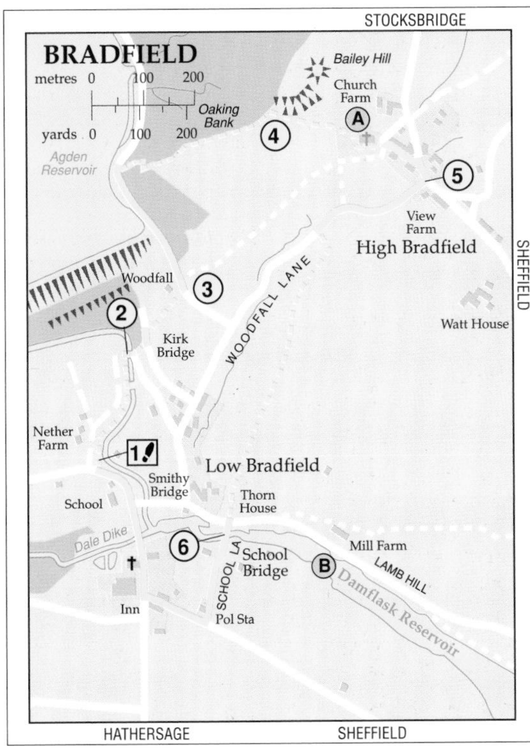

Village life in Bradfield still centres largely around the Parish Church of St Nicholas (top), with its fine views over the valley, and the village green (above), where cricket is played.

WALK DIRECTIONS

①

Turn right from the car park in Low Bradfield and follow the track beside it to a footbridge. Do not cross the bridge but continue straight on the narrow path (signposted High Bradfield).

②

At a second footbridge, turn right over it and up a flight of steps, over a stone stile, and bear left up more steps to reach a road.

③

Turn left here by the dam of Agden Reservoir. Where the path curves to the right, turn right steeply up by Oaking Bank Plantation, at a sign to Bailey Hill. At the top, ahead is Bailey Hill, now partly obscured by trees.

④

Turn right over a stile towards the churchyard. Climbing a stone stile by the Watch House - built to deter body-snatchers - turn right and left along Towngate into High Bradfield.

⑤

Turn right down Woodfall Lane and as the lane curves left, turn left at a footpath sign to Low Bradfield over a stile. This path crosses several fields to Lamb Hill.

⑥

Walled School Lane enters New Road by the Police Station. Here turn right, then right again to the car park.

CALDBECK
CUMBRIA

On B5299, 11 miles SW of Carlisle

A typical stone-built Cumbrian village situated at the most northerly point of the Lake District National Park. There are extensive views to the south over the Caldbeck Fells at the 'back o' Skiddaw'. In earlier times Caldbeck was a largely self-sufficient village and supported a considerable amount of industry. It boasted a brewery that supplied 16 inns and alehouses and had 13 mills which were powered by the Cald Beck (i.e. cold stream), from which the village takes its name. Many of these buildings survive as handsome relics of a bygone era.

Caldbeck is named after this 'cold stream'.

POINTS OF INTEREST

Ⓐ

The Packhorse Bridge. This dates from the 15th century and is good example of a type once found throughout northern England. The pronounced arch was easy to build and is immensely strong. Next to the bridge on the right-hand bank is an old well.

Ⓑ

The Parish Church. The church is unusual in being dedicated to St Kentigern, better known as St Mungo, a Scottish missionary who became the patron saint of the City of Glasgow. He is reputed to have preached at Caldbeck when on a journey from Scotland to Wales in AD533. The church dates from Norman times and was restored in 1512, 1727 and 1932. The churchyard is remarkable for the size of the gravestones, which are beautifully laid out in serried ranks. It contains the graves of John Peel and the Maid of Buttermere.

Ⓒ

Priest's Mill. A handsome building originally built in 1740 as a corn mill for the church. The water-wheel is still *in situ*. but the building has been restored and converted to a mining museum.

Ⓓ

The Brewery. The handsome old brewery buildings near the bridge once supplied the 16 pubs and beer houses in the village.

WALK DIRECTIONS

①

From the car park, cross the road and follow the metalled bridleway opposite past a row of old cottages to a packhorse bridge that crosses the beck.

②

Cross the bridge, enter the churchyard and visit the church and John Peel's grave (a conspicuous white tombstone set against the right-hand wall of the churchyard, at 2 o'clock when viewed from the church porch). Nearby is the grave of the 'Buttermere Beauty'. Return to the bridge, but instead of crossing it, turn right and follow the path behind the church to Priest's Mill.

③

After visiting the Museum of Mining in Priest's Mill, turn left and follow the un-metalled lane to the road. Turn right and walk past the church and the handsome 18th-century rectory (note the Gothic windows) to the Oddfellows Arms.

④

Keep the public house on your right and continue along the main road (there is a clog-maker's sign on an old mill on the left).

⑤

Take the first turning on the right and pass the old brewery buildings to cross the bridge. After the lane bears to the right, turn right into the car park.

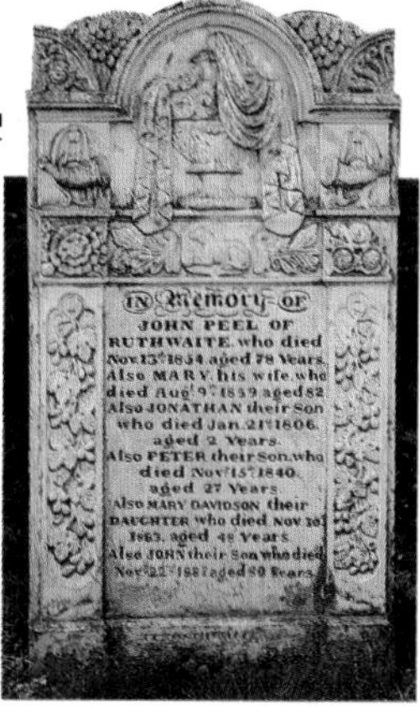

The tomb of John Peel. He was immortalised in the song D'ye ken John Peel.

THE MAID OF BUTTERMERE

Mary Robinson was the daughter of the landlord of the Fish Inn, Buttermere. She was born in 1779 and when still a young girl gained an astonishing reputation as a beauty. Wordsworth wrote a poem about her, and she became a significant tourist attraction.

She was courted by many but married a scoundrel named John Hatfield who had deserted two previous wives. He was apprehended not long after his marriage to Mary, and in 1803 was hanged for forgery. Poor Mary became a *cause célèbre*, but after the fuss died down she moved to Caldbeck and married a farmer. She died in 1837.

INFORMATION
Length of walk: ¾ mile
Approximate time: 1 hour

TERRAIN:
Mostly level.

PARKING:
There is a National Park car park on B5299 near the bridge.

OPEN:
Priest's Mill Mining Museum, Tue-Sun and bank hols., 10.30am-5pm.

REFRESHMENTS:
Monoleys, the Old Smithy coffee shop in Priest's Mill and the Oddfellows Arms.

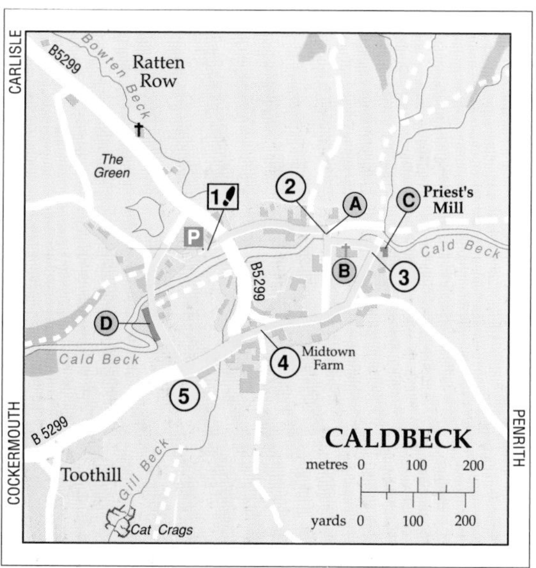

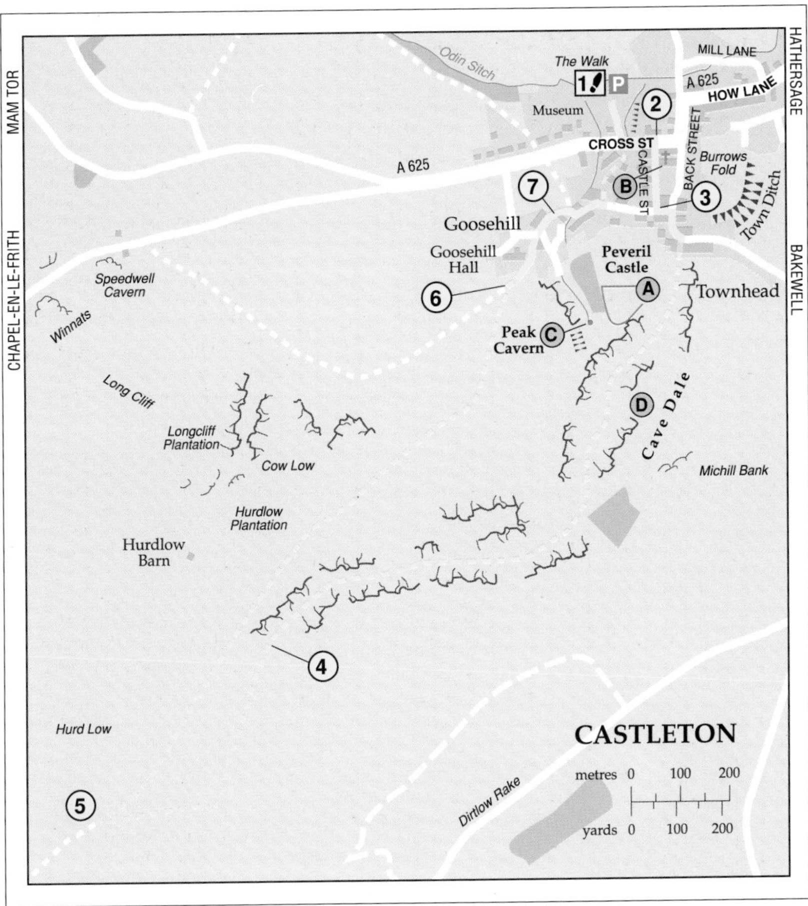

CASTLETON

DERBYSHIRE

On A625 between Hathersage and Chapel-en-le-Frith, 1½ miles W of Hope

CASTLETON, on the Great Divide between the limestone White Peak and gritstone Dark Peak, is the stronghold of the Peak's underground kingdom. Water flowing off the acid shales and grits disappears under the permeable limestones forming spectacular caves, many of which are open to the public. Other spectacular geological features, such as the Winnats Pass and Cave Dale, and the 'Shivering Mountain', Mam Tor, are all within easy walking distance of the village. The natural features of Cave Dale and the gorge of Peak Cavern were used by William Peveril, son of William the Conqueror, as natural fortifications for his apparently impregnable castle, overlooking the village after which it was named.

BLUE JOHN

Castleton's limestone caverns are famous for this rare type of fluorspar, first recorded in the 1600s. The story that the Romans exploited it centuries before is no longer taken seriously. It has to be mined by hand, laboriously and expensively: blasting ruins it.

Visitors to Castleton's gift shops can buy jewellery, ornaments, small bowls and other souvenirs made of Blue John. A good museum display can be admired at the Ollerenshaw Collection in Castleton. The famous circular table top here was made of Blue John from the Bull Beef vein in the Blue John Cavern, which the Ollerenshaw family has owned for many years. Blue John is still mined in Treak Cliff Cavern, which is open to the public. Not far away at Chatsworth, the Duke of Devonshire owns the largest Blue John vase in existence.

POINTS OF INTEREST

Ⓐ

Peveril Castle. William Peveril's castle, reached up a steep zig-zag path from the village, is the finest medieval landmark in the Peak. Constructed soon after the Conquest, it was designed to allow Peveril to oversee the King's Royal Forest of the Peak, a medieval hunting reserve. The present keep dates from 1175 and was built under the instruction of Henry II, who had accepted the submission of King Malcolm of Scotland here in 1157. Henry also laid down the grid-iron pattern of Castleton's streets, within the enclosing Town Ditch.

St Edmund's Parish Church. One of the most interesting parish churches in the Peak, Castleton's original church may have been the garrison church for the castle. The zig-zag decorated Norman chancel arch echoes exactly that at the castle entrance, suggesting the same architect. The 17th-century box pews and the copy of a 1611 Breeches Bible in the church library add further interest to the church, which was heavily restored in 1837. It is the scene on Oak Apple Day (29 May) of the climax of the ancient Castleton Garlanding Ceremony, when the bell-like 'garland', having been paraded through the village over the head of the 'Garland King', is hoisted to the top of the church tower.

The ruined keep of Peveril Castle overlooks the village to which it gave its name. The castle is now in the care of English Heritage.

(C)

Peak Cavern. One of Britain's most impressive cave entrances, Peak Cavern is also one of the traditional Wonders of the Peak. Formerly known as 'The Devil's Arse', it was once the subterranean home of a community of rope-makers, who found that the damp atmosphere of the cave enhanced the binding process. The smoke from the chimneys of their cottages still blackens the cavern roof. Later visitors included Celia Fiennes, Daniel Defoe, Lord Byron and Queen Victoria.

Cave Dale. These impressive limestone gorges were probably first formed underwater in a tropical sea some 330 million years ago. The harder 'reef' limestones were laid down on the edge of a shallow lagoon, and have resisted the later forces of erosion, including the meltwaters of Ice Age glaciers. Cave Dale gets its name from the numerous caves which lead off from it, and runs directly above and parallel with Peak Cavern hundreds of feet beneath.

WALK DIRECTIONS

(1)

From the car park, turn left into Cross Street, noting the embankments of the ancient Town Ditch on the left. Turn right opposite the Bull's Head into Castle Street.

Walk past the Information Centre and St Edmund's Parish Church and into the Market Place. To visit the castle, go straight on past the Youth Hostel and take the zig-zag path which winds up from the custodian's house, with increasingly extensive views across the Hope Valley to the Mam Tor-Lose Hill ridge.

Turn left past the war memorial into Bargate, and immediately right into the narrow entrance to Cave Dale (signposted). Over a stile between narrowing crags, the dale opens up, with Peveril Castle frowning down to the right.

Soot blackens the roof of Peak Cavern (left), a reminder of its former rope-making inhabitants.

Winnats Pass (below) east of Castleton, is a Site of Special Scientific Interest.

Follow the path to a metal gate, where the gradient becomes less steep, and follow a broken drystone wall through a succession of metal gates until the confluence with a path coming in from the left.

Turn sharply right and into a walled lane leading back to the village over Cow Low. Descend past Hurdlow Barn and Hurdlow Plantation to your left, with the limestone crags of The Winnats Pass beyond.

Join the path coming from the left down from The Winnats and Speedwell Cavern to re-enter Castleton at Goosehill, with Goosehill Hall to the left. Descend to Goosehill Bridge, which is convenient for a visit to the yawning mouth of Peak Cavern, to the right, the largest cave entrance in Britain and once the home of a community of rope-makers.

Walk down the footpath beside Peakshole Water to Newhall Bridge turning right into Cross Street back to the car park.

INFORMATION

Length of walk: 2 miles
Approximate time: 2-3 hours

TERRAIN:

Some steep climbs which can be muddy. Several gates, stiles and cattle grids. Not suitable for pushchairs or wheelchairs.

PARKING:

Use the main car park in the village.

OPEN:

Ollerenshaw Collection. Open daily, all year. Admission charge.
Peveril Castle. Open daily except winter Mons. Charge.
National Park Information Centre. Open daily, Easter-Oct and winter weekends.
Blue John, Speedwell and Treak Cliff Caverns. Open daily. Charge.
Peak Cavern. Open daily, Apr-Oct. Admission charge.
Castleton Village Museum. Limited opening. Charge.

MAM TOR

Another Wonder of the Peak, Mam Tor (the name is thought to mean 'Mother Mountain') is crowned by a large hillfort, one of the most impressive and highest (1,695ft) in the Pennines. The unstable east face, formed of a layer-cake succession of shales and grits, gives it the name of the Shivering Mountain. The main A625 Chapel-en-le-Frith road was finally swept away by these constant landslips in 1977. It is thought that the late Bronze Age or early Iron Age people who built the Mam Tor hillfort used the precipitous east face as part of the defences for their 16-acre fort.

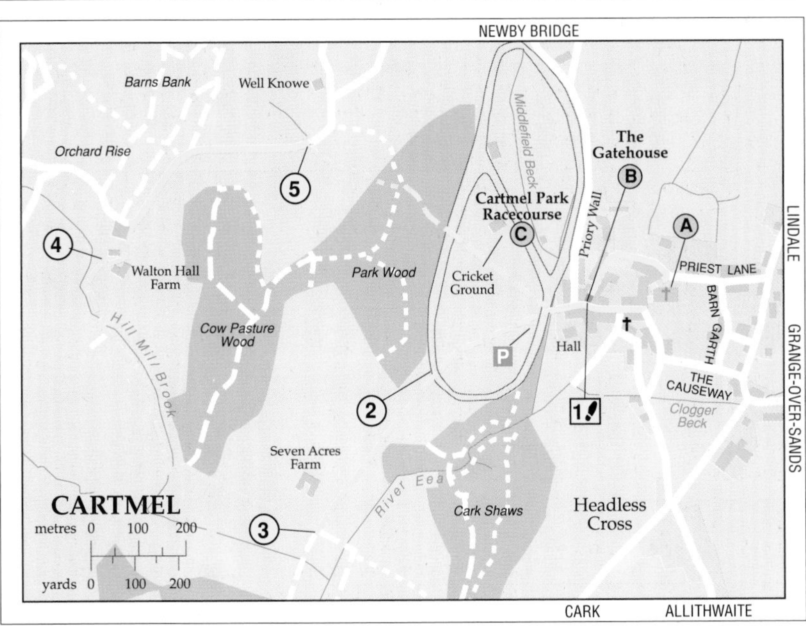

CARTMEL

CUMBRIA

Off A590, 3 miles S of High Newton

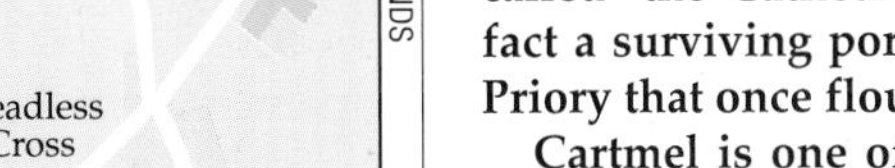

CARTMEL lies in a lovely undulating stretch of countryside between the edge of the Lake District Mountains and the sandy estuaries of Furness. The village is dwarfed by its massive Priory Church, often called `the Cathedral of the Lakes', which is in fact a surviving portion of the great Augustinian Priory that once flourished in this valley.

Cartmel is one of the most ancient villages in Cumbria, first mentioned in the 7th century when King Ecgrith of Cumbria gave the village 'and all its Britons' to the Northumbrian missionary St Cuthbert, presumably to found a church.

INFORMATION
Length of walk:
1½ miles (including stroll round Cartmel)
Approximate time:
1 hour

TERRAIN:
Easy – farm tracks and field paths, with one narrow and steep section impossible for pushchairs and wheelchairs, but quite suitable for children.

PARKING:
Park in the racecourse car park, a large field signed to the left of the post office from the Square (closed on race days).

Cartmel Priory Church contains many treasures: superb Renaissance screens, stained-glass windows and carved miserichords on the choir stalls.

WALK DIRECTIONS

For a short walk round the village, take the lane under the Gatehouse arch, turning right into Priest Lane to emerge at the back of the Priory. Turn right through the churchyard to pass the entrance to the Priory Church and back into the Square.

For the main part of the walk, from the car park go straight ahead to the gate at the far side, and take the middle track across open fields ahead. Go through the red gate, and continue straight ahead along the track.

Walk past Seven Acres Farm, but before going through the gate ahead, turn right and walk alongside the wall, before joining a track. Keep to the left of the deciduous wood, and continue on the track, which bends round the Walton Hall Farm.

Keep to the right past the farmhouse on to a metalled lane; turn right following the narrow lane for about 500yds over a low rise.

Where the land bends left, turn right, through a gap stile signposted for Cartmel. Follow the wall along the edge of the field, then go over a rocky hummock before descending into Park Wood, through a narrow gap stile.

Continue straight ahead, descending through the woods along a twisting path, through the iron gate at the bottom and across the racecourse, heading for the bench and pole by the car park.

POINTS OF INTEREST

Cartmel Priory Church. Cartmel Priory was founded in 1188 by William Marshall, Earl of Pembroke, for Augustinian Canons who developed the church in magnificent late Norman and Perpendicular Gothic style as part of a great monastery. At the Dissolution in 1537, the Priory Church was not destroyed or abandoned, but remained as the area's Parish Church. Notable features include the unusual tower set diagonally on its staging, a 13th-century choir, a wonderful 15th-century east window with original glass, many fine memorials, and the Cromwell Door in the south-west corner with holes said to have been made by parishioners firing at Cromwell's soldiers in 1643. The graveyard contains memorials to many people who over the centuries have drowned crossing Morecambe Bay sands.

The Gatehouse. The Priory Gatehouse, with its pointed arch, leading off the Square, dates from around 1330, and served as the village Grammar School between 1624 and 1790. Containing a small art gallery it is now owned by the National Trust, and is open to the public. Traces of the Priory Wall are still to be seen in the village, with fragments incorporated into surviving cottages.

Cartmel Park Racecourse. This traditional country racecourse hosts the popular Cartmel Steeplechase race meetings every Spring and Summer Bank Holiday. (At such times stewards accompany people using the right-of-way across the course.)

CHIPPING

LANCASHIRE

About 5 miles N of Longridge, on minor roads between Garstand and Clitheroe

THIS working village lies around little Chipping Brook in the foothills of the massive fell country of the Forest of Bowland, overlooked by the magnificent green expanse of Longridge Fell. The name Chipping means `market' in Old English, which indicates the antiquity of this settlement, and there has been a church here since AD597. Though no market or fair survive (the last were held earlier this century), Chipping was for many centuries a centre of the wool industry. Fleeces from local fell sheep were spun and woven in the village, creating a flourishing cottage industry in the 17th century.

POINTS OF INTEREST

Ⓐ

John Brabin's School. It is worth wandering down Windy Street, to the south of the village, to see the old village school with its handsome porch, paid for by money in the will of John Brabin, a prosperous Chipping weaver and dyer, who died in 1683. Almhouses nearby were also endowed in Brabin's will.

The school is now a youth club, and Brabin's former home in Talbot Street is now the village post office and a craft centre.

Ⓑ

The Church of St Bartholomew. The present church has a 15th-century tower, the remainder being rebuilt in 1506 and heavily restored in 1873. Controversy came to Chipping church in the 18th century. John Milner, the Vicar, was a close friend of John Wesley and accompanied him on his preaching journeys through the North of England, but when Wesley made a second visit to Chipping in 1753 he was shouted down by a group of irate anti-Methodist parishioners and had to complete his sermon in the vicarage.

Ⓒ

Berry's Furniture Factory. Chipping has been celebrated for over 100 years as a centre for the manufacture of chairs - in particular the traditional Lancashire 'spindle back' chair. In the factory premises in the old mill hardwood timber is seasoned ready for working into high-quality furniture. There are memorials to two members of the Berry family who were both craftsman chairmakers, in the Parish Church.

Chipping's old school dates from post 1683.

WALK DIRECTIONS

①

Leave the car park at the bottom left-hand corner, by the church.

②

Turn left at the crossroads past the church and walk along Talbot Street. Pass some stone cottages, shops, inns and old watermill, formerly Chipping Mill.

③

At the fork of the road, take the narrower lane left which climbs gently uphill. Keep to the right hand side of the lane. Follow the lane for about 500yds past the entrance to Leagram Hall on the left.

④

Turn left along the tarmac drive (cattle grid) through Leagram Park, which follows the edge of the grounds before curving left past woodland towards Chipping Laund Farm. There are superb views of the wild Bowland Fells from the section of path which runs north of Chipping Laund Farm, among them (from left to right) Wolf Fell, Burnslack, Fair Oak and, on the opposite side of the Hodder Valley, Birkett Fell.

⑤

Continue past the farm bearing left towards Birchen Lee. Ignore the track off to the right.

⑥

Go past the farm and barns at Birchen Lee. The track, now concrete surfaced, dips down past a shallow wooded ravine. Keep ahead through gates to pass in front of the next farm ahead.

⑦

Beyond the farm the track dips down into another shallow ravine to a stream and swings right, uphill. On the corner, before reaching Dobson's Brook, take a faint path left which leads to woodland in the centre of which there is a footbridge. Cross and follow the path out of the wood.

⑧

Turn right above the wood to follow the faint path running parallel to Nan King's Wood and the stream, the line of path about 50yds above the stream. Stiles in the walls indicate the line of path which now climbs a low hillock away from the stream, soon giving good views of Chipping and its church before descending, quite sharply, to a stile opposite the mill pond.

⑨

Turn left past Berry's factory down to Kirkgate and the car park.

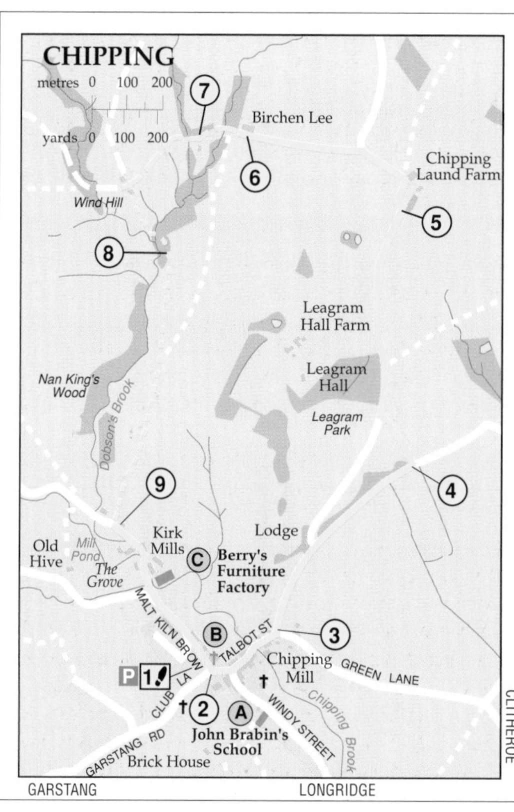

INFORMATION
Length of walk: 2½ miles
Approximate time: 1½ hours

TERRAIN:
Easy, but some gentle climbing. Suitable for children, but not for wheelchairs or push-chairs after Birchen Lee Farm, though an alternative return route could be taken via farm tracks and lanes (additional 1½ miles).

PARKING:
Park at the village car park immediately to the west of the church, reached off Club Lane/ Garstang Road.

INFORMATION
Length of walk:
1 mile (with optional 3-mile return walk to Ingleborough Cave)
Approximate time:
½ hour

TERRAIN:
Suitable for wheelchairs or pushchairs (also to Ingleborough Cave).

PARKING:
Park in the village car park by the Yorkshire Dales National Park Information Centre. There are toilets here.

OPENING TIMES:
Ingleborough Estate and Cave is open daily throughout the year from 10.30am. Charge.

CLAPHAM

NORTH YORKSHIRE

Off A65, 7 miles W of Settle

CLAPHAM Beck, which flows out of the extensive cave system under Ingleborough, divides Clapham village in two. The Beck forms a little ravine, lined with shrubs, around which is situated one of the most delightfully intimate of Yorkshire Dales villages, whose grey stone cottages and houses seem to echo the simple grandeur of the surrounding limestone uplands.

Although this walk is barely a mile long, it can easily form the prelude to an additional three-mile lake and beckside walk through the Ingleborough Estate to Ingleborough Show Cave.

WALK DIRECTIONS

(1)

Turn left at the Information Centre, passing the old Market Cross on the wall on the right.

(2)

At the bridge at the main road, by the New Inn, cross to continue along the same side of the beck, along The Green for 270yds, to the footbridge on the right which leads to Station Road.

(3)

Turn right to return to the bridge along Station Road, this time continuing up the left-hand side of the stream, along Riverside, past cottages and the two footbridges over the beck to the top of the village opposite the waterfalls.

(4)

Continue left at the top of the village to the woodyard. If you are continuing into the Ingleborough Estate a small toll is payable.

(5)

Return to the top of the village, crossing the road bridge to the church.

(6)

Turn right along Church Avenue, passing Ingleborough Hall, back to the Car Park.

POINTS OF INTEREST

(A)

The Manor House. The little Tudor Manor House with its lintel dated 1701 is now the National Park Centre. Excellent displays of geology and local history are now held here.

(B)

The Old Market Cross. The old weathered market cross, moved here from the main road some years ago, is built into the beckside wall. It is many years since a market was last held here, though fairs were held as late as this century. The New Inn on the main road is the survivor of two inns at Clapham on what was the busy Leeds-Kendal turnpike road, now by-passed by the A65.

(C)

The Church of St James. Only the tower of Clapham Church is medieval, probably of the Perpendicular (14th-century) period, the rest of the building being of the Regency period (1814) and unusually light in design. There are memorials to the Farrer family, but none to Reginald, who converted to Buddhism before his death. There is a memorial to him, appropriately enough, in the garden of Ingleborough Hall.

(D)

Ingleborough Hall. This elegant neo-classical country house, with its giant Doric columns, dates from between 1820 and 1830, the period when the Farrer brothers were redeveloping the estate. An unusual feature in the entrance hall are pillars of black 'Dent' marble from nearby Dentdale quarries. The house and its extensive grounds is now an outdoor education centre serving schools in the Yorkshire region.

THE FARRER FAMILY

The Farrer family first settled in Clapham in the 18th century, but it was London financier Oliver Farrer (known as 'Penny Bun' Farrer because of his frugal habits) who built up the family fortune and bought and developed his Yorkshire estates.

His nephews, Oliver and James William, redesigned Clapham in the 1830s and created the lake and dam above the village. This provided an early source of hydro-electric power for the village and still powers the estate-owned sawmill.

Reginald Farrer (1880-1920) was perhaps the most famous member of the family. A distinguished botanist and plant collector who helped popularise rock gardening in Britain, he introduced many exotic species to this country – the descendants of which still grace Kew Gardens and the Royal Botanic Gardens in Edinburgh. He died of typhoid while on a botanic expedition in the Burmese mountains at the tragically early age of 40.

A stone bridge over Clapham Beck connects the two halves of the village.

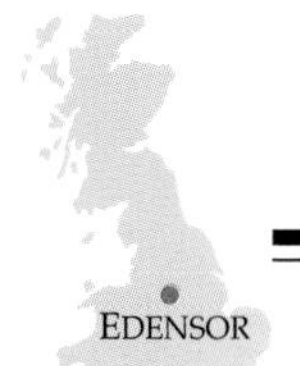

EDENSOR

DERBYSHIRE

Off B6012, between Rowsley and Baslow, 4 miles E of Bakewell

EDENSOR (pronounced 'Ensor') is a 19th-century estate village in Chatsworth Park. It replaced the demolished cottages of the original village, which was mentioned in Domesday but which had offended the view of the fourth Duke of Devonshire.

POINTS OF INTEREST

Chatsworth House. The present classical Palladian-style building dates from between 1678 and 1707, and is largely the work of the fourth Duke of Devonshire. It replaced an earlier Tudor Chatsworth built by the legendary Bess of Hardwick. The interior is a treasure house of works of art from around the world. The park is the work of Capability Brown, and the gardens were laid out by Sir Joseph Paxton, who also designed London's Crystal Palace.

(B)

Queen Mary's Bower. This strange open-roofed and moated structure at the entrance to the House was a kind of belvedere or summerhouse traditionally favoured by Mary, Queen of Scots during her several enforced stays at Chatsworth between 1570 and 1581. This and the Hunting Tower, seen above the woods beyond the House, are the only remaining structures left from Bess of Hardwick's original Tudor Chatsworth.

Edensor Village. In 1839, the sixth Duke of Devonshire employed architect John Robertson to create a new Edensor across the road from Chatsworth House. He is said to have consulted a popular architectural pattern book and used every conceivable style, from mock-Tudor to Swiss chalet and pseudo-Italian villa, to create an extraordinary pot-pourri of *cottage ornée* designs.

The Church of St Peter. The drastic redesign by Sir George Gilbert Scott in 1867 gave Edensor a church which overshadows the tiny village. There are many links and memorials to the Cavendish family, including the grave of Joseph Paxton. At the top of the churchyard are the Cavendish family graves. Kathleen Kennedy, sister of US President John Kennedy, who was married to the Marquis of Hartington, is also buried in the churchyard.

A majestic view of the west front of Chatsworth House.

WALK DIRECTIONS

(1)

From the car park, cross the road by the cattle grid and walk through a white gate down to the river by the ruined watermill.

(2)

Turn left and follow the riverside path with fine views of Chatsworth House across the river to the right.

(3)

Walk up to the bridge leading to the House past Queen Mary's Bower to your left.

(4)

Otherwise, turn left and immediately take the path leading up right through some fine beeches. This path drops down towards Edensor, crossing the road by a large tree encircled by a seat.

(5)

After exploring the village and church, turn left up the steep stone steps just beyond the church to emerge out on open pasture again. The path contours slowly up the hill between the oval Maud's Plantation and another, with extensive views of Chatsworth House and parkland and the moors beyond to the left.

(6)

On reaching New Piece Wood, turn left to walk downhill on the path, finally dropping steeply down to reach the car park again.

INFORMATION
Length of walk: 2 miles
Approximate time: 2 hours (more if you visit the house).

TERRAIN:
Field path walking, not suitable for pushchairs or wheelchairs.

PARKING:
In the large free car park at Calton Lees, at the southern entrance to the park.

OPEN:
Chatsworth House and gardens. Daily Apr-Oct. Charge. Also, Chatsworth Farm and Adventure Playground, open Apr-Sep.

REFRESHMENTS:
Chatsworth House.

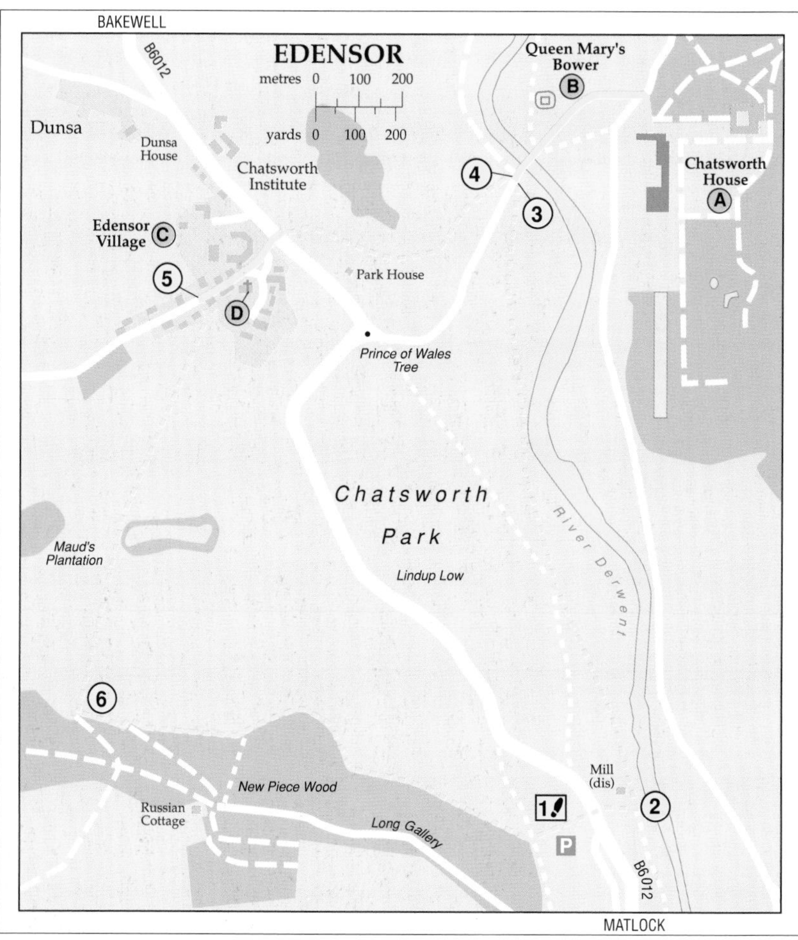

DENT
CUMBRIA

On a minor road, 6 miles SW of Sedbergh

DENT Town, as it is most correctly known, is the only community of any size in the whole of Dentdale. Its first settlers were the Vikings, who came to what is now Cumbria via Ireland during the 9th and 10th centuries. Their system of creating scattered freehold homesteads owned by `statesmen' or owner-farmers is still evident in a landscape of narrow farms each situated close to a hillside spring and with its share of good valley bottom land and rough pasture divided by drystone walls. Dent Town was the natural focal point of this community. With its narrow cobbled street, quiet courts and alleyways, and ancient church, the village retains its medieval flavour

The clock on the church tower in Dent is a reminder that time seems to have stopped in this quaint little village.

POINTS OF INTEREST

Adam Sedgwick of Dent. The Shap granite fountain in the centre of Dent's main street was erected to commemorate the life of geologist Professor Adam Sedgwick (1785-1873), who was born in the village. Sedgwick, for 55 years Woodwardian Professor of Geology at Cambridge University, was one of the greatest field geologists of his time. He was also a gifted teacher and lecturer (Charles Darwin was one of his pupils, though Sedgwick was later to be a stern critic of Darwinism), a personal friend of both Queen Victoria and Prince Albert, and a great benefactor of his local Dale. The account of his early memories of life in the dale, contained in the *Memorial by the Trustees of Cowgill Chapel*, published when he was in his 80s, is still regarded as a classic of local history.

St Andrew's Church. St Andrew's Church is a simple, but dignified Dales church which has its origin in Norman times, though with a new tower in the late 18th century and heavily restored in Victorian times. Only a blocked door remains of the original church, though much 15th-century Perpendicular work survives. There is a memorial to Professor Adam Sedgwick in the south wall, and to other members of the Sedgwick family, several of whom, including Adam's own father, were Vicars of Dent.

THE PENNINE FAULT

The deep valley formed by Barbondale and across to Helm Knott lies along one of the most important geological fault lines of the Pennines. Here, the typical Carboniferous rocks of the Yorkshire Dales – limestones and gritstones – yield to the harder and older Silurian slates of the Lake District, creating an area of complex geological shift and instability.

If you look carefully at the area west of Gawthrop on this walk, you will see a change in the landscape, both in terms of shape and texture. The smooth summits of the fellsides of the higher valley contrast with the darker, spikier and uneven land-scape formations of the lower dale. Adam Sedgwick first discovered this great fault line during his original field work and research into the geology of the Lake District and the Pennines during the early 1830s. It was first described in his paper to the Geological Society of London, published in 1835.

This granite slab is both a memorial to Adam Sedgwick and a fountain.

Cobbled streets like this one (right) lend Dent its unique charm.

(C)

Dent Grammar School. The tiny two-storey building in Dent churchyard, just to the rear and right of the church, is the 17th-century Grammar School, originally founded to teach local boys to read and write and to master church Latin and some mathematics. Adam Sedgwick was a pupil here as a child, being taught by his father Richard, Vicar of Dent, whose duties included teaching at the school. Adam continued his education at nearby Sedbergh School before going on to Trinity College, Cambridge.

Hall Lane. This narrow lane has changed little since the days of pack-ponies and wheeled carts and is lined with traditional tall hedgerows rich in wildflowers, typical of this part of Dentdale.

High Hall Farm, whose Tudor chimneys are visible from the lane, is now in use as a rare breeds farm.

Grey stone and white-washed cottages are typical of Dent, a quiet little village in the valley of the Dee.

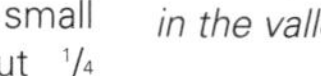

INFORMATION
Length of walk:
$2^1/_2$ miles
Approximate time:
2 hours

TERRAIN:
Riverside paths, tracks, quiet lanes and field paths. One short uphill stretch. Suitable for older children but not for wheelchairs or pushchairs because of some narrow sections of path.

PARKING:
Park in Dent Car Park (off Main Street).

WALK DIRECTIONS

From Dent Car Park turn left along the cobbled street, but take the enclosed way left across the churchyard, past the front of the church. Continue straight ahead down steps and turn left into the main road, walking down to Church Bridge.

Cross the bridge over the River Dee, taking the gap stile on the left at the far side of the bridge, down steps into the field. Follow the hedge and riverside, but where the river bends away to the left, keep straight ahead to a stile in the hedge and wall.

Turn left in to Hall Lane, a narrow, partially surfaced lane between tall hedgerows. Follow the lane, which goes below farms and eventually alongside the river, to the main Sedbergh road at Barth Bridge.

Cross the bridge - pausing to enjoy the clear waters of the Dee - and after about 100yds cross a stile on the right to take the path leading to Gawthrop.

(5)

The path goes over two more stiles, joins a small brook and after about $^1/_4$ mile, meets a lane in Gawthrop.

Turn right and at a crossroads in a few yards look for a lane ahead signed 'Dent $^3/_4$'. Follow this lane as it becomes a farm track past cottages into the farm.

Keep directly ahead through the farm gate, and keep on the path along the hedge below an embankment, through another gate ahead to a stile. There are superb views here along Dentdale and across Dent Town.

Keep walking in the same direction, to the next gate and down to Mill Beck Farm. Go through the farmyard and past the main farm buildings, turning left along the waymarked path down the field to the left.

At the right-hand corner of the field, before a grey bungalow, take the path right which leads over stiles to emerge at a barn at Laning Farm. Bear left to walk round the outside of the barn to the farm buildings ahead, past the caravan site. Turn left to the car park at the centre of Dent.

THE TERRIBLE KNITTERS OF DENT

Until the 19th century Dent was a self-sufficient community, sustained by agriculture and a prolific hand-knitting industry. Stockings, caps and gloves were made from the rough local wool and sold at nearby Kendal market. Along the narrow, cobbled main street are tall houses whose upper storeys had balconies where the 'terrible knitters of Dent' ('terrible' refers to the speed of their knitting) sat hard at work during the summer months.

During the winter, whole families worked around the fireside, to earn some 'knitting brass' to help a subsistence income. With the coming of the Industrial Revolution and the growth of the steam-powered mills in the West Riding, the trade ceased and Dent reverted to a quiet backwater, its population steadily declining.

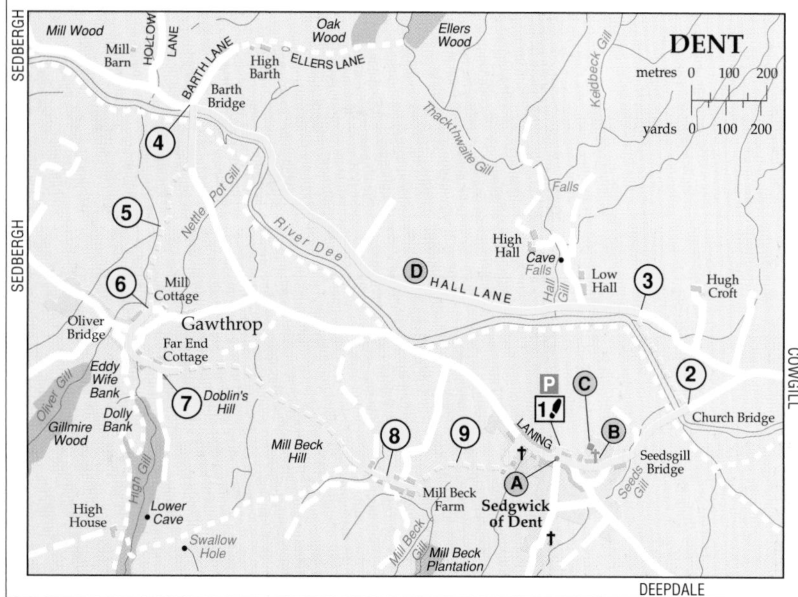

ELSDON

NORTHUMBERLAND

On B6341, 12 miles SW of Rothbury

'CAPITAL' of Redesdale until its prosperous cattle droving and packhorse trading routes were bypassed during the 19th century, Elsdon today is a peaceful, unspoilt village clustered around a church and extensive green. Only one of three pubs remain and the Rector's school is now closed, but against a background of the Northumberland National Park's remote moorlands, the centuries of violent border warfare and subsequent prosperity are much in evidence.

POINTS OF INTEREST

A

Elsdon Tower. This 14th-century vicar's Pele Tower, occupies a dominant position above the village. Decorated externally with the Arms of the Lords of Redesdale, it has walls up to 8ft thick and originally comprised a tunnel-vaulted stable with domestic and living quarters above.

B

St Cuthbert's Church. Predominantly 14th-century, Elsdon's parish church bears testimony to a turbulent border history – a mass grave, probably containing casualties of the Battle of Otterburn (1388), was uncovered during 19th-century building work, and horse skulls discovered in the bell turret suggest earlier pagan sacrifices.

Elsdon Castle. Built in the late 11th century, the earthworks, once crowned with a timber keep and stockade, today present an excellent example of a 'motte and bailey' castle.

Village Green. Extending to seven acres and including St Cuthbert's Church, the village green remains Elsdon's focal point. Annual fairs and a weekly market started in the late 13th century have long been forgotten, but the stone 'pinfold' (cattle pound) and a commemorative oak tree on the site of a cock-fighting pit remain in evidence of busier times.

The old stone cattle pen on Elsdon village green, with St Cuthbert's in the distance

INFORMATION
Length of walk:
1¾ miles
Approximate time:
1¼ hours

TERRAIN:
Tarmac roads and enclosed farmland. Seven gates and one cattle grid/gate. Unsuitable for wheelchairs and pushchairs but suitable for children.

PARKING:
The walk begins outside the Bird in Bush public house on the west side of the village green, park on the road near here.

OPEN:
Elsdon Tower gardens, Apr-Sep. Charge. (Elsdon Tower by appointment only).

REFRESHMENTS:
Public house in village; tearoom at Soppit Farm, 1 mile W of village on B6341.

WALK DIRECTIONS

1

Cross the main road and walk north (uphill), past the old Rector's school on your left, to Elsdon Tower.

Either detour around the Tower gardens (open seasonally), or bear sharp right and walk downhill to the main road. Here, turn right to visit St Cuthbert's church or left to continue the walk.

Cross the bridge and turn right along the Hudspeth/Eastnook road, but before reaching the gate bear left on a rough track to pass the village hall on your right. Walk along the tarmac road, through a gate and then uphill to The Mote

At the house walk on across the yard and through a wooden hurdle into the paddock, noting Elsdon Castle on your left. Cross the paddock, go through a gate, then bear diagonally right across the field, passing a disused quarry to your left, to gates and low trees seen ahead.

Go through the left-hand gate and continue with the fence on your right. From the next gate bear right along the surfaced road, walk downhill, through a gate and past Landshot Glebe, and turn right at the road junction.

6

Walk on towards Elsdon village, across a cattle grid and eventually to a gate. Beyond the gate bear left along the main road, cross the bridge then turn left along the Newcastle/Morpeth road.

After approximately 30yds turn left again to walk in front of the houses. Continue to the village shop.

8

Bear right (around the pinfold), cross the road and walk on to finish the visit at the Bird in Bush public house, with the village green on the right.

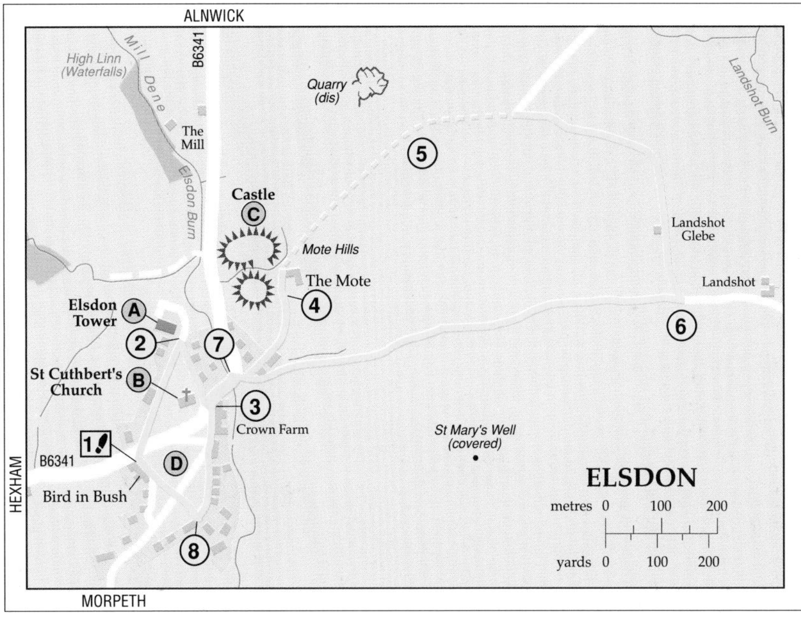

ESCOMB

CO DURHAM

Off B6282, 2 miles W of Bishop Auckland

TUCKED away down a cul-de-sac close to the River Wear is a village that still retains a link with early Christianity. At the foot of the hill is the simple stone Saxon church, surrounded by a circular wall enclosing the churchyard. Facing the church are modern houses and a small green. The banks of the nearby river offer an opportunity to discover a wide variety of wild flowers.

POINTS OF INTEREST

St John's Church. The north-east of England retains a number of places associated with early Christianity, including Jarrow, Lindisfarne, Monkwearmouth and Escomb, which has one of the finest examples of an Anglo-Saxon church in Britain. It has stood here for over 1,300 years. Many of the stones used to build the church were taken from the Roman fort at Binchester, north of Bishop Auckland, and one stone carries the mark of the VI Legion.

(B)

The Graveyard. Here there is the gravestone of Michael Robson Elliot. He died when there was an explosion of `fire damp' in Woodhouse Close colliery on 8 January 1840. Death through accident and explosion was quite common in these communities.

The Stockton to Darlington Railway was built because of the wealth of coal in this area. It became the first passenger-carrying steam railway, but the main commercial reason for building the line was to take the coal from nearby Witton Park to the Tees for onward shipment.

Wear Valley Way. This is a 46-mile long-distance walk that begins at Killhope Wheel, high on the Pennines at the head of the Wear Valley. The walk follows the river part of the way and takes in the surrounding countryside with features such as disused mineral railways and Hamsterley Forest. Then it returns to the River Wear for its final few miles through Escomb to the finish at Willington.

Wild Flowers on the river bank. The banks of the River Wear at Escomb and the return path offer a wide variety of wild flowers in summer. In early July white campion, common sorrel, wild strawberry, birds' foot trefoil, wild rose, meadow cranesbill, foxglove, lady's bedstraw, wood forget-me-not and ox-eye daisy can be seen.

SACRED SIMPLICITY

When the church at Escomb was built, the village was in the kingdom of Northumbria, which played a leading role in the Christian conversion of England.

In AD597 a band of missionaries from Rome arrived in Kent, at Canterbury. In AD625 the Christian daughter of the Kentish king came north to marry King Edwin of Northumbria, who duly became a Christian himself. His son and successor, Oswald, sent for monks from Iona in Scotland. They, together with St Aidan, founded the monastery at Lindisfarne.

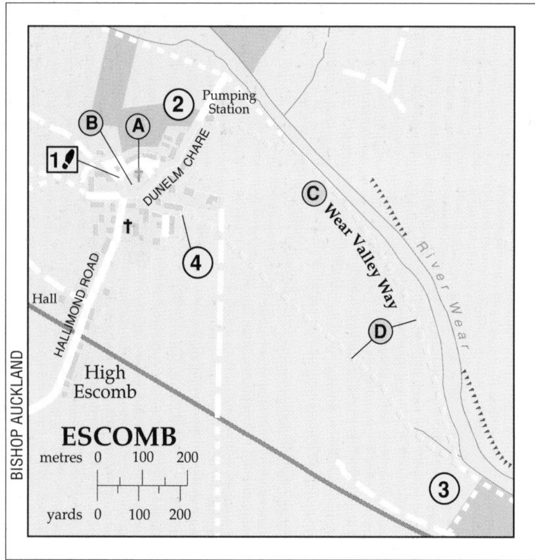

WALK DIRECTIONS

After parking your car, visit the church. Then take the road out of the bottom right-hand corner of the road on which you came into the village, Dunelm Chare.

(2)

Ten yards after the road becomes a rough track, turn right through a squeeze stile beside a gate. Follow the track, keeping the hedge on your right, until you can turn right on to a riverside path. Follow this along the riverside to a footbridge.

Cross the footbridge and turn right along the track. A series of stiles leads back to Escomb.

(4)

The path passes above some farm buildings on the right and enters Escomb along Bede Close. Continue back to the church and Saxon Green.

The River Wear (above). The Anglo-Saxon church (left) at Escomb.

INFORMATION
Length of walk: 1½ miles
Approximate time: 1¼ hours

TERRAIN:
Suitable for children. Unsuitable for pushchairs and wheelchairs.

PARKING:
Park on the roadside.

OPEN:
St John's Church (obtain key from 22 Saxon Green, Escomb).

REFRESHMENTS:
One inn.

EYAM

DERBYSHIRE

On B6521, 4 miles W of Baslow

EYAM (pronounced 'Eem') has not changed much since the fateful event which made it famous more than three centuries ago. The visitation of the Great Plague in 1665-66 prompted the villagers into a noble act of self-imposed quarantine which decimated their community, but achieved the objective of halting the spread of the deadly virus. There are many reminders of those days, from the notices on the cottages of the victims to the registers in the church and perhaps most touching, the isolated family graves in the surrounding fields. The ancient Saxon cross in the churchyard tells of earlier times, while all around are reminders of the lead-mining industry which was the keystone of the local economy.

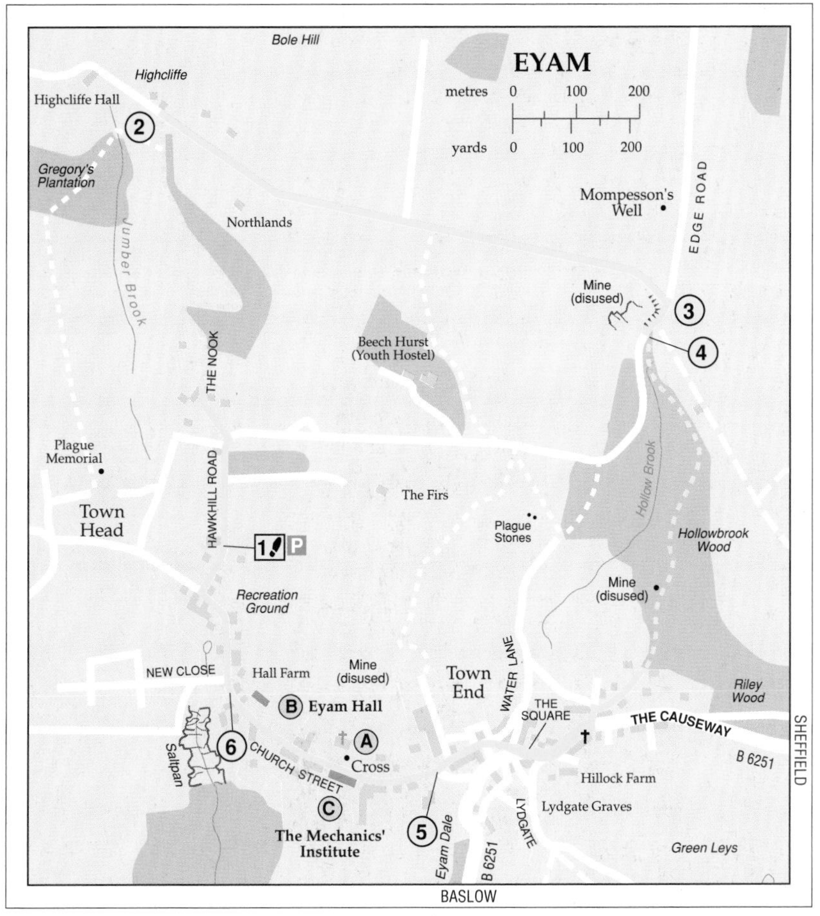

INFORMATION
Length of walk: $2\frac{1}{2}$ miles
Approximate time: 2 hours

TERRAIN:
Easy field and track walking, with some climbs and stiles which would make it difficult for pushchairs and wheelchairs.

PARKING:
Park in the car park on Hawkhill Road.

REFRESHMENTS:
Pubs in Eyam.

WALK DIRECTIONS

From the car park, turn right up the hill and where the road bends right, go left up the narrow lane known as The Nook. This is a steep climb, with fine views back to Eyam.

Turn right on reaching the metalled road at the top. After about $\frac{1}{2}$ a mile, you pass close to Mompesson's Well, a spring covered by a carved gritstone slab where food was left for the quarantined villagers during the Plague. The money left in payment was disinfected by the running water, or vinegar. William Mompesson was the rector of Eyam during the time of the Plague.

At the road junction, turn right down the hill, and after passing a small lane on the left leading to Hollowbrook Barn and Riley House (where there are more Plague family memorials), a signpost points left down into Furness, or Hollowbrook, Wood.

This well-defined path leads on to a lane leading back into Eyam village, which you enter by The Causeway, which leads down to The Square. The old Bull Ring is preserved in The Square, where bull-baiting contests once took place.

Keep right into Church Street, to pass the church on the right with the Mechanics' Institute opposite (now a bank). Pass the village stocks on the left with the Old Market behind. Opposite is the 17th-century Eyam Hall (private).

Keep straight on past the post office, and turn right into Hawkhill Road and back to the car park, on the edge of the recreation ground.

Many cottages were infected by the plague (above). This cottage (right) is where it first struck in Eyam.

This complex 18th-century sundial is fixed above the chancel door of St Lawrence's, the parish church.

POINTS OF INTEREST

St Lawrence's Parish Church. This mainly 13th-century church has been much restored, but retains many items which suggest an even earlier building. In the churchyard near the south door stands the famous truncated Saxon Cross, which has been dated to the early 9th century, and there is a Saxon, as well as a Norman, font inside the church.

Above the chancel door is a complex sundial, dated 1775, and there are many interesting gravestones in the churchyard, including the table tomb of Katherine Mompesson, the rector's wife, who was another Plague victim. Mompesson's Chair, rescued from a Liverpool antique shop by a former rector, stands in the chancel, and the carved Jacobean pulpit must have been used by the leader of 'the epic sacrifice'.

Eyam Hall. One of the finest Stuart houses in the Peak, Eyam Hall was built by Thomas Wright in 1676, while the Plague was still a vivid memory in the village. Set back behind a walled garden, the tiny gables on the front are no more than decorative details, but the overall impression is of a harmonious whole.

The Mechanics' Institute. This is the scene every spring of the Barmote Court, where the ancient laws affecting lead mining are still administered. The fields around Eyam are still pitted with the remains of lead-mining activity, which reached its heyday in the 18th and 19th centuries.

WELL-DRESSING IN DERBYSHIRE

Flowers often figure prominently in rural folklore where customs have remained unchanged for generations. It is particularly true of the custom of dressing wells as an appreciation of the gift of water.

Eyam is one of a number of villages in the Peak District which continue the ancient custom of well-dressing. Although wells and springs have been regarded with religious awe since far back in the past, the dressing is believed to have originated from the culture of Mediterranean countries where water was valued for cleansing, healing and refreshment, and may have been introduced during the Roman occupation of Britain.

With the rise of Christianity, the saints of the early church replaced the original pagan goddesses and nymphs who were their previous guardians. The offering of flowers placed at the wells in the springtime, to celebrate the festivals of *Floralia* or *Fontinalia*, therefore disappeared.

It was revived in the early 17th century in the Peak District village of Tissington, reputably by a certain Mary Twigg. Garlands of flowers were hung up at the wells as a thanksgiving because they did not run dry during the severe drought of 1615. The idea spread to other villages and in the 19th century became much more elaborate. Complicated pictures were made by pressing flower petals, ferns, mosses, lichen, bark and greenery into damp clay, held in a wooden frame.

Today, boards, which form the basis of the frames, are pierced with holes and studded with nails to key the clay, then placed on trestles or bales of straw to facilitate the work of 'petalling'. The subject is outlined by piping with seeds, rice and alder cones, and filled in with more durable materials such as leaves and lichens. Finally the delicate work of petalling is carried out. The petals are inserted from the bottom of the picture like tiles on a roof, so that the paler parts are covered by the next and succeeding layers. This also allows rain or moisture to drain off.

This colourful custom has continued to the present day and more than 30 Derbyshire and Staffordshire towns and villages dress their wells during the spring and summer. The pictures are traditionally on religious themes and often carry Biblical texts or improving exhortations. Placed by the well, they have become a major Peak District tourist attraction.

The festival in Eyam is held on the first Sunday in September, the week after the annual Plague commemoration service.

Well-dressing is still practised in Bakewell (below), and Eyam (above) where it coincides with the plague commemoration service.

The village's grey-stone buildings (above) surround its village green. Inset, a steam locomotive on the Deviation Line.

GOATHLAND

NORTH YORKSHIRE

Off A169, 10 miles SW of Whitby

THIS moorland village can be reached from Pickering or Grosmont by the North York Moors Railway, a privately owned line on which both steam and diesel services operate. The first railway line through the village was built in 1836 but was horse drawn until 1847, and the track forms the early part of the walk. The deviation line built in 1865 and still in use today is followed on the return.

Goathland's stone houses stand well back from the roads and sheep crop the grass. There are nine small waterfalls in the narrow wooded valleys around the village.

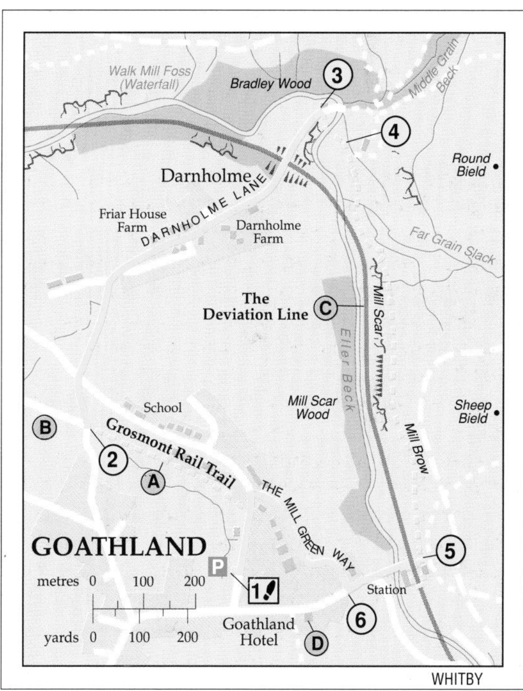

POINTS OF INTEREST

Ⓐ

Railway Incline. Part of the original 1836 line built by George Stephenson. The wagons were hauled up the incline by rope. Because of the delays and accidents this caused, it was decided to build the deviation line that opened in 1865. A trail now passes along the original line to Grosmont.

The North York Moors Crosses Walk. The start and finishing point for this 54-mile walk, which sets off down the incline, is at Goathland Village Hall. The walk is an annual event organised by the local rescue team. The circuit of the moors passes 13 crosses or shafts of crosses which acted as waymarkers for travellers. The winner runs the route in about eight hours, while slower walkers will take up to 22 hours.

The Deviation Line. The 1-in-49 incline connecting Grosmont and Goathland offers a fine sight, as steam engines haul their carriages through excellent scenery. The line was closed in 1965 but was reopened by enthusiasts eight years later. Goathland Station was moved from Incline Top to its present site when the Deviation Line opened. There is a small shop on the platform.

Plough Stots. A group of local people perform a long sword dance at local shows, traditionally on Plough Monday, (the first Monday after 6 January) but nowadays more usually on the nearest Saturday. The dancers are accompanied by a musician, people performing a play and the plough stots dragging their plough. The swords are displays in the bar of the Goathland Hotel.

INFORMATION
Length of walk:
$1^3/_4$ miles
Approximate time:
$1^1/_2$ hours

TERRAIN:
Suitable for children, unsuitable for push-chairs and wheelchairs; two footbridges and a series of steps.

PARKING:
Use the car park in the centre of the village.

OPEN:
North York Moors Railway. Daily. Charge.

REFRESHMENTS:
A number of inns and cafés.

EVENTS:
Plough Stots. First Saturday after 6 Jan, check locally. North York Moors Crosses Walk. Second or third weekend in Jul.

WALK DIRECTIONS

From the car park turn left and in 50yds turn left through a kissing-gate, sign-posted Grosmont Rail Trail. Follow the track to a gate and descend part of the incline to a road.

②

Turn right and follow a flagged path beside the road to a crossroads. Walk down Darnholme Lane, opposite, and eventually you cross the railway and descend into Darnholme.

③

Halfway down the hill, bear right on a signposted public footpath beside railings. This sweeps right to a foot-bridge; cross over Eller Beck and continue for 20yds.

④

Turn right along the path which leads to a series of steps by a drystone wall. Continue at the top for 600yds alongside the devia-tion line and then fork right, down to Goathland station.

⑤

Turn right through a white gate and left along the platform to a footbridge. Return along the opposite platform and turn left along the road, passing over a bridge with pleasant river views.

⑥

Turn right along The Mill Green Way which leads to a track along the original roadway. At the road, turn left back to the car park.

GRASSINGTON

NORTH YORKSHIRE

On B6265, 9 miles N of Skipton

LYING along a natural limestone shelf in the hillside above the River Wharfe, Grassington, a former lead-mining town, is everything a Dales village should be. Amid beautiful riverside scenery and open moorland, the extensive remains of the leadmines where local people earned a perilous living can still be seen. The leadminers' cottages now house the Upper Wharfedale Museum with its display on local farming, mining and geology.

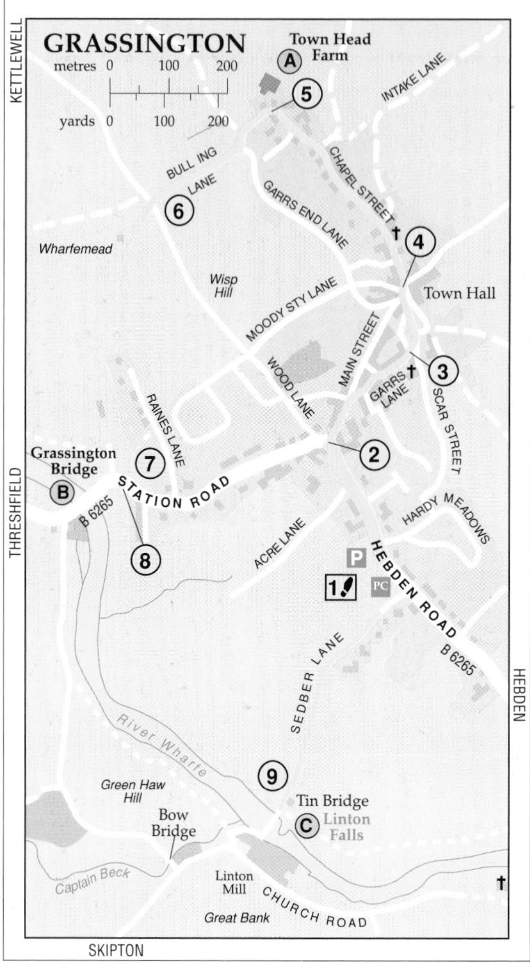

INFORMATION
Length of walk:
1 mile
Approximate time:
45 minutes

TERRAIN:
Easy – narrow paths and lanes, suitable for children, but a number of stiles make it difficult for pushchairs beyond Point 7 (from where a return could be made back to the car park along Wood Lane).

PARKING:
Park in the National Park Car Park on the Hebden road (Toilets and Information Centre).

OPEN:
Upper Wharfedale Museum: Sun 2-5pm, daily during main holiday period, Thu 7-9pm.

POINTS OF INTEREST

Ⓐ

Town Head Farm. Town Head Farm is a beautiful example of a 17th-century yeoman's (freeholder's) farmhouse, with traditional narrow mullioned windows and drip stones, cottage garden, and nearby dovecote in a barn. Many exceptionally fine farmhouses in the Yorkshire Dales date from this period, which reflected the relative prosperity in the latter part of the 17th century, as trade increased and with it demand for farm produce. The farm belongs to the Trustees of Fountaines Hospital, a charity established in 1721 under the will of one Richard Fountaine, a local man who made his fortune in London, to use the income of this and other lands to help the poor people of the parish.

Grassington Bridge. Dating from the 17th century, though with additions every century since, Grassington Bridge is an imposing structure with 'breakwaters' to reduce the destructive power of the fast-flowing river.

Ⓒ

Linton Falls. This superb series of waterfalls is caused by the North Craven Fault which crosses Wharfedale at this point, exposing underlying Carboniferous limestones and creating this spectacular natural feature. From medieval times onwards there was a water-powered wool and later cotton mill here as well as a pioneering hydro-electric plant built early this century, and the weirs that provided a head of water are still in place.

WALK DIRECTIONS

①

Take the kissing-gate into Hebden Road to the left of the toilet block and turn left to enter Grassington Square.

②

Walk through the Square, keeping to the right-hand side past the Museum and the Black Horse Hotel along Garrs Lane.

The series of waterfalls at Linton were created by the North Craven Fault as it crosses Wharfedale. The shallow stretches of river are popular with both dippers and mallards.

③

Where a track forks left past some cottages (Water Lane), continue along beside an extensive barn (Pletts Barn) to arrive at the Town Hall.

④

At the Town Hall head straight on, along Chapel Street. Follow the street past cottages to Town Head Farm.

⑤

Follow the lane as it swings left downhill, and at the crossroads turn left and then immediately right into Bull Ing Lane.

⑥

At the next crossroads, take the track between the stone walls opposite. This leads to a gate into a field. Walk down the field diagonally left but soon bear sharp left below housing and above farm buildings to reach a gate in the bottom left-hand corner of the field.

Turn right along the track to the main road just above Grassington Bridge.

⑧

Cross the busy road with great care to a gap stile in the wall almost directly opposite. Follow the path above and parallel to the riverside over a tiny foot-bridge and a stile to Linton waterfalls.

Cross the stile into the narrow enclosed path to the footbridge to view the Falls. Turn left, following the enclosed way uphill through kissing-gates. A kissing-gate at the top of the hill leads into the car park.

On Grasmere lake, just south of the main village settlement, the public can hire rowing boats to view the small solitary island. This was a favourite summer haunt of the Wordsworths.

GRASMERE

CUMBRIA

On A591, 4 miles N of Ambleside

LYING in a great natural bowl between the green, craggy mountains, few villages in England enjoy a more dramatic setting than Grasmere. Rough-slate cottages, an ancient church and the nearby lake have the intense beauty of a romantic painting, and many artists and poets have been inspired by this spectacular landscape. Yet there is one name that will forever be associated with Grasmere – William Wordsworth (1770-1850), one of England's greatest poets. Wordsworth lived for most of his long life in and around Grasmere, and now lies buried with his wife, sister Dorothy and two of his children under simple gravestones in the little churchyard. Shops, cottages, galleries, hotels and inns of bluish-green Lakeland slate crowd along Grasmere's busy Broadgate and around the village centre. A pleasant village green is to be found at the junction of Broadgate and College Street, whilst around the back of the village, the Rothay serpentines past attractive fields before flowing into Grasmere lake. The village is the idyllic setting, in late August, for the famous Grasmere Sports.

WALK DIRECTIONS

1

Make your way to the National Park Information Centre in Red Bank Road, in the village centre, to start the walk. Take the main road leading south out of Grasmere towards Ambleside. Immediately out of the village, turn left at the footpath sign at the school entrance and bus stop. (For Dove Cottage, continue another 500yds along Stock Lane towards Town End, keeping to the right-hand side to face oncoming traffic. Dove Cottage lies immediately opposite the junction with the main A591. Return the same way to continue the walk).

2

Go through the school yard at the front of the school, to the lane at the far side, passing the old Workman's Reading Room.

3

Leave the lane at the gates to go into the field, following the tractor tracks through the fields. In about 400yds, go through the kissing-gate by the small wood (on the

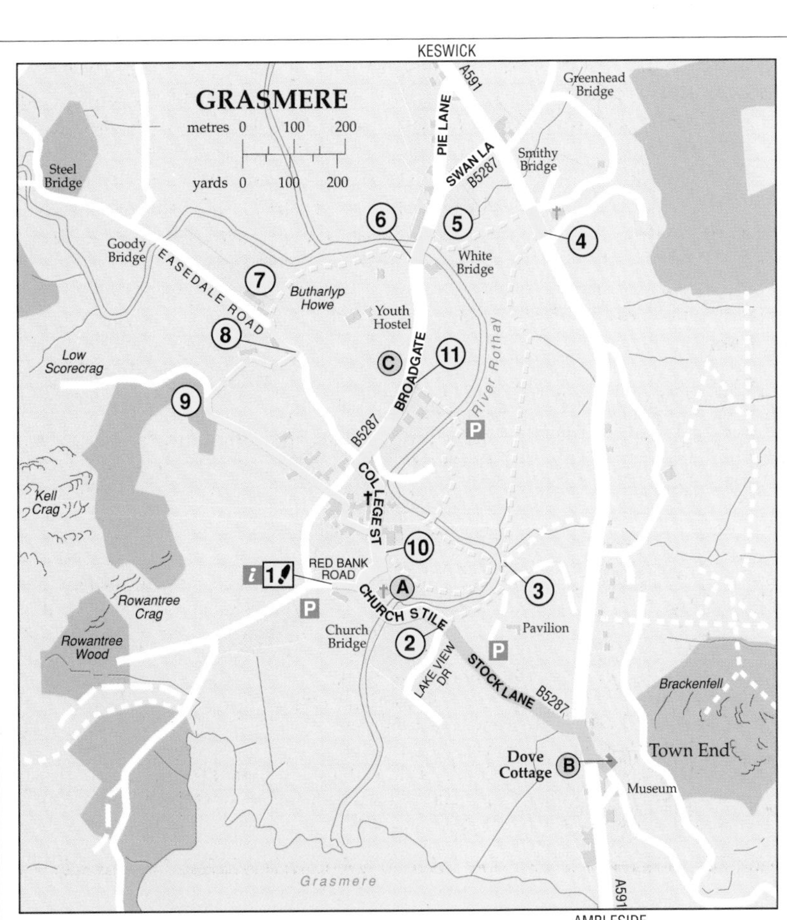

INFORMATION
Length of walk: $2^1/_2$ miles (3 miles if a visit to Dove Cottage is included)
Approximate time: $1^1/_2$ hours (not including Dove Cottage)

TERRAIN:
Easy. Suitable for children; difficult but not impossible for pushchairs because of uneven ground and some kissing-gates.

PARKING:
There are three car parks in the village. All are busy in the summer months.

OPEN:
Dove Cottage Museum and Wordsworth Museum: Daily, except Christmas and mid-Jan–mid-Feb.

REFRESHMENTS:
A good selection of hotels, inns and cafés.

right), before the path bends towards the main Keswick road.

Go through the metal gate, up on to the road and turn left. In a few yards, take the next left turning, which is a surfaced path.

The path widens to a track by the River Rothay, which bends round to join the road, Swan Lane. At the road turn left and cross over the bridge.

Take the path on the right by the river. The path bends through the trees and climbs slightly. Where the path splits, take the wider left-hand path.

Descend by the houses bordered by the metal fence set into the stone wall. At the narrow road, turn left.

Continue down this narrow road for about 80yds and then turn right through an iron gate, marked by a lamp-post opposite (a signpost is also concealed on top of the wall). Continue straight ahead until you are level with the border between the two gardens, then bear left keeping to the right of the two trees in the middle of the field, before joining the path.

Where the path ends at the metalled lane, turn left, down towards the village, going over the cattle grid.

The annual Rushbearing Festival.

A riverside path starts before the church gates on the left. Follow it alongside and across the stream, ending in the car park behind Grasmere Hall.

Turn left at the main road, Broadgate, going left again down College Street on the left side of the Green to reach the village centre, and lower car park.

Dorothy and William Wordsworth were born in Cockermouth, but spent most of their lives in Grasmere and Rydal.

THE WORDSWORTHS AND THE LAKES

William Wordsworth is imperishably linked with the Lake District, which he dearly loved and where he spent most of his life. An insatiable walker, he covered the fells minutely and exhaustively on foot, and besides his poems he wrote on of the earliest guidebooks to the area.

Wordsworth and his much-loved sister Dorothy were born in Cumbria, at Cockermouth, in 1770 and 1771 respectively, and William went to the grammar school at Hawkshead. Brother and sister set up house together in Dove Cottage at Grasmere at Christmas time in 1799. When Wordsworth married Mary Hutchinson domestic harmony was not disturbed and all three lived together.

Dorothy's *Grasmere Journals* gives a vivid picture of cottage life in this remote area at the beginning of the 19th century.

As children were born to William and Mary, Dove Cottage became too small. The household moved to another house in Grasmere, Allan Bank, for a time and then to the parsonage, before moving away to Rydal Mount, just outside Ambleside in 1808. Dorothy later fell ill, became an invalid and suffered from severe mental problems. Her brother died in 1850, she lived on until 1855, Mary until 1859. All three lie buried close together now, in Grasmere churchyard.

POINTS OF INTEREST

Grasmere Church. Dedicated to St Oswald, the 7th-century King of Northumbria, the oldest part of Grasmere church dates from the 13th century. Its outer walls and tower are built with massive rough cast stone, whilst the interior is equally impressive. Eight of the yew trees in the churchyard were planted by Wordsworth himself, and the poet's prayer book is on display in a showcase behind the choir stalls.

The ancient custom of rushbearing is still carried out here on the Saturday nearest St Oswald's day – 5 August – when new rushes are scattered on what were once earth floors. Despite being the Poet Laureate, William Wordsworth is buried in the simplest of graves in Grasmere churchyard. He lies with his wife Mary and his beloved sister Dorothy, who inspired much of his finest work. Close by are three of their children – John, Dora and Thomas. A stone nearby recalls his brother John who was drowned off Portland, Dorset, in 1805 and who is buried in Lyme Regis.

Dove Cottage. Dove Cottage was originally an inn known as the Dove and Olive Bough. William Wordsworth and his sister Dorothy lived here between 1799-1808, paying an annual rent of just £8, and it was here that William brought his young wife Mary Hutchinson when he married in 1802 and where three of their children – John, Dora and Thomas – were born. Some of Wordsworth's finest verse, including *Resolution and Independence*, *Intimations of Immortality* and *The Prelude* (1805) was written at Dove Cottage, which has now been carefully restored to its original appearance. Guided tours are available. Nearby is the Wordsworth Museum, filled with manuscripts, paintings, and memorabilia of the Wordsworths and many of their fellow 'romantics'. There is also a restaurant and bookshop.

Broadgate. Grasmere's winding main street, Broadgate, has shops, houses, galleries, hotels and guest houses all built with the blue-green slate which gives such a distinctive feel to this part of Lakeland. The word 'gate' in the street name doesn't refer to a gate in the usual sense but is derived from Old Norse, 'Gata' meaning way or road, and reflects Viking influence. The small building by the church lych-gate served as the village school between 1660 and 1854, and is now celebrated as the home of the popular 'Sarah Nelson's Original Grasmere Gingerbread' made to a secret recipe.

HAWORTH

WEST YORKSHIRE

On A6033, 3 miles S of Keighley

THE village of Haworth, which huddles on the edge of grey moorland, enjoys worldwide fame thanks to the novels of the Brontë sisters. Because of its many Brontë connections, Haworth is popular with visitors, and can become very crowded at holiday times and summer weekends, the main street bristling with souvenir and antique shops, cafés and pubs. Essentially though, its character as an early industrial Pennine village remains unspoiled.

The old Haworth is evident not only around the famous cobbled main street and stone cottages, but along paved paths and tracks between old farms and along the valley bottoms, over packhorse bridges and past quiet millponds. Down in the valley is Haworth station; a stop on the Keighley and Worth Valley Railway.

Haworth village is a place of steep streets and dark stone buildings.

WALK DIRECTIONS

From the Parsonage Museum, turn right past the church and into the cobbled Main Street.

Descend the street, but after 150yds look for a broad opening on the left signed Toilets. Follow this track, which becomes Butt Lane, entering Central Park by an entrance on the right.

Walk along the edge of the park, past the children's playground, down the steps on to the street (Belle Isle Road) opposite Haworth Station. Turn right and continue to the end of the street parallel with the railway until you reach Bridgehouse Lane.

Turn left, going over the railway bridge to the junction. Take the road on the right, Brow Road, following it past the War Memorial round a bend, past Butterfield Mill, beyond which there is a signed path for Upper Gate, Oxenhope through a narrow gap and up steps.

The path goes through a narrow stile and becomes a fieldpath, partially flagged, along the side of a millrace, Bridgehouse Beck. Continue along the millrace before crossing it at a footbridge. Follow the yellow waymarks by the riverside.

The path curves to reach a narrow packhorse bridge, known as Donkey bridge. Do not cross the bridge but continue down the valley. The path curves away from the stream for a short distance before joining a bridlepath from the right.

Ignore an enclosed path to the left, crossing the stream

INFORMATION
Length of walk:
2 miles if the walk is terminated at Oxenhope, returning by steam train. Otherwise $3^1/_2$ miles.
Approximate time:
$1^1/_2$ hours to Oxenhope: $2^1/_2$ hours for round trip.

TERRAIN:
Narrow paths with stiles and one moderate climb. Not suitable for wheelchairs, pushchairs or younger children.

PARKING:
Park at the Parsonage Museum (if full, there are other well-signed car parks around the village).

OPEN:
The Brontë Parsonage Museum. Daily throughout the year. Check opening times locally. Charge.
Oxenhope Railway Museum. Weekends throughout the year, and daily Jul-Aug and main holiday weeks. Charge.

REFRESHMENTS:
The village is well supplied with pubs and cafés.

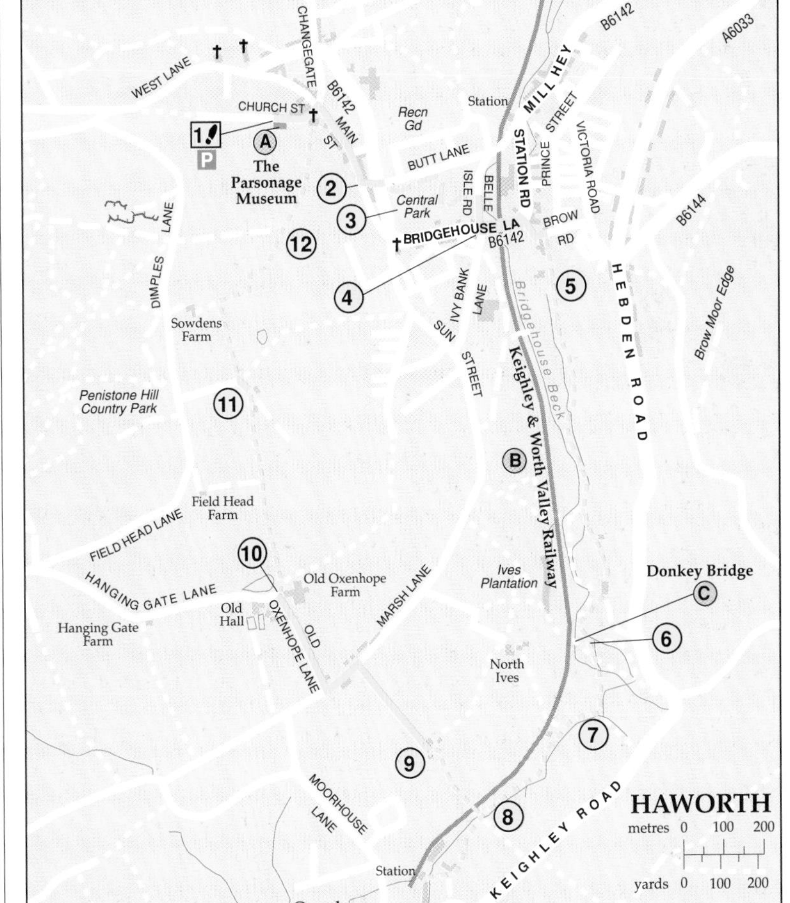

again. The path winds past the sewage works, recrosses the stream and, ignoring a junction of paths, keeps parallel to the railway to Oxenhope Railway Station and Museum.

If you are walking back to Haworth, retrace your steps to the junction of paths, this time turning left over a footbridge over the railway. The path bears to the left over a stile and goes up the hill on the left side of the field.

Go through a gate and up a track on to the road. Turn left along the road for 100yds, then right up Old Oxenhope Lane.

At the bend past the farm turn right and take the path on the left of the field, following the yellow waymarks through the walled pathway. Cross the green lane, keeping to the right of the field, and descend to the lane by some houses.

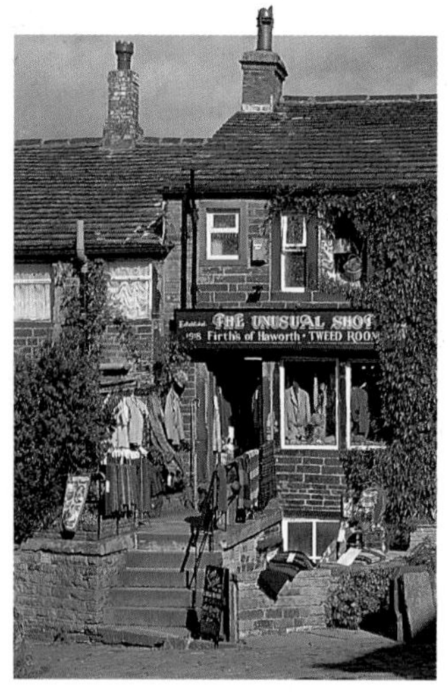

Being the home of the famous Brontës, Haworth has developed a whole new industry – tourism.

Turn left at the lane and go through the metal gate on the right. Turn right down the walled pathway at the street lamp.

Continue straight ahead at the crossroads, descending by the churchyard on to the main street.

POINTS OF INTEREST

The Parsonage Museum. Under the care of the Brontë Society, the 18th-century Parsonage, overlooking the churchyard, has become one of England's most famous literary shrines. Inside the house, rooms have been restored and furnished to look as they would have appeared at the time the Brontë children were growing up there in the 1830s. In the museum extension at the rear of the house there are displays of Brontë memorabilia and manuscripts, together with an important library of first editions and correspondence.

The Keighley and Worth Valley Steam Railway. One of Britain's finest preserved lines, this $4^1/_2$-mile, steeply graded branch railway operates steam services between Keighley, Haworth and Oxenhope. This is not just a museum railway, but a working public transport service, and at busy times it is possible to avoid congestion and restricted parking in Haworth by taking the 'park and ride' service either from Keighley or Ingrow on the A6035 main Halifax road from Keighley or from Oxenhope (large free car parks), travelling into the village by steam train.

Oxenhope Station has a Museum containing a number of superbly preserved steam locomotives, the most famous of which is the Lancashire and Yorkshire Railway 0-6-0 Goods locomotive, built in 1887, which appeared in the popular film *The Railway Children*, which was shot on location along Keighley and the Worth Valley Railway.

Locomotives operate between Haworth, Keighley and Oxenhope on the Keighley and Worth Valley Railway.

Donkey Bridge. A superb example of a single span packhorse bridge over Bridgehouse Beck, probably dating from the late 17th or early 18th century. It was used by trains of packponies carrying raw wool or finished cloth to and from outlying farms and cottages where handloom weaving was an important source of income. Paved flagstone causeways or 'causeys' often indicate such routes and there are many examples in the Haworth area.

THE BRONTËS

The three literary sisters, Charlotte, Emily and Anne Brontë, born at Thornton, Yorkshire, lived most of their short lives at Haworth parsonage with their stern and mildly eccentric father, Patrick Brontë, a clergyman of Irish descent, and their brother Branwell, whose lesser talents were lost through unrequited love, drink and opium. Mrs Brontë died of cancer in 1821, leaving six children under the age of eight. The two oldest sisters, Maria and Elizabeth, died in childhood.

The great Brontë novels – among them *Jane Eyre, Villette* and perhaps above all *Wuthering Heights* – record an England in the turmoil of the Industrial Revolution.

The entire Brontë family, except Anne, are buried in a vault in Haworth parish church. The church is not the one the sisters knew; the structure was rebuilt in the Victorian period. The vaults remain, and the approximate position of the Brontë's resting place is marked by a plaque commemorating Charlotte and Emily. Anne is buried at Scarborough.

Patrick Branwell Brontë erased himself from the portrait which he painted of his sisters – from the left; Anne, Emily and Charlotte.

HAWKSHEAD

CUMBRIA

Off B5285, 5 miles S of Ambleside

LYING between two great lakes, Windermere and Coniston, Hawkshead was almost certainly a Norse or Viking settlement, its name being derived from one *Haukr* who built what was originally a stockaded settlement in Grisedale Forest.

Thimble Hall, with its overhanging top storey, was given with others to the National Trust by Mrs W. Heelis, better known as Beatrix Potter. As a child, Wordsworth lived in the village and attended the village school, and his experiences inspired part of his autobiographical poem *The Prelude*.

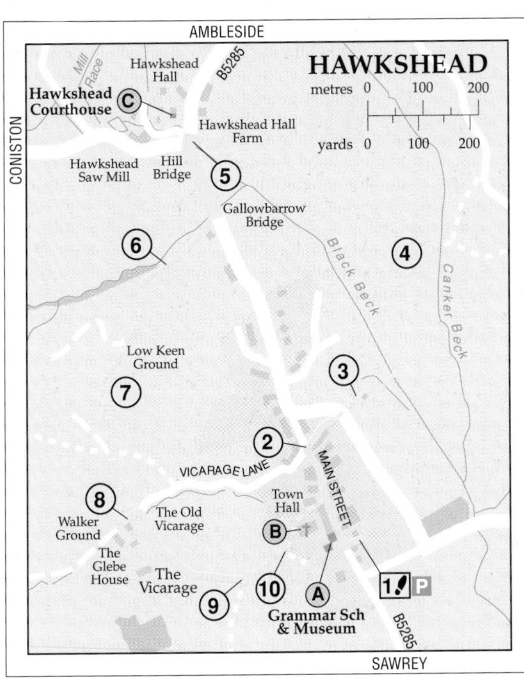

INFORMATION
Length of walk: 1¾ miles
Approximate time: 1¼ hours

TERRAIN:
Fieldpaths and tracks, but with one short climb.

PARKING:
Park in the main car park by the National Park Centre.

OPEN:
Hawkshead Grammar School Museum: April-end Oct, Mon, Tue, Thu, Sat 10am-5pm; Sun 12.30am-5pm.
Hawkshead Courthouse: Daily 10.00am-5pm; key from the National Trust shop in the village.

WALK DIRECTIONS

From the car park, walk to the main entrance. The Old Grammar School (Museum) lies directly ahead. Turn right along Main Street into the centre of the village. At a fork, bear right and go through a small pedestrianised area.

Immediately past the Red Lion Inn, turn right, down the signposted lane. Go through the wooden gate and cross the road on to the signposted path opposite.

The path bends round a house before crossing over a bridge. Turn left, walking through the field as the path swings to the right.

Before a kissing-gate, at a stone bridge crossing over a ditch, leave the path by turning 90° to the left, crossing the field, and head towards the corner of the field.

Go through the double gate on to the road. To visit the Courthouse, go right for 100yds. Then retrace your steps and follow the road for about 100yds. Turn right at the large stone gateposts up the signposted track.

⑥

The track ascends through a wood, and after two bends it forks. Turn left off the track through two stone gateways on the right, to the right of the trees, as indicated by an arrow on one of the trees. The path then bends left up to a gate.

⑦

Continue straight ahead through the next gate and join a track, maintaining the same direction.

⑧

The track soon joins a lane. Turn left, then right at the next junction, the track being signposted for Hawkshead. The way is flanked by stone causeway flags with the Vicarage and its grounds on the right.

The path then bends to the left, as Hawkshead Church comes into view.

At the junction of paths, go through the gate on the left, down into the churchyard. Turn left, and go through the wooden gates into the village centre. Turn right for the National Park Centre and car park.

The old square at Hawkshead is surrounded by whitewashed buildings which are typical of the area. Hawkshead was founded in the 10th century.

POINTS OF INTEREST

Hawkshead Grammar School and Museum. Edwin Sandys, from nearby Esthwaite Hall, who became Archbishop of York, endowed this little school in 1585 for the education of local boys. William Wordsworth was a pupil here from 1778 to 1787. Wordsworth came to Hawkshead as a child of eight, and stayed with Mrs Ann Tyson, whose cottage still survives near the junction of Vicarage Lane and Wordsworth Street.

The Parish Church. Built of local stone in a traditional style, Hawkshead Church dates from the late 15th century, the oldest part probably being the tower. The nave was rebuilt in the late 16th century thanks to the munificence of Edwin Sandys, who dedicated a small chapel to his parents. There are some fascinating 17th- and 18th-century wall paintings, whilst a showcase includes measures used at Hawkshead's weekly market and annual fairs. In the north-west end of the church a 'Burial in Wool' certificate is displayed, a requirement following a 1666 Parliamentary decree that corpses should be shrouded in wool to help the wool trade.

Hawkshead Courthouse. Dating from the 15th century, this little courthouse is the only surviving part of the large Manor House owned by the monks of Furness Abbey. The monks were industrious and wealthy. As well as having large herds of sheep, they made charcoal from the forest and smelted iron in little 'bloomeries' or outdoor furnaces, traces of which survive today. A single room of the Manor House – the pre-Reformation Courthouse – survives.

KETTLEWELL

NORTH YORKSHIRE

On B6160, 15 miles N of Skipton

KETTLEWELL'S name is derived from Ketel, a Norse-Irish Viking chieftain who owned the village before the Norman Conquest, but it was almost certainly an Anglian settlement judging by the many lynchets (ploughing terraces) still visible on the hillsides nearby.

In the 12th century it was partly owned by the monks of Coverham Abbey. In later years it became a centre both for cotton weaving, when an old water-powered corn mill by the beck was converted in 1806, and for lead, with mines on the moors and a smelt mill above the village.

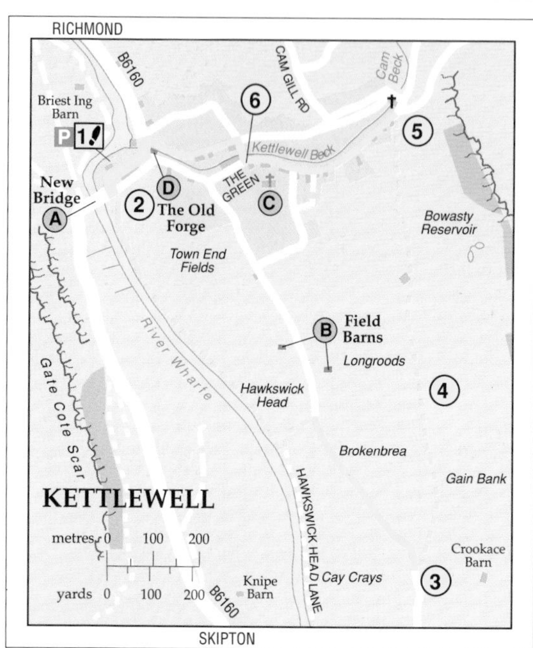

INFORMATION
Length of walk:
2 miles
Approximate time:
1 hour

TERRAIN:
Easy, but lots of very narrow stiles which take time to negotiate. Suitable for children, but not with pushchairs.

PARKING:
Park in the car park near New Bridge.

REFRESHMENTS:
Inns and cafés in the village.

The main road only touches the southern edge of this village, which is a good base for exploring.

WALK DIRECTIONS

From the car park cross the road and turn right towards the bridge but before reaching it take the path left signposted Lovers Lane towardsthe riverside.

Follow the riverside path over a series of six stiles. Turn left where the path meets a walled footpath at a stile by a gate, signed 'To Road'. Turn right along the road for 200yds.

3

Turn sharp left at the next bend in the road, following the footpath signs to Kettlewell. Continue over a series of stiles through the edge of three fields, before going through a gate on the left (waymarked).

Carry on in the same direction towards the village, on the edge of the fields, following the yellow waymarks.

Cross over the high wooden stile, and turn left where the path meets the metalled lane. Continue down the lane into the village, parallel with the course of the stream Kettlewell Beck (Cam Beck), past the church and into the village centre.

Turn right over the bridge across Kettlewell Beck and first left by the post office to the main road. Turn left over Townfoot bridge to the car park.

POINTS OF INTEREST

Kettlewell Bridge. Kettlewell Bridge (New Bridge) was built to replace an ancient ford over the River Wharfe. It is a particularly fine example of a traditional Dales' bridge and still carries the original masons' marks on its stonework, even though it had to be extensively rebuilt a few years ago, having become dangerous.

Field Barns. The return part of the walk back to Kettlewell passes a number of narrow fields and scattered stone barns, built in the days before the tractor. Hay was stored in the barns and cattle accommodated close to their source of food. Changing farming methods have now made many of these barns redundant.

St Mary's Church. St Mary's Church was built in 1820 to replace the original Norman church which had been demolished the previous year. The present tower dates from this time, but nave and chancel were rebuilt again between 1882 and 1885. Only the circular font remains from the original church, decorated with the crest of the Percy family and dating from the 12th or 13th centuries.

The Old Forge. In the last century the Forge not only undertook all the usual work of a village blacksmith's shop, including the shoeing of both horses and drovers' cattle and the making and repair of harnesses and hinges, but also served the needs of local leadminers. Here tools were made, and equipment sharpened or repaired.

HUTTON-LE-HOLE

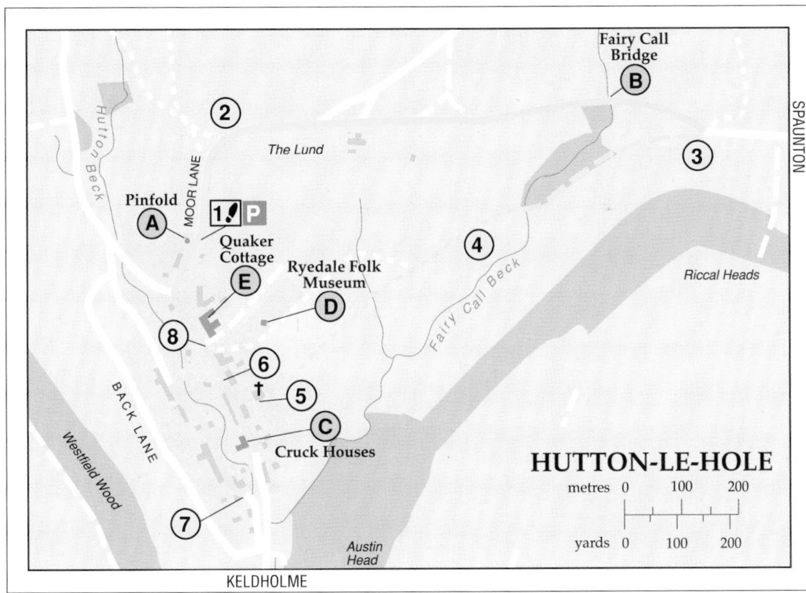

HUTTON-LE-HOLE

NORTH YORKSHIRE

Off A170, 8 miles NW of Pickering

Hutton Beck flows through the village, dividing the green.

NESTLING in a hollow on the North York Moors is the delightful village of Hutton le Hole. Hutton Beck tumbles its way through the village, crossing the green where a footbridge links the two streets. Sheep roam freely, keeping grass on the green cropped short. Many of the stone-built houses have interesting histories and some still retain features of cruck construction. The Ryedale Folk Museum, with extensive grounds, lies in the village centre.

WALK DIRECTIONS

(1)

From the bottom of the car park, turn right and cross the road to the pinfold. Turn right beside the road.

Follow the road (Moor Lane) as it swings round to the right and continue along it, ignoring forks to the left, for 700yds to Fairy Call Bridge.

About 100yds after Fairy Call Bridge, turn sharp right at a public footpath sign.

The path leads through a conifer wood to a footbridge, and a series of stiles lead back across the fields to Hutton le Hole.

As you approach the village, turn left at the stone wall near the bowling green, then turn right to the road. Turn right to the telephone box.

Take the tarmac path opposite the telephone box which crosses the green to a footbridge, then forks left to the road where you turn left.

Bear left at Ford Cottage and join a tarmac path to a small bridge. Turn left and pass Burnley House Hotel and continue through the village to the Ryedale Folk Museum.

Turn right when leaving the museum, past the inn and Quaker Cottage to the car park.

Hutton's village shop is housed in a sturdy stone cottage so typical of this region.

INFORMATION
Length of walk:
2 miles
Approximate time:
3 hours

TERRAIN:
Suitable for children. Unsuitable for wheelchairs and pushchairs except in the village; 4 stiles and 2 footbridges.

PARKING:
Park in the main car park at the north end of the village.

OPEN:
Ryedale Folk Museum. Daily, Easter-Oct. Charge.

REFRESHMENTS:
Cafés and one inn.

EVENTS:
Merrills Championship, Second weekend in Sep.

POINTS OF INTEREST

(A)

Pinfold. The stone-walled, circular enclosure near the car park is a pinfold where stray animals were impounded. A Pinder was appointed by the manor court, and his duty was to capture the strays in the pinfold and collect fines from owners who wished to retrieve their animals.

Fairy Call Bridge. The bridge was built in 1890 to replace a ford. It takes its name from a legend which held that the fairies were responsible for blowing out lantern lights on dark, wintry nights.

Cruck Houses. A number of houses in the village retain features of this old method of construction. A pair of curved timbers, connected at the top, formed one end of the building, with another pair at the other end. The area between, known as a bay, became the house. Walling would be added

George Fox, founder of the Society of Friends.

MEETINGS OF FRIENDS

The Society of Friends, popularly known as Quakers, was founded in the 17th century by George Fox, who believed that priests, services and creeds stood as obstacles between human beings and their God. The Quakers met in earnest silence, without ceremony, singing or prayers, in the confident expectation that God would duly move one of those present to bear witness. They were fiercely persecuted, but gained support, especially in the north of England. Hutton le Hole, concealed from the eye of authority the North Riding moors, had a Friends' meeting place in the early days.

The oldest house in the village, dated 1695, belonged to John Richardson, a zealous Quaker who began preaching in his teens and went to America, where he rode thousands of miles to spread the Friends' message. He was an ally of William Penn, founder of the state of Pennsylvania. He returned to England and spent his last days in Hutton, dying in 1753. He lies buried not far away, at Kirbymoorside.

The Quakers have always been pacifists, strong supporters of the temperance movement, the emancipation of women, prison reform and the abolition of capital punishment.

and connecting timber would carry the roof, originally made of heather thatch. Some 'long houses', based on Viking ideas, consisted of four or more bays. There would be living quarters, stables and byres for the cattle all under the same roof.

Good examples of cruck houses in Hutton le Hole include Burnley House Hotel, which dates to at least the 16th century. The datestone of 1787 on the south wall, above the door, is from a rebuilding by John and Lydia Featherstone. At the west end the outline of the cruck gable can be seen. Further south is Moorside Cottage – a former cruck house with a cross passage, which is a feature of this type of house. The crucks were reused as window lintels.

The last house, Primrose Hill Farm, is a long house 72ft in length. At the southern end is Primrose Hill Cottage, once the farm's turf house, increasing the length of the building to 97ft.

Ⓓ

Ryedale Folk Museum. The museum incorporates extensive grounds where local buildings have been restored and furnished in contemporary styles. There is an Elizabethan manor house, cruck cottages, craft workshops displaying tools of various trades, cart sheds and other farm buildings. There are many reminders of the life and folklore of this area. The museum stages frequent working demonstrations of crafts, and hosts the World Championships of the ancient board game of Merrills, which has been played in this area for centuries. There are three parts to the game. Firstly, the two opponents take it in turns to place their nine pegs on the board, trying to make a line of three. If they succeed, they can remove an opponent's peg. When all the pegs are placed, they begin the second part, moving pegs along lines to make a line of three to reduce their opponent to less than three pegs, when the game is won. The third part is when one player only has three pegs and he can move anywhere on the board, possibly changing the outcome of the game.

Ⓔ

Quaker Cottage. The houses on the right after the Crown Inn are of interest. The Hammer and Hand was built in 1784 as an inn and blacksmith's shop. The carved lintel over the door carries the arms of the Blacksmith Company of London; three hammers and a phoenix in flames, with the couplet 'By hammer and hand, All arts do stand'.

The next building is Quaker Cottage, a long house that was 60ft long and 22ft wide. The datestone refers to John Robinson, who built this house. His daughter Ann married John Richardson, a Quaker, in 1705. John Richardson had been to America and was a close friend of William Penn, who founded Pennysylvania. After his wife died, he again travelled to America on a voyage that lasted eleven weeks, returning to Hutton le Hole some two years later. He spent nearly 50 years of his life in the cottage.

The oldest building in the village is Quaker Cottage (inset) built by John Richardson in 1695. George Fox (below), founder of the Quakers, preaching in a tavern.

INFORMATION
Length of walk:
2 miles
Approximate time:
1¼ hours

TERRAIN:
Easy, with one short ascent of about 40yds. Unsuitable for pushchairs and wheelchairs.

PARKING:
Park close to one of the greens.

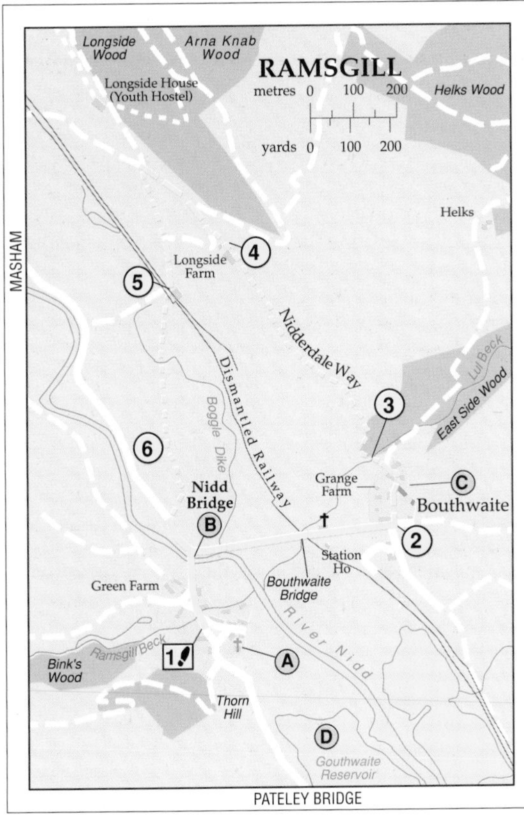
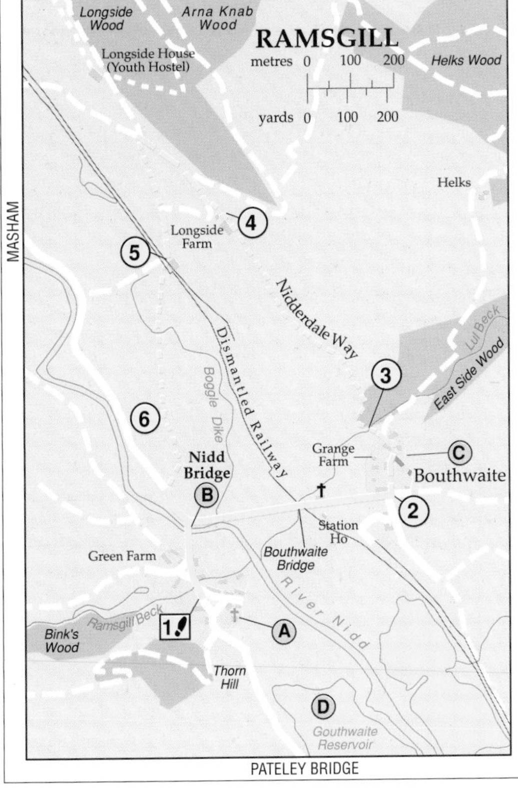

RAMSGILL

NORTH YORKSHIRE

Off B6165, 4 miles N of Pateley Bridge

LYING in a sheltered position close to Gouthwaite Reservoir in Upper Nidderdale, the village is rich in historical associations, most notably with the monks of Byland Abbey, King Edward II and Eugene Aram, a notorious 18th-century murderer. In 1202 Roger de Mowbray confirmed a gift of pasture for cattle and hogs in Nidderdale to the monks of Byland Abbey, who established a grange at Ramsgill to administer their estates. A corn mill and a little chapel close to the site of the present church were built. After the Dissolution, the estate was eventually purchased in 1546 by the Yorke family, at that time London merchants, whose arms are borne by the village inn, which was rebuilt in 1843.

WALK DIRECTIONS

From the top green, follow the road northwards towards Lofthouse. Immediately over the river bridge turn right down the narrow metalled lane to Bouthwaite marked 'unsuitable for motor traffic'.

After ½ a mile, the lane reaches Bouthwaite hamlet. Turn left at the bend, taking the signposted Nidderdale Way, up the track through the hamlet and past a farm. Go through the gate marked with a yellow arrow, taking the left fork after the gate.

Cross the bridge, and bend right along the barbed-wire fence and up the stony track shaded by trees. Continue on the track, past the stile, following the wall as the track becomes a path and levels off. Keep to the right of the row of hawthorns, continuing straight ahead. Go through the next field, keeping to the left side, and over the next stile. Pass Longside farm, keeping above it.

Descend to the track, and continue to the gate before the old youth hostel. Then turn sharply back left, down to the farm below on the valley floor.

Bend right on the track after the gate, and at the double gate take the left-hand gate, which is waymarked. Bend left to a waymarked step stile to the right of a tree. Go over a bridge crossing a ditch and a stile, then veer slightly to the right across a field. Head towards a stone stile at a corner of the field.

Bear left after the stile, keeping by the hedge over two more stiles.

After the second stile, follow the stone wall to the road. Turn left and follow the road into Ramsgill. Visit the church before returning to your car.

The peaceful scene around the village green at Ramsgill, Nidderdale

POINTS OF INTEREST

(A)

Ramsgill Church. Ramsgill Church was rebuilt (1842) in the Early English style thanks to the generosity of the Yorke family. A small gable from the original monastic chapel was incorporated in the churchyard wall on the eastern side. The church overlooks one of the two village greens.

Nidd Bridge. Until the late 17th century, there was no crossing of the River Nidd at this point except by ford, and it was along this ancient road from Kirkby Malzeard that King Edward II rode with his retinue in the autumn of 1323, calling at the Abbot's Grange in 'Rammesgill'. The bridge was probably erected in the 1660s.

Bouthwaite Grange. This hamlet was a Grange farm of nearby Fountains Abbey, rivals of the Byland Monks, who owned much of the moorland above Nidderdale. After the Dissolution it passed to the Inman family, one of whom, known as 'Bold Robin of Bouthwaite', is said to have slain several thieves with a dagger which was kept in the family for many years.

Gouthwaite Reservoir. When this reservoir was built in the 1890s, it drowned Gouthwaite Hall, a famous Elizabethan house. The reservoir was built to supply the city of Bradford and holds about 1,500 million gallons of water. It is now a major nature reserve, and an important habitat for migrant birds in winter.

REETH

NORTH YORKSHIRE

On B6270, 12 miles W of Richmond

LYING along a terrace on the slopes of evocatively-named Mount Calva, close to where Arkengarthdale meets Swaledale, the former market town of Reeth overlooks and owes allegiance to both dales. Its history is intimately linked to two important Dales industries – sheep farming, which continues, and lead-mining, long since vanished, but whose remains still scatter the nearby hillsides.

Much of the filming for the popular TV series *All Creatures Great and Small* takes place in the village, which has some exceptionally interesting shops, chapels and cottages dating from the 17th century to late Victorian times.

POINTS OF INTEREST

Ⓐ

Reeth Green. In 1695 a charter was granted to Philip, Lord Wharton to hold a Friday market in Reeth and four fairs each year for the buying and selling 'of all manner of cattle, goods and merchandise.'

Though the market has long vanished, and the Fair (in the form of Reeth Show) only takes place once a year in September, the extensive Green remains, complete with village pump, war memorial and magnificent views across Swaledale and to Fremington Edge, giving Reeth very much the feel of an important town and the 'capital' of mid-Swaledale. The number of inns and hotels around the Green also testifies to the village's former importance in the days of lead-mining, as do the number of chapels – Swaledale was a strong bastion of Methodism from the 18th century onwards.

Reeth Bridge. This fine stone humpback bridge over the Arkle Beck was formerly known as Fremington Bridge, and is built in traditional style, probably dating from the 18th century. The long building at the other side of the bridge, now part of a garage, was formerly a water-powered sawmill and also of 18th century origin.

Ⓒ

Swaledale Folk Museum. This small but compact local museum contains outstanding collections of material illustrating various aspects of Dales history, concentrating in particular on life in the dale last century. There are exhibits relating to lead-mining, knitting, local crafts, pubs and poor law, brass bands and Dales medicine.

The magnificent view from Reeth's extensive village green over the houses and up into the dales. Once an important centre of farming and industry the village is now best known for its scenery. The green is fringed by houses and at its lower end the former Methodist Schoolroom contains the Swaledale Folk Museum.

INFORMATION
Length of walk:
1 mile
Approximate time:
1 hour

TERRAIN:
Village streets with some cobbled stretches: suitable for pushchairs.

PARKING:
Park in the village centre, on the cobbled area in front of the shops.

OPEN:
Swaledale Folk Museum: Daily, Easter–mid-Oct, 10.30am-6pm.

REFRESHMENTS:
A good selection of pubs and cafés in the village.

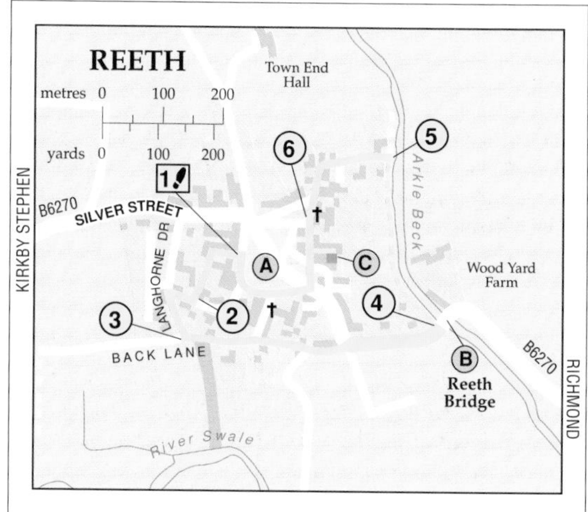

WALK DIRECTIONS

①

Walk down the narrow lane which lies between the King's Arms Hotel and the Black Bull.

②

At the T-junction, turn right, turning left at the next junction into Langhorne Drive.

③

Follow this around to the left to join Back Lane. Follow Back Lane to its junction with the main road below the village and continue along the main road as far as Reeth Bridge.

④

Take the enclosed path on the left immediately before the bridge and walk along it beside Arkle Beck.

After about 300yds, turn left along a track which leads back to Reeth Green.

⑥

For the museum, keep left past the Methodist Church and Vicarage, bearing left again to the cottages containing the Swaledale Folk Museum (signposted).

Paintings, pottery and local crafts are exhibited for sale in Reeth's local shops or galleries, which are also centred around the village green.

RIBCHESTER

LANCASHIRE

On B6245 between Blackburn and Longridge, about 7 miles N of Blackburn

RIBCHESTER might appear to be of Roman origin, its Roman name *Bremetennacum* meaning the walled town by the Ribble. In fact it is far older, going back to mid Bronze Age times, around 2000BC, and recent research has established both Bronze and Iron Age burial remains. The Romans probably established their fort on an existing settlement.

INFORMATION
Length of walk:
2 miles
Approximate time:
1½ hours

TERRAIN:
Suitable for children, but difficult for pushchairs on the return leg owing to stiles.

PARKING:
Park in the village car park opposite the playing fields – signed from the main Longridge road.

OPEN:
The Roman Museum. Daily Mar-Nov 2-5pm Jun-Aug 11.30am-5.30pm Dec-Feb Sun 2-5pm.

POINTS OF INTEREST

The White Bull Inn. A fine early Georgian inn, dated 1707, with a square projecting porch complete with handsome classical columns, probably from Roman buildings. The inn was formerly used as a courthouse for the village.

This white bull is one of Lancashire's best inn signs.

(B)

Ribchester Roman Museum of Antiquities. As well as the Roman Granary, the recently expanded museum includes Roman altars, pottery, glasswear, jewellery, domestic items, a replica of a superb ceremonial helmet found at Ribchester (now in the British Museum) and models of the original fort based on archaeological evidence.

Ribchester Roman Fort. The original late 1st-century Roman fort of *Bremetennacum* lay around an area covered by the present church, museum and riverside, and there is little to be seen except part of the Roman granaries, which have been recently excavated. These lie alongside the museum and can be viewed from there. The remains of the 2nd-century Bath House which consist of a furnace room and three heating flues, can be reached from the riverside on the walk.

St Wilfred's Church. The first reference to the church at Ribchester, which was built on the Roman fort, comes in 1246 when its Rector was drowned whilst trying to cross the river.

Parts of the church date from his period, including a 13th-century doorway with moulded arches, and both the chancel and the nave. The tower dates from the late 15th century as does the font. The west gallery is supported by round stone pillars reputed to be Roman.

Ribchester Ferry. The Ribchester Ferry is mentioned in a document dated 1355, when one Adam Biby of Ribchester granted 'the fferiman' William de Braddley the right to operate the boat across the river.

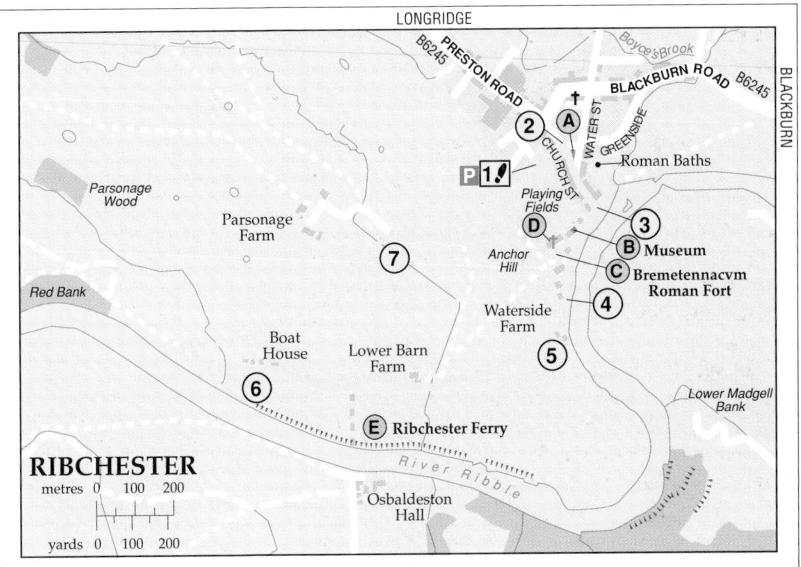

WALK DIRECTIONS

Turn left out of the car park to Church Street.

(2)

Turn right down Church Street to its junction with Water Street, past 18th-century weavers' cottages and the White Bull Inn.

(3)

At the bottom of Church Street at the riverside, turn left along the footpath down to the Roman Bath House. Retrace your steps back to Church Street. Continue along Church Street as it bends along the riverside to the church. The Ribchester Museum of Roman Antiquities is in a small building on the right in Churchgate.

(4)

The walk continues along the track which provides an extension to Church Street along the riverside. This leads into the farmyard of Waterside Farm. Keep straight ahead across the yard to the gate at the far side, continuing along the track.

(5)

Follow the track for about ½ mile past Lower Barn Farm. A white-painted stile on the left leads to an optional fieldpath across to the edge of the river where once a ferry crossed to Osbaldeston Hall (view-point). Retrace your steps to the Lower Barn Farm track and continue past the farm buildings known as Boat House, where once the ferry boats were kept, to pass through a fieldgate.

(6)

The track is now unenclosed along the edge of a field. Look along the hedge on the right, to see a stile leading into the second, higher field. This indicates the path back to Ribchester. Keep the hedge on the right over more stiles until, opposite Parsonage Farm, the way goes through a white-painted stile to the other side of the hedge.

(7)

Cross the next field to a stile and join a track. Turn right along the track which curves past the playing fields to the car park.

ROBIN HOOD'S BAY

NORTH YORKSHIRE

On B1447, 5 miles S of Whitby

THE picturesque houses in this cramped fishing village huddle together in the valley formed by Kings Beck. Locally the village is referred to as Bay or Bay Town. The maze of houses stand either side of narrow passageways and occur in a random manner at many varying elevations. Two centuries ago smuggling was rife in the village, and it is said that a bolt of silk could be passed from the houses near the sea to the cliff top without seeing daylight; via interconnecting doors and cellars.

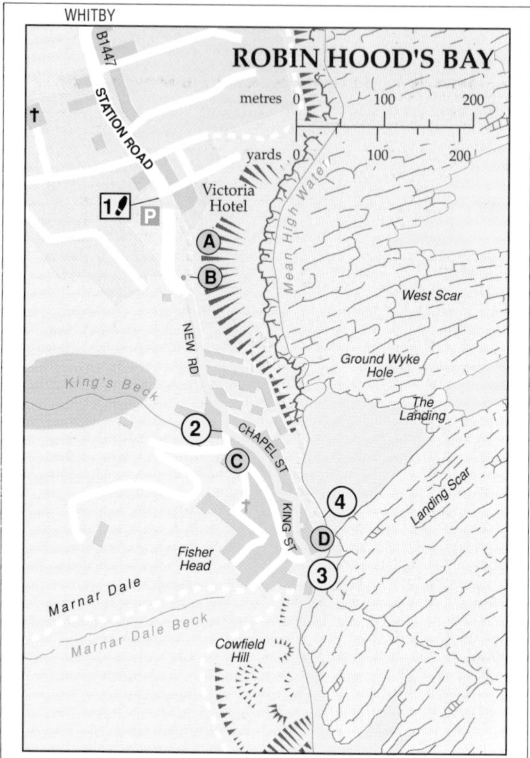

INFORMATION

Length of walk: 1 mile
Approximate time: 1 hour

TERRAIN:
The route is hilly. A 1-in-3 hill is used for the descent and an easier gradient for the return. There is a good surface throughout and pushchairs can be taken, provided great care is taken on the descent. There are a number of steps, so not suitable for wheelchairs.

PARKING:
Park at the car park opposite the Victoria Hotel.

OPEN:
The Smuggling Experience, Apr-end Sep. Charge.

REFRESHMENTS:
There are several inns, cafés and restaurants in the village.

This dramatic view over Robin Hood's Bay can be seen from the Cleveland Way footpath. This great bay sweeps 3 miles south, contained in a steep bowl of farmland. Ravenscar is found at the southern end.

WALK DIRECTIONS

(1)

From the roundabout take the cliff top path to Bank Top, where there is a former sea mine. This is an excellent viewpoint. Descend the steep hill, passing the Laurel Inn.

(2)

Turn left just before reaching the bridge along flagged and cobbled Chapel Street. The street turns left into King Street where you can turn right down to The Dock, outside the Bay Hotel. A slipway descends to the seashore and you now have an opportunity to explore the maze of side streets in the centre of the village.

(3)

To return to the car park, walk back up King Street. Immediately after passing Ye Dolphin Hotel, turn right along a path which descends by steps to the sea wall.

(4)

Turn left along the sea wall and at the end climb further steps. The path climbs the hillside to the top of The Bank, passing a picnic site. Turn right back to the car park.

POINTS OF INTEREST

(A)

Viewpoint. From the cliff top there is an extensive view over the bay. To the right is the older part of the village in the valley, with Fylingdales Moor behind rising to nearly 1,000ft above sea level. At the southern end of the bay is Ravenscar, standing 600ft above the sea.

(B)

Sea Mine. On the cliff top is a former sea mine, now used as a collecting box for the Shipwrecked Mariners Society. Many such mines were released into the North Sea in both World Wars with the intention of sinking coastal shipping, and numerous ships went down along this coast.

(C)

Chapel Street and the Village Centre. Smuggling reached its peak in Robin Hood's Bay in the late 17th and early 18th century. Ships from the continent would wait offshore to meet local fishing boats, which bought the goods and smuggled them ashore. As well as spirits, other highly taxed items imported included tea, playing cards, spinning wheels and chocolate. In 1775, seven soldiers and their sergeant were billeted in the village to try to suppress this illegal trade.

(D)

King Street and the Sea Wall. King Street was the main road out of the village until 1780, when part of the road became washed into the sea. Over the years the waves have eroded the cliffs causing some of the houses to be undercut and slide into the sea. The sea wall now takes the brunt of the storms, preventing other parts of the village falling into the bay. Leo Walmsley, the writer, lived in the third house above the post office, in King Street from 1894 to 1913. There is a plaque over the door. He incorporated the village in a number of his books under the pseudonym 'Bramblewick'.

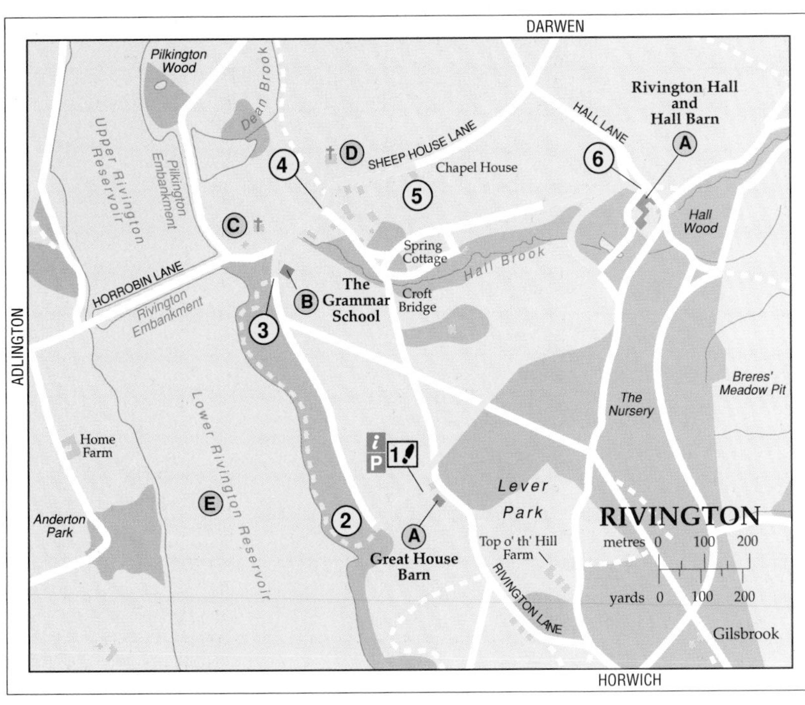

RIVINGTON

LANCASHIRE

On an unclassified road, 2 miles E of Adlington on A6

RIVINGTON lies on the edge of the West Pennine Moors, immediately above Rivington and Anglezarke Reservoirs and close to Lever Park. Rivington Pike to the east, was one of the chain of hilltop beacons used for giving the alarm across country from early medieval times onwards. A stack of wood was kept ready and on 19 July 1588 the flames flared on the Pike to signal the sighting of the Spanish Armada. Stones from the base of the beacon were used to build the tower on the Pike in 1733. This was wild and lonely country for centuries and there is still much unspoiled landscape here. Rivington village is a charming hamlet around a crossroads and triangular village green, with a post office and a delightful Tudor church whose detached bellhouse is unique in Lancashire. If you look over the wall from the Vicarage garden you see the old village stocks, whilst the Unitarian Chapel, also overlooking the Green, dates from 1702.

INFORMATION
Length of walk:
1½ miles
Approximate time:
1 hour

TERRAIN:
Tracks and stony paths. Suitable for children and for pushchairs with care. Unsuitable for wheelchairs.

PARKING:
There is no parking in Rivington village. The nearest car park is at Great House Barn (information centre, picnic area).

REFRESHMENTS:
At both Great House Barn (toilets) and Hall Barn.

WALK DIRECTIONS

From the Great House Barn car park, descend through the children's playground to a surfaced path before a fence.

Turn right down a stone-edged path which runs alongside Lower Rivington Reservoir. After about 400yds the path rises up a slope to meet a track.

Turn left here and walk 50yds down the road. Turn right to the centre of Rivington village.

At the village green, take the left fork (the Belmont road). Immediately after the last house (Chapel House) turn right and go through the left-hand of the two stiles opposite.

Follow the grassy track, which becomes a wide tree-lined stony track leading up to Rivington Hall Barn.

From Hall Barn, follow the tarmac drive down to Great House Barn, taking a path on the left-hand side, past the junction, to return to the car park.

Rivington's picturesque triangular village green showing the post office and the old village stocks in the foreground.

Rivington Hall is a fine Georgian house with brick façade of five bays and two storeys, behind which there is older stone work. In fact there is a low six-light window which may have been constructed as long ago as 1694.

LORD LEVERHULME, THE SOAP KING

William Mesketh Lever, born in Bolton in 1851, made his fortune marketing and eventually manufacturing soap under the famous 'Sunlight' name. In 1885 he bought a factory in Warrington, but demand was more than the factory could meet, so he moved in 1888 to a new site in the Wirral where he established Port Sunlight, a factory and model village, and the remarkable Lever Brothers empire, now known as Unilever.

In 1900 he purchased the Rivington estates where he built a country house (burnt down by a suffragette in 1913 but rebuilt). In 1911 he was created Lord Leverhulme, joining his wife's surname, Hulme, to his own. He continued to live at Rivington until his death in 1925. He also laid out extensive terraced gardens.

Leverhulme, a notable philanthropist, gave much of his 400-acre estate to the public during his own lifetime, and the gardens and house were acquired by Liverpool Corporation in 1947, who demolished the house, despite public protest. The magnificent terraced gardens, however, survive, now carefully restored to their former glory.

POINTS OF INTEREST

Rivington Hall and the Barns. Rivington Hall, a handsome Georgian house, was built in 1780 by John Andrews, owner of the estate, incorporating parts of an earlier building. There are two magnificent barns – Hall Barn by Rivington Hall, and Great House Barn at the start of the walk. Both are almost certainly of ancient origin, possibly Anglo-Saxon; built with massive wooden supports or crucks supporting immense roofs, and originally used for housing livestock. However, little of the original structures remain, the barns having being largely rebuilt in the early 18th century and again by Lord Leverhulme, the soap magnate, in 1900.

Since that time, they have been popular among generations of walkers and cyclists as sources of refreshment and entertainment. Refreshment facilities remain and there is a Pennine Moors Visitor Centre in Great House Barn. The old building with mullioned windows close by, once Great House Farm, is now a craft shop and Rangers' Office.

The Grammar School. The village school, downhill from the church, was originally the Grammar School, designed quite literally to teach local boys `grammar' or Latin. It was built in 1656 and expanded in 1703.

Rivington Church. The church is a Tudor one, whose detached bellhouse is unique in Lancashire. With a gabled roof, it was built in 1549 to contain a single bell, but is in fact large enough to hold a full peal. Though usually closed to the public, the interior of the church also has some interesting features, including a 15th-century chancel screen and memorials of the Pilkington family, including a family tree painted on the north door, showing Richard Pilkington and his twelve children. There are a number of interesting gravestones in the churchyard, many of them 17th-century.

This chapel was founded in 1662 as a Unitarian Church.

The Chapel. The little stone-roofed Chapel above the Village Green dates from 1703, and still has many of its original fittings, including a high panelled pulpit and pews, one of which is a canopied pew of the Willoughby family. Lord Willoughby of Parnham was brought here for burial in 1619, before the chapel was built, in a funeral procession which took three weeks to reach Rivington from London.

Lower Rivington Reservoir. This reservoir forms part of a series of eight built between 1847 and 1875 to provide the city of Liverpool with badly needed fresh water supplies, replacing inadequate local wells. The total capacity of the reservoir system is 18,000 megalitres (1 megalitre = 220,000 gallons) and it supplies about 52 megalitres a day; mainly to Liverpool, but also to St Helens, Wigan and Leigh.

THE UNITARIANS

In 16th-century Europe there were Protestants who denied that Jesus was divine and rejected the Christian doctrine of the Trinity. Their ideas influenced the Unitarian movement in England, which grew out of the religious disputes of the 17th century that helped to lose King Charles I his head.

After the restoration of Charles II, the Act of Uniformity of 1662 drove 2,000 clergymen from their parishes. Among them was the Reverend Samuel Newton of Rivington. Eventually dissenters were able to build their own chapels.

In the 18th century the scientist and dissenting minister Joseph Priestley preached that Jesus was human and that God the Father was the only deity in whom good sense and the Bible required belief. Others agreed and the first Unitarian church in England was founded in London by Theophilus Lindsey, a clergyman who broke away from the Church of England in 1773. Support grew and a national Unitarian association was founded in 1825, which a hundred years later blended into the General Assembly of Unitarian and Free Churches.

Studley Roger has the neat housing typical of estate villages.

STUDLEY ROGER

NORTH YORKSHIRE

Off B6265, 3 miles W of Ripon

STUDLEY Roger is an 18th-century estate village on the edge of Studley Royal Estate, a magnificent deer park and ornamental garden which is better known as the setting for Fountains Abbey, the largest Cistercian ruin in Western Europe. This walk along the edge of the deer park and through the lovely Valley of the Seven Bridges takes in the whole of this delightful, one-street village which was built to house estate workers at the time that the Royal Park was being laid out.

WALK DIRECTIONS

Make for the top of the car park and a wooden gate signposted to St Mary's Church. Walk straight ahead up the hill to the church – its spire soon comes into view.

At the church, turn right down the metalled, unfenced track. Continue along this track (Ripon Cathedral coming into view ahead), for ½ mile, over the Cocked Hat crossroads. The deer park is on the right.

The stunning 19th-century church is surrounded by estate cottages.

Take a grassy path on the left, 100yds after a small, dry valley runs in alongside the track. The path runs between a small caged tree and a line of three very large trees. It continues towards a gate.

Go through the tall kissing-gate (approximately 200yds to the left of the Park's main entrance), then follow the barbed-wire fence to a wooden gate.

Walk down a short walled lane into the village of Studley Roger. Turn right on the lane through the village past the Park's entrance gates, and walk straight ahead at the junction down Plumpton Lane (marked 'No Through Road'). Continue along the track, ignoring a turn-off left, ascending a gentle slope.

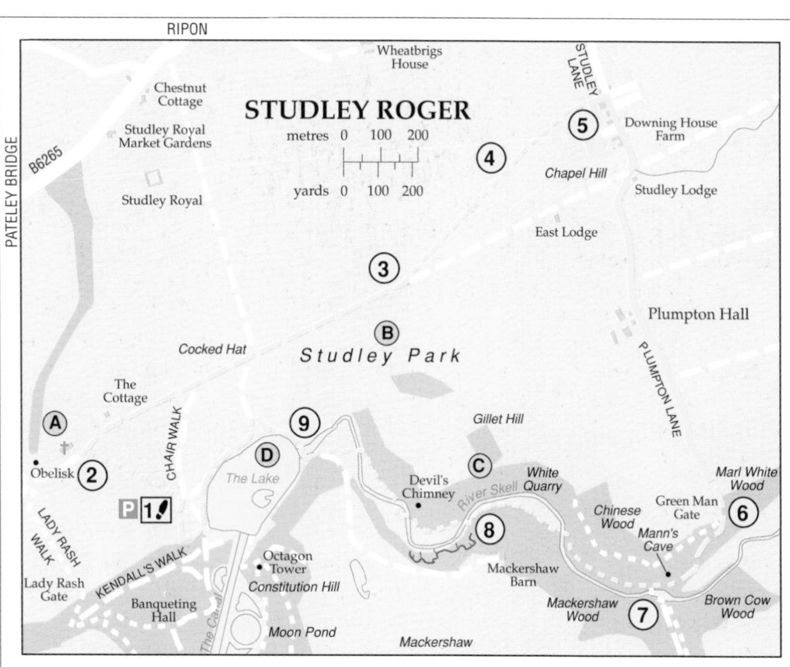

6

The track then bears right into the woods and descends into a small valley. Keep to the main track as you re-enter the woodland, ignoring the bridge on your left.

Continue along the track as it runs along beside the River Skell and go through a kissing-gate. Cross over the bridge and follow the track as it winds up the valley.

8

The track crosses the river by a stone bridge again as limestone cliffs come into view, and re-crosses twice more. After the fifth bridge, continue up to the weir, and cross it by a low wooden footbridge.

9

Follow the track round the lake to the entrance of Fountains Abbey, and ascend the steps back to the car park.

INFORMATION
Length of walk:
3 miles
Approximate time:
2 hours

TERRAIN:
Stony tracks and kissing-gates make it difficult for pushchairs and wheelchairs, otherwise easy walking.

PARKING:
Park in the National Trust car park at Studley Royal (eastern entrance to Fountains Abbey) – fee payable, but free to NT members.

OPEN:
St Mary's Church.
Daily, 1-5pm.

POINTS OF INTEREST

St Mary's Church. Built by the Marquis of Ripon at Studley Royal between 1871 and 1878, this estate and village church in High Victorian neo-Gothic style is considered to be one of the masterpieces of its architect, William Burges. It is richly decorated, and supports a 152ft spire. Among features of note are the splendid west doorway, some superb stained glass windows and the Chancel. Both the roof of the Choir and the Sanctuary contain richly gilded figures. One of the focal points of the entire church is the magnificent Italian marble tomb, erected in 1908 for the Marquis and Marchioness of Ripon and their families.

The Church, declared redundant in 1970, is maintained by the Historic Buildings and Monuments Commission and is open to the public between 1pm and 5pm daily.

The Deer Park. Studley Royal Deer Park covers some 400 acres of beautiful parkland and scattered woodland. Herds of three species of deer are to be seen roaming freely – the Red Deer, one of the two surviving native British species and the largest native British mammal, Fallow Deer, thought to have been introduced by the Romans, and Sika Deer from Japan and Manchuria. The herds are carefully managed by the National Trust.

The park also has some exceptionally handsome specimen trees, including avenues of beech and stately oaks, a huge Spanish chestnut and a Wellingtonia planted by Princess Alexandra, later the consort of King Edward VII.

The tall obelisque west of the church is another 18th-century folly, but note how perfectly it aligns along the tree-lined drive with the park's entrance gate and the distant view of Ripon Cathedral. The faint line of the North York Moors can be seen beyond. The crossing of tracks mid way along the Park (now part of the entrance drive) was formerly known as `the Cocked Hat' because of its unusual and distinctive shape.

The Valley of the Seven Bridges. The beautiful valley of the River Skell, enclosed by low cliffs of magnesian limestone, is full of features of interest, most notably a water-sink hole near the third bridge, and a particularly attractive woodland, including a Chinese wood on the right. The series of imitation packhorse bridges and the Devil's Chimney, a stone tower built as a folly, are all features built purely to improve the picturesque qualities of the landscape.

The Lake. This is a purely artificial lake, created by Aislabie by building a dam across the River Skell and with an ornamental cascade at its head. It was also carefully planted with shrubbery and with an ornamental octagonal tower to add to the effect of the view at the entrance to the Water Gardens. It is now a sanctuary for a variety of waterfowl, particularly mallard, Eider duck, swans and Canada geese.

JOHN AISLABIE AND STUDLEY ROYAL

Studley Roger is really a hamlet rather than a village, originally built to house estate workers at the time that Great Studley or Studley Royal Park was being laid out by John Aislabie in the early 18th century. This explains the uniformity of style of the stone cottages, harmonising with the neo-classical Gateway to the Park with its magnificent ornamental iron gates.

John Aislabie was a Chancellor of the Exchequer who was expelled from Parliament in 1720 after the South Sea Bubble scandal and returned disgraced, but still fabulously wealthy, to develop his Yorkshire estates. The house that formed the centrepiece of the Studley Royal estate was destroyed by fire in 1945, only the stable block (built 1716-20) remaining. The deer park, ornamental gardens and Fountains Abbey itself, founded in 1132, form part of a major National Trust property which has recently been designated a World Heritage Site. Studley Royal's landscape gardener, William Fisher, set out the park between 1720 and 1740.

Plumpton Hall, on the edge of Studley Roger village is a fine example of a small, unspoiled Georgian country house. It is still a private house.

Studley Royal Park was landscaped in the 18th century and has many features typical of the period, including various temples (left) and the unusual temple folly (inset).

LEAD MINING

Tideswell lies at the heart of Peakland lead-mining country, and the bumps and hollows in the fields all around are evidence of the work of 't'owd man' – the local name for the miners. These men were governed by a set of laws famous for their severity and administered by ancient Barmote Courts. Tideswell was in the King's Field, owned by the monarch. Mining explains the presence of many fine houses in the area.

This Norman font, found at Ashover, is a unique piece of lead work.

TIDESWELL

DERBYSHIRE

On B6049, 8 miles E of Buxton

TIDESWELL'S magnificent pinnacled parish church, often referred to as 'the Cathedral of the Peak', was built within a single period of about 60 years, spanning the Decorated and Perpendicular styles. The grey, workmanlike village stands at over 1,000ft on the limestone plateau, and has been an important marketing centre for lead and wool at least since 1251, when it was awarded its charter for a market and fair. Further evidence of Tideswell's medieval importance is that Edward I stayed here for three days in 1275, while hunting in his Royal Forest of the Peak.

WALK DIRECTIONS

From the car park, turn left towards the village centre.

At the war memorial, bear right up a narrow lane and pass the post office into Commercial Road to visit the church.

Opposite the church, take a narrow winding 'ginnel' which emerges at a sharp bend in Church Lane.

Follow Church Lane for $^3/_4$ mile towards Litton. The stone-walled lane must be much younger than the surrounding fields, as it bisects their grid-iron pattern.

Keep straight ahead over a junction of lanes to enter Litton past the small, modern church.

Leave Litton by the cross steps and bear left past the post office to descend by the lane towards Litton Dale, a shallow dry depression in the limestone plateau. The drystone walls on the right 'fossilise' medieval strip cultivations.

Just past Dale House, a minor lane leads off to the right past a house called Dale View. This lane then drops down above the end of wooded Tideswell Dale by a lane called The Lodge.

The Lodge, eventually leads down on to the Buxton Road, and you re-enter Tideswell by Town End before continuing back into Queen Street.

INFORMATION
Length of walk:
2 miles
Approximate time:
1-1$^1/_2$ hours

TERRAIN:
Mainly on quiet lanes, but with some steep steps leaving the village. Suitable for children and push-chairs, if the steps can be negotiated.

PARKING:
Park in the cobbled parking area of Cherry Tree Square, just off Queen Street.

REFRESHMENTS:
Several pubs and cafés in Tideswell, and a pub in Litton.

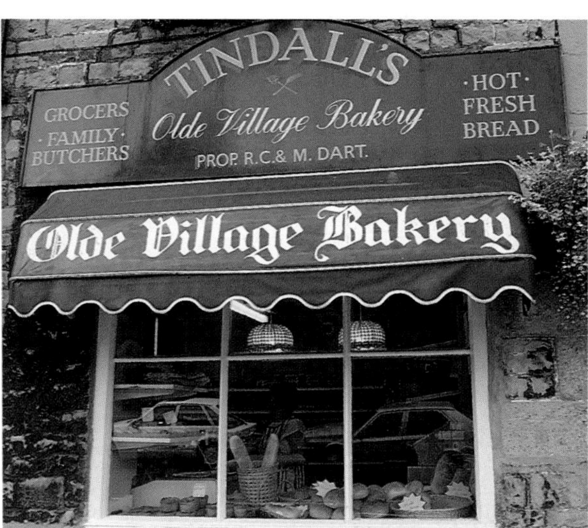

Many of the buildings in this village are a lot older than they look.

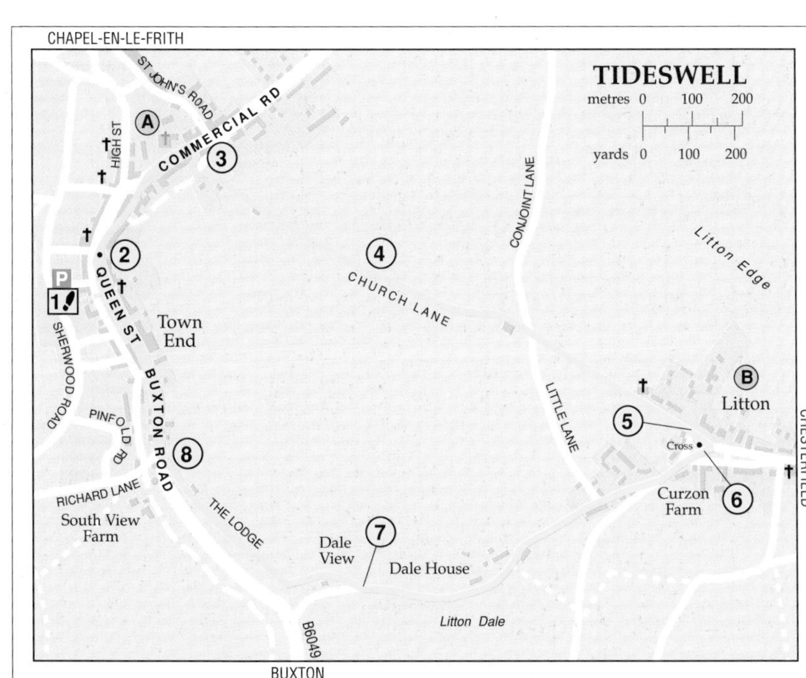

POINTS OF INTEREST

Ⓐ

Tideswell Parish Church. One of the finest churches in the Peak, it was built between 1320 and 1380 on the wealth gained from the industries of lead and wool. The light and airy chancel, lit by decorated windows and clear, medieval glass, is balanced by two transepts, containing brasses commemorating Sir Sampson Meverill, Knight Constable of England, who died in 1462; and Bishop Robert Purseglove (d.1579) who founded the Grammar School in his home village.

Ⓑ

Litton. The village has a fine collection of 17th- and 18th-century houses. The weathered market cross steps at the western end of the green may indicate a busier past. The ancient Red Lion Inn is a popular hostelry.

Warkworth's market place, complete with its village cross.

WARKWORTH
NORTHUMBERLAND

On A1068, 7 miles SE of Alnwick

ON the southern boundary of Northumberland's `Heritage Coast', Warkworth, dominated by its castle, occupies a penninsula formed by a looping meander of the River Coquet. This defensive character reflects centuries of border warfare.

Given to Lord Percy of Alnwick in 1332, Warkworth Castle, overlooking the River Coquet, dominates Warkworth.

INFORMATION
Length of walk: 1¾ miles.
Approximate time: 1¼ hours

TERRAIN:
Surfaced roads and paths, 3 gates. North end of village and river bank walk (loose surface; access from Hotspur Court near Market Place) suitable for wheelchairs. Suitable for pushchairs and children.

PARKING:
Park tidily in the village. The walk begins outside the post office in Castle Street.

OPEN:
Warkworth Castle. Easter-Oct Daily. Oct-Easter Tue-Sun (except Christmas holidays). Charge.
Warkworth Hermitage. Easter-Oct weekends. Access by boat from castle. Charge.

WALK DIRECTIONS

(1)

From the post office walk uphill (towards the castle), cross the road and where the road bears left continue straight on through a gap in the wall.

Walk on 50yds to a fork in the path – bear left, up some steps and then left again to the castle entrance or right (downhill) to continue the walk.

Bear left on a gravel path beside the River Coquet, pass the rowing boat landing-stage, and continue along the river bank to a gate. Walk on across a field then bear right along the tarmac road for 100yds. Warkworth Hermitage lies partially hidden in the trees across the river.

Retrace your route to the boat landing-stage, beyond which continue left along the river bank. On reaching the houses turn right along a lane, continue forwards to pass the toilets on your left, and walk through the arch of Hotspur Court and on into Castle Street.

Turn left, continue on through the market place, then turn right through a narrow metal gate into the churchyard to view the church. Continue past the church entrance, go through a second gate and proceed along St Lawrence Terrace to Bridge Street.

Turn left, go through the gatehouse arch, and cross the old stone bridge. Turn sharp right and recross the River Coquet on the modern road bridge.

Bear right along Bridge Street and follow the main road on up Castle Street to the post office.

POINTS OF INTEREST

Warkworth Castle. Dating in part from the 12th century, with later additions including its magnificent keep, Warkworth Castle was owned by Northumberland's Percy family for over six centuries and is today an English Heritage property. It was popularised by Shakespeare in his work *Henry IV*.

(B)

Warkworth Hermitage. Beside the River Coquet is the small 14th-century chapel, with associated living quarters, of Warkworth Hermitage. Legend tells of it being hewn out of the rock cliff and lived in by Sir Bertram of Bothal as penance for accidentally killing the woman he loved.

St Lawrence's Church. Pre-dated by an 8th-century Saxon church, built by King Ceolwulf of Northumbria and probably later destroyed by Danish raiders, Warkworth's present church is largely Norman, (early 12th-century), with some later additions. Earliest features include the nave, Northumberland's longest at 27 metres, and the chancel. The chancel has a vaulted roof, associated diagonal ribbing possibly having been a precaution against fire damage during the centuries of border troubles. Exposed frequently to cross-border violence St Lawrence's was the scene of a terrible massacre by the Scots in 1174, when 300 villagers were killed by the Earl of Fife.

(D)

Coquet Bridge. Along with its gatehouse, Warkworth's 14th-century cobbled stone bridge, one of very few fortified bridges remaining in Britain, provided an outer defence to the village and castle. It carried all traffic over the Coquet for almost 600 years until its replacement in 1965.

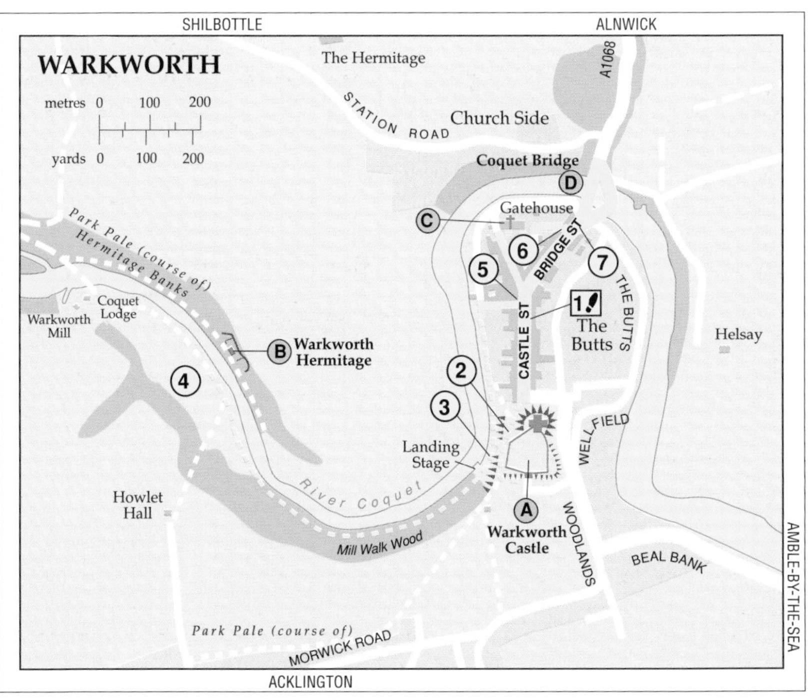

WALES

•

PORTMEIRION, GWYNEDD

•

Lovely the woods, waters, meadows, coombes, vales,
All the air things wear that build this world of Wales;
GERARD MANLEY HOPKINS – IN THE VALLEY OF THE ELWY

•

WALES

The Celts, a mid-European Iron Age people whose name is now synonymous with Wales, took over Britain from Bronze Age folk in the last centuries before the birth of Christ. They farmed the fertile valleys of Wales, converting the hill tops into the hill forts that are so recognisably a feature of the Iron Age. When the Romans came to Britain their first major battle was at Maiden Castle, one of Britain's biggest hill forts.

The Romans pushed west, finding stern resistance to the invasion from the two predominant tribes of Wales, the Silures and the Ordovices. These tribes were led by Caratacus, who fought for several years performing brave deeds before being betrayed and captured by the Romans, who were so impressed by his fighting qualities and his dignity as a prisoner that he was taken to Rome as an honoured guest, and lived out his years at peace in that far-off city. Caerwent was built by the Romans in the heart of Silure country, but it dates from a later time, when the tribe was living at peace with its new masters.

When the Romans departed, the next enemies to threaten the British Celts were the Saxons. These invaders pushed the Celts west, finally cutting off the Welsh Celts – whom they never subdued – from those of the other parts of Britain. The Welsh name for Wales, *Cymru*, is from the Celtic word for fellow countryman, Wales deriving from the Saxon *Wallas* meaning foreigner. Behind Offa's Dyke the Celtic Welsh continued on their own path, one that involved frequent tribal battles with princedoms forming and reforming as leaders died.

When the Normans arrived at Offa's Dyke they found not one country, but many little countries, making it easier for them to subdue Wales, though the task was still a difficult one. In South Wales the Normans had quick successes. In Carew and Manorbier castles were built to subdue the locals, but Bosherston is as Norman English as any village east of the Dyke. The further north the Normans went, the more difficulties they had. Tretower is sited where they needed to hold a pass over the Black Mountains, while New Radnor was a wholly new village, growing up on a grid pattern at the foot of the hill topped off by the local Marcher lord's castle.

The Marcher lords, who lived on the *March*, or border, of the two countries, controlled the Welsh for the king. As a rule they did it harshly, a harshness that led to frequent rebellions. That led by Llywelyn the Great was the most successful and Dolwyddelan Castle dates from then – though the village is largely later, from a time when North Wales slate was the economic backbone of the country. The rebellion of Llywelyn the Last induced Edward I to secure the country for good, and this he did with his great *Ring of Stone* castles, including Harlech, where the castle held the western edge of Gwynedd, and Beaumaris, which secured Anglesey, the Granary of Wales.

However, though the Normans brought battle and domination, they also brought their monastic tradition to Wales, as can be seen at Talley, where the ruins of a fine monastery rest in a beautiful valley. Here is buried Dafydd ap Gwilym, the greatest of medieval Welsh poets. Poetry has a long tradition in Wales, stretching back to the Celtic bards. The most brilliant of modern Welsh poets, Dylan Thomas, lived and worked at sleepy Laugharne until his untimely death.

After the Edwardian castles were built there was one more major rebellion – that led by Owain Glyndwr, in which both New Radnor and Harlech saw action – before the crowning of Henry Tudor as Henry VII effectively united England and Wales. The Welsh returned to their farming: Dinas Mawddwy is a typical market village. Not until the late 19th century did the country's mineral wealth bring industrialisation. In the south the industries were coal and iron; in the north it was slate. In the slate village of Dolwyddelan, it is noticeable that the two halves of the country were united by the presence of Nonconformist chapels in the villages, the chapels siding with the people when the established church took the side of the landlords.

Later, as tourism replaced industry, villages such as Betws-y-Coed became popular with the seekers of wild Wales. Finally, to bring the story up to date there is Portmeirion, a folly village that can be seen as representing the leisure activity focus of modern Wales.

A widespread species, the small tortoishell butterfly is a common visitor to gardens and villages in Wales. It breeds several times a year and is therefore present right through from spring to autumn, when it feeds on michelmas daisies. The eggs are laid on nettles and so the species has a preference for overgrown gardens and rough borders.

BEAUMARIS

GWYNEDD

On A545, 5 miles NE of Menai Bridge

BEAUMARIS (the name means 'beautiful marsh') occupies the eastern corner of the Isle of Anglesey. It was once a stopping point for pleasure steamers out of Liverpool and, set on the waters of the Menai Straits, is one of the most historic sites in Wales.

POINTS OF INTEREST

Beaumaris Castle. Following the defeat of Llywelyn the Last, Edward I of England decided that never again would the Welsh princes rise up and trouble his western border. To ensure this he built his 'Ring of Stone' around Gwynedd, the Welsh stronghold. Beaumaris was the last of the Ring, and the largest, and as it was on a site never previously defended, the designer was given free reign. He was James of St George, the greatest of castle builders, and Beaumaris is believed to be his masterpiece. In order that sea supply could break any siege he chose this site on the extreme tip of Anglesey, but on the calmer, mainland side. The site was marshy – in Norman French a good, or beautiful marsh, ('a beau maris') which allowed the digging of a surrounding sea moat. Unfortunately there was a Welsh village nearby, but the villagers were 'persuaded' to move to the western shore where a new borough was built for them and where Newborough now stands.

Master James' great work took only three years to build and is superbly constructed. Within the encircling moat, and rising directly from it for maximum security, is a wall guarded by 16 round towers. At the southern edge there was a sea gate with a fortified dock. Inside the wall was a 'ward',

ANGLESEY, MAM CYMRU

Anglesey is one of the most historically interesting parts of Wales. Here are found the Neolithic burial chambers of Bryn Celli Ddu and Barclodiad y Gawres, two of the finest sites in Britain. In the days when the Celts controlled Wales – and the rest of Britain – the island was the centre for Druidism, that mysterious priesthood that had absolutely nothing to do with the origins of Stonehenge.

When the Romans invaded Britain in AD43 they soon realised that they needed to neutralise the powerful Druids, and advanced on Anglesey. In AD60 an army under Suetonius Paulinus arrived at the Menai Straits. They were faced with a Celtic army among whom moved the Druids, calling for the vengeance of the gods to fall upon the invaders. Tacitus, the Roman historian, paints a vivid picture, admitting that the Romans were at first very afraid. But they were also professional soldiers and the Druids' ritual cursing proved no match for the Roman short sword.

When later invaders, the Normans, arrived on the borders of Wales, Anglesey assumed a new importance. The island is very fertile, unlike the nearby mountains of Snowdonia, and the Princes of Gwynedd used both Anglesey and the hills to good effect. Operating from the royal palace at Aberffraw on the western coast, they harried the Norman armies, then withdrew behind the mountains that were hard to penetrate and produced vile weather. Safely on Anglesey, the Gwynedd armies ate their fill while the Norman soldiers, far from home, were cold, wet and hungry. Consequently, Anglesey soon became known as the Granary of Wales or, more simply, Mam Cymru, the Mother of Wales.

Llywelyn the Great campaigned from Anglesey, as did his grandson Llywelyn the Last – so called because he was the last of the true-born Princes of Wales. Edward I, having defeated the last Llywelyn, set up his 'Ring of Stone' castles to hold the area; Conwy to hold the crossing of the River Conwy, Caernarfon and Harlech behind the Snowdonia wall, and Beaumaris to hold Mam Cymru.

The main entrance of Beaumaris Castle, approached over its moat. Built in the 14th century to guard the Menai Strait, it has a separate defensive wall.

The last of a chain of castles built by Edward I along the north and west coast of Wales, Beaumaris, seen here against the backdrop of the Snowdonia Range, is of concentric construction, perfect in symmetry.

a stretch of flat land that had to be crossed to reach the inner defences and which could be raked by fire from both sides. The inner defences consisted of another complete wall, also tower defended. This inner wall was higher than the outer so that if the outer were taken, the castle defenders could fire down on to the enemy.

Oddly the castle was never fully completed, but its defences where tested during the Owain Glyndwr rebellion. Glyndwr's men besieged Beaumaris, but were unable to take it. Later, during the Civil War, Beaumaris was heavily defended, but the fighting never reached it.

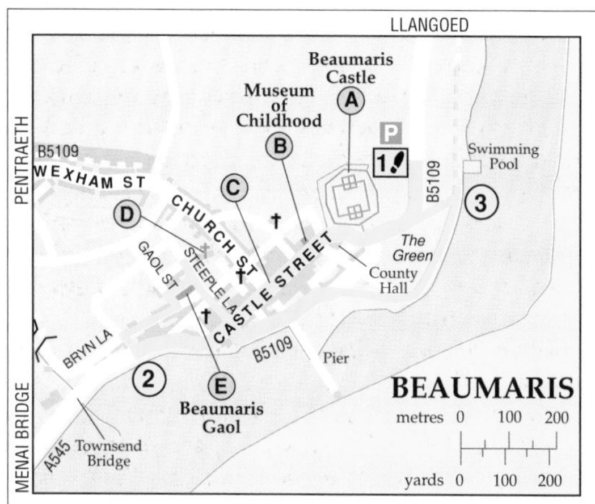

WALK DIRECTIONS

Walk out of the car park and turn right past the children's playground to reach the castle. After a visit continue into Castle Street passing the County Hall and the Bull's Head Inn. To the left is the Museum of Childhood. Walk past Church Street and turn right into Steeple Lane to visit the church. To the left is the huge wall of Beaumaris Gaol, reached from Bunker's Hill. Go left into Gaol Street and, at the T-junction, right into Rosemary Lane. The first turning on the left now leads to the sea front.

Turn left along the front to visit the Victorian pier, continuing beyond to reach The Green.

At the far side of The Green there is a narrow kissing-gate in the wall beside the Timelock, with its *son et lumiere* show of the history of North Wales. Through the gate a short walk leads to seats high above the Menai Straits.

Retrace your steps to the gate and continue around The Green to reach the car park.

The 15th-century Tudor Rose, found in Castle Street, is one of the oldest domestic buildings in Anglesey.

INFORMATION
Length of walk: 2 miles
Approximate time: 1 hour (excluding castle and museum)

TERRAIN:
Suitable for children, pushchairs and wheelchairs at all times of the year, except for the final short climb on the hills above the Menai Straits. This is not suitable for wheelchairs.

PARKING:
Parking is relatively easy in Beaumaris, either in the village itself or on the sea front. There is also a large car park on the far side of the castle from the village. It is assumed below that the latter is used.

OPEN:
The castle. Daily Oct-Mar 9.30am-4pm, Sun 2-4pm; Mar-Oct 9.30am-6.30pm Sun 2-6.30pm. Charge.
The Museum of Childhood. Daily Easter-Jan 10am-6pm, Sun 12 noon-5pm. Charge.
The Timelock. Daily Easter-Oct 10am-5pm. Charge.

REFRESHMENTS:
Selection of pubs and cafés in the village.

Museum of Childhood. This delightful museum spans one and a half centuries of toys and games and has many items that are very rare as well as entertaining. The collections include music boxes and magic lanterns, clockwork trains, teddy bears and dolls. There is a fine rocking horse – with free rides for the under fives – while the shop has many toys for sale including some of interest to the collector.

Castle Street. The County Hall is 16th-century and legend has it that Judge Jeffreys held a Bloody Assize there, though this has little support in fact. Further on is the Bull's Head Inn, built in 1472 though rebuilt before it became the headquarters of General Mytton when his Parliamentarians were besieging the Castle. Later both Dr Johnson and Charles Dickens stayed there. The Inn contains what is claimed to be Britain's oldest door. Look out too for the 15th-century Tudor Rose, one of Anglesey's oldest houses.

The George and Dragon Inn in Church Street is believed to be older than The Bull's Head, some of the interior walls being of wattle and daub, but no definite record exists before the end of the 16th-century.

St Mary's Church. The church is 14th-century and holds, in the porch, the stone sarcophagus of Joan, daughter of King John and wife of Llywelyn the Great. Before being placed in its present position, the coffin was used as a horse trough. Also in the church is a fine effigy of a courtly couple and a good early 16th-century brass. The hut in the churchyard was used by a nightwatchman placed there to deter bodysnatchers in the 19th-century.

Beaumaris Gaol. Despite its imposing appearance, the gaol was one of the most progressive prisons in Britain when it was built in 1829. The Gaol Act of 1823 called for the segregation of men and women, separate cells for prisoners, and a degree of hygiene previously unheard of. The reasons were not wholely humanitarian, it having been recognised that the old gaols were a breeding ground for more crime. The old Beaumaris gaol was pulled down and this one built, though in 1874 it had been replaced by one in Caernarfon.

Visitors can judge for themselves whether the prison was humane: the punishment cell would imply otherwise, although the condemned cell is twice the size of other cells. Only two men were hanged at Beaumaris, one of whom died protesting his innocence and cursing the church clock, which he could see from the scaffold. The clock has not kept proper time since! The executions were in public, people owning houses overlooking the scaffold making a fortune from selling the right to stand in their gardens.

This village, set in the heart of the Gwydir Forest, has long been a popular mountain resort.

BETWS-Y-COED

WALES

BETWS-Y-COED

GWYNEDD

On A5, beside the River Conwy

THE name of the village means 'the prayer-house in the woods'. The house referred to was an early monastic building, and the woods can still be seen growing thick on the sides of the Conwy, Lledr and Llugwy valleys that meet at the town. It used to be said that a squirrel could travel from Dolgarrog to Dolwyddelan, a distance of about 15 miles, without touching ground. The three rivers meeting here, or rather the bridges over them, are the reasons for the village's existence.

Betws would still be a quiet river-crossing village had it not been for the arrival of the railway and the recognition of the great beauty of its setting. The railway still operates: this is as close as you can get to the National Park's hills by rail, the village justifying its name of Gateway to Snowdonia.

INFORMATION
Length of walk:
1 mile (2 miles if Waterloo Bridge is visited)
Approximate time:
1 hour ($1\frac{1}{2}$ hours if Waterloo Bridge is visited)

TERRAIN:
Suitable for children at all times of year. The railway footbridge may cause difficulties for pushchairs and wheelchairs.

PARKING:
There is a car park next to the railway station and another near the railway museum. Elsewhere, it can be difficult to park in Betws during high summer.

OPEN:
The Railway Museum. Daily Easter-Oct, 10am-5.30pm. Charge.
The Motor Museum. Daily. Charge.
The RSPB centre and Living Aquarium. Daily. Easter-Oct 10am-6pm. Oct-Easter 9.30am-4pm. Charge for Aquarium only.

REFRESHMENTS:
Good selection of pubs and cafés.

POINTS OF INTEREST

Ⓐ

Museums. The Railway Museum, across the track from the station, has model railways and memorabilia of the days of steam. It also has a buffet car café. The RSPB Visitor Centre is a mine of information on Snowdonia's bird life, while the Motor Museum next door has a collection of vintage and newer cars.

The Betws Bridges. The Afon Llugwy, draining down from high Snowdonia, is crossed by Pont y Pair, the Bridge of the Cauldron, a 15th-century structure of great beauty. The Lledr's bridge, just south of the village, is equally good, but it is the Waterloo Bridge of Thomas Telford that takes the eye. Telford was the finest road engineer of his day, the bridge over the Menai Straits to Anglesey being considered his masterpiece. The Betws iron bridge is almost as good. The 105ft span is liberally decorated with the emblems of the four home countries, and in case the visitor was in any doubt about the name, both sides of the bridge explain that it was built in the year of the battle, 1815.

Churches. Betws has two churches. The loop of this walk goes around St Mary's built in 1873 in mock Early English style, in local stone and Cornish black serpentine. Older, and more elegant, is St Michael's, close to the suspension bridge. This is 14th-century and is used only for funerals. The effigy of a knight inside is believed to be of Gruffydd ap Dafydd Goch, (Griffith, the son of Red David). Gruffydd was the grandson of Prince Dafydd, brother of Llywelyn the Last, who survived his brother by just one year, being captured in a skirmish near Shrewsbury in 1283 and beheaded. Gruffydd's home was at Fedw Deg, a mile from the Ledr bridge and still inhabited.

WALK DIRECTIONS

From the station car park walk along the metalled path to the Information Centre, RSPB Visitor Centre, Living Aquarium and Motor Museum. Go left at the end of this path on another path that reaches the main road over a bridge.

②

Turn right to reach Pont y Pair bridge. From there retrace the route and continue along the main road. Go right on the square-shaped crescent road that leads around the church and continue, passing the road back to the car park to reach the next road to the left.

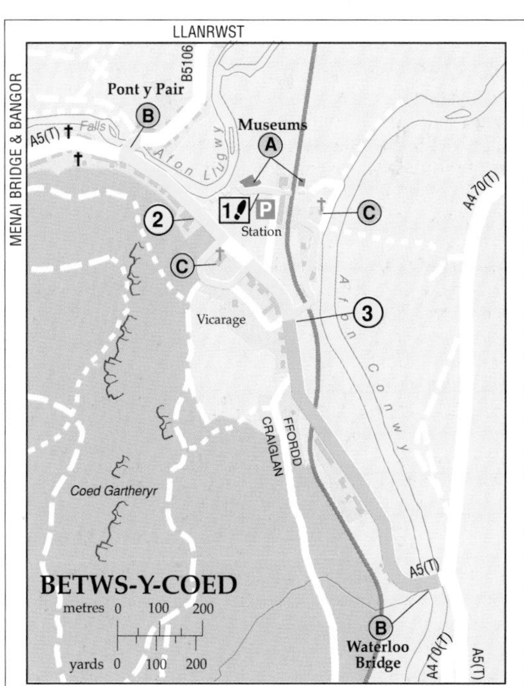

③

To extend the walk continue along the main road to Waterloo Bridge before returning to this point. Otherwise, cross the railway and go along the road to reach another church and fine footbridge, right. Stay with the road as it bears left, then right to reach the Railway Museum. After visiting the museum go over the station footbridge back to the start point.

BOSHERSTON

WALES

BOSHERSTON
DYFED

Off B4319, 4 miles S of Pembroke

THE village lies close to one of the loveliest parts of the Pembrokeshire Coast National Park, and is noted for a delightful series of man-made lily ponds.

The church is 13th-century Norman, and has a fine stained glass window depicting St Govan. It also has a good hagioscope or squint, a passage in the chancel wall that allowed those in the side chapel to see the altar. Outside is an ancient cross, perhaps as old as the church itself.

POINTS OF INTEREST

St Michael's Church. The village church, built towards the end of the 13th century, contains a stained glass window depicting St David and St Govan, who carries a model of his tiny chapel. The 14th-century Preaching Cross in the churchyard may have been adapted from an older Crucifixion, the evidence visible in the face in the centre. Possibly dismantled at the Reformation, the original shaft appears to have been lost and replaced by the present stumpy one.

Bosherston Lily Ponds. The Stackpole Estate was owned by the Scottish Earls of Cawdor until it was transferred to the National Trust, and it was members of this family who dammed the valleys of three streams bound for Broad Haven to form the lily ponds. The ponds cover 80 acres and are nationally important because of the underlying calcareous marls. The ponds hold perch, roach, tench and pike. The lilies are at their best in June. The lucky visitor will see the electric blue flash of a kingfisher, while in the colder months there is a good collection of winter migrants. The ponds are also associated with the Arthurian legend; one version of the story has Bedivere throwing the sword Excalibur into what was then a single lake as he had been instructed to by the dying Arthur following the final battle against Modred.

WALK DIRECTIONS

①

After visiting the church, turn left down the stony track to reach the first lily pond. Now bear right and walk along the southern shore of the pond to reach the three-way sign and footbridge at its far end.

②

Pass over the footbridge to follow the right edge of the lily pond. The path crosses two more bridges in quick succession, then follows the pond edge to reach another bridge, beyond which the stony track leads straight back to the car park.

For an optional extra route from point 2, follow the stream leaving the lily pond south across the beach to a flight of steps. Ascend to the Broad Haven car park and walk along the coastal path marked by white posts. At a Y-junction there is the option to turn left for St Govan's Head, but the main option continues ahead to steps that lead down to St Govan's Chapel. To return to the lily ponds simply retrace your steps to point 2.

This tiny village is flanked by 80 acres of ponds, whose lilies make a spectacular display, especially in June.

INFORMATION
Length of walk:
2 miles (5 miles if the longer route is taken)
Approximate time:
1 hour (2½ hours if the longer route is taken)

TERRAIN:
Care must be taken with children on the optional route as the cliff edge on the coastal section of the walk is abrupt and unprotected. The circuit of the lily ponds is suitable for pushchairs and wheelchairs, and these can also easily reach the cliffs. The Broad Haven section of the walk is unsuitable for both.

PARKING:
There are car parks at Bosherston church and at St Govan's Head. The directions assume the church car park is used.

REFRESHMENTS:
One inn and a teashop.

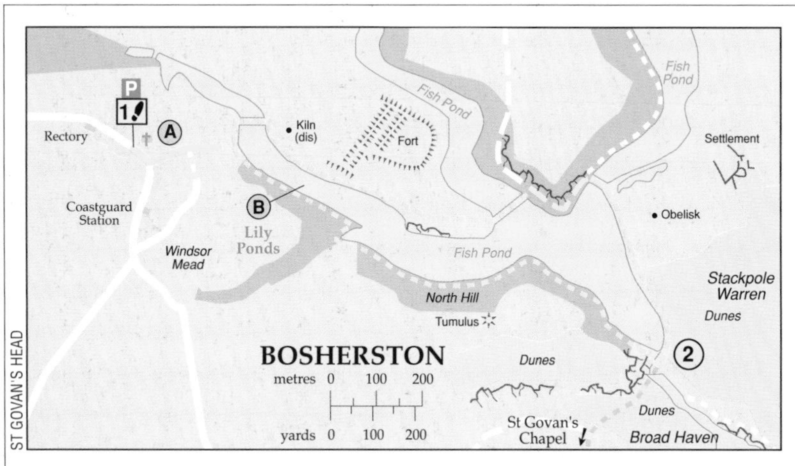

ST GOVAN'S CHAPEL

The chapel is reached by a stone stairway. Legend has it that if you count the steps as you descend and then again on the way up, you will not arrive at the same number. The chapel is named for Gobhan or Govan, 6th-century abbot of Dairinis in Wexford, Ireland, who landed here having sailed across the Celtic Sea in his coracle. His hermitage cell was formed by cutting into the rock, and this cell can still be reached from the chapel built of local stone by his followers. The cleft in the cell's rock wall is said to have hidden Govan when raiders landed nearby.

The bell cote once held a silver bell which was stolen by raiders whose ship was later wrecked. Sea nymphs rescued and returned the bell, but to protect it they placed it in a rock. If you find the right rock, the bell will ring when you strike it.

CAREW

WALES

CAREW

DYFED

Off A477, 3 miles E of Pembroke

THE three villages of Carew (Caeriw) that straddle the main road offer one of inland Pembrokeshire's most appealing walks. At the centre is a fine castle and a most interesting sea mill.

Carew's magnificent Celtic cross is believed to be 11th-century.

WALK DIRECTIONS

Make your way to the picnic area then go east along the side of the mill-pond – with excellent views of the castle – to reach the main road (A4075). Turn right to reach Carew village. The turning left after the church allows a view of the Flemish chimney, a 17th-century tapering chimney rising from a pair of stone bread ovens. Turn right to visit the Castle. Return to the main street and turn right. To the right now is Carew Cross. Go past this and down to the A477. Cross this with care to reach the lane to Carew Cheriton.

Opposite the church is a footbridge. Go over this and turn right along Paddock Lane to reach Milton near the water works complex. At the T-junction go right, pass the lovingly restored village water pump, and continue to reach the A477. Cross the road to reach the village pub.

From the pub follow the lane over a bridge and beside the playground to return to the A477. A few yards along the road, pass over a stile on the left. The footpath is well signed by yellow arrows. Follow it, reaching Radford Pill down some steps. The Pill is an inlet of the sea. The quarry here provided building stone which was shipped out from the Pill. Go over a stile and continue on the obvious path to reach the steps on to a lane.

Turn right, then first left to reach Carew French Tidal Mill. Cross the dam to reach a path along the mill-pond that leads back to the picnic area.

POINTS OF INTEREST

Carew Castle. It is likely that the strategic importance of the Carew site was recognised well before the first recorded castle. Indeed, the name itself is believed to derive from *caer*, a Welsh word often used for hillforts. In this low-lying place a real hillfort is unlikely to have been built, but some sort of protection for the ford of the important local river could have existed in earlier times. It is likely that there was a Roman fort on the site, but the first castle that we can be sure of was built around 1100 when the local land was given to Gerald de Windsor by Rhys ap Tewdr, Prince of Deheubarth as part of the dowry for his daughter, Nesta, on her marriage to Gerald. A later owner of the castle was Sir Nicholas de Carew whose effigy, it is believed, can be seen in the church of Carew Cheriton. Later still, Rhys ap Thomas owned the castle and here he held the tournament that is thought to have been the greatest ever seen in Wales.

Sir John Perrot, an illegitimate son of Henry VIII, converted the castle from medieval fortress to Elizabethan mansion by adding the north wing that dominates the view across the mill-pond. The more ancient castle section can be seen from the dam of the sea mill. Sir John died a natural death in the Tower of London after he had been accused of treason and the castle went into a decline that was hastened by siege and counter-siege during the Civil War. Today Carew is a beautiful and interesting ruin.

Carew Cross. Believed by many to be the most important early Christian cross in Wales, and certainly one of the most impressive, Carew Cross commemorates Maredudd, son of Edwin. Maredudd was joint ruler, with his brother, of the princedom of Deheubarth, as this area of south-west Wales was called in medieval times. Maredudd – a great grandson of Hywel Dda,

CAREW'S GREAT TOURNAMENT

Henry Tudor returned from exile in Brittany on 7 August 1485. By 21 August he was king.

When Henry landed in Pembroke *en route* to Bosworth Field and victory over Richard III it is believed that he stayed at Carew Castle as a guest of Rhys ap Thomas. Rhys came from a family that was staunchly Lancastrian so this was, perhaps, not surprising. However, Rhys had only a few years previously been in the pay of Richard III, and had vowed to him that Henry would only enter Wales over his (Rhys') body. The story is that to appease his conscience when Henry landed in Pembroke that Rhys hid under Mullock Bridge near Dale as Henry rode over it, so that the man soon to be Henry VII could indeed ride into Wales over his body.

Rhys added 500 men to Henry's army and at Bosworth he fought with ferocious bravery. Some said that it was Rhys who killed Richard. Whatever the truth of that, when Henry had been made king he did not forget Rhys, making him a Knight of the Garter, a great honour.

To celebrate, Sir Rhys held a Tournament at Carew. The event lasted for five days around 23 April 1507, that being St George's Day, the patron saint of the Order of the Garter. The Tournament started with a banquet and after several days of jousting and sword fighting displays, ended with a day's hunting. It was, by common consent, the greatest Tournament ever staged in Wales.

The grandeur of the once palatial Carew Castle is reflected by the creek at high tide.

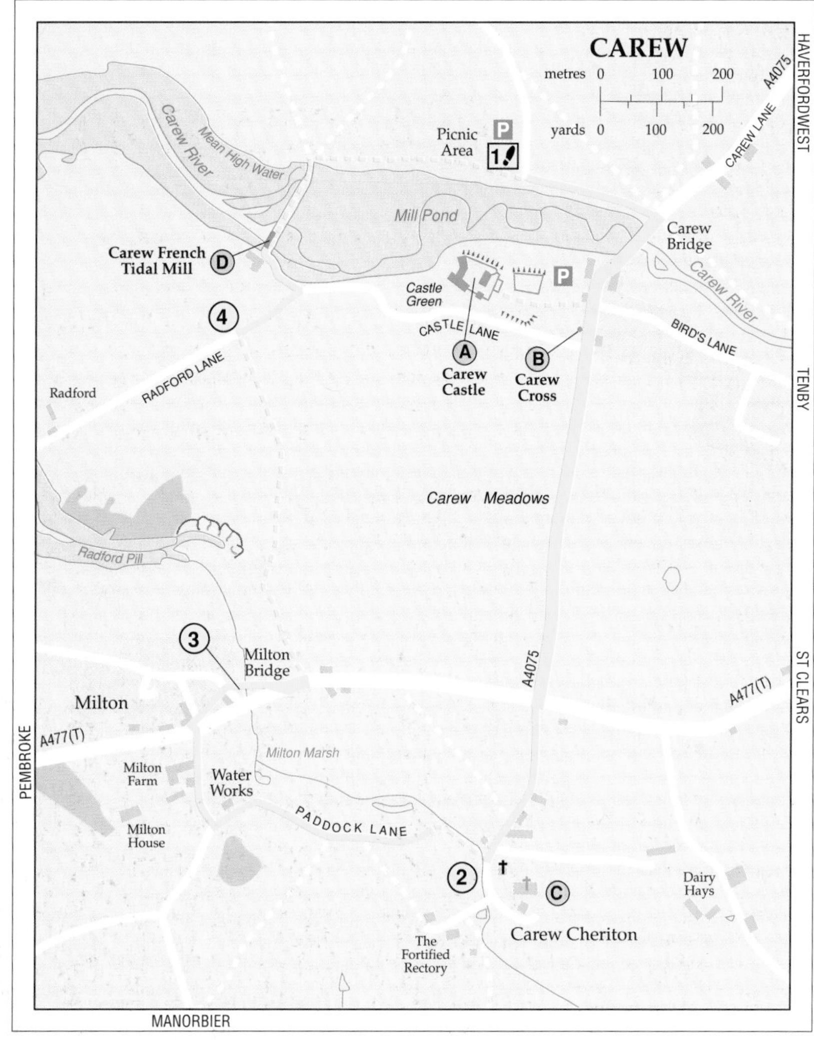

Hywel the Good, one of the greatest of Welsh rulers – was killed in battle in 1035. The huge cross – it is just over 13½ft high – is intricately made, the finely worked Celtic wheel-cross being tenon-jointed to the richly inscribed, and massive, shaft. The shaft itself is carved with various motifs, including plaits and swastikas.

Carew Cheriton Church. The church of St Mary is late 14th century and contains an effigy that is believed to be that of Sir Nicholas de Carew, who is known to have been buried here. Sir Nicholas served Edward I well, fighting with distinction for him in Ireland. The 14th-century Chantry Chapel in the churchyard is now the Sunday School.

Carew French Tidal Mill. It is known that a sea mill existed at Carew in Elizabethan times, as a record exists of one John Bartlett leasing the site for an annual rent of £10. The present building is 19th century and the visitor can see the flour-grinding equipment that was used until the outbreak of World War I. The mill – the only complete sea mill that now exists in Wales – was powered by tidal water, a series of sluices allowing the incoming tide to fill the mill-pond and then releasing the water on the ebb when the water head was high. The released water drove water wheels which turned the grindstones. It is not certain whether the name refers to the fact that an early mill was of French design or construction, or because it used imported French grindstones rather than British stones. The visitor to the mill can not only see the interesting grinding machinery, but also has a superb view of the castle.

This ivy-clad, 14th-century chantry chapel stands in the churchyard of St Mary's, the village church. It is now the Sunday school.

INFORMATION
Length of walk:
2½ miles
Approximate time:
2 hours

TERRAIN:
Suitable for children at all times of year. Not suitable for pushchairs or wheelchairs. Two stiles, two sets of steps and a footbridge.

PARKING:
Parking is available at the castle or at the picnic area across the mill-pond from the castle.

OPEN:
The Castle and Mill. Easter-Oct, daily from 10am-5pm. Charge.

REFRESHMENTS:
There is a village pub.

PRINCESS NESTA, THE HELEN OF WALES

Nesta, the daughter of Rhys ap Tewdr who gave Carew to Gerald de Windsor as a wedding gift, was a princess whose beauty – she really was known as the Helen of Wales – was matched by her fertility. She had at least five children by Gerald, one of whom, a daughter named Angharad, was the mother of Gerald of Wales, perhaps the most famous of all travellers through the Principality, a man we shall meet again in Manorbier. She was then kidnapped by Owain ap Cadwgan who was so captivated by her beauty that he invaded Carew Castle to capture her.

The story goes that one night, fired by accounts of Nesta's beauty and further inflamed by a sight of her, he gathered together a band of young Welshmen as crazy as himself. Having dug their way under the castle gate he started a fire and in the confusion that followed kidnapped Nesta, though it does seem that she was not too reluctant to be captured. The whole of Wales was in an uproar and Henry I, Nesta's ward, was furious. Owain took her back to his stronghold near Dinas Mawddwy and there Nesta bore him at least two children. The relationship did not last however, Gerald bringing an army north to kill Owain and to rescue his wife. Owain in the turmoil fled to Ireland. Soon after, Gerald died, and Nesta married Stephen of Cardigan and had yet more children.

CAERWENT

GWENT

Off A48, 4 miles SW of Chepstow

THIS pleasant little village close to the River Severn's M4 bridge is almost completely surrounded by one of Britain's finest Roman remains, the *Venta Silurum* town wall. Caerwent's main street marks the approximate line of the Roman central avenue.

POINTS OF INTEREST

Venta Silurum. When the Romans invaded Britain in AD43, (the landing of Julius Caesar in 55BC having been only an investigation) they rapidly moved west until they reached the Severn. Beyond the Severn they found war-like Celtic tribes, the Silures and Ordovices, who fought a vigorous guerilla campaign, retreating often into rugged hills and vile weather. Eventually, however, the Romans subdued the Celts and introduced them to the joys of the *Pax Romana*. The Silures took to it well and by AD75 the Romans felt secure enough to consider building a market town as opposed to another fort.

Here, at Caerwent, they built *Venta Silurum*, the market of the Silures. The *Venta* has passed to us as Gwent, the name for the new local county, and the *went* was added to the Celtic name for a fort, *caer*. The Roman town covered 44 acres, a good size for Britain, and had the usual buildings – forum, public baths, amphitheatre, temple – as well as numerous town houses on the normal grid array. The whole was enclosed within a huge square of walls 25ft high and 10ft thick. Even today the southern and western walls (the best preserved) rise nearly 20ft in places. Much later a series of bastions (half-round towers), were added to the walls, probably to take *ballistae*, the rock-throwing Roman artillery.

Visitors can walk the walls and see the remains of the Roman temple in the main street – reached from either the church or the base of the Roman Wall – but it is the church porch where some of the most important remains are to be found. There is a small altar stone dedicated to Mars Ocelus, a Romano-Celtic god, and an inscribed stone. The inscription indicates that the stone was the base for a statue to Claudius Paulinus who became Governor of Britain in AD219.

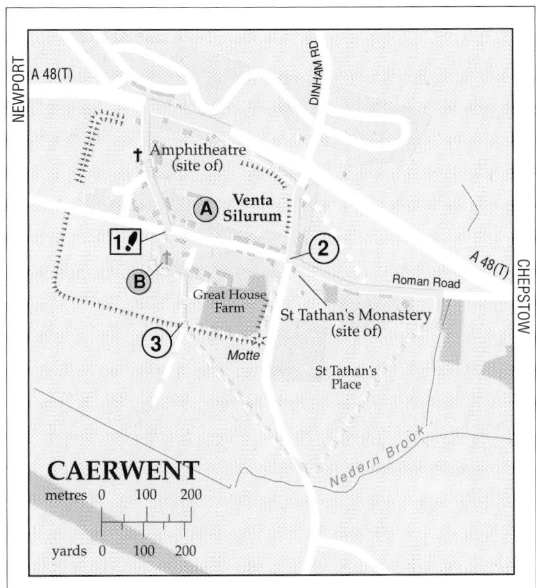

INFORMATION
Length of walk:
1 mile (1½ miles if longer route is taken)
Approximate time:
1½ hours (2 hours if longer route is taken)

TERRAIN:
Suitable for children at all times of year. Unsuitable for pushchairs and wheelchairs due to stiles and several stepped sections. One stile on the short walk, four on the longer version.

PARKING:
Parking is not easy, but with care can be accomplished in several places within the village.

REFRESHMENTS:
Village inns.

WALK DIRECTIONS

Start from the church. From the church lych-gate cross the road, go past the war memorial and down to the main A48. Here, go right along the front of the North Gate Inn and bear right down the lane with the '30 mph' and other road signs. At the T-junction turn right, passing the Burton almshouses to reach the main village street.

For the shorter walk, cross the street and go up the steps on to the Roman wall. Follow the wall ahead and then turn right at the corner to reach a track.

For the longer walk go left at point 2, along the street passing the site of St Tathan's monastery, left, to reach Highfield on the right. Turn right into this, past Brookside Stores to the left, and bear right at a fork to reach the village hall. Climb over the stile in front of the hall and take the field path. Bear left at a path fork just beyond a hedge gap and reach a stile to a road. Cross and go right, and after a few yards cross another stile on the left. Climb over and cross the field diagonally to a stile at the base of the wall, as for the shorter walk.

The walls of Venta Silurum, second largest civilian settlement in the south west and the only civilian town built by the Romans in Wales.

③

Go right, up the track towards a farm. At the 'Private Roadway' sign, go left over a stone stile to reach the church.

Ⓑ

The Church of St Stephen and St Tathan. After the Romans had left Britain Caerwent became home, at the end of the 6th century, to Tathan, an Irish monk. He was granted land and founded a monastery here, though nothing remains of it. Excavations did reveal a skeleton in a stone coffin which was assumed to be Tathan and the remains were reburied in the 13th-century church. The church has a joint dedication, to Celtic Tathan and Norman Stephen. Tathan's new resting place can be seen in the south aisle. The large stone coffin lid built into the wall has nothing to do with Tathan, and is known as the Bishop's Stone.

DINAS MAWDDWY

WALES

DINAS MAWDDWY
GWYNEDD

On A470, 8 miles S of Dolgellau

ONE of the most beautifully placed villages in Wales, Dinas Mawddwy is located where the Afon Cerist joins the Afon Dyfi (the River Dovey). The view up the Dyfi Valley towards the river's birthplace, the high Arans, is breathtaking.

`Dinas' means fortress, an apt name here as legend has it that King Arthur's final battle against Mordred was fought at Maes-y-Camlan to the south of the village. A couple of centuries ago Dinas Mawddwy was an important market town, with over 1,000 inhabitants and an annual round of cattle, sheep and horse fairs.

The Red Lion Hotel is not only the oldest building in the village, it also has a large and unique collection of brasses.

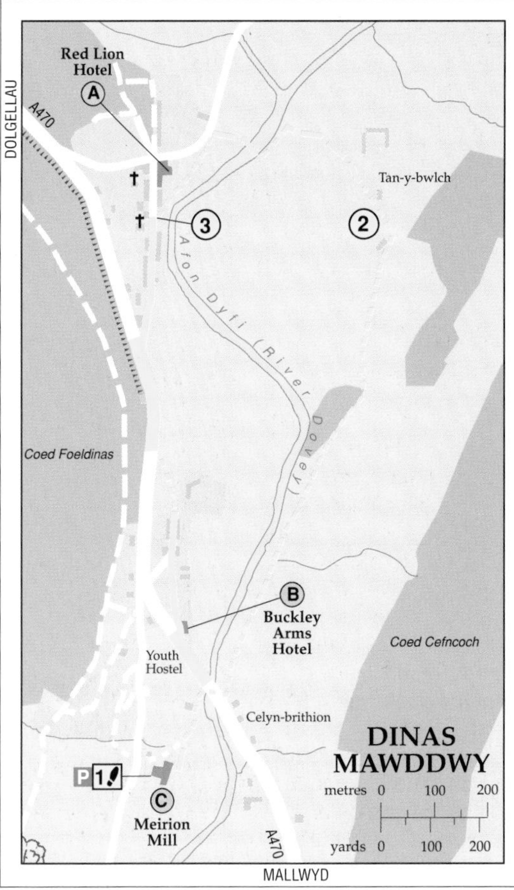

INFORMATION
Length of walk:
1½ miles
Approximate time:
1 hour

TERRAIN:
Suitable for children at all times of year. The section between Tan-y-bwlch and Dinas Mawddwy is not suitable for pushchairs or wheelchairs. Several kissing-gates, a stepped section and one footbridge.

PARKING:
Parking is usually straightforward in the village, and there is a car park at Meirion Mill. The directions assume the mill car park is used.

OPEN:
Meirion Mill. Daily. Easter-Oct. No Charge.

REFRESHMENTS:
Inns and cafés in the village.

POINTS OF INTEREST

Ⓐ

The Red Lion Hotel. This is the oldest building in the village, dating back to the time of Henry I. Henry's illegitimate son, Robert, was a frequent visitor according to legend. His interest in the village was more accurately an interest in the infamous Nesta, known for her beauty as the Helen of Wales. She had been brought here by Owain ap Cadwgan – but was visited by Robert – and lived, again so legend has it, in the shop that is the last house of the terrace on the left as you enter Dinas on the walk.

Ⓑ

Buckley Pines Hotel. As Dinas' importance declined there were several efforts to revive its fortunes, most notably the building of a railway by Edmund Buckley, a Manchester businessman who lived locally in the mid-19th century. Buckley went bankrupt, but his name lives on in the Buckley Pines Hotel. The trees that stand between the Hotel and the road are the unusual Noble Fir. At the right time of year they shed cones that are almost a foot long.

Ⓒ

Meirion Mill. The mill has a café in what was the Dinas station, the line going from here to Cemmas Road, about 7 miles down the Dyfi valley. A small section of line still exists near the mill, though it is doubtful whether full restoration will ever add Dinas Mawddwy to the list of the Great Little Trains of Wales. The mill itself is woollen rather than flour, and has an interesting range of items – clothes and blankets – made on the site using old Dobcross looms.

WALK DIRECTIONS

From the mill car park, cross the old Dyfi bridge to reach the A470. Cross this road with care to reach the signposted gate into Celyn-brithion campsite. Follow the track beyond the campsite, beside the Dyfi, to reach Tan-y-bwlch.

Pass to the left of Tan-y-bwlch, going through a gate to the river. Go left along beside the river for a short way to a footbridge. Cross, and turn left along the river again, then bear right to reach Dinas Mawddwy.

Go left along the road through the village to reach the A470. Turn left, past the garage, to reach a signed path which leads down some steps to the left. Follow the path through two kissing-gates to reach a road near the village school. Go right along the road to the A470. Turn left and then cross the road with care to reach Meirion Mill and the car park.

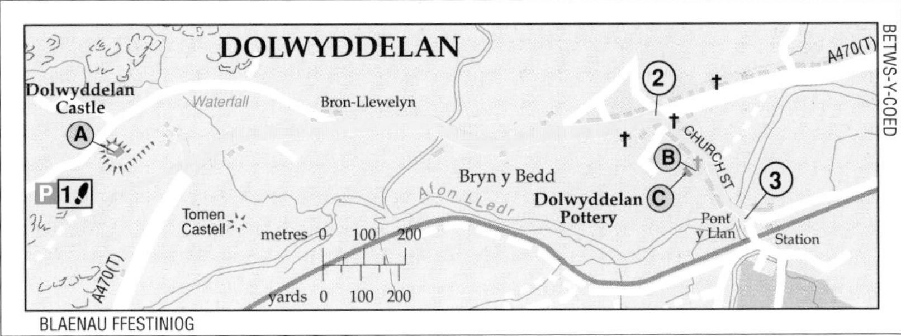

DOLWYDDELAN

GWYNEDD

On A470, mid-way between Betws-y-Coed and Blaenau Ffestiniog

THE village grew up around a church founded by Gwyddelan, a 6th-century Celtic saint. The 'dol' of the name means meadow. In later years it had a brief spell of prosperity resulting from its slate quarry. The castle is unusual in being Welsh, not an English castle in Wales as are Harlech and Beaumaris.

There may have been an even earlier hamlet here as Sarn Helen, the best known of North Wales' Roman roads, came this way, crossing the Lledr here and heading south.

A stretch of the Afon Lledr towards Foel Gynnud.

POINTS OF INTEREST

Dolwyddelan Castle. Tradition has it that Llywelyn the Great was born at Dolwyddelan Castle, though most scholars now believe this is to be incorrect. It is likely however that what we see was built by him, using the site and stone of an earlier fortress that defended the Lledr valley route between the Conwy Valley and old Merioneth. The Welsh held it only until 1283, when it was captured by Edward I. Edward had no use for it: the site was strategically less important than those of Caernarfon, Conwy and Harlech, and the buildings themselves lacked the sophistication of the English castle designs. Dolwyddelan consisted of a wall around a courtyard with one keep and a single tower, little enough by the standards of the day. In addition, the rocky outcrop on which it stands, though difficult to overcome, meant that the castle had little chance of withstanding a siege as there was no hope of supplies being obtained.

Behind the castle rises the mountain wall of Moel Siabod. This peak is seen at its best from the A5 near Capel Curig, where it appears as a shapely cone. From this side it can be seen that it is, in fact, a tent-shaped ridge.

The Church of St Gwyddelan. The church that Gwyddelan founded stood on Bryn y Bedd, but a later one was abandoned when the present village church was built in the early 16th century. Inside are many interesting items. The bell is 7th-century and is probably the one Gwyddelan himself brought from Ireland. The church has a fine brass to Meredydd ap Ieuan, who constructed the new building, and an interesting dragon carved in a beam on the northern side. The carved oak rood screen may have come from the earlier church.

Elsewhere, the village is non-Conformist. On the main road just off the walk's route, towards Betws-y-Coed, is the double-doored, massive Moriah Calvinistic Methodist Chapel, while on the corner is one of almost Romanesque design, with a Norman door.

Dolwyddelan Pottery. In the old school beside the church is an interesting small pottery. Visitors can watch potters at work, buy finished goods and have a relaxing cup of tea.

INFORMATION
Length of walk: 2½ miles
Approximate time: 1½ hours (add time to visit the Castle and Pottery)

TERRAIN:
Suitable for children, pushchairs and wheelchairs at all times of year.

PARKING:
Car parking is usually straightforward in Dolwyddelan itself, though as the walk is out and back, the castle car park can also be used. The directions below assume the castle car park as start point.

OPEN:
Castle. Daily, Oct-Mar 9.30am-4pm, Sun 2-4pm; Mar-Oct 9.30am-6.30pm, Sun 2-6.30pm.
Pottery. Daily except Sun from Easter-Oct.
Pottery shop. Daily except Sun in Nov, Dec and from Feb-Easter.

REFRESHMENTS:
Inns and a café in the village.

WALK DIRECTIONS

From the castle car park walk along the obvious path to reach the farm road. Go left here to visit the Castle, behind which rises Moel Siabod to the height of 2,860ft. Retrace your steps and continue down to the main road. Turn left and head for Dolwyddelan village. Close to the first houses in the village look to the right to see Bryn y Bedd, the hill of graves, which was the site of the Celtic village's cemetery. Continue along the road into Dolwyddelan.

At the post office turn right down Church Street to reach the church and pottery, to the right, and Pont y Llan over the Afon Lledr.

Pont y Llan is an excellent triple-arched bridge, heavily buttressed upstream. The somewhat indistinct Roman numerals seem to imply a building date of 1808, but it looks older.

To return to the car park, simply reverse the outward route.

HARLECH

WALES

HARLECH
GWYNEDD

Off A496, across Tremadog Bay from Porthmadog

THIS huddle of houses standing in the shadow of a castle, at the sea's edge with a backdrop of craggy hills, is as perfect as a film set. Add a history as wide and interesting as Harlech's and you have the perfect spot for an afternoon.

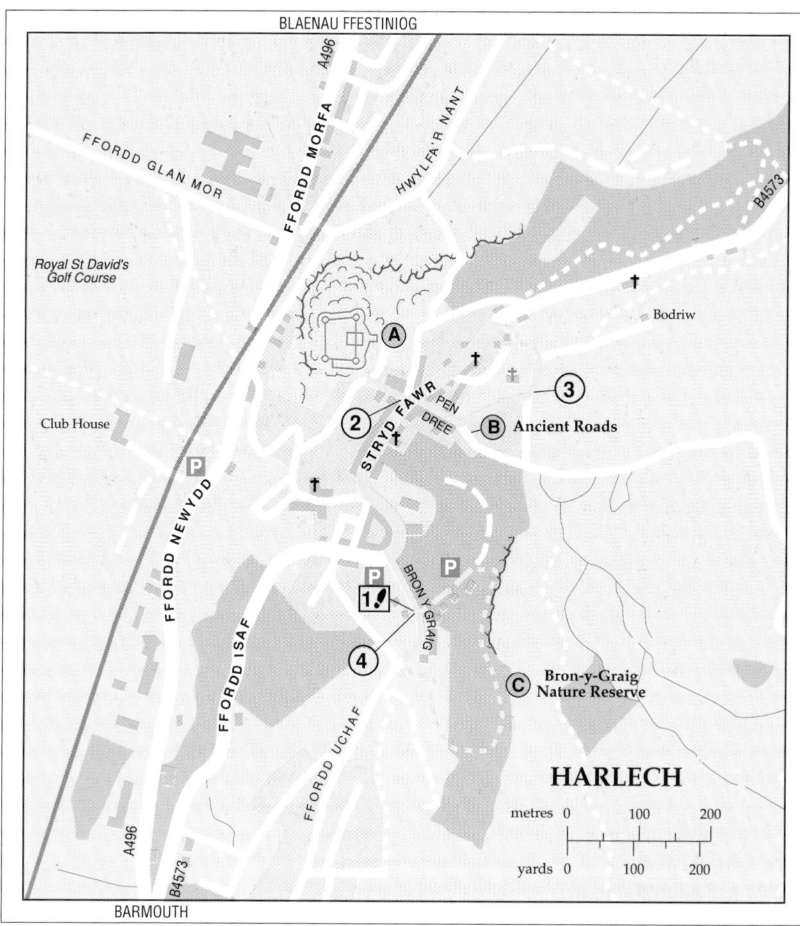

POINTS OF INTEREST

Ⓐ

Harlech Castle. Started in 1283, Harlech Castle has all the advantages of a naturally defensive site plus the useful ability to be supplied from the sea. Visitors to the castle will notice, at the base of the rock, the walls that defended the sea gate. Now, seven centuries later, the advance of the Morfa Harlech dunes has pushed the sea some distance away from the gate. The castle design is simpler than Beaumaris; the outer wall has no defending towers, because the inner castle is taller, and its corner towers were used to defend the outer wall.

Harlech first saw action in the Glyndwr rebellion and then played a part in the Wars of the Roses, when it was held for Lancaster and besieged by the Yorkists under the Earl of Pembroke. Legend says that during this siege the song *Men of Harlech* was first sung. Ultimately the siege succeeded.

Ancient Roads. The road that rises steeply from the Castle is the first section of a Bronze Age route that crossed the low passes at the northern end of the Rhinogs, the rugged hills behind Harlech. The road is still discernible along its length, and at times it is even possible to see the slabs of stone laid to help ancient travellers cross boggy sections. So good was the route that it was used by stagecoaches in the 18th and 19th centuries.

Bron-y-Graig Nature Reserve. The Reserve makes the very best of the local geology, plant and bird life. There are many native British trees, including the fine horse chestnut at the entrance. Fixed on the trees are many nest boxes which have been set up to attract tawny owls, robins, flycatchers (both pied and spotted) and several species of tit. The Reserve's birds also include five species of warbler - willow, wood, garden, chiff-chaff and blackcap - and the goldcrest, britain's smallest bird. A leaflet on the walk is available from the Tourist Information Centre in the main street.

WALK DIRECTIONS

①

From the car park go back down Bron y Graig to Ffordd Isaf and go right along it to the crossroads.

Turn left to reach the castle. Return to the crossroads and go steeply up Pen Dree – which is opposite if you have visited the castle, and to the right if you have not. Take the first turning left and go along to the T-junction next to the chapel (dated 1820). Below is the castle framed against the waters of Tremadog Bay. Beyond are, to the left, the Rivals on the Lleyn Peninsula, then the peaks of Moel Hebog, the high Snowdonia peaks, the Moelwyns and the hills above Blaenau Ffestiniog.

③

Turn left, and where the lane bears right to Bodriw, go left down a stony track. This becomes steeper and finishes down steps on to a road. Be cautious when you step into the road. Turn left to return to Harlech and retrace the route to the car park.

④

At the car park entrance look for the Nature Trail sign on the horse chestnut opposite. This is the start of the trail. Follow the signs around the trail to exit on to a road. Go right and right again at the junction to regain the car park.

Harlech Castle with the sea in the distance.

INFORMATION

Length of walk:
2 miles
Approximate time:
1½ hours, plus time to visit the castle

TERRAIN:
Suitable for children at all times of year. The stepped section will be difficult for pushchairs and wheelchairs but can be avoided.

PARKING:
There are two car parks in Harlech but the directions use the upper park. This is reached by going on up Bron y Craig and then bearing left.

OPEN:
The castle. Daily, all year. Oct-Mar 9.30am-4pm, Sun 2-4pm; Mar-Oct 9.30am-6.30pm, Sun 2-6.30pm. Also April-Sep Sun from 9.30am. Charge.

REFRESHMENTS:
Inns and cafés in the village.

LAUGHARNE

WALES

LAUGHARNE
DYFED

On A4066, reached from the main A40 West Wales road at St Clears

IN a delightful setting where the little River Coran reaches the estuary of the River Taf, Laugharne (Lacharn) will always be associated with Dylan Thomas, who spent his final years in the village and is buried in the churchyard. It is thought by many to be the model for Llaregyb in *Under Milk Wood.*

Brown's Hotel in the centre of the village was Dylan Thomas' favourite pub during his stays. Though it is the Boathouse that is the poet's shrine, he actually spent time in several houses in Laugharne. It was from Sea View that he made one particularly sad departure from the village, being forced to leave after he had sold all the family furniture and still been unable to settle his debts. In happier times he had been visited there by Augustus John. Happier times were also associated with the gazebo of the Georgian mansion in the castle grounds. The house was occupied by the writer Richard Hughes who lent the gazebo to Dylan. There he wrote *Portrait of the Artist as a Young Dog.*

The ancient village of Laugharne still retains several old customs. The head of the Corporation that governs it, the Portreeve, is elected on Big Court Day, the first Monday after St Michael and All Angels, and holds office for six months, the next election being on the Monday after Low Sunday. The Portreeve wears a chain of gold cockleshells, the shellfish having once been the source of wealth in the village. In addition, on the Whit Monday of every third year, the Bounds of the village are beaten on the Common Walk, a 20-mile hike following a specified route and stopping at 24 'hoisting places'. These all have names and anyone on the walk who does not know the name of the place is quickly hoisted upside down and given three strokes of the Constable's cane.

The castle, of which only ruins survive, comprises two 12th-century towers and traces of Sir John Perrot's Tudor mansion conversion.

INFORMATION
Length of walk:
2 miles (4 miles if the headland walk is followed)
Approximate time:
2 hours (3 hours if the headland walk is followed, more if Dylan's Boathouse is visited)

TERRAIN:
Apart from the short-cut track from Dylan's Boathouse to the church the route is suitable for children, pushchairs and wheel-chairs at all times of the year. The short-cut track is passable, but stony, and can be a little muddy and overgrown.

PARKING:
Car parking is easiest in the large area beside the estuary just below the castle, reached from The Grist.

OPEN:
Dylan's Boathouse. Daily, Easter-9 Nov, 10am-6pm. Charge. Laugharne Castle is in the care of *Cadw* and is being prepared for full visitor access. It will be open at standard times, and there will be an admission charge.

REFRESHMENTS:
Selection of inns and cafés in the village.

WALK DIRECTIONS

With The Grist behind you, head to the far left corner of the parking area where a ford gives access to a path beneath the castle. Where this path forks, go up on the left fork to reach Market Lane. Turn right to reach Victoria Street and follow this to the entrance to Laugharne Park caravan site.

From the Park follow the lane, right, to Dylan's Boathouse. To return retrace your steps to the park entrance. Now take the signed footpath that goes up the left side of the Park. The path is obvious, the sign beside the gate marked 'Farm Entrance Keep Clear'. Do not go through this gate. Follow the track, bearing left at one point to where it ends at a T-junction with a tarmac lane.

Go up the steps opposite to reach the church. After visiting Dylan's grave – reached across the footbridge – go out of the churchyard into the church car park and on to Clifton Street. Turn left and follow the street – it soon becomes King Street. Note the superb Great House to the right with its elegant door. Continue to the Town Hall, which once housed the village gaol. Bear right into Wogan Street and follow it to The Grist, where there is an ancient cross.

To extend the walk follow Gosport Street past the Corporation Arms Hotel. Go uphill and round a right-hand bend to reach the last house in Laugharne, to the left. There turn left, signed for Sir John's Hill Farm. Bear right at a junction and walk up the lane towards the farm. There are fine views of the castle from here. Just before the farm is reached, a signed pathway goes off to the right. Walk up along this. The route now bears left around Sir John's Hill (subject of one of Dylan's most powerful poems) and then goes above the estuary to return to the car park. In the estuary are Green Banks where once there was a small quay but where oystercatchers, curlews, sandpipers and ducks now congregate. The beginning and the end of this optional route are shown on the map. It is waymarked along its length.

The Bell House, just below Dylan's Boathouse, contained a bell for summoning the ferry for the crossing to Llanstephan.

POINTS OF INTEREST

Laugharne Castle. There was a castle at Laugharne as early as the 12th century, though of that only a pair of towers remain. It was built by Rhys ap Gruffydd, the last Prince of the area, the Normans taking over the whole of South Wales early in their march west. Rhys received Henry II in the castle, and King Street was named to commemorate the royal visit in 1172. Sadly, Rhys's castle was a victim of the uprising under Llywelyn the Great and was badly damaged in 1215, and again a half-century later. After this second destruction the Normans rebuilt the castle in solid fashion. Later, in Tudor times, the building was completely remodelled by Sir John Perrott, reputedly an illegitimate son of Henry VIII. The present ruinous state is due to bombardment by Cromwellian troops during the Civil War.

The Boathouse where Dylan finally settled. Much of his famous poem Under Milk Wood *was written here.*

St Martin's Church. The yew trees that surround the church are believed to be at least 500 years old. Inside, opposite the south door, is the Oberammergau carving, a superb representation of St Martin of Tours – to whom the church is dedicated – giving his cloak to a beggar. The carving was brought from the German village of Passion Play fame in the late 19th century. Be sure to see the reredos screen behind the altar. The church also has a replica of the plaque to Dylan Thomas in Poet's Corner, Westminster Abbey. Outside, in the new section of the churchyard reached across the footbridge is Dylan's grave.

The Village Cross. In The Grist (the square) there is an ancient cross. The base is thought to be 13th- or 14th-century, but the cross itself is more recent. Until last century Laugharne funerals processed three times round the cross.

DYLAN THOMAS

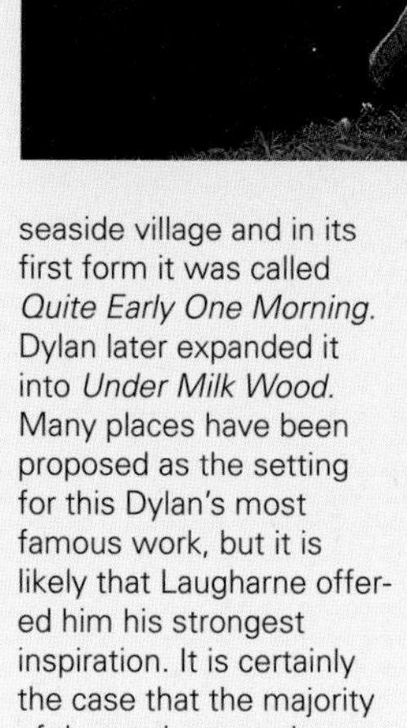

Dylan Thomas was born in Swansea on 27 October 1914, son of the senior English teacher at Swansea Grammar School. As a schoolboy he excelled at English, writing poems in exercise books at all times of the day. Some later scholars have maintained that much of Dylan's work was written before he was 21 and that in later years he only refined his early poetry. After leaving school Dylan worked for a time as a reporter on the local newspaper, but then moved to London where he shared a house with several artistic friends. The poet's first work was published in 1934 and was immediately highly praised. In 1937 he married Catlin McNamara and after spells in London and Oxfordshire they lived in the Boathouse at Laugharne, Dylan writing in what was originally the garage. From 1944 he worked intermittently on a radio script about a Welsh seaside village and in its first form it was called *Quite Early One Morning.* Dylan later expanded it into *Under Milk Wood.* Many places have been proposed as the setting for this Dylan's most famous work, but it is likely that Laugharne offered him his strongest inspiration. It is certainly the case that the majority of the work was written at the Boathouse, a place Dylan referred to as his 'sea-shaken house on a breakneck of rocks'.

Dylan Thomas made four visits to America to give recitals of his work, on the last of which he died, on 9 November 1953, in a New York hospital where he was taken after going into a drink-induced coma. His body was brought back to Laugharne and placed beneath a simple white cross.

The sculptor Jonah Jones used green Welsh slate for the plaque to him in Poet's Corner, Westminster Abbey. The stone is inscribed with two lines from his poem *Fern Hill:*

Time held me green
and dying
Though I sang in my
chains like the sea

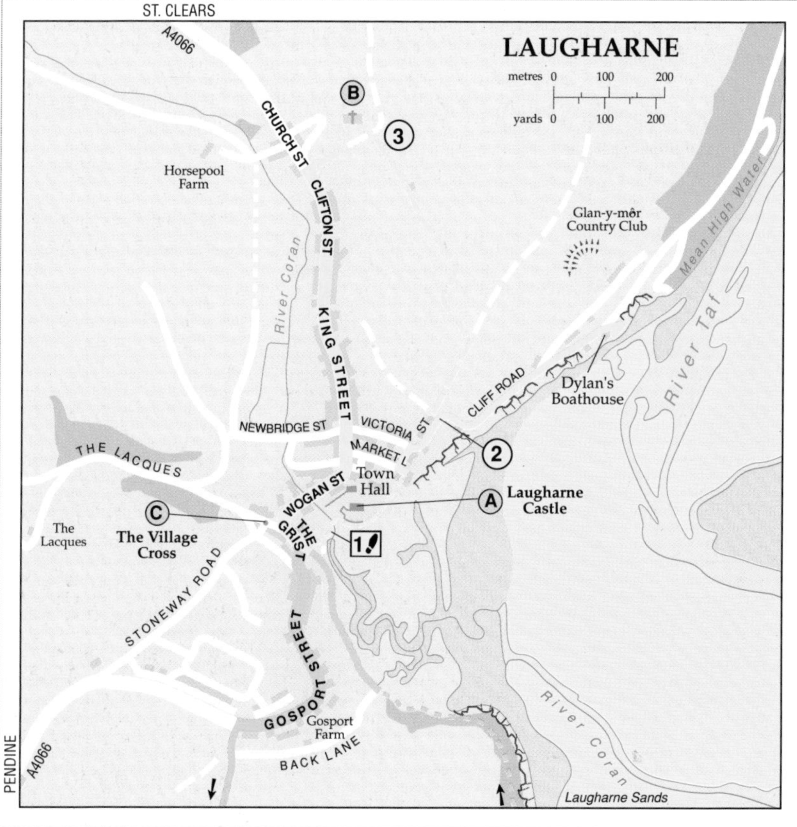

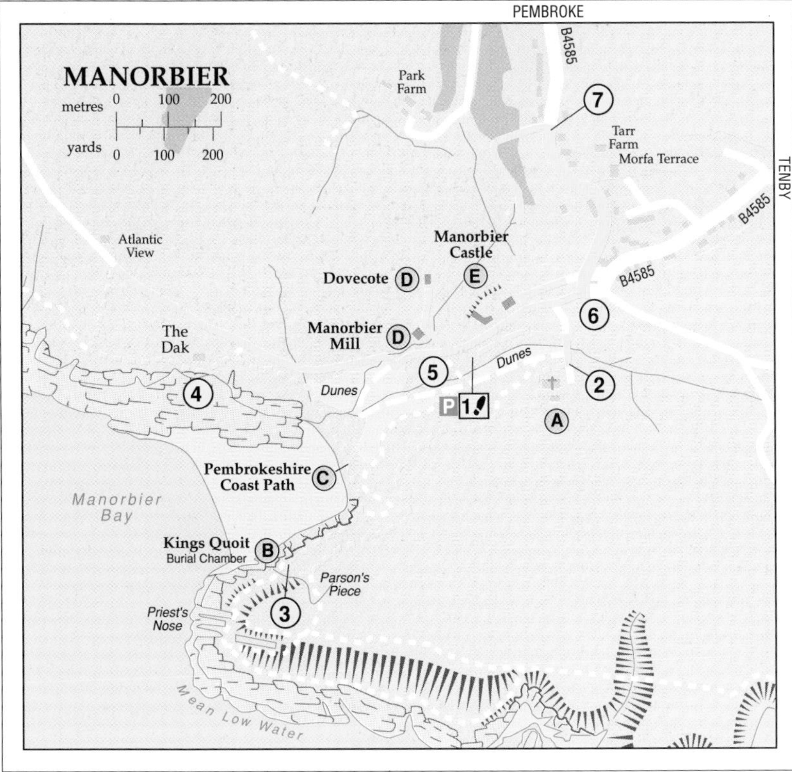

MANORBIER

DYFED

On B4585 that loops off the A4139, 3 miles W of Tenby

THE fascinating little village of Manorbier (Maenorbyr) is arranged on two sides of a tiny valley cut down to the Pembrokeshire Coast. The castle was the birthplace of Gerald of Wales, one of the earliest and most interesting of travellers to the Principality.

POINTS OF INTEREST

St James' Church. Though the earliest part of the church dates from the mid-12th century, and so pre-dates the castle, it is a real mixture of styles and dates. Look especially for the superb 14th-century oak loft, one of the very best pieces of ancient wood carving in the county, and for the effigy of a 14th-century knight. Some have suggested that the knight is a member of the de Barri family whose most famous son was Gerald of Wales. Gerald recalls in his writing how he once hid in the church when Norman Manorbier was attacked by the Welsh.

King's Quoit. About 5,000 years ago the farmers of the Neolithic (New Stone) Age made man's first permanent impression on the landscape with their burial chambers. These were formed from slabs of local stone earthed over to form a long barrow. King's Quoit is such a burial chamber, its name being an interesting link between the Celts of Wales and those of Cornwall, where the chambers are also frequently called quoits. In Wales the 'official' name for such chambers is *cromlech*, a

WALK DIRECTIONS

With your back to the sea, walk to the far right-hand corner of the car park where there is an iron rail stile. Go over and turn right up the lane that rises steeply to the church.

Go into the graveyard next to the church, walk up the left side and then right along the top to a stile. Climb over and keep to the field edge, right, to reach the headland. Now follow the obvious path through the bracken to King's Quoit.

At King's Quoit you join the Pembrokeshire Coast Path, a long-distance footpath. Go right towards Manorbier Bay, down some steps. Follow the beach, or continue on the footpath so as to cross the valley stream by footbridge. Follow the path to The Dak, a house which in summer becomes a café.

Beyond the Dak the path wanders close to a crumbling cliff edge. Please be cautious, especially if you are with children. Thankfully this awkward section is only a few yards long. Just before you reach the next Coast Path stile, take the path that rises to the right, going steeply up through the bracken. At the road turn right, back down to Manorbier Bay. Follow the road to the car park entrance, and there turn left to visit the old mill and dovecote, reached beyond a gate by the waterworks.

(5)

Go back to the road and turn left and up into the village, ignoring a gateway, left, to the castle.

(6)

Bear left on the Pembroke road to pass the main entrance to the castle. Bear left again, staying with the Pembroke road to go out of the village.

(7)

Look for a post box on the left side of the road, just before some houses. Take the signed footpath found beside it. The early narrow path is stony and falls steeply. At the right time of year vegetation is prolific and the smell of wild garlic is overpowering. It is altogether delightful. Turn left at a T-junction along a path that is equally green, but more open. Go over a stile by a gate and take an obvious path over a field to reach an enclosed path beyond a stile. Soon you will need to duck underneath a low-slung hawthorn tree. Walk past an old ruin to reach the main path to the castle.

To return to the start, leave the castle grounds by way of the side entrance on to the village road, close to the car park entrance.

The shore at Manorbier is part of the Pembrokeshire Coast National Park.

Manorbier Castle was converted into a fortress mansion.

name that has now passed into common usage. King's Quoit originally comprised a capstone, 16¾ft long, 8½ft wide and 1¾ft thick, supported on three upright stones, all the stones being of the local sandstone. The capstone weighs around 30 tons. It is interesting just to stand and contemplate the effort required to lift such a stone into position.

Unfortunately one of the uprights has now collapsed, but the burial chamber is still an impressive sight. It is believed that the collapse was a natural event, but since many other cromlechs have been undermined by digging for the treasure that local folklore usually maintains is buried underneath, it is possible that nature was given a hand.

Pembrokeshire Coast Path. The coastline of the old county of Pembrokeshire was designated as Britain's fifth, and smallest, National Park in 1952. Work began almost immediately on creating the footpaths necessary to allow a continuous walk along the coast. In 1970 the route was finally opened, becoming, at the time, Britain's third long distance footpath. The walker on the path can complete a 190 mile trip from St Dogmael's on the old Cardiganshire border to Amroth where Pembrokeshire once met Carmarthenshire.

Manorbier Mill and Dovecote. The ruins of the village's old mill can be seen among the undergrowth. In ancient times the villagers would have had their flour milled here. The mill was water driven, the wheel shaft still being visible even though the wheel has gone. The remnants of millstones can also be seen. Further on is a Norman dovecote, a delightful round structure, small by the standards of the day, but still large enough to meet the needs of the manor's family.

Manorbier Castle. Gerald of Wales, who was born here, described it thus; 'The castle...is excellently well defended by turrets and bulwarks, and is situated on the summit of a hill extending on the western side to the sea-port, having on the northern and southern sides a fine fish-pond under its walls, as conspicuous for its grand appearance as for the depth of its waters, and a beautiful orchard on the same side, enclosed on one part by a vineyard and on the other by a wood, remarkable for the projection of its rocks and the height of its hazel trees'. Gerald goes on to tell of 'a rivulet of never-failing water' of the surrounding country 'well supplied with corn, sea fish...and what is preferable to every other advantage'. He was clearly in love with both castle and village. His account ends 'It is evident, therefore, that Maenorr Pirr' (the ancient name) 'is the pleasantest spot in Wales'.

The lordship of Manorbier was granted to the de Barri family by Earl Roger de Montgomery after the conquest of this part of Wales. One of the descendants of the first holder of the lordship, William de Barri, married Angharad, a daughter of Nesta, Helen of Wales. Gerald of Wales, named for his grandfather, was the fourth son of that marriage. The Castle was started in the early 12th century, work continuing for several centuries. By the time the de Barri line had died out and the Castle had passed to the Crown, it had been converted into a mansion, this area of Wales having long been subdued. Today the Castle, which is in private hands, is a superb example of Norman fortress mansion architecture.

GERALD OF WALES

Gerald de Barri was born at Manorbier in about 1145. He became a churchman having been made Archdeacon of Brecon when he accompanied Archbishop Baldwin through Wales in 1188 in an effort to drum up support for the Third Crusade. After this trip Gerald wrote *The Journey through Wales*, the most famous of his books. Three quarters Norman and one quarter Welsh, Gerald – known as Geraldus Cambrensis, in his day, the Latin translating as Gerald of Wales – was intent upon becoming Bishop of St Davids, dreaming of a Welsh church independant of Canterbury. Sadly he was seen as too difficult and too dynamic and he eventually died in obscurity in 1223, possibly in Lincoln, far from his beloved Wales. Nevertheless he has achieved lasting fame with his travelogues which are not only a mine of information but excellently written.

INFORMATION
Length of walk:
3 miles
Approximate time:
2 hours

TERRAIN:
Suitable for children at all times of year, but not suitable for push-chairs or wheelchairs. Three stiles, steps and one footbridge.

PARKING:
There is a National Trust car park below Manorbier castle. The toilet block here is built around the remains of the village miller's house.

OPEN:
The castle. Daily Easter-Sep. 11am-6pm. Charge.

REFRESHMENTS:
Village inn and The Dak (summer only).

NEW RADNOR

WALES

NEW RADNOR

POWYS

On B4372, 7 miles NW of Kington

NEW Radnor (Maesyfed) was laid out on the grid system that was standard for villages that grew up around castles on new sites. The Elizabethan traveller, John Leland, wrote in the early 16th century that it was `metely well walled... There is an old church standing now as a chapel by the castle... The building of the town is in some part metely good, in most part but rude, many houses being thatched. The castle is in ruin... The Town was defaced in Henry IV days by Owain Glyndwr.'

Unfortunately for New Radnor it did not gain from the creation of the Welsh Counties, and as other county towns grew in importance and size, it fell into a partial decline from which it has never really recovered. As a result, time has virtually stood still in the village for several centuries, leaving a pattern of houses little changed from medieval times.

POINTS OF INTEREST

Ⓐ

New Radnor Castle. The village of Old Radnor, set on its rocky ridge, has an ancient history, though when the Normans came they built their castle to the west, at New Radnor. This new site was the first village on *The Journey through Wales* of Gerald of Wales and Archbishop Baldwin. The finest castle here was built in the 13th century on the site of the first Norman castle. This newer castle was the one devastated by Owain Glyndwr.

The earliest Norman castle was almost certainly of motte-and-bailey type, constructed of earth and timber. Later, as time allowed and techniques improved, stone was used to produce outer defences. The original motte remained but was topped by a new stone keep.

The ridge on which the castle was built was known, in Welsh, as Crug Eryr, the rock of the eagle. In complete contrast to this delightful description is one of the castle and town that predates that of Leland quoted earlier. It noted that much of the once-beautiful town had `...fallen down, decayed and at times remain unre-edified, lying as desolate and void grounds, and many of them adjoining nigh unto the high streets, replenished with much other filth and uncleanness, with pits, cellars, and vaults lying open and uncovered...'

OWAIN GLYNDWR AND THE MARCHER LORDS

When the Normans invaded England, they quickly moved westward to reach the border that separated old Saxon England and Celtic Wales. There the Normans stopped, reluctant at that stage to invade and fight in another hostile country. The Norman kings needed to secure the border as the Welsh made frequent raids over it – an irritation that could not be tolerated. Their solution was to create the Marcher lords, the March being the border between the two peoples. A Marcher lord's land was defined on its eastern (English) border, but undefined to the west. That way he was allowed to take anything he felt he could hold. As most of the lords were men of high ambition, there were constant disputes and fights.

Owain Glyndwr was different from many Welsh princes. He was literate and sophisticated, had been raised in the English court and fought for the king. He was also middle-aged. Owain's Marcher neighbour, Lord Grey, wanted the Welshman's land. Given the job of asking Owain to attend court he failed to pass the message on, told the King Owain was defying him and used this excuse to invade Owain's estate in September 1400. Owain's followers persuaded him to take the title Prince of Wales and a long and bloody rebellion began.

Owain's men fought as guerillas, using the cover of the Welsh hills and weather to avoid pitched battles. Early in 1401 Owain's men stormed and sacked many of the villages that had grown up around Marcher castles. One that was devastated and burned was New Radnor.

The great octagonal memorial to Sir George Cornewall Lewis.

WALK DIRECTIONS

Walk east along High Street, passing Broad Street to the right to reach Mutton Dingle Lane, to the left. The signed path to the left here is a short cut, skirting the bottom of the old castle mound to reach the church. Go up Mutton Dingle Lane to reach a rickety gate on the left with a yellow arrow marker.

For an optional excursion walk a little further on to reach a marked bridleway to the right. Follow this around Knowle Hill on to the flank of the Radnor Forest. The bridleway leads to Jack's Green Farm, its latter part running between a Forestry Commission plantation to the left and Knowle Hill to the right. Buried among the trees to the left is a small pond. Unfortunately the only reasonable way to return is along the outward route to reach the rickety gate.

Go through the gate and go right and up – not down and left on the obvious path – on a path that reaches the outer ramparts of the old castle. When the first rampart is reached, go half left to reach the castle mound, from the top of which there is a marvellous view over the village. The line of the old town wall can be seen on the right side of the village. It lies below the raised hedge that leaves the B4372 to the right of the church and goes through a right angle leftward to aim for, but not reach, the main village street near the Cornewall Lewis monument.

From the mound the short-cut footpath can be seen (down and left) while a gate to the church can be seen down and right. Go down to the church gate but please take care, the mound is steep and, in wet weather, very slippery. If in doubt retreat to easier ground to reach the gate. From the church follow the main path to reach High Street.

Cross to reach Rectory Lane and follow this to a T-junction with Broad Street. Turn right to the Cornewall Lewis monument.

From the monument turn sharp left up Water Street, named for the delightful stream that runs down it to the right. The houses on that side are reached over tiny clapper bridges. Bear left with the road to reach Broad Street and go right there back to High Street.

The Eagle Hotel stands on the site of the old prison.

WALES

St Mary's Church. Though built in Gothic style, the church actually dates from 1843. At that time an earlier, late medieval church was completely demolished. This vandalism was referred to by no less an authority than Sir Nicholas Pevsner as 'an extreme case of unsuitable rebuilding'. Pevsner believed that the new church had no redeeming features, expressing enthusiasm only for the two well-worn effigies that were certainly retained from the original building. These effigies – one of a knight, the other of a woman – are believed to be from the 12th or 13th centuries.

Gerald recounts a local anecdote about the castellan, or captain, of the New Radnor castle in the time of Henry I. The captain spent a night in the local church, (probably not the village church) together with his dogs, and for this irreverence his dogs were driven mad and he was struck blind.

Another local tale is of a king from a much later period. Charles I stayed locally on the night of 6 August 1645 and was poorly fed at an inn called The Bush. Even the miserly ration of cheese he was offered was taken from him before he had eaten properly. The King, not amused, noted that the place should really be called Beggar's Bush, and so it still is, the name having been transferred to a small hamlet a few miles north-east of New Radnor.

The Cornewall Lewis Monument. The 77ft monument at the bottom of Water Street is to Sir George Cornewall Lewis, a mid-Victorian Chancellor of the Exchequer. It was erected in 1864 in what is termed the 'florid' style!

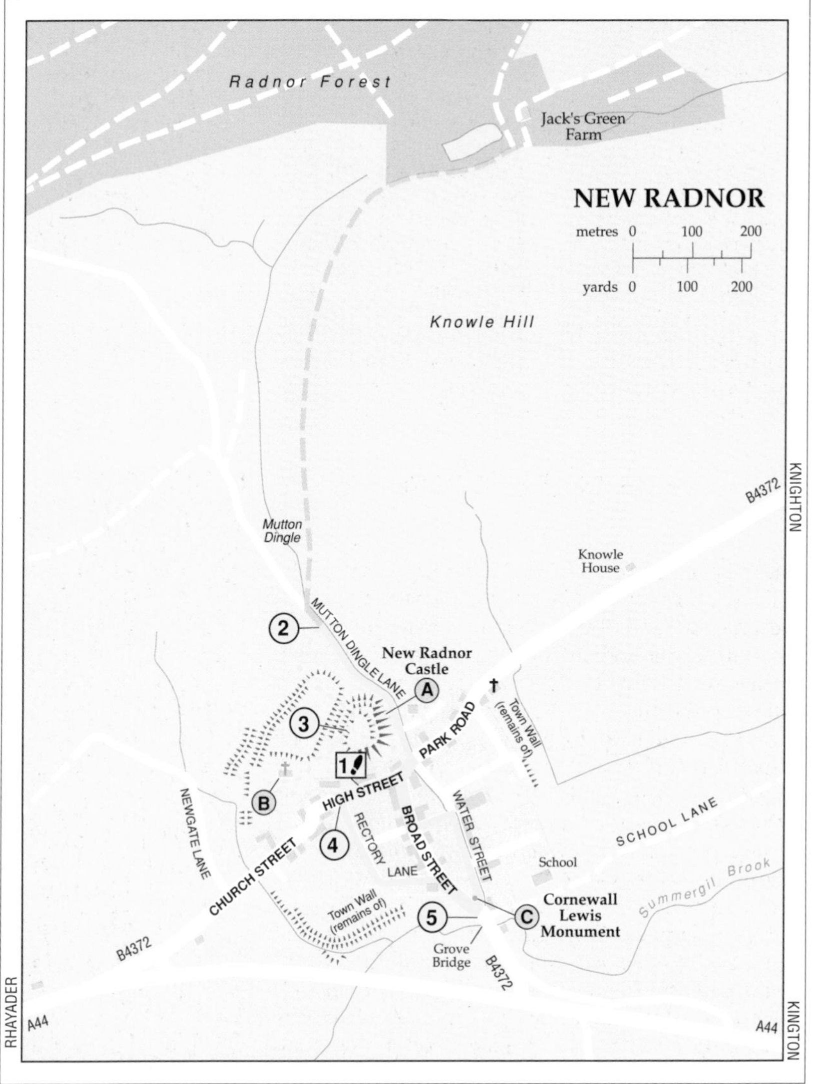

Looking down on New Radnor with the Victorian St Mary's church to the left.

INFORMATION
Length of walk: $2^1/_2$ miles
Approximate time: 2 hours

TERRAIN:
The old castle section is not suitable for pushchairs or wheelchairs and has one very steep descent that could be a hazard to children.

PARKING:
There is no car park in New Radnor, but parking within the village is relatively easy. In the directions below it is assumed the visitor is starting in the High Street, outside the post office.

REFRESHMENTS:
Village Inns.

MADOCKS' COB

William Madocks was an entrepreneur who saw the advantages of a port on the River Glaslyn's estuary. He therefore reclaimed 7,000 acres of land in the estuary by building the Cob, a huge embankment across the river's mouth. He then built Portmadoc as the port for the Blaenau Ffestiniog quarries, naming it after himself, and his new village of Tremadoc, under what were once sea cliffs, and are now marooned inland. Some years ago, anxious that the town should not bear the name of an Englishman, the council of Portmadoc changed the name to Porthmadog, effectively naming it after Madog, a legendary Welsh giant said to have discovered America. The change was hardly necessary: William Madocks was born in Llandwrnod in what was then Denbighshire.

A statue of Atlas supporting the world, in Portmeirion.

Portmeirion village with its unusual architecture.

PORTMEIRION

GWYNEDD

1M S of A487, 1M W of Penrhyndeudraeth

NOTHING can prepare the first-time visitor for the shock of discovering Portmeirion. Set in the Snowdonia National Park, an area of mountains, slate quarries and typically Welsh scenery, an ornate Italian village suddenly appears among the trees.

POINTS OF INTEREST

The Village of Portmeirion. In the last years of the 19th century two landscape gardeners, Mr J Westmacott and Sir William Fothergill Cook, introduced rhododendron and other Himalayan shrubs to Y Gwyllt, cleared land and generally tidied up the area – as they saw it. It was they who demolished Gruffydd's castle – because they feared it would attract visitors to their land! When Sir Clough Williams-Ellis bought the land in the 1920s it comprised a landscaped wilderness, an old fishing port, and a few buildings. With these he started to create one of the finest follies in Britain. The name is an amalgamation of Portofino, an Italian village he had fallen in love with at first sight, and *Meirionydd*, the Welsh name for the old country of Merionethshire in which the land stood.

Concerned that he might not live to see his work completed (as it turned out he lived to the great age of 92) Sir Clough built quickly rather than permanently. His designs transformed into buildings almost overnight, at times by the use of wood, wattle and daub and other fast techniques. As an example, the dome of the Pantheon was built of green painted plywood. Much of his earliest building work has now been consolidated.

Sir Clough also rescued parts of other doomed buildings for incorporation into Portmeirion. One of the best examples is his incorporation of the vaulted plaster ceiling and wall panelling from the 16th-century Emral Hall in Clwyd into Portmeirion's Town Hall.

For many, a visit to Portmeirion will bring back memories of Patrick McGoohan's cult TV series *The Prisoner*. The house of Number Six has been taken over by an appreciation group who have filled it with mementoes of the programme.

Castell Deudraeth. Before William Madocks reclaimed the land that lies north of the Porthmadog Cob (see box above) the tongue of land on which Portmeirion sits poked its way far out into Cardigan Bay. Its thickly forested end was called *Y Gwyllt*, the wilderness. In this wilderness,

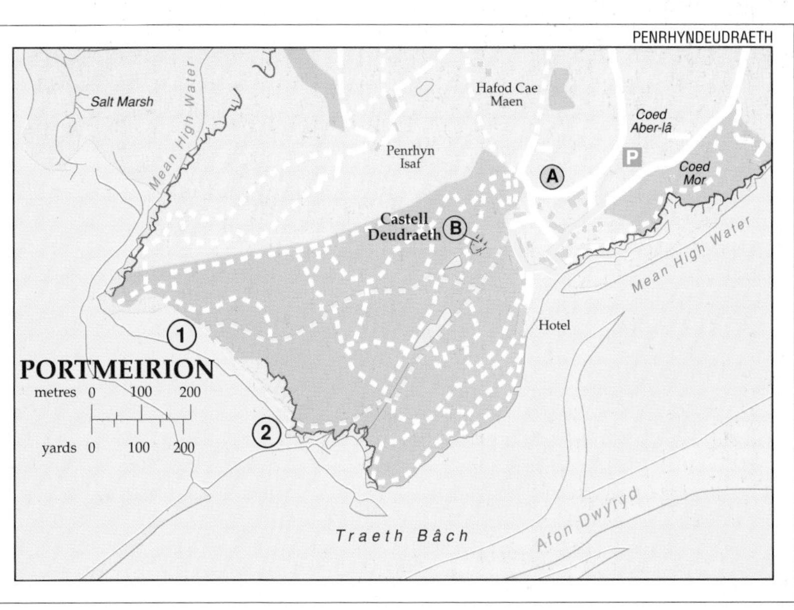

according to Gerald of Wales, the 12th-century traveller born in Manorbier, Gruffydd ap Cynon, Prince of Gwynedd, built a castle. Gerald was writing in 1186 and it is now thought likely that the first castle, of which only a few stones survive on the outcrop just to the west of Portmeirion, was built around 1130. Visitors to the site pass another Castell Deudraeth; although a Victorian sham it is a fine work.

The last of Gruffydd's castle was pulled down in the mid-nineteenth century; an act of genuine vandalism. Some years before the destruction there lived in the village of Iber Ia (where Portmeirion now stands) a big man from the south of Wales whose name has come down only as Yr Hwntw Mawr – the Big South Walian! The man was helping to build Madocks' Cob. One day he robbed the farm of Penrhyn Isaf, killing a girl who surprised him. Pursued to Aber Ia, he tried to escape by crossing the sands of the Dwyryd estuary towards Harlech. The locals cut off his exit routes and the exhausted man was caught. He was tried, convicted and publicly hanged in Dolgellau.

SIR CLOUGH WILLIAMS-ELLIS

The architect of Portmeirion was born in 1883 and had a most distinguished career. In the first third of this century he wrote a book, *England and the Octopus*, that called for the owners of country houses who were unable to afford their upkeep to use the land for the benefit of the whole community. At the time it was a revolutionary concept, only the recent Green movement suggesting that Williams-Ellis was, indeed, ahead of his time. As an architect he is perhaps best known for his transformation of Castell Coch, north of Cardiff, and for his work on the New Towns that grew up after the Second World War, Stevenage in particular. For his services to architecture and the environment Clough Williams-Ellis was knighted in 1971. He died in 1978 having lived long enough to see the 50th anniversary of the 'birth' of Portmeirion.

He fulfilled his wish to create a seaside resort free from advertisements and careless building. He combed more than two-dozen possible sites scattered between the Hebrides and Scillies, and had almost abandoned hope when, in 1925, the craggy, little peninsula became available.

INFORMATION

Length of walk:
Almost any length from about ½ mile to 20 miles!
Approximate time:
At least ½ day.

TERRAIN:
Within the village and for most of the forest walks the walking is excellent and is suitable for children, pushchairs and wheelchairs. Some of the less-frequented paths, and some paths in very wet weather, are not easy. There are also sections of stepped path.

PARKING:
From Minffordd on the A487 a road takes the visitor directly to the car park for Portmeirion.

OPEN:
Daily throughout the year. Charge.
Guests at Portmeirion's hotel can enjoy the village before and after the day-visitors have left.

REFRESHMENTS:
Cafés and restaurants in the village.

WALK DIRECTIONS

From the car park the village is reached straightforwardly. No directions are needed for an exploration, the visitor being left to explore at will.

The estate grounds have two marked paths, both starting from the Triumphal Arch found close to the top, northern, end of the village. The shorter walk, taking about 15 minutes, threads its way through the best of the estate's azaleas and rhododendrons. The longer walk is signed for the beach and takes a marked path behind the restaurant. After about 100yds go right on a marked path to the viewpoint at the northern end of the village's beach. From the end of the walk the beach itself is reached. Go left and walk along the beach towards the village to reach, after about 300yds, steps to the left. Take these and follow the marked path back to the start point.

Please note that the beach connection between (1) and (2) cannot be followed at all tides, and that it involves steps on to the beach itself.

The whole village is set in 175 acres of sub-tropical grounds with coastal cliffs and wooded gardens.

THE FFESTINIOG RAILWAY

What is perhaps the best of the Great Little Trains of Wales runs over Madocks' Cob from Porthmadog, passing Minffordd and Penrhynddeudraeth before going on to Blaenau Ffestiniog. The narrow-gauge line was originally built in 1836 to carry slates from the Blaenau quarries to the Porthmadog docks for shipment and only had steam trains – as opposed to horse drawn trucks – many years after it began. The line closed in 1946, but today the line is operated by enthusiasts who carry out all necessary repair and maintenance work from the Boston Lodge building on the end of the Cob.

TALLEY

WALES

TALLEY
DYFED

Off B4302, 7 miles N of Llandeilo

THE tiny village of Talley (Talyllychau) huddles close to ruins of an old monastery set beside lakes in a fine open valley. In the churchyard is the reputed grave of Dafydd ap Gwilym, greatest of Celtic poets.

INFORMATION
Length of walk:
3/4 mile
Approximate time:
1 hour (plus time in the Abbey ruins)

TERRAIN:
Suitable for children at all times of year. The kissing-gate will cause problems for push-chairs and wheelchairs.

PARKING:
Parking is difficult in Talley, though it can be accomplished with luck. If you are a patron you might, perhaps, use the Inn car park.

OPEN:
The Abbey ruins. Daily. Charge.

REFRESHMENTS:
One inn.

The scant remains of Talley Abbey.

WALK DIRECTIONS

The walk begins at the Abbey. Go through the gate beside the Abbey into the churchyard. The memorial stone to Dafydd ap Gwilym can be found on the far side of the church, beside the path; the only one facing the church rather than facing the lakes. Walk beside the wall between the chapel and Abbey to a gate to a path beside the lake. At the end of this a fine rotating kissing-gate gives access to a path on to the road.

Turn right, passing the Inn to reach a crossroads.

③

Turn right and follow the road back to the Abbey, bearing right where a road joins from the left.

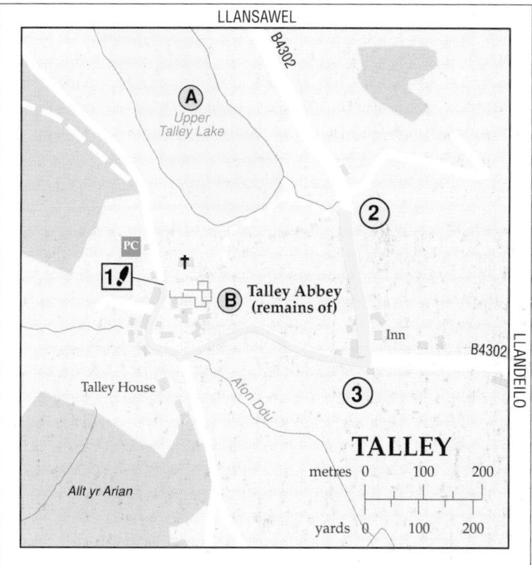

PHYSICIANS OF MYDDFAI

East of Talley rises Mynydd Ddu, the Black Mountain, below which lies Llyn y Fan Fach, famous as the watery home of the Lady of the Lake.

An old folk story tells of a woman who emerged from the lake to marry a local man, retreating to the lake when he struck her three times, but returning from time to time to teach her sons the secrets of herbal medicine. The sons grew up to become the first Physicians of Myddfai.

Myddfai is a small village near Llandovery and did indeed produce a quite remarkable line of medieval doctors. Legend has it that many of them were taught here at Talley Abbey.

Many of their medieval remedies sound a great deal worse than the diseases they were said to cure. For example; *'To extract a tooth painlessly make a powder from newts and "those nasty beetles which are found in ferns during summer" and rub it on the tooth.' 'To see things invisible to others rub a paste of cat's gall and hen's fat on your eyes.'*

DAFYDD AP GWILYM

The greatest of all medieval Welsh poets was born at Penrhyncoch near Aberystwyth. Dafydd was both a humourist and a ladies' man, and has several reputed burial sites in mid-Wales, most famously here at Talley and at the Abbey of Strata Florida. Many say that this was due to his having had a sweetheart in most villages in the area, all of whom claimed to have been the dearest in his life so that he chose their village as his burial site! Dafydd is best remembered for his poems and prose – poems on love and humorous themes.

POINTS OF INTEREST

The Talley Lakes. The two lakes are of glacial formation. The valley was dammed by moraines brought down by an Ice Age glacier, the lakes filling the valley behind the dam. Between the two lakes the natural hummock of morainic land was reinforced to form a motte and bailey castle in early Norman times. The name Talley is a corruption of the Welsh *Talyllychau*, the head of the lakes. The lakes themselves are popular with birdwatchers, being home to, amongst other species, great crested grebes.

Talley Abbey. The abbey was founded in 1120 by Rhys ap Gruffydd, Lord Rhys of Dinefwr, for the Premonstratensian Order. This order of White Canons was formed at Prémontré in France as an offshoot of the Cistercians. There were several White Canon abbeys in England, but Talley was the only Welsh house. Lord Rhys also founded the abbeys of Whitland and Strata Florida. Though Whitland was Cistercian, there was great rivalry between it and Talley. Talley claimed that Whitland had stolen some of its land, and canons journeyed to Canterbury to obtain a ruling from the Archbishop. When the Whitland monks ignored this, the Canons travelled to Rome, though still to no effect.

It is said that when Henry Tudor landed at Aberporth on a visit that preceded his 'invasion' of 1485, he was brought here to talk with the Abbot and the Lord of Dinefwr, another Rhys. Legend has it he stayed in the house in the village still known as King's Court. What he heard at Talley persuaded Henry to fight Richard III and when he returned to do so Rhys fought bravely at Bosworth Field, receiving a Knighthood for his services. In gratitude to the Welsh who had helped him reach Talley, the new Henry VII granted money for the building of a church tower in every parish from Aberporth to Talley. These were all built in 1485 with the exception of Talley, where the locals used the Abbey church and had no need of a tower. Instead they were granted £6 per year 'for ever'. This money was paid until early this century, when the Welsh church was dis-established.

After the Dissolution, when there were only eight canons at the Abbey, the building fell into disrepair. The church became ruinous and a new one with, unusually, two doors and box pews inside, was built for the village in 1773.

TRETOWER

WALES

TRETOWER
POWYS

On A479 Crickhowell-Talgarth Road

THE tiny village of Tretower (Tretwr) is hemmed in by the Black Mountains to the east and wooded Myarth to the west. Here, where the Rhiangoll stream meets the Usk Valley, the Normans built a defensive castle, beside which stands one of the finest manorial houses in Wales.

The interior of Tretower Court, a 14th-century, fortified manor.

POINTS OF INTEREST

Ⓐ

Tretower Castle. In the late 11th century the Norman advance into Wales had stopped, the newly created Marcher lordships (see New Radnor, page 231-232) holding the boundary between the Masters of England and their unruly neighbours. Recognising the importance of the Usk Valley the Normans sought to protect it from flanking attacks by sealing the Rhiangoll Valley and, therefore, the pass over the Black Mountains. To do this they established a castle at Tretower.

The earliest building was a motte-and-bailey (see also New Radnor) the motte being reinforced in the early 12th century by a square shell keep built of stone. This castle was then attacked and captured by the Welsh, possibly by Llywelyn the Great himself, during one of the numerous border wars of the time. When the Normans regained control, instead of repairing the damaged keep they built a huge, solid, three-storey round tower among its ruins, a unique solution to a well-known problem. The central tower is almost all that remains today, though sections of the original domestic buildings, including the kitchen, are grouped around it.

Ⓑ

Tretower Court. When a few centuries had passed and the area was less prone to insurrection, the Norman lords decided to build a more luxurious mansion. Looking at the Court it is easy to imagine the joy that the lady of the manor must have felt when she moved out of the cramped and miserable castle into this new, light and airy building.

The Normans, unlike the Welsh, tried to dissociate their living and defensive buildings, and the Court is clearly not a fortress, though the gatehouse would have made all but a small army despondent. Inside, the court has a central courtyard, the two storeyed building around it being galleried. Of all the rooms, none of which are furnished, the Great Hall captures the imagination with its space and superb roof timbers. Overall, Tretower Court is one of the most elegant buildings in Wales.

INFORMATION
Length of walk: 2 miles
Approximate time: 1 hour

TERRAIN:
The track on to the Black Mountains is steep and stony to start with, and overgrown with bracken in summer. Children will have no difficulties, but those with pushchairs and wheelchairs will have problems.

PARKING:
Parking in Tretower is a problem for which there is no easy solution, the Court and Castle having no car park and parking on the main road being inadvisable. However, near the church, and near the Court, it is usually possible to park without causing a nuisance.

OPEN:
Tretower Court and Castle. In the care of Cadw. Daily all year. Oct-Mar 9.30am-4pm (Sun 2-4pm), Mar-Oct 9.30am-6.30pm (Sun 2-6.30pm). Charge

REFRESHMENTS:
Village inns and cafés.

WALK DIRECTIONS

①

From the church go back to the main road. Cross and take the track between Pen Isaf Pentre and Lilac Cottage. The way is stony and rises quite steeply to a T-junction of tracks.

②

Go right – there is a yellow arrow, but one points along the left route too! – and follow the bracken-shrouded lane to a gate. Pass through on to a farm road and go right along it. There are superb views of the village from here, and of the flank of the Black Mountains.

③

At a T-junction go right and downhill to the main road.

④

Turn right, back into the village and turn down left to reach the Court and Castle. After a visit turn back towards the church, turning left in front of it and going along the road to Zoar Chapel on the right.

⑤

Turn right and follow the lane to the main road. Go right and return back into the village to finish the walk.

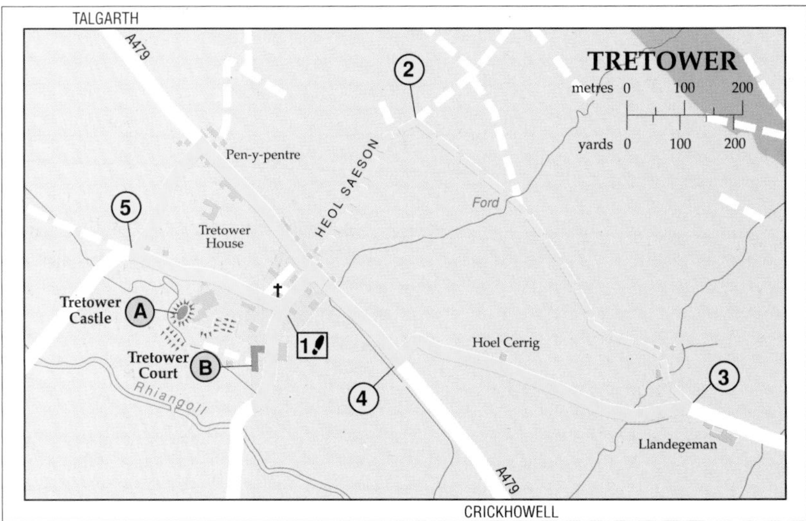

SCOTLAND

•

CULROSS, SCOTLAND

•

Oh, Scotia! My dear, my native soil!
For whom my warmest wish to Heaven is sent!
Long may thy hardy sons of rustic toil
Be blest with health, and peace, and sweet content!
ROBERT BURNS

•

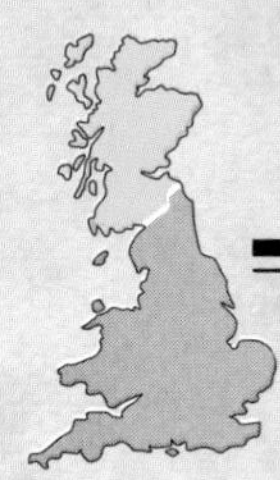

SCOTLAND

Widespread and common in lowland Scotland, the spear thistle can be found along hedges and in rough fields. A popular flower with butterflies.

One of the great delights of Scotland is the variety of scenery and architecture which can be found within a relatively small compass, and the 15 villages presented here fully reflect that variety. They all have associations with Scotland's dramatic and often turbulent history, and two themes that run through them are the status of the burgh and the close link with a noble family and its seat.

The establishment of burghs dates back to the time of King David I (1124-1153), a period when trading and commerce developed rapidly in Scotland. Burghs, originally strongholds, became places of commerce and trade, recognised by the granting of charters which brought the right to hold regular markets and to trade with other burghs. The title of `Royal Burgh' brought additional privileges, including that of being able to export produce overseas. In all cases the burgh had to pay taxes to the Crown, but the status of burgh was eagerly sought.

The development of many of these trading burghs, such as Culross with coal and Portsoy with marble, was linked to a local family (the Bruces and the Ogilvies respectively). Falkland is a Royal Burgh because the king had his summer palace, to which he repaired for sport and recreation, built there in the shadow of the Fife hills. A much more recent royal association comes with Braemar, site of an 11th-century stronghold but brought to the wider public's notice largely through the acquisition by Queen Victoria and Prince Albert of Balmoral, a few miles down the Dee Valley.

Communities such as Blair Atholl and Glamis have long lived in the benevolent shadow of the 'great house' nearby – Blair Castle is the seat of the Dukes of Atholl, chiefs of the Clan Murray, and at Glamis Castle, still the family home of the Earls of Strathmore and Kinghorne, Queen Elizabeth the Queen Mother spent a very happy childhood. The village of Fochabers was moved bodily by the Duke of Gordon in the late 18th century from outside the walls of Gordon Castle to a new site a mile away, where it was replanned on a rectangular grid pattern.

David I also established many religious foundations, and there are links with those times in many villages, perhaps most notably at New Abbey, where the magnificent remains of Sweetheart Abbey still dominate the village.

Scotland is a mountainous country, and trading routes have always held great importance. Many settlements grew up on crossing-places or staging-points on these routes, as at Aberfoyle, Braemar, Fort Augustus, Taynuilt and West Linton. The fort named after Augustus, Duke of Cumberland, was one of those hastily put up by the British government in the 18th century to try to quell the Jacobite Risings which came so near to restoring the Stuarts to the throne. An earlier restoration, of Charles II after the period of the Commonwealth, is marked at Coldstream, from where General Monk's army – later to become known as the Coldstream Guards – marched on London.

Architecturally, local stone has always been important, and the vernacular buildings display a pleasing sympathy with the landscape and a number of individual characteristics including crow-stepped gables and, in Fife, the distinctive red pantiled roofs imported from Holland. The great houses such as Falkland, Blair and Glamis are fit to compare with any in Europe in terms of architecture, decoration and interior furnishings.

Above all, the villages of Scotland must be seen as part of the landscape of the country. In this small selection (and how difficult it has been to choose just 15!) there are magnificent coastal scenes at Portsoy and St Abbs; superb mountain backdrops at Blair Atholl, Braemar, Fort Augustus and Taynuilt; lesser but still fine hills at Aberfoyle, Falkland, New Abbey and West Linton.

Islands have a special magic and fascination and Arran is one of the finest of all. Not for nothing is it called `Scotland in Miniature'; few people go there once. Lamlash is included here as much for its wonderful situation as for any other reason. It summarises so much of what Scotland has to offer. The religious association comes with Holy Island in Lamlash Bay and the 'great house', Brodick Castle, is just a few miles up the road.

All these villages repay time spent exploring them. Pointers are given to some of the main points of interest, but the visitor blessed with curiosity can always find out more. Some fall naturally into pairs – Culross and Falkland make a superb day, for instance, as do Fochabers and Portsoy, Coldstream and St Abbs. It is our hope that the 15 villages in this section will both prove enjoyable in their own right and will act as a spur to further exploration of Scotland, a joyous task that never ends.

A corner of Main Street, Aberfoyle, showing an interesting mix of roof profiles. The road to David Marshall Lodge goes up to the left. The walk starts and finishes near this point.

INFORMATION
Length of walk: $2\frac{1}{2}$ miles
Approximate time: 2 hours

TERRAIN:
Mainly paths and forest tracks, with slopes and steps which make the walk unsuitable for pushchairs and wheelchairs. Both are catered for, however, in short walks from the David Marshall Lodge.

PARKING:
Park in the large free car park off Main Street.

OPEN:
David Marshall Lodge (Queen Elizabeth Forest Park Visitor Centre). Easter-mid-Oct. Daily, 10am-6pm. A Scottish Wool Centre is due to open in the village in 1991.

REFRESHMENTS:
A wide selection of hotels, pubs and cafés in the village. Café at the David Marshall Lodge.

SCOTLAND

ABERFOYLE

CENTRAL

On A821, 10 miles W of Callander

LIKE many other Scottish settlements, Aberfoyle grew from a number of separate `townships', and here as elsewhere you will find placenames such as Milton (where the mill turned) and Kirkton (where the church stood). Aberfoyle's mill was on the Avondhu, the black stream, which joins with the Duchray Water a little west of the village to form the infant River Forth, and the village was also important as a crossing-point on the river.

The former industries of iron-working and slate quarrying have been replaced by forestry and tourism, the latter dating from 1810, when Sir Walter Scott set his epic poem *The Lady of the Lake* in this area and started a rush of visitors which continues to this day. Aberfoyle also has the distinction of sitting on the Highland Fault, a geological boundary which runs across Scotland from the Clyde to the North Sea.

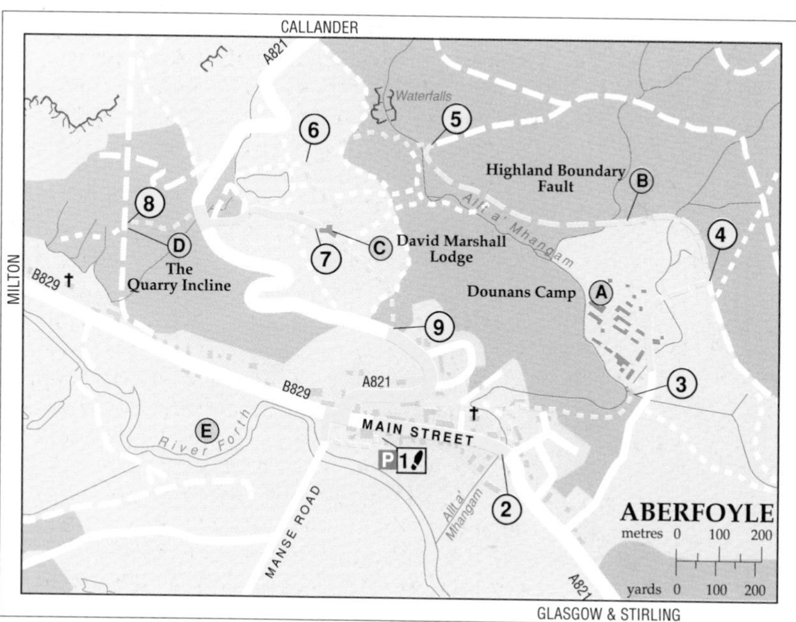

WALK DIRECTIONS

1

From the car park, with its superb view westwards to Ben Lomond, turn right (east) along Main Street, passing on the right the neat, small fire station, and on the left an interesting terrace of houses with mock half-timbered gables – a rather odd feature for a Scottish village.

In 200yds a track on the left leads up to the plain Episcopal Church of St Mary's, half-hidden in trees. It replaced the much older church at Kirkton across the River Forth.

2

Cross the Allt a'Mhangam burn and immediately turn left up a short road. Past the last house (Kincraig) look for a small path on the right going uphill. Continue past a road-end and follow this very pleasant path as it winds round with the burn below to your left.

3

Cross a footbridge over a ditch to enter the grounds of Dounans. Walk ahead over grass for a short distance to join a road and turn left. Follow the road through the camp buildings. It becomes a track, passes to the right of a canoeing pond, and swings right to cross a wooden barrier. Just after the barrier, turn left up a path for 70yds.

4

At the wide forest track, turn left. The hill of Craigmore is prominent ahead. Pass the Highland Boundary Fault notice and carry on. At the `trail end' notice do not turn left but continue for a further 200yds.

5

Where the track curves right, turn left (signposted `footpath to David Marshall Lodge'). Cross the footbridge and turn right. You are now on the Waterfall Trail and soon reach the foot of the lovely Fall of the Little Fawns, with a 55ft drop. Continue uphill on the path – informative notices tell you about the woods and the wildlife. The area is typical of the way much of Scotland would have appeared up to 300 years ago.

6

At a junction, turn left on to a boardwalk. Go straight on at the next junction and follow the path up to the David Marshall Lodge.

7

After visiting the Lodge, walk out along the vehicle exit road to the A821. Cross the road with care, turn right, and in 30yds turn left on to a path. Take the left fork of the path and in 300yds look for an old gatepost, which marks the line of the quarry incline tramway. This is an optional diversion, but very worthwhile both for a pleasant walk and because of the interest of the quarry, formerly an integral part of village life.

8

Return to the Lodge by the same route, but divert right after the first car parking area to see the large boulder marking the visit by the Queen Mother in 1973 to celebrate the Forestry Commission's one millionth acre of planting in Scotland. Take the path right of the Lodge to the viewpoint indicator.

From the rear corner of the Lodge, a stepped path leads steeply downhill (past a seat) through the woods – a delightful walk with lovely views. Across the village is wooded Doon Hill, where the Reverend Robert Kirk is said to have been spirited away by fairies in 1691 after first befriending them and then revealing their secrets in a book. To break the spell, a knife had to be thrown over his head. However, when he did appear in his own kirk at his daughter's christening, the congregation were so amazed that no-one took the necessary action, and he vanished, never to be seen again.

At the road, turn left and walk down to the village. On the right is the village hall, built 'in proud and grateful memory of the men of this parish who died in the service of their country during the war of 1939-1945' – a very practical and lasting memorial.

At the junction with Main Street is the Bailie Nocol Jarvie Hotel. It is on the site of a much older inn, but is named after a character in Scott's novel *Rob Roy*. Cross the road and walk down Manse Road for a few yards, turning left along the banks of the Forth to re-enter the car park.

Tree-fringed Loch Ard with the peak of Ben Lomond in the distance.

POINTS OF INTEREST

Dounans Camp. Dounans was built in 1939 and during the war housed first evacuee children from Glasgow and later refugees from occupied Holland. Since 1947 it has been a residential camp offering outdoor and environmental education to children of all ages and increasingly to adult groups. It is one of four such ventures run by the Scottish National Camps Association (now called Scottish Centres). The mound on which the swings are placed was the site of the ancient Dunance Castle, of which nothing now remains.

In July 1990, Dounans was the scene for the Challenger Trophy, a four-day event for teams from business organisations all over Europe. This was the first time the event had been held in the UK, and it was a great success. Powergen came first of the 92 teams entered.

Highland Boundary Fault. Between points 4 and 5 on the walk you will find a marker informing you that you are crossing the line of the Highland Boundary Fault, which runs from the Clyde to the North Sea. You pass from Achray Sandstone back to Leny Gritstone. It is believed that the Fault occurred about 500 million years ago, and geologists still come to the area to study it. Further information can be found at the David Marshall Lodge, starting point for the full Highland Fault Trail, of which this walk includes a small part.

David Marshall Lodge. The Lodge was constructed by the Carnegie Trust and presented to the Forestry Commission for public use in 1960. A new wing was added in 1978. The Lodge contains very informative displays about the area, its industries, landscape, geology and wildlife, with a fine audio-visual presentation in the small cinema and much

Children play below the Fall of the Little Fawns.

excellent literature. It is named after David Marshall, Chairman of the Carnegie Trust from 1950-55.

The Lodge serves as the Visitor Centre for the Queen Elizabeth Forest Park, and here you can learn about the work of the Forestry Commission and the importance of forestry in this area. The large windows offer panoramic views of the woods all around, and there are several fine short walks from the Lodge.

The Quarry Incline. Slate was quarried on Craigmore from the mid-18th century until 1958. It was a highly skilled operation, and a good team could turn out 1,500 slates a day. The inclined plane seen on the walk led down from the quarry to the site of the school, from where another line linked up with the railway yard, which occupied the site of today's car park.

The inclined plane operated a system whereby full wagons going down lifted the empty wagons coming back up. The rate of descent was controlled by brakes at the top of the plane. It is fascinating to stand on the line of the plane and imagine the wagons rattling and creaking as they ran up and down. The quarry provided much employment.

River Forth. Aberfoyle is the first crossing-point on the River Forth, here a clear stream vastly different in character from the great river that runs past Edinburgh to its mighty Firth. A little way down-stream from Aberfoyle, the Forth runs through Flanders Moss, a vast boggy expanse of flat ground formerly of considerable strategic importance. Ways of crossing it were known only to a few and it held up more than one army in the turbulent times of Scotland's past.

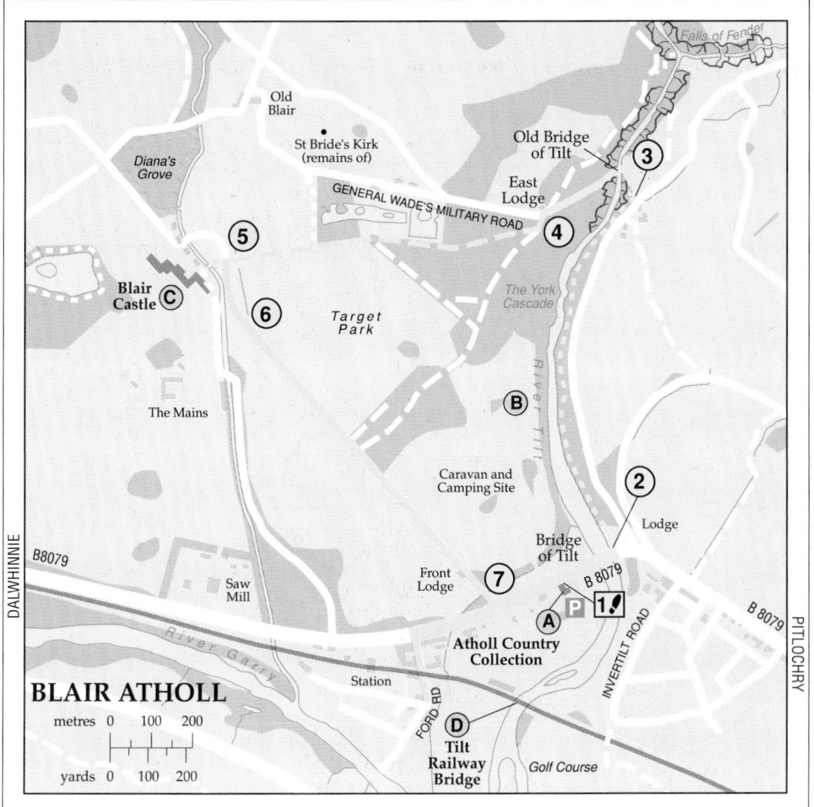

BLAIR ATHOLL

TAYSIDE

On B8079 off A9, 6 miles N of Pitlochry

BLAIR Atholl takes its name from Gaelic words meaning 'the field of New Ireland' – a reference, perhaps, to the original settlers here. There were Kings of Atholl in Pictish times, and the Atholl line retained rights of regality as late as 1747, when they were removed by the Westminster Parliament.

The Earls (later Dukes) of Atholl have been based at Blair Castle for 700 years, although the first fortification on this site was started by their enemy John Comyn or Cumming of Badenoch. Blair Castle today is the most visited historic house in Scotland, and Atholl Estates are still major employers in the area.

INFORMATION
Length of walk: 2½ miles
Approximate time: 1½ hours (the Castle will take several hours to see properly).

TERRAIN:
Roads, tracks and riverside path. Manageable for pushchairs (one flight of steps) but not for wheelchairs.

PARKING:
Use the car park at the Atholl Country Collection, where there are picnic tables.

OPEN:
Open: Blair Castle. Easter-late Oct. Daily 10am-5pm (Sun in Apr, May and Oct, afternoons only). Charge. Atholl Country Collection. Apr-mid Oct. Daily 1.30-5.30pm also Jul-Aug 9.30am-12.30pm. Charge.
The Old Mill: Apr-Oct weekdays 10am-5.30pm Sun 12noon-5.30pm.

REFRESHMENTS:
Two hotels, the Old Mill tearoom, and a café in the Castle.

WALK DIRECTIONS

After parking, visit the Atholl Country Collection and if you wish, the nearby Craft Centre, where mountain bikes can be hired during the summer months. Return to the main road, turn right and continue ahead to the Bridge of Tilt.

Cross the road and go down the short flight of steps to the path beside the River Tilt. This charming tree-lined path winds along with the river rushing by on the left through an increasingly rocky gorge. There are several lovely spots where small waterfalls are visible, and seats have been provided in a number of places. In about ½ a mile the path climbs above the river to meet a lane.

Turn left and left again at the fork to cross the Old Bridge of Tilt. This has been a crossing-point for centuries, and was once known as Black Bridge. General Wade built the first stone bridge here in the mid 18th century; his was superseded by a later bridge that has recently been renovated.

Blair Castle, with the peaks of Beinn a'Ghlo behind.

Follow the lane round to the left under an old footbridge.

At East Lodge turn left on to a track. In 20yds take the first path on the right and follow it – you should see a yellow post marked 4 after about 100yds. The broad path passes an old walled garden with a neglected lily pond and later a statue of the naked Hercules in heroic pose dated 1743.

Go through a gate, across the drive and over a footbridge to reach the Castle. From this point there is a signposted optional short walk to Diana's Grove. At the end of your visit, return to the main drive and then turn right.

Walk down the full length of the drive. Pass on the left the Target Park, sometimes used for International Scout Jamborettes, then a fine view of Beinn a'Ghlo opens up. The nearest peak is Carn Liath (grey cairn). Continue past the caravan park to the main entrance.

Turn right, cross the road, and in 250yds turn left to cross the railway to the Old Mill, where flour is still ground by water power and some of the resultant delicious produce is on sale in the tearoom. Return to the main road and turn right to the car park. As you cross the railway look east to Joseph Mitchell's ornate railway bridge over the Tilt.

POINTS OF INTEREST

Atholl Country Collection. The collection fully lives up to its motto of 'the friendly museum with something for everyone'. It largely concentrates on village and rural life, with plenty of artefacts from bygone days; a crofter's kitchen, the kirk and the smiddy, even a Highland cow in a byre. Outside the museum there is a scented Jacobean rose of the type said to have been worn by Bonnie Prince Charlie's supporters.

The most arresting exhibit is undoubtedly the vast Caledonian Challenge Shield. Admitted to the Guinness Book of Records as Britain's Largest Trophy, this carved oak monster, 9ft 6in high and 6ft wide, is an extraordinary thing to find in a small country museum. It was designed by J. Clark Stanton in 1861 as a trophy for rifle shooting at five distances up to 600yds, to encourage good marksmanship. It is still shot for annually, but instead of being displayed in the town of domicile of the winner as was previously the case, it now stays here to amaze the visitor.

The River Tilt rushes over its rocky bed.

River Tilt. At Blair Atholl the Tilt joins the Garry at the end of its journey from the heart of the Grampian Mountains. Glen Tilt, through which the river runs, has been a through-route to Deeside for centuries. Mary, Queen of Scots enjoyed a famous hunt here and a later monarch, Queen Victoria, knew the glen well and loved its wild scenery. It is a public right of way. Notice at Old Bridge of Tilt the signpost erected by the Scottish Rights of Way Society, the oldest amenity body in the country, with its laconic message 'To Deeside by Glen Tilt'. This is a tough two-day hike of over 30 miles!

Blair Castle. This magnificent building is a clan centre, home, fortress and a sophisticated business operation. Its history goes back to 1269 when John Comyn (or Cumming) of Badenoch tried to establish a stronghold here while the Earl of Atholl was away Crusading. Much of what we see today dates from the 18th century when the 2nd Duke of Atholl reshaped his fortress into a Georgian mansion on the grand scale.

A century later the 7th Duke restored the castellations and added the present entrance and the superb ballroom. The visitor is given a full tour of 32 rooms containing splendid armour, weapons, portraits, china and tapestries, plus a display of the natural history of the area. The 10th Duke lives in the castle. He is the titular head of Clan Murray and as such the castle is the clan's spiritual home.

Blair Castle hosts many events each year including musical festivals and competitions, scout assemblies, a three-day eventing competition in September, and of course the parades of the Atholl Highlanders. It proudly claims to be Scotland's most-visited historic house.

Tilt Railway Bridge. The railway from Perth to Inverness was constructed in the 1860s. It was a major engineering feat, the line rising to over 1,500ft on the Drumochter Pass and having to cross many rapid waters by bridge or viaduct. The engineer Joseph Mitchell, from Manchester, was given the job of bridging the Garry at Blair Atholl.

He ran into considerable opposition from the then Duke, who was opposed to railways and only agreed to the line passing through on condition that the structures were harmonious with the surroundings. Mitchell had an ally in the Duchess, who intervened on his behalf, but he allowed himself the comment that the bridge was 'somewhat more ornate than was necessary'.

It has nonetheless left us with a splendid monument to Victorian design and engineering. The bridge has a single diamond lattice truss span of 150ft with stone abutments and rises 40ft above the river.

A full parade of the Atholl Highlanders outside Blair Castle.

THE ATHOLL HIGHLANDERS

The Duke of Atholl is the only person in Britain permitted to retain his own private army, a privilege dating back to the time when Atholl was like a small kingdom within Scotland. The Athollmen always supported their Duke in battle, right up to the time of the Jacobite Risings when they fought at Culloden, gallantly but in vain, on Prince Charles's side. That year, 1746, Blair Castle was the last place in Britain to undergo a siege.

Even with the suppression of the Highlanders the tradition continued, men of Atholl fighting in the American Wars, but their time as a ceremonial bodyguard for the Duke can be said to date from 1839 when the Duke's heir, Lord Glenlyon, went to the Eglinton Tournament – his portrait is in the castle. This was a genuine tournament, not a display, and a number of those taking part, including Glenlyon, were injured. He took with him 70 men and four pipers, who six years later, in 1845, received personal Colours from Queen Victoria. These Colours can be seen in the castle today.

Since then the Atholl Highlanders have regularly paraded for and marched with their Duke, mounting bodyguard for members of royalty and other notable visitors to Blair Atholl. At present there are about 45 in the company, all local men, and they have a fine pipe band. The dates when they parade at the castle are advertised well in advance, and they make a magnificent spectacle, proudly upholding a tradition which has lasted for centuries.

BRAEMAR

GRAMPIAN

SCOTLAND

On A93, 58 miles W of Aberdeen and 51 miles N of Perth

AT 1,100ft above sea level, Braemar is one of the highest villages in Britain. It sits at the confluence of the River Dee and the Clunie Water and has been important strategically and as a meeting place of routes through the mountains for many centuries. Until relatively recently Braemar was regarded as two separate villages, Castleton on the right bank of the Clunie and Auchendryne on the left.

WALK DIRECTIONS

From the car park, climb the steps to the Glenshee Road and turn left. Walk down the road for 300yds to reach the Invercauld Arms Hotel.

Return past the Invercauld Festival Theatre and take the first left (Castleton Terrace/Place). Take the second turning on the right.

At the junction with the main road turn right. The first building on the right is the cottage where Robert Louis Stevenson stayed in 1881 and where he drafted *Treasure Island.*

Cross the road. By the gates of Invercauld Galleries take the narrow path leading back to the car park. Walk ahead to see Kindrochit Castle. After viewing the castle, walk down the road into the village.

Turn left into the village centre. On the right of the square is the handsome Fife Arms Hotel, with (opposite) its former mews.

Return to Mar Road and turn left, passing the police station and on the right, St Andrew's Catholic Church.

Turn left into Broombank Terrace and walk through the Memorial Park, going round to the left of the arena.

(6)

Leave the park on its south side at a gate opposite a cottage and turn right. At the road end follow the track right, keeping the fence on your right, and continue to Chapel Brae. Turn left.

(7)

You soon reach a pond, Poll na Ceire, on the left. Climb the knoll above the pond – it gives a fine view over the village.

Return to the road and turn left. It soon becomes a track. At a fork go straight on to reach the sign for the National Nature Reserve.

Turn right down another track to reach the Linn of Dee Road. Turn right and walk back into the village.

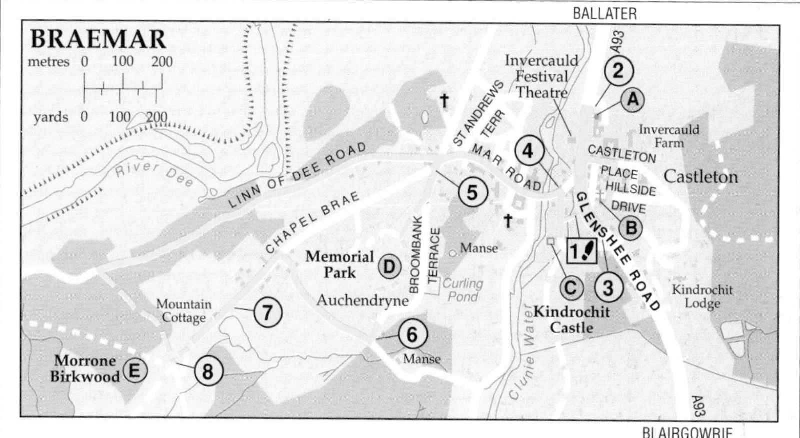

POINTS OF INTEREST

The Site of the 1715 Rising. There were several attempts to restore the Stuarts to the throne of Great Britain. Where the Invercauld Arms Hotel now stands, the Earl of Mar raised the standard for the Old Pretender (known to his followers as King James VIII and III) to start the 1715 Rising. A plaque in the hotel commemorates the event, and at the roadside opposite is a memorial stone erected in 1953.

Episcopal Church of St Margaret. The church we see today was opened in 1897. The finest feature is the great East Window, which includes Biblical scenes; portraits of the saints including St Margaret and St Andrew, patron saint of Scotland; and the Royal Arms of Queen Victoria.

Kindrochit Castle. This ancient fortification dates from the 11th century, when King Malcolm Canmore established a stronghold here. The castle remained an important site for 400 years.

The Memorial Park. There is evidence that Malcolm Canmore held contests at Kindrochit to find the strongest and fleetest men for his army, and such gatherings have been a feature of Highland life for many centuries.

The splendid natural arena in Braemar was given to the Braemar Royal Highland Society in 1906 by the then Duke of Fife, and it received the name of the Princess Royal and Duke of Fife Memorial Park. It is still the scene of the Braemar Gathering, held each year on the first Saturday in September and always attended by members of the Royal Family.

Morrone Birkwood. The birch woodland on the lower steps of Morrone (big hill) is designated as a National Nature Reserve. Believed to be the finest upland birchwood of its type in Britain, the wood has largely retained the appearance it would have had 10,000 years ago, following the last Ice Age.

Turreted Braemar Castle is a popular attraction.

INFORMATION

Length of walk:
2 miles
Approximate time:
1½ hours

TERRAIN:
One section of rough track, otherwise easy going. Suitable for children and for push-chairs with care: suitable for wheelchairs by turning back into the village at point (7).

PARKING:
Use the signposted car park near the junction of Mar Road and the Glenshee Road.

OPEN:
Braemar Castle. May-early Oct. Daily except Fri, 10am-6pm. Charge.

REFRESHMENTS:
Hotels and cafés.

SCOTLAND

COLDSTREAM
BORDERS

On A697, 15m W of Berwick-upon-Tweed

COLDSTREAM was for centuries the first crossing place on the River Tweed west of Berwick, and for that reason it held a particular military significance. King James IV of Scotland forded the river with his army in 1513 on his way to defeat and death at Flodden Field, a few miles over the border, and in 1660 General Monk started his march to London to restore Charles II to the crown from Coldstream.

Smeaton's fine old bridge over the Tweed has marked Scotland's boundary with England for well over two centuries.

POINTS OF INTEREST

Ⓐ

Coldstream Museum. The museum includes many items of local life, donated by the people of Coldstream, and also exhibits on the Coldstream Guards and their history. A scroll marks the occasion in August 1968 when the regiment was presented with the Freedom of the Burgh.

The Coldstream Guards were not raised in Coldstream, but became associated with the burgh after General Monk's march to London in 1660, which started here. Monk's aim was to restore Charles II to the throne. In this he was successful, and the regiment thereafter became known, formally, as the Second Foot Guards, but affectionately as the Coldstream Guards. The museum is on the site of their original headquarters.

Ⓑ

Coldstream Bridge. The fine five-arched bridge, designed by John Smeaton (perhaps better known as a lighthouse builder) was completed in 1766 at a cost of £6,000, and for many years was maintained by the Tweed Bridges Trustees. A plaque marks Robert Burns' crossing in 1787 – his first venture into England – and records that he knelt in prayer for a blessing on his native land.

The small building on the Scottish side of the bridge, originally a tollhouse, achieved notoriety as a marriage-house rivalling that at Gretna Green. Until 1856 couples could be married under Scots Law simply by making a declaration before witnesses; thereafter the law required a minimum period of three weeks' residence.

Ⓒ

Parish Church. The spacious church contains the laid-up Colours of the Second Battalion, Coldstream Guards, together with a side drum and a bugle, marking the close association between burgh and regiment

WALK DIRECTIONS

①

From the car park, turn right into High Street. Cross the Leet Water and take the first turning on the left to recross the burn.

②

Turn right over this bridge and almost immediately left into Duke Street.

③

At the end of Duke Street, turn right and walk down to the broad Market Square. Keep left to reach the Coldstream Museum, and carry on to reach the riverside path on Tweed Green.

④

Turn left and walk along this surfaced path, with its splendid views across the Tweed to the Cheviot Hills. The path was once called Nuns' Walk, the only reminder that there was a Cistercian foundation here at one time.

Before long there is a fine view of Coldstream Bridge; the path then passes above a high, unprotected drop down to the river. It is perfectly safe but children need to be kept in check.

⑤

Join the road and turn right to Coldstream Bridge. The middle of the bridge is the border between Scotland and England.

⑥

Return by the same route to pass the imposing monument to Charles Marjoribanks, Berwickshire's first MP after the Reform Act of 1832, and continue along High Street. On the left opposite the Town Hall is Henderson Park. It was created to commemorate the visit of the Queen and the Duke of Edinburgh here in 1962.

Pass the parish church and turn right opposite the Newcastle Arms Hotel into Duns Road. Turn left into Home Place.

Turn left into Home Park and follow the path round the left-hand side of the park back to the car park. The name is a reminder that Lord Home, the former Prime Minister Sir Alec Douglas-Home, has his seat at the Hirsel, a few miles to the west.

INFORMATION
Length of walk:
$1\frac{3}{4}$ miles
Approximate time:
$1\frac{1}{2}$ hours

TERRAIN:
Roads and good paths. Suitable for pushchairs and wheelchairs.

PARKING:
Use the signposted car park (toilets) off High Street, by Home Park.

OPEN:
Coldstream Museum. Apr-Oct, Tue-Sun 2-5pm, also 10am-1pm Jul-Aug. Charge.

REFRESHMENTS:
Cafés and inns.

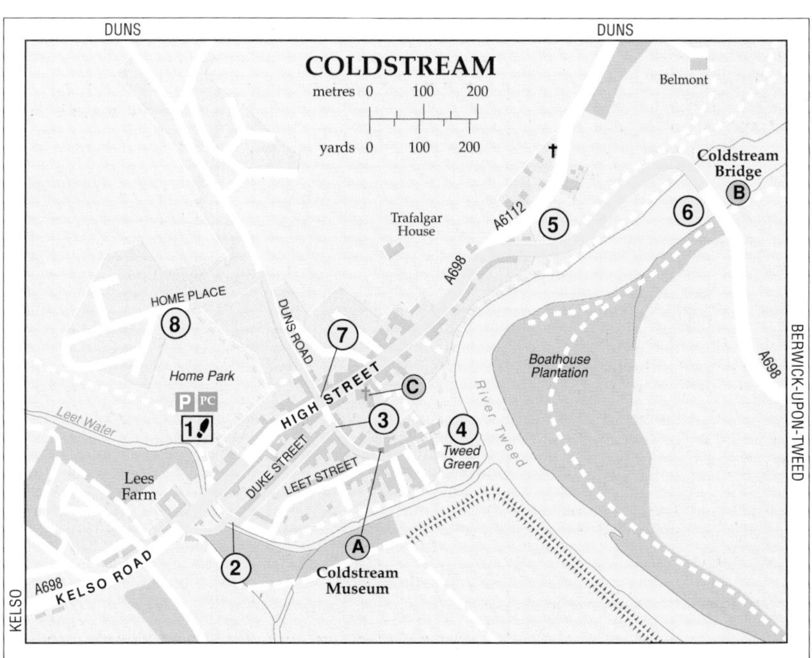

SCOTLAND

CULROSS

FIFE

On B9037, 4 miles E of Kincardine Bridge

CULROSS is reputed to have been the birthplace, in the 6th century, of St Mungo, patron saint of Glasgow. A thousand years later it was a place of great industry, a Royal Burgh with a thriving trade in salt and coal and a reputation for producing the best iron baking girdles in Scotland. Ships from many countries filled its harbour. One man, Sir George Bruce, is especially associated with its development. He built Culross Palace, a grand house very characteristic of the period.

By a miracle – perhaps wrought by St Mungo – much of medieval Culross has survived, and through the energetic and imaginative efforts of the National Trust for Scotland in particular, today's visitor is still able to capture the feeling of wandering the lanes of a 16th-century burgh. Up on the hill are the remains of another great Cistercian abbey, parts of which still serve the parish.

Pantiled roofs, crow-stepped gables and narrow cobbled streets, typical of Culross.

WALK DIRECTIONS

From the car park, walk left with the Firth of Forth on your left. You can either use the road or the shore path, though the latter may be overgrown in places.

In 200yds, turn right up the narrow paved way known as the Slate Loan. It was formerly used for transporting slate from a quarry on the hill. The open area to the left of the lower part of the loan, known as the Play Field, was used for mystery plays and other performances in medieval times.

In ¼ of a mile, where a lane comes in from the right, bear left on a wide grassy path to reach the West Church. The graveyard is still used, and commands a splendid view across the Firth of Forth. Return to the start of the path and turn left along the lane for 600yds. This was the old road to Kincardine, and can still be followed for much of its original length.

④

Turn right at a junction and walk downhill to reach Culross Abbey. The Abbey House next to it was built in 1608 for Lord Kinloss, Master of the Rolls and Sir George Bruce's elder brother, but he died before it was completed. It may have been designed by Inigo Jones. The house originally had three storeys but is now reduced to two levels.

After leaving the Abbey, continue down Kirk Street. The first and very narrow opening on the left is Cat Close, said to be the haunt of a ghostly, but friendly, Cistercian monk. A little further on, a gap in the wall permits a fine view of the two famous Forth bridges. As you enter the burgh, on your right is the Tanhouse, formerly used for tanning hides, and on your left is Snuff Cottage. Continue to wander down the brae, reaching The Study on the right, and admiring the many other old buildings.

At the foot of the brae, go right to visit the Town House then walk along Sandhaven to Culross Palace before returning to the car park.

INFORMATION
Length of walk:
1¾ miles
Approximate time:
1¼ hours

TERRAIN:
The walk includes steep lanes, some of them cobbled, and a short length of grassy track. Pushchairs could manage it with an effort, but wheelchairs should stay in the village centre.

PARKING:
Use the car park on the foreshore (toilets).

OPEN:
Culross Palace (NTS). Apr-Sep, weekdays 9.30am-7pm, Sun 2-7pm; Oct-Mar weekdays 10am-4pm, Sun 2-4pm. Charge.
Town House (NTS). Easter and 1 May-30 Sep. Daily 11am-1pm, 2-5pm. Charge.
The Study (NTS). See locally for times of opening.
Culross Abbey. All reasonable times. No charge.

REFRESHMENTS:
One inn. NTS are hoping to open Bessie Bar's Hall as a tearoom in the near future.

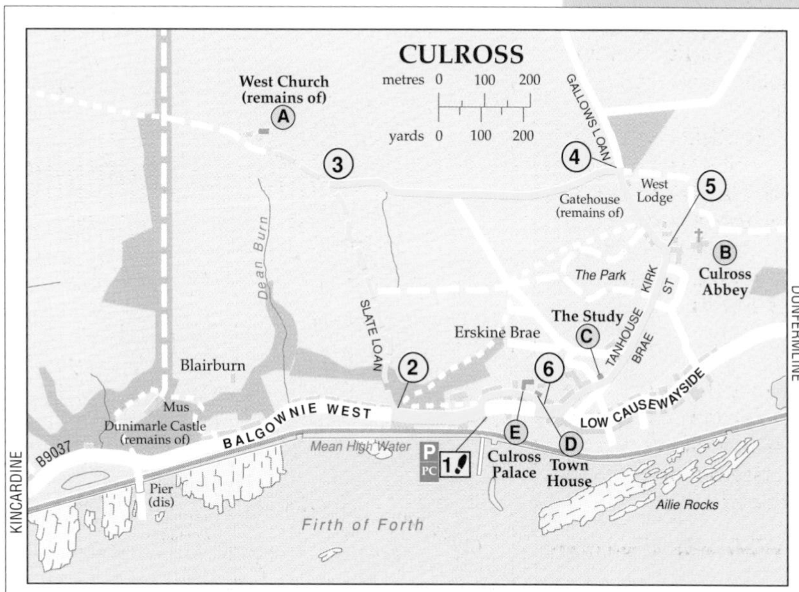

The corbelled outlook tower of The Study is a noted Culross feature.

POINTS OF INTEREST

West Church. It is believed that parts of this ancient place of worship date from the 12th century. The east and south walls, measuring approximately 70 x 20ft, remain. Notice the two large stones sculptured with crosses which are incorporated into the wall and doorway; they may originally have been tombstones.

This was the original parish church for the burgh, and its lovely burial ground is still occasionally used. It lost its status in 1633 when the Abbey Church took over as the place of worship for the inhabitants of Culross. Nearby, though not now visible, was the Monks' Well, the source of water for the Abbey gardens and orchard, once the pride of the area.

Culross Abbey. The Abbey was one of a number of Cistercian foundations in Scotland established during the 13th century. In this case the founder was Malcolm, Earl of Fife, in 1217. The site is reputed to have held a church in the 6th century, in St Mungo's time.

By the time of the Reformation in 1589, much of the Abbey was in a ruinous state, although the choir continued to be used for worship, as it is today. Off the North Transept is a Tomb House built in 1642 for the splendid tomb of Sir George Bruce. Both transepts were renovated in 1905. The church entrance incorporates the stone screen which would originally have divided the choirs of the monks and the lay brethren.

The Study. This distinctive early 17th-century building is noted for its corbelled outlook tower. It is said to have been used by Bishop Leighton of Dunblane when he visited Culross. Inside, there are old panelled walls and a fine painted ceiling.

It is intriguing to imagine what the Bishop might have seen as he looked out. There would have been much bustle and movement up and down the street, with market traders crying their wares. Out in the harbour ships would be loading up with salt and coal. The burgh would have been a noisy place by day, and not a very pleasant one either by modern standards – waste was simply flung out of windows in buckets, and the sides of the street were running channels. These things were part of the life of a prosperous burgh.

Town House. The Town House dates from 1626, though the tower was added later, in 1783. It was the place of meeting for the town's council and also served as the Tolbooth, where goods were measured and weighed. The house now contains a NTS information centre and exhibition, with an audio-visual display on Culross and its history and much interesting literature available.

Culross Palace. The palace is in fact a splendid town house, very characteristic of the period with its stepped gables and pantiled roofs around an open courtyard. It was built for Sir George Bruce in 1597 and extended in 1611. The oldest part is to the west of the courtyard, and the initials GB and the date 1597 can be seen over one of the windows.

The southern extension contained a long gallery – the present timber partitions were added later. The northern wing includes the kitchen and bakery, and on its first floor a reinforced strong room with an inner door of iron. No doubt Sir George kept his money and other valuables here. In several of the rooms are walls and ceilings with tempera and oil paintings.

Culross Palace was the first property acquired by the infant National Trust for Scotland in 1932, one year after the Trust's formation. It is one of nearly 40 buildings in Culross which the Trust has been responsible for saving and restoring – a magnificent record of achievement.

THE MERCHANT OF CULROSS

George Bruce was very much a man of his time. A descendant of King Robert the Bruce, he was born in 1548 at Blairhall, north of Culross. He is said to have had 'great knowledge and skill in machinery' and in 1575 was granted a Charter to mine coal on the Abbey lands at Culross. He felt sure there was coal under the waters of the Firth, and in a bold venture, had his men dig a Moat Pit with a high, circular stone wall, below the high water mark. They went 40ft down into the rock, and found the coal seam. It stretched for a mile, and the venture had paid off.

Coal was needed abroad and so Bruce applied to James VI for a Royal Charter for Culross – necessary for a burgh involved in export. The king agreed, and Bruce paid the £1,000 Scots for the charter himself, though the town council later paid him back. In 1617 James VI visited Culross and was taken into the mine from the landward side. When he emerged at the Moat Pit he thought he had been the victim of a trick, and cried out 'Treason', but was reassured when one of George Bruce's vessels came to fetch him safely back to dry land.

By this time George Bruce had built Culross Palace, and had been knighted by the king in 1611. He died in 1624.

Culross Palace retains many of its original features dating from the late 16th century.

FALKLAND

FIFE

On A912, 5 miles N of Glenrothes

FALKLAND, nestling at the foot of the Lomond Hills, became a Royal Burgh in 1458, and for the following two centuries its magnificent Palace was a favourite retreat for the kings and queens of Scotland. The Palace is very much a part of the Burgh and many of the fine old buildings that still remain were occupied by merchants and traders whose lives were bound up with that of the court.

Much of the old Burgh still remains, and many buildings have been superbly well restored. A walk round Falkland throws up endless items of interest and truly has the air of a walk through the history of medieval Scotland.

WALK DIRECTIONS

From the car park, follow the signposted route through the archway of the Hunting Lodge Hotel and cross High Street to visit Falkland Palace, the Chapel Royal, and the Palace grounds with the Royal Tennis Court.

On leaving the Palace, recross the street. Almost every building here is of interest. Moncrieffe House, with the last remaining thatched roof in Falkland, is 17th-century.

Across the road, Saddler's House, the gift shop and St Andrew's House make a fine group. Two of them have marriage lintels (e.g. GL/BD 1777), a feature of many houses in Falkland.

On the corner of Back Wynd is the Town Hall. In medieval burghs, a wynd was a narrow street connecting wider ones. After visiting the Town Hall, cross to the Church and the Bruce Fountain.

Cross the square, noting the cobbled shape of the Mercat Cross on the roadway, and walk up CrossWynd.

Turn right into Brunton Street. Brunton House was once the home of the Simson family, who were falconers to the king. Over the door is their coat of arms, with a falcon, and the date 1712. Keep right into the short alley called Rotten Row. As with its more famous counterpart in London's Hyde Park, it is thought the name is a corruption of *Route du Roi*, the King's Way.

Turn left into High Street. Immediately on the left is the unique electricity sub-station. Walk along the street. Weaver's Cottage (also restored by NTS) was indeed once used for weaving – the small, irregular windows and thick walls are typical of the vernacular building of the period. A little further along on the left is the entrance to the old burial ground.

At West Port go left with the road and in 100yds (before the entrance to Millfield House) turn left again into Back Dykes, an unsurfaced track. New houses on the right maintain the Fife tradition of red pantiled roofs.

INFORMATION
Length of walk:
1 mile
Approximate time:
1 hour

TERRAIN:
Generally suitable for pushchairs and wheel-chairs, though the tour of the Palace involves stairs.

PARKING:
Large car park in Back Wynd, with toilets.

OPEN:
Falkland Palace (NTS). 1 Apr-31 Oct weekdays, 10am-6pm, Sun 2-6pm. Combined admission charge with Town Hall. Falkland Town Hall (NTS). 1 April-31 Oct, weekdays 10am-6pm, Sun 2-6pm.

REFRESHMENTS:
Good selection of teashops and inns.

Falkland contains many quiet corners ideal for exploration on foot. In this view the spire of the parish church, which was gifted to the Burgh by the Bruce family, rises above the houses.

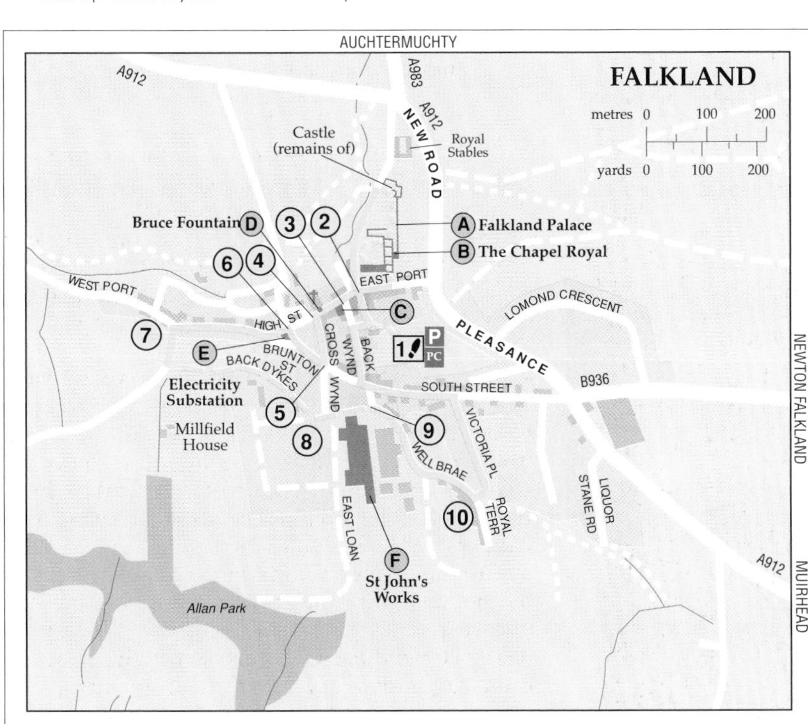

POINTS OF INTEREST

Falkland Palace. Falkland's royal associations date from the 1450s, when James II gave the Palace to his wife, Mary of Gueldres. Much of what we see today, however, is 16th-century. James IV and V both spent considerable time here and the Palace was enlarged, extended and improved for them.

Falkland was not a stronghold but a place of retreat and recreation for the royal family and their retinue, and it was designed for those purposes, with fine furnishings and embellishments. The Royal Tennis Court, the oldest in Britain, dating from 1539, is still in use today. One room has the Royal Bed of State made for James VI in Aberdeen. Around it are angels to guard him, the four Christian virtues of Truth, Justice, Virtue and Wisdom, and an intriguing word puzzle.

Falkland Palace, a royal retreat in medieval times, is now in the care of the National Trust for Scotland.

The Palace was greatly restored 100 years ago by the 3rd Marquess of Bute, who acquired the title of Hereditary Keeper, still held today by one of his descendants, Major Michael Crichton Stuart. In 1952 he appointed the National Trust for Scotland as Deputy Keeper of the Palace, allowing the Crichton Stuarts to retain part of the Palace as their family home.

Ⓑ

The Chapel Royal. Within the Palace is the beautiful chapel, still in regular use as the place of worship for Catholics in Falkland. It was started in 1520, and the Royal Pews can still be seen. On one wall are `windows', painted to exactly match the real windows opposite. This wall now bears superb Flemish tapestries telling the story of Joseph and his brothers.

The painted wooden ceiling has Stuart arms and emblems, and another notable feature is the Madonna made of cartridge cases by Polish servicemen who were stationed in the area during World War II.

Ⓒ

Falkland Town Hall. The imposing Town Hall was built in 1801 and was the regular meeting place for the town council until local government reorganisation in 1975. Over the pediment is the Burgh crest of the stag and oak tree. The Latin motto translates as `Learn justice and take heed to despise not Christ'. The building also served as a prison and was once used for religious services.

The Town Hall was acquired by the National Trust for Scotland in 1986 and it now houses an excellent exhibition which not only describes the long history of Falkland but shows how it is a thriving community today.

THE BRUCE FAMILY IN FALKLAND

In the 1830s, Margaret Bruce inherited Falkland from her uncle, Professor John Bruce, who died childless. She was already wealthy when she married Onesiphorus Tyndall, a barrister. He added her name to his own and they settled in Falkland, commissioning William Burn to build House of Falkland for them at the foot of the Lomond Hills. It is now used as a school.

The Bruces carried out extensive tree planting and many other improvements. In 1849 they commissioned William Bryce to build a new and splendid parish church, and a few years later provided the Bruce Fountain for public use. Mrs Bruce donated a field to the cricket club in 1860 – one of the earliest clubs in Scotland and still going today. The hotel was at that time known as the Bruce Arms.

Margaret Bruce's initials and the date 1869 (the year of her death) can be seen on a building in High Street. Onesiphorus died in 1855. There were no children, and in 1887 the estates were sold to the Marquess of Bute. In gratitude for all his good works, the people of Falkland built a tower as a monument to Onesiphorus Bruce on Black Hill. It was described as `an inadequate tribute to the memory of a good man'.

Parish Church and Bruce Fountain. The parish church is on the site of an earlier building dating from 1620. The present church was built in 1849-50 to a design by William Bryce, the money being provided by Onesiphorus Tyndall Bruce (see box), whose statue in bronze is in the grounds. The church is an imposing Victorian Gothic style with a tall stepped spire.

The Bruce Fountain stands in front of the church. It boasts four fine heraldic lions, two of which carry the Bruce coat of arms. It dates from 1856 and was another of the gifts from the Bruce family to the burgh.

Ⓔ

Electricity Substation. This unusual building stands in High Street at its junction with Rotten Row. It is an 18th-century house whose appearance has been preserved despite its modern purpose. At one time the ground floor was used as a reading room: Thomas Drysdale, a local stonemason, reading newspapers and other literature to people of the burgh who could not read themselves.

Ⓕ

St John's Works. This building was opened in the 1870s as a power-loom factory, employing up to 400 people, including many children. It was then known as 'the Bruce factory'.

At the beginning of the 20th century the works changed from weaving to producing floor-cloth, under the management of Mr Charles Jackson. He brought orphan boys from London to work here, boarding them out in homes and hostels. In the 1930s the factory was taken over by the Scottish Co-operative Wholesale Society for the manufacture of linoleum.

With the move towards fitted carpets, the demand for linoleum died out and the factory closed in 1966, to reopen shortly afterwards when Smith Anderson of Leslie took it over for the manufacture of paper and paper bags, much of the output being from recycled material.

The Bruce Fountain, which stands in front of the parish church.

⑧

At a T-junction turn left past a small green and at the crossroads go straight over, with St John's Works on the right. An enticing sign says `Footpath to Lomond Hills' and there rising above the village is the bulk of East Lomond, once a royal hunting ground.

⑨

Fork right into Well Brae. At the road end look right to Royal Terrace to see a stepped row of former weavers' cottages. Turn left into Victoria Place.

⑩

Follow this road to its junction with South Street and turn left. At the crossroads turn right into Back Wynd. The area ahead was the Horsemarket, where animals would have been bought and sold at the markets and fairs held regularly in the Burgh following the granting of the Charter in 1458. Return along Back Wynd to the car park.

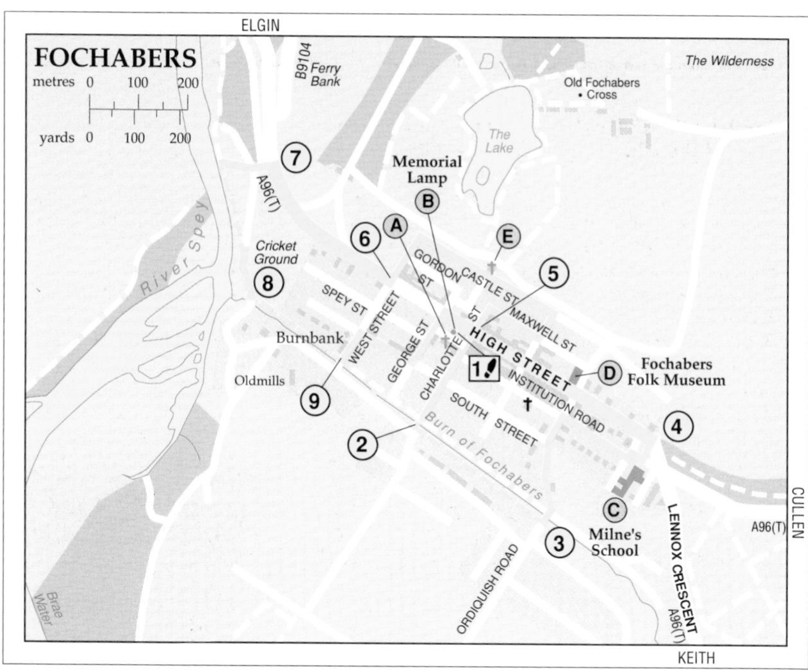

FOCHABERS

GRAMPIAN

At junction of A96 and A98, 10m E of Elgin

THE history of Fochabers is intimately bound to a great house and the family which lived there and owned much of the land around it. Gordon Castle was one of the finest buildings in Scotland, and was the home of the Dukes of Gordon (later Dukes of Richmond and Gordon) until 1938, when the 9th Duke sold the estate to the Crown Commissioners to pay death duties.

In 1776, in more prosperous times, the 4th Duke of Gordon wished to enlarge his policies, and had the entire village of Fochabers – a burgh of Barony since 1598 – moved from its position near the castle to its present site. He engaged the architect John Baxter to replan it on a rectangular pattern, which is still its basic shape today. Much of this 'New Town' has survived, and the superb folk museum, a goldmine of treasures for the curious, tells the story of Fochabers (the name may mean `below the well') through photographs and mementos.

Baxter is still a name closely associated with Fochabers: the world-famous soups, preserves and other fine products come from a large factory across the River Spey from the village. It has an interesting visitor centre and provides another link with Gordon Castle, its founder having worked there as a gardener.

INFORMATION
Length of walk: 1½ miles
Approximate time: 1 hour

TERRAIN:
Mainly village streets, where a circuit for wheelchairs could very easily be devised. Some paths which pushchairs should manage without too many problems.

PARKING:
There is some parking in The Square, otherwise park tidily in one of the surrounding streets.

OPEN:
Fochabers Folk Museum. Apr-Oct, Daily 9.30am-1pm, 2-6pm. Nov-Mar, Daily 9.30pm-1pm, 2-5pm. Charge. Baxters Visitor Centre. Mar-Dec. Weekdays 10am-4.30pm plus Easter weekend and weekends from May-Sep, Sat 11am-5.30pm, Sun 12.30-4.30pm.

REFRESHMENTS:
Cafés and hotels.

WALK DIRECTIONS

The walk starts from The Square, where you can admire the Bellie Kirk and the fine Memorial Lamp. Walk to the east side of The Square and turn right down Charlotte Street, named after the daughter of the 4th Duke.

Cross the Burn of Fochabers by the White Bridge. Turn left on the path beside the burn, through The Planting, a pleasant tree-shaded stroll.

At the road turn left over the Black Bridge. Walk towards the village and just past the police station turn right along Institution Road. Walk to its end to reach Milne's School. Walk round the square in front of the school to admire its classical façade and exit through the gateway on to High Street.

Turn left and walk along High Street, admiring the old buildings. The fine Public Institute was opened in 1905, the money being raised by the inhabitants by various means, including a Grand Bazaar held at Gordon Castle. At the corner with East Street is the Fochabers Folk Museum. Continue along, noting on a house near the Red Lion inn the initials JA on a lintel. James Allan was one of the first `tenementers' of the New Town in 1776. Tenements had a regular size of 45x150ft: a plan can be seen in the museum.

Reach the Gordon Arms Hotel, another building dating from 1776, and turn right into The Square. Continue into Maxwell Street, turn left into Westmorland Street and left again into

The broad River Spey at Fochabers, a few miles from its estuary.

Castle Street, where there were once public baths, the charge being a penny for a cold bath and two pence for a hot one! In Castle Street is the Gordon Chapel. Follow the street as it turns left to West Street.

 6

Turn right and cross the road to reach the attractive Fochabers Cricket Ground, passing a fountain erected in memory of Major Allan Wilson, killed in action in Matabeleland in 1893.

 7

Take the first turning left (signposted to the putting green) and turn right by the small car parking area along a path to reach the River Spey. Turn left and walk along by the river. This is the Speyside Way, a footpath which runs from Spey Bay up into the Cairngorms.

 8

At a footbridge, go left following the Speyside Way marker and follow this shady path along behind the houses in Burnbank.

 9

At the road, turn left. Take the first right (South Street) back into the grid of the New Town, and turn left into George Street to return to The Square.

The Gordon Chapel, which originally had a private entrance for the Duke and his family at the rear.

POINTS OF INTEREST

 A

Bellie Kirk. The kirk (the name may come from *Baile-lith*, a place of flooding) was the last major work of John Baxter, a famous architect of his day. It was completed in 1798 and its handsome portico and tall spire give a classical elegance to the small square. The clock shows the date of completion. The buildings to either side – originally the manse and the school/courthouse – were designed to match and to complete a harmonious group with the church.

 B

Memorial Lamp. This handsome object marks the coming of electricity to Fochabers. In 1904, the 7th Duke provided the castle and village with its own hydro-electric power scheme, the water coming by canal from the Spey some two miles south of the village. On cold winter nights a bellringer went round the houses calling 'no light tonight due to the grue' – 'grues' or pieces of ice blocked the water intake to the power station in times of hard frost. In time, the Duke's power was replaced by grid electricity, but the memorial remains 'in appreciation of his generosity' as its inscription says.

 C

Milne's School. The old school provides a link between Fochabers and New Orleans. Designed by Thomas Mackenzie with columns and castellations, it opened in 1846, the money coming from a bequest by Alexander Milne, a native of Fochabers who in his youth was dismissed from service for refusing to have his hair cut and emigrated to the USA, where he made a fortune building the port of New Orleans. He clearly bore no grudge against his birthplace! Part of New Orleans is still called Milneburg, and the name appears, slightly corrupted, in *Milenburg Joys*, a well-known piece by the great jazz pianist Jelly Roll Morton.

A new Milne's High School has recently opened on a site to the south of the village, continuing the link with the benefactor.

The 19th-century buildings of Milne's School.

 D

Fochabers Folk Museum. The museum is housed in the former Pringle Church, erected in 1900 with £3,000 given by Alexander Pringle, a Fochabers man who had a distinguished career in the inland revenue. The church closed for worship in 1954 and the building was acquired by the Christie family in 1983. Part of it is an antiques shop and part the wonderful folk museum; a veritable treasure trove of memorabilia of Fochabers life.

 E

Gordon Chapel. The chapel, the Episcopal Church for the village, was opened in 1834. It was originally within the castle grounds, having a private entrance at the rear for the ducal party. There was a school on the ground floor. The chapel went to the Crown with the castle in 1938 but was bought back by the parishioners, led by Mr and Mrs William Baxter of the food company, in 1950.

THE BAXTERS OF FOCHABERS

George Baxter began his career as a gardener at Gordon Castle. With the active encouragement of the Duke, he borrowed £10 (no mean sum in 1868) and opened a shop in Fochabers, growing his own produce on a piece of land he had cleared himself. His wife Margaret, a fine cook, started making jams and jellies in copper pans, the method that is used to this day.

The business was continued and expanded by the second generation of Baxters, William and Ethel. In 1914, again with the then Duke's encouragement, a new factory site was opened across the Spey, using local stone and timbers from a ship washed ashore in Spey Bay. It was Ethel who introduced the famous Royal Game Soup, in 1929. Growth and success continued with William's sons Gordon and Ian and their wives Ena and Margaret, and today the fourth generation of Baxters are all involved in the business.

Baxters supply produce to the present Royal Family, and on one day of the year only they bottle plums by special request of Her Majesty The Queen. A handsome visitor centre was opened next to the factory in 1986, and tours of the plant are very popular. Visitors can see the original Victorian kitchen and the old shop.

Baxters visitor centre, where the food company started over 100 years ago.

FORT AUGUSTUS

HIGHLAND

On A82, 35 miles S of Inverness

THE settlement of Fort Augustus, at the southern end of Loch Ness, was anciently called Kilcumein. Its situation at the confluence of strategic routes from all four compass points led General George Wade to make it his headquarters after the 1715 rising. He supervised the building of the fort, naming it after William Augustus, Duke of Cumberland.

Communications are still a vital part of life in Fort Augustus: it is an important staging post on the Caledonian Canal.

INFORMATION
Length of walk:
2½ miles (not including options)
Approximate time:
2 hours (not including options).

TERRAIN:
Suitable for pushchairs, except the Torr a' Choiltreich option. Not suitable for wheelchairs.

PARKING:
Large car park on A82 just north of the canal crossing, with toilets and tourist information centre.

OPEN:
The Abbey and School. Group tours only. Phone (0320) 6232 for further details. The Abbey Church is open at all reasonable times.

REFRESHMENTS:
Pubs and cafés.

POINTS OF INTEREST

Ⓐ

St Benedict's Abbey and School. The Abbey and School stand on the site of the fort which gave the village its modern name. The fort remained in military use until 1854. The 14th Lord Lovat bought the buildings in 1867, and nine years later his son gave them to the Benedictine Order. The monks founded the school – an independent secondary school intended mainly for Scottish Catholic boys.

The Abbey Church features a variety of architectural styles, but is largely in the English Gothic style designed by Pugin 100 years ago.

Ⓑ

Cille-chumein Burial Ground. Fort Augustus was originally named Kilchumein after St Cumein, a follower of Columba, and this spot still bears that name. Among those buried is John Anderson, friend of Robert Burns, whom the poet immortalised in the poem *John Anderson, My Jo.*

Ⓒ

Caledonian Canal. Thomas Telford's great feat of engineering was completed, with many trials and setbacks, in 1822, after nearly 20 years of work. The canal provided a safe and relatively sheltered route from the North Sea to the Western Ocean.

The Caledonian Canal near Fort Augustus.

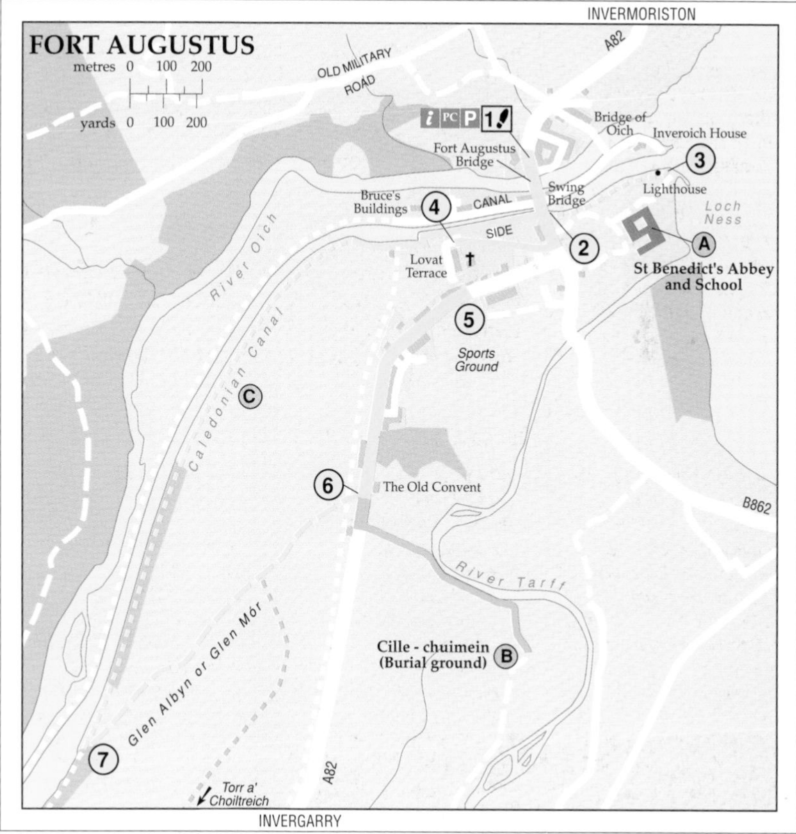

WALK DIRECTIONS

①

From the car park, turn right and cross the River Oich and the bridge over the canal.

②

Take the path on the left immediately after crossing the canal. The path ends at a point giving a superb view up Loch Ness.

③

Return to the road and turn left. In 150yds turn right to pass behind the Lovat Arms Hotel and continue forward.

④

At the entrance to the secondary school take the path on the left (Lovat Terrace). Swing right with the path and turn left to reach the main road.

⑤

Turn right and walk down the main road for ½ mile.

⑥

At the derestricted sign, turn right. Cross the campsite to the golf clubhouse, go through a small green gate and continue on the clear track at the left-hand side of the golf course. After leaving the golf course it carries on through woods, following the course of a power line.

Option 1: A few yards past the campsite turn-off, a sign points left to Cille-chumein burial ground. Walk down the lane to view the burial ground and return by the same route.

Option 2: After 250yds on the track by the golf course, at a gate, a path goes left and climbs to the summit of Torr á Choiltreich. Take the left fork at all junction paths to reach the summit. Return by the same path to rejoin the main walk alongside the golf course.

⑦

Where the track meets the Caledonian Canal, turn back right and walk alongside the canal. The path goes through four gates, leaves the golf course, and passes a mooring area to arrive at the series of locks connecting the canal with Loch Ness. Continue down the locks and turn left at the road back to the car park.

GLAMIS

TAYSIDE

Off A94, 5m W of Forfar

THE small village of Glamis, set in the beautiful Angus countryside in the fertile Vale of Strathmore, sits at the southern edge of the policies of Glamis Castle, home of the Lords of Glamis (later Earls of Strathmore and Kinghorne) since 1372 and the childhood home of Queen Elizabeth the Queen Mother. The life of the village and the life of the great house have been intertwined for the whole of that period, and they still are today.

Glamis Castle, childhood home of Queen Elizabeth the Queen Mother, dates originally from 1372.

WALK DIRECTIONS

From the castle car park, take the tour of Glamis Castle. (Please note that there is a charge for both the park and the castle.) On leaving the castle, turn left following the signposts to visit the Italian Garden and Nature Trail.

(2)

Return to the castle and walk down the main drive. Part way down is a restored 'doocot'. The flesh from these birds was a staple part of the diet in earlier times.

(3)

Before the drive enters woodland, turn left along a road that curves back into the village by St Fergus's Church. On leaving the church, walk ahead for 200yds along Kirkby Road to visit the Angus Folk Museum.

Take the first left past the Folk Museum to reach the Square (public toilets). Turn right past the Mercat Cross and the Strathmore Arms and follow the road round to the right to reach the main entrance to the castle.

(5)

Turn right through the superb De'il Gates with their heraldic beasts and satyrs, back to the castle.

POINTS OF INTEREST

(A)

Glamis Castle. Glamis has played a leading role in Scottish history for at least nine centuries. It is known that King Malcolm II had a hunting lodge here, and Duncan's Hall in the castle commemorates the killing of Duncan by Macbeth, although the murder itself took place not at Glamis but near Elgin. Malcolm II, however, did die here after being wounded in battle in 1034.

King Robert II raised Glamis to a barony in the late 14th century and granted it to his son-in-law, Sir John Lyon. The line he founded, later joined with the Bowes family, still holds Glamis today.

Italian Garden and Nature Trail. The Italian Garden, laid out by the 14th Earl, includes herbaceous borders, a fountain, arches of trees and two attractive stone gazebos with seats. The wrought iron gates at the entrance were made by local blacksmith George Sturrock to mark the Queen Mother's 80th birthday.

The Nature Trail, of half a mile in length, shows some examples of the many types of trees at Glamis. Rhododendrons add colour in spring, and birds seen include wood pigeons, chaffinches, tits and the shy goldcrest.

St Fergus's Church. The parish church for Glamis, with its handsome stepped spire, dates from 1792 and replaced a much older building. It is a mix of Gothic and Romanesque architecture.

In the garden of the manse opposite the church is an ancient Celtic standing stone.

Angus Folk Museum. The museum is housed in a row of six cottages built for estate workers in 1793 and typical of the area with their thick walls, small windows and Angus stone roof, the slates held in place by wooden pegs.

The six cottages have been made into one long display encompassing a manse parlour, dairy, laundry, schoolroom, kitchen, nursery, and 'Madge's Room', which was moved here in its entirety from a cottage at Craichie. There are numerous display cases and across the road is an agricultural section.

INFORMATION
Length of walk:
$2^{1}/_{2}$ miles
Approximate time:
2 hours

TERRAIN:
Suitable for children. Mostly suitable for pushchairs and wheelchairs, though not in parts of the castle.

PARKING:
Use the castle car park (charge) unless visiting at a time when the castle is closed, in which case park next to the church in the village.

OPEN:
Glamis Castle. Easter and the end of Apr-mid Oct. Daily 12 noon-5.30pm (last tour 4.45pm). Charge.
Angus Folk Museum (NTS). Easter, May and Sep. Daily 12 noon-5pm. Jun-Aug Daily 11.30am-5.30pm. Charge.

REFRESHMENTS:
Tearoom and pub in the village. Restaurant at the castle.

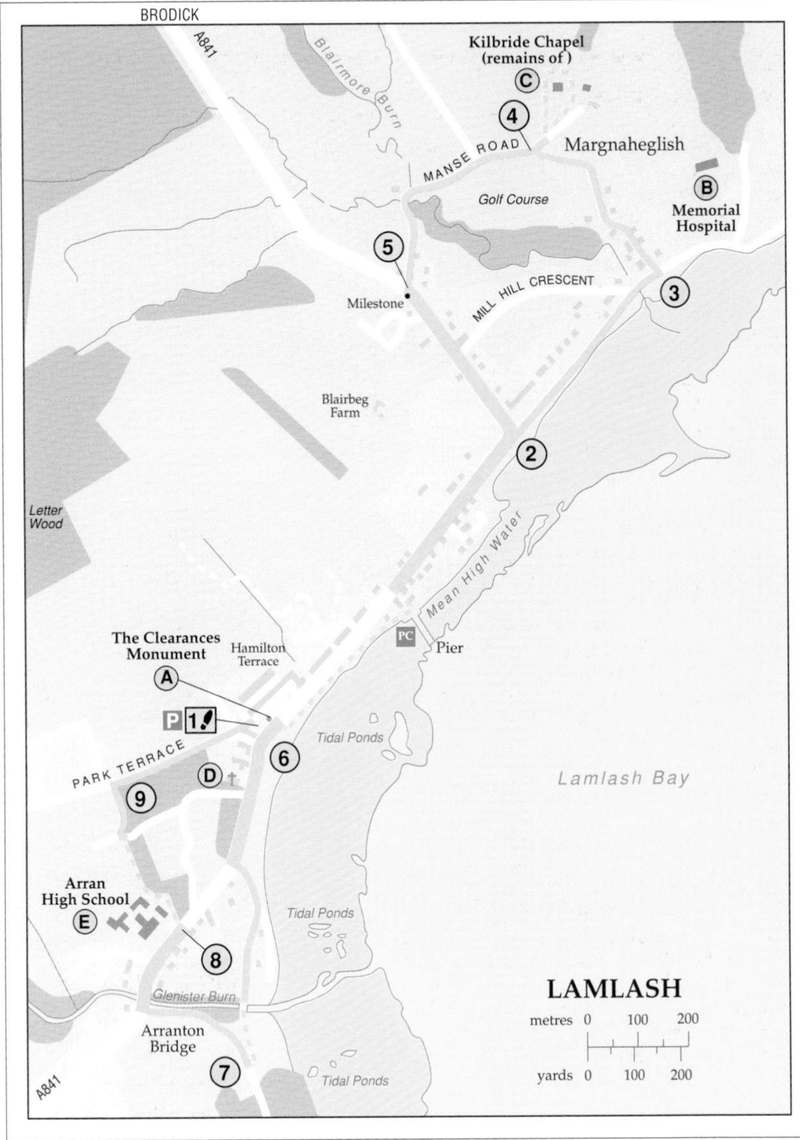

LAMLASH

STRATHCLYDE

On A841, 5 miles S of Brodick, which is reached by regular ferries from Ardrossan

THE village of Lamlash, on the Isle of Arran, is strung out around the beautiful curve of Lamlash Bay, with Holy Island prominent offshore. Both the island and the village are associated with St Molaise, a Scot who established a place of worship on Holy Island in the 7th century.

WALK DIRECTIONS

①

From the car park, turn left and in a few yards reach the Clearances Monument. Cross the road and walk along the grass verge next to the sea, passing behind a boatyard to reach the pier (toilet). Turn left up to the road and continue along it.

②

Where the main road swings left, carry on along the shore road.

③

Take the second turning on the left, signposted to the hospital. The road winds up through a new housing estate, passing the turnoff to the hospital.

④

At a T-junction turn right for a few yards to reach the cemetery and the remains of Kilbride Chapel, reached by a gate. Leave by the gate at the far side to walk back through the cemetery to the road. Turn right and follow the road across part of the very hilly golf course and round a left-hand bend back to the A841.

⑤

Cross the road, noting the very old milestone, and walk down the pavement to the sea. Turn right and walk back to the car park.

⑥

For the short southern loop, continue past the car park and in 100yds reach the parish church. Keep to the shore side of the road and take the path with the tennis courts on your right. At the end of the courts take the gravel path on the right, not the surfaced path – it is a dead end. Continue across the footbridge over the Glenlister Burn.

⑦

In another 100yds, turn back right on a track to reach the road at Arranton Bridge. Turn right past Arran High School.

⑧

Immediately past the school, take the enclosed path on the left and follow it around the school grounds and along the right-hand edge of a small park to reach a T-junction.

⑨

Turn right and follow Park Terrace back to the car park.

INFORMATION
Length of walk: 2½ m
Approx time: 1½ hrs

TERRAIN:
Northern loop suitable for pushchairs and wheelchairs. Southern loop suitable only for pushchairs.

PARKING:
Use of car park close to the village green is assumed.

REFRESHMENTS:
Good selection of pubs and cafés.

POINTS OF INTEREST

Ⓐ

The Clearances Monument. On 25 April 1829, 12 families, mainly from Sannox, sailed from Lamlash on the brig *Caledonia* bound for Canada. They were part of the clearance of thousands of people from the Highlands and Islands, so that the land could be given over to more profitable enterprises.

Ⓑ

Memorial Hospital. In its splendid situation overlooking Lamlash Bay, the hospital was opened in 1922 as a memorial to those who gave their lives in the 1914-18 War.

Ⓒ

Kilbride Chapel. In the burial ground are the remains of the 14th-century pre-Reformation Chapel of St Bride. The chapel walls contain several sculptured stones and the graves include that of Lady Charlotte Erskine (1771-1857), eldest daughter of John, Earl of Mar.

Ⓓ

Parish Church. The church just south of the village green was built with funds provided by the 12th Duke of Hamilton, and was presented to the parish by him in 1884. Its features include six beautiful stained glass windows, a carillon with nine bells, and a two-manual organ.

Ⓔ

Arran High School. The school was completed in 1939 but was almost immediately requisitioned by the Navy as a barracks and canteen serving the many ships which used Lamlash Bay during World War Two. It reopened as a school in 1946.

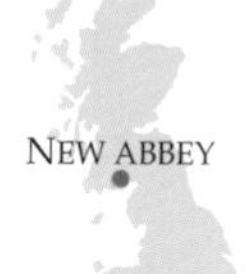

SCOTLAND

NEW ABBEY

DUMFRIES AND GALLOWAY

On A710, 7 miles S of Dumfries

NEW Abbey is a compact village with a charming main street. It is dominated by the powerful ruin of Sweetheart Abbey, a Cistercian foundation of 1273.

New Abbey's old Corn Mill, a superb restoration job.

POINTS OF INTEREST

St Mary's Catholic Church. This interesting chapel with its house attached was built by Rev T.P. Bagnall in 1824. Money for many of its features, including the alter and reredos, was given by Lord and Lady Herries.

The Abbot's Tower. The tower was built by the last abbot of Sweetheart Abbey, Gilbert Broun of Carsluith, an outspoken opponent of the Reformation. He used the tower as his base in the latter part of the 16th century as he travelled and worked for the cause of the counter-Reformation.

Shambellie House. Formerly the home of the Stewarts of Shambellie, the house dates from the mid-19th century and was designed in Scottish Baronial style. It is now a Museum of Costume run by the National Museums of Scotland.

(D)

New Abbey Corn Mill. A mill on this site is mentioned in documents from 1559, but the present attractive buildings are late 18th century, no doubt erected as part of improvements being carried out by the Stewarts of Shambellie. The mill continued in operation until the 1940s.

(E)

Sweetheart Abbey. The impressive ruins of this ancient Cistercian foundation date from 1273, when it was established as a daughter house to Dundrennan by the Lady Devorgilla as a lasting memorial to her husband, John Balliol, who had died four years earlier. The Abbey was named Dulce Cor – sweet heart – by the monks after Devorgilla's death in 1290.

WALK DIRECTIONS

From the car park, return to the main road and continue forward round a left-hand bend. In another 100yds turn right on to a surfaced path across a field to the parish church. Turn left to pass in front of the church and rejoin the main road.

Cross the road, turn left, and in 20yds turn right along a walled path. On the left is St Mary's Catholic Church. Bear left to walk up beside a playing field, and continue on the path between a wall and fence, with the Abbey and churchyard to your left.

(3)

At the Abbey Wall, go through the kissing-gate and turn right. In 100yds go through another gate on to a track and in 20yds go through the gate on the right and cross the footbridge over New Abbey Pow. Pass the cottage (the former Lint Mill) and walk up the lane.

At the left-hand bend, go ahead through Landis churchyard to view the Abbot's Tower. Return to the road, turn right and follow it along round a bend and past Shambellie Grange.

At the A710, cross with care and walk down the road. The Scots pines on the left were planted in 1775-1780 by the Stewart family of Shambellie House.

Turn right after 400yds to visit Shambellie House. After your visit, return to the road, turn right and walk over New Abbey Bridge into the village.

(7)

Visit the corn mill, and afterwards divert round the back of the building to see the mill stream, pond and a fine little green. Walk up the main street and continue to the Abbey, the climax of the walk.

INFORMATION
Length of walk: 2½ miles
Approx time: 2 hrs

TERRAIN:
Suitable for pushchairs, but wheelchairs should stay in the village.

PARKING:
Next to the Abbey.

OPEN:
Sweetheart Abbey. Apr-Sep weekdays 9.30am-7pm, Sun 2-7pm. Oct-Mar weekdays 10am-4pm, Sun 2-4pm. Charge. Corn Mill. Hours as for Abbey. Charge. Shambellie House. May-mid Sep, Thu-Mon 10am-5.30pm (Sun 12noon-5.30pm). No charge.

REFRESHMENTS:
Two pubs and the Abbey Coffee Shop.

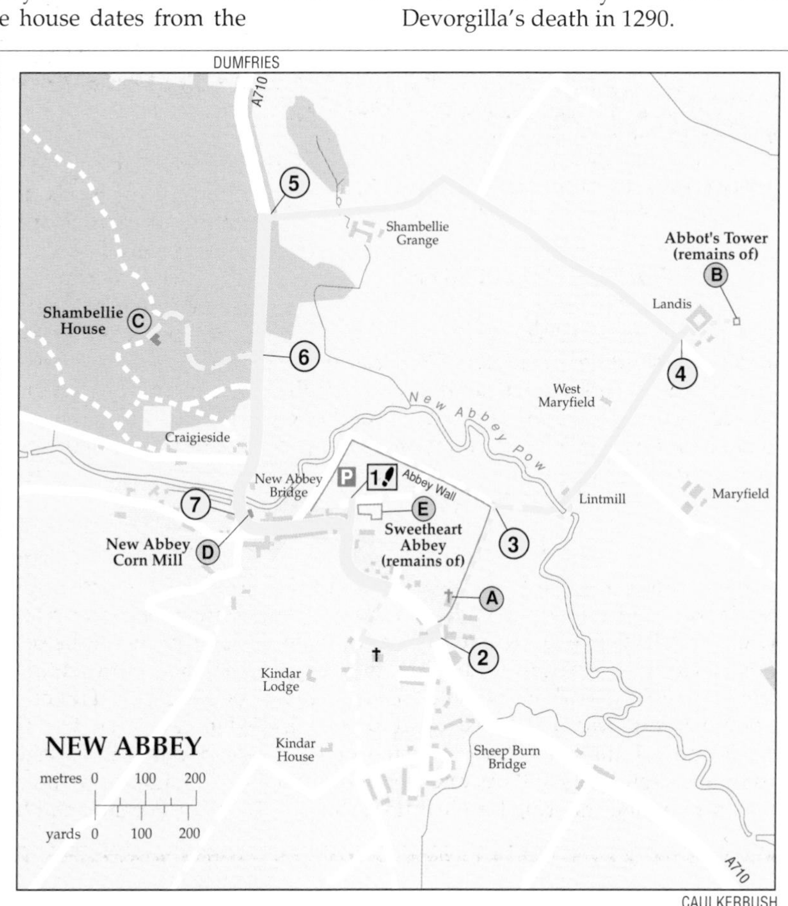

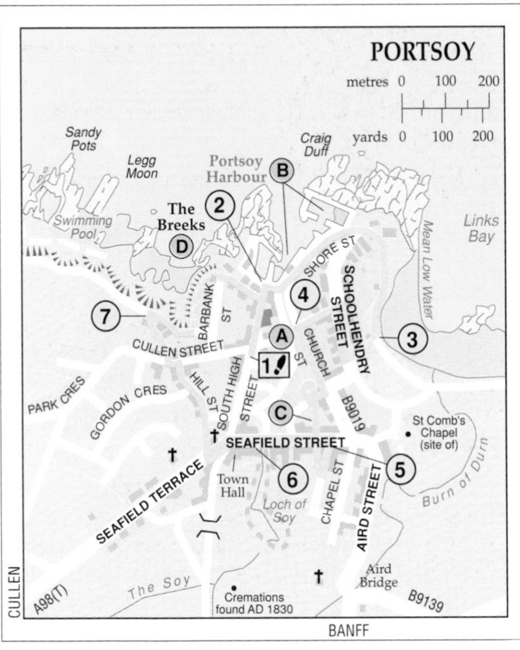

INFORMATION

Length of walk:
1½ miles

Approximate time:
1 hour

TERRAIN:
Steep slopes and steps make this walk difficult for pushchairs and unsuitable for wheelchairs. Children should manage it without difficulty, however.

PARKING:
There is some parking in the square, where the walk starts. Otherwise use one of the nearby streets.

REFRESHMENTS:
Several cafés and pubs in the village.

PORTSOY

GRAMPIAN

On A98, 5m W of Banff

PORTSOY was declared a Burgh of Barony by Mary, Queen of Scots in 1550. The charter was granted to the Ogilvies of Boyne, who in about 1580 built Boyne Castle, now ruined, a little east of the village. The old harbour dates from 1692 when it was developed by the then Lord Boyne both for fishing and for the export of Portsoy marble. The new harbour dates from 1825 and is still used by fishing boats today.

WALK DIRECTIONS

From the square, walk down North High Street past the former Star Inn to the harbour. The Portsoy marble shop is on the left, in Corf House, a fine late 18th-century building. At the foot of North High Street is a group of former warehouses and tenements which have been refurbished as modern accommodation. This new development received a Saltire Society design award in 1967.

Walk right, along the harbour wall, past the Shore Inn and round to the new harbour. Looking back you will notice how the end wall of the old harbour has the stone unusually laid vertically. Pass to the right of Sutherland's fish market and continue round into Links Bay. To the right here is the old Salmon House of 1834, the date shown on the carving of the 'king of fish' on its wall.

At Links Cottage, by the caravan park, go right and climb the steps to reach Schoolhendry Street. Turn right and in 200yds turn left down an alley and then down some steps to reach Church Street.

Turn left. In 150yds on the left is Soy House, the oldest building in Portsoy, dating from the 1690s. Take the next right (Shillinghill), cross the humpback bridge and immediately go right down steps and right again on to the old railway line. Follow it under two bridges and at the first gap in the wall on the left turn sharply back left up a lane to reach Seafield Street (the A98).

Turn left. On the right in 100yds is the former parish church, now the parish hall, with its chiming clock. Turn left by the Co-op shop to reach Loch Soy, which formerly fed an oatmeal mill but is now the centrepiece of an attractive park. The short walk round the loch is an optional extra which is well worth taking.

Portsoy Harbour, with the village rising behind it.

Continue along Seafield Street past the Town Hall, and cross to pass the Episcopal Church and turn right into Hill Street, where no. 15 has a splendid painted iron balcony rail. At the T-junction turn left into Cullen Street and immediately right to reach the clifftop above the Breeks. There are fine views west to Redhythe Point.

Turn right along the clifftop path and follow it round a small bay. At a lane go straight ahead. At the end turn right back to the square.

POINTS OF INTEREST

Star Inn. The building dates from 1727. It can easily be picked out by its corner lantern and also the pend arch leading to its former cobbled courtyard. It is said to have been a centre for smuggling in earlier times, but now, following restoration, it is used for housing.

Portsoy Harbour. The old harbour dates from 1692 when it was built by Patrick Ogilvie, Lord Boyne. Portsoy marble was exported from here to many places including France. With the growth of herring fishing, the harbour became too small, and the new harbour was developed by Lord Seafield in 1825 and rebuilt after storm damage in 1839. Lobster and crab boats still operate from here and it is a popular mooring for pleasure craft.

(C)

The Old Railway. The line from Banff to Portsoy opened in 1859, the full line to Elgin not opening until 1886, at which time a new station was built. It survives as a large Scout hut in the Loch Soy park. The steep branch line serving the harbour also closed in the 1880s but the line was not lifted until 1910. It makes an unusual and evocative short walk and it is easy to imagine the little goods engines puffing up and down here. The old station is in commercial use and can be seen on the right after passing underneath Seafield Road (the second bridge).

The Breeks. This area to the west of Portsoy Harbour is the source of the serpentine green marble, once the basis for a considerable industry. The marble can be seen in the walls of a house on the left as you enter Loch Soy park. It was very popular in France and was used for two chimneypieces in the Palace of Versailles. The marble is still worked here but on a much smaller scale, and souvenirs and jewellery can be bought in the Portsoy marble shop on the harbour front.

SCOTLAND

WEST LINTON

BORDERS

On A702, 15 miles S of Edinburgh

WEST Linton, on the eastern edge of the Pentland Hills, was an important market village on the cattle and sheep droving routes which crossed the hills on their way south. At their height these droves were carrying 30,000 sheep and cattle each year, and the status of the village can be gauged from the old saying `It's as big as a Linton market'.

INFORMATION
Length of walk:
2 miles
Approximate time:
1½ hours

TERRAIN:
Village section suitable for pushchairs and wheelchairs, but the north-western loop would be difficult for either. It is however quite easy for children.

PARKING:
Park tidily in the village.

OPEN:
Village information centre, Raemartin Square. Certain times in summer – enquire locally.

REFRESHMENTS:
Two inns and the Old Bakehouse Tearoom.

The Clock Tower in West Linton, with the 'Lady' Gifford statue.

WALK DIRECTIONS

①

Start from Raemartin Square and turn right into Main Street. On the right as you walk down the street is `Lady' Gifford's Clock Tower. Further down is the parish church, and right at the south end of the village is the former tollhouse. At the fork keep right and cross the bridge.

②

Turn right immediately over the bridge on to the path alongside the burn. The path continues to a small weir and the former ford.

③

Recross the burn and take the lane straight ahead. Opposite the corner of Raemartin Square turn left on a gravel path. Turn right at Uplyne Cottage and past Ravelston go left into a narrow lane which emerges on Upper Green.

④

Walk across Upper Green, climb the steps to the main road, and turn left. In 100yds take the second right (signposted to the golf course).

⑤

Pass the entrance to Medwyn House, formerly a coaching inn, and the turnoff to the golf course. In a further 200yds, turn right (signposted to Carlops).

⑥

Walk down this pretty lane. Do not be put off by the intimidating `Private Road' signs – this is a right of way. Cross the old bridge over the Lyne Water. You are now on the Roman Road. The lane winds uphill.

⑦

At the end of a field, about 250yds from the bridge and where the lane bends left, turn right on to a small path. In 200yds it joins another path coming in from the left. Follow the path high above the Lyne Water.

⑧

The path swings left, away from the burn. In 100yds turn left on a narrow fenced path and walk up to The Loan, an unsurfaced road. Turn right and continue down to the main road.

⑨

Cross the road and turn right. Turn left along past the post office to join the Edinburgh Road. At the top of Main Street turn left into Deanfoot Road, right into Croft Road, and in 200yds take the path on the right to return to Main Street opposite Raemartin Square.

POINTS OF INTEREST

The Clock Tower. This much-altered monument started out in 1660 as a statue erected by James Gifford to honour his wife. On the four corners of the pedestal were small statues of their children. The birth of a fifth child was marked by adding another small statue - on the mother's head!

'Lady' Gifford for a time adorned a drinking fountain and then in 1894 the monument was adapted to incorporate the former school clock.

Ⓑ

St Andrew's Church. The church was started in 1782 and was enlarged a century later with bigger windows, a gallery and a spire added. The interior features fine wood carvings by two local women. The Romanesque font was constructed of pieces of stone found in the area.

The boundary wall contains two bee-boles, in which the ministers or their wives would keep bee-skeps to provide them with honey.

Ⓒ

Tollhouse. In earlier times many roads had tollhouses. This example, on the turnpike from Blyth Bridge to Carlops, dates from the early 19th century.

Ⓓ

Roman Road. The substantial nature of the old bridge over the Lyne Water at the northern end of the walk shows the importance of this route, and indeed it can be traced back to Roman times. This was their road from the Clyde Valley to Edinburgh.

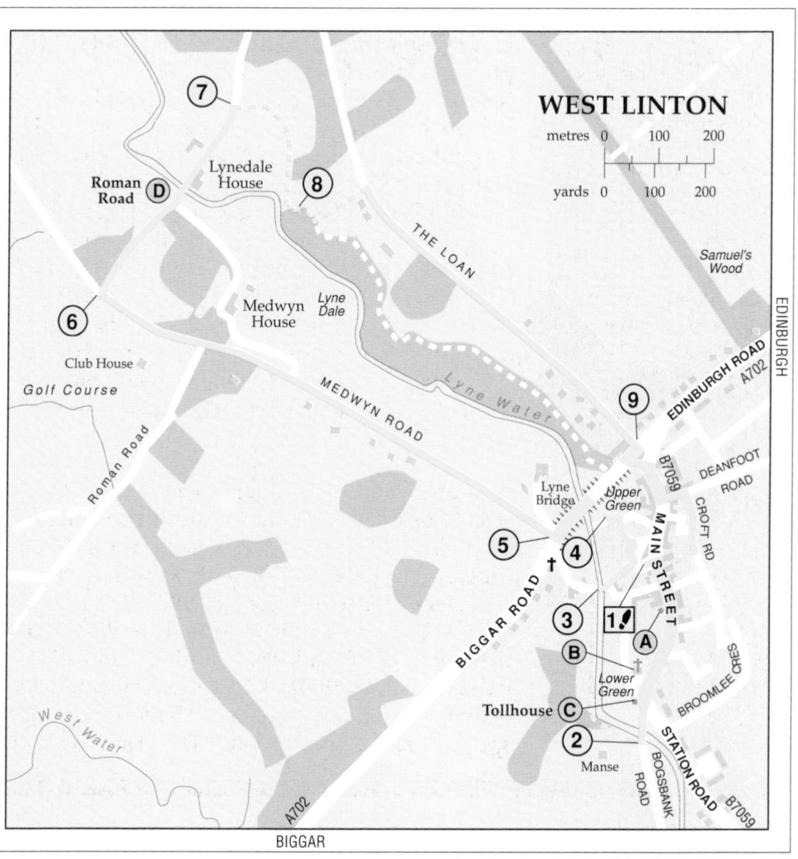

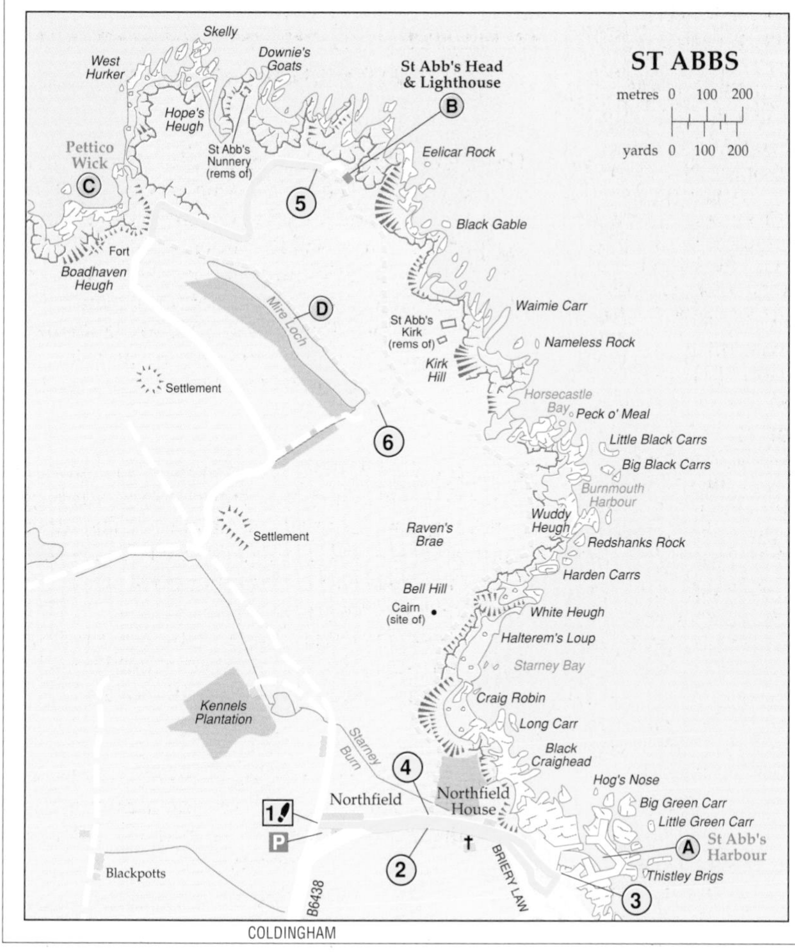

ST ABBS

BORDERS

Off A1107, 12m N of Berwick-upon-Tweed

ST Abbs takes its name from Ebba or Aebbe, daughter of Edilfred, King of Northumbria, who founded a nunnery here in the 7th century. The remains of a later foundation bearing her name can be seen in Coldingham, a mile to the west. Later the village became one of a number of harbours on the Berwickshire coast used by fishermen. Small boats still work from here today, though Eyemouth, to the south, has a much larger fleet.

This is a particularly fine stretch of coastline, and the area north of the village, including St Abb's Head, is now a National Nature Reserve. The walk out to the head and back is splendid at any time of the year.

The village of St Abbs slopes steeply down to its picturesque small harbour.

INFORMATION
Length of walk:
4 miles
Approximate time:
2½ hours

TERRAIN:
Steep streets and steps in the village: paths to St Abb's Head and back with some ascent and descent. Not suitable for pushchairs or wheelchairs, but no problem for older children.

PARKING:
There is limited parking in the village, but it is easier to park at the St Abb's Head Visitor Centre at Northfield, and this is recommended. The walk starts from there.

OPEN:
St Abb's Head Visitor Centre (NTS/SWT). All year. Free parking, tearoom, toilets, art gallery.

REFRESHMENTS:
Tearooms at Northfield and in the village.

POINTS OF INTEREST

St Abbs Harbour. Berwickshire has long been the home of fishing fleets. St Abbs is one of the smaller harbours, but boats still work from here, catching lobsters and crabs in creels or going further out for prawns. Careful navigation is needed to enter the tight confines of the harbour, which is also used as a base by divers. One of the offshore rocks is evocatively known as the Hog's Nose while another is called Thistly Brigs.

The full story of fishing along this coast is very well told in Eyemouth Museum, which also records the awful events of 14 October 1881, when a fierce storm battered over 30 boats to destruction. In all, 192 men lost their lives. The museum includes a 15ft tapestry depicting the disaster. It was sewn by local women, descendants of men lost in the tragedy.

St Abb's Head and Lighthouse. The 192 acres which form the National Nature Reserve (declared as such in 1983) were purchased by the National Trust for Scotland in 1980 and are managed by the Trust jointly with the Scottish Wildlife Trust.

St Abbs is noted for its superb birdlife. On the cliffs here are found large nesting populations of guillemots, razorbills, kittiwakes, fulmars, shags, eiders and a few puffins. Many other inland species use the grazing land. The best time for the seabirds is the summer, when there can be as many as 50,000 here, nesting on the smallest of ledges on the high cliffs. During the winter the birds spend nearly all their time at sea.

There is a wide variety of flowering plants and grasses including less-common species such as purple milk-vetch, and on Kirk Hill an area has been fenced off to protect the rock rose, the principal food for the caterpillars of the rare Northern Brown Argus butterfly. St Abb's Head

itself is formed from ancient lavas (see Pettico Wick, below).

The lighthouse was built in 1862 and is still manned. It is a very important beacon and sighting point for shipping entering the Firth of Forth, and the keepers also control unmanned lights on the Island of May and the Bell Rock. The area around the cliffs is a voluntary Marine Nature Reserve which aims to help conserve the equally fascinating and diverse sealife.

Pettico Wick. This lovely small bay provides a grandstand from which to see the geology of the cliffs in both directions. To the north, stretching up to Fast Castle Head, the rock is grey and clearly banded, formed from muds and oozes on an ocean floor some 450 million years ago and later buckled by forces whose power is almost beyond comprehension.

To the south, at and beyond St Abb's Head, are more rugged cliffs of pink and purple lavas which were ejected by volcanoes, probably about 50 million years after the grey rocks were formed.

These harder volcanic rocks form steeper cliffs which are much more suitable for seabird nesting sites. At Pettico Wick you stand on the line of an ancient earth movement which is called the St Abb's Head fault.

Mire Loch. Unlike the dramatic cliffs you have just left, this is a man-made feature. The fault line provided the valley, but the loch is less than 100 years old, being formed after a dam was built here. It now provides a splendid wetland habitat for plants – on the way to it you pass glorious, huge bulrushes. Water birds include swans and mallard, and in summer the kittiwakes come from their cliff sites to bathe here. The slopes have numerous rabbit burrows, in some of which wheatears have taken advantage of the natural cover to nest.

The lighthouse tops the cliff at St Abbs Head.

WALK DIRECTIONS

From the visitor centre, take the path signposted to St Abb's Head.

At the wall of Northfield House, do not turn left but continue down the road into the village, following as it drops to the harbour, where there is always activity to catch the eye. The harbour is one of the few safe havens on a dangerous coast.

③

At the end of the road, turn right up the steps. Turn right on the road at the top and walk along it; there are fine views down to the harbour and out to sea. Rejoin the inward route past the church on its hilltop site.

Take the signposted path to St Abb's Head and follow it all the way to the lighthouse. The path dips and climbs, affording superb views of the coastline and the restless, ever-changing sea.

At the far side of the first inlet, Halterem's Loup, are the eroded pinnacles of White Heugh. The rocks are white with seabird deposits. Continue over Wuddy Heugh and drop down to Burnmouth Harbour, where fishing boats used to shelter, and Horsecastle Bay, where there is a gradation of lichens common on these coasts: black on the rocks below high water mark, yellow a little higher up, and grey on the sheltered rocks well above the waterline.

Fishermen knew every rock along this coast, and named many of them. The walk passes Redshanks Rock, Big and Little Black Carrs, the Peck o'Meal, and oddest of all, Nameless Rock! After Horsecastle Bay the path skirts Kirk Hill, where St Aebbe's original foundation is thought to have been, and climbs up to the lighthouse on St Abb's Head itself, with its wonderful views in all directions and its permanent and noisy seabird population.

From the lighthouse, follow the road inland to Pettico Wick. At the lowest point of the road here, turn left off it and take the path which runs down the left-hand side of Mire Loch.

At the end of Mire Loch, go left for a short distance to rejoin the outward route, and walk back to the visitor centre.

ST AEBBE

Aebbe (or Ebba) was the daughter of King Edilfred of Northumbria. It is said that she took to sea to escape the unwelcome attentions of the King of Mercia, and was cast ashore at or near the headland which now bears her name. She founded a combined nunnery and monastery, an unusual thing for the time, and ruled it as abbess until she died in 683. St Cuthbert, of Lindisfarne visited her in 661. The buildings were destroyed by raiders, possibly Vikings, in the late 9th century.

The remains of a later foundation also bearing her name can be seen in Coldingham village, but the ruins on Nunnery Point, north of the lighthouse, once thought to be associated with St Aebbe, have recently been dated only to medieval times.

Looking to the cliffs at White Heugh. The National Nature Reserve is noted for the number and variety of its birdlife, and the rocks are stained white with bird droppings.

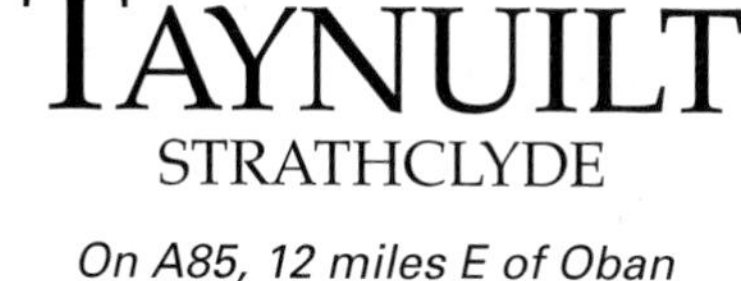

TAYNUILT

STRATHCLYDE

SCOTLAND

On A85, 12 miles E of Oban

SET on the banks of Loch Etive and overlooked by the sharp peaks of Ben Cruachan, present-day Taynuilt is a quieter place than in former times, when it was one of the principal iron-smelting centres in Scotland. Cannon balls, thought to have been used at the Battle of Trafalgar, were made at Taynuilt. The village was originally called Muckairn, which may derive from 'hogs dens' or from the Gaelic *Moadh-Eaharan*, the field of Edgar, a prince of ancient times.

Home to a close-knit community, Taynuilt has a lively annual calendar including a Highland Games in August. There is a strong church congregation and a fine new primary school. The walk visits the iron furnaces, now a scheduled ancient monument, an award-winning tearoom, a unique brewery and an unusual monument to one of our great national heroes.

WALK DIRECTIONS

From the station, walk back up towards the A85 and take the last turning on the left before the main road to view the church.

Return to the village street and turn right. Most of the houses are made of Cruachan granite from the Inverawe Quarry, which closed in 1945. The only older building is the present confectioners. Turn right up the lane past Graham's shop, go over a stile and climb the knoll both to see Nelson's Monument and to enjoy the views, with Cruachan prominent to the south-east. Notice that the last house in the lane is called Clach a' Charraigh (Rock Pillar). Return to the road and turn right.

Cross the railway bridge and continue, crossing the bridge over the chuckling River Nant. Glen Nant, where the river has its source, is a beautifully wooded nature reserve and is well worth a visit. At the guesthouse called Alandon, go straight on up a path to rejoin the road by the Roman Catholic Church.

At the church take the left fork (really straight on) down a quiet lane with views of Airds Bay and Loch Etive opening up. Gulls and oystercatchers are likely to be your companions, and the tidal ponds often hold swans. Notice the smart wall plaque at Brochroy Farm. Leave the road to walk down Kelly's Pier and enjoy the fine views out across the loch to Bonawe.

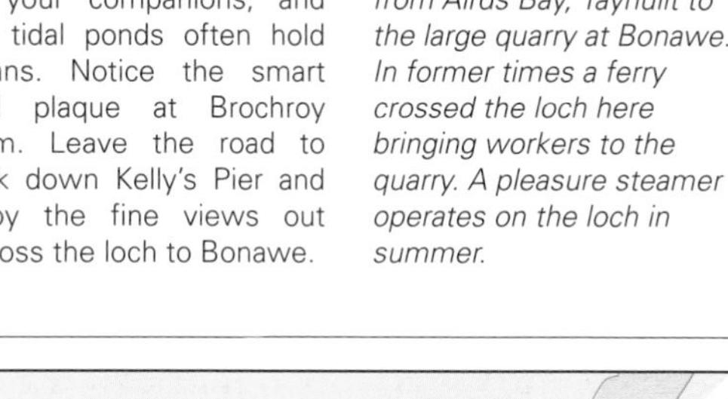

Looking across Loch Etive from Airds Bay, Taynuilt to the large quarry at Bonawe. In former times a ferry crossed the loch here bringing workers to the quarry. A pleasure steamer operates on the loch in summer.

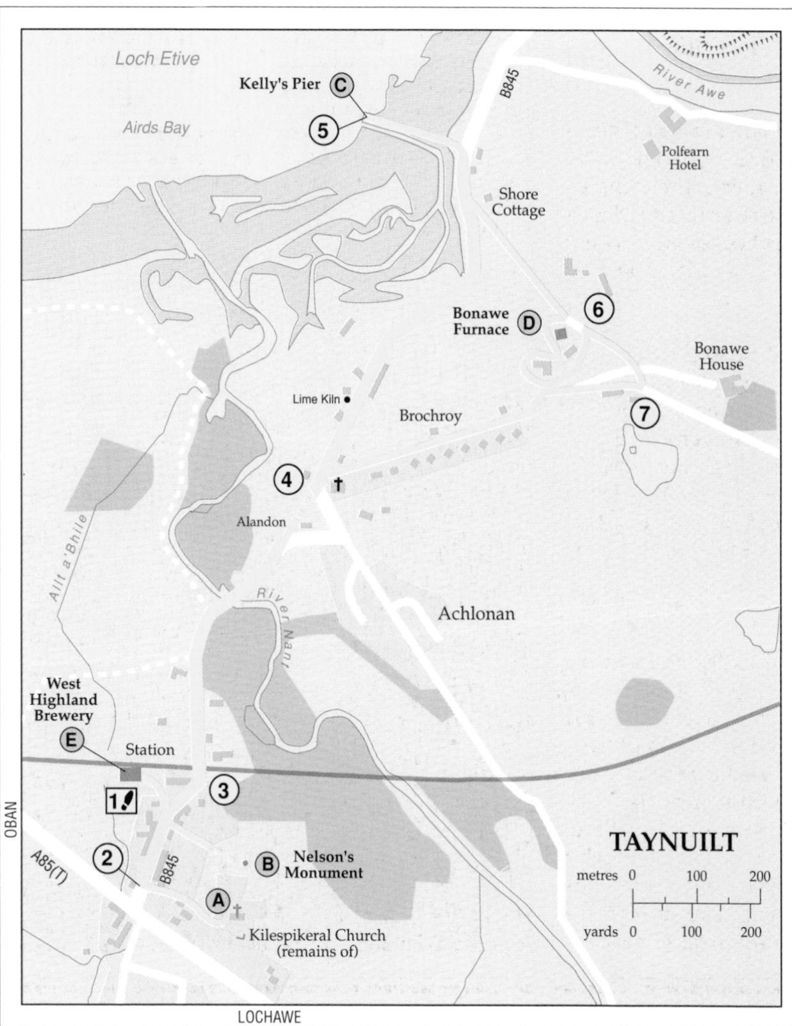

INFORMATION
Length of walk:
2½ miles
Approximate time:
1½ hours

TERRAIN:
Minor roads, lanes and a track. Suitable for children and for push-chairs (except the optional lade walk and the short section to the Nelson Monument).

PARKING:
Park tidily in the station area.

OPEN:
Bonawe Furnace. Apr-Sep Mon-Sat 9.30am-7pm, Sun 2-7pm. Charge. Toilets.
Loch Etive Cruises operate from the jetty at the end of the B845 (not on the walk). Twice daily 3-hour cruises up Loch Etive, May-Sep. Charge. Toilets on board.

REFRESHMENTS:
A splendid tearoom, a brewery selling its own beer, and a hotel serving coffees, teas and bar meals.

The monument to Nelson, moved to its present site by workers at the furnace in 1805, commands superb views across Loch Etive. Far right: the buildings at Taynuilt Station, on the Oban line, have been converted into a brewery and bar.

5

Returning to the road, retrace your steps for a few yards and then fork left at the Bonawe Furnace sign-post to pass Shore Cottage. This lovely little place won for its owner, Mrs Lily McNaught, the Egon Ronay Tearoom of the Year Award in 1989. Mrs McNaught travelled to the Ritz in London to receive her award, but it's doubtful whether she got a better tea than you will find here by Loch Etive. Continue along the track for 250yds to the entrance to the Bonawe Furnace.

6

After looking round the furnace, leave by the gate marked for the walk down the old lade to the river. You can walk down the lade and back as an optional extra: it adds a mile to the walk. Otherwise, turn right up the track. On the left is Bonawe House, built for the mine manager who gave his name to Kelly's Pier.

7

Turn right to pass a group of cottages built for workers at the furnace, and still happily lived in today, and walk through the pleasant settlement of Brochroy, with detached houses and a number of fine gardens, back to the RC church. Here you join the outward route to return to the station and its brewery, where there is a strong temptation to take refreshment at the end of the walk.

POINTS OF INTEREST

A

Muckairn Church. The present parish church, built in 1829, stands close to the site of the original place of worship, which was called Killespickerill - possibly deriving from Earailt or Harold, Bishop of Argyll in 1227. Little remains of this church, which was the Bishop's seat for 30 years, but it is clear that Christian worship has been continuous here for well over 700 years. The present church is fairly plain inside, with an atmosphere of peace very appealing to the visitor. The burial ground formerly contained incised stones mentioned by antiquaries at the turn of the century.

B

Nelson's Monument. This rough granite pillar 12ft high stands on Cnoc Aingeal (Hill of Sacrificial Fires) and has an extraordinary history. It stood for centuries in a field near Airds Bay House. On hearing of Nelson's victory at Aboukir, or perhaps Trafalgar, workers at the Furnace mounted the 4-ton stone on wooden rollers and dragged it nearly a mile to its present site.

The Second Statistical Account of 1840 describes this action as `not in the best possible taste'! The inscription on the stone (originally, it is believed, raised in memory of the Celtic St Nessog) reads: `To the memory of Lord Nelson this stone was erected by Lorn Furnace workmen 1805'. It is thought to have been the first monument to Nelson erected anywhere in Britain – a most unusual find in a West Highland village.

C

Kelly's Pier. From the old jetty, now grass-grown and little used, look to the right across Loch Etive to the village of Bonawe and its massive quarry. The name Bonawe originally applied to the Taynuilt side of the loch, coming as it does from the Gaelic *Bun Atha* – Mouth of the Awe. This was once the main crossing-point, by ferry, to Appin and the road north.

When the ferry operated, men from Taynuilt crossed to work at the quarry, but this is no longer the case. The quarry produced top quality granite setts which were used in many large public works such as the entrances to the Mersey Tunnel and the King George V Bridge in Glasgow. It now produces crushed stone. The pier, named after a former furnace manager, once saw 3-masted sailing ships bringing in ore from Cumberland for use in the furnace.

D

Bonawe Furnace. The furnace here was the first successful operation of its kind in Scotland. It opened in 1753 and employed up to 600 men. It had its own doctor, schoolmaster, blacksmith and carpenter. The furnace was established by the Newland Company of Coniston in Cumbria because of the abundance of good timber in the area, the ore being brought by ship to Kelly's Pier (C above). The charcoal produced at Bonawe was of the highest quality, and the iron was renowned for its quality too. The furnace closed down in 1874. It is now a scheduled Ancient Monument with well laid out displays and interpretive panels.

E

West Highland Brewery. The railway to Oban was opened in 1880, and Taynuilt Station was built at that time. Like so many of its type, it is a pleasing Victorian building. The company constructing the railway faced many difficulties both financially and in engineering their way through the West Highland landscape.

The line survived the drastic cuts of the 1960s and there are still regular trains to Glasgow, but the station buildings have been put to other uses as the West Highland Brewery and Tap. Beer brewed on the premises is sold at the bar and comes in various strengths up to West Highland Severe, which will be relished by real-ale lovers – but not if you are driving afterwards! This walk would in fact make a very pleasant day out from Oban using the train to get to Taynuilt.

INDEX

The Automobile Association would like to thank the following photographers, libraries and associations for their assistance in the preparation of this book.

AEROFILMS *8* Combe Martin, *9* Ayot St Lawrence, Albury.
J ALLAN CASH PHOTO LIBRARY *28* Buckfast Railway.
BAXTERS OF SPEYSIDE LTD *250* Baxters Shop.
COLLECTIONS *15* Ickwell Market Day.
DEVIZES MUSEUM *5* Collared Urn.
DORSET COUNTY LIBRARY *42* Purbeck Marblers.
THE FRANCIS FRITH COLLECTION *3* Castle Combe.
INTERNATIONAL PHOTOBANK *39* Clovelly, *41* Corfe Castle.
MARY EVANS PICTURE LIBRARY *14* Harvest Home.
MUSEUM OF ENGLISH RURAL LIFE *12* Smithy.
NATURE PHOTOGRAPHERS LTD *Cover* small tortoiseshell (A Wharton), *20* small brown, *134* goldfinch, *174* meadow cranesbill (P R Sterry), *216* small tortoiseshell, *238* spear thistle (E A Janes).
ROYAL COMMISSION OF HISTORICAL MONUMENTS AIR PHOTO LIBRARY *6* Wharram Percy.
SPECTRUM COLOUR LIBRARY *136* Abbots Bromley.
THE HULTON PICTURE CO *228* Dylan Thomas.
THE MANSELL COLLECTION LTD *7* Lanark, *83* George Bernard Shaw, *124* Gilbert White, *130* Sir Francis Dashwood, *147* Nelson, *198* Dorothy & William Wordsworth, *200* Brontë Sisters, *204* George Fox.
A TRYNER *155* Cromford.
V&A Museum *98* Vale of the Stour.
WEST AIR PHOTOGRAPHY *24* Avebury.
ANDY WILLIAMS PHOTO LIBRARY *Cover* Wendens Ambo.

All remaining pictures are held in the Associations own photo library (AA PHOTO LIBRARY), with contributions from:

A Baker, P Baker, J Beazley, A W Besley, M Birkitt, E A Bowness, J Carney, P Eden, R Fletcher, D Forss, J Gravell, V Greaves, S King, A Lawson, S & O Mathews, E Meacher, A Molyneux, R Newton, D Noble, G Rowatt, A Souter, R Surman, T Teegan, T D Timms, M Trelawny, W Voysey, R Weir, T Wood, T Woodcock.